Algebra 1
Concepts and Skills

Volume 2
Chapters 7-12

McDougal Littell
A HOUGHTON MIFFLIN COMPANY
Evanston, Illinois • Boston • Dallas

ISBN: 0-618-10648-0   23456789–DWO–06 05 04 03 02 01

Internet Web Site: http://www.mcdougallittell.com

About the Authors

▶ **RON LARSON** is a professor of mathematics at Penn State University at Erie, where he has taught since receiving his Ph.D. in mathematics from the University of Colorado in 1970. He is the author of a broad range of instructional materials for middle school, high school, and college. Dr. Larson has been an innovative writer of multimedia approaches to mathematics, and his Calculus and Precalculus texts are both available in interactive form on the Internet.

▶ **LAURIE BOSWELL** is a mathematics teacher at Profile Junior-Senior High School in Bethlehem, New Hampshire. A recipient of the 1986 Presidential Award for Excellence in Mathematics Teaching, she is also the 1992 Tandy Technology Scholar and the 1991 recipient of the Richard Balomenos Mathematics Education Service Award presented by the New Hampshire Association of Teachers of Mathematics.

▶ **TIMOTHY D. KANOLD** is Director of Mathematics and a mathematics teacher at Adlai E. Stevenson High School in Lincolnshire, Illinois. In 1995 he received the Award of Excellence from the Illinois State Board of Education for outstanding contributions to education. A 1986 recipient of the Presidential Award for Excellence in Mathematics Teaching, he served as President of the Council of Presidential Awardees of Mathematics.

▶ **LEE STIFF** is a professor of mathematics education in the College of Education and Psychology of North Carolina State University at Raleigh and has taught mathematics at the high school and middle school levels. He is the 1992 recipient of the W. W. Rankin Award for Excellence in Mathematics Education presented by the North Carolina Council of Teachers of Mathematics, and a 1995–96 Fulbright Scholar to the Department of Mathematics of the University of Ghana.

All authors contributed to planning the content, organization, and instructional design of the program, and to reviewing and writing the manuscript. Ron Larson played a major role in writing the textbook and in establishing the program philosophy.

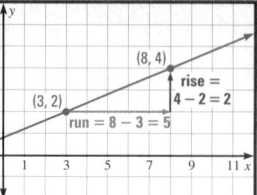

▶ REVIEWERS

Pauline Embree
Mathematics Department Chair
Rancho San Joaquin Middle School
Irvine, CA

Diego Gutierrez
Mathematics Teacher
Crawford High School
San Diego, CA

The reviewers read and commented on textbook chapters in pre-publication format, particularly with regard to classroom needs.

▶ TEACHER PANEL

Courteney Dawe
Mathematics Teacher
Placerita Junior High School
Valencia, CA

Diego Gutierrez
Mathematics Teacher
Crawford High School
San Diego, CA

Dave Dempster
Mathematics Teacher
Temecula Valley High School
Temecula, CA

Roger Hitchcock
Mathematics Teacher
Buchanan High School
Clovis, CA

Pauline Embree
Mathematics Department Chair
Rancho San Joaquin Middle School
Irvine, CA

Louise McComas
Mathematics Teacher
Fremont High School
Sunnyvale, CA

Tom Griffith
Mathematics Teacher
Scripps Ranch High School
San Diego, CA

Viola Okoro
Mathematics Teacher
Laguna Creek High School
Elk Grove, CA

The Teacher Panel helped plan the content, organization, and instructional design of the program.

CALIFORNIA CONSULTING MATHEMATICIANS

Kurt Kreith
Professor of Mathematics
University of California, Davis

Don Chakerian
Professor of Mathematics
University of California, Davis

The California Consulting Mathematicians prepared the *Mathematical Background Notes* preceding each chapter in the Teacher's Edition of this textbook.

VOLUME 1

CHAPTER 1

Connections to Algebra

Getting Ready

VOLUME 1

CHAPTER 2

Properties of Real Numbers

STUDENT HELP

Study Tip *66, 86, 93, 94, 101, 102, 108, 109, 113, 114*
Skills Review *66, 111*
Reading Algebra *65, 71, 107*
Writing Algebra *94*
Vocabulary Tip *100*
Look Back *72, 79, 84, 87, 97, 99, 119, 120*
Keystroke Help *80*
Test Tip *126*

APPLICATION HIGHLIGHTS

Helicopters *63, 75*
Nome, Alaska *67*
Stars *69*
Space Shuttle *73*
Planets *75*
Golf Scores *82*
Stock Market *88*
Water Cycle *90*
Flying Squirrels *95*
Rappelling *97*

 **INTERNET**

63, 67, 69, 73, 75, 80, 90, 91, 95, 97, 101, 104, 108, 115, 117, 127

ASSESSMENT

VOLUME 1

CHAPTER 3

Solving Linear Equations

VOLUME 1

CHAPTER 4

Graphing Linear Equations and Functions

ASSESSMENT

VOLUME 1

VOLUME 1

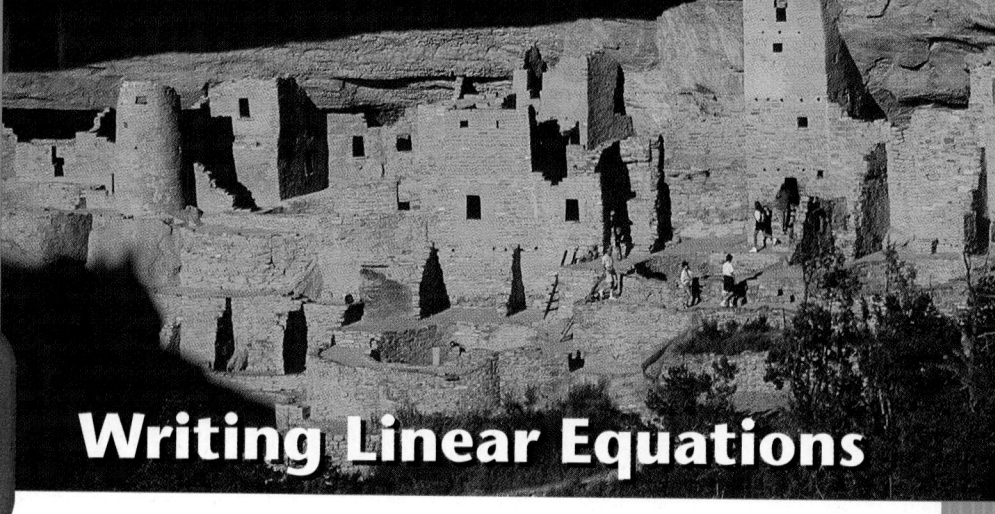

CHAPTER 5

Writing Linear Equations

VOLUME 1

CHAPTER
6

Solving and Graphing Linear Inequalities

STUDENT HELP

Study Tip *324, 330, 337, 338, 342, 343, 344, 348, 349, 350, 356, 362, 363, 368, 369*
Skills Review *340*
Reading Algebra *323*
Writing Algebra *325, 331*
Vocabulary Tip *367*
Keystroke Help *374*
Test Tip *380*

APPLICATION HIGHLIGHTS

Music *321*
Astronomy *325, 359*
Mercury *327*
Fly-fishing *338*
Mountain Plants *343*
Steel Arch Bridge *346*
Water Temperature *352*
Poodles *357*
Fireworks *365*
Nutrition *371*

INTERNET

321, 327, 332, 337, 340, 346, 347, 349, 359, 365, 369, 371, 372, 374, 381

ASSESSMENT

VOLUME 2

CHAPTER 7

Systems of Linear Equations and Inequalities

VOLUME 2

> **Key Skills Review**
>
> *Volume 2 includes key skills review and assessment material for Chapters 1–6 of Volume 1. This material begins on p. xxvii of Volume 2.*

VOLUME 2

CHAPTER 8

Exponents and Exponential Functions

VOLUME 2

STUDENT HELP

APPLICATION HIGHLIGHTS

 **INTERNET**

VOLUME 2

CHAPTER 9

Quadratic Equations and Functions

VOLUME 2

CHAPTER

10

Polynomials and Factoring

ASSESSMENT

STUDENT HELP

APPLICATION HIGHLIGHTS

 **INTERNET**

VOLUME 2

CHAPTER 11

Rational Expressions and Equations

ASSESSMENT

VOLUME 2

CHAPTER 12

Radicals and More Connections to Geometry

STUDENT HELP

Study Tip *692, 693, 699, 717, 724, 726, 736, 741*
Reading Algebra *710*
Vocabulary Tip *722, 731*
Look Back *698, 715, 726, 742*
Test Tip *752*

APPLICATION HIGHLIGHTS

Centripetal Force *689, 706*
Dinosaurs *696*
Sailing *700*
De-icing Planes *708*
Penguins *718*
Diving *720*
Staircase Design *728*
Soccer *732*
Maps *734*
Pony Express *739*

 INTERNET

689, 693, 696, 702, 705, 708, 712, 720, 725, 728, 732, 734, 737, 739, 742, 743, 744

ASSESSMENT

VOLUME 2

Contents of Student Resources

Pre-Course Test

This Pre-Course Test covers pre-book skills that are necessary for both Volumes 1 and 2. It does not test material taught in Volume 1. See pages R2–R3 to test material from Volume 1.

DECIMALS

Skills Review
pp. 759–760

Find the sum, difference, product, or quotient.

1. $3.4 + 6.005$ **2.** $27.77 - 18.09$ **3.** 23.7×13.67 **4.** $9.744 \div 0.87$

FACTORS AND MULTIPLES

Skills Review
pp. 761–762

Find the greatest common factor of the pair of numbers.

5. $8, 28$ **6.** $36, 42$ **7.** $54, 81$ **8.** $50, 150$

Find the least common multiple of the pair of numbers.

9. $6, 7$ **10.** $10, 15$ **11.** $24, 38$ **12.** $12, 36$

Find the least common denominator of the pair of fractions.

13. $\frac{1}{2}, \frac{7}{10}$ **14.** $\frac{5}{8}, \frac{6}{7}$ **15.** $\frac{5}{9}, \frac{7}{12}$ **16.** $\frac{11}{20}, \frac{15}{32}$

FRACTIONS

Skills Review
pp. 763–766

Find the reciprocal of the number.

17. 12 **18.** $\frac{3}{16}$ **19.** $\frac{9}{5}$ **20.** $2\frac{1}{3}$

Add, subtract, multiply, or divide. Write the answer in simplest form.

21. $\frac{3}{4} - \frac{1}{4}$ **22.** $\frac{1}{2} + \frac{1}{8}$ **23.** $\frac{6}{7} + \frac{5}{9}$ **24.** $11\frac{1}{4} - 2\frac{5}{8}$

25. $\frac{1}{2} \times \frac{6}{11}$ **26.** $\frac{7}{11} \div \frac{3}{5}$ **27.** $\frac{4}{15} \div \frac{8}{3}$ **28.** $4\frac{1}{8} \times \frac{2}{3}$

FRACTIONS, DECIMALS, AND PERCENTS

Skills Review
pp. 768–769

Write the percent as a decimal and as a fraction in simplest form.

29. 7% **30.** 26% **31.** 48% **32.** 84%

Write the decimal as a percent and as a fraction in simplest form.

33. 0.08 **34.** 0.15 **35.** 0.47 **36.** 0.027

Write the fraction as a decimal and as a percent.

37. $\frac{9}{10}$ **38.** $\frac{4}{5}$ **39.** $\frac{7}{8}$ **40.** $\frac{11}{20}$

COMPARING AND ORDERING NUMBERS

Skills Review
pp. 770–771

Compare the two numbers. Write the answer using <, >, or =.

41. 138 and 198

42. 781 and 718

43. 8.4 and 8.2

44. -7.88 and -4.88

45. $\frac{5}{12}$ and $\frac{3}{4}$

46. $\frac{3}{6}$ and $\frac{4}{8}$

47. $\frac{5}{3}$ and $1\frac{1}{2}$

48. $16\frac{2}{3}$ and $16\frac{7}{8}$

Write the numbers in order from least to greatest.

49. 47, 74, 44, 77

50. 80, 808, 88, 8

51. 0.19, 0.9, 0.49, 0.4

52. $-6.5, -5.4, 6.4, -6$

53. $\frac{5}{8}, \frac{4}{7}, \frac{3}{5}, \frac{1}{2}$

54. $\frac{9}{7}, \frac{6}{4}, \frac{5}{4}, \frac{6}{13}$

55. $1\frac{5}{9}, 1\frac{3}{4}, \frac{13}{11}, \frac{7}{5}$

56. $-16\frac{1}{4}, -15\frac{1}{9}, -16\frac{1}{8}, -15\frac{2}{3}$

PERIMETER, AREA, AND VOLUME

Skills Review
pp. 772–773

Find the perimeter.

57. a triangle with sides of length 18 feet, 27 feet, and 32 feet

58. a square with sides of length 4.7 centimeters

Find the area.

59. a square with sides of length 13 yards

60. a rectangle with length 7.7 kilometers and width 4.5 kilometers

Find the volume.

61. a cube with sides of length 19 meters

62. a rectangular prism with length 5.9 inches, width 8.6 inches, and height 1.2 inches

DATA DISPLAYS

Skills Review
pp. 777–779

63. The list below shows the distribution of gold medals for the 1998 Winter Olympics. Choose an appropriate graph to display the data. ▶Source: International Olympic Committee

Germany 12	Norway 10	Russia 9	Canada 6
United States 6	Japan 5	Netherlands 5	Austria 3
South Korea 3	Finland 2	France 2	Italy 2
Switzerland 2	Bulgaria 1	Czech Republic 1	

MEASURES OF CENTRAL TENDENCY

Skills Review
p. 780

Find the mean, median, and mode(s) of the data set.

64. 1, 3, 3, 3, 4, 5, 6, 7, 7, 9

65. 17, 22, 36, 47, 51, 58, 65, 80, 85, 89

66. 5, 23, 12, 5, 9, 18, 12, 4, 10, 21

67. 101, 423, 564, 198, 387, 291, 402, 572, 222, 357

Pre-Course Practice

This Pre-Course Practice reviews pre-book skills that are necessary for both Volumes 1 and 2. It does not review material taught in Volume 1. See pages R4–R7 to review Volume 1.

DECIMALS

Skills Review pp. 759–760

Find the sum or difference.

1. $14 + 7.1$

2. $11 - 0.003$

3. $19.76 + 48.19$

4. $73.8 - 6.93$

5. $10.2 + 3.805 + 1.1$

6. $7.2 - 3.56$

Find the product or quotient.

7. 17×3.9

8. 6.08×3.15

9. 15.2×5.02

10. 0.019×0.27

11. 45.28×16.1

12. $26.01 \div 5.1$

13. $7.03 \div 1.9$

14. $21.84 \div 0.84$

15. $0.0196 \div 0.056$

FACTORS AND MULTIPLES

Skills Review pp. 761–762

List all the factors of the number.

1. 12

2. 41

3. 54

4. 126

Write the prime factorization of the number if it is not a prime number. If a number is prime, write *prime*.

5. 54

6. 60

7. 35

8. 47

List all the common factors of the pair of numbers.

9. $16, 20$

10. $24, 36$

11. $28, 42$

12. $60, 72$

Find the greatest common factor of the pair of numbers.

13. $8, 12$

14. $10, 25$

15. $15, 24$

16. $24, 30$

17. $36, 42$

18. $54, 81$

19. $68, 82$

20. $102, 214$

Find the least common multiple of the pair of numbers.

21. $9, 12$

22. $8, 5$

23. $14, 21$

24. $24, 8$

25. $12, 16$

26. $70, 14$

27. $36, 50$

28. $22, 30$

Find the least common denominator of the pair of fractions.

29. $\dfrac{5}{8}, \dfrac{5}{6}$

30. $\dfrac{5}{12}, \dfrac{7}{8}$

31. $\dfrac{7}{12}, \dfrac{9}{20}$

32. $\dfrac{5}{6}, \dfrac{8}{15}$

33. $\dfrac{3}{4}, \dfrac{15}{28}$

34. $\dfrac{9}{11}, \dfrac{8}{13}$

35. $\dfrac{5}{6}, \dfrac{20}{27}$

36. $\dfrac{17}{40}, \dfrac{27}{52}$

FRACTIONS

Skills Review
pp. 763–766

Find the reciprocal of the number.

1. 8

2. $\dfrac{1}{16}$

3. $\dfrac{9}{5}$

4. $3\dfrac{4}{7}$

Add or subtract. Write the answer as a fraction or a mixed number in simplest form.

5. $\dfrac{7}{12} - \dfrac{1}{12}$

6. $\dfrac{1}{8} + \dfrac{3}{8}$

7. $\dfrac{9}{10} + \dfrac{3}{10}$

8. $\dfrac{5}{15} - \dfrac{2}{15}$

9. $\dfrac{1}{3} + \dfrac{2}{9}$

10. $\dfrac{17}{20} - \dfrac{3}{5}$

11. $\dfrac{1}{6} + \dfrac{5}{8}$

12. $1\dfrac{2}{3} - \dfrac{8}{9}$

Multiply or divide. Write the answer as a fraction or a mixed number in simplest form.

13. $\dfrac{3}{5} \times \dfrac{1}{2}$

14. $\dfrac{2}{3} \times \dfrac{3}{8}$

15. $\dfrac{3}{5} \times 1\dfrac{1}{2}$

16. $2\dfrac{2}{3} \times 3\dfrac{3}{8}$

17. $\dfrac{2}{5} \div \dfrac{4}{5}$

18. $\dfrac{2}{3} \div \dfrac{8}{9}$

19. $5\dfrac{1}{4} \div \dfrac{7}{8}$

20. $4\dfrac{4}{5} \div 1\dfrac{1}{3}$

Add, subtract, multiply, or divide. Write the answer as a fraction or a mixed number in simplest form.

21. $\dfrac{2}{3} + \dfrac{5}{6}$

22. $9\dfrac{3}{8} - 5\dfrac{1}{4}$

23. $8\dfrac{2}{5} + 5\dfrac{3}{8}$

24. $\dfrac{4}{5} \times \dfrac{1}{4}$

25. $1\dfrac{2}{3} \div 1\dfrac{1}{4}$

26. $5\dfrac{3}{8} \times 3\dfrac{3}{4}$

27. $\dfrac{1}{4} \div \dfrac{1}{5}$

28. $1\dfrac{2}{3} - \dfrac{3}{4}$

FRACTIONS, DECIMALS, AND PERCENTS

Skills Review
pp. 768–769

Write the percent as a decimal and as a fraction or a mixed number in simplest form.

1. 8%

2. 25%

3. 38%

4. 73%

5. 135%

6. 350%

7. 6.4%

8. 0.15%

Write the decimal as a percent and as a fraction or a mixed number in simplest form.

9. 0.44

10. 0.09

11. 0.13

12. 0.008

13. 1.6

14. 3.04

15. 6.6

16. 4.75

Write the fraction or mixed number as a decimal and as a percent. Round decimals to the nearest thousandth. Round percents to the nearest tenth of a percent.

17. $\dfrac{3}{5}$

18. $\dfrac{5}{8}$

19. $\dfrac{17}{25}$

20. $\dfrac{11}{12}$

21. $5\dfrac{1}{5}$

22. $2\dfrac{1}{4}$

23. $3\dfrac{1}{16}$

24. $8\dfrac{3}{7}$

continued from page xxi

COMPARING AND ORDERING NUMBERS

Skills Review
pp. 770–771

Compare the two numbers. Write the answer using <, >, or =.

1. 13,458 and 14,455

2. 907 and 971

3. -8344 and -8434

4. -49.5 and -49.05

5. 0.58 and 0.578

6. 0.0394 and 0.394

7. $\frac{15}{16}$ and $\frac{9}{10}$

8. $\frac{13}{20}$ and $\frac{1}{4}$

9. $\frac{9}{24}$ and $\frac{3}{8}$

10. $7\frac{1}{4}$ and $7\frac{1}{5}$

11. $-2\frac{11}{16}$ and $-3\frac{2}{9}$

12. $18\frac{2}{3}$ and $18\frac{5}{8}$

Write the numbers in order from least to greatest.

13. 1507, 1705, 1775, 1075

14. 38,381, 30,831, 38,831, 30,138

15. $-0.019, -0.013, -0.205, -0.035$

16. 6.034, 6.30, 6.33, 6.34

17. $\frac{1}{2}, \frac{2}{7}, \frac{5}{11}, \frac{5}{8}$

18. $\frac{4}{5}, \frac{3}{4}, \frac{3}{7}, \frac{4}{9}$

19. $-\frac{4}{2}, -\frac{2}{3}, -\frac{4}{3}, -\frac{3}{2}$

20. $\frac{3}{8}, \frac{5}{4}, \frac{7}{9}, 1\frac{4}{7}$

21. $1\frac{3}{5}, \frac{7}{5}, \frac{5}{3}, 1\frac{4}{5}$

22. $15\frac{5}{9}, 14\frac{2}{3}, 14\frac{5}{7}, 15\frac{5}{8}$

PERIMETER, AREA, AND VOLUME

Skills Review
pp. 772–773

Find the perimeter.

1.
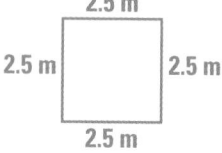
2.5 m, 2.5 m, 2.5 m, 2.5 m

2.
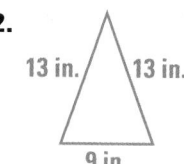
13 in., 13 in., 9 in.

3.
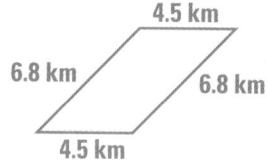
4.5 km, 6.8 km, 6.8 km, 4.5 km

4. a rectangle with length of 12.5 centimeters and width of 11.6 centimeters

5. a regular pentagon with sides of length 19 feet

Find the area.

6. a square with sides of length 1.67 yards

7. a rectangle with length 1.4 inches and width 2.8 inches

8. a triangle with base 15 centimeters and height 10 centimeters

Find the volume.

9. a cube with sides of length 34 feet

10. a rectangular prism with length 18 meters, width 6 meters, and height 3 meters

11. a rectangular prism with length 6.5 millimeters, width 5.5 millimeters, and height 2.2 millimeters

DATA DISPLAYS

In Exercises 1 and 2, use the table shown below. Hurricane categories are determined by wind speed, with Category 5 the most severe.

U.S. Mainland Hurricane Strikes by Category from 1900–1996					
Category	One	Two	Three	Four	Five
Number	57	37	47	15	2

1. The data range from 2 to 57. The scale must start at 0. Choose a reasonable scale for a bar graph.

2. Draw a bar graph to display the number of hurricane strikes by category.

In Exercises 3 and 4, use the table shown below.

U.S. Mainland Hurricane Strikes by Decade from 1900–1989									
Decade	1900–1909	1910–1919	1920–1929	1930–1939	1940–1949	1950–1959	1960–1969	1970–1979	1980–1989
Number	16	19	15	17	23	18	15	12	16

▶ Source: National Hurricane Center

3. The data range from 12 to 23. The scale must start at 0. Choose a reasonable scale for a histogram.

4. Draw a histogram to display the number of hurricane strikes by decade.

Choose an appropriate graph to display the data. Draw the graph.

5.

Reported House Plant Sales for One Week				
Type	Violets	Begonias	Coleus	Orchids	Cacti
Number	90	46	39	70	60

6.

Republicans in the Senate by Congress Number						
Congress	100th	101st	102nd	103rd	104th	105th	106th
Republicans	45	45	44	43	52	55	55

▶ Source: *Statistical Abstract of the United States: 1999*

MEASURES OF CENTRAL TENDENCY

Find the mean, median, and mode(s) of the data set.

1. 1, 3, 7, 2, 6, 3, 7, 9, 4, 7

2. 16, 19, 15, 17, 23, 18, 15, 12, 16, 7

3. 10, 48, 86, 32, 58, 73, 89, 39, 59, 27

4. 53, 54, 53, 45, 45, 44, 43, 52, 55, 55

Getting Ready

A Guide to Student Help

▶ *Each chapter begins with a Study Guide*

CHAPTER PREVIEW
gives an overview of
what you will be
learning.

KEY WORDS
lists important new
words in the chapter.

READINESS QUIZ
checks your under-
standing of words and
skills that you will use
in the chapter, and
tells you where to
go for review.

STUDY TIP
suggests ways to
make your studying
and learning easier.

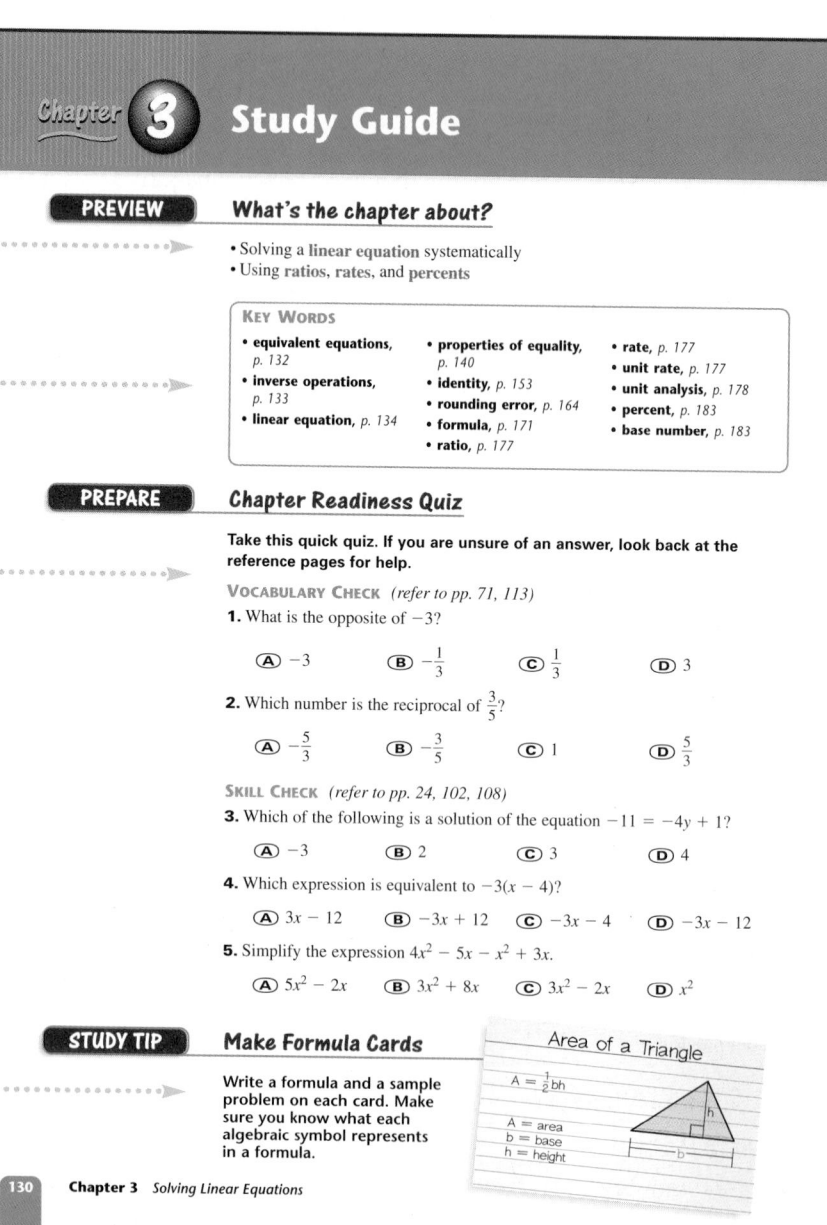

Chapter **3** **Study Guide**

PREVIEW   **What's the chapter about?**

• Solving a linear equation systematically
• Using ratios, rates, and percents

KEY WORDS

• **equivalent equations,**
  p. 132
• **inverse operations,**
  p. 133
• **linear equation,** p. 134

• **properties of equality,**
  p. 140
• **identity,** p. 153
• **rounding error,** p. 164
• **formula,** p. 171
• **ratio,** p. 177

• **rate,** p. 177
• **unit rate,** p. 177
• **unit analysis,** p. 178
• **percent,** p. 183
• **base number,** p. 183

PREPARE   **Chapter Readiness Quiz**

Take this quick quiz. If you are unsure of an answer, look back at the
reference pages for help.

VOCABULARY CHECK *(refer to pp. 71, 113)*

1. What is the opposite of -3?

   (A) -3 (B) $-\frac{1}{3}$ (C) $\frac{1}{3}$ (D) 3

2. Which number is the reciprocal of $\frac{3}{5}$?

   (A) $-\frac{5}{3}$ (B) $-\frac{3}{5}$ (C) 1   (D) $\frac{5}{3}$

SKILL CHECK *(refer to pp. 24, 102, 108)*

3. Which of the following is a solution of the equation $-11 = -4y + 1$?

   (A) -3 (B) 2   (C) 3   (D) 4

4. Which expression is equivalent to $-3(x - 4)$?

   (A) $3x - 12$ (B) $-3x + 12$ (C) $-3x - 4$ (D) $-3x - 12$

5. Simplify the expression $4x^2 - 5x - x^2 + 3x$.

   (A) $5x^2 - 2x$ (B) $3x^2 + 8x$ (C) $3x^2 - 2x$ (D) x^2

STUDY TIP   **Make Formula Cards**

Write a formula and a sample
problem on each card. Make
sure you know what each
algebraic symbol represents
in a formula.

Area of a Triangle

$A = \frac{1}{2}bh$

A = area
b = base
h = height

130   **Chapter 3** *Solving Linear Equations*

▶ Student Help notes throughout the book

STUDY TIPS help you understand and apply concepts and avoid common errors.

MORE EXAMPLES indicates that there are more worked-out examples on the Internet.

READING ALGEBRA guides you in reading and understanding your textbook.

Student Help

▶ READING ALGEBRA
Order is important for subtraction. "4 less than a number" means $y - 4$, *not* $4 - y$.

SKILLS REVIEW refers you to the pages where you can go for review and practice of topics from earlier courses.

Student Help

▶ SKILLS REVIEW
For help with writing fractions in lowest terms, see p. 763.

HOMEWORK HELP tells you which textbook examples may help you with homework exercises, and lets you know when there is extra help on the Internet.

Student Help

▶ HOMEWORK HELP
Extra help with problem solving in Exs. 34–39 is available at www.mcdougallittell.com

Other notes included are:
- **WRITING ALGEBRA**
- **KEYSTROKE HELP**
- **TEST TIP**
- **LOOK BACK**

VOCABULARY TIPS explain the meaning and origin of words.

Student Help

▶ VOCABULARY TIP
Equation comes from a Latin word that means "to be equal".

SIMPLIFIED EXPRESSIONS The distributive property allows you to *combine like terms* by adding their coefficients. An expression is **simplified** if it has no grouping symbols and if all the like terms have been combined.

Student Help

▶ STUDY TIP
In Example 2 the distributive property has been extended to three terms:
$(b + c + d)a = ba + ca + da$

EXAMPLE 2 Combine Like Terms

Simplify the expression.

a. $8x + 3x$ **b.** $2y^2 + 7y^2 - y^2 + 2$

Solution

a. $8x + 3x = (8 + 3)x$ Use distributive property.

$= 11x$ Add coefficients.

b. $2y^2 + 7y^2 - y^2 + 2 = 2y^2 + 7y^2 - 1y^2 + 2$ Coefficient of $-y^2$ is -1.

$= (2 + 7 - 1)y^2 + 2$ Use distributive property.

$= 8y^2 + 2$ Add coefficients.

Student Help

▶ MORE EXAMPLES
More examples are available at www.mcdougallittell.com

EXAMPLE 3 Simplify Expressions with Grouping Symbols

Simplify the expression.

a. $8 - 2(x + 4)$ **b.** $2(x + 3) + 3(5 - x)$

Solution

a. $8 - 2(x + 4)$

$= 8 - 2(x) + (-2)(4)$ Use distributive property.

$= 8 - 2x - 8$ Multiply.

$= -2x + 8 - 8$ Group like terms.

$= -2x$ Combine like terms.

b. $2(x + 3) + 3(5 - x)$

$= 2(x) + 2(3) + 3(5) + 3(-x)$ Use distributive property.

$= 2x + 6 + 15 - 3x$ Multiply.

$= 2x - 3x + 6 + 15$ Group like terms.

$= -x + 21$ Combine like terms.

Checkpoint ✓ Simplify Expressions

Simplify the expression.

3. $5x - 2x$ **4.** $8m - m - 3m + 5$ **5.** $-x^2 + 5x + x^2$

6. $3(y + 2) - 4y$ **7.** $9x - 4(2x - 1)$ **8.** $-(z + 2) - 2(1 - z)$

Getting Ready

Key Skills Review

▶ A Note to the Student

Your teacher may suggest that you use the materials in the following Key Skills Review section, pages R1–R74, in preparation for your work in Chapters 7–12 of *Algebra 1, Concepts and Skills*, Volume 2. These materials review and practice skills that were used or introduced in Chapters 1–6 of *Algebra 1, Concepts and Skills*, Volume 1.

For each lesson in Chapters 1–6, key examples and practice exercises are provided. Answers to all practice exercises are provided on pages R76–R91.

Also included in this Key Skills Review section are a Pre-Course Test and a Pre-Course Practice section, both with references to lessons in Volume 1; Chapter Tests for Chapters 1–6; an End-of-Course Test for Volume 1; and an End-of-Course Test for Volume 2.

▸ *Description of Resources*

Pre-Course Test The Pre-Course Test on pages R2 and R3 checks understanding of the key skills from *Algebra 1, Concepts and Skills*, Volume 1. If you have difficulty with a question, you can go the Pre-Course Practice on pages R4–R7 for additional practice or to the Key Skills Review on pages R8–R70 for reteaching and practice.

Pre-Course Practice The Pre-Course Practice on pages R4–R7 contains additional practice on the key skills found in the Pre-Course Test (Expressions, Equations, and Variables; Solving Linear Equations; Graphing Linear Equations; Writing Linear Equations; Linear Inequalities). The practice items are also referenced to lessons in *Algebra 1, Concepts and Skills*, Volume 1.

Key Skills Review The Key Skills Review on pages R8–R70 contains worked examples and exercises that review the key skills from each lesson of Volume 1, Chapters 1–6. A chapter test is provided to assess the key skills from each chapter.

End-of-Course Test, Volume 1 The End-of-Course Test on pages R71 and R72 checks mastery of the key skills of *Algebra 1, Concepts and Skills*, Volume 1, Chapters 1–6: Variables and Expressions; Operations on Real Numbers; Equations and Inequalities; Ratios, Rates, and Percents; Writing Linear Equations; Graphing Linear Equations and Inequalities; Absolute Value Equations and Inequalities.

End-of-Course Test, Volume 2 The End-of-Course Test on pages R73 and R74 checks mastery of the key skills of *Algebra 1, Concepts and Skills*, Volume 2, Chapters 7–12: Systems of Equations and Inequalities; Exponents and Scientific Notation; Quadratic Equations; Polynomials; Rational and Radical Expressions and Equations.

Contents of Key Skills Review

EXPRESSIONS, EQUATIONS, AND VARIABLES

Evaluate the expression for the given value of the variable.
(Lessons 1.1, 1.2, 1.3)

1. $x \div 4$ when $x = 28$

2. $(b - 7) + 2b$ when $b = 8$

3. $2x - 5$ when $x = 12$

4. $9x^2$ when $x = 3$

5. $5y - (2y + y)$ when $y = 3$

6. $(4b)^2$ when $b = 2$

Write the phrase or sentence as a variable expression, equation, or inequality. (Lesson 1.5)

7. Fifteen minus the quotient of a number and three

8. Six less than five times a number is 39.

9. A number, plus 24 is greater than or equal to 54.

10. GYMNASTICS Cara is a gymnast who has scored 9.55 on her first vault, and 8.95 on her second vault. What score must she make on her third vault to have an average score of at least 9.2? *(Lesson 1.6)*

In Exercises 11 and 12, use the table showing the favorite ice-cream flavors of students in an eighth-grade class. (Lesson 1.7)

11. Draw a bar graph of the data.

12. Use the bar graph to determine the most popular ice-cream flavor.

Flavor of Ice Cream	Number of Students
Chocolate	11
Vanilla	8
Strawberry	2
Chocolate Chip	4
Pistachio	1

13. Draw a line graph to represent the function given by the input-output table. *(Lesson 1.8)*

Input x	1	2	3	4	5	6
Output y	14	12	10	8	6	4

Evaluate the expression. (Lessons 2.3, 2.4)

14. $3 + 5 - 12$

15. $25 - [2(3 + 7)]$

16. $30 \div [(5 - 3)3]$

17. $3 + (-7) + (-13)$

18. $12[(-2 + 8) \div 3]$

19. $4.1 - (-4.4) - 2.4$

Simplify the expression. (Lessons 2.5, 2.6, 2.7)

20. $5(a - 5)$

21. $4(7 + d)$

22. $(4 - r)(-6)$

23. $5a + 8 + 8a$

24. $5(y + 3) + 4(y + 4)$

25. $5(4 + 3x) - 9(3x + 3)$

SOLVING LINEAR EQUATIONS

Solve the equation. (Lessons 3.1–3.5)

26. $3c = -36$

27. $4y - 3(y + 8) = 12$

28. $\frac{1}{4}v + 3 = 2$

29. $-14 = -3x + 2 + x$

30. $3(2 - x) + x = 13$

31. $8 - 7x = -6$

Solve the equation. Round the result to the nearest hundredth. (Lesson 3.6)

32. $22x - 35 = 106$

33. $8.2x - 9.3x = 81.6$

34. $4.91 - 0.78x = 1.52x$

SOLVING A RATE FORMULA The formula for distance is given by $d = rt$, where r is the rate of travel (speed) and t is the travel time. *(Lesson 3.7)*

35. Solve this formula for r.

36. Use the result to find the rate of an automobile which travels 348 miles in 5 hours and 48 minutes.

GRAPHING EQUATIONS AND FUNCTIONS

Plot and label the ordered pairs in a coordinate plane. (Lesson 4.1)

37. $A(0, 3)$, $B(-2, -1)$, $C(2, 0)$

38. $A(-4, 1)$, $B(-1, 5)$, $C(0, -4)$

Graph the equation. (Lesson 4.2, 4.4, 4.7)

39. $y - 5x = -2$

40. $4y - 2x = 8$

41. $x + 4y = 4$

WRITING EQUATIONS AND FUNCTIONS

Write the equation of the line in slope-intercept form. (Lesson 5.1)

42. $m = 3$, $b = 2$

43. $m = 0$, $b = 6$

44. $m = -1$, $b = -\dfrac{2}{5}$

Write in slope-intercept form the equation of the line that passes through the given point and has the given slope. (Lesson 5.2)

45. $(-1, -3)$, $m = \dfrac{1}{2}$

46. $(2, 3)$, $m = 1$

47. $(1, -4)$, $m = -4$

48. $(2, 6)$, $m = 2$

Write in point-slope form the equation of the line that passes through the given points. (Lesson 5.3)

49. $(-3, 2)$, $(4, -1)$

50. $(-2, 5)$, $(2, 4)$

51. $(2, 3)$, $(0, 4)$

52. $(1, 1)$, $(8, 7)$

Write in standard form an equation of the line that passes through the given point and has the given slope. (Lesson 5.4)

53. $(6, 8)$, $m = 2$

54. $(1, 5)$, $m = \dfrac{2}{5}$

55. $(-4, 3)$, $m = -1$

INEQUALITIES

Solve the inequality. (Lessons 6.1–6.5, 6.7)

56. $\dfrac{3}{4}x + 6 \le 3$

57. $7 - x > 12$

58. $4x + 3 \le 3x - 1$

59. $-(4 - x) \ge 2(3 - x)$

60. $-3x - 7 > 7x + 11$

61. $-6 \le \dfrac{1}{4}(3 - x) \le 12$

62. $8 < 3x - 4 < 17$

63. $2x + 1 \ge 7$ or $-3x - 4 \ge 2$

64. $|8 - 2x| \ge 12$

EXPRESSIONS, EQUATIONS, AND VARIABLES

Evaluate the expression for the given value of the variable. (Lesson 1.1)

1. $b - 12$ when $b = 43$

2. $12 + x$ when $x = 4$

3. $12n$ when $n = 4$

4. $\dfrac{y}{15}$ when $y = 30$

Write the expression in exponential form. (Lesson 1.2)

5. eight squared

6. $9 \cdot 9 \cdot 9 \cdot 9$

Evaluate the expression. Then simplify the answer. (Lesson 1.3)

7. $9 + 12 - 4$

8. $7 + 56 \div 8 - 2$

9. $4 \cdot 2 - 5$

10. $3 + 13 - 6$

11. $(28 \div 4) + 3^2$

12. $2[(2 + 3)^2 - 10]$

Write the sentence as an equation or an inequality. Let x represent the number. (Lesson 1.5)

13. A number divided by 6 is less than 15.

14. A number plus 10 is greater than or equal to 46.

15. The product of 10 and a number is 40.

16. A number minus 6 is 15.

In Exercises 17 and 18, use an algebraic model to solve the problem. (Lesson 1.6)

17. Two runners who live 10 miles apart leave home and start running towards each other at the same time. One runner runs 4 miles per hour, and the other runs 6 miles per hour. How long after the runners begin running will they meet?

18. Andrea has 4 shelves on the wall of her room. The distance between the shelves is the same as the distance between the floor and the bottom shelf. The distance between the ceiling and the top shelf is 2 ft 4 in. The ceiling in the room is 9 ft high. What is the distance between the shelves?

In Exercises 19 and 20, use the table at the right showing survey results for the number of hours of TV watched each week. (Lesson 1.7)

19. Draw a bar graph of the data.

20. Use the bar graph to determine which group watches TV the most hours per week.

Classification	Hours
Women	30
Men	22
Teens	34
Children	25

Determine if each relation is a function. (Lesson 1.8)

21.

Input x	11	12	13	20
Output y	−2	−1	0	7

22.

Input x	−2	−3	6	−2
Output y	−1	0	3	1

Evaluate the expression. (Lessons 2.3, 2.4)

23. $-3 + 18 + (-6)$

24. $9 + (-10) + 2$

25. $7 + 6.5 + (-3.5)$

26. $-2 - 7 - (-8)$

27. $-5.7 - (-3.1) - 8.6$

28. $-3 - \left(-\frac{1}{4}\right) - \frac{1}{2}$

29. $2 - (-4) + (-7)$

30. $\frac{5}{7} + \left(-\frac{4}{7}\right) - \left(-\frac{6}{7}\right)$

31. $46 - 17 - (-2)$

32. $11 - (-23) - 77$

33. $2.3 - (-9.5) + (-1.6)$

34. $-8 + (-3.1) - 6.2$

Simplify the expression. (Lesson 2.5)

35. $-5(-b)$

36. $-3(6)$

37. $-6(-2)$

38. $-9(-4)(-x)$

39. $(-x)^4$

40. $-6(2)(r)(t)$

Use the distributive property to rewrite the expression without parentheses. (Lesson 2.6)

41. $8(x + 3)$

42. $(a - 6)4$

43. $-7(y - 5)$

Simplify the expression. (Lesson 2.7)

44. $2a + 4a$

45. $t^2 - 9 + t^2$

46. $2x^2 + 4z - x^2 + 3z$

47. $15p + 3(6 - p)$

48. $-9(y + 11) + 6$

49. $3(b + 4) - 6(b - 2)$

Find the quotient. (Lesson 2.8)

50. $8 \div (-2)$

51. $-7 \div 7$

52. $-5 \div \left(-\frac{1}{2}\right)$

53. $\frac{1}{2} \div \left(-\frac{3}{4}\right)$

SOLVING LINEAR EQUATIONS

Solve the equation. (Lessons 3.1, 3.2, 3.3)

1. $4 + y = 12$

2. $t - 2 = 1$

3. $-14 = r + 5$

4. $a - (-9) = -2$

5. $6a = -102$

6. $-7n = 49$

7. $10d = -10$

8. $47 = \frac{r}{6}$

9. $3 = \frac{3}{5}t$

10. $2t - 5 = 13$

11. $12 + 9h = 30$

12. $8y - 10 - 12y = -18$

13. $6(5t - 3) + 2 = 14$

14. $7r - 8(r + 3) = 1$

15. $\frac{2}{3}(x + 1) = 10$

Solve the equation. (Lessons 3.4, 3.5)

16. $2p + 5 = -p - 4$

17. $13c = 15c + 14$

18. $8v - 3 - 5v = 2v + 7$

19. $9 - 4t = 6t + 2 - 3t$

20. $5 + 4(x - 1) = 3(2 + x)$

21. $-3(4 - r) + 4r = 2(4 + r)$

22. $8n + 4(-5 - 7n) = -2(n + 1)$

23. $x - 5(x + 2) = x + 3(3 - 2x)$

24. $\frac{1}{2}(2j - 4) = 3(j + 2) - 3j$

25. $\frac{1}{3}(6y - 3) = 6(2 + y) - 5y$

continued on next page

continued from page R5

Solve the equation. Round to the nearest hundredth. (Lesson 3.6)

26. $7c + 19 = 11$

27. $213d + 51d = -26$

28. $3.6a + 7.5 = 8.2a$

29. $18s - 8 = 4s - 3$

30. $2.24b - 33.52 = 8.91b$

31. $3.2f - 4.9 = 8.4f + 6.7$

Solve the formula for the indicated variable. (Lesson 3.7)

32. Solve for h: $A = \frac{1}{2}bh$

33. Solve for L: $P = 2L + 2W$

Find the unit rate. (Lesson 3.8)

34. Earn $50.75 for working 7 hours

35. 16 grams of protein in 8 cups of cereal

Solve the percent problem. (Lesson 3.9)

36. 15% of 320 meters is what length?

37. What number is 30% of 150?

GRAPHING LINEAR EQUATIONS

Plot and label the ordered pairs in a coordinate plane. (Lesson 4.1)

1. $A(-4, 1)$, $B(0, 2)$, $C(0, -3)$

2. $A(-1, -5)$, $B(0, -7)$, $C(1, 6)$

3. $A(-1, 1)$, $B(1, 3)$, $C(-1, -6)$

4. $A(2, -6)$, $B(5, 0)$, $C(0, -4)$

Rewrite the equation in function form. (Lesson 4.2)

5. $2x + y = 0$

6. $5x - 2y = 20$

7. $-4x - 8y = 32$

Graph the equation. (Lesson 4.3)

8. $x = -5$

9. $y = 2$

10. $x = 4$

Find the *x*-intercept and the *y*-intercept of the line. Graph the equation. Label the points where the line crosses the axes. (Lesson 4.4)

11. $y = 3x + 6$

12. $y - 4x = -8$

13. $x - y = 10$

Find the slope of the line passing through the points. (Lesson 4.5)

14. $(0, 0)$, $(5, 2)$

15. $(-3, 1)$, $(-5, -4)$

16. $(3, 3)$, $(-6, -4)$

The variables *x* and *y* vary directly. Use the given values to write an equation that relates *x* and *y*. (Lesson 4.6)

17. $x = 3$, $y = 9$

18. $x = 5$, $y = 40$

19. $x = 15$, $y = 60$

Rewrite the equation in slope-intercept form. Identify the slope and *y*-intercept. (Lesson 4.7)

20. $y - 4 = 3x$

21. $x = -y + 2$

22. $2x + y = 6$

Graph the function. (Lesson 4.8)

23. $f(x) = -5x$

24. $f(x) = 4x - 7$

25. $f(x) = -6x + 5$

WRITING LINEAR EQUATIONS

Write the equation in slope-intercept form of the line described below. (Lesson 5.1)

1. slope $= -2$, y-intercept $= 1$

2. slope $= -5$, y-intercept $= 0$

Write in slope-intercept form the equation of the line that passes through the given point and has the given slope. (Lesson 5.2)

3. $(2, 3)$, $m = 1$

4. $(-6, 4)$, $m = 0$

5. $(1, -4)$, $m = -4$

Write in slope-intercept form the equation of the line that passes through the two points. (Lesson 5.3)

6. $(10, -3)$ and $(5, -2)$

7. $(6, 2)$ and $(7, 5)$

8. $(4, 4)$ and $(-7, 4)$

Write in standard form an equation of the line that passes through the point and has the given slope. (Lesson 5.4)

9. $(6, 8)$, $m = 2$

10. $(4, 1)$, $m = -\dfrac{1}{2}$

11. $(1, 5)$, $m = \dfrac{2}{5}$

LINEAR INEQUALITIES

Solve the inequality. (Lessons 6.1, 6.2, 6.3)

1. $a + 2 < 7$

2. $-3 + m \le -11$

3. $-13 > b - 1$

4. $\dfrac{1}{3}f \ge -7$

5. $-\dfrac{3}{4}d \le -27$

6. $105 > -15a$

7. $5 \le -\dfrac{x}{2} + 4$

8. $-4x + 2 \ge 14$

9. $-x - 4 > 3x - 12$

10. $-(-x + 8) > -10$

11. $-10 \le -2(2x - 9)$

12. $x + 3 \le 2(x - 7)$

Solve the inequality. (Lessons 6.4, 6.5)

13. $-5 < x - 8 < 4$

14. $-10 < 2x + 8 \le 22$

15. $-10 \le -4x - 18 \le -2$

16. $5x > 25$ or $2x + 9 < -1$

17. $-3 > x + 6$ or $-x < 4$

18. $2 - x < -3$ or $2x + 14 < 12$

Solve the equation. If the equation has no solution, write *no solution*. (Lesson 6.6)

19. $|x| = 14$

20. $|x + 8| = -43$

21. $|x - 9| = 24$

Solve the inequality. Then graph the solution. (Lesson 6.7)

22. $|3x - 12| \le 9$

23. $|x - 4| > 1$

24. $|x + 7| < 2$

Graph the inequality. (Lesson 6.8)

25. $x \le -|4|$

26. $3x + y > 1$

27. $y - 5x \ge 0$

Variables in Algebra

Goal

Evaluate variable expressions.

Key Words

- variable
- value
- variable expression
- numerical expression
- evaluate

A **variable** is a letter used to represent one or more numbers called the **values** of the variable. A **variable expression** consists of constants, variables, and operations. To **evaluate**, or find the value of, a variable expression, you can substitute numbers for the variables. Then simplify the **numerical expression**.

EVALUATING EXPRESSIONS

Evaluate the expression $5n$ when $n = 11$.

Write the expression.	$5n$	The expression $5n$ means 5 times n.
Substitute numbers.	$5 \cdot 11$	
Simplify.	55	

Student Help

▶ **WRITING ALGEBRA**
The multiplication symbol $\times$ is usually not used in algebra because of the possible confusion with the variable x.

EXAMPLE

Evaluate the variable expression when $x = 3$.

a. 11 minus x **b.** 12 times x **c.** 15 divided by x **d.** x plus 8

$11 - x$ $12x$ $\dfrac{15}{x}$ $x + 8$

$11 - 3 = 8$ $12(3) = 36$ $\dfrac{15}{3} = 5$ $3 + 8 = 11$

1.1 Exercises

State the meaning of the variable expression and name the operation.

1. $\dfrac{x}{2}$ **2.** $2 + x$ **3.** $2x$ **4.** $x - 2$

Evaluate the expression for the given value of the variable.

5. $x + 17$ when $x = 3$ **6.** $8x$ when $x = 6$ **7.** $10 - y$ when $y = 5$

8. $13 + y$ when $y = 10$ **9.** $(12)(f)$ when $f = 3$ **10.** $48 - b$ when $b = 11$

11. $\dfrac{b}{12}$ when $b = 48$ **12.** $\dfrac{81}{n}$ when $n = 9$ **13.** $3a$ when $a = 8$

14. UNIT ANALYSIS Evaluate the expression $(8 \text{ weeks})\left(\dfrac{7 \text{ days}}{1 \text{ week}}\right)$.

15. DRIVING DISTANCE You are driving through the state of California at a speed of 55 miles per hour. How far do you travel in 6 hours? Use the formula $d = rt$, or distance = rate $\times$ time.

16. PERIMETER The perimeter of a triangle with side lengths a, b, and c is $P = a + b + c$. Find P when $a = 3$ feet, $b = 4$ feet, and $c = 5$ feet.

17. AREA The area of a triangle with base b and height h is $A = \dfrac{1}{2}bh$. Find the area of a triangle (in square inches) when $b = 6$ inches and $h = 5$ inches.

1.2 Exponents and Powers

Goal
Evaluate a power.

Key Words
- power
- exponent
- base
- grouping symbols

An expression like 2^5 is called a **power**. The **exponent** 5 represents the number of times the **base** 2 is used as a factor.

two to the fifth power $= 2^5 = 2 \cdot 2 \cdot 2 \cdot 2 \cdot 2$

You can evaluate variable expressions that contain exponents. Some expressions involve *grouping symbols*.

GROUPING SYMBOLS

Parentheses ( ) and brackets [ ] are **grouping symbols**. They tell you the order in which to do the operations. You must do the operations within the set of grouping symbols first. Consider $(4 \cdot 5) + 8$ and $4 \cdot (5 + 8)$:

First multiply. Then add.   **First add. Then multiply.**

$(4 \cdot 5) + 8 = 20 + 8 = 28$ $4 \cdot (5 + 8) = 4 \cdot 13 = 52$

Expressions with powers also involve grouping symbols: $3x^4 = 3(x^4)$.

Student Help

▶ READING ALGEBRA
You can read x^2 as "x squared." You can read x^3 as "x cubed."

EXAMPLE

Evaluate the variable expression when $x = 2$ and $y = 4$.

a. $x^5 = 2^5$
$= 2 \cdot 2 \cdot 2 \cdot 2 \cdot 2$
$= 32$

b. $5y^2 = 5(4^2)$
$= 5(4 \cdot 4)$
$= 5(16)$
$= 80$

c. $(x^3) + (y^2) = (2^3) + (4^2)$
$= (2 \cdot 2 \cdot 2) + (4 \cdot 4)$
$= 8 + 16$
$= 24$

d. $(x + y)^2 = (2 + 4)^2$
$= (6)^2$
$= 6 \cdot 6$
$= 36$

1.2 Exercises

Write the expression in exponential form. Then evaluate the power.

1. 6 squared

2. five cubed

3. three to the fourth power

4. $2 \cdot 2 \cdot 2 \cdot 2 \cdot 2 \cdot 2$

Evaluate the expression for the given value(s) of the variable(s).

5. x squared when $x = 8$ **6.** $3x^3$ when $x = 2$ **7.** $7t^5$ when $t = 2$

8. $(2a)^3$ when $a = 4$ **9.** $(5n)^4$ when $n = 2$ **10.** $(6 + y)^2$ when $y = 4$

11. $(x + y)^2$ when $x = 3, y = 4$ **12.** $(a^2) - (b^3)$ when $a = 10, b = 4$

13. INTERIOR DESIGN The floor of a kitchen is 18 feet long by 18 feet wide. How many square feet of tile are needed to cover the floor? Use the formula $A = s^2$, or area = side length squared.

Order of Operations

Goal

Use the established order of operations.

Key Words

- order of operations
- left-to-right rule

In arithmetic and algebra there is an **order of operation**s to evaluate an expression involving more than one operation.

ORDER OF OPERATIONS

STEP ❶ First do operations that occur within grouping symbols.

STEP ❷ Then evaluate powers.

STEP ❸ Then do multiplications and divisions *from left to right*.

STEP ❹ Finally, do additions and subtractions *from left to right*.

Student Help

▶ STUDY TIP

A fraction bar can act as a grouping symbol. You can evaluate the numerator and denominator separately, then divide: $\frac{2+4}{3-1} =$ $(2+4) \div (3-1)$.

EXAMPLE

Evaluate the expression.

a. $2 + 24 \cdot 2 = 2 + (24 \cdot 2)$ Do multiplication first.

$= 2 + 48$ Multiply 24 times 2.

$= 50$ Add 2 and 48.

b. $12 \div 3 \cdot 2 = (12 \div 3) \cdot 2$ Work from left to right.

$= 4 \cdot 2$ Divide 12 by 3.

$= 8$ Multiply 4 times 2.

c. $665 - 5(4 + 3)^2 = 665 - 5(7)^2$ Add within grouping symbols.

$= 665 - 5 \cdot 49$ Evaluate power.

$= 665 - 245$ Multiply.

$= 420$ Subtract.

1.3 Exercises

Evaluate the expression.

1. $18 \div 6 - 3$

2. $10 - 3 + 5$

3. $3 \cdot 7^2$

4. $16 + 8 \div 4$

5. $12 \div 3 \cdot 4$

6. $24 - 2 + 12$

7. $(14 - 11)^3 + 6$

8. $8 - (5 - 2) + 2^2$

9. $8 + 3^2 - (8 - 4)$

10. $\frac{4 + 6}{7 - 2}$

11. $\frac{3 \cdot 5}{25 - 10}$

12. $\frac{8^2}{4 \cdot 4}$

13. $\frac{5 \cdot 4}{6 + 2^2 - 5}$

14. $\frac{22 + 3}{2^2 + 12 - 11}$

15. $\frac{20 - 3^2 + 1}{13 - 9}$

Evaluate the variable expression when $x = 4$.

16. $x^3 - 6$

17. $x^2 + 8x$

18. $x + 5x^3$

19. $\left(\frac{32}{x} - 4\right) \cdot 3$

20. $\frac{x}{2} \cdot 19$

21. $\frac{5x}{x^2 - 3 + 7}$

1.4 Equations and Inequalities

Goal

Check solutions of equations and inequalities.

Key Words

- equation
- solution
- inequality

EQUATIONS AND INEQUALITIES

EQUATION	INEQUALITY
An **equation** is a statement formed by placing an equal sign between two expressions: $5x + 3 = 12$	An **inequality** is a statement formed by placing an inequality symbol between two expressions: $5 < 6$

A **solution** is a number that produces a true statement when it is substituted for the variable in an equation or inequality.

EXAMPLE 1

Use a mental math question to solve the equation.

EQUATION	QUESTION	SOLUTION
$x + 2 = 8$	What number plus 2 gives 8?	$6 + 2 = 8$, so $x = 6$.
$x - 5 = 8$	What number minus 5 gives 8?	$13 - 5 = 8$, so $x = 13$.
$4x = 20$	4 times what number gives 20?	$4 \cdot 5 = 20$, so $x = 5$.
$\frac{x}{2} = 8$	What number divided by 2 gives 8?	$\frac{16}{2} = 8$, so $x = 16$.

Student Help

▶ READING SYMBOLS

symbol	meaning
$=$	is equal to
$<$	is less than
$\leq$	is less than or equal to
$>$	is greater than
$\geq$	is greater than or equal to

EXAMPLE 2

Check to see if $y = 5$ is or is not a solution of the inequality.

INEQUALITY	SUBSTITUTE	SIMPLIFY	CONCLUSION
$y + 6 \geq 12$	$5 + 6 \overset{?}{\geq} 12$	$11 \not\geq 12$	False, 5 is *not* a solution.
$3y - 4 < 15$	$3(5) - 4 \overset{?}{<} 15$	$11 < 15$	True, 5 is a solution.

1.4 Exercises

Use mental math to solve the equation.

1. $3 + a = 10$ **2.** $\frac{x}{5} = 5$ **3.** $5p = 150$ **4.** $\frac{48}{n} = 8$

5. $a + 16 = 24$ **6.** $13 - n = 11$ **7.** $4x = 100$ **8.** $y - 3 = 21$

Check to see if $b = 6$ is or is not a solution of the equation or inequality.

9. $b + 9 = 15$ **10.** $24 - 4b = 0$ **11.** $7b < 64$

12. $2b + 5 = 12$ **13.** $b - 5 = 1$ **14.** $\frac{b}{3} = 18$

15. $7 \geq \frac{30}{b}$ **16.** $16 - b \leq 10$ **17.** $b^2 + 8 = 48$

18. $5b + 9 = 54$ **19.** $15 \leq b^2$ **20.** $4b + 6 > 81$

1.5 Translating Words into Mathematical Symbols

Goal
Translate words into mathematical symbols.

Key Words
- translate
- phrase
- sentence

TRANSLATING VERBAL PHRASES

To **translate** a verbal **phrase** into an algebraic expression, look for words that indicate mathematical operations.

PHRASE	TRANSLATION
A number *plus* nine	$n + 9$
Four *less than* a number	$n - 4$
The *quotient* of a number and 3	$\dfrac{n}{3}$
A number *multiplied* by 7	$7n$

Phrases are translated into variable or numerical expressions. **Sentences** are translated into equations or inequalities.

Student Help

▶ READING ALGEBRA
Order is important for subtraction and division. For example, "4 less than a number" means $y - 4$, *not* $4 - y$.

EXAMPLE

Write the sentence as an equation or an inequality. Let *x* represent the number.

SENTENCE	TRANSLATION
The *sum* of 8 and a number *is less than* 11.	$8 + x < 11$
The *difference* between 9 and a number *is* 2.	$9 - x = 2$
The *product* of 12 and a number *is equal to* 36.	$12x = 36$
8 *divided by* a number *is* 4.	$\dfrac{8}{x} = 4$
A number *increased by* 2 is less than 14.	$x + 2 < 14$
15 *minus* a number *is greater than or equal to* 12.	$15 - x \geq 12$

1.5 Exercises

Write the sentence as an equation or inequality. Let *x* represent the number.

1. A number decreased by 6 is 18.   **2.** A number times 7 is less than 21.

3. 4 less than a number is 12.   **4.** The sum of 3 and a number is 5.

5. The product of 3 and a number is greater than 24.

6. 45 divided by a number is greater than or equal to 15.

7. A number increased by 12 is less than or equal to 32.

8. The quotient of 48 and a number is less than 8.

9. ADMISSION PRICES The organizers of a fireworks display charge $20 for each carload of people. There are five people in your car. If you share the cost evenly, how much does each person pay?

A Problem Solving Plan Using Models

1.6

Goal
Model and solve real-life problems.

Key Words
• modeling
• verbal model
• algebraic model

Writing algebraic expressions, equations, or inequalities that represent real-life situations is called **modeling**. First you write a **verbal model** using words. Then you translate the verbal model into an **algebraic model**.

A PROBLEM SOLVING PLAN USING MODELS

VERBAL MODEL	Ask yourself what you need to know to solve the problem. Then write a verbal model that will give you what you need to know.
LABELS	Assign labels to each part of your verbal model.
ALGEBRAIC MODEL	Use the labels to write an algebraic model based on your verbal model.
SOLVE	Solve the algebraic model and answer the original question.
CHECK	Check that your answer is reasonable.

EXAMPLE 1

The price of one computer is $999. It costs $199 less than another computer. What is the price of the more expensive computer?

VERBAL MODEL

$$\boxed{\text{Lower price}} = \boxed{\text{Higher price}} - \boxed{\text{Difference in prices}}$$

LABELS

Lower price = 999   (dollars)
Higher price = x (dollars)
Difference in prices = 199   (dollars)

ALGEBRAIC MODEL

$999 = x - 199$ Write algebraic model.
$1198 = x$ Solve using mental math.

ANSWER ▶ The price of the more expensive computer is $1198.

CHECK ✓ Check the reasonableness of the answer: $999 = 1198 - 199$ ✓

In the Problem Solving Plan above, the last step is to **check your answer**. Always check your results against the wording of the original problem. Does your answer make sense? You might need to round your answer to make it reasonable.

For example, suppose you want to know how many cars are needed for 32 people to travel to an outing at a lake. You can divide.

$$(32 \text{ people}) \div \left(\frac{5 \text{ people}}{1 \text{ car}}\right) = 6\frac{2}{5} \text{ cars}$$

An answer of $6\frac{2}{5}$ cars would make no sense, however. You would need to take 7 cars.

EXAMPLE **2**

You want to buy a $255 CD player. You can earn $30 each time you work at the video store. How many times must you work at the video store in order to earn $255?

| **VERBAL MODEL** | **Pay received each time you work** $\cdot$ | **Number of times worked** = | **Total earned** |

LABELS   Pay each time you work = 30   (dollars per time)
Number of times worked = x (times)
Total earned = 255   (dollars)

ALGEBRAIC MODEL $30 \cdot x = 255$ Write algebraic model.
$x = 8.5$ Solve using mental math.

ANSWER ▶ You need to work in the video store 9 times to earn $255.

CHECK ✓ Check your answer with the words in the problem.

The answer is reasonable because $30 \cdot 9 = 270, which is just $15 more than the amount you need to buy the CD player.

1.6 **Exercises**

1. Order the steps for a general problem solving plan.

A. Assign values to the labels.   **B.** Solve the algebraic model.

C. Answer the original question.   **D.** Write a verbal model.

E. Check your solution.   **F.** Write an algebraic model.

SNOWBOARDING In Exercises 2–6, use the following information.
At your local store, snowboards with bindings cost $685. Snowboards without bindings cost $529. You worked for 10 months and saved $55 a month and you have enough to buy the snowboard without the bindings. How much would you have needed to save each month to buy the other snowboard?

2. Write a verbal model that relates the number of months worked, the amount you would have needed to save each month, and the price of the snowboard with the bindings.

3. Assign labels to the verbal model. Use s to represent the unknown value.

4. Use the labels to translate your verbal model into an equation.

5. Use mental math to solve the equation.

6. Check that your answer is reasonable.

 **Tables and Graphs**

Goal

Organize data using a table or graph.

Key Words

- data
- bar graph
- line graph

Data are information, facts, or numbers that describe something. One way to represent certain data is with a **bar graph**. A bar graph uses the lengths of bars to represent numbers and can be used to compare data.

EXAMPLE **1**

The following table shows statistics for the home run leaders in the American and National Leagues for 1995–1999. The graph shows the information from the table.

Number of Home Runs Hit		
Year	American League leader	National League leader
1995	50	40
1996	52	47
1997	56	49
1998	56	70
1999	48	65

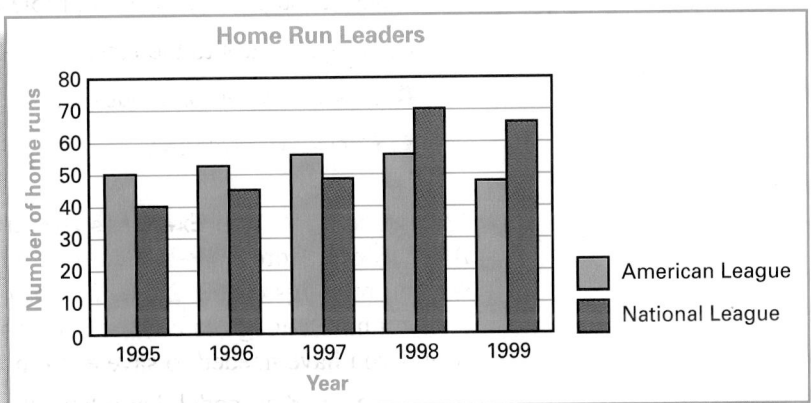

The bar graph can help you make a quick visual comparison. For example, the American League leaders hit more home runs than the National League leaders from 1995 to 1997, but in 1998 and 1999 the National League's number was greater than that of the American League.

The table can help you make a precise numerical comparison. For example, in 1998, the National League leader hit 14 more home runs than the American League leader: $70 - 56 = 14$.

Student Help

▶**SKILLS REVIEW**
For help with drawing bar graphs and line graphs to display data, see pages 777–779.

Another way to represent data is to use a **line graph**. A line graph provides a way of showing how one or more quantities change over a particular period of time.

EXAMPLE 2

Look at the graph below. During which one-year interval did the unemployment rate decrease the most?

To find the one-year interval in which the California unemployment rate decreased the most, find the steepest downward segment on the graph. The unemployment rate decreased the most between 1996 and 1997.

California Unemployment Rates	
Year	Percent of population unemployed
1995	7.8%
1996	7.2%
1997	6.3%
1998	5.9%
1999	5.2%

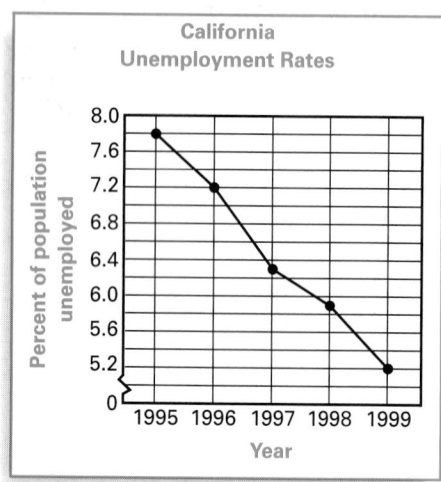

California Unemployment Rates

1.7 Exercises

1. Look at the line graph in Example 2. The zigzag line on the vertical axis shows a break where part of the scale is not shown. Because of this break in the scale, a reader might misinterpret the graph at quick glance and think that the unemployment rate in 1999 was almost 0%.

   a. Redraw the line graph from Example 2 so that the scale on the vertical axis has no break.

   b. Compare the two graphs. At a quick glance, does the unemployment rate in 1999 seem as low on your graph as it did in Example 2?

Use the table showing the heights of the tallest buildings in some cities in the United States.

2. Draw a bar graph of the data.

3. Which of these cities has the tallest building?

4. A building 609 m tall has been proposed for Chicago. How much taller would that building be than the tallest building in the bar graph?

Tall Buildings in the United States	
Los Angeles	310 m
Houston	305 m
Chicago	442 m
New York City	417 m
Atlanta	312 m

An Introduction to Functions

Goal
Use four different ways to represent functions.

Key Words
- function
- input
- output
- input-output table
- domain
- range

A **function** is a rule that establishes a relationship between two quantities, called the **input** and the **output**. For each input, there is exactly one output—even though two different inputs may give the same output. One way to describe a function is to make an **input-output table**. The collection of all input values is the **domain** of the function and the collection of all output values is the **range** of the function.

DESCRIBING FUNCTIONS

WORDS	You are in a hot-air balloon at a height of 200 feet. You begin to rise higher at a rate of 18 feet per minute for a period of 5 minutes.	EQUATION	$h = 200 + 18t$, where $t \geq 0$ and $t \leq 5$

INPUT-OUTPUT TABLE		GRAPH	

Input t	Output h
0	200
1	218
2	236
3	254
4	272
5	290

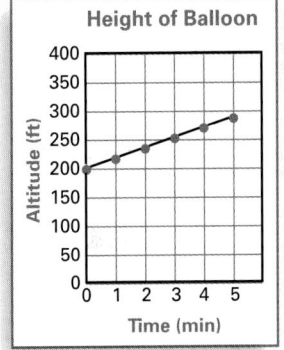

Height of Balloon

EXAMPLE 1

To make an input-output table for the function $y = 6x + 5$, evaluate the expression $6x + 5$ for the given input values. Then make the table.

INPUT (x)	FUNCTION	OUTPUT (y)
$x = 2$	$y = 6(2) + 5$	$y = 17$
$x = 4$	$y = 6(4) + 5$	$y = 29$
$x = 6$	$y = 6(6) + 5$	$y = 41$
$x = 8$	$y = 6(8) + 5$	$y = 53$

Input x	2	4	6	8
Output y	17	29	41	53

The range for the input values in the table is 17, 29, 41, and 53.

EXAMPLE **2**

You hire an electrician to install an electrical outlet in a wall. The electrician charges $68 for materials plus $40 an hour for service. The electrician says that the job will take at least 1 hour but no more than 3 hours. Write an equation to represent the function.

VERBAL MODEL	**Total cost**	=	**Cost of materials**	+	**Cost per hour**	.	**Number of hours worked**

LABELS

Total cost = C (dollars)
Cost of materials = **68**   (dollars)
Cost per hour = **40**   (dollars per hour)
Number of hours worked = h (hours)

ALGEBRAIC MODEL

$C = 68 + 40 \cdot h$ Write algebraic model.

ANSWER ▶ The function can be represented by the equation

$C = 68 + 40h$, where $h \geq 1$ and $h \leq 3$.

1.8 Exercises

Make an input-output table for the function. Use 0, 1, 2, 3, 4, and 5 as values for x.

1. $y = 4x + 8$ **2.** $y = 29 - 5x$ **3.** $y = 3(12 - x)$

In Exercises 4–6, use the algebraic model from Example 2.

4. Make a table of input h and output C for $h = 1$, 1.5, 2, 2.5, and 3.

5. Draw a line graph that represents the function.

6. What is the minimum amount the electrician will charge? What is the maximum amount?

7. SNOWBOARDING While you are on vacation, you want to rent snowboard equipment. It costs $65 a day to rent the equipment.

   a. Write an equation where R is the total rental cost and d is the number of days.

   b. Make an input-output table to find the cost of renting the equipment for 1, 2, 3, and 4 days.

   c. Draw a graph that represents the function.

8. PICTURE FRAMES The perimeter P for rectangular picture frames with side lengths $4w$ and $5w$ is given by the function $P = 8w + 10w$. Make an input-output table that shows the perimeter when $w = 1$, 2, 3, 4, and 5. Then determine the range of the function from the values in the table.

Evaluate the variable expression when *x* = 5 and *y* = 2.

1. $3y + 4x$

2. $2x^2 - 6y$

3. $\dfrac{18}{y} + 3x$

4. $(27 - x) \div y$

5. $7y^2$

6. $(7y)^2$

7. $(x + y)^2$

8. $x^2 + y^2$

Evaluate the expression.

9. $(16 - 4) \cdot 3^2$

10. $6^2 + 8 \cdot 5$

11. $(16 + 8) \div (4 + 2)$

Check to see if *b* = 4 *is* or *is not* a solution of the equation or inequality.

12. $b + 11 = 15$

13. $\dfrac{36}{b} = 8$

14. $17 - b = 13$

15. $5b > 20$

16. $15 + b < 24$

17. $64 \div b \le 18$

Write the sentence as an equation or an inequality. Let *x* represent the number.

18. The quotient of 32 and a number is 8.

19. The sum of a number and 6 is less than 11.

20. The difference of 42 and a number is 17.

21. The product of 7 and a number is greater than or equal to 54.

In Exercises 22–26, use the following information.
The school store sold sweatshirts at a price of $60 each. The store's sales of sweatshirts totaled $900. How many sweatshirts did the store sell?

22. Write a verbal model.

23. Assign labels to the verbal model. Use *x* to represent the unknown value.

24. Use the labels to translate the verbal model into an equation.

25. Solve your equation.

26. Check that your answer is reasonable.

For Exercises 27 and 28, use the table showing the lengths of the longest bridges in the United States.

27. Draw a bar graph of the data.

28. Which two bridges are closest in length?

29. Make an input-output table for $y = 3x + 4$ where $x = 0, 1, 2,$ and 3. Then determine the range of the function for the input values in the table.

Longest Bridges in the United States	
Verrazano-Narrows	4260 ft
Golden Gate	4200 ft
Mackinac Straits	3800 ft
George Washington	3500 ft

2.1 The Real Number Line

Goal
Graph, compare, and order real numbers.

Key Words
- real number
- real number line
- positive number
- negative number
- integer
- whole number
- graph of a number

Positive numbers are numbers that are greater than zero. **Negative numbers** are numbers that are less than zero. Zero is neither positive nor negative. You can **graph** positive and negative numbers on a **real number line**.

EXAMPLE 1

Write the numbers $-\frac{5}{2}$, 1, -3, 0, and 0.5 in increasing order.

Graph the numbers on the number line. $-\frac{5}{2} = -5 \div 2 = -2.5$

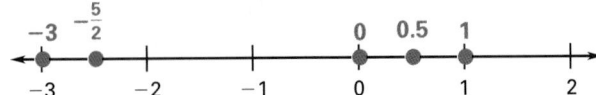

On a number line, numbers to the left are *less than* numbers to the right. Numbers to the right are *greater than* numbers to the left.

ANSWER ▶ From the graph, you can see that the order is -3, $-\frac{5}{2}$, 0, 0.5, 1.

Student Help

▶ **STUDY TIP**
The scale marks on the real number line in Example 1 are equally spaced and represent the set of **integers**: . . . -3, -2, -1, 0, 1, 2, 3, ...

EXAMPLE 2

A weather research station recorded the temperature each day at noon for a week: $-17°C$, $-21°C$, $-22°C$, $-9°C$, $1°C$, $-3°C$, $-12°C$. Which noon temperature was the coldest?

First graph the temperatures on a number line.

ANSWER ▶ The coldest temperature was $-22°C$.

2.1 Exercises

Use a number line to write the numbers in increasing order.

1. $-6, -2, 5$

2. $0, -4, 4$

3. $3, -4, -9, 2, -3$

4. $-2, -3, -\frac{3}{4}$

5. $-10, 3, \frac{6}{4}, -0.25$

6. $7, -3, \frac{1}{2}$

7. $-1.2, -4.3, 6, 8, -1.4$

8. $-3, \frac{3}{4}, 4, -\frac{3}{2}, -2$

Complete the statement using < or >. Use a number line.

9. -5 ? -7

10. 0 ? -7

11. 8.7 ? -8.9

12. $\frac{1}{4}$? $\frac{1}{2}$

13. **TEMPERATURE** A weather research station in the Arctic recorded the temperature each day at noon for a week: $10°F$, $-6°F$, $17°F$, $20°F$, $-15°F$, $3°F$, $-2°F$. Which noon temperature was the coldest? the warmest?

2.2 Absolute Value

Goal
Find the opposite and the absolute value of a number.

Key Words
- opposite
- absolute value
- counterexample

THE ABSOLUTE VALUE OF A NUMBER

The **absolute value** of a number is its distance from zero on a number line. The symbol $|a|$ represents the absolute value of a.

- If a is a positive number, then $|a| = a$. **Example:** $|2.5| = 2.5$
- If a is zero, then $|a| = 0$. **Example:** $|0| = 0$
- If a is a negative number, then $|a| = -a$. **Example:** $|-2.1| = -(-2.1) = 2.1$

EXAMPLE 1

Evaluate the expression.

a. $|6| = 6$ **b.** $|-3.4| = -(-3.4) = 3.4$ **c.** $-|-9| = -(9) = -9$

EXAMPLE 2

Use mental math to solve the equation.

a. $|x| = 9$

Ask, "What numbers are 9 units from 0?" Both 9 and -9 are 9 units from 0, so there are two solutions: 9 and -9.

b. $|x| = -8$

The absolute value of a number is never negative because a distance is never negative. There is no solution.

2.2 Exercises

Student Help

▶ STUDY TIP
Two numbers that are the same distance from 0 on a number line but on opposite sides of 0, like -5 and 5, are **opposites**.

Find the opposite of the number.

1. 2 **2.** -4 **3.** -3.5 **4.** $\dfrac{1}{3}$

Evaluate the expression.

5. $|-16|$ **6.** $|5|$ **7.** $-|-4.9|$ **8.** $|-3.5|$

9. $|0|$ **10.** $-\left|-\dfrac{5}{8}\right|$ **11.** $-|12.3|$ **12.** $-\left|\dfrac{2}{9}\right|$

Use mental math to solve the equation. If there is no solution, write *no solution*.

13. $|x| = 12$ **14.** $|x| = -5$ **15.** $|x| = 8.8$ **16.** $|x| = \dfrac{3}{4}$

17. Determine whether the statement is *always*, *sometimes*, or *never* true. Explain.

The absolute value of a number is positive.

2.3 Adding Real Numbers

Goal
Add real numbers using a number line or the rules of addition.

Key Words
- closure property
- commutative property
- associative property
- identity property
- inverse property

You can use rules and properties of addition to add real numbers.

RULES OF ADDITION

To add two numbers with the *same sign*:

STEP ❶ *Add* their absolute values.
STEP ❷ *Attach* the common sign.

To add two numbers with *opposite signs*:

STEP ❶ *Subtract* the smaller absolute value from the larger one.
STEP ❷ *Attach* the sign of the number with the larger absolute value.

EXAMPLE 1

a. Find the sum $-8 + (-12)$.

-8 and -12 have the same sign.
$|-8| + |-12| = 8 + 12 = 20$
$-8 + (-12) = -20$

b. Find the sum $7 + (-13)$.

7 and -13 have opposite signs.
$|-13| - |7| = 13 - 7 = 6$
$7 + (-13) = -6$

Student Help

▶ VOCABULARY TIP
See page 799 and the Glossary for statements of properties such as those mentioned in Example 2.

EXAMPLE 2

Use properties of addition to find the sum.

$$5.5 + (-8) + (-5.5) = (-8) + 5.5 + (-5.5) \quad \text{Commutative property}$$
$$= -8 + [5.5 + (-5.5)] \quad \text{Associative property}$$
$$= -8 + 0 \quad \text{Inverse property}$$
$$= -8 \quad \text{Identity property}$$

2.3 Exercises

Match the property with the statement that illustrates it.

1. Inverse property

2. Associative property

3. Identity property

4. Commutative property

A. $4 + (-3) = -3 + 4$

B. $6 + (-6) = 0$

C. $-16 + 0 = -16$

D. $(-6 + 7) + 3 = -6 + (7 + 3)$

Find the sum.

5. $8 + (-5)$

6. $0 + (-5)$

7. $-4 + 3$

8. $13 + (-9)$

9. $-7 + 12$

10. $-11 + (-23)$

11. $48 + (-59)$

12. $-16 + (-8)$

13. $5 + (-11)$

Find the sum. Use the properties of addition.

14. $-8 + 5 + (-2)$

15. $6 + (-16) + 5$

16. $6 + 9 + (-6)$

2.4 Subtracting Real Numbers

Goal

Subtract real numbers using the subtraction rule.

Key Words

• term

SUBTRACTION RULE

Adding the opposite of a number is equivalent to subtracting the number.

To subtract b from a, add the opposite of b to a.

$$a - b = a + (-b) \qquad \textbf{\textit{Example:}} \; 4 - 6 = 4 + (-6) = -2$$

The result is the difference of a and b.

EXAMPLE 1

a. $11 - 13 = 11 + (-13)$ Add the opposite of 13.

         $= -2$ Use rules of addition.

b. $12 - 9 = 12 + (-9)$ Add the opposite of 9.

        $= 3$ Use rules of addition.

c. $-5 - (-8) = -5 + 8$ Add the opposite of -8.

         $= 3$ Use rules of addition.

Student Help

▶ **READING ALGEBRA**
In Example 2, the **terms** of the expression $4 + 8 + (-3.5)$ are the parts being added: 4, 8, and -3.5.

EXAMPLE 2

Evaluate the expression $4 - (-8) - 3.5$.

$$4 - (-8) - 3.5 = 4 + 8 + (-3.5) \qquad \text{Add the opposites of } -8 \text{ and } 3.5.$$

$$= 12 + (-3.5) \qquad \text{Add 4 and 8.}$$

$$= 8.5 \qquad \text{Add 12 and } -3.5.$$

2.4 Exercises

Evaluate the expression.

1. $-5 - 2$ **2.** $-5 - 8$ **3.** $3 - 12$

4. $0 - (-9)$ **5.** $-7 - 11.6$ **6.** $4 - (-11) - 8$

7. $-9 - 11 - (-6.5)$ **8.** $5 - \frac{1}{4} - 8$ **9.** $7 - (-1.5) - 2.3$

10. Evaluate the function $y = -x - 5$ when $x = -2, -1, 0, 1,$ and 2. Organize your results in an input-output table.

11. STOCK MARKET The daily closing prices for a company's stock are given in the table. Find the change in the closing price since the previous day.

Date	Jan. 12	Jan. 13	Jan. 14	Jan. 15	Jan. 16
Closing Price	25.15	24.19	26.33	25.18	23.22
Change	——	?	?	?	?

2.5 Multiplying Real Numbers

Goal

Multiply real numbers using the rule for the sign of a product.

Key Words

- closure property
- commutative property
- associative property
- identity property
- property of zero
- property of negative one

You can use rules and properties of multiplication to multiply real numbers.

> **RULES FOR THE SIGN OF A PRODUCT OF NONZERO NUMBERS**
>
> - A product is negative if it has an *odd* number of negative factors.
>   **Example:** $(-4)^3 = -64$ Three negative factors, so product is negative.
> - A product is positive if it has an *even* number of negative factors.
>   **Example:** $-2\left(-\dfrac{1}{2}\right)\left(\dfrac{1}{3}\right) = \dfrac{1}{3}$ Two negative factors, so product is positive.

EXAMPLE 1

Simplify the expression.

a. $-5(8x) = -40x$ One minus sign, so product has one minus sign.

b. $-4(-x)^3 = (-4)(-x)(-x)(-x)$ Write the power as a product.

$= 4x^3$ Four minus signs, so product has no minus sign.

EXAMPLE 2

Use properties of multiplication to find the product.

$(-1)(5)(1) = (-5)(1)$ Property of negative one

$= -5$ Identity property

2.5 Exercises

Student Help

▶ VOCABULARY TIP
See page 799 for statements of properties, such as the multiplication property of zero.

Name the property shown by the statement.

1. $0 \cdot 18 = 0$ **2.** $-1 \cdot 4 = -4$ **3.** $1 \cdot (-4) = -4$

4. $7 \cdot (-24) = -24 \cdot 7$ **5.** $-8(6 \cdot 3) = (-8 \cdot 6)3$

Simplify the expression.

6. $8(-4)$ **7.** $-5(5)$ **8.** $-9(-9)$

9. $2(-3)\left(\dfrac{1}{3}\right)$ **10.** $(-2)^3$ **11.** $-7(-9)(d)$

12. $8(-d)(-d)(-d)$ **13.** $9(-x)^4$ **14.** $-x(-x)(x)(-x)$

Evaluate the expression for the given value of the variable.

15. $-5(-b)(-b)$ when $b = -8$ **16.** $8(-4)(x)$ when $x = -2$

2.6 The Distributive Property

Goal

Use the distributive property.

Key Words

• distributive property

To distribute means to give something to each member of a group. The **distributive property** is an important algebraic property.

THE DISTRIBUTIVE PROPERTY

• The product of a and $(b + c)$:

$a(b + c) = ab + ac$ *Example:* $8(d + 2) = 8d + 16$

$(b + c)a = ba + ca$ *Example:* $(d + 5)9 = 9d + 45$

• The product of a and $(b - c)$:

$a(b - c) = ab - ac$ *Example:* $7(d - 8) = 7d - 56$

$(b - c)a = ba - ca$ *Example:* $(d - 9)4 = 4d - 36$

Student Help

▶ **STUDY TIP**
Be careful when using the distributive property with negative factors. Forgetting to distribute the negative sign is a common error.

EXAMPLE

Use the distributive property to rewrite the expression without the parentheses.

a. $-7(y + 3) = -7(y) + (-7)(3)$ Distribute -7 to each term.

$= -7y - 21$ Multiply.

b. $(x + 6)(-8) = (x)(-8) + (6)(-8)$ Distribute -8 to each term.

$= -8x - 48$ Multiply.

c. $-(4 - 4x) = -1(4) - (-1)(4x)$ Distribute -1 to each term.

$= -4 + 4x$ Multiply.

d. $(4 - x)(-5) = (4)(-5) - (x)(-5)$ Distribute -5 to each term.

$= -20 + 5x$ Multiply.

2.6 Exercises

Use the area model shown.

1. Write two expressions for the area of the rectangle.

2. Write an algebraic statement that shows that the two expressions from Exercise 1 are equal.

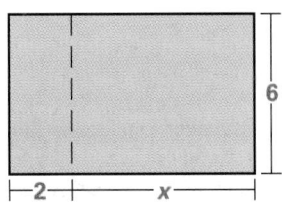

Use the distributive property to rewrite the expression without the parentheses.

3. $3(y + 6)$ **4.** $(x + 1)11$ **5.** $-4(y - 2)$

6. $(x + 5)(-2)$ **7.** $10(y - 6)$ **8.** $8(x + 4)$

9. $(a - 7)6$ **10.** $-(9 - 2y)$ **11.** $(3 + x)(-3)$

12. $(x - 8)(2)$ **13.** $(x + 5)(-2)$ **14.** $(-3 - x)(-3)$

Key Skills Review   **R25**

2.7 Combining Like Terms

Goal

Simplify an expression by combining like terms.

Key Words

- coefficient
- like terms
- simplified expression

Like terms are terms in an expression that have the same variable raised to the same power. In a term that is the product of a number and a variable, the number is called the **coefficient** of the variable.

$$-x^2 + 5x$$

-1 is the coefficient of x^2. ⟶ ⟵ 5 is the coefficient of x.

The distributive property allows you to combine like terms by adding their coefficients. An expression is **simplified** if it has no grouping symbols and if all the like terms have been combined.

EXAMPLE

Simplify the expression by combining like terms.

a. $5x + 6x + x = (5 + 6 + 1)x$ Use distributive property.

$= 12x$ Add coefficients 5, 6, and 1.

b. $3y^2 + 5y^2 - y + 6y$

$= 3y^2 + 5y^2 - 1y + 6y$ Coefficient of $-y$ is -1.

$= (3 + 5)y^2 + (-1 + 6)y$ Use distributive property.

$= 8y^2 + 5y$ Add coefficients.

c. $3(x + 6) - 4(6 - x)$

$= 3(x + 6) + (-4)(6 - x)$ Use subtraction rule to simplify.

$= 3(x) + 3(6) + (-4)(6) - (-4)(x)$ Use distributive property.

$= 3x + 18 - 24 + 4x$ Multiply.

$= 7x - 6$ Combine like terms.

2.7 Exercises

Simplify the expression. If not possible, write *already simplified*.

1. $6x + 2x$ **2.** $2d - 8d$ **3.** $-5h - 6 + 5h$

4. $15 - 11f + f + 15$ **5.** $3b^2 + b + 8$ **6.** $12h - 4h + 12h^2$

7. $15d + 5(d + 6)$ **8.** $24x - 2(x - 3)$ **9.** $-3(3f + 6) - f$

10. $8(5b + 4) + 12$ **11.** $9(x - 8) + 5(x + 5)$ **12.** $3(s - 3) - 7(1 - s)$

13. TRANSPORTATION It takes you 50 minutes to get to school. You spend t minutes riding the school bus at an average speed of 0.3 mile per minute. The rest of the time is spent walking at 0.05 mile per minute. Which function correctly represents the total distance you travel?

    A. $d = 0.3(50 - t) + 0.05t$ **B.** $d = 0.3t + 0.05(50 - t)$

14. Simplify the correct function from Exercise 13. If you ride the bus for 30 minutes, how far away is your school?

2.8 Dividing Real Numbers

Goal

Divide real numbers and use division to simplify algebraic expressions.

Key Words

- reciprocal

Two numbers whose product is 1 are called **reciprocals**.

DIVISION RULE

To divide a number a by a nonzero number b, multiply a by the reciprocal of b. The result is the quotient of a and b.

$$a \div b = a \cdot \frac{1}{b} \qquad \textbf{\textit{Example:}} \ -2 \div 5 = -2 \cdot \frac{1}{5} = -\frac{2}{5}$$

EXAMPLE

Simplify the expression.

a. $12 \div (-6) = 12 \cdot \left(-\frac{1}{6}\right) = -2$

The quotient of two numbers with opposite signs is negative.

b. $-8 \div \left(-1\frac{1}{3}\right) = -8 \div \left(-\frac{4}{3}\right) = -8 \cdot \left(-\frac{3}{4}\right) = 6$

The quotient of two numbers with the same sign is positive.

c. $\dfrac{24x - 6}{2} = (24x - 6) \div 2$ Rewrite fraction as a division.

$\qquad = (24x - 6) \cdot \dfrac{1}{2}$ Multiply by reciprocal.

$\qquad = 24x \cdot \dfrac{1}{2} - 6 \cdot \dfrac{1}{2}$ Use distributive property.

$\qquad = 12x - 3$ Multiply.

2.8 Exercises

Find the reciprocal of the number.

1. 24 **2.** -8 **3.** $-\frac{1}{2}$ **4.** $2\frac{1}{3}$

Simplify the expression.

5. $16 \div (-2)$ **6.** $-36 \div (-9)$ **7.** $-36 \div 9$

8. $-\frac{1}{2} \div 5$ **9.** $2 \div \frac{-3}{4}$ **10.** $-10 \div \left(-2\frac{1}{2}\right)$

11. $-56 \div \frac{-7}{8}$ **12.** $-\frac{1}{2} \div \frac{5}{8}$ **13.** $45 \div \left(-1\frac{4}{5}\right)$

14. $\dfrac{15x - 5}{5}$ **15.** $\dfrac{-36 - c}{-4}$ **16.** $\dfrac{48y - 120}{12}$

17. Evaluate the expression $\dfrac{-w}{2z + 1}$ when $w = -5$ and $z = \frac{1}{3}$.

18. Is the statement *always*, *sometimes*, or *never* true? Explain. For every number a, there is a unique number $\frac{1}{a}$ such that $a \cdot \frac{1}{a} = 1$ and $\frac{1}{a} \cdot a = 1$.

Student Help

▶ **STUDY TIP**

Remember that quotient = dividend ÷ divisor. You can check your solution by showing quotient • divisor = dividend.

Use a number line to write the numbers in increasing order.

1. $4, -3, 0, -6, 2$

2. $3.1, 2.8, -4.2, -1.4$

3. $\frac{2}{3}, -\frac{3}{4}, -\frac{4}{5}, \frac{1}{4}$

4. $3, -\frac{1}{2}, 0, \frac{4}{5}$

Evaluate the expression.

5. $|8|$

6. $|-12|$

7. $|0|$

8. $-|-18|$

Use mental math to solve the equation. If there is no solution, write *no solution*.

9. $|x| = 9$

10. $|x| = 0$

11. $|x| = -7$

12. $-|x| = -5$

Evaluate the expression.

13. $9 + (-15)$

14. $9 + 11 + (-9)$

15. $7 + (-12) + 18$

16. $-14 + 25$

17. $-7 - 21$

18. $0 - (-13)$

19. $21 - (-9) - 15$

20. $-11 - 19 - 14$

Simplify the expression.

21. $6(-9)$

22. $(-12)(-4)$

23. $5(-c)(-c)(-c)$

24. $(-3)(-m)^6$

25. $4(-3)(x)(-x)$

26. $6(y + 7)$

27. $8(d - 5)$

28. $-3(x - 7)$

Simplify the expression by combining like terms.

29. $5d - 3 + 6d$

30. $7x + 4 - 3x - 11$

31. $8x^2 - 11 + 3x^2 + 7$

32. $14 + 5m^3 - 11m^3 + 9$

33. $5(3 - 2x) + 3x$

34. $-4(4a - 3) + 2(6 + 2a)$

Find the quotient.

35. $24 \div (-4)$

36. $-81 \div (-3)$

37. $-18 \div \frac{3}{4}$

38. $-42 \div \left(-\frac{6}{7}\right)$

Simplify the expression.

39. $\frac{12 + 4x}{4}$

40. $\frac{42x - 27}{3}$

41. $\frac{81n + 18}{-9}$

42. $\frac{-36d + 54}{-6}$

3.1 Solving Equations Using Addition and Subtraction

Goal
Solve linear equations using addition and subtraction.

Key Words
- equivalent equations
- transforming equations
- inverse operations
- properties of equality (See page 799.)
- linear equation

Linear equations are **equivalent equations** if they have the same solution(s). You can use *inverse operations* to write equivalent equations with the variable isolated on one side. **Inverse operations** are two operations that undo each other, such as addition and subtraction.

TRANSFORMING EQUATIONS

OPERATION	ORIGINAL EQUATION		EQUIVALENT EQUATION
• Add the same number to *each* side. (Add. Prop. of Equality)	$x - 2 = 7$	Add 2.	$x = 9$
• Subtract the same number from *each* side. (Sub. Prop. of Equality)	$x + 4 = 10$	Subtract 4.	$x = 6$

EXAMPLE

Solve. You may need to simplify one or both sides first.

a.
$$x - 6 = -14$$
$$x - 6 + 6 = -14 + 6$$
$$x = -8$$

b.
$$-9 = x - (-5)$$
$$-9 = x + 5$$
$$-9 - 5 = x + 5 - 5$$
$$-14 = x$$

CHECK ✓
$$x - 6 = -14$$
$$-8 - 6 \stackrel{?}{=} -14$$
$$-14 = -14 ✓$$

CHECK ✓
$$-9 = x - (-5)$$
$$-9 \stackrel{?}{=} \mathbf{-14} - (-5)$$
$$-9 \stackrel{?}{=} -14 + 5$$
$$-9 = -9 ✓$$

Student Help

▶ STUDY TIP
Always use substitution in the *original* equation to check each solution.

3.1 Exercises

Solve the equation. Check your solution in the original equation.

1. $n + 7 = -9$　　**2.** $m + 3 = 1$　　**3.** $x - 16 = 7$

4. $a - (-12) = 20$　　**5.** $6 = y - 21$　　**6.** $-44 = t - 10$

7. $q - 9 = 0$　　**8.** $14 + x = 4$　　**9.** $18 = c + 12$

10. $\frac{1}{4} + x = \frac{5}{4}$　　**11.** $\frac{7}{8} = \frac{2}{8} + y$　　**12.** $s + \frac{3}{10} = \frac{1}{10}$

13. $5 - 1 = x + 15$　　**14.** $9 + (-4) = s$　　**15.** $11 = 5 - 3 + y$

16. SAVING MONEY You want to purchase a CD for $16 but you have only $12. Write and solve an equation to find out how much money you need to save to purchase the CD.

Solving Equations Using Multiplication and Division

Goal

Solve linear equations using multiplication and division.

Key Words

- inverse operations
- transforming equations
- reciprocal
- properties of equality
  (See page 799.)

Multiplication and division are *inverse operations* that can help you to isolate the variable on one side of an equation. Multiplication and division undo each other.

TRANSFORMING EQUATIONS

OPERATION	ORIGINAL EQUATION		EQUIVALENT EQUATION
• Multiply *each* side of the equation by the same nonzero number. (Mult. Prop. of Equality)	$\frac{x}{3} = 2$	Multiply each side by 3.	$x = 6$
• Divide *each* side of the equation by the same nonzero number. (Div. Prop. of Equality)	$5x = 15$	Divide each side by 5.	$x = 3$

Student Help

▶ STUDY TIP
To solve an equation with a fractional coefficient, multiply each side of the equation by the **reciprocal** of the fraction.

EXAMPLE

Solve the equation. Use inverse operations to isolate the variable *x*.

a. $-3x = 1$

$$\frac{-3x}{-3} = \frac{1}{-3}$$

$$x = -\frac{1}{3}$$

b. $\frac{x}{6} = -30$

$$6\left(\frac{x}{6}\right) = 6(-30)$$

$$x = -180$$

c. $12 = \frac{3}{4}x$

$$\frac{4}{3}(12) = \frac{4}{3}\left(\frac{3}{4}x\right)$$

$$16 = x$$

3.2 Exercises

Solve the equation. Check your solution in the original equation.

1. $4x = -16$
2. $81 = 9y$
3. $5w = 35$
4. $8p = -56$

5. $6d = 30$
6. $-2a = 3$
7. $7x = 70$
8. $60 = 15y$

9. $\frac{t}{7} = -3$
10. $7 = \frac{t}{-3}$
11. $\frac{y}{8} = 12$
12. $\frac{n}{12} = 24$

13. $\frac{2}{9}x = 0$
14. $\frac{3}{4}d = 6$
15. $-8 = \frac{1}{2}n$
16. $15 = \frac{3}{5}z$

17. TICKET PRICE You buy six tickets for a concert that you and your friends want to attend. The total charge for all of the tickets is $72.
Use the verbal model to write and solve an equation to find the price of one concert ticket.

$$\boxed{\text{Number of tickets bought}} \cdot \boxed{\text{Cost per ticket}} = \boxed{\text{Total paid}}$$

3.3 Solving Multi-Step Equations

Goal

Use two or more steps to solve a linear equation.

Key Words

• like terms
• distributive property

Solving a linear equation may require more than one step. Use the steps you already know for transforming an equation. Simplify one or both sides of the equation first, if needed. Then use inverse operations to isolate the variable.

EXAMPLE

Solve the equation.

a.

$5x + 3 = 38$	Original equation
$5x + 3 - 3 = 38 - 3$	Subtract 3 from each side to undo addition.
$5x = 35$	Simplify both sides.
$\dfrac{5x}{5} = \dfrac{35}{5}$	Divide each side by 5 to undo the multiplication.
$x = 7$	Simplify.

b.

$13 = 2x - 5(x + 4)$	Original equation
$13 = 2x - 5x - 20$	Use distributive property.
$13 = -3x - 20$	Combine like terms to simplify.
$13 + 20 = -3x - 20 + 20$	Add 20 to each side to undo subtraction.
$33 = -3x$	Simplify.
$\dfrac{33}{-3} = \dfrac{-3x}{-3}$	Divide each side by -3 to undo the multiplication.
$-11 = x$	Simplify.

3.3 Exercises

Solve the equation. Check your solution.

1. $2x - 5 = 7$ **2.** $6y - 2 = -8$ **3.** $5 - 2z = 9$

4. $4 + 6x = 12$ **5.** $-3x + 5 = 4$ **6.** $8 - 7x = -6$

7. $\frac{1}{3}(1 + 2a) = 5$ **8.** $\frac{1}{2}(x - 40) = 12$ **9.** $\frac{3}{5}(x + 2) = 9$

10. $10s + 5 - 4s = 13$ **11.** $7 + 3a - 5 = 14$

12. $3(2 - w) = 12$ **13.** $3k + 3 - 4k + 8 = 7$

14. $y + 3(y - 1) = -11$ **15.** $-x + 2(1 + 3x) = 16$

16. **CAMERA** You want to buy a camera for $78. You have already saved $36. You plan to save $8 each week. In how many weeks will you be able to buy the camera? Choose the equation that represents this situation. Solve the equation. Explain what the answer means.

A. $78 = 8x + 36$ **B.** $8x - 78 = 36$

Student Help

▶ **STUDY TIP**
In Exercises 7–9 you can clear the equation of fractions by multiplying by the reciprocal first.

3.4 Solving Equations with Variables on Both Sides

Goal

Solve equations that have variables on both sides.

Key Words

- identity
- variable terms
- coefficient

Some equations have variables on both sides. To solve these equations, you can first collect the **variable terms** on one side of the equation.

EXAMPLE 1

Solve $-5x + 2 = -3x - 8$.

Since variables represent numbers, you can transform an equation by adding and subtracting variable terms. Look at the coefficients of the x-terms. Since the coefficient -3 is greater than -5, collect the x-terms on the right side.

$-5x + 2 = -3x - 8$	Write original equation.
$-5x + 2 + 5x = -3x - 8 + 5x$	Add $5x$ to each side.
$2 = 2x - 8$	Combine like terms.
$2 + 8 = 2x - 8 + 8$	Add 8 to each side.
$10 = 2x$	Simplify both sides.
$\dfrac{10}{2} = \dfrac{2x}{2}$	Divide each side by 2.
$5 = x$	Simplify.

ANSWER ▶ The solution is 5.

So far you have seen linear equations that have only *one* solution. Some linear equations have *no* solution. An **identity** is an equation that is true for all values of the variable, so an identity has *many* solutions.

EXAMPLE 2

Solve the equation if possible. Determine whether it has *one solution, no solution*, or is an *identity*.

a. $n - 2n + 3 = 3 - n$ **b.** $8 + 6x = 6x - 1$ **c.** $-7 + 4b = 6b - 5$

a.	
$n - 2n + 3 = 3 - n$	Write original equation.
$-n + 3 = 3 - n$	Combine like terms.
$-n + 3 + n = 3 - n + n$	Add n to each side
$3 = 3$	Combine like terms.

ANSWER ▶ The equation $3 = 3$ is always true, so all values of n are solutions. The original equation is an *identity*.

b.	
$8 + 6x = 6x - 1$	Write original equation.
$8 + 6x - 6x = 6x - 1 - 6x$	Subtract $6x$ from each side.
$8 \neq -1$	Combine like terms.

ANSWER ▶ The equation $8 = -1$ is never true no matter what the value of x. The original equation has *no solution*.

continued

EXAMPLE **2** *continued*

c. $-7 + 4b = 6b - 5$ Write original equation.

$-7 + 4b - 4b = 6b - 5 - 4b$ Subtract $4b$ from each side.

$-7 = 2b - 5$ Combine like terms.

$-7 + 5 = 2b - 5 + 5$ Add 5 to each side.

$-2 = 2b$ Simplify both sides.

$\dfrac{-2}{2} = \dfrac{2b}{2}$ Divide each side by 2.

$-1 = b$ Simplify both sides.

ANSWER ▶ The original equation has *one solution*: -1.

CHECK ✓ Check the solution in the original equation.

$-7 + 4b = 6b - 5$ Write original equation.

$-7 + 4(-1) \stackrel{?}{=} 6(-1) - 5$ Substitute -1 for each b.

$-7 + (-4) \stackrel{?}{=} -6 - 5$ Simplify both sides.

$-11 = -11$ ✓   Solution is correct.

3.4 Exercises

Solve the equation. Check your solution in the original equation.

1. $3x + 2 = x$ **2.** $2x + 16 = -6x$ **3.** $6y = 10 - 4y$

4. $4x - 2x = 15 - 3x$ **5.** $9 - 4m = -5m$ **6.** $3 - 2x = 9 - 8x$

7. $8x - 4 = 3(x - 2)$ **8.** $t + 1 = 3t - 5$ **9.** $5z + 6 = 2z + 3 - z$

Solve the equation if possible. Determine whether the equation has *one solution*, *no solution*, or is an *identity*.

10. $6m - 5 = 7m + 7 - m$ **11.** $10 - 8a = 2(5 - 4a)$

12. $3(x - 4) = 2x + 16$ **13.** $4x - 7 = x + 12 + 3x$

14. $5x - x = 3(x - 1)$ **15.** $3t + 8 = 5t + 8 - 2t$

16. **BUSINESS** A toy company spends $1800 each day on plant costs plus $4 per toy for labor and materials. The toys sell for $12 each. How many toys must the company sell in one day to equal its daily costs?

17. **TRANSPORTATION** Judy and Mary are sisters. They left school at 3:00 P.M. and bicycled home along the same bike path. Judy bicycled at a speed of 12 mi/h. Mary bicycled at 9 mi/h. Judy got home 15 minutes before Mary did. How long did it take Judy to get home?

18. **TRANSPORTATION** A truck traveling 45 mi/h and a train traveling 60 mi/h cover the same distance. The truck travels 2 hours longer than the train. How many hours did each travel?

3.5 More on Linear Equations

Goal
Solve more complicated equations that have variables on both sides.

Key Words
- inverse operations
- distributive property

You have learned several ways to transform an equation into an equivalent equation.

STEPS FOR SOLVING LINEAR EQUATIONS

1. **Simplify** each side by distributing and/or combining like terms.
2. **Collect** variable terms on the side with the greater coefficient.
3. **Use** inverse operations to isolate the variable.
4. **Check** your solution in the *original* equation.

EXAMPLE 1

Solve $n + 3(n + 2) = 2(n + 8)$.

Use the distributive property to remove parentheses.

$n + 3(n + 2) = 2(n + 8)$	Write original equation.
$n + 3n + 6 = 2n + 16$	Use distributive property.
$4n + 6 = 2n + 16$	Combine like terms.
$2n + 6 = 16$	Subtract 2n from each side.
$2n = 10$	Subtract 6 from each side.
$n = 5$	Divide each side by 2.

ANSWER The solution is 5. Check this in the original equation.

Student Help

▶ **STUDY TIP**
Simplify an equation before you decide whether to collect the variable terms on the right side or the left side.

EXAMPLE 2

A video store has two payment plans. You can become a member by paying a one-time $15 new member fee and rent each video for a fee of $2 each. As a nonmember, it will cost you $4 each to rent the first two videos. Thereafter each video rental will cost $3. Compare the costs of the two payment plans.

First write a verbal model in which the plans would be the same.

VERBAL MODEL

$$\boxed{\text{New member fee}} + \boxed{\text{Member's fee per video}} \cdot \boxed{\text{Number of rentals}} =$$

$$\boxed{\text{cost of first two videos}} + \boxed{\text{Nonmember's fee per video}} \cdot \left(\boxed{\text{Number of rentals}} - 2\right)$$

LABELS

Now assign labels.

New member fee = **15**	(dollars)	
Member's fee per video rental = **2**	(dollars)	
Cost of first two videos = **8**	(dollars)	
Nonmember's fee per video rental = **3**	(dollars)	
Number of video rentals = **n**		

continued

Student Help

▶**STUDY TIP**
In Example 2, you can use a table of values for numbers above and below 13 videos to help you decide which is the better option.

EXAMPLE 2 *continued*

ALGEBRAIC MODEL

Write and solve an algebraic model.

$15 + 2 \cdot n = 8 + 3 \cdot (n - 2)$	Write linear equation.
$15 + 2n = 8 + 3(n - 2)$	Simplify.
$15 + 2n = 8 + 3n - 6$	Use distributive property.
$15 + 2n = 3n + 2$	Simplify.
$15 = n + 2$	Subtract $2n$ from each side.
$13 = n$	Subtract 2 from each side.

ANSWER ▶ If you plan to rent a total of 13 videos, the cost would be the same as a member or a nonmember. If you plan to rent fewer than 13 videos, it would cost less as a nonmember. If you plan to rent more than 13 videos, it would cost less to become a member.

3.5 Exercises

Solve the equation.

1. $(-4 + y)10 = 2y$

2. $3(x + 3) = 2(x - 5)$

3. $9(b - 4) = 5(b - 2)$

4. $6(3 - x) = 2(x + 1)$

5. $-4(3 - n) = 11(2n - 3)$

6. $2(k + 5) = 3 - (2k + 5)$

7. $4(x - 1) = 13 - 2(x - 4)$

8. $3(2x - 3) = -2(3x + 16) - 1$

9. $-2(x - 5) - 3x = -3(3x + 1)$

10. $\frac{1}{2}(8n - 2) = 16 - 30n$

11. BUSINESS You own a small business that produces stadium cushions. Your costs are $2200 plus $6 in materials for each cushion. You sell each cushion for $10. How many cushions must be sold to cover your costs?

12. VIDEO GAMES You want to join a video game club to buy video games. The video game club has a membership fee of $50 and each video game costs $25. A video game store charges $40 for the first two video games you buy and $30 for each game after that.

a. How many video games do you have to buy for the costs of both options to be the same?

b. You are buying 5 video games. Your friend says that it is more economical to buy the video games from the video store. Is your friend correct?

13. DANCE CLUB You are considering joining one of two dance clubs. At Club 1, there is no membership fee and lessons cost $7 per session. At Club 2, there is an annual membership fee of $30, and lessons cost $5 per session. Explain how you would decide which club to join.

3.6 Solving Decimal Equations

Goal
Find exact and approximate solutions of equations that contain decimals.

Key Words
• rounding error

You may be required to round decimal answers, especially in real-world problems where the exact answer is not practical.

EXAMPLE

Solve $3.57x - 37.4 = 0.23x + 8.32$. Round to the nearest hundredth.

$3.57x - 37.4 = 0.23x + 8.32$	Write original equation.
$3.34x - 37.4 = 8.32$	Subtract $0.23x$ from each side.
$3.34x = 45.72$	Add 37.4 to each side.
$x = \dfrac{45.72}{3.34}$	Divide each side by 3.34.
$x \approx 13.68862275$	
$x \approx 13.69$	Round to nearest hundredth.

ANSWER ▶ The solution is approximately 13.69.

CHECK ✓ When you substitute a rounded answer into the original equation, the two sides of the equation may not be exactly equal, but they should be approximately equal.

$3.57x - 37.4 = 0.23x + 8.32$	Write original equation.
$3.57(\mathbf{13.69}) - 37.4 \stackrel{?}{=} 0.23(\mathbf{13.69}) + 8.32$	Substitute 13.69 for each x.
$11.4733 \approx 11.4687$ ✓	Rounded answer is reasonable.

3.6 Exercises

Solve the equation. You may want to use a calculator. Round the result to the nearest hundredth. Check the rounded solution.

1. $17x - 33 = 114$ **2.** $-3x + 51 = 104$ **3.** $-18 + 41a = 57$

4. $31 = 44 - 12m$ **5.** $25 = 14 - 10d$ **6.** $99 = 100t + 56$

7. $238 = 79x - 43$ **8.** $28 - 68c = 241$ **9.** $3(31 - 12x) = 82$

10. $15.97 - 2.36x = 18.66x - 12$ **11.** $9.2x + 5.3 = 7.4x - 8.8$

12. $38.5x + 2.4 = -31.7 + 41.8x$ **13.** $-6.41x + 5.42 = 8.21x + 3.08$

In Exercises 14 and 15, remember to write the percent in decimal form. To review this skill, see page 768.

14. NEWSPAPER ROUTE Bonnie and Marti deliver newspapers. Bonnie's monthly earnings are 15% more than Marti's. They have combined monthly earnings of $53.47. How much does Marti earn each month?

15. MUSIC CONCERT Concert organizers pay musicians a guaranteed payment of $12,000, plus 16% of all ticket sales greater than $30,000. If the organizers paid the musicians $14,166.40 for a weekend concert, how much did the organizers collect from ticket sales?

3.7 Formulas

Goal

Solve a formula for one of its variables.

Key Words

• formula

A **formula** shows the relationship between two or more variables. A table of key formulas is shown on page 798 of your textbook. You can transform a formula to describe one quantity in terms of the others.

EXAMPLE 1

Transform the distance formula $d = rt$ to find a formula for the travel time t in terms of distance and average speed.

$d = rt$	Write original formula.
$\dfrac{d}{r} = \dfrac{rt}{r}$	Divide each side by r.
$\dfrac{d}{r} = t$	Simplify.

ANSWER ▶ The formula for travel time is $t = \dfrac{d}{r}$.

EXAMPLE 2

The formula for the perimeter of a rectangle with length ℓ and width w is $P = 2\ell + 2w$.

a. Find the formula for length ℓ in terms of perimeter P and width w.

$P = 2\ell + 2w$	Write original formula.
$P - 2w = 2\ell$	Subtract $2w$ from each side.
$\dfrac{P - 2w}{2} = \ell$	Divide each side by 2.

b. Substitute into the new formula to find the length of a rectangle that has a perimeter of 28 feet and a width of 5 feet.

$$\ell = \frac{P - 2w}{2} = \frac{28 - 2(5)}{2} = 9$$

ANSWER ▶ The length of the rectangle is 9 feet.

3.7 Exercises

Solve the formula for the indicated variable.

1. $x + y = 20$; y **2.** $4m - n = 6$; n **3.** $2(t + r) = 5$; t

4. $z - a = y$; z **5.** $mx - k = y$; x **6.** $A = \ell w$; w

7. $A = \dfrac{1}{2}bh$; b **8.** $P = 2\ell + 2w$; w **9.** $C \approx 3.14d$; d

10. TEMPERATURE Solve the formula $C = \dfrac{5}{9}(F - 32)$ for F to find the Fahrenheit temperature F for a given Celsius temperature C. Use the result to find the Fahrenheit temperature equivalent to 49°C.

11. TRAVEL You travel 121.5 miles to an amusement park in 2.25 hours. Transform the formula $d = rt$ to find a formula for average speed. Use the result to find your average speed for the trip.

Ratios and Rates

Goal

Use ratios and rates to solve real-life problems.

Key Words

- ratio
- rate
- unit rate
- unit analysis

The **ratio of *a* to *b*** is $\frac{a}{b}$. If *a* and *b* are measured in different units, then $\frac{a}{b}$ is called the **rate of *a* per *b***. Rates are often expressed as *unit rates*. A **unit rate** is a rate of one given unit, such as 60 miles per 1 gallon.

EXAMPLE 1

The baseball team won 12 out of its 18 games. Find the ratio of wins to losses in simplest form.

$$\text{Ratio} = \frac{\text{games won}}{\text{games lost}} = \frac{12 \text{ games}}{6 \text{ games}} = \frac{12}{6} = \frac{2}{1}$$

ANSWER ▶ The win-loss ratio is $\frac{2}{1}$, which is read as "two to one."

EXAMPLE 2

Your car travels 264 miles on 12 gallons of gasoline. Find the unit rate in miles per gallon.

To find the unit rate, divide the number of miles traveled by the number of gallons of gasoline used.

$$\text{Rate} = \frac{264 \text{ miles}}{12 \text{ gallons}} = 22 \text{ miles/gallon}$$

ANSWER ▶ The unit rate is 22 miles per gallon.

Writing the units when comparing each quantity of a rate is called **unit analysis**. You can multiply and divide units just like you multiply and divide numbers. When solving a rate problem, you can use unit analysis to help determine the units for rate.

EXAMPLE 3

Use unit analysis to convert the units.

  a. 5 hours to minutes

    Use the fact that 60 minutes = 1 hour, so $\frac{60 \text{ minutes}}{1 \text{ hour}}$ equals 1.

    $5 \text{ hours} = 5 \text{ hours} \cdot \frac{60 \text{ minutes}}{1 \text{ hour}} = 300 \text{ minutes}$

    ANSWER ▶ 5 hours equals 300 minutes.

  b. 48 ounces to pounds

    Use the fact that 1 pound = 16 ounces, so $\frac{1 \text{ pound}}{16 \text{ ounces}}$ equals 1.

    $48 \text{ ounces} = 48 \text{ ounces} \cdot \frac{1 \text{ pound}}{16 \text{ ounces}} = 3 \text{ pounds}$

    ANSWER ▶ 48 ounces equals 3 pounds.

Student Help

▶ **WRITING ALGEBRA**
You can express a ratio as a fraction in simplest form, such as $\frac{5}{8}$. You can also write this ratio as 5 to 8 or 5 : 8.

EXAMPLE 4

Average mileage is a unit rate that compares miles traveled to amount of gasoline used. Estimate the number of miles you can drive a compact car with an average mileage of 23.6 miles per gallon on a full 16 gallon tank. Round your answer to the nearest mile.

Multiply the rate by 16 gallons to estimate the distance you can drive.

$$\text{distance} = \left(23.6\ \frac{\text{mi}}{\text{gal}}\right)(16\ \text{gal}) \qquad \text{Substitute rate and gallons.}$$

$$= (23.6\ \text{mi})(16) \qquad \text{Use unit analysis.}$$

$$= 377.6\ \text{mi} \qquad \text{Multiply.}$$

ANSWER ▶ You can drive about 378 miles.

3.8 Exercises

Write the ratio in simplest form.

1. $\dfrac{25}{45}$ **2.** $\dfrac{15}{60}$ **3.** $\dfrac{21}{63}$ **4.** 8 to 24

5. 2 to 10 **6.** 36 to 48 **7.** 60 : 24 **8.** 16 : 12

Find the unit rate.

9. Earn $20 for working 5 hours **10.** 42 gallons in 7 minutes

11. Descend 144 feet in 3 seconds **12.** $12 for 60 pencils

13. $4 for 16 juice boxes **14.** 245 miles in 35 hours

Student Help

▶**STUDY TIP**
For help with converting units, see the Table of Measures on page 802.

Convert the units. Round the result to the nearest tenth.

15. 175 days to weeks **16.** 8 years to months

17. 3488 minutes to hours **18.** 108 ounces to pounds

19. 480 yards to feet **20.** 3000 meters to kilometers

21. 17 miles to yards **22.** 988 inches to yards

CARS In Exercises 23 and 24, use the following information.
A subcompact car travels 190 miles and uses about 7.1 gallons of gasoline. A compact car travels 150 miles and uses about 6.3 gallons of gasoline.

23. For each car, find the average mileage for a gallon of gasoline. Round your results in miles per gallon to the nearest tenth. Which car has the better fuel economy?

24. Use the results from Exercise 23 to estimate the number of miles you can drive each car on 12 gallons of gasoline. Round your answers to the nearest mile.

3.9 Percents

Goal
Solve percent problems.

Key Words
- percent
- base number

A **percent** is a ratio that compares a number to 100. In a percent problem, the **base number** is the number that is being compared to.

PERCENT EQUATION

VERBAL MODEL	Number being compared to base = Percent · Base number

| ALGEBRAIC MODEL | $a = \dfrac{p}{100} \cdot b$ |

EXAMPLE

Solve the percent problem for the missing number.

a. What number is 10% of 60?

Write labels.
Number compared to base = a

Percent = $p\% = 10\% = \textbf{0.10}$

Base number = $b = \textbf{60}$

Solve for a.

$a = \dfrac{p}{100} \cdot b$

$a = (0.10)(60)$

$a = 6$

ANSWER ▶ 10% of 60 is 6.

b. 24 is what percent of 32?

Write labels.
Number compared to base = $a = \textbf{24}$

Percent = $p\% = \dfrac{p}{100}$

Base number = $b = \textbf{32}$

Solve for p.

$a = \dfrac{p}{100} \cdot b$

$24 = \dfrac{p}{100}(32)$

$\dfrac{24}{32} = \dfrac{p}{100}$

$0.75 = \dfrac{p}{100}$

$75 = p$

ANSWER ▶ 24 is 75% of 32.

Student Help

▶ **STUDY TIP**
You can write a percent as a fraction, as a decimal, or as number followed by a percent symbol %. For example, you can write thirty percent as $\dfrac{30}{100}$, 0.30, or 30%.

3.9 Exercises

1. What number is 25% of 80?

2. 1% of what number is 7?

3. 5 is what percent of 10?

4. 80% of 49 is what number?

5. 120% of what number is 60?

6. What percent of 40 is 29?

7. 15% of 60 is what number?

8. 4 is what percent of 20?

9. What percent of 5 is 3?

10. 66 is 120% of what number?

11. What number is 40% of 30?

12. 25% of what number is 11?

13. **DISCOUNT** When an item is on sale, the difference between the regular price and the sale price is the *discount*. A \$32 watch is on sale at 30% off. Find the amount of the discount. Then find the sale price of the watch with the discount.

Solve the equation. If necessary, round the result to the nearest hundredth.

1. $x + 21 = 36$ **2.** $n - 14 = 2$ **3.** $a - 22 = -41$ **4.** $17 + b = -12$

5. $5c = 135$ **6.** $8d = -112$ **7.** $\frac{x}{12} = 7$ **8.** $\frac{3}{4}a = 42$

9. $2y - 5 = 17$ **10.** $4z + 13 = 37$ **11.** $10a - 7 = 63$ **12.** $3m + 30 = 51$

13. $2a - (3a + 2) = -7$ **14.** $5(x + 2) - 10 = 5$ **15.** $4(y - 1) - 2y = 6$

16. $2c + 16 = c + 2$ **17.** $-6b + 5 = -7b$ **18.** $3(n - 4) = 2n + 5$

19. $3(y - 2) + y = 2(y + 1)$ **20.** $5(x + 2) = x + 6(x - 3)$ **21.** $3(m + 2) = 3(m - 2) + 3m$

22. $0.12n = 1.9 - 0.10n$ **23.** $0.8 + 0.24z = 0.3z$ **24.** $0.03d = 0.15(4 - d)$

Solve the equation if possible. Determine whether the equation has *one solution*, *no solution*, or is an *identity*.

25. $7(c - 5) = 2(c + 5)$ **26.** $2(m - 5) = 3m + 4 - m$

27. $2(3c + 9) = 3(2c + 6)$ **28.** $4(t + 2) = 5t + 3$

29. $2(8y + 6) = 2(9 + 6y)$ **30.** $5(2x + 3) = 10(x + 1)$

Solve the formula for the indicated variable.

31. $C = 2\pi r$; r **32.** $P = a + b + c$; b **33.** $F = ma$; m

34. $I = Prt$; P **35.** $V = \pi r^2 h$; h **36.** $A = \frac{1}{2}bh$; h

Write the ratio in simplest form.

37. $\frac{18}{34}$ **38.** $\frac{69}{30}$ **39.** 27 to 33   **40.** 90 to 36

Find the unit rate.

41. 450 miles in 9 hours   **42.** 88 feet in 2 minutes   **43.** $6 for 8 cans

Convert the units.

44. 42 weeks to days

45. 304 ounces to pounds (1 pound = 16 ounces)

46. 9 miles to yards (1 mile = 1760 yards)

Solve the percent problem.

47. What percent of 75 is 15?   **48.** 60% of what number is 90?

49. 14 is what percent of 56?   **50.** What is 20% of 500?

4.1 The Coordinate Plane

Goal

Plot points in a coordinate plane.

Key Words

- coordinate plane
- origin
- x-axis, y-axis
- ordered pair
- x-coordinate
- y-coordinate
- quadrant
- scatter plot

A **coordinate plane** is formed by two real number lines that intersect at a right angle at the **origin**. The horizontal axis is the **x-axis** and the vertical axis is the **y-axis**. Each point in a coordinate plane corresponds to an **ordered pair** of real numbers. In an ordered pair, the first number is the **x-coordinate** and the second number is the **y-coordinate**.

EXAMPLE

Plot the point in the coordinate plane. Then name the quadrant the point is in.

a. To plot the point $(-3, 1)$, start at the origin. Move **3 units** to the left and **1 unit** up. Point $(-3, 1)$ is in Quadrant II.

b. To plot the point $(3, -2)$, start at the origin. Move **3 units** to the right and **2 units** down. Point $(3, -2)$ is in Quadrant IV.

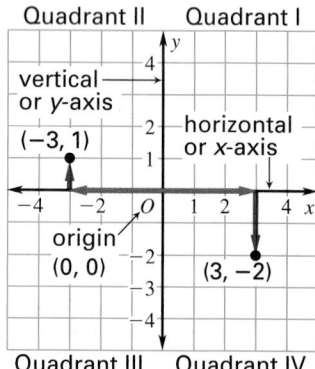

4.1 Exercises

Write the ordered pairs for the points labeled A, B, and C. Then name the axis the point is on or the quadrant the point is in.

1.

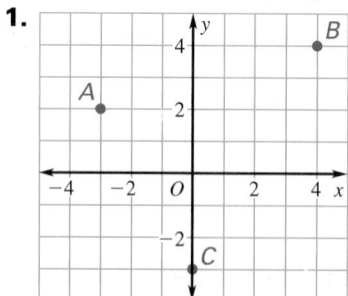

2.

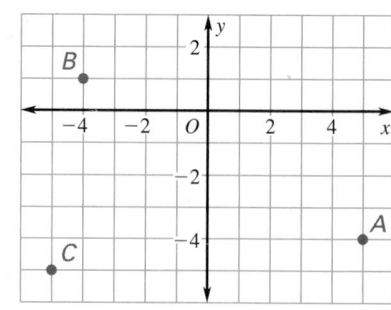

Plot and label the ordered pairs in a coordinate plane.

3. $A(2, 3)$, $B(5, 4)$, $C(-3, -2)$

4. $D(-3, -3)$, $E(-4, -2)$, $F(0, 5)$

5. $G(5, -1)$, $H(-1, 5)$, $J(-5, -1)$

6. $K(-3, -4)$, $L(5, 1)$, $M(3, 0)$

7. $N(-4, 3)$, $P(4, 1)$, $R(3, 4)$

8. $S(5, 3)$, $T(-1, -5)$, $U(-3, -1)$

9. Make a scatter plot of the data in the table. Use the horizontal axis to represent time. Is there a relationship between distance and time?

Time t (hours)	1	4.5	6	3.5
Distance d (miles)	2	8	11	14

4.2 Graphing Linear Equations

Goal
Graph a linear equation using a table of values.

Key Words
- linear equation
- solution of an equation
- function form
- graph of an equation

A **linear equation** in x and y is an equation that can be written in the form $Ax + By = C$, where A and B are not both zero. The **graph of a linear equation** is a straight line. When you are graphing an equation, first write it in **function form** with one of its variables isolated on one side of the equation.

EXAMPLE

Find solutions of $-4x + y = -3$. Then graph the equation.

❶ Rewrite the equation in function form, if necessary, to make it easier to substitute values into the equation.

$$-4x + y = -3 \qquad \text{Write original equation.}$$
$$y = 4x - 3 \qquad \text{Add 4x to each side.}$$

❷ Choose any values for x and substitute them into the equation to find the corresponding y-values. Make a table of values.

x	$y = 4x - 3$
-2	$y = 4(-2) - 3 = -11$
-1	$y = 4(-1) - 3 = -7$
0	$y = 4(0) - 3 = -3$
1	$y = 4(1) - 3 = 1$
2	$y = 4(2) - 3 = 5$

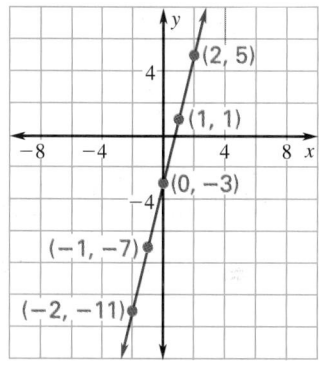

❸ Plot the points and draw a line through them, as shown above.

4.2 Exercises

Determine whether the ordered pair is a solution of the equation.

1. $4x + 3y = 1, (4, -5)$ **2.** $x + 3y = 6, (0, 2)$ **3.** $y = -2x + 5, (-2, 7)$

Use a table of values to graph the equation. Rewrite the equation in function form if necessary.

4. $y = 2x - 4$ **5.** $y = 5 - 3x$ **6.** $y = 6x - 3$

7. $y = -x + 2$ **8.** $y = 2x - 1$ **9.** $y - x = -2$

10. $4x + 2y = 6$ **11.** $-x + 2y = 8$ **12.** $4x + 3y = 24$

13. ADMISSIONS Ticket sales for the school show were $500. Tickets cost $2 for students and $5 for adults. If x represents the number of students and y represents the number of adults, then the solutions of $2x + 5y = 500$ represent the possible numbers of each kind of ticket sold. Make a table of values and graph the equation.

Key Skills Review

4.3 Graphing Horizontal and Vertical Lines

Goal

Graph horizontal and vertical lines.

Key Words

- horizontal line
- vertical line
- coordinate plane
- x-coordinate
- y-coordinate
- constant function
- domain
- range

EQUATIONS OF HORIZONTAL AND VERTICAL LINES

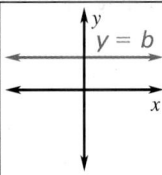

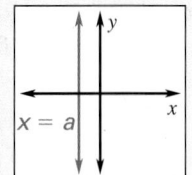

In the coordinate plane, the graph of $y = b$ is a horizontal line.

In the coordinate plane, the graph of $x = a$ is a vertical line.

EXAMPLE

Graph the equation $y = 3$.

The equation does not have x as a variable. The y-coordinate is always 3, regardless of the value of x. For instance, here are some points that are solutions of the equation:

$(-2, 3)$, $(0, 3)$, and $(3, 3)$

ANSWER ▶ The graph of the equation $y = 3$ is a horizontal line 3 units above the x-axis.

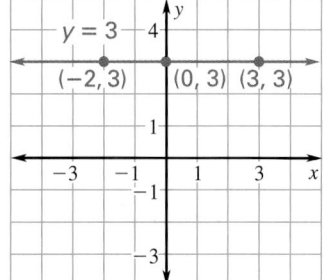

4.3 Exercises

Graph the equation.

1. $y = 2$ **2.** $x = -2$ **3.** $y = -6$ **4.** $x = 5$

5. $x = -3$ **6.** $y = \dfrac{1}{2}$ **7.** $x = \dfrac{3}{2}$ **8.** $y = -4$

Write the equation of the line in the graph.

9.

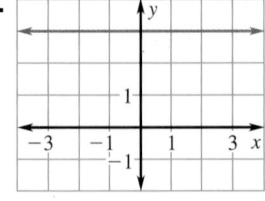

10.

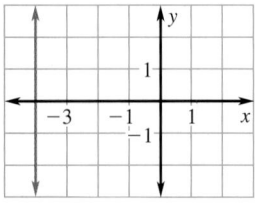

11.

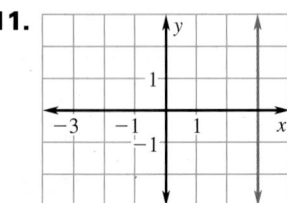

12.

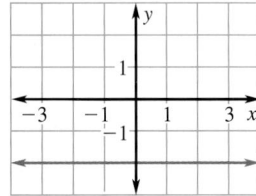

4.4 Graphing Lines Using Intercepts

Goal
Find the intercepts of the graph of a linear equation and then use them to make a quick graph of the equation.

Key Words
- x-intercept
- y-intercept
- x-axis
- y-axis

An **x-intercept** is the x-coordinate of a point where a graph crosses the x-axis. In other words, the x-intercept is the value of x when $y = 0$. A **y-intercept** is the y-coordinate of a point where a graph crosses the y-axis. In other words, the y-intercept is the value of y when $x = 0$. You can use the intercepts to make a quick graph.

EXAMPLE

Graph the equation $3x + 4y = 12$.

❶ **Find** the intercepts.

$3x + 4y = 12$	Write original equation.
$3x + 4(0) = 12$	Substitute 0 for y.
$x = 4$	The x-intercept is 4.
$3x + 4y = 12$	Write original equation.
$3(0) + 4y = 12$	Substitute 0 for x.
$y = 3$	The y-intercept is 3.

❷ **Draw** a coordinate plane that includes the points (4, 0) and (0, 3).

❸ **Plot** the points (4, 0) and (0, 3) and draw a line through them.

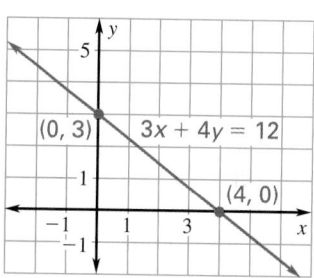

4.4 Exercises

Find the x-intercept of the graph of the equation.

1. $x - 4y = 3$ **2.** $2x + 3y = -6$

3. $3x + 2y = 9$ **4.** $-6x + 5y = 84$

5. $-5x + 4y = 40$ **6.** $3x - 2y = 15$

Find the y-intercept of the graph of the equation.

7. $3x + 5y = 15$ **8.** $y - 3x = 6$

9. $-2y + 12 = 3x$ **10.** $2x - 3y = 18$

11. $2x + 12y = -48$ **12.** $-x + 8y = 40$

Find the intercepts of the graph of the equation. Use the intercepts to help you find an appropriate scale on each axis. Graph the equation.

13. $y = 3 - x$ **14.** $y = -3 + 2x$

15. $y = -3x + 7$ **16.** $4x + 3y = 24$

17. $-9x + 2y = 36$ **18.** $5x - y = 10$

4.5 The Slope of a Line

Goal

Find the slope of a line.

Key Words

- rise
- run
- slope

The **slope** of a line is the ratio of the vertical rise to the horizontal run between any two points on the line.

THE SLOPE OF A LINE

The slope m of the line that passes through the points (x_1, y_1) and (x_2, y_2) is

$$m = \frac{\text{rise}}{\text{run}} = \frac{\text{change in } y}{\text{change in } x} = \frac{y_2 - y_1}{x_2 - x_1}.$$

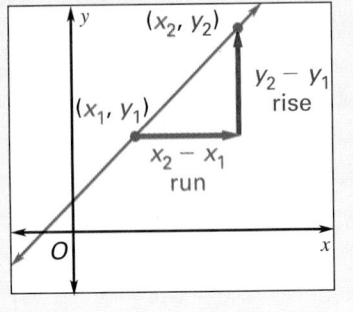

You can use the slope of a line to describe the steepness and direction of the line.

- A line with positive slope *rises* from left to right. (See above.)
- A line with negative slope *falls* from left to right. (See Example 1.)
- A line with zero slope is *horizontal*. (See part (a) of Example 2.)
- A line with undefined slope is *vertical*. (See part (b) of Example 2.)

EXAMPLE 1

Find the slope of the line that passes through the points (–1, 2) and (2, –3).

Let $(x_1, y_1) = (-1, 2)$ and $(x_2, y_2) = (2, -3)$.

$$m = \frac{y_2 - y_1}{x_2 - x_1}$$ Subtract y-values. Use the same order to subtract x-values.

$$= \frac{-3 - 2}{2 - (-1)}$$ Substitute values.

$$= \frac{-3 + (-2)}{2 + 1}$$

$$= \frac{-5}{3}$$ Simplify.

$$= -\frac{5}{3}$$ Slope is negative.

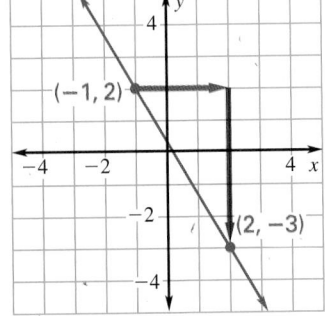

ANSWER ▶ The slope of the line is $-\frac{5}{3}$. The line falls from left to right.

When you use the formula for slope, you must subtract the coordinates in the same order in both the numerator and the denominator.

Student Help

▶ **READING ALGEBRA**
In the slope formula, x_1 is read as "x sub one" and y_1 is read as "y sub one."

EXAMPLE 2

Find the slope of the line.

a.

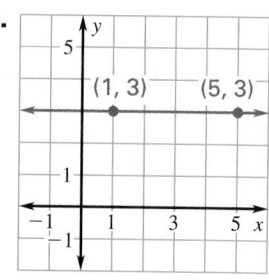

b.

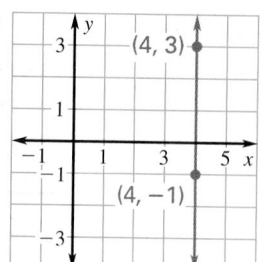

$$m = \frac{y_2 - y_1}{x_2 - x_1}$$

$$= \frac{3 - 3}{5 - 1}$$

$$= \frac{0}{4}$$

$$= 0$$

ANSWER ▶ The slope is 0.

$$m = \frac{y_2 - y_1}{x_2 - x_1}$$

$$= \frac{3 - (-1)}{4 - 4}$$

$$= \frac{3 + 1}{4 - 4}$$

$$\cancel{\frac{4}{0}}$$ Division by zero is undefined.

ANSWER ▶ The slope is undefined.

4.5 Exercises

Plot the points and draw the line that passes through them. Without finding the slope, determine whether the slope is *positive, negative, zero,* or *undefined*.

1. $(5, 4), (4, 3)$ **2.** $(2, 4), (-1, 5)$ **3.** $(5, 3), (5, -4)$

4. $(-3, 1), (2, 3)$ **5.** $(1, 1), (4, -3)$ **6.** $(-4, 2), (1, 2)$

Find the slope of the line that passes through the points.

7. $(-3, 0)$ and $(1, 4)$ **8.** $(-4, 1)$ and $(2, -1)$ **9.** $(0, 5)$ and $(6, 1)$

10. $(4, 1)$ and $(6, 1)$ **11.** $(-7, -1)$ and $(2, 5)$ **12.** $(3, 2)$ and $(3, 3)$

13. $(0, 0)$ and $(4, 5)$ **14.** $(0, 0)$ and $(-1, -3)$ **15.** $(-3, -2)$ and $(1, 6)$

16. $(-6, 1)$ and $(-6, 4)$ **17.** $(0, -10)$ and $(-4, 0)$ **18.** $(1, -2)$ and $(-2, -2)$

19. **ROAD GRADES** A road rises 15 feet vertically for every 70 feet it runs horizontally. Another road rises 12 feet vertically for every 60 feet it runs horizontally. Which road is steeper? Explain.

Direct Variation

Goal

Write and graph equations that represent direct variation.

Key Words

- direct variation
- constant of variation
- origin

When two quantities y and x have a constant ratio k, they are said to have **direct variation.** The constant k is called the **constant of variation.**

Model for Direct Variation: $y = kx$ or $\dfrac{y}{x} = k$, where $k \neq 0$.

You read the equation $y = kx$ as "y varies directly with x."

EXAMPLE

The variables x and y vary directly. Suppose $y = 150$ when $x = 6$.

a. Write an equation that relates x and y.

Because x and y vary directly, the equation is in the form of $y = kx$.

$y = kx$	Write model for direct variation.
$150 = k(6)$	Substitute 6 for x and 150 for y.
$25 = k$	Divide each side by 6.

ANSWER ▶ An equation that relates x and y is $y = 25x$.

b. Find the value of y when $x = -2$.

$y = 25x$	Write original equation.
$y = 25(-2)$	Substitute -2 for x.
$y = -50$	Simplify.

ANSWER ▶ When $x = -2$, $y = -50$.

4.6 Exercises

The variables x and y vary directly. Use the given values to write an equation that relates x and y.

1. $x = 3, y = 9$ **2.** $x = 5, y = 40$ **3.** $x = 15, y = 60$

4. $x = 2, y = -6$ **5.** $x = -2, y = -2$ **6.** $x = 2, y = 6$

7. $y = 9, x = -6$ **8.** $x = 8, y = -7$ **9.** $x = 9, y = -10$

Graph the equation.

10. $y = -4x$ **11.** $y = 2x$ **12.** $y = -x$ **13.** $y = \dfrac{2}{3}x$

Student Help

▶ STUDY TIP
The graph of $y = kx$ is a line through the origin. The slope of the graph of $y = kx$ is k.

14. **WEATHER** The time it takes you to hear thunder varies directly with your distance from the lightning. If you are 2 miles from where lightning strikes, you will hear thunder about 10 seconds after you see the lightning.

a. Write an equation for the relationship between the time t (in seconds) it takes you to hear thunder and your distance d (in miles) from the lightning.

b. Use the equation to find about how far you are from lightning if you hear thunder 7 seconds after you see lightning.

4.7 Graphing Lines Using Slope-Intercept Form

Goal

Graph a linear equation in slope-intercept form.

Key Words

- slope
- *y*-intercept
- slope-intercept form
- parallel lines

You can graph the equation of a line given its slope and *y*-intercept.

SLOPE-INTERCEPT FORM OF THE EQUATION OF A LINE

The linear equation $y = mx + b$ is written in **slope-intercept form,** where m is the slope and b is the *y*-intercept.

$$\text{slope} \searrow \quad \swarrow \text{ } y\text{-intercept}$$
$$y = mx + b$$

EXAMPLE

Graph the equation $-3x + y = -1$.

❶ Rewrite the equation in slope-intercept form.

$$-3x + y = -1$$
$$y = 3x - 1$$

❷ Find the slope, 3, and the *y*-intercept, -1.

❸ Plot the point $(0, b)$ when b is -1.

❹ Use the slope to locate a second point on the line.

$$m = \frac{3}{1} = \frac{\text{rise}}{\text{run}} \quad \rightarrow \quad \frac{\text{move 3 units up}}{\text{move one unit right}}$$

❺ Draw a line through the two points.

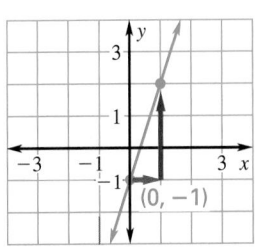

4.7 Exercises

Rewrite the equation in slope-intercept form. Find the slope and the *y*-intercept of the graph of the equation.

1. $2x = y + 7$ **2.** $y = 3$ **3.** $y - 4 = 3x$

4. $2x - 3y = 12$ **5.** $2x + y = 6$ **6.** $-7x - y = -49$

7. $18 - y - 4x = 0$ **8.** $2x + 3y - 24 = 0$ **9.** $3x + 4y = -20$

Graph the equation.

10. $y = 2x - 3$ **11.** $y = x + 2$ **12.** $y = -x + 3$

13. $y = 3x - 5$ **14.** $x + y = 0$ **15.** $-x + 2y = 6$

16. Two nonvertical lines are **parallel** if they have the same slope and different *y*-intercepts. Which lines in Exercises 10–15 are parallel? Explain.

17. SAVING Carlos has saved $225 for a used car. He plans to save $8 a week. After *x* weeks, Carlos will have saved *y* dollars where $y = 8x + 225$. Graph the model. Explain what the *y*-intercept and slope mean in this situation.

4.8 Functions and Relations

Goal

Decide whether a relation is a function and use function notation.

Key Words

• relation
• function
• vertical line test
• function notation
• linear function

IDENTIFYING FUNCTIONS

A **relation** is any set of ordered pairs. A relation is a function if for every input there is exactly one output. The relation at the far right is not a function because the input 1 has two outputs: 3 and 6.

	Functions		Not Functions	
	Input	Output	Input	Output

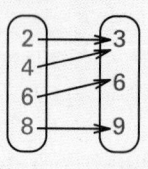 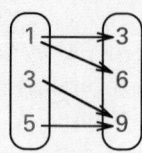

When you graph a function or relation, the input is given by the horizontal axis and the output is given by the vertical axis. A graph is a function if no vertical line intersects the graph at more than one point.

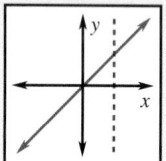 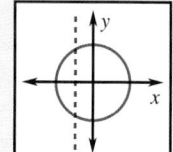

The letter f is commonly used to name a function. To write the equation for a function using **function notation,** you use $f(x)$ in place of y. The symbol $f(x)$ is read as "the value of f at x" or simply "f of x." It *does not mean f times x.*

You can evaluate a function for a given value by substituting the given value for the variable and simplifying. For example, you can find the value of $f(x) = 3x - 2$ when $x = -3$ as follows.

$$f(-3) = 3(-3) - 2 = -11, \text{ so when } x = -3, f(x) = -11.$$

4.8 Exercises

Evaluate the function when $x = -3$, $x = 0$, and $x = 3$.

1. $f(x) = 2x + 5$ **2.** $g(x) = -x - 1$ **3.** $h(x) = 5x - 1$

Student Help

▶ STUDY TIP
The collection of all input values is the domain. The collection of all output values is the range.

Determine whether the relation is a function. Explain your reasoning. If it is a function, give the domain and the range.

4.

Input	1	6	10	1
Output	−3	−2	0	3

5.

Input	−4	−1	0	2
Output	−4	−4	−4	−4

Use the vertical line test to determine whether the graph represents a function. Explain your reasoning.

6. 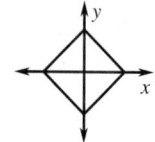   **7.** 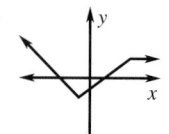   **8.**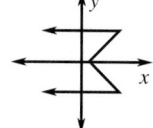

Plot and label the ordered pairs in a coordinate plane.

1. $A(3, 6)$, $B(0, -3)$, $C(-2, -5)$, $D(6, 0)$ **2.** $E(4, -2)$, $F(-3, 1)$, $G(-1, -5)$, $H(2, 6)$

Determine whether the ordered pair is a solution of the equation.

3. $y - 3x = 10$; $(-1, 7)$ **4.** $y = 5 - 2x$; $(1, 3)$ **5.** $y = 3x - 2$; $(-2, 0)$

Rewrite the equation in function form. Then use a table of values to graph the equation.

6. $2x + y = 6$ **7.** $y - 4x = -1$ **8.** $3x - y = 5$

Graph the equation.

9. $y = 6$ **10.** $x = -4$ **11.** $x = 2$ **12.** $y = -9$

Find the intercepts of the graph of the equation. Graph the equation.

13. $y = 4 - 2x$ **14.** $2y - x = 4$ **15.** $3x + 2y = 6$

Find the slope of the line that passes through the points.

16. $(2, 7)$ and $(4, 3)$ **17.** $(2, -4)$ and $(5, -6)$ **18.** $(6, 7)$ and $(4, 4)$

The variables *x* and *y* vary directly. Use the given values to write an equation that relates *x* and *y*.

19. $x = 5$, $y = 30$ **20.** $x = 8$, $y = -32$ **21.** $x = 3$, $y = 5$ **22.** $x = 12$, $y = -4$

Rewrite the equation in slope-intercept form. Find the slope and *y*-intercept. Then graph the equation.

23. $y - 5x = 2$ **24.** $4y - 4 = 3x$ **25.** $\frac{1}{5}x = y - \frac{1}{2}$

Evaluate the function for the given value of the variable.

26. $f(x) = 5 - 2x$; $x = 8$ **27.** $f(x) = 7x + 1$; $x = 4$ **28.** $f(x) = 4 + 3x$; $x = -6$

Decide whether the relation is a function. If it is a function, give the domain and range.

29.

Input	Output
-1	1
1	1
2	4
-2	4

30.

Input	Output
4	2
4	-2
9	3
9	-3

5.1 Slope-Intercept Form

Goal

Use slope-intercept form to write an equation of a line.

Key Words

- slope
- y-intercept
- slope-intercept form

A **coordinate plane** is formed by two real number lines that intersect at a right angle at the **origin**. The horizontal axis is the **x-axis** and the vertical axis is the **y-axis**. Each point in a coordinate plane corresponds to an **ordered pair** of real numbers. In an ordered pair, the first number is the **x-coordinate** and the second number is the **y-coordinate**.

EXAMPLE

Write the equation of the line shown in the graph using slope-intercept form.

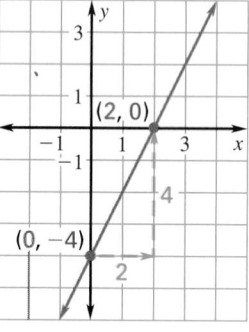

❶ **Find** the slope m of the line. Use any two points on the graph.

Let $(0, -4)$ be (x_1, y_1) and let $(2, 0)$ be (x_2, y_2).

$$m = \frac{\text{rise}}{\text{run}} = \frac{y_2 - y_1}{x_2 - x_1} = \frac{0 - (-4)}{2 - 0} = 2$$

❷ **Use** the graph to find the y-intercept. The y-intercept b is -4.

❸ **Substitute** slope 2 for m and -4 for b in the equation $y = mx + b$.

ANSWER ▶ The equation of the line is $y = 2x - 4$.

> **Student Help**
>
> ▶ STUDY TIP
> Recall that the y-intercept is the y-coordinate of the point where the line crosses the y-axis.

5.1 Exercises

Write in slope-intercept form the equation of the line described below.

1. $m = 3, b = -2$ **2.** $m = 1, b = 2$ **3.** $m = -1, b = 3$

4. $m = -2, b = 0$ **5.** $m = 2, b = -6$ **6.** $m = 3, b = -1$

7. $m = \frac{3}{2}, b = 3$ **8.** $m = -\frac{1}{4}, b = 1$ **9.** $m = -\frac{1}{3}, b = -1$

Write in slope-intercept form the equation of the line shown in the graph.

10.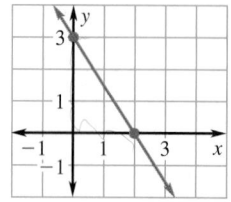

11.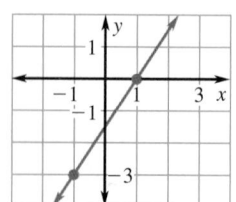

12.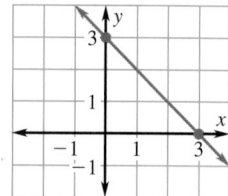

13. The graph shows square $ABCD$. Write the slope-intercept form of the equations of the lines that contain the sides of the square. Compare the equations of the parallel sides. What do you notice?

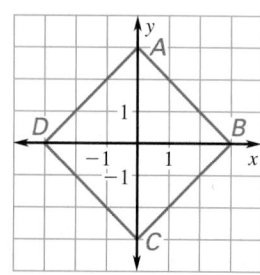

5.2 Point-Slope Form

Goal

Use point-slope form to write the equation of a line.

Key Words

- slope
- point-slope form

POINT-SLOPE FORM

The **point-slope form** of the equation of the line through (x_1, y_1) with slope m is $y - y_1 = m(x - x_1)$.

EXAMPLE

Write in point-slope form the equation of the line that passes through the point $(-4, 1)$ with slope 3. Then rewrite the equation in slope-intercept form.

❶ Write the point-slope form.

$$y - y_1 = m(x - x_1)$$

❷ Substitute 3 for m, -4 for x_1, and 1 for y_1.

$$y - 1 = 3[x - (-4)]$$

❸ Simplify the equation.

$$y - 1 = 3(x + 4)$$

❹ Distribute the 3.

$$y - 1 = 3x + 12$$

❺ Add 1 to each side.

$$y = 3x + 13$$

ANSWER ▶ An equation of the line in point-slope form is $y - 1 = 3(x + 4)$. An equation of the line in slope-intercept form is $y = 3x + 13$.

5.2 Exercises

Write in point-slope form the equation of the line. Then rewrite the equation in slope-intercept form.

1. $(0, 3)$, $m = -2$ **2.** $(-1, -1)$, $m = 1$ **3.** $(2, -2)$, $m = 0$

4. $(-7, 5)$, $m = -1$ **5.** $(-4, 0)$, $m = \dfrac{1}{2}$ **6.** $(3, -6)$, $m = 4$

7. $(-3, 6)$, $m = 2$ **8.** $(3, 2)$, $m = 1$ **9.** $(4, -2)$, $m = -1$

Write the equation of the line in point-slope form. Remember that you can calculate slope as $m = \dfrac{\text{rise}}{\text{run}}$.

10. 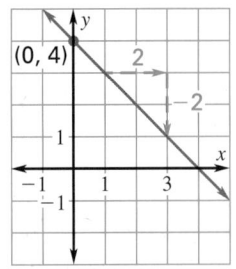   **11.** 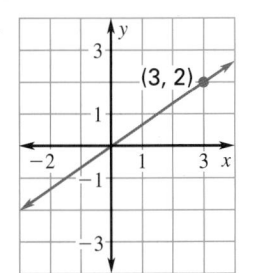   **12.**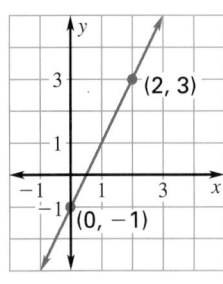

Write in slope-intercept form the equation of the line that is parallel to the given line and passes through the given point.

13. $y = 3x - 5$, $(1, 1)$ **14.** $y = \dfrac{1}{2}x + 4$, $(-6, 3)$ **15.** $y = \dfrac{3}{5}x$, $(-10, -2)$

16. $y = -6x + 4$, $(1, 3)$ **17.** $y = 2x - 7$, $(0, 8)$ **18.** $y = -x + 3$, $(5, 0)$

Writing Linear Equations Given Two Points

Goal
Write an equation of a line given two points on the line.

Key Words
- slope
- slope-intercept form
- point-slope form

You can write the equation of a line if you know two points on the line. First, use the two points to find the slope. Then if you know the *y*-intercept, use the slope-intercept form to write the equation. Otherwise, use the point-slope form to write the equation.

EXAMPLE

Write in slope-intercept form the equation of the line that passes through the points (−2, 1) and (−4, −3).

❶ **Find** the slope. Use $(x_1, y_1) = (-2, 1)$ and $(x_2, y_2) = (-4, -3)$.

$$m = \frac{y_2 - y_1}{x_2 - x_1}$$ Write formula for slope.

$$= \frac{-3 - 1}{-4 - (-2)}$$ Substitute.

$$= 2$$ Simplify.

❷ **Write** the equation of the line. You do not know the *y*-intercept, so use the point-slope form.

$$y - y_1 = m(x - x_1)$$ Write point-slope form.

$$y - 1 = 2[x - (-2)]$$ Substitute 2 for *m*, −2 for x_1, 1 for y_1.

$$y - 1 = 2x + 4$$ Simplify and use the distributive property.

$$y = 2x + 5$$ Add 1 to each side.

ANSWER ▶ The equation of the line is $y = 2x + 5$.

5.3 Exercises

Write the equation of the line in slope-intercept form.

1.
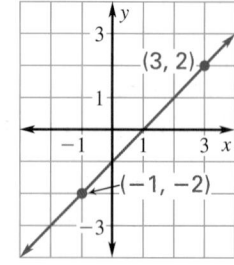

2.
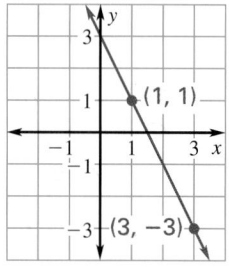

3.
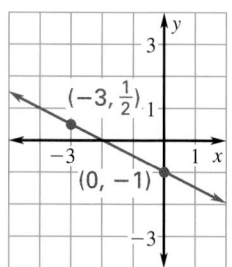

Write in slope-intercept form the equation of the line that passes through the given points.

4. (−1, 1) and (2, 8) **5.** (0, 3) and (4, −1) **6.** (2, 0) and (−4, −3)

7. (3, 1) and (−3, 5) **8.** (1, −4) and (−2, 8) **9.** (0, −4) and (3, 2)

10. (−1, 1) and (0, −1) **11.** (−2, −1) and (4, 2) **12.** (1, 1) and (4, 4)

13. (1, 2) and (2, 4) **14.** (1, 3) and (3, 3) **15.** (1, −2) and (3, −2)

5.4 Standard Form

Goal

Write an equation of a line in standard form.

Key Words

- standard form
- slope-intercept form
- point-slope form
- integer
- coefficient

Equations can be written in slope-intercept form, point-slope form, or *standard form*. For example, here are three equations that can be written for the line that contains the points $(-3, 4)$ and $(0, 10)$.

SLOPE-INTERCEPT FORM	POINT-SLOPE FORM	STANDARD FORM
$y = 2x + 10$	$y - 4 = 2(x + 3)$	$2x - y = -10$

STANDARD FORM

The **standard form** of an equation of a line is $Ax + By = C$, where A and B are both not zero.

In standard form, the variable terms are on the left side and the constant term is on the right side of the equation.

EXAMPLE 1

Write $y = \frac{3}{4}x - 2$ in standard form with integer coefficients.

❶ **Write** original equation. $\qquad y = \frac{3}{4}x - 2$

❷ **Multiply** each side by 4 to clear the equation of fractions. $\qquad 4y = 4\left(\frac{3}{4}x - 2\right)$

❸ **Use** the distributive property. $\qquad 4y = 3x - 8$

❹ **Subtract** $3x$ from each side. $\qquad -3x + 4y = -8$

ANSWER ▶ In standard form, an equation is $-3x + 4y = -8$.

Student Help

▶ **VOCABULARY TIP**
Recall that a coefficient can be thought of as "the number in front of a variable". For example, $\frac{3}{4}$ is the coefficient in the variable expression $\frac{3}{4}x$.

In standard form, the variable terms are on the left side and the constant term is on the right side of the equation.

EXAMPLE 2

Write in standard form an equation of the line passing through $(5, -8)$ with a slope of -3. Use integer coefficients.

❶ **Write** the point-slope form. $\qquad y - y_1 = m(x - x_1)$

❷ **Substitute** -3 for m, 5 for x_1, and -8 for y_1. $\qquad y - (-8) = -3(x - 5)$

❸ **Simplify** the equation. $\qquad y + 8 = -3(x - 5)$

❹ **Use** the distributive property. $\qquad y + 8 = -3x + 15$

❺ **Subtract** 8 from each side. (Slope-intercept form) $\qquad y = -3x + 7$

❻ **Add** $3x$ to each side. (Standard form) $\qquad 3x + y = 7$

ANSWER ▶ In standard form, an equation is $3x + y = 7$.

Recall that the slope of a horizontal line is zero and the slope of a vertical line is undefined.

EXAMPLE 3

Write an equation of the blue line in standard form.

a.

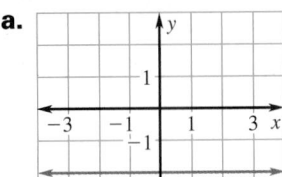

b.

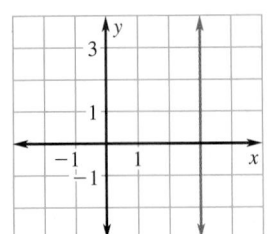

a. Each point on this horizontal line has a *y*-coordinate of −2. So, the equation of the line is $y = -2$.

b. Each point on this vertical line has an *x*-coordinate of 3. So, the equation of the line is $x = 3$.

5.4 Exercises

Write the equation in standard form with integer coefficients.

1. $y = -3x + 4$ **2.** $y = 2x - 7$ **3.** $y = -\frac{1}{3}x - 2$

4. $y = -\frac{3}{4}x + \frac{5}{4}$ **5.** $y = \frac{3}{8} - \frac{1}{8}x$ **6.** $y = \frac{2}{5}x$

Write in standard form an equation of the line that passes through the given point and has the given slope. Use integer coefficients.

7. $(-4, 3), m = -1$ **8.** $(0, 5), m = 2$ **9.** $(3, -1), m = 0$

10. $(0, 2), m = \frac{4}{5}$ **11.** $(-2, -7), m = -\frac{3}{2}$ **12.** $(5, -8), m = -3$

Write in standard form an equation of the line that passes through the two points. Use integer coefficients.

13. $(2, 4), (5, 6)$ **14.** $(-3, 3), (6, 7)$ **15.** $(-2, -1), (2, -3)$

Write an equation of the blue line in standard form.

16.

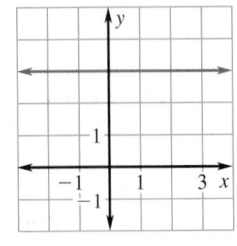

17.

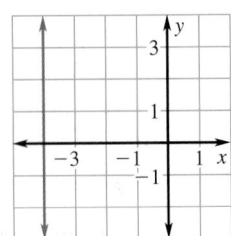

18.

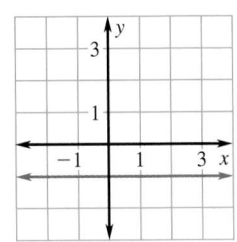

5.5 Modeling with Linear Equations

Goal
Write and use a linear equation to solve a real-life problem.

Key Words
• linear model
• rate of change

A **linear model** is a linear function that is used to model a real-life situation. A **rate of change** compares two quantities that are changing. Slope is often used to describe a real-life rate of change.

EXAMPLE 1

From 1996 to 2000, the population of Johnson County increased steadily by about 6250 people per year. In 2000, the population of Johnson County was estimated to be 120,000 people. Write a linear model for the population of Johnson County. Let $t = 0$ represent 1996.

The rate of increase is 6250 per year, so the slope is $m = 6250$. The year 2000 is represented by $t = 4$. Therefore, $(t_1, y_1) = (4, 120{,}000)$ is a point on the line.

❶ Write the point-slope form. $\qquad y - y_1 = m(t - t_1)$

❷ Substitute 6250 for m, 4 for t_1 $\qquad y - 120{,}000 = (6250)(t - 4)$
and 120,000 for y_1.

❸ Use the distributive property. $\qquad y - 120{,}000 = 6250t - 25{,}000$

❹ Add 120,000 to each side. $\qquad y = 6250t + 95{,}000$

ANSWER ▶ A linear model for the population of Johnson County is $y = 6250t + 95{,}000$, where $t = 0$ represents 1996.

CHECK ✓ Check the linear model by showing that the point $(4, 120{,}000)$ is a solution.

$y = 6250t + 95{,}000$	Write linear model.
$120{,}000 \stackrel{?}{=} 6250(4) + 95{,}000$	Substitute 120,000 for y and 4 for t.
$120{,}000 \stackrel{?}{=} 25{,}000 + 95{,}000$	Multiply.
$120{,}000 = 120{,}000$ ✓	Linear model is correct.

Once you have written a linear model, you can use the model to predict unknown values. When you do this, you are assuming that the pattern established in the past will continue in the future.

EXAMPLE 2

Use the linear model in Example 1 to estimate what the population of Johnson County will be in the year 2004.

Because $t = 0$ represents the year 1996, 2004 is represented by $t = 8$.

❶ Write the linear model. $\qquad y = 6250t + 95{,}000$

❷ Substitute 8 for t. $\qquad y = (6250)(8) + 95{,}000$

❸ Simplify. $\qquad y = 50{,}000 + 95{,}000 = 145{,}000$

ANSWER ▶ You can predict that the population of Johnson County in 2004 will be about 145,000.

EXAMPLE 3

You are buying grapes and tomatoes for a school party. The grapes cost $3 per pound. The tomatoes cost $2 per pound. You have $45 to spend. Write an equation that models the different amounts (in pounds) of grapes and tomatoes you can buy.

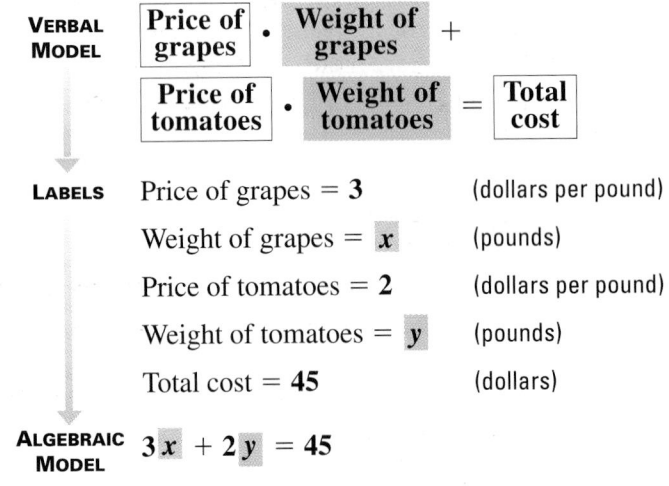

VERBAL MODEL

Price of grapes	·	Weight of grapes	+

Price of tomatoes	·	Weight of tomatoes	=	Total cost

LABELS

Price of grapes = **3**   (dollars per pound)

Weight of grapes = **x**   (pounds)

Price of tomatoes = **2**   (dollars per pound)

Weight of tomatoes = **y**   (pounds)

Total cost = **45**   (dollars)

ALGEBRAIC MODEL $3x + 2y = 45$

5.5 Exercises

SNOWBOARD RENTAL In Exercises 1–6, use the following information.
Renting a snowboard at a local ski resort costs $30 plus $10 per day. The linear model for this situation relates the total cost of renting a snowboard, y, with the number of days rented, x.

1. What number corresponds to the slope in the linear model?

2. What number corresponds to the y-intercept in the linear model?

3. Use the slope and y-intercept form to write a linear model.

4. Graph the linear model from Exercise 3.

5. Use the linear model to find the cost of renting the snowboard for 3 days.

6. If you had $90 to spend, for how many days could you rent a snowboard?

7. Copy the table. Use the model from Example 3 to complete the table that illustrates several different amounts of grapes and tomatoes you can buy.

Grapes (pounds), x	3	6	9	12	15
Tomatoes (pounds), y	?	?	?	?	?

8. You are buying hamburger and shrimp for a barbecue. The hamburger costs $4 per pound and the shrimp costs $6 per pound. You have $80 to spend. Write an equation that models the different amounts (in pounds) of hamburger and shrimp that you can buy.

5.6 Perpendicular Lines

Goal
Write equations of perpendicular lines.

Key Words
• perpendicular lines

Two lines in a plane are **perpendicular** if they intersect at a right, or 90°, angle. In a coordinate plane, two nonvertical lines are perpendicular if and only if the product of their slopes is -1, as in the graph shown.

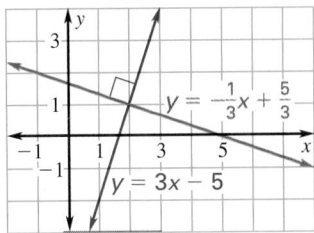

$$y = -\frac{1}{3}x + \frac{5}{3}$$
$$y = 3x - 5$$

EXAMPLE

Write in slope-intercept form the equation of the line passing through $(5, 6)$ and perpendicular to the line $y = -\frac{1}{2}x + 3$.

The slope of the given line is $-\frac{1}{2}$. To be perpendicular, the line through $(5, 6)$ should have a slope of $m = 2$.

❶ **Write** the point-slope formula. $y - y_1 = m(x - x_1)$

❷ **Substitute** 2 for m, 5 for x_1, and 6 for y_1. $y - 6 = 2(x - 5)$

❸ **Use** the distributive property. $y - 6 = 2x - 10$

❹ **Add** 6 to each side. $y = 2x - 4$

ANSWER ▶ The equation of the line perpendicular to the line $y = -\frac{1}{2}x + 3$ is $y = 2x - 4$.

5.6 Exercises

Determine whether the lines are perpendicular.

1. $y = 4x + \frac{3}{4}$, $y = -\frac{1}{4}x + 4$ **2.** $y = 3x - 4$, $y = \frac{1}{3}x + 2$

3. $x = 2$, $y = 9$ **4.** $y = -x + 5$, $y = x + 5$

Write in slope-intercept form the equation of the line passing through the given point and perpendicular to the given line.

Student Help

▶ STUDY TIP
Horizontal and vertical lines are perpendicular to each other.

5. $(0, 0)$, $y = 2x + 7$ **6.** $(4, 6)$, $y = x - 3$

7. $(-3, 2)$, $y = 6$ **8.** $(8, 1)$, $y = -\frac{4}{5}x$

9. $(1, 6)$, $y = -4x - \frac{5}{2}$ **10.** $(6, 5)$, $y = 3x - 1$

Write in slope-intercept form the equation of the line passing through the two points. Show that the line is perpendicular to the given line.

11. $(-6, -4)$ and $(0, 0)$, $y = -\frac{3}{2}x - 3$

12. $(4, -7)$ and $(7, 5)$, $y = -\frac{1}{4}x$

Write in slope-intercept form the equation of the line described below.

1. $m = 4, b = -2$

2. $m = -3, b = 8$

3. $m = \frac{3}{4}, b = -5$

4. $m = -\frac{2}{3}, b = 3$

Write in point-slope form the equation of the line that passes through the given point and has the given slope.

5. $(0, -2); m = 4$

6. $(5, 0); m = -2$

7. $(2, 5); m = 1$

8. $(-3, 6); m = 3$

Write in slope-intercept form the equation of the line that passes through the given points.

9. $(-4, 0)$ and $(0, 3)$

10. $(2, 0)$ and $(0, -4)$

11. $(2, 5)$ and $(-3, -3)$

12. $(4, 9)$ and $(-2, 4)$

13. $(-5, 7)$ and $(-3, -2)$

14. $(-4, -1)$ and $(-6, -9)$

Write the equation in standard form with integer coefficients.

15. $y = 3x + 9$

16. $y = -5x + 10$

17. $y = -4x - 12$

Write in standard form an equation of the line that passes through the given point and has the given slope. Use integer coefficients.

18. $(4, 6); m = -3$

19. $(-2, 0); m = 5$

20. $(-4, -1); m = -8$

Write in standard form an equation of the line that passes through the two points. Use integer coefficients.

21. $(6, 2)$ and $(5, 4)$

22. $(0, -8)$ and $(6, 9)$

23. $(-4, 1)$ and $(9, -5)$

In Exercises 24–26, use the following information.

Julie bought a new car in 1997. The car cost $24,000. In 2001, the value of the car was $15,740.

24. Write a linear model for the value of the car after t years. Let $t = 0$ represent 1997.

25. Graph the linear model.

26. Use the linear model to find the value of the car after 10 years.

Determine whether the lines are perpendicular.

27. $y = \frac{3}{4}x - 3; y = \frac{4}{3}x + 3$

28. $y = \frac{3}{2}x + 2; y = -\frac{2}{3}x + 5$

29. $x = 6; y = -4$

6.1 Solving Inequalities Using Addition or Subtraction

Goal

Solve and graph one-step inequalities in one variable using addition or subtraction.

Key Words

- graph of an inequality
- equivalent inequalities
- addition property of inequality
- subtraction property of inequality

A *solution* of an inequality in one variable is a value of the variable that makes the inequality true. To solve such an inequality, you may have to rewrite it as a simpler *equivalent inequality*. **Equivalent inequalities** have the same solutions. Adding the same number to, or subtracting the same number from, each side of an inequality in one variable produces an equivalent inequality.

PROPERTIES OF INEQUALITY

ADDITION PROPERTY OF INEQUALITY

For all real numbers a, b, and c: If $a > b$, then $a + c > b + c$.
                                          If $a < b$, then $a + c < b + c$.

SUBTRACTION PROPERTY OF INEQUALITY

For all real numbers a, b, and c: If $a > b$, then $a - c > b - c$.
                                          If $a < b$, then $a - c < b - c$

These properties are also true for $\geq$ and $\leq$ inequalities.

Student Help

▶ **STUDY TIP**
To check solutions, choose numbers that make the arithmetic easy. For the Example, you could check 10 as a value of y.

$$10 + 4 \overset{?}{\geq} 12$$
$$14 \geq 12 \checkmark$$

EXAMPLE

Solve $y + 4 \geq 12$. Then graph the solution on a number line.

$y + 4 \geq 12$	Write original inequality.
$y + 4 - 4 \geq 12 - 4$	Subtract 4 from each side. (Subtraction Property of Inequality)
$y \geq 8$	Simplify.

ANSWER ▶ The solution is all real numbers greater than or equal to 8. The graph of the solution is shown below.

6.1 Exercises

Solve the inequality. Then match the solution with its graph.

1. $q - 1 \leq -2$

2. $n + 4 \geq 3$

3. $x + 9 < 8$

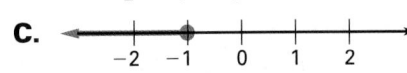

A.
B.
C.

Solve the inequality. Then graph the solution.

4. $x - 1 > 10$ **5.** $w + 4 \leq 9$ **6.** $h + 3 \geq 1$

7. $-5 > b - 1$ **8.** $0 \leq x + 7$ **9.** $n - 5 > 3$

10. $35 < m - 20$ **11.** $3 + k \geq -5$ **12.** $y - 3 < 28$

13. $2 < s - 8$ **14.** $h - 2 \geq -1$ **15.** $-6 > n - 5$

6.2 Solving Inequalities Using Multiplication or Division

Goal

Solve and graph one-step inequalities in one variable using multiplication or division.

Key Words

- multiplication property of inequality
- division property of inequality

You can solve an inequality by multiplying or dividing each side by the same number. When the number is negative, you must *reverse*, or change the direction of, the inequality.

PROPERTIES OF INEQUALITY

MULTIPLICATION PROPERTY OF INEQUALITY

For all real numbers a and b, and for $c > 0$:

If $a > b$, then $ac > bc$.

If $a < b$, then $ac < bc$.

For all real numbers a and b, and for $c < 0$:

If $a > b$, then $ac < bc$.

If $a < b$, then $ac > bc$.

DIVISION PROPERTY OF INEQUALITY

For all real numbers a and b, and for $c > 0$:

If $a > b$, then $\dfrac{a}{c} > \dfrac{b}{c}$.

If $a < b$, then $\dfrac{a}{c} < \dfrac{b}{c}$.

For all real numbers a and b, and for $c < 0$:

If $a > b$, then $\dfrac{a}{c} < \dfrac{b}{c}$.

If $a < b$, then $\dfrac{a}{c} > \dfrac{b}{c}$.

EXAMPLE

Solve $-2x \le 6$.

$-2x \le 6$ Write original inequality.

$\dfrac{-2x}{-2} \ge \dfrac{6}{-2}$ Divide each side by -2 and reverse the inequality. (Division Prop. of Inequality)

$x \ge -3$ Simplify.

ANSWER ▶ The solution is all real numbers greater than or equal to -3.

6.2 Exercises

Tell whether the graph is the graph of the solution of the inequality.

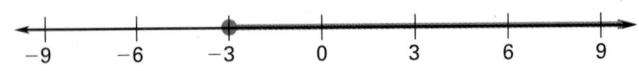

1. $-2x \le 6$ **2.** $-x \ge 3$ **3.** $\dfrac{x}{3} \le -1$ **4.** $-\dfrac{2}{3}x \le 2$

Solve the inequality. Then graph the solution.

5. $4d \le -28$ **6.** $3y < 27$ **7.** $2 < -8s$ **8.** $-h \ge 4$

9. $\dfrac{u}{7} > 5$ **10.** $\dfrac{1}{5}x > 5$ **11.** $\dfrac{1}{2}k \ge -45$ **12.** $5 > -\dfrac{p}{3}$

13. $84 \ge -4t$ **14.** $0 < -7b$ **15.** $24 < -3x$ **16.** $-2m \ge 9$

Solving Multi-Step Inequalities

Goal

Solve and graph multi-step inequalities in one variable.

Key Words

- multi-step inequality

The inequalities in Lessons 6.1 and 6.2 could be solved in one step using one operation. A multi-step inequality requires more than one operation.

EXAMPLE 1

Solve $-6 - x > 3$.

$-6 - x > 3$	Write original inequality.
$-x > 9$	Add 6 to each side.
$x < -9$	Multiply each side by -1 and reverse the inequality.

ANSWER ▶ The solution is all real numbers less than -9.

Student Help

▶ **STUDY TIP**
To avoid concerns about reversing the inequality, first collect variable terms on the side whose variable term has the greater coefficient.

EXAMPLE 2

Solve $8z - 6 \geq 3z + 12$.

$8z - 6 \geq 3z + 12$	Write original inequality.
$5z - 6 \geq 12$	Subtract $3z$ from each side.
$5z \geq 18$	Add 6 to each side.
$z \geq 3.6$	Divide each side by 5.

ANSWER ▶ The solution is all real numbers greater than or equal to 3.6.

6.3 Exercises

1. Describe the steps you would use to solve the inequality $4j + 5 \geq 23$.

Match the inequality with its graph.

2. $2 - 2x > 4$

A.

3. $2x + 2 > 4x$

B.

4. $-2(x - 2) > 4$

C.

Solve the inequality.

5. $5 \leq 11 + 3h$ **6.** $3(y - 5) > 6$ **7.** $-4x - 2 < 8$

8. $6 + 4r \geq 15 - 2r$ **9.** $5 - 2n \leq 3 - n$ **10.** $-(6b - 2) > 0$

11. $2(q - 3) < 8$ **12.** $8 - 4s > 16$ **13.** $2y - 5 > 9 + y$

14. $2(m - 8) - 3m < -8$ **15.** $3(2y - 4) \leq 2(y - 5)$

16. COUNTY FAIR A county fair charges $4.00 for admission and $.75 for each ride ticket. You have $20.00. How many ride tickets can you buy? Write and solve an inequality for this situation. Interpret the result.

6.4 Solving Compound Inequalities Involving "And"

Goal

Solve and graph compound inequalities involving *and*.

Key Words

• compound inequality

A compound inequality consists of two inequalities connected by the word *and* or the word *or*. A compound inequality with *and* can be written as:

$$0 \le x \text{ and } x < 5 \qquad\qquad 0 \le x < 5$$

$$x \text{ is greater than or equal to 0 and less than 5}$$

A number is a solution of a compound inequality with *and* if the number is a solution of *both* inequalities.

Student Help

▶ **STUDY TIP**
To perform any operation on a compound inequality with *and*, you must perform the operation on all *three* expressions.

EXAMPLE

Solve $-4 < r - 5 \le -1$. Then graph the solution.

Method 1 Separate the inequality. Solve the two parts separately.

$-4 < r - 5$	*and*	$r - 5 \le -1$	Separate inequality.
$-4 + 5 < r - 5 + 5$	*and*	$r - 5 + 5 \le -1 + 5$	Add 5 to each side.
$1 < r$	*and*	$r \le 4$	Simplify.
	$1 < r \le 4$		Write compound inequality.

Method 2 Isolate the variable between the inequality symbols.

$-4 < r - 5 \le -1$	Write original inequality.
$-4 + 5 < r - 5 + 5 \le -1 + 5$	Add 5 to each expression.
$1 < r \le 4$	Simplify.

ANSWER ▶ The solution is all real numbers greater than 1 and less than or equal to 4. The graph of the solution is shown below.

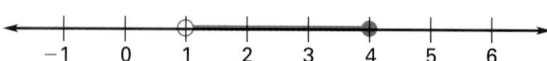

6.4 Exercises

Write an inequality that represents the statement.

1. x is greater than or equal to 1 and less than 6.

2. x is less than or equal to -3 and greater than -5.

Write an inequality that describes the graph.

3.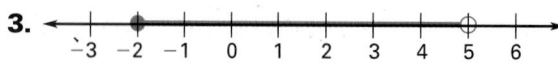

4.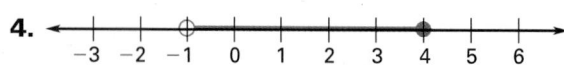

Solve the inequality. Then graph the solution.

5. $-3 < j + 2 < 7$

6. $3 \ge 4r - 5 \ge -1$

7. $-3.8 < 2r + 0.2 \le -2.8$

8. $1.5 < w + 3 < 6.5$

9. $-12 < 2x - 6 < 4$

10. $-2 \le 3x - 8 \le 10$

11. $-4 < 3 - x < 2$

12. $-10 \le 6 - 2x < 8$

6.5 Solving Compound Inequalities Involving "Or"

Goal

Solve and graph compound inequalities involving *or*.

Key Words

• compound inequality

In Lesson 6.4 you studied compound inequalities that involve the word *and*. In this lesson you will study compound inequalities that involve the word *or*.

EXAMPLE

Solve the compound inequality $4x + 2 < 6$ or $5x - 6 > 9$. Then graph the solution.

A solution of this compound inequality is a solution of either of its parts. Solve each of the parts using the methods of Lesson 6.3.

$4x + 2 < 6$	*or*	$5x - 6 > 9$	Write original inequality.
$4x + 2 - 2 < 6 - 2$	*or*	$5x - 6 + 6 > 9 + 6$	Isolate x.
$4x < 4$	*or*	$5x > 15$	Simplify.
$\dfrac{4x}{4} < \dfrac{4}{4}$	*or*	$\dfrac{5x}{5} > \dfrac{15}{5}$	Solve for x.
$x < 1$	*or*	$x > 3$	Simplify.

ANSWER ▶ The solution is all real numbers less than 1 or greater than 3. The graph of the solution is shown below.

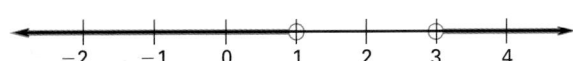

Student Help

▶ **STUDY TIP**
A number is a solution of a compound inequality with *or* if the number is a solution of *either* inequality.

6.5 Exercises

Match the inequality with its graph.

1. $x < -1$ or $x \geq 4$

2. $4 < x$ or $-1 > x$

A.

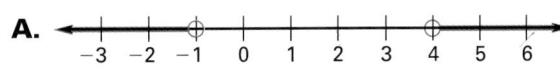

B.

Write an inequality that represents the set of numbers.

3. All real numbers less than -6 or greater than or equal to 12.

4. All real numbers greater than or equal to 9 or less than -7.

Solve the inequality. Then graph the solution.

5. $x - 5 > 0$ or $x + 1 \leq -2$

6. $6 + 5x > 1$ or $-4 - x > 0$

7. $5 - x \leq 2$ or $2x + 5 < 1$

8. $6 - a \leq 1$ or $3a \leq 12$

9. $25g < 400$ or $100 < 4g$

10. $4 + k > 3$ or $6k < -30$

11. $6 - 2x > 20$ or $8 - x \leq 0$

12. $-3x - 7 \geq 8$ or $-2x - 11 \leq -31$

13. An equilateral triangle has a side length of $(2x - 3)$ inches. Suppose its perimeter is less than 15 inches or greater than 27 inches. Describe the possible values of x.

Solving Absolute-Value Equations

Goal

Solve absolute-value equations in one variable.

Key Words

- absolute-value equation

An **absolute-value equation** is an equation of the form $|ax + b| = c$. You can solve this type of equation by solving two related linear equations.

SOLVING AN ABSOLUTE-VALUE EQUATION

For $c \geq 0$, x is a solution of $|ax + b| = c$ if x is a solution of
$$ax + b = c \text{ or } ax + b = -c.$$
For $c < 0$, the absolute-value equation $|ax + b| = c$ has no solution, since absolute value always indicates a number that is not negative.

EXAMPLE 1

Solve the equation.

a. $|x| = 9$

There are two values of x that have an absolute value of 9.
$$|x| = 9$$
$$x = 9 \text{ or } x = -9$$

ANSWER ▶ The equation has two solutions: 9 and -9.

b. $|x| = -11$

The absolute value of a number is never negative.

ANSWER ▶ The equation $|x| = -11$ has *no* solution.

EXAMPLE 2

Solve $|x - 6| = 12$.

Because $|x - 6| = 12$, the expression $x - 6$ is equal to 12 *or* -12.

$x - 6$ IS POSITIVE	*or*	$x - 6$ IS NEGATIVE
$x - 6 = 12$		$x - 6 = -12$
$x - 6 + 6 = 12 + 6$		$x - 6 + 6 = -12 + 6$
$x = 18$	*or*	$x = -6$

ANSWER ▶ The equation has two solutions: 18 and -6.

CHECK ✓

$$|x - 6| = 12 \qquad\qquad |x - 6| = 12$$
$$|18 - 6| \stackrel{?}{=} 12 \qquad\qquad |-6 - 6| \stackrel{?}{=} 12$$
$$|12| \stackrel{?}{=} 12 \qquad\qquad |-12| \stackrel{?}{=} 12$$
$$12 = 12 ✓ \qquad\qquad 12 = 12 ✓$$

Student Help

▶ **STUDY TIP**
Check the solutions to an absolute-value equation by substituting each solution in the original equation.

EXAMPLE 3

Solve $|3x - 6| - 7 = 17$.

First isolate the absolute-value expression on one side of the equation.

$$|3x - 6| - 7 = 17$$
$$|3x - 6| - 7 + 7 = 17 + 7$$
$$|3x - 6| = 24$$

Because $|3x - 6| = 24$, the expression $3x - 6$ is equal to 24 or -24.

$3x - 6$ IS POSITIVE	*or*	$3x - 6$ IS NEGATIVE
$3x - 6 = 24$		$3x - 6 = -24$
$3x - 6 + 6 = 24 + 6$		$3x - 6 + 6 = -24 + 6$
$3x = 30$		$3x = -18$
$\dfrac{3x}{3} = \dfrac{30}{3}$		$\dfrac{3x}{3} = \dfrac{-18}{3}$
$x = 10$	*or*	$x = -6$

ANSWER ▶ The equation has two solutions: 10 and -6.

CHECK ✓ $|3(\mathbf{10}) - 6| - 7 = |24| - 7 = 24 - 7 = 17$
$|3(\mathbf{-6}) - 6| - 7 = |-24| - 7 = 24 - 7 = 17$

Student Help

▶ **STUDY TIP**
Make sure that an equation involving absolute value is in the form $|ax + b| = c$ before splitting it into two equations.

6.6 Exercises

Tell how many solutions the equation has.

1. $|x| = 7$ **2.** $|x| = -4$ **3.** $|x| = 0$

Write the two linear equations you would use to solve the equation.

4. $|x + 4| = 8$ **5.** $|5x - 3| = 12$ **6.** $|2x + 2| - 1 = 9$

Solve the equation and check your solution. If the equation has no solution, write *no solution*.

7. $|x| = 5$ **8.** $|x + 1| = 7$ **9.** $|x - 1| = 7$

10. $|4 - 5x| = 23$ **11.** $|-2x + 9| = 7$ **12.** $|5 - 2x| = 7$

13. $|7 - 3x| + 10 = 4$ **14.** $|3x - 2| - 2 = 5$

15. $6 + |-x - 5| = 9$ **16.** $|3x - 7| + 2 = 4$

Match the absolute-value equation with its graph.

17. $|x + 3| = 6$ **18.** $|x - 3| = 6$

A.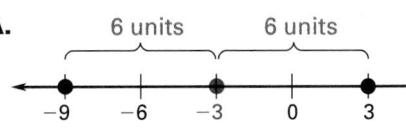

B.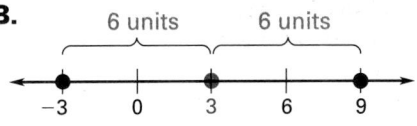

Solving Absolute-Value Inequalities

Goal
Solve absolute-value inequalities in one variable.

Key Words
• absolute-value inequality

To solve an absolute-value inequality, you solve two related inequalities. The inequalities for < and > inequalities are shown. Similar rules apply for ≤ and ≥.

$$|ax + b| < c \qquad\qquad |ax + b| > c$$

means   means

$$ax + b < c \quad and \quad ax + b > -c \qquad ax + b > c \quad or \quad ax + b < -c$$

EXAMPLE

Solve $|x + 4| \geq 6$. **Then graph the solution.**

The solution consists of all numbers x whose distance from -4 is greater than or equal to 6. The inequality involves ≥ so the related inequalities are connected by *or*.

		Write original inequality.
$|x + 4| \geq 6$		Write original inequality.
$x + 4 \geq 6$ or $x + 4 \leq -6$		Write related inequalities.
$x + 4 - 4 \geq 6 - 4$ or $x + 4 - 4 \leq -6 - 4$		Subtract 4 from each side.
$x \geq 2$ or $x \leq -10$		Simplify.

ANSWER ▶ The solution is all real numbers less than or equal to -10 or greater than or equal to 2. The graph of the solution is shown below.

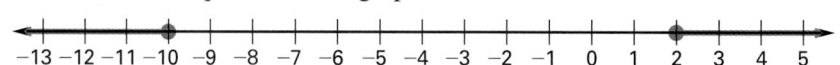

Check the solution by testing one value from each region of the graph.

Student Help

▶ **STUDY TIP**
The expression inside the absolute-value symbols can be positive or negative. When you rewrite the expression for the negative value, reverse the inequality.

6.7 **Exercises**

Match the absolute-value inequality with its compound inequality.

1. $|x + 3| < 8$ **A.** $-8 \leq x + 3 \leq 8$

2. $|x + 3| \geq 8$ **B.** $x + 3 \geq 8$ *or* $x + 3 \leq -8$

3. $|x + 3| \leq 8$ **C.** $x + 3 < 8$ *and* $x + 3 > -8$

Solve the inequality. Then graph and check the solution.

4. $|x| \geq 2$ **5.** $|x| < 4$ **6.** $|2x| > 8$

7. $|x + 8| < 9$ **8.** $|x + 12| < 36$ **9.** $|x + 1| > 17$

10. $|10 - 4x| < 2$ **11.** $|1 + 2x| \leq 9$ **12.** $|18 + 2x| \leq 14$

13. $|x - 12| - 2 \geq 4$ **14.** $|2x - 3| + 2 < 7$ **15.** $|3x + 2| + 5 > 16$

16. Complete the statement with *always*, *sometimes*, or *never*. Explain your answer.

A solution of the inequality $|3 - 2x| \geq 9$ will __?__ be negative.

R68   **Key Skills Review**

6.8 Graphing Linear Inequalities in Two Variables

Goal

Graph linear inequalities in two variables.

Key Words

- linear inequality in two variables

When you graph the solutions of a linear inequality in two variables, you get a *half-plane*. This is a region of a coordinate plane bounded by the graph of the linear equation that corresponds to the linear inequality. A dashed boundary line indicates that the points on the line are *not* solutions of the inequality. A solid boundary line indicates that the points on the line *are* solutions.

EXAMPLE

Graph the inequality $3x - y \geq -3$ using the slope-intercept form of the corresponding equation.

Write the corresponding equation in slope-intercept form.

$3x - y = -3$	Write corresponding equation.
$-y = -3x - 3$	Subtract $3x$ from each side.
$y = 3x + 3$	Multiply each side by -1.

Student Help

▶ STUDY TIP
You can use any point that is not on the line as a test point to decide which half-plane to shade. It is often convenient to use the origin because 0 is substituted for each variable.

❶ **Graph** the corresponding equation $y = 3x + 3$. The graph of the line has a slope of 3 and a y-intercept of 3. The inequality is $\geq$, so use a solid line.

❷ **Test** a point. The origin $(0, 0)$ is a solution: $3(0) - 0 = 0$ and $0 \geq -3$. Since $(0, 0)$ lies below the line, the graph of $3x - y \geq -3$ is all points *on* or *below* the line.

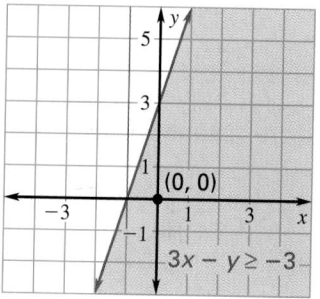

❸ **Shade** the half-plane below the line.

ANSWER ▶ The graph of $3x - y \geq -3$ is all points on or below the graph of the line $3x - y = -3$. Check by testing any point below the line.

6.8 Exercises

1. Does the graph of $y > -2$ lie above or below the graph of the horizontal line $y = -2$?

2. Does the graph of $x \leq 4$ lie to the right or to the left of the vertical line $x = 4$?

3. Check whether the ordered pair $(3, 2)$ is a solution of $x - 3y \leq 4$.

Graph the inequality.

4. $y \geq -1$ **5.** $x < 3$ **6.** $5y \geq 10$

7. $y - 2x < 3$ **8.** $3x + y \geq 4$ **9.** $x - y < 1$

10. $x - 2y \leq 1$ **11.** $x + y > 2$ **12.** $3x - y \geq 0$

13. $4x + y < -2$ **14.** $2x + 3y \geq 6$ **15.** $x - 4y > 3$

Solve the inequality. Then graph the solution.

1. $x + 6 > 11$

2. $n - 4 < -8$

3. $m - 3 \leq -5$

4. $b + 8 \geq 6$

5. $5c \geq 20$

6. $3x < -18$

7. $\frac{1}{2}w > 3$

8. $\frac{y}{4} \leq -2$

9. $8 - x \geq 7$

10. $3a + 4 < -8$

11. $6 + 4b > -10$

12. $12x - 36 \leq 3x$

13. $5c < 2(c - 9)$

14. $-6z - 16 \geq 6z + 8$

15. $-5 \leq -5 + h < 3$

16. $-3 < 2n + 1 < 7$

17. $-7 \leq -1 - 3x \leq 8$

18. $m - 1 \leq -3$ or $m - 1 > 3$

19. $1 + 2d < -9$ or $1 + 2d > 9$

20. $6n < -18$ or $-12 + 4n > 0$

21. $4x - 1 \leq 3$ or $3x \geq x + 8$

Solve the equation and check your solution. If the equation has no solution, write *no solution*.

22. $|2x - 5| = 7$

23. $|6z - 3| = 9$

24. $|3c + 4| = -10$

25. $|1 - 3x| + 5 = 7$

26. $|4a + 9| + 3 = 0$

27. $|2n - 9| - 1 = 0$

Solve the inequality. Then graph the solution.

28. $|3 + a| < 4$

29. $|-2 - m| \geq 4$

30. $|2 - x| - 3 < 1$

31. $|12 - 3h| > 6$

32. $|2z + 1| \geq 1$

33. $|2d - 1| \leq 3$

Graph the inequality.

34. $x + 2y \leq 4$

35. $2x + 3y > 18$

36. $2x - y > 5$

VARIABLES AND EXPRESSIONS

Evaluate the variable expression when $w = 4$, $x = -2$, $y = 5$, and $z = -6$.

1. $w + z$ **2.** $x - y$ **3.** $2y + z$ **4.** xz

5. $z \div w$ **6.** w^3 **7.** $-y^2$ **8.** $9x^4$

9. $2(z + 4w)$ **10.** $10 \div y - z$ **11.** $9 + w \div x$ **12.** $(wz + x)3$

OPERATIONS ON REAL NUMBERS

Use a number line to write the numbers in increasing order.

13. $5, -9, 0, 6, 11, -3$ **14.** $6.3, 0.6, -1.3, 4.1, -0.7$ **15.** $\dfrac{3}{4}, \dfrac{5}{2}, -\dfrac{2}{3}, -\dfrac{5}{4}, \dfrac{4}{5}$

Evaluate the expression.

16. $|6|$ **17.** $|0|$ **18.** $|-8|$ **19.** $|-4|$

20. $-7 + 11$ **21.** $15(-3)$ **22.** $8 - (-9)$ **23.** $-5 - 12$

24. $25 \div (-5)$ **25.** $(-4)12$ **26.** $16 + (-16)$ **27.** $(-8) \div 8$

EQUATIONS AND INEQUALITIES

Solve the equation or inequality. For the inequalities, graph the solution. If there is no solution, write *no solution*.

28. $2x = 30$ **29.** $\dfrac{1}{8}m = 3$ **30.** $-4d < 20$ **31.** $c - 3 \geq 1$

32. $3k - 1 > 2$ **33.** $3y = 2y + 7$ **34.** $2b + 6 = 5b$ **35.** $-3a + 4 > -8$

36. $\dfrac{1}{4}m - 3 = 19$ **37.** $2.5z - 1.5 = 5z + 3.5$ **38.** $2w + 4 \leq 2w - 7$

39. $5n > 6(n - 1)$ **40.** $5(2z - 1) - 4z = 16 + 5z$ **41.** $4(c - 5) = 2(2c + 6)$

RATIOS, RATES, AND PERCENTS

Write the ratio in simplest form.

42. $\dfrac{6}{30}$ **43.** $\dfrac{25}{150}$ **44.** $\dfrac{24}{36}$

45. 18 to 90 **46.** 84 to 12

47. A soccer team played 24 games and won 18. Find the ratio of wins to games played.

48. June has 9 sweaters with buttons and 6 sweaters that are pullovers. Find the ratio of sweaters with buttons to pullovers.

continued on next page

Find the unit rate.

49. 550 miles in 11 hours

50. $5.70 for 6 cans

51. 84 gallons in 7 minutes

52. A car traveled 459 miles on 17 gallons of gasoline.

53. A 10,000 gallon swimming pool was filled in 250 minutes.

Solve the percent problem.

54. Find 35% of 220.

55. Find 25% of 480.

56. What percent of 75 is 51?

57. What percent of 180 is 99?

58. 64% of what number is 80?

59. 18% of what number is 63?

WRITING LINEAR EQUATIONS

Write in slope-intercept form the equation of the line that passes through the given points.

60. $(0, 1), (4, 7)$

61. $(0, -3), (4, -1)$

62. $(3, -2), (6, 0)$

63. $(2, 5), (6, 7)$

64. $(2, -1), (3, -3)$

65. $(-4, 6), (-2, 1)$

66–68. Write in standard form the equations of the lines from Exercises 63–65.

GRAPHING LINEAR EQUATIONS AND INEQUALITIES

Graph the equation or inequality.

69. $x = -3$

70. $y = -3x + 5$

71. $y = \frac{1}{3}x - 4$

72. $y \geq 2$

73. $y < 3x$

74. $y \leq -2x - 6$

ABSOLUTE VALUE EQUATIONS AND INEQUALITIES

Solve the equation or inequality. For the inequalities, graph the solution. If there is no solution, write *no solution*.

75. $|x - 2| = 7$

76. $|m + 5| = 22$

77. $|3d - 4| = 5$

78. $|y + 2| < 5$

79. $|4x + 5| \geq 19$

80. $|2z - 7| > 17$

SYSTEMS OF EQUATIONS AND INEQUALITIES

Graph the linear system.

1. $x - 2y = 2$
$2x + y = 9$

2. $6x + y = 2$
$6x + y = 6$

3. $y \le 3x + 1$
$y < x - 1$

4. $x + y \ge 1$
$x - y < -4$

Solve the linear system.

5. $3x + 4y = 4$
$y = x - 6$

6. $x - 3y = 8$
$4x + 5y = -2$

7. $13x + 5y = -11$
$13x + 11y = 7$

8. $3x - 5y = -35$
$-2x + 5y = 30$

9. $3x + 4y = 11$
$4x - 3y = 23$

10. $-3x + 5y = -7$
$9x + 2y = 38$

EXPONENTS AND SCIENTIFIC NOTATION

Write the expression as a single power of the base. Use only positive exponents.

11. $2^8 \cdot 2^3$

12. $7^5 \cdot 7^7$

13. $4^4 \cdot 4^{-2}$

14. $8^{-8} \cdot 8^6$

15. $\dfrac{3^5}{3^{-6}}$

16. $\dfrac{2^9}{2^3}$

17. $\dfrac{2^{-2}}{2^{-5}}$

18. $\dfrac{3^{-4}}{3^6}$

Simplify the expression. Use only positive exponents.

19. $x^3 \cdot x^6$

20. $(c^0)^4$

21. $(-2n^2)^5$

22. $3b^4 \cdot (-4b^8)$

23. $\dfrac{m^3}{m^{-5}}$

24. $\dfrac{5ab^5}{a^0 b^{-3}}$

25. $\left(\dfrac{2a^3}{b^4}\right)^5$

26. $\left(\dfrac{c^4}{c^7}\right)^{-4}$

Write the number in decimal form.

27. 4.9×10^6

28. 2.21×10^8

29. 5.7×10^{-7}

30. 8.34×10^{-4}

Write the number in scientific notation.

31. 8,970,000,000

32. 45,000,000

33. 0.0000000276

34. 0.00000731

35. You open a savings account with $400. The account pays 3% annual interest. Write an exponential growth model to find the amount in the account after 8 years.

36. You buy a new car for $24,000. The car depreciates 10% per year. Write an exponential decay model to find the value of the car after 6 years.

continued on next page

QUADRATIC EQUATIONS

Solve the equation. If there is no real solution, write *no real solution*.

37. $x^2 - 3x - 18 = 0$

38. $x^2 - 64 = 36$

39. $5x^2 + 3x + 2 = 0$

40. $(4x - 1)(x - 4) = 0$

41. $x^2 + 4x + 1 = 0$

42. $x^2 + 10x + 25 = 0$

Sketch the graph of the function.

43. $y = x^2 - 8x + 15$

44. $y = -x^2 + x - 2$

45. $y = x^2 + 6x + 9$

POLYNOMIALS

Find the sum, difference, or product.

46. $(y^2 + 3y + 7) + (-y^2 - 11y)$

47. $(-5x^2 + x - 3) + (11x^2 + 7x - 8)$

48. $(11m^2 - m + 8) - (19 + 5m - m^2)$

49. $(a^2 + 3a - 2) - (9a^2 + 5a - 8)$

50. $(3x - 2)(5x + 4)$

51. $(n + 9)(n - 9)$

52. $(2x - 5)(x^2 + x + 1)$

Factor the expression completely.

53. $x^2 + 5x + 6$

54. $n^2 + 11n + 18$

55. $x^2 + 10x + 25$

56. $5a^2 - 7a + 2$

57. $3x^2 + x - 2$

58. $4c^3 - 5c^2 - 6c$

RATIONAL AND RADICAL EXPRESSIONS AND EQUATIONS

Simplify the expression.

59. $\dfrac{5}{x + 3} + \dfrac{3}{x - 4}$

60. $\dfrac{x}{x - 2} + \dfrac{1}{x}$

61. $\dfrac{x}{x + 1} - \dfrac{2}{x + 1}$

62. $\dfrac{3x + 6}{x - 3} \cdot \dfrac{x^2}{x + 2}$

63. $\dfrac{1}{3x^2} \div \dfrac{x - 2}{12x}$

64. $\dfrac{4}{n + 1} \div \dfrac{2}{3n + 3}$

65. $14\sqrt{3} - 19\sqrt{3}$

66. $5\sqrt{2} + 3\sqrt{50}$

67. $8^{1/3} \cdot 8^{4/3}$

68. $\sqrt{33} \cdot \sqrt{3}$

69. $\dfrac{3}{4 + \sqrt{7}}$

70. $(7 - \sqrt{5})^2$

Solve the equation.

71. $\dfrac{x}{x + 2} = \dfrac{2}{x - 1}$

72. $\sqrt{2x - 6} = 4$

Answers for Key Skills Review

Answers for all practice exercises in the Key Skills Review section are provided, as follows.

Answers

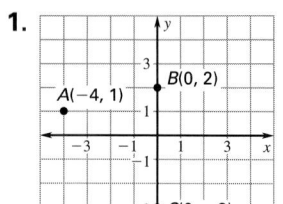

Volume 2
Pre-Course Practice

Expressions, Equations, and Variables (R4–R5)

1. 31 **2.** 16 **3.** 48 **4.** 2 **5.** 8^2 **6.** 9^4 **7.** 17

8. 12 **9.** 3 **10.** 10 **11.** 16 **12.** 30

13. $x \div 6 < 15$ **14.** $x + 10 \geq 46$ **15.** $10x = 40$

16. $x - 6 = 15$ **17.** 1 hour

18. 20 in. or 1 ft 8 in.

19.

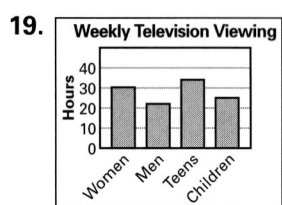

20. teens **21.** function; exactly one y-value is assigned to each x-value **22.** not a function; the two y-values -1 and 1 are assigned to the single x-value -2 **23.** 9 **24.** 1 **25.** 10 **26.** -1

27. -11.2 **28.** $-3\frac{1}{4}$ **29.** -1 **30.** 1 **31.** 31

32. -43 **33.** 10.2 **34.** -17.3 **35.** $5b$

36. -18 **37.** 12 **38.** $-36x$ **39.** x^4 **40.** $-12rt$

41. $8x + 24$ **42.** $4a - 24$ **43.** $-7y + 35$

44. $6a$ **45.** $2t^2 - 9$ **46.** $x^2 + 7z$ **47.** $12p + 18$

48. $-9y - 93$ **49.** $-3b + 24$ **50.** -4 **51.** -1

52. 10 **53.** $-\frac{2}{3}$

Solving Linear Equations (R5–R6)

1. 8 **2.** 3 **3.** -19 **4.** -11 **5.** -17 **6** -7

7. -1 **8.** 282 **9.** 5 **10.** 9 **11.** 2 **12.** 2

13. 1 **14.** -25 **15.** 14 **16.** -3 **17.** -7

18. 10 **19.** 1 **20.** 5 **21.** 4 **22.** -1 **23.** 19

24. 8 **25.** 13 **26.** -1.14 **27.** -0.10 **28.** 1.63

29. 0.36 **30.** -5.03 **31.** -2.23 **32.** $h = \dfrac{2A}{b}$

33. $L = \dfrac{P - 2W}{2}$ **34.** \$7.25/h **35.** 2 g/c

36. 48 m **37.** 45

Graphing Linear Equations (R6–R7)

1.

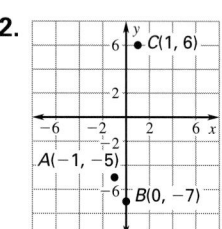

2.

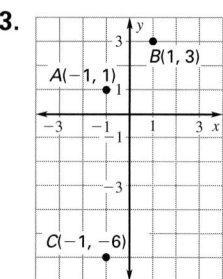

3.

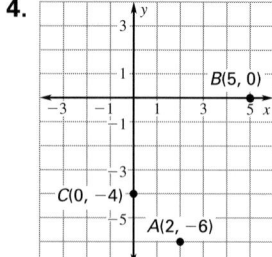

4.

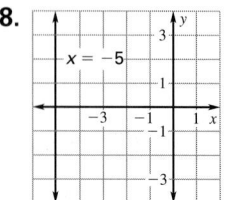

5. $y = -2x$ **6.** $y = \frac{5}{2}x - 10$ **7.** $y = -\frac{1}{2}x - 4$

8.

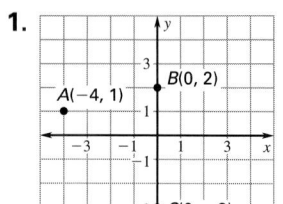

9.

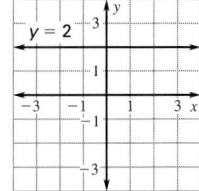

10.

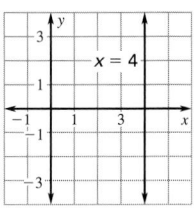

11. x-intercept: -2, y-intercept: 6;

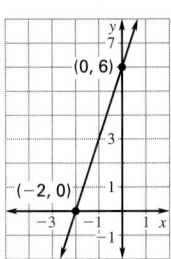

12. x-intercept: 2, y-intercept: -8;

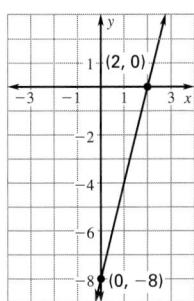

13. x-intercept: 10, y-intercept: -10;

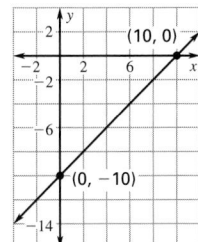

14. $\frac{2}{5}$ **15.** $\frac{5}{2}$ **16.** $\frac{7}{9}$ **17.** $y = 3x$ **18.** $y = 8x$
19. $y = 4x$ **20.** $y = 3x + 4$;
$m = 3, b = 4$
21. $y = -x + 2$; $m = -1, b = 2$
22. $y = -2x + 6$; $m = -2, b = 6$

23.

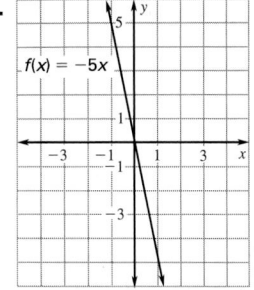

24.

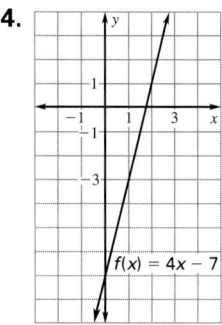

25.

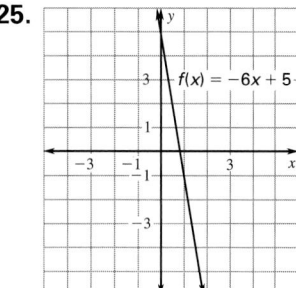

Writing Linear Equations (R7)

 1. $y = -2x + 1$ **2.** $y = -5x$ **3.** $y = x + 1$
 4. $y = 4$ **5.** $y = -4x$ **6.** $y = -\frac{1}{5}x - 1$
 7. $y = 3x - 16$ **8.** $y = 4$ **9.** $2x$
$- y = 4$
10. $x + 2y = 6$ **11.** $2x - 5y = -23$

Linear Inequalities (R7)

 1. $a < 5$ **2.** $m \leq -8$ **3.** $b < -12$ **4.** $f \geq -21$
 5. $d \geq 36$ **6.** $a > -7$ **7.** $x \leq -2$ **8.** $x \leq -3$
 9. $x < 2$ **10.** $x > -2$ **11.** $x \leq 7$ **12.** $x \geq 17$
13. $3 < x < 12$ **14.** $-9 < x \leq 7$ **15.** $-4 \leq x \leq -2$
16. $x > 5$ or $x < -5$ **17.** $x < -9$ or $x > -4$
18. $x < -1$ or $x > 5$ **19.** $14, -14$
20. no solution **21.** $33, -15$

22. $1 \le x \le 7$;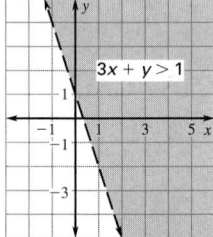

23. $x > 5$ or $x < 3$;

24. $-9 < x < -5$;

25.

$x \le -|4|$

26.

$3x + y > 1$

27.

$y - 5x \ge 0$

Chapter 1

Lesson 1.1 (R8)

1. x divided by 2; division   **2.** 2 plus x; addition
3. 2 times x; multiplication   **4.** x minus 2;
subtraction   **5.** 20   **6.** 48   **7.** 5   **8.** 23   **9.** 36
10. 37   **11.** 4   **12.** 9   **13.** 24   **14.** 56 days
15. 330 miles   **16.** 12 feet   **17.** 15 square inches

Lesson 1.2 (R9)

1. $6^2 = 36$ **2.** $5^3 = 125$ **3.** $3^4 = 81$ **4.** $2^6 = 64$
5. 64   **6.** 24   **7.** 224   **8.** 512   **9.** 10,000
10. 100   **11.** 49   **12.** 36   **13.** 324 square feet

Lesson 1.3 (R10)

1. 0   **2.** 12   **3.** 147   **4.** 18   **5.** 16   **6.** 34
7. 33   **8.** 9   **9.** 13   **10.** 2   **11.** 1   **12.** 4   **13.** 4
14. 5   **15.** 3   **16.** 58   **17.** 48   **18.** 324   **19.** 12
20. 38   **21.** 1

Lesson 1.4 (R11)

1. 7   **2.** 25   **3.** 30   **4.** 6   **5.** 8   **6.** 2   **7.** 25
8. 24   **9.** solution   **10.** solution   **11.** solution
12. not a solution   **13.** solution   **14.** not a
solution   **15.** solution   **16.** solution   **17.** not a
solution   **18.** not a solution   **19.** solution
20. not a solution

Lesson 1.5 (R12)

1. $x - 6 = 18$ **2.** $7x < 21$ **3.** $x - 4 = 12$
4. $3 + x = 5$ **5.** $3x > 24$ **6.** $\dfrac{45}{x} \geq 15$

7. $x + 12 \leq 32$ **8.** $\dfrac{48}{x} < 8$

9. $\dfrac{\$20 \text{ per car}}{5 \text{ people per car}} = \$4 \text{ per person}$

Lesson 1.6 (R13–R14)

1. D, A, F, B, C, E
2.

Number of months worked	·	Amount saved each month	=	Cost of snowboard with bindings

3. Number of months worked = 10 (months)
Amount saved each month = s (dollars per month)
Cost of snowboard with bindings = 685 (dollars)

4. $10s = 685$ **5.** \$68.50   **6.** $10(68.5) = 685$,
so the answer is reasonable.

Lesson 1.7 (R15–R16)

1. a.

b.   The 1999 unemployment rate in the
redrawn graph looks much higher than in the graph
in Example 2.

2.

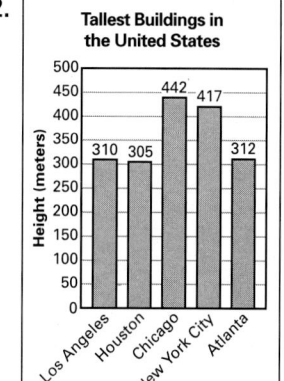

3. Chicago

4. 167 m

Lesson 1.8 (R17–R18)

1.

Input x	0	1	2	3	4	5
Output y	8	12	16	20	24	28

2.

Input x	0	1	2	3	4	5
Output y	29	24	19	14	9	4

3.

Input x	0	1	2	3	4	5
Output y	36	33	30	27	24	21

4.

Input h (hours)	1.0	1.5	2.0	2.5	3.0
Output C (dollars)	108	128	148	168	188

5.

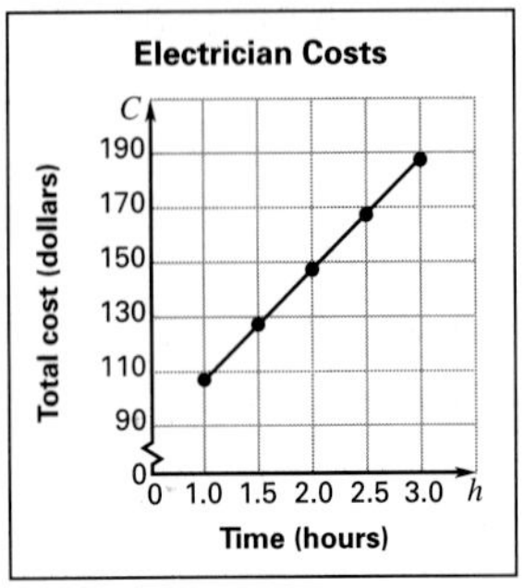

Electrician Costs

6. $108, $188

7. a. $R = 65d$

b.

Input d (days)	1	2	3	4
Output R (dollars)	65	130	195	260

c.

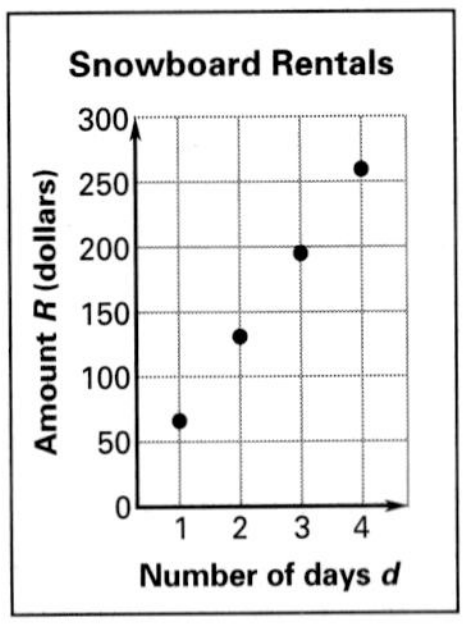

Snowboard Rentals

8. $P = 8w + 10w$

Input w	1	2	3	4	5
Output P	18	36	54	72	90

The range for the input values in the table is 18, 36, 54, 72, and 90.

Chapter 2

Lesson 2.1 (R20)

1. $-6, -2, 5$ **2.** $-4, 0, 4$ **3.** $-9, -4, -3, 2, 3$
4. $-3, -2, -\frac{3}{4}$ **5.** $-10, -0.25, \frac{6}{4}, 3$
6. $-3, \frac{1}{2}, 7$ **7.** $-4.3, -1.4, -1.2, 6, 8$
8. $-3, -2, -\frac{3}{2}, \frac{3}{4}, 4$ **9.** $>$ **10.** $>$ **11.** $>$
12. $<$ **13.** $-15°\,\text{F}; 20°\,\text{F}$

Lesson 2.2 (R21)

1. -2 **2.** 4 **3.** 3.5 **4.** $-\frac{1}{3}$ **5.** 16 **6.** 5
7. -4.9 **8.** 3.5 **9.** 0 **10.** $-\frac{5}{8}$ **11.** -12.3
12. $-\frac{2}{9}$ **13.** $-12, 12$ **14.** no solution
15. $-8.8, 8.8$ **16.** $-\frac{3}{4}, \frac{3}{4}$
17. sometimes; the absolute value of a number is either a positive number or zero.

Lesson 2.3 (R22)

1. B   **2.** D   **3.** C   **4.** A   **5.** 3 **6.** -5 **7.** -1
8. 4 **9.** 5 **10.** -34 **11.** -11 **12.** -24
13. -6 **14.** -5 **15.** -5 **16.** 9

Lesson 2.4 (R23)

1. -7 **2.** -13 **3.** -9 **4.** 9 **5.** -18.6 **6.** 7
7. -13.5 **8.** $-3\frac{1}{4}$ **9.** 6.2

10.

Input x	-2	-1	0	1	2
Output y	-3	-4	-5	-6	-7

11. $-0.96, 2.14, -1.15, -1.96$

Lesson 2.5 (R24)

1. property of zero   **2.** property of negative one
3. identity property   **4.** commutative property
5. associative property   **6.** -32 **7.** -25 **8.** 81
9. -2 **10.** -8 **11.** $63d$ **12.** $-8d^3$ **13.** $9x^4$
14. $-x^4$ **15.** -320 **16.** 64

Lesson 2.6 (R25)

1. $(2 + x)6$ and $2(6) + x(6)$
2. $(2 + x)6 = 2(6) + x(6)$
3. $3y + 18$ **4.** $11x + 11$ **5.** $-4y + 8$
6. $-2x - 10$ **7.** $10y - 60$ **8.** $8x + 32$
9. $6a - 42$ **10.** $-9 + 2y$ **11.** $-9 - 3x$
12. $2x - 16$ **13.** $-2x - 10$ **14.** $9 + 3x$

Lesson 2.7 (R26)

1. $8x$ **2.** $-6d$ **3.** -6 **4.** $-10f + 30$
5. already simplified   **6.** $12h^2 + 8h$ **7.** $20d + 30$
8. $22x + 6$ **9.** $-10f - 18$ **10.** $40b + 44$
11. $14x - 47$ **12.** $10s - 16$ **13.** B
14. $d = 0.25t + 2.5$; 10 miles

Lesson 2.8 (R27)

1. $\frac{1}{24}$ **2.** $-\frac{1}{8}$ **3.** -2 **4.** $\frac{3}{7}$ **5.** -8
6. 4 **7.** -4 **8.** $-\frac{1}{10}$ **9.** $-\frac{8}{3}$ or $-2\frac{2}{3}$ **10.** 4
11. 64 **12.** $-\frac{4}{5}$ **13.** -25 **14.** $3x - 1$
15. $9 + \frac{c}{4}$ **16.** $4y - 10$ **17.** 3
18. sometimes; the value of a cannot be zero since there is no division by zero.

Chapter 3

Lesson 3.1 (R29)

1. -16 **2.** -2 **3.** 23 **4.** 8 **5.** 27 **6.** -34

7. 9 **8.** -10 **9.** 6 **10.** 1 **11.** $\frac{5}{8}$

12. $-\frac{1}{5}$ **13.** -11 **14.** 5 **15.** 9

16. $12 + x = 16$; $4

Lesson 3.2 (R30)

1. -4 **2.** 9 **3.** 7 **4.** -7 **5.** 5

6. $-1\frac{1}{2}$ **7.** 10 **8.** 4 **9.** -21 **10.** -21

11. 96 **12.** 288 **13.** 0 **14.** 8 **15.** -16 **16.** 25

17. $6x = 72$; $12

Lesson 3.3 (R31)

1. 6 **2.** -1 **3.** -2 **4.** $1\frac{1}{3}$ **5.** $\frac{1}{3}$ **6.** 2

7. 7 **8.** 64 **9.** 13 **10.** $1\frac{1}{3}$ **11.** 4

12. -2 **13.** 4 **14.** -2 **15.** $2\frac{4}{5}$

16. A; $x = 5\frac{1}{4}$; You will be able to buy the camera in 6 weeks.

Lesson 3.4 (R32–R33)

1. -1 **2.** -2 **3.** 1 **4.** 3 **5.** -9 **6.** 1

7. $-\dfrac{2}{5}$ **8.** 3 **9.** $-\dfrac{3}{4}$ **10.** no solution

11. identity **12.** one solution; 28

13. no solution **14.** one solution; -3

15. identity **16.** 225 toys

17. $\frac{3}{4}$ hour $= 45$ minutes

18. Train travels 6 hours; truck travels 8 hours

Lesson 3.5 (R34–R35)

1. 5 **2.** -19 **3.** $6\frac{1}{2}$ **4.** 2 **5.** $1\frac{1}{6}$

6. -3 **7.** $4\frac{1}{6}$ **8.** -2 **9.** $-3\frac{1}{4}$

10. $\frac{1}{2}$ **11.** 550 cushions **12. a.** 14 video games

b. Yes. **13.** If you expect to take fewer than 15 lessons, it is cheaper to join Club 1. If you intend to take exactly 15 lessons, it does not matter which club you join. If you expect to take more than 15 lessons, it is cheaper to join Club 2.

Lesson 3.6 (R36)

1. 8.65 **2.** -17.67 **3.** 1.83 **4.** 1.08 **5.** -1.1

6. 0.43 **7.** 3.56 **8.** -3.13 **9.** 0.31 **10.** 1.33

11. -7.83 **12.** 10.33 **13.** 0.16 **14.** $24.87

15. $43,540

Lesson 3.7 (R37)

1. $y = 20 - x$ **2.** $n = 4m - 6$ **3.** $t = \dfrac{5 - 2r}{2}$

4. $z = a + y$ **5.** $x = \dfrac{y + k}{m}$ **6.** $w = \dfrac{A}{1}$

7. $b = \dfrac{2A}{h}$ **8.** $w = \dfrac{P - 21}{2}$ **9.** $d \approx \dfrac{C}{3.14}$

10. $F = \dfrac{9}{5}C + 32$; $120.2°\text{F}$

11. $r = \dfrac{d}{t}$; 54 miles per hour

Lesson 3.8 (R38–R39)

1. $\frac{5}{9}$ **2.** $\frac{1}{4}$ **3.** $\frac{1}{3}$ **4.** 1 to 3 **5.** 1 to 5

6. 3 to 4 **7.** $5 : 2$ **8.** $4 : 3$ **9.** $4 per hour

10. 6 gal/min **11.** 48 ft/sec

12. $.20 per pencil **13.** $.25 per juice box

14. 7 miles/hour **15.** 25 weeks

16. 96 months **17.** 58.1 hours

18. 6.8 pounds **19.** 1440 feet **20.** 3 kilometers

21. 29,920 yards **22.** 27.4 yards

23. Subcompact car: 26.8 miles per gallon, compact car: 23.8 miles per gallon; the subcompact car.

24. about 322 miles; about 286 miles

Lesson 3.9 (R40)

1. 20 **2.** 700 **3.** 50% **4.** 39.2 **5.** 50

6. 72.5% **7.** 9 **8.** 20% **9.** 60% **10.** 55

11. 12 **12.** 44 **13.** $9.60; $22.40

Chapter 4

Lesson 4.1 (R42)

1. $A(-3, 2)$, quadrant II; $B(4, 4)$, quadrant I;
$C(0, -3)$, y-axis   **2.** $A(5, -4)$, quadrant IV;
$B(-4, 1)$, quadrant II, $C(-5, -5)$, quadrant III

3.
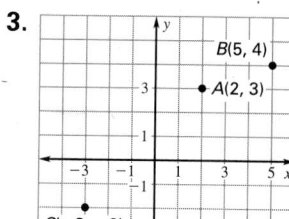

4.
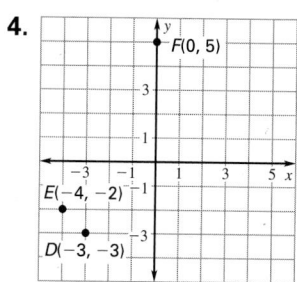

5.
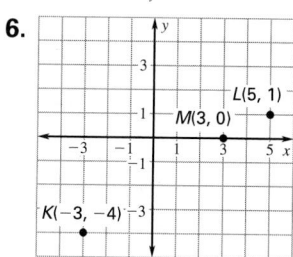

6.
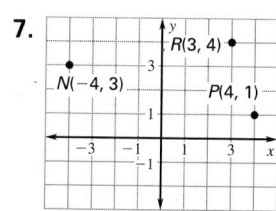

7.
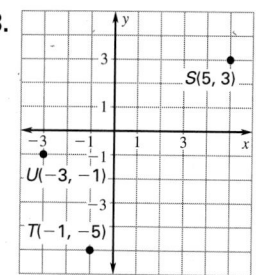

8.
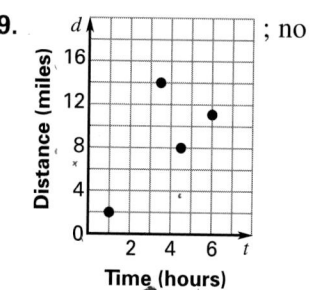

9. ; no
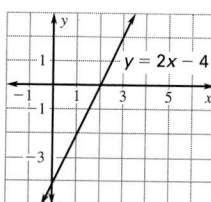

Lesson 4.2 (R43)

1. yes   **2.** yes   **3.** no

4. equation in function form;
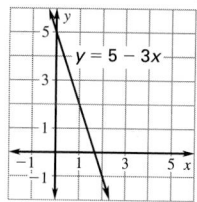

5. equation in function form;
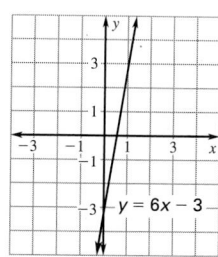

6. equation in function form;
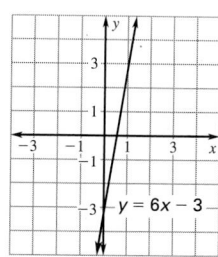

7. equation in function form;

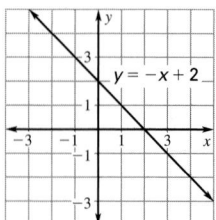

$y = -x + 2$

8. equation in function form;

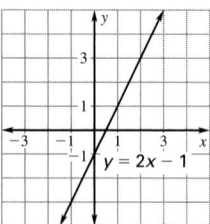

$y = 2x - 1$

9. $y = x - 2$;

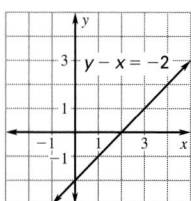

$y - x = -2$

10. $y = -2x + 3$;

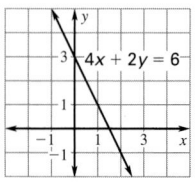

$4x + 2y = 6$

11. $y = \dfrac{1}{2}x + 4$;

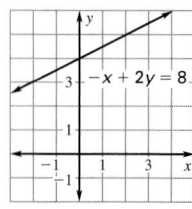

$-x + 2y = 8$

12. $y = -\dfrac{4}{3}x + 8$;

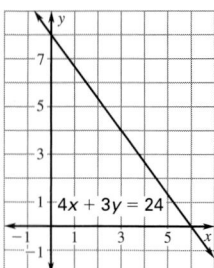

$4x + 3y = 24$

13. Tables will vary.

Student tickets	250	200	150	100	50	0
Adult tickets	0	20	40	60	80	100

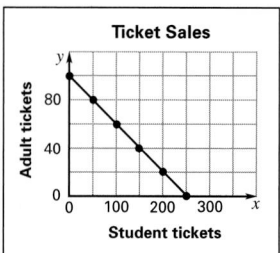

Lesson 4.3 (R44)

1.

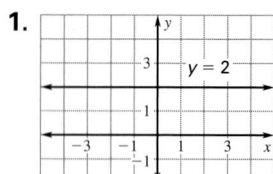

$y = 2$

2.

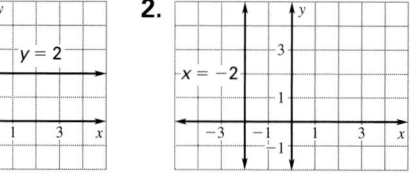

$x = -2$

3.

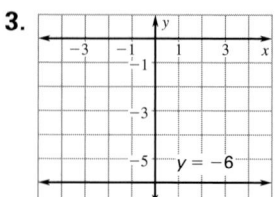

$y = -6$

4.

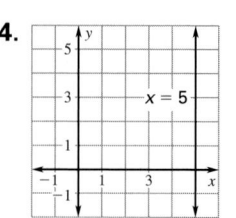

$x = 5$

5.

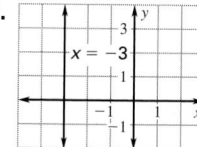

6.

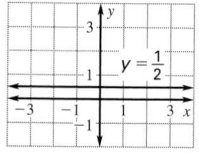

7.

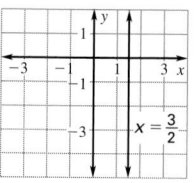

8.

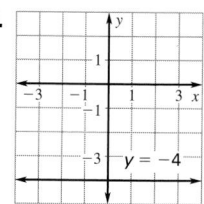

9. $y = 3$ **10.** $x = -4$ **11.** $x = 3$ **12.** $y = -2$

Lesson 4.4 (R45)

1. 3   **2.** -3 **3.** 3   **4.** -14 **5.** -8 **6.** 5

7. 3   **8.** 6   **9.** 6   **10.** -6 **11.** -4 **12.** 5

13. x-intercept $= 3$, y-intercept $= 3$;

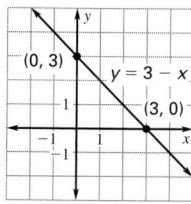

14. x-intercept $= \frac{3}{2}$, y-intercept $= -3$;

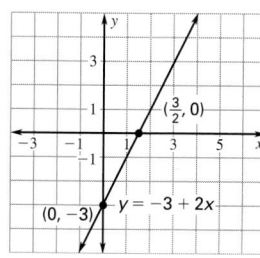

15. x-intercept $= \frac{7}{3}$, y-intercept $= 7$;

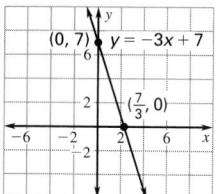

16. x-intercept $= 6$, y-intercept $= 8$;

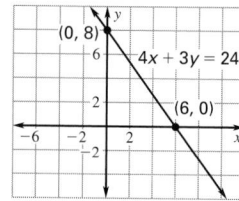

17. x-intercept $= -4$, y-intercept $= 18$;

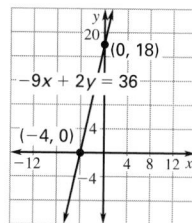

18. x-intercept $= 2$, y-intercept $= -10$;

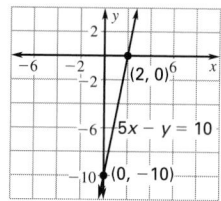

Lesson 4.5 (R46–R47)

1.

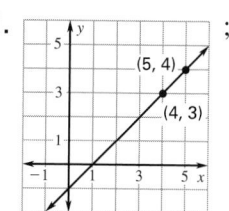

; positive

2.

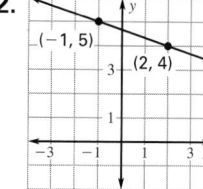

; negative

3. 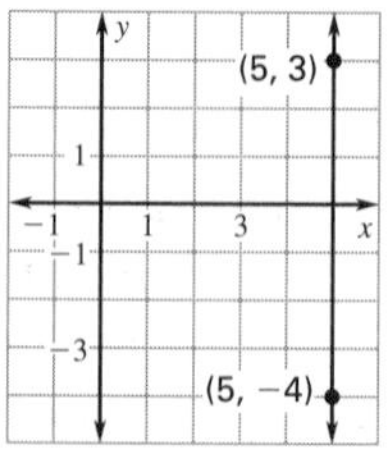

; undefined

4. 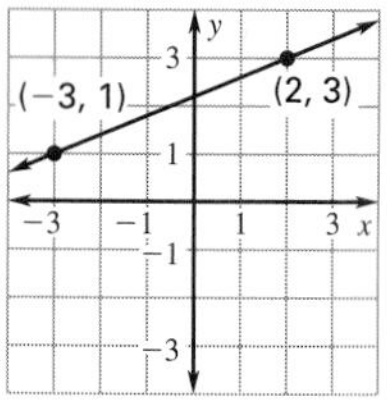

; positive

5. 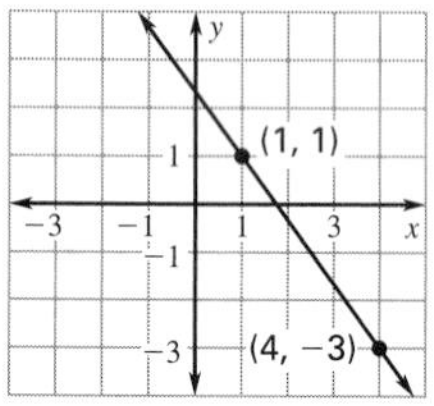

; negative

6. 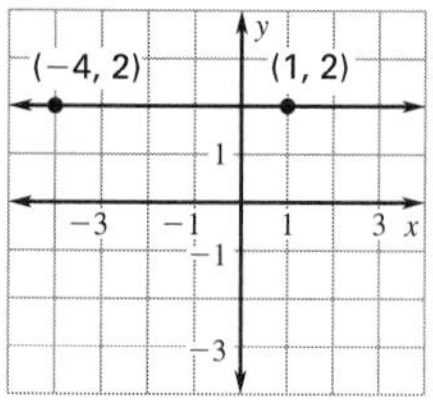

; zero

7. 1 **8.** $-\frac{1}{3}$ **9.** $-\frac{2}{3}$ **10.** 0 **11.** $\frac{2}{3}$

12. undefined **13.** $\frac{5}{4}$ **14.** 3 **15.** 2

16. undefined **17.** $-\frac{5}{2}$ **18.** 0

19. Slope of first road: $\frac{3}{14}$; slope of second road: $\frac{1}{5}$; since $\frac{3}{14} > \frac{1}{5}$, the first road is steeper.

Lesson 4.6 (R48)

1. $y = 3x$ **2.** $y = 8x$ **3.** $y = 4x$ **4.** $y = -3x$
5. $y = x$ **6.** $y = 3x$ **7.** $y = -\frac{3}{2}x$ **8.** $y = -\frac{7}{8}x$
9. $y = -\frac{10}{9}x$

10. 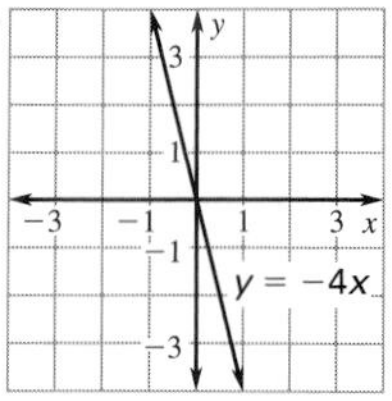

11. 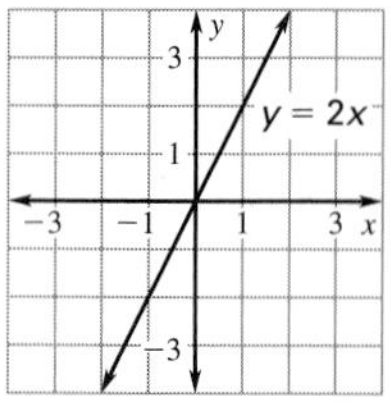

12. 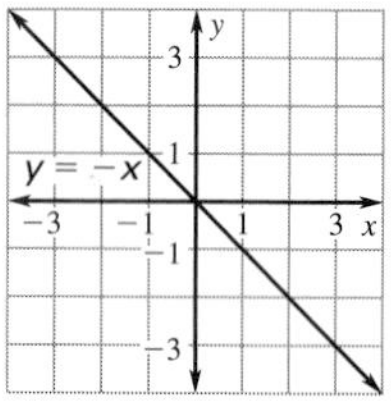

13. 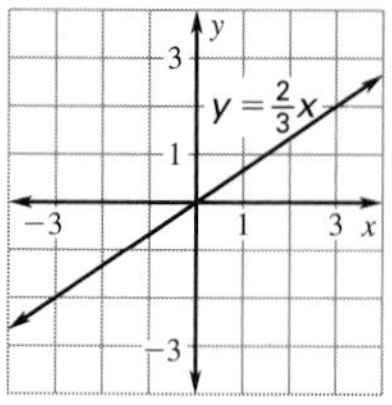

14. a. $t = 5d$ **b.** $d = 1.4$ miles

Lesson 4.7 (R49)

1. $y = 2x - 7$, 2, −7
2. equation is in slope-intercept form; 0, 3
3. $y = 3x + 4$; 3, 4
4. $y = \frac{2}{3}x - 4$; $\frac{2}{3}$, − 4
5. $y = -2x + 6$, −2, 6
6. $y = -7x + 49$; −7, 49
7. $y = -4x + 18$; −4, 18
8. $y = -\frac{2}{3}x + 8$; $-\frac{2}{3}$, 8
9. $y = -\frac{3}{4}x - 5$; $-\frac{3}{4}$, −5

10. 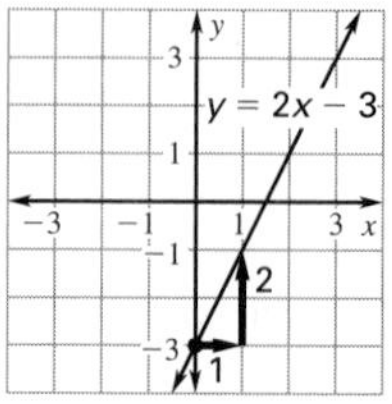

11. 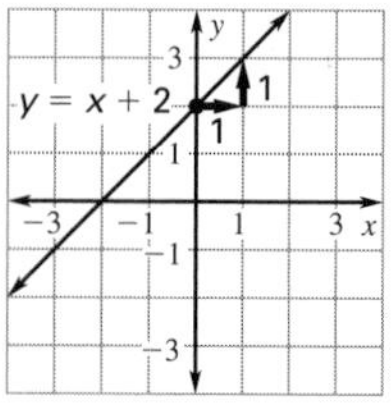

ANSWERS

12.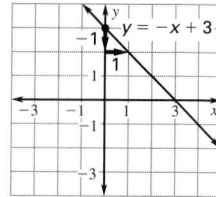

13.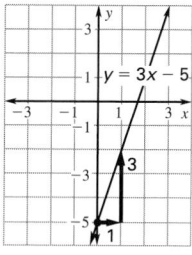

14.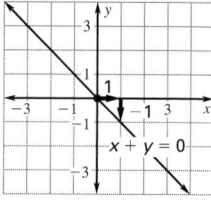

15.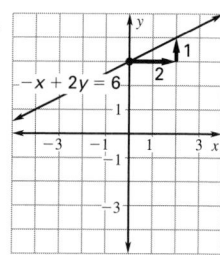

1. $-1, 5, 11$ **2.** $2, -1, -4$ **3.** $-16, -1, 14$

4. No; for one input, 1, there is more than one output, -3 and 3   **5.** Yes, for each input there is one output, domain: $-4, -1, 0, 2$; range: -4
6. No; a vertical line can intersect the graph more than once.   **7.** Yes; a vertical line intersects the graph only once.   **8.** No; a vertical line can intersect the graph more than once.

16. Equations 12 and 14 are parallel. They have the same slope, -1, but different y-intercepts: 3 and 0

17. 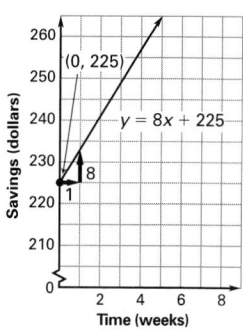   The slope is 8: the savings rate per week; the y-intercept is 225: the amount Carlos first saved.

Chapter 5

Lesson 5.1 (R52)

1. $y = 3x - 2$ **2.** $y = x + 2$ **3.** $y = -x + 3$

4. $y = -2x$ **5.** $y = 2x - 6$ **6.** $y = 3x - 1$

7. $y = \frac{3}{2}x + 3$ **8.** $y = -\frac{1}{4}x + 1$

9. $y = -\frac{1}{3}x - 1$ **10.** $y = -\frac{3}{2}x + 3$

11. $y = \frac{3}{2}x - \frac{3}{2}$ **12.** $y = -x + 3$

13. Parallel sides $\overline{AB}$ and $\overline{DC}$: $y = -x + 3$,
$y = -x - 3$; Parallel sides $\overline{DA}$ and $\overline{CB}$:
$y = x + 3$, $y = x - 3$; The slopes of the parallel
lines are equal.

Lesson 5.2 (R53)

1. $y = -2x + 3$ **2.** $y = x$ **3.** $y = -2$

4. $y = -x - 2$ **5.** $y = \frac{1}{2}x + 2$ **6.** $y = 4x - 18$

7. $y = 2x + 12$ **8.** $y = x - 1$ **9.** $y = -x + 2$

10. $y - 4 = -1(x - 0)$ **11.** $y - 2 = \frac{2}{3}(x - 3)$

12. $y - 3 = 2(x - 2)$ **13.** $y = 3x - 2$

14. $y = \frac{1}{2}x + 6$ **15.** $y = \frac{3}{5}x + 4$

16. $y = -6x + 9$ **17.** $y = 2x + 8$

18. $y = -x + 5$

Lesson 5.3 (R54)

1. $y = x - 1$ **2.** $y = -2x + 3$

3. $y = -\frac{1}{2}x - 1$ **4.** $y = \frac{7}{3}x + \frac{10}{3}$

5. $y = -x + 3$ **6.** $y = \frac{1}{2}x - 1$

7. $y = -\frac{2}{3}x + 3$ **8.** $y = -4x$ **9.** $y = 2x - 4$

10. $y = -2x - 1$ **11.** $y = \frac{1}{2}x$ **12.** $y = x$

13. $y = 2x$ **14.** $y = 3$ **15.** $y = -2$

Lesson 5.4 (R55–R56)

1–18. Standard forms may vary.

1. $3x + y = 4$ **2.** $-2x + y = -7$

3. $x + 3y = -6$ **4.** $3x + 4y = 5$

5. $x + 8y = 3$ **6.** $-2x + 5y = 0$

7. $x + y = -1$ **8.** $-2x + y = 5$

9. $y = -1$ **10.** $-4x + 5y = 10$

11. $3x + 2y = -20$ **12.** $3x + y = 7$

13. $-2x + 3y = 8$ **14.** $-4x + 9y = 39$

15. $x + 2y = -4$ **16.** $y = 3$ **17.** $x = -4$

18. $y = -1$

Lesson 5.5 (R57–R58)

1. 10 **2.** 30 **3.** $y = 10x + 30$

4. $y = 10x + 30$;

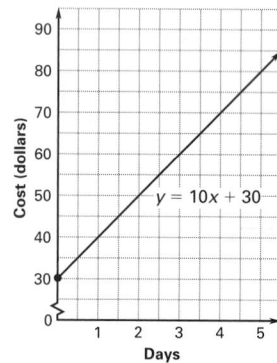

5. $60 **6.** 6 days

7.

Grapes (pounds), x	3	6	9	12	15
Tomatoes (pounds), y	18	13.5	9	4.5	0

8. $4x + 6y = 80$

Lesson 5.6 (R59)

1. yes **2.** no **3.** yes **4.** yes **5.** $y = -\frac{1}{2}x$

6. $y = -x + 10$ **7.** $x = -3$ **8.** $y = \frac{5}{4}x - 9$

9. $y = \frac{1}{4}x + \frac{23}{4}$ **10.** $y = -\frac{1}{3}x + 7$

11. $y = \frac{2}{3}x$; the product of the slopes of the lines
is $\frac{2}{3} \cdot (-\frac{3}{2}) = -1$ so the lines are perpendicular. **12.** $y = 4x - 23$; the product of the slopes
of the lines is $4 \cdot (-\frac{1}{4}) = -1$ so the lines are
perpendicular.

Chapter 6

Lesson 6.1 (R61)

1. $q \le -1$; C

2. $n \ge -1$, A

3. $x < -1$, B

4. $x > 11$;
```
 +——+——+——+——+——○——+——+——+——→
 7   8   9  10  11  12  13
```

5. $w \le 5$;
```
 +——+——+——+——+——●——+——+——
 0   1   2   3   4   5   6   7
```

6. $h \ge -2$;
```
 +——+——●——+——+——+——+——+——→
-4  -3  -2  -1  0   1   2   3   4
```

7. $b < -4$;
```
 ←——+——○——+——+——+——+——+——+——+——
-6  -5  -4  -3  -2  -1  0   1   2
```

8. $x \ge -7$;
```
 +——+——+——●——+——+——+——+——→
-10 -9  -8  -7  -6  -5  -4  -3  -2
```

9. $n > 8$;
```
 ←——+——+——+——○——+——+——+——+——
 4   5   6   7   8   9  10  11  12
```

10. $m > 55$;
```
 ←——+——+——○——+——+——+——+——→
40  45  50  55  60  65  70  75  80
```

11. $k \ge -8$;
```
 ←——+——●——+——+——+——+——+——→
-12 -10 -8  -6  -4  -2  0   2   4
```

12. $y < 31$;
```
 +——+——○——+——+——+——+——
28  29  30  31  32  33  34  35
```

13. $s > 10$;
```
 +——+——+——+——+——○——+——+——→
 0   2   4   6   8  10  12  14
```

14. $h \ge 1$;
```
 ←——+——+——●——+——+——+——→
-3  -2  -1  0   1   2   3   4
```

15. $n < -1$;
```
 ←——+——+——+——○——+——+——+——
-5  -4  -3  -2  -1  0   1   2
```

Lesson 6.2 (R62)

1. yes   **2.** no   **3.** no   **4.** yes

5. $d \le -7$;
```
 ←——●——+——+——+——+——+——→
-8  -7  -6  -5  -4  -3  -2  -1
```

6. $y < 9$;
```
 ←——+——+——+——○——+——+——
 5   6   7   8   9  10  11  12
```

7. $s < -\frac{1}{4}$;
```
 ←——+——+——+——○——+——+——
   -\frac{3}{2}  -1  -\frac{1}{2}  0   \frac{1}{2}
```

8. $h \le -4$
```
 ←——+——+——●——+——+——+——+——
-8  -7  -6  -5  -4  -3  -2  -1  0
```

9. $u > 35$;
```
 +——+——+——○——+——+——+——+——→
20  25  30  35  40  45  50  55  60
```

10. $x > 25$;
```
 ←——+——+——+——+——○——+——+——+——→
 0   5  10  15  20  25  30  35  40  45
```

11. $k \ge -90$;
```
 +——●——+——+——+——+——+——+——→
-100 -90 -80 -70 -60 -50 -40 -30 -20
```

12. $p > -15$;
```
 ←——+——○——+——+——+——+——+——→
-25 -20 -15 -10 -5  0   5  10  15
```

13. $t \ge -21$;
```
 ←——+——●——+——+——+——+——+——→
-27 -24 -21 -18 -15 -12 -9  -6
```

14. $b < 0$;
```
 ←——+——+——+——○——+——+——+——
-4  -3  -2  -1  0   1   2   3   4
```

15. $x < -8$;
```
 ←——+——+——+——○——+——+——+——
-16 -14 -12 -10 -8  -6  -4  -2  0
```

16. $m \le -4\frac{1}{2}$;
```
 ←——+——+——●——+——+——+——
-6      -5      -4      -3      -2
```

Lesson 6.3 (R63)

1. $4j + 5 \ge 23$ Write original inequality.
   $4j \ge 18$ Subtract 5 from each side.
   $j \ge 4.5$ Then divide each side by 4.

2. B   **3.** C   **4.** A   **5.** $h \ge -2$ **6.** $y > 7$

7. $x > -2\frac{1}{2}$ **8.** $r \ge 1\frac{1}{2}$ **9.** $n \ge 2$ **10.** $b < \frac{1}{3}$

11. $q < 7$ **12.** $s < -2$ **13.** $y > 14$ **14.** $m > -8$

15. $y \le \frac{1}{2}$

16. $0.75x + 4 \le 20$; $x \le 21\frac{1}{3}$; You can buy up to 21 ride tickets.

Lesson 6.4 (R64)

1–4. Statements of inequalities may vary.

1. $x \ge 1$ and $x < 6$ **2.** $-5 < x \le -3$

3. $x \ge -2$ and $x < 5$ **4.** $-1 < x \le 4$

5. $-5 < j < 5$;
```
 +——+——○——+——○——+——+——
-15 -10 -5  0   5  10  15
```

6. $1 \le r \le 2$;
```
 ←——+——+——●——●——+——+——→
-2  -1  0   1   2   3   4
```

7. $-2 < r \le -1.5$;
```
 ←○——+——+——●——+——→
  -2    -1.8    -1.6    -1.4
```

8. $-1.5 < w < 3.5$;

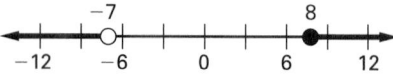

9. $-3 < x < 5$;

10. $2 \le x \le 6$;

11. $1 < x < 7$;

12. $-1 < x \le 8$;

Lesson 6.5 (R65)

1. B   **2.** A   **3.** $x < -6$ or $x \ge 12$

4. $x \ge 9$ or $x < -7$

5. $x \le -3$ or $x > 5$;

6. $x < -4$ or $x > -1$;

7. $x < -2$ or $x \ge 3$;

8. $a \ge 5$ or $a \le 4$;

9. $g < 16$ or $g > 25$;

10. $k > -1$ or $k < -5$;

11. $x < -7$ or $x \ge 8$;

12. $x \le -5$ or $x \ge 10$;

13. x is between 1.5 and 4 or x is greater than 6.

Lesson 6.6 (R66–R67)

1. two   **2.** none   **3.** one

4. $x + 4 = 8, x + 4 = -8$

5. $5x - 3 = 12; 5x - 3 = -12$

6. $2x + 2 = 10 ; 2x + 2 = -10$

7. $5, -5$ **8.** $6, -8$ **9.** $8, -6$

10. $-\frac{19}{5}, \frac{27}{5}$ **11.** $1, 8$ **12.** $-1, 6$ **13.** no solution

14. $3, -\frac{5}{3}$ **15.** $-8, -2$ **16.** $\frac{5}{3}, 3$ **17.** A   **18.** B

Lesson 6.7 (R68)

1. C   **2.** B   **3.** A

4. $x \ge 2$ or $x \le -2$;

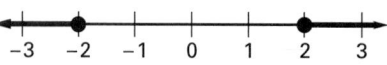

5. $-4 < x < 4$;

6. $x > 4$ or $x < -4$;

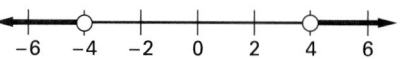

7. $-17 < x < 1$;

8. $-48 < x < 24$;

9. $x < -18$ or $x > 16$;

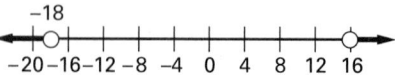

10. $2 < x < 3$;

11. $-5 \le x \le 4$;

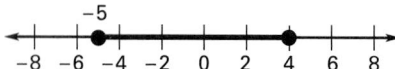

12. $-16 \le x \le -2$;

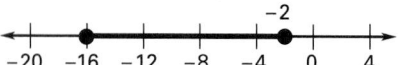

ANSWERS

13. $x \leq 6$ or $x \geq 18$;

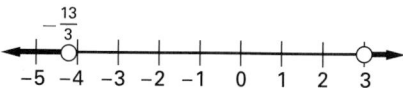

14. $-1 < x < 4$;

15. $x < -\frac{13}{3}$ or $x > 3$;

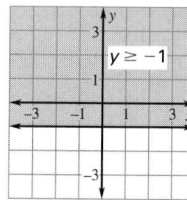

16. sometimes; $x \geq 6$ or $x \leq -3$

Lesson 6.8 (R69)

1. above **2.** to the left

3. $3 - 3(2) = 3 - 6 = -3$; Since $-3 \leq 4$, the point $(3, 2)$ is a solution of $x - 3y \leq 4$.

4.   **5.**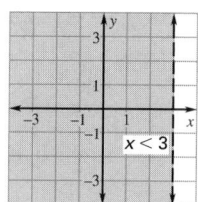

6. 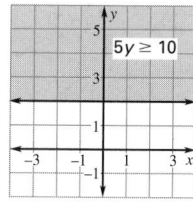 **7.**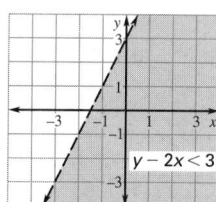

8. 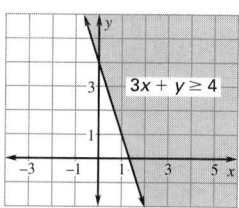 **9.**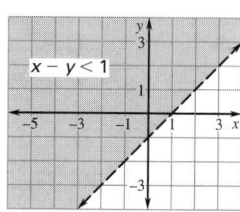

10. 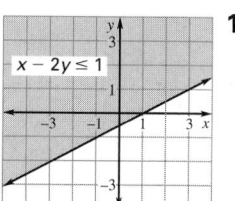 **11.**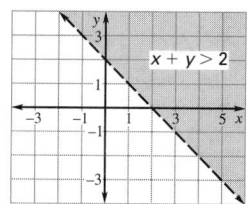

12.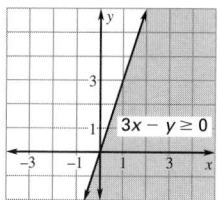

13.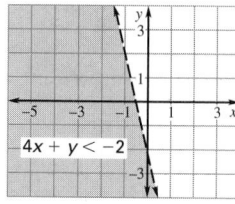

14.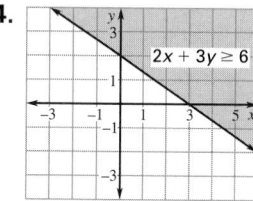

15.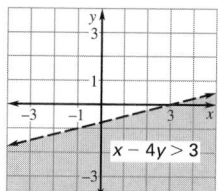

Algebra 1

Concepts and Skills

Volume 2

Chapters 7-12

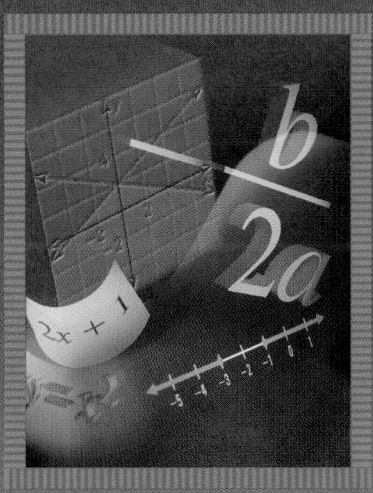

McDougal Littell

A HOUGHTON MIFFLIN COMPANY

Evanston, Illinois • Boston • Dallas

Systems of Linear Equations and Inequalities

▷ How can you analyze the need for low-income housing?

To see how the need for low-income rental housing changes over time, you can construct a model. The graph below shows the number of households with annual earnings of $12,000 or less that need to rent housing and the number of rental units available that they can afford.

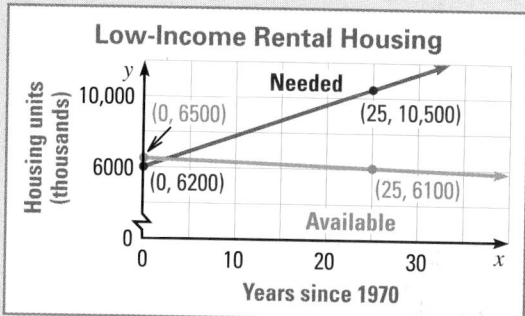

Low-Income Rental Housing

In this chapter you will learn how to use pairs of linear equations, as well as inequalities, to analyze problems.

Think & Discuss

Use the graph to answer the following questions.

1. How many low-cost housing units were available in 1995?

2. In 1995 how much greater was the need for low-income housing than the availability of low-cost units?

Learn More About It

You will use a linear system to analyze the need for low-income housing in Exercises 32 and 33 on page 413.

APPLICATION LINK More about housing is available at www.mcdougallittell.com

PREVIEW

What's the chapter about?

- Graphing and solving **systems of linear equations**
- Determining the number of **solutions of a linear system**
- Graphing and solving **systems of linear inequalities**

KEY WORDS

- **system of linear equations**, *p. 389*
- **solution of a linear system**, *p. 389*
- **point of intersection**, *p. 389*

- **linear combination**, *p. 402*
- **system of linear inequalities**, *p. 424*
- **solution of a system of linear inequalities**, *p. 424*

PREPARE

Chapter Readiness Quiz

Take this quick quiz. If you are unsure of an answer, look back at the reference pages for help.

VOCABULARY CHECK *(refer to pp. 134, 153)*

1. Which of the following is *not* a linear equation?

   A $2x + y = 5$ **B** $x = 3$

   C $y = 2x^2 - 1$ **D** $y = 3x$

2. Which equation is an identity?

   A $7x + 6 = 5(2x + 1)$ **B** $5(2x + 4) = 2(10 + 5x)$

   C $-8x + 4 = -2(4x + 4)$ **D** $-4(2 - 3x) = -8 - 12x$

SKILL CHECK *(refer to pp. 146, 367)*

3. What is the solution of the equation $2x + 6(x + 1) = -2$?

   A -1 **B** $-\dfrac{3}{8}$ **C** $\dfrac{1}{2}$ **D** 1

4. Which ordered pair is a solution of the inequality $7y - 8x > 56$?

   A $(0, 8)$ **B** $(0, 0)$ **C** $(-6, 1)$ **D** $(-7, 2)$

STUDY TIP

List Kinds of Problems

In your notebook keep a list of different types of problems and how to solve them.

Mixture Problems (p. 410)

$$x + y = 90 \longleftarrow \text{volume of mixture}$$

$$0.2x + 0.5y = 36 \longleftarrow \text{acid in mixture}$$

Since at least one of the variables has a coefficient of 1, use the substitution method to solve.

7.1 Graphing Linear Systems

Goal
Estimate the solution of a system of linear equations by graphing.

Key Words
- system of linear equations
- solution of a linear system
- point of intersection

How many hits are you getting at your Web site?

In this chapter you will study *systems of linear equations*. In Example 3 you will use two equations to predict when two Web sites will have the same number of daily visits.

Two or more linear equations in the same variable form a **system of linear equations**, or simply a *linear system*. Here is an example of a linear system.

$$x + 2y = 5 \qquad \text{Equation 1}$$
$$2x - 3y = 3 \qquad \text{Equation 2}$$

A **solution of a linear system** in two variables is a pair of numbers *a* and *b* for which $x = a$ and $y = b$ make each equation a true statement.

Such a solution can be written as an ordered pair (a, b) in which *a* and *b* are the values of *x* and *y* that solve the linear system. The point (a, b) that lies on the graph of each equation is called the **point of intersection** of the graphs.

Student Help

▶ MORE EXAMPLES

More examples are available at www.mcdougallittell.com

EXAMPLE 1 Find the Point of Intersection

Use the graph at the right to estimate the solution of the linear system. Then check your solution algebraically.

$$3x + 2y = 4 \qquad \text{Equation 1}$$
$$-x + 3y = -5 \qquad \text{Equation 2}$$

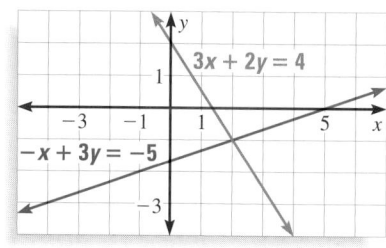

Solution

The lines appear to intersect at the point $(2, -1)$.

CHECK ✓ Substitute 2 for *x* and -1 for *y* in each equation.

EQUATION 1	EQUATION 2
$3x + 2y = 4$	$-x + 3y = -5$
$3(2) + 2(-1) \stackrel{?}{=} 4$	$-(2) + 3(-1) \stackrel{?}{=} -5$
$6 - 2 \stackrel{?}{=} 4$	$-2 - 3 \stackrel{?}{=} -5$
$4 = 4$ ✓	$-5 = -5$ ✓

ANSWER ▶ Because the ordered pair $(2, -1)$ makes each equation true, $(2, -1)$ is the solution of the system of linear equations.

SOLVING A LINEAR SYSTEM USING GRAPH-AND-CHECK

STEP ❶ **Write** each equation in a form that is easy to graph.

STEP ❷ **Graph** both equations in the same coordinate plane.

STEP ❸ **Estimate** the coordinates of the point of intersection.

STEP ❹ **Check** whether the coordinates give a solution by substituting them into each equation of the original linear system.

EXAMPLE 2 Graph and Check a Linear System

Use the graph-and-check method to solve the linear system.

$$x + y = -2 \qquad \textbf{Equation 1}$$
$$2x - 3y = -9 \qquad \textbf{Equation 2}$$

Solution

Student Help

▶ **LOOK BACK**
For help with writing equations in slope-intercept form, see p. 243.

❶ **Write** each equation in slope-intercept form.

EQUATION 1	EQUATION 2
$x + y = -2$	$2x - 3y = -9$
$y = -x - 2$	$-3y = -2x - 9$
	$y = \dfrac{2}{3}x + 3$

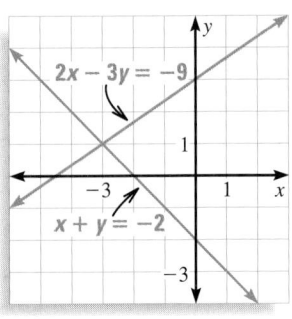

❷ **Graph** both equations.

❸ **Estimate** from the graph that the point of intersection is $(-3, 1)$.

❹ **Check** whether $(-3, 1)$ is a solution by substituting -3 for x and 1 for y in each of the original equations.

EQUATION 1	EQUATION 2
$x + y = -2$	$2x - 3y = -9$
$-3 + 1 \overset{?}{=} -2$	$2(-3) - 3(1) \overset{?}{=} -9$
$-2 = -2$ ✓	$-6 - 3 \overset{?}{=} -9$
	$-9 = -9$ ✓

ANSWER ▶ Because the ordered pair $(-3, 1)$ makes each equation true, $(-3, 1)$ is the solution of the linear system.

Checkpoint ✓ Graph and Check a Linear System

Use the graph-and-check method to solve the linear system.

1. $x + y = 4$
$2x + y = 5$

2. $x - y = 5$
$2x + 3y = 0$

3. $x - y = -2$
$x + y = -4$

Link to
Careers

WEBMASTERS build Web
sites for clients. They design
Web pages and update
content.

More about
Webmasters at
www.mcdougallittell.com

EXAMPLE 3 Write and Solve a Real-Life Linear System

WEBMASTER You are the Webmaster of the Web sites for the science club and for the math club. Assuming that the number of visits at each site can be represented by a linear function, use the information in the table to predict when the number of daily visits to the two sites will be the same.

Club	Current daily visits	Increase (daily visits per month)
Science	400	25
Math	200	50

Solution

VERBAL MODEL

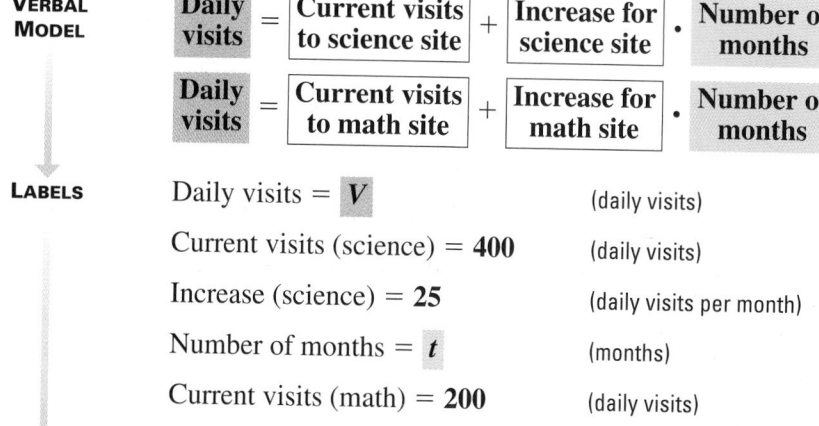

$$\boxed{\text{Daily visits}} = \boxed{\text{Current visits to science site}} + \boxed{\text{Increase for science site}} \cdot \boxed{\text{Number of months}}$$

$$\boxed{\text{Daily visits}} = \boxed{\text{Current visits to math site}} + \boxed{\text{Increase for math site}} \cdot \boxed{\text{Number of months}}$$

LABELS

Daily visits = V (daily visits)

Current visits (science) = **400** (daily visits)

Increase (science) = **25** (daily visits per month)

Number of months = t (months)

Current visits (math) = **200** (daily visits)

Increase (math) = **50** (daily visits per month)

ALGEBRAIC MODEL

$V = 400 + 25t$ **Equation 1 (science)**

$V = 200 + 50t$ **Equation 2 (math)**

Graph both equations. The point of intersection appears to be (8, 600).

CHECK ✓ Check this solution in each of the original equations.

Equation 1 $600 \stackrel{?}{=} 400 + 25(8)$

         $600 = 400 + 200$ ✓

Equation 2 $600 \stackrel{?}{=} 200 + 50(8)$

         $600 = 200 + 400$ ✓

ANSWER ▶ According to the model, the sites will have the same number of visits in 8 months.

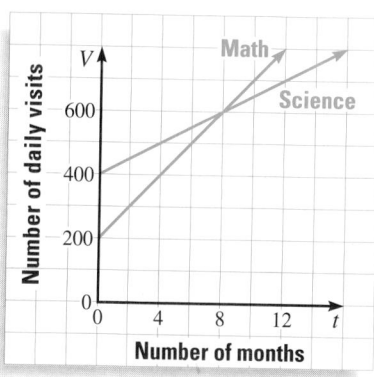

Student Help

▶**READING ALGEBRA**
The graph at the right tells you that in 8 months both sites should have the same number of daily visits, 600.

Checkpoint ✓ **Write and Solve a Real-Life Linear System**

4. The Spanish club Web site currently receives 500 daily visits. If the number of daily visits increases by 20 each month, when will the Spanish club site have the same number of daily visits as the science club site?

Exercises

Guided Practice

Vocabulary Check

1. Explain what it means to solve a linear system using the graph-and-check method.

2. Use the graph at the right to find the point of intersection for the system of linear equations.
$$y = -x + 2$$
$$y = x + 2$$

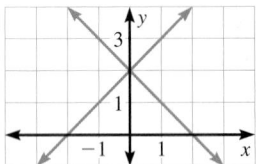

Skill Check

In Exercises 3–6, use the linear system below.
$$-x + y = -2$$
$$2x + y = 10$$

3. Write each equation in slope-intercept form.

4. Graph both equations in the same coordinate plane.

5. Estimate the coordinates of the point of intersection.

6. Check the coordinates algebraically by substituting them into each equation of the original linear system.

Practice and Applications

CHECKING SOLUTIONS **Check whether the ordered pair is a solution of the system of linear equations.**

7. $3x - 2y = 11$
$-x + 6y = 7$ $(5, 2)$

8. $6x - 3y = -15$
$2x + y = -3$ $(-2, 1)$

9. $x + 3y = 15$
$4x + y = 6$ $(3, -6)$

10. $-5x + y = 19$
$x - 7y = 3$ $(-4, -1)$

11. $-15x + 7y = 1$
$3x - y = 1$ $(3, 5)$

12. $-2x + y = 11$
$-x - 9y = -15$ $(6, 1)$

FINDING POINTS OF INTERSECTION **Use the graph given to estimate the solution of the linear system. Then check your solution algebraically.**

13. $-x + 2y = 6$
$x + 4y = 24$

14. $2x - y = -2$
$4x - y = -6$

15. $x + y = 3$
$-2x + y = -6$

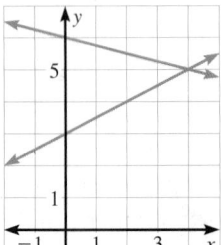

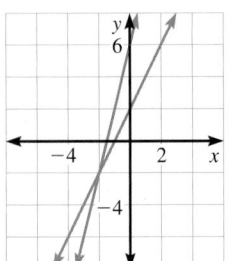

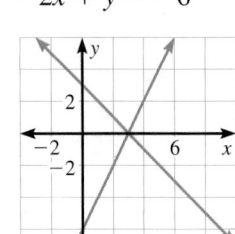

Student Help

▶ **HOMEWORK HELP**
Example 1: Exs. 7–15
Example 2: Exs. 16–24
Example 3: Exs. 25–28

GRAPH AND CHECK Estimate the solution of the linear system graphically. Then check the solution algebraically.

16. $y = -x + 3$
$y = x + 1$

17. $y = -6$
$x = 6$

18. $y = 2x - 4$
$2y = -x$

19. $2x - 3y = 9$
$x = -3$

20. $5x + 4y = 16$
$y = -16$

21. $x - y = 1$
$5x - 4y = 0$

22. $3x + 6y = 15$
$-2x + 3y = -3$

23. $y = -2x + 6$
$y = 2x + 2$

24. $5x + 6y = 54$
$-x + y = 9$

25. CARS Car model A costs $22,000 to purchase and $.12 per mile to maintain. Car model B costs $24,500 to purchase and $.10 per mile to maintain.

Use the graph to determine how many miles each car must be driven for the total costs of the two models to be the same.

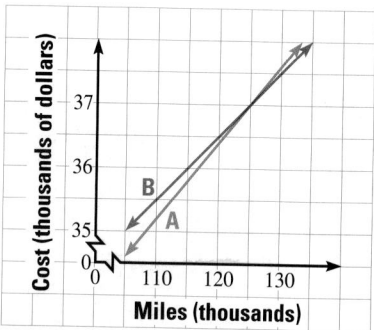

26. AEROBICS CLASSES A fitness club offers an aerobics class in the morning and in the evening. Assuming that the number of people in each class can be represented by a linear function, use the information in the table below to predict when the number of people in each class will be the same.

Class	Current attendance	Increase (people per month)
Morning	40	2
Evening	22	8

27. **History Link** The fast-changing world of the 1920s produced new roles for women in the workplace. From 1910 to 1930 the percent of women working in agriculture decreased, while the percent of women in professional jobs increased, as shown in the table.

Job type	Percent holding that job type in 1910	Average percent increase per year from 1910 to 1930
Agriculture	22.4%	−0.7%
Professional	9.1%	0.25%

Assuming that both percentages can be represented by a linear function, use the information in the table above to estimate when the percent of women working in agriculture equaled the percent of women working in professional jobs between 1910 and 1930.

WOMEN'S EMPLOYMENT
In 1870 only 5% of all office workers were women. By 1910 that number had risen to 40%.

28. PERSONAL FINANCE You and your sister are saving money from your allowances. You have $25 and save $3 each week. Your sister has $40 and saves $2 each week. After how many weeks will you and your sister have the same amount of money?

29. CHALLENGE You know how to solve the equation $x + 2 = 3x - 4$ algebraically. This equation can also be solved by graphing the following system of linear equations.

$$y = x + 2$$
$$y = 3x - 4$$

a. Explain how the system of linear equations is related to the original equation given.

b. Estimate the solution of the linear system graphically.

c. Check that the x-coordinate from part (b) satisfies the original equation by substituting the x-coordinate for x in $x + 2 = 3x - 4$.

Standardized Test Practice

30. MULTIPLE CHOICE Which ordered pair is a solution of the following system of linear equations?

$$x + y = 3$$
$$2x + y = 6$$

Ⓐ $(0, 3)$ Ⓑ $(1, 2)$ Ⓒ $(2, 1)$ Ⓓ $(3, 0)$

31. MULTIPLE CHOICE Which system of linear equations is graphed?

Ⓕ $\begin{array}{l} -x + 2y = 2 \\ -3x + 4y = 2 \end{array}$ Ⓖ $\begin{array}{l} x + 2y = 2 \\ x - 2y = 0 \end{array}$

Ⓗ $\begin{array}{l} -2x + y = 1 \\ -4x + 3y = 2 \end{array}$ Ⓙ $\begin{array}{l} 2x + y = 1 \\ 4x + 3y = 2 \end{array}$

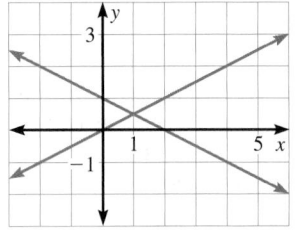

Mixed Review

SOLVING EQUATIONS Solve the equation. *(Lesson 3.3)*

32. $3x + 7 = -2$ **33.** $15 - 2a = 7$ **34.** $2y + 3y = 5$

35. $21 = 7(w - 2)$ **36.** $-2(t - 5) = 26$ **37.** $4(2x + 3) = -4$

WRITING EQUATIONS Write in slope-intercept form the equation of the line that passes through the given point and has the given slope. *(Lesson 5.2)*

38. $(3, 0)$, $m = -4$ **39.** $(-4, 3)$, $m = 1$ **40.** $(1, -5)$, $m = 4$

41. $(-4, -1)$, $m = -2$ **42.** $(2, 3)$, $m = 2$ **43.** $(-1, 5)$, $m = -3$

44. SUSPENSION BRIDGES The Verrazano-Narrows Bridge in New York is the longest suspension bridge in North America, with a main span of 4260 feet. Let x represent the length (in feet) of every other suspension bridge in North America. Write an inequality that describes x. Then graph the inequality. *(Lesson 6.1)*

Maintaining Skills

DECIMAL OPERATIONS Perform the indicated operation. *(Skills Review pp. 759, 760)*

45. $3.71 + 1.054$ **46.** $10.35 + 5.301$ **47.** $2.5 - 0.5$

48. $(2.1)(0.2)$ **49.** $\dfrac{0.3}{0.03}$ **50.** $\dfrac{5.175}{1.15}$

USING A GRAPHING CALCULATOR
Graphing Linear Systems

You can use a graphing calculator to graph linear systems and to estimate their solution.

Sample

Use a graphing calculator to estimate the solution of the linear system.

$$y = -0.3x + 1.8 \qquad \text{Equation 1}$$
$$y = 0.6x - 1.5 \qquad \text{Equation 2}$$

Solution

Student Help

▶ **KEYSTROKE HELP**

 See keystrokes for several models of calculators at www.mcdougallittell.com

① Enter the equations.

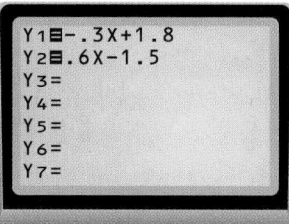

② Set an appropriate viewing window to graph both equations.

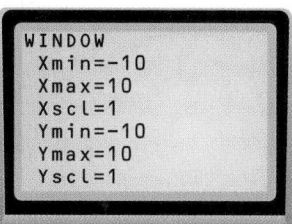

③ Graph both equations. You can use the direction keys to move the cursor to the approximate intersection point.

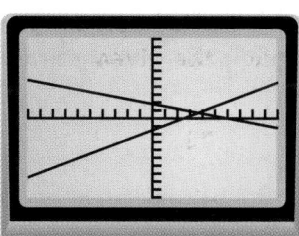

④ Use the *Intersect* feature to estimate a point where the graphs intersect. Follow your calculator's procedure to display the coordinate values.

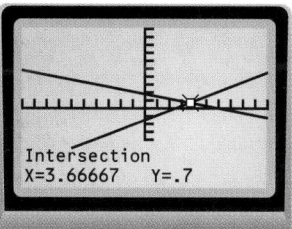

ANSWER ▶ The solution of the linear system is approximately (3.7, 0.7).

Try These

Use a graphing calculator to estimate the solution of the linear system. Check the result in each of the original equations.

1. $y = x + 6$
$y = -x - 1$

2. $y = -3x - 2$
$y = x + 8$

3. $y = -0.25x - 2.25$
$y = x - 1.25$

4. $y = 1.33x - 20$
$y = 0.83x - 8.5$

7.2 Solving Linear Systems by Substitution

Goal
Solve a linear system by substitution.

Key Words
• substitution method

How many softballs were ordered?

In Exercise 29 you will solve a linear system to analyze a problem about ordering softballs. You will use a method called the *substitution method*.

There are several ways to solve a linear system without using graphs. In this lesson you will study an algebraic method known as the *substitution method*.

EXAMPLE 1 **Substitution Method: Solve for y First**

Solve the linear system.

$$-x + y = 1 \qquad \text{Equation 1}$$
$$2x + y = -2 \qquad \text{Equation 2}$$

Solution

❶ **Solve** for y in Equation 1.

$$-x + y = 1 \qquad \text{Original Equation 1}$$
$$y = x + 1 \qquad \text{Revised Equation 1}$$

❷ **Substitute** $x + 1$ for y in Equation 2 and find the value of x.

$$2x + y = -2 \qquad \text{Write Equation 2.}$$
$$2x + (x + 1) = -2 \qquad \text{Substitute } x + 1 \text{ for } y.$$
$$3x + 1 = -2 \qquad \text{Combine like terms.}$$
$$3x = -3 \qquad \text{Subtract 1 from each side.}$$
$$x = -1 \qquad \text{Divide each side by 3.}$$

❸ **Substitute** -1 for x in the revised Equation 1 to find the value of y.

$$y = x + 1 = -1 + 1 = 0$$

❹ **Check** that $(-1, 0)$ is a solution by substituting -1 for x and 0 for y in each of the original equations.

ANSWER ▶ The solution is $(-1, 0)$.

Student Help

> **STUDY TIP**
> When using substitution, you will get the same solution whether you solve for *y* first or *x* first. You should begin by solving for the variable that is easier to isolate.

EXAMPLE 2 **Substitution Method: Solve for *x* First**

Solve the linear system.

$$2x + 2y = 3 \qquad \textbf{Equation 1}$$
$$x - 4y = -1 \qquad \textbf{Equation 2}$$

Solution

❶ *Solve* for *x* in Equation 2 because it is easy to isolate *x*.

$x - 4y = -1$	Original Equation 2
$x = 4y - 1$	Revised Equation 2

❷ *Substitute* $4y - 1$ for *x* in Equation 1 and find the value of *y*.

$2x + 2y = 3$	Write Equation 1.
$2(4y - 1) + 2y = 3$	Substitute $4y - 1$ for *x*.
$8y - 2 + 2y = 3$	Use the distributive property.
$10y - 2 = 3$	Combine like terms.
$10y = 5$	Add 2 to each side.
$y = \dfrac{1}{2}$	Divide each side by 10.

❸ *Substitute* $\dfrac{1}{2}$ for *y* in the revised Equation 2 to find the value of *x*.

$$x = 4y - 1 = 4\left(\dfrac{1}{2}\right) - 1 = 2 - 1 = 1$$

❹ *Check* by substituting 1 for *x* and $\dfrac{1}{2}$ for *y* in the original equations.

ANSWER ▶ The solution is $\left(1, \dfrac{1}{2}\right)$.

 **Substitution Method**

Name the variable you would solve for first. Explain.

1. $3x - y = -9$
$2x + 4y = 8$

2. $x + 3y = -11$
$2x - 5y = 33$

3. $x - 3y = 0$
$x - 2y = 10$

SUMMARY

Solving a Linear System by Substitution

STEP ❶ *Solve* one of the equations for one of its variables.

STEP ❷ *Substitute* the expression from Step 1 into the other equation and solve for the other variable.

STEP ❸ *Substitute* the value from Step 2 into the revised equation from Step 1 and solve.

STEP ❹ *Check* the solution in each of the original equations.

EXAMPLE **3** **Write and Use a Linear System**

MUSEUM ADMISSIONS In one day the National Civil Rights Museum in Memphis, Tennessee, admitted 321 adults and children and collected $1590. The price of admission is $6 for an adult and $4 for a child. How many adults and how many children were admitted to the museum that day?

Solution

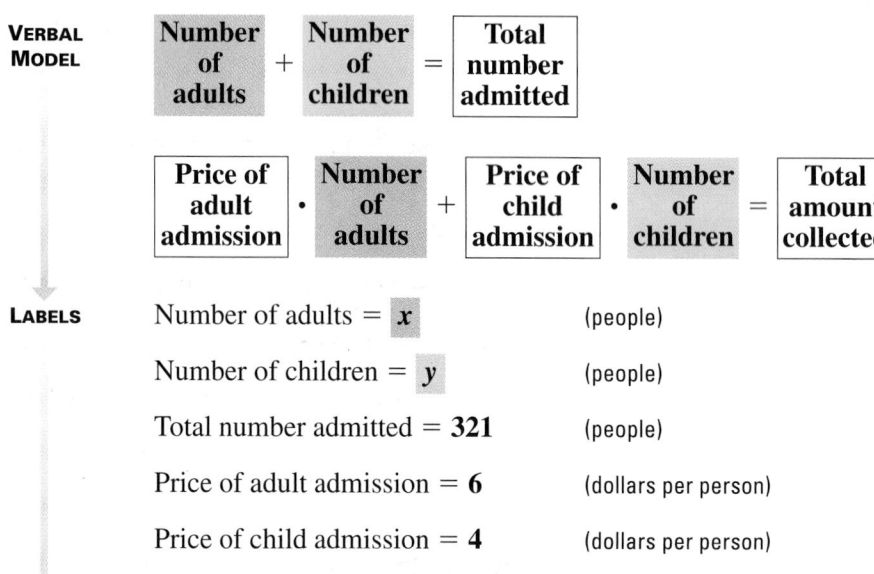

VERBAL MODEL

| Number of adults | + | Number of children | = | Total number admitted |

| Price of adult admission | · | Number of adults | + | Price of child admission | · | Number of children | = | Total amount collected |

LABELS

Number of adults = x (people)

Number of children = y (people)

Total number admitted = **321**   (people)

Price of adult admission = **6**   (dollars per person)

Price of child admission = **4**   (dollars per person)

Total amount collected = **1590**   (dollars)

ALGEBRAIC MODEL

$x + y = 321$ **Equation 1 (Number admitted)**

$6x + 4y = 1590$ **Equation 2 (Amount collected)**

Use the substitution method to solve the linear system.

$x = -y + 321$	Solve Equation 1 for x. (Revised Equation 1)
$6(-y + 321) + 4y = 1590$	Substitute $-y + 321$ for x in Equation 2.
$-6y + 1926 + 4y = 1590$	Use the distributive property.
$-2y + 1926 = 1590$	Combine like terms.
$-2y = -336$	Subtract 1926 from each side.
$y = 168$	Divide each side by -2.
$x = -(168) + 321 = 153$	Substitute 168 for y in revised Equation 1.

ANSWER ▶ 153 adults and 168 children were admitted to the National Civil Rights Museum that day.

Checkpoint ✓ **Write and Use a Linear System**

4. In one day a movie theater collected $4275 from 675 people. The price of admission is $7 for an adult and $5 for a child. How many adults and how many children were admitted to the movie theater that day?

7.2 Exercises

Guided Practice

Vocabulary Check

1. What four steps do you use to solve a system of linear equations by the substitution method?

2. When solving a system of linear equations, how do you decide which variable to isolate in Step 1 of the substitution method?

Skill Check

In Exercises 3–6, use the following system of equations.

$$3x + 2y = 7 \qquad \text{Equation 1}$$
$$5x - y = 3 \qquad \text{Equation 2}$$

3. Which equation would you use to solve for y? Explain why.

4. Solve for y in the equation you chose in Exercise 3.

5. Substitute the expression for y into the other equation and solve for x.

6. Substitute the value of x into your equation from Exercise 4. What is the solution of the linear system? Check your solution.

Use substitution to solve the linear system. Justify each step.

7. $3x + y = 3$
   $7x + 2y = 1$

8. $2x + y = 4$
   $-x + y = 1$

9. $3x - y = 0$
   $5y = 15$

Practice and Applications

CRITICAL THINKING **Tell which equation you would use to isolate a variable. Explain.**

10. $2x + y = -10$
   $3x - y = 0$

11. $m + 4n = 30$
   $m - 2n = 0$

12. $5c + 3d = 11$
   $5c - d = 5$

13. $3x - 2y = 19$
   $x + y = 8$

14. $4a + 3b = -5$
   $a - b = -3$

15. $3x + 5y = 25$
   $x - 2y = -10$

SOLVING LINEAR SYSTEMS **Use the substitution method to solve the linear system.**

16. $y = x - 4$
   $4x + y = 26$

17. $s = t + 4$
   $2t + s = 19$

18. $2c - d = -2$
   $4c + d = 20$

19. $2a = 8$
   $a + b = 2$

20. $2x + 3y = 31$
   $y = x + 7$

21. $p + q = 4$
   $4p + q = 1$

Student Help

▶ **HOMEWORK HELP**
  Example 1: Exs. 10–27
  Example 2: Exs. 10–27
  Example 3: Exs. 28–34

22. $x - 2y = -25$
   $3x - y = 0$

23. $u - v = 0$
   $7u + v = 0$

24. $x - y = 0$
   $12x - 5y = -21$

25. $m + 2n = 1$
   $5m + 3n = -23$

26. $x - y = -5$
   $x + 4 = 16$

27. $-3w + z = 4$
   $-9w + 5z = -1$

28. TICKET SALES You are selling tickets for a high school play. Student tickets cost $4 and general admission tickets cost $6. You sell 525 tickets and collect $2876. Use the following verbal model to find how many of each type of ticket you sold.

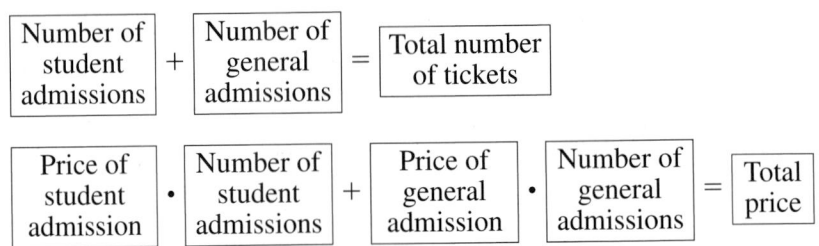

29. SOFTBALL You are ordering softballs for two softball leagues. The size of a softball is measured by its circumference. The Pony League uses an 11 inch softball priced at $3.50. The Junior League uses a 12 inch softball priced at $4.00. The bill smeared in the rain, but you know the total was 80 softballs for $305. How many of each size did you order?

30. *Geometry Link* The rectangle at the right has a perimeter of 40 centimeters. The length of the rectangle is 4 times as long as the width. Find the dimensions of the rectangle.

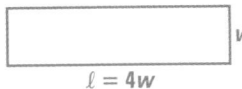

$\ell = 4w$

31. INVESTING One share of ABC stock is worth three times as much as XYZ stock. An investor has 100 shares of each. If the total value of the stocks is $4500, how much money is invested in each stock?

Link to
Sports

RUNNING In Exercises 32 and 33, use the following information.
You can run 200 meters per minute uphill and 250 meters per minute downhill. One day you run a total of 2200 meters in 10 minutes.

32. Assign labels to the verbal model below. Then write an algebraic model.

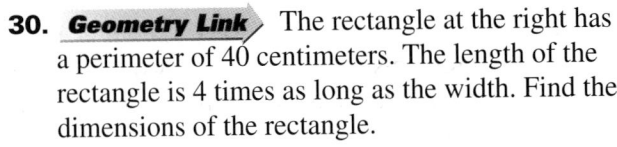

33. Find the number of meters you ran uphill and the number of meters you ran downhill.

34. ERROR ANALYSIS Find and correct the error shown below.

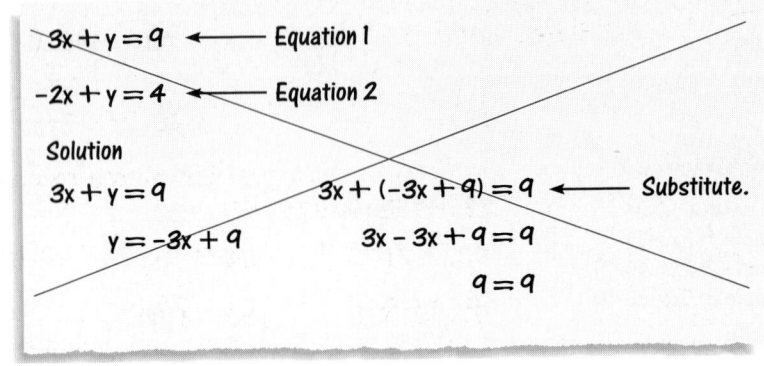

35. MULTIPLE CHOICE Which linear system has the solution $(6, 6)$?

- **A** $4x - 3y = -1$
  $-2x + y = -3$

- **B** $x + y = 12$
  $3x - 2y = 6$

- **C** $3x + y = 4$
  $4x - 3y = 1$

- **D** $4x + 3y = 0$
  $2x - y = 0$

36. MULTIPLE CHOICE Which linear system has been correctly solved for one of the variables from the following system?

$$2x - y = -1$$
$$2x + y = -7$$

- **F** $2x - y = -1$
  $y = 2x - 7$

- **G** $2x - y = -1$
  $y = -2x + 7$

- **H** $y = 2x + 1$
  $2x + y = -7$

- **J** $y = -2x - 1$
  $2x + y = -7$

37. MULTIPLE CHOICE Your math test is worth 100 points and has 38 problems. Each problem is worth either 5 points or 2 points. How many problems of each point value are on the test?

- **A** 5 points: 54
  2 points: 46

- **B** 5 points: 46
  2 points: 54

- **C** 5 points: 30
  2 points: 8

- **D** 5 points: 8
  2 points: 30

Mixed Review

SIMPLIFYING EXPRESSIONS **Simplify the expression.** *(Lesson 2.7)*

38. $4g + 3 + 2g - 3$

39. $3x + 2 - (5x + 2)$

40. $6(2 - m) - 3m - 12$

41. $4(3a + 5) + 3(-4a + 2)$

GRAPHING LINES **Write the equation in slope-intercept form. Then graph the equation.** *(Lesson 4.7)*

42. $6x + y = 0$

43. $8x - 4y = 16$

44. $3x + y = -5$

45. $5x + 3y = 3$

46. $x + y = 0$

47. $y = -4$

SOLVING AND GRAPHING **Solve the inequality. Then graph the solution.** *(Lessons 6.4, 6.5)*

48. $-5 < -x \le 1$

49. $-14 \le x + 5 \le 14$

50. $-2 < -3x + 1 < 10$

51. $x + 6 < 7 \; or \; 4x > 12$

52. $3x - 2 \ge 4 \; or \; 5 - x > 9$

Maintaining Skills

COMMON FACTORS **List all the common factors of the pair of numbers.** *(Skills Review p. 761)*

53. 3, 21

54. 4, 28

55. 21, 27

56. 10, 50

57. 12, 30

58. 18, 96

59. 78, 105

60. 84, 154

7.3 Solving Linear Systems by Linear Combinations

Goal
Solve a system of linear equations by linear combinations.

Key Words
• linear combination

How can a farmer find the location of a beehive?

In Exercise 44 you will solve a linear system to find the location of a beehive. You will use a method called *linear combinations*.

Sometimes it is not easy to isolate one of the variables in a linear system. In that case it may be easier to solve the system by *linear combinations*. A **linear combination** of two equations is an equation obtained by (1) multiplying one or both equations by a constant if necessary and (2) adding the resulting equations.

EXAMPLE 1 Add the Equations

Solve the linear system.

$$4x + 3y = 16 \qquad \textbf{Equation 1}$$
$$2x - 3y = 8 \qquad \textbf{Equation 2}$$

Solution

① *Add* the equations to get an equation in one variable.

$4x + 3y = 16$	Write Equation 1.
$2x - 3y = \ \ 8$	Write Equation 2.
$6x \qquad = 24$	Add equations.
$x = 4$	Solve for x.

② *Substitute* 4 for x into either equation and solve for y.

$4(4) + 3y = 16$	Substitute 4 for x.
$y = 0$	Solve for y.

③ *Check* by substituting 4 for x and 0 for y in each of the original equations.

ANSWER ▶ The solution is $(4, 0)$.

 **Add the Equations**

Solve the linear system. Then check your solution.

1. $3x + 2y = 7$
$-3x + 4y = 5$

2. $4x - 2y = 2$
$3x + 2y = 12$

3. $5x + 2y = -4$
$-5x + 3y = 19$

Sometimes you can solve by adding the original equations because the coefficients of a variable are already opposites, as in Example 1. In Example 2 you need to multiply both equations by an appropriate number first.

EXAMPLE 2 *Multiply Then Add*

Solve the linear system.

$$3x + 5y = 6 \qquad \text{Equation 1}$$
$$-4x + 2y = 5 \qquad \text{Equation 2}$$

Solution

❶ *Multiply* Equation 1 by 4 and Equation 2 by 3 to get coefficients of x that are opposites.

$3x + 5y = 6$	**Multiply by 4.** ➤	$12x + 20y = 24$
$-4x + 2y = 5$	**Multiply by 3.** ➤	$-12x + 6y = 15$

❷ *Add* the equations and solve for y.

$$26y = 39 \qquad \text{Add equations.}$$
$$y = 1.5 \qquad \text{Solve for } y.$$

❸ *Substitute* 1.5 for y into either equation and solve for x.

$$-4x + 2(\mathbf{1.5}) = 5 \qquad \text{Substitute 1.5 for } y.$$
$$-4x + 3 = 5 \qquad \text{Multiply.}$$
$$-4x = 2 \qquad \text{Subtract 3 from each side.}$$
$$x = -0.5 \qquad \text{Solve for } x.$$

❹ *Check* by substituting -0.5 for x and 1.5 for y in the original equations.

ANSWER ▶ The solution is $(-0.5, 1.5)$.

Checkpoint ✓ *Multiply Then Add*

Solve the linear system. Then check your solution.

4. $2x - 3y = 4$
$-4x + 5y = -8$

5. $3x + 4y = 6$
$2x - 5y = -19$

6. $6x + 2y = 2$
$-3x + 3y = -9$

SUMMARY

Solving a Linear System by Linear Combinations

STEP ❶ *Arrange* the equations with like terms in columns.

STEP ❷ *Multiply*, if necessary, the equations by numbers to obtain coefficients that are opposites for one of the variables.

STEP ❸ *Add* the equations from Step 2. Combining like terms with opposite coefficients will eliminate one variable. Solve for the remaining variable.

STEP ❹ *Substitute* the value obtained in Step 3 into either of the original equations and solve for the other variable.

STEP ❺ *Check* the solution in each of the original equations.

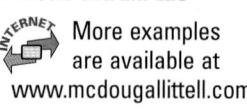
EXAMPLE 3 **Solve by Linear Combinations**

Solve the linear system. $3x + 2y = 8$ **Equation 1**
                             $2y = 12 - 5x$ **Equation 2**

Solution

1 **Arrange** the equations with like terms in columns.

  $3x + 2y = 8$ Write Equation 1.

  $5x + 2y = 12$ Rearrange Equation 2.

2 **Multiply** Equation 2 by -1 to get the coefficients of y to
be opposites.

  $3x + 2y = 8$ $3x + 2y = 8$

  $5x + 2y = 12$ **Multiply by −1.**⇒ $-5x - 2y = -12$

3 **Add** the equations. $-2x = -4$ Add equations.

                                            $x = 2$ Solve for x.

4 **Substitute** 2 for x into either equation and solve for y.

  $3x + 2y = 8$ Write equation 1.

  $3(2) + 2y = 8$ Substitute 2 for x.

  $6 + 2y = 8$ Multiply.

  $2y = 2$ Subtract 6 from each side.

  $y = 1$ Solve for y.

ANSWER ▶ The solution is $(2, 1)$.

5 **Check** the solution in each of the original equations.

First check the solution in Equation 1.

  $3x + 2y = 8$ Write Equation 1.

  $3(2) + 2(1) \stackrel{?}{=} 8$ Substitute 2 for x and 1 for y.

  $6 + 2 \stackrel{?}{=} 8$ Multiply.

  $8 = 8$ ✓   Add.

Then check the solution in Equation 2.

  $2y = 12 - 5x$ Write Equation 2.

  $2(1) \stackrel{?}{=} 12 - 5(2)$ Substitute 2 for x and 1 for y.

  $2 \stackrel{?}{=} 12 - 10$ Multiply.

  $2 = 2$ ✓   Subtract.

Checkpoint ✓ **Solve by Linear Combinations**

Solve the linear system. Then check your solution.

7. $2x + 5y = -11$ **8.** $-13 = 4x - 3y$ **9.** $4x + 7y = -9$
  $5y = 3x - 21$ $5x + 2y = 1$ $3x = 3y + 18$

Guided Practice

Vocabulary Check

1. When you use linear combinations to solve a linear system, what is the purpose of using multiplication as a first step?

Skill Check

ERROR ANALYSIS In Exercises 2 and 3, find and correct the error.

2.

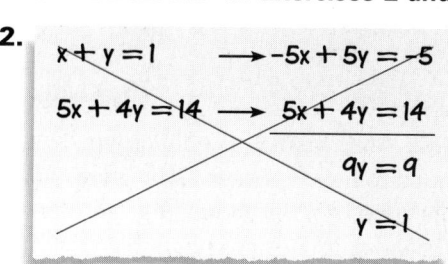

3.

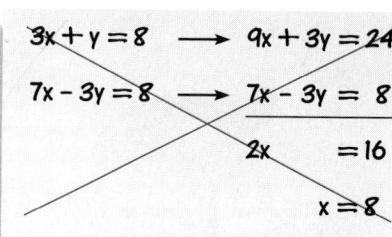

Describe the steps you would use to solve the system of equations using linear combinations. Then solve the system. Justify each step.

4. $x + 3y = 6$
$x - 3y = 12$

5. $3x - 4y = 7$
$2x - y = 3$

6. $2y = 2x - 2$
$2x + 3y = 12$

Practice and Applications

USING ADDITION Use linear combinations to solve the linear system. Then check your solution.

7. $x + y = 4$
$x - y = -10$

8. $a - b = 8$
$a + b = 20$

9. $2x + y = 4$
$x - y = 2$

10. $m + 3n = 2$
$-m + 2n = 3$

11. $p + 4q = 23$
$-p + q = 2$

12. $3v - 2w = 1$
$2v + 2w = 4$

13. $g + 2h = 4$
$-g - h = 2$

14. $13x - 5y = 8$
$3x + 5y = 8$

USING MULTIPLICATION AND ADDITION Use linear combinations to solve the linear system. Then check your solution.

15. $x + 3y = 3$
$x + 6y = 3$

16. $v - w = -5$
$v + 2w = 4$

17. $2g - 3h = 0$
$3g - 2h = 5$

18. $x - y = 0$
$-3x - y = 2$

19. $2a + 6z = 4$
$3a - 7z = 6$

20. $5e + 4f = 9$
$4e + 5f = 9$

21. $2p - q = 2$
$2p + 3q = 22$

22. $9m - 3n = 20$
$3m + 6n = 2$

Student Help

▶ **HOMEWORK HELP**
Example 1: Exs. 7–14,
31–42
Example 2: Exs. 15–22,
31–42
Example 3: Exs. 23–42

ARRANGING LIKE TERMS Use linear combinations to solve the linear system. Then check your solution.

23. $x - 3y = 30$
$3y + x = 12$

24. $3b + 2c = 46$
$5c + b = 11$

25. $y = x - 9$
$x + 8y = 0$

26. $m = 3n$
$m + 10n = 13$

27. $2q = 7 - 5p$
$4p - 16 = q$

28. $2v = 150 - u$
$2u = 150 - v$

29. $g - 10h = 43$
$18 = -g + 5h$

30. $5s + 8t = 70$
$60 = 5s - 8t$

31. $x + 2y = 5$
$\quad\ 5x - y = 3$

32. $-3p + 2 = q$
$\quad\ -q + 2p = 3$

33. $t + r = 1$
$\quad\ 2r - t = 2$

34. $3g - 24 = -4h$
$\quad\ -2 + 2h = g$

35. $x + 1 = 3y$
$\quad\ 2x = 7 - 3y$

36. $4a = -b$
$\quad\ a - b = 5$

37. $2m - 4 = 4n$
$\quad\ m - 2 = n$

38. $3y = -5x + 15$
$\quad\ -y = -3x + 9$

39. $3j + 5k = 19$
$\quad\ j - 2k = -1$

40. $6x + 2y = 5$
$\quad\ 8x + 2y = 3$

41. $3x + 7y = 6$
$\quad\ 2x + 9y = 4$

42. $5y - 20 = -4x$
$\quad\ 4y = -20x + 16$

Link to
Science

VOLUME AND MASS
Legend has it that
Archimedes (above) was
asked to prove that a
crown was not pure gold.
Archimedes compared the
volume of water displaced by
the crown with the volume
displaced by an equal mass
of gold. The volume of water
displaced was *not* the same,
proving that the crown was
not pure gold.

EXAMPLE *Write and Use a Linear System*

VOLUME AND MASS A gold crown, suspected of containing some silver, was found to have a mass of 714 grams and a volume of 46 cubic centimeters. The density of gold is about 19 grams per cubic centimeter. The density of silver is about 10.5 grams per cubic centimeter. What percent of the crown is silver?

Solution

VERBAL MODEL

| Gold volume | + | Silver volume | = | Total volume |

| Gold density | · | Gold volume | + | Silver density | · | Silver volume | = | Total mass |

LABELS

Volume of gold = **G** $\qquad$ (cubic centimeters)

Volume of silver = **S** $\qquad$ (cubic centimeters)

Total volume = **46** $\qquad$ (cubic centimeters)

Density of gold = **19** $\qquad$ (grams per cubic centimeter)

Density of silver = **10.5** $\qquad$ (grams per cubic centimeter)

Total mass = **714** $\qquad$ (grams)

ALGEBRAIC MODEL

$$G + S = 46 \qquad \textbf{Equation 1}$$

$$19\,G + 10.5\,S = 714 \qquad \textbf{Equation 2}$$

Use linear combinations to solve for *S*.

$$
\begin{array}{ll}
-19G - 19S = -874 & \text{Multiply Equation 1 by } -19. \\
\underline{19G + 10.5S = 714} & \text{Write Equation 2.} \\
-8.5S = -160 & \text{Add equations.} \\
S \approx 18.8 & \text{Solve for } S.
\end{array}
$$

ANSWER ▶ The volume of silver is about 19 cm³. The crown has a volume of 46 cm³, so the crown is $\frac{19}{46} \approx 41\%$ silver by volume.

MODELING Use the example on the previous page as a model for Exercise 43.

43. VOLUME AND MASS A bracelet made of gold and copper has a mass of 46 grams. The volume of the bracelet is 4 cubic centimeters. Gold has a density of about 19 grams per cubic centimeter. Copper has a density of about 9 grams per cubic centimeter. How many cubic centimeters of copper are mixed with the gold?

44. BEEHIVE A farmer is tracking two wild honey bees in his field. He maps the first bee's path to the hive on the line $7y = 9x$. The second bee's path follows the line $y = -3x + 12$. Their paths cross at the hive. At what coordinates will the farmer find the hive?

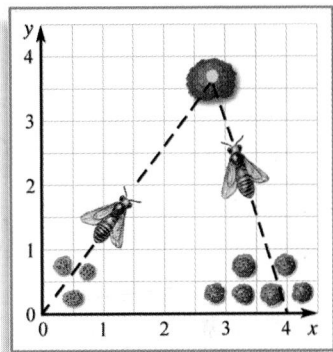

45. *History Link* The first known system of linear equations appeared in Chinese literature about 2000 years ago. Solve this problem from the book *Shu-shu Chiu-chang* which appeared in 1247.

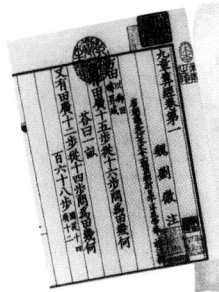

A storehouse has three kinds of stuff: cotton, floss silk, and raw silk. They take inventory of the materials and wish to cut out and make garments for the army. As for the cotton, if we use 8 rolls for 6 men, we have a shortage of 160 rolls; if we use 9 rolls for 7 men, there is a surplus of 560 rolls.... We wish to know the number of men [we can clothe] and the amount of cotton [we will use]. . .

$$x = \frac{8y}{6} - 160$$

$$-x = -\frac{9y}{7} - 560$$

$$\overline{}$$

$$0 = \frac{8y}{6} - \frac{9y}{7} - 720$$

46. CHALLENGE Solve for x, y, and z in the system of equations. Explain each step of your solution.

$$3x + 2y + z = 42$$
$$2y + z + 12 = 3x$$
$$x - 3y = 0$$

Standardized Test Practice

47. MULTIPLE CHOICE Solve the system and choose the true statement.

$$x + y = 4$$
$$x - 2y = 10$$

(**A**) The value of x is greater than y.   (**B**) The value of y is greater than x.

(**C**) The values of x and y are equal.   (**D**) None of these

48. MULTIPLE CHOICE Solve the system and choose the true statement.

$$3x + 5y = -8$$
$$x - 2y = 1$$

(**F**) The value of x is greater than y.   (**G**) The value of y is greater than x.

(**H**) The values of x and y are equal.   (**J**) None of these

WRITING EQUATIONS Write in slope-intercept form the equation of the line that passes through the given point and has the given slope, or that passes through the given points. *(Lessons 5.2, 5.3)*

49. $(-2, 4)$, $m = 3$ **50.** $(5, 1)$, $m = 5$ **51.** $(9, 3)$, $m = -3$

52. $(-2, -1)$ and $(4, 2)$ **53.** $(6, 5)$ and $(2, 1)$ **54.** $(4, -5)$ and $(-1, -3)$

CHECKING SOLUTIONS Check whether each ordered pair is a solution of the inequality. *(Lesson 6.8)*

55. $3x - 2y < 2$; $(1, 3)$, $(2, 0)$ **56.** $5x + 4y \geq 6$; $(-2, 4)$, $(5, 5)$

SOLVING LINEAR SYSTEMS Use the substitution method to solve the linear system. *(Lesson 7.2)*

57. $-6x - 5y = 28$
     $x - 2y = 1$

58. $m + 2n = 1$
    $5m - 4n = -23$

59. $g - 5h = 20$
    $4g + 3h = 34$

SIMPLIFYING FRACTIONS Decide whether the statement is *true* or *false*. Explain. *(Skills Review p. 763)*

60. $\dfrac{1}{4} = \dfrac{3}{12}$ **61.** $\dfrac{5}{7} = \dfrac{25}{35}$ **62.** $\dfrac{6}{16} = \dfrac{3}{7}$

63. $\dfrac{2}{11} = \dfrac{10}{55}$ **64.** $\dfrac{9}{7} = \dfrac{18}{15}$ **65.** $\dfrac{250}{350} = \dfrac{2}{3}$

Quiz 1

Estimate the solution of the linear system graphically. Then check the solution algebraically. *(Lesson 7.1)*

1. $3x + y = 5$
    $-x + y = -7$

2. $x - 2y = 0$
    $3x - y = 0$

3. $2x + 3y = 36$
    $-2x + y = -4$

Use substitution to solve the linear system. *(Lesson 7.2)*

4. $4x + 3y = 31$
    $y = 2x + 7$

5. $-12x + y = 15$
    $3x + 2y = 3$

6. $x + 2y = 14$
    $2x + 3y = 18$

Use linear combinations to solve the linear system. *(Lesson 7.3)*

7. $2x + 3y = 36$
    $2x - y = 4$

8. $x + 7y = 12$
    $3x - 5y = 10$

9. $3x - 5y = -4$
    $-9x + 7y = 8$

Choose a method to solve the linear system. *(Lessons 7.1–7.3)*

10. $2x + 3y = 1$
    $4x - 2y = 10$

11. $x + 18y = 18$
    $x - 3y = -3$

12. $5x - 3y = 7$
    $x + 3y = 5$

13. COMPACT DISCS A store is selling compact discs for $10.50 and $8.50. You buy 10 discs for $93. Write and solve a linear system to find how many compact discs you bought at each price. *(Lessons 7.1–7.3)*

7.4 Linear Systems and Problem Solving

Goal
Use linear systems to solve real-life problems.

Key Words
- substitution method
- linear combinations method

How many violins were sold?

In Example 1 you will use a system of linear equations to find the number of violins a store sold. Once you have written a linear system that models a real-life problem, you need to decide which solution method is most efficient.

EXAMPLE 1 Choosing a Solution Method

VIOLINS In one week a music store sold 7 violins for a total of $1600. Two different types of violins were sold. One type cost $200 and the other type cost $300. How many of each type of violin did the store sell?

Solution

VERBAL MODEL

$$\boxed{\text{Number of type A}} + \boxed{\text{Number of type B}} = \boxed{\text{Total number sold}}$$

$$\boxed{\text{Price of type A}} \cdot \boxed{\text{Number of type A}} + \boxed{\text{Price of type B}} \cdot \boxed{\text{Number of type B}} = \boxed{\text{Total sales}}$$

LABELS

Number of type A = x (violins)

Number of type B = y (violins)

Total number sold = **7**   (violins)

Price of type A = **200**   (dollars per violin)

Price of type B = **300**   (dollars per violin)

Total sales = **1600**   (dollars)

ALGEBRAIC MODEL

$$x + y = 7 \qquad \text{Equation 1}$$

$$200x + 300y = 1600 \qquad \text{Equation 2}$$

The coefficients of x and y are 1 in Equation 1, so use the substitution method. You can solve Equation 1 for x and substitute the result into Equation 2. After simplifying, you will obtain $y = 2$. Then substitute this y-value into the revised Equation 1 and simplify to obtain $x = 5$.

ANSWER ▶ The store sold 5 type A violins and 2 type B violins.

Student Help

▶ **STUDY TIP**
Examples 1 and 2 are called *mixture problems*. Mixture problems often have one equation of the form

$$x + y = \text{amount}$$

and another equation in which the coefficients of x and y are not 1.

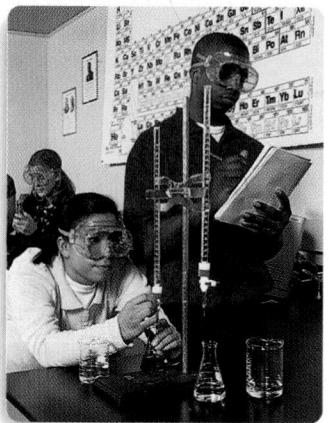

Link to Science

CHEMISTRY To test the acidity of a substance, scientists use litmus paper. When the paper comes in contact with acid, it turns red.

EXAMPLE 2 Solve a Mixture Problem

CHEMISTRY You combine 2 solutions to form a mixture that is 40% acid. One solution is 20% acid and the other is 50% acid. If you have 90 milliliters of the mixture, how much of each solution was used to create the mixture?

Solution

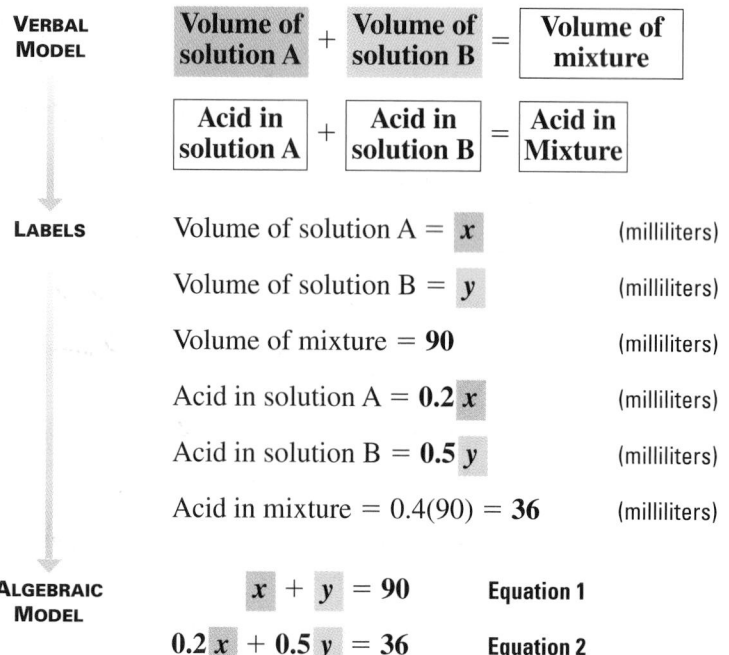

VERBAL MODEL

| Volume of solution A | + | Volume of solution B | = | Volume of mixture |

| Acid in solution A | + | Acid in solution B | = | Acid in Mixture |

LABELS

Volume of solution A = x	(milliliters)
Volume of solution B = y	(milliliters)
Volume of mixture = **90**	(milliliters)
Acid in solution A = **0.2** x	(milliliters)
Acid in solution B = **0.5** y	(milliliters)
Acid in mixture = 0.4(90) = **36**	(milliliters)

ALGEBRAIC MODEL

$$x + y = 90 \qquad \text{Equation 1}$$

$$0.2x + 0.5y = 36 \qquad \text{Equation 2}$$

Solve Equation 1 for x and multiply each side of Equation 2 by 10 so that it contains only integers. Then use substitution to solve the system.

$x = 90 - y$	Revised Equation 1
$2x + 5y = 360$	Revised Equation 2
$2(90 - y) + 5y = 360$	Substitute $90 - y$ for x in Revised Equation 2.
$180 - 2y + 5y = 360$	Use the distributive property.
$3y = 180$	Combine like terms.
$y = 60$	Solve for y.
$x = 90 - 60 = 30$	Substitute 60 for y in Revised Equation 1.

ANSWER ▶ 30 mL of solution A and 60 mL of solution B were used.

Checkpoint ✓ **Solve Mixture Problems**

1. A store sold 32 pairs of jeans for a total of $1050. Brand A sold for $30 per pair and Brand B sold for $35 per pair. How many of each brand were sold?

2. A 10-pound mixture of peanuts and cashews sells for $5.32 per pound. The price of peanuts is $3.60 per pound and the price of cashews is $7.90 per pound. How many pounds of each type are in the mixture?

EXAMPLE 3 Compare Two Salary Plans

SALES JOBS Job A offers an annual salary of $30,000 plus a bonus of 1% of sales. Job B offers an annual salary of $24,000 plus a bonus of 2% of sales. How much would you have to sell to earn the same amount in each job?

Solution

VERBAL MODEL

Total earnings = Job A salary + 1% · Total sales

Total earnings = Job B salary + 2% · Total sales

LABELS

Total earnings = y (dollars)

Total sales = x (dollars)

Job A salary = 30,000   (dollars)

Job B salary = 24,000   (dollars)

ALGEBRAIC MODEL

$y = 30,000 + 0.01x$ **Equation 1 (Job A)**

$y = 24,000 + 0.02x$ **Equation 2 (Job B)**

It is convenient to use the linear combinations method.

$-y = -30,000 - 0.01x$ Multiply Equation 1 by −1.

$y = 24,000 + 0.02x$ Write Equation 2.

$0 = -6000 + 0.01x$ Add Equations.

$x = 600,000$ Solve for x.

Substitute $x = 600,000$ into Equation 1 and simplify to obtain $y = 36,000$.

ANSWER ▶ You would have to sell $600,000 of merchandise to earn $36,000 in each job.

When a linear system has a solution (a, b), this solution can be found by substitution or by linear combinations.

SUMMARY

Ways to Solve a System of Linear Equations

SUBSTITUTION requires that one of the variables be isolated on one side of the equation. It is especially convenient when one of the variables has a coefficient of 1 or −1.
(Examples 1–3, pp. 396–398)

LINEAR COMBINATIONS can be applied to any system, but it is especially convenient when a variable appears in different equations with coefficients that are opposites.
(Examples 1–3, pp. 402–404)

GRAPHING can provide a useful method for estimating a solution.
(Examples 1–3, pp. 389–391)

Guided Practice

Vocabulary Check   **1.** Describe a system that you would use linear combinations to solve.

Skill Check   **Choose a method to solve the linear system. Explain your choice.**

2. $x + y = 300$
$x + 3y = 18$

3. $3x + 5y = 25$
$2x - 6y = 12$

4. $2x + y = 0$
$x + y = 5$

5. Solve Example 3 on page 411 using the substitution method.

POCKET CHANGE **In Exercises 6–8, use the following information.**
You have $2.65 in your pocket. You have a total of 16 coins, with only quarters and dimes. Let q equal the number of quarters and d equal the number of dimes.

6. Complete: ___?___ + ___?___ = 16

7. Complete: $25q +$ ___?___ $= 265$

8. Use the equations you wrote in Exercises 6 and 7 to find how many of each coin you have.

Practice and Applications

COMPARING METHODS **Solve the linear system using both methods described on page 411. Then represent the solution graphically.**

9. $x + y = 2$
$6x + y = 2$

10. $x - y = 1$
$x + y = 5$

11. $3x - y = 3$
$-x + y = 3$

CHOOSING A SOLUTION METHOD **Choose a solution method to solve the linear system. Explain your choice, but do not solve the system.**

12. $6x + y = 2$
$9x - y = 5$

13. $2x + 3y = 3$
$5x + 5y = 10$

14. $\quad\;\; -3x = 36$
$-6x + y = 1$

15. $2x - 5y = 0$
$x - y = 3$

16. $3x + 2y = 10$
$2x + 5y = 3$

17. $x + 2y = 2$
$x + 4y = -2$

SOLVING LINEAR SYSTEMS **Choose a solution method to solve the linear system. Explain your choice, and then solve the system.**

18. $2x + y = 5$
$x - y = 1$

19. $2x - y = 3$
$4x + 3y = 21$

20. $x - 2y = 4$
$6x + 2y = 10$

21. $3x + 6y = 8$
$-6x + 3y = 2$

22. $x + y = 0$
$3x + 2y = 1$

23. $2x - 3y = -7$
$3x + y = -5$

24. $8x + 4y = 8$
$-2x + 3y = 12$

25. $x + 2y = 1$
$5x - 4y = -23$

26. $6x - y = 18$
$8x + y = 24$

27. You have 7 packages of paper towels. Some packages have 3 rolls, but some have only 1 roll. There are 19 rolls altogether.

28. You buy 5 pairs of socks for $19. The wool socks cost $5 per pair and the cotton socks cost $3 per pair.

29. You have only $1 bills and $5 bills in your wallet. There are 7 bills worth a total of $19.

A. $x + y = 7$
$x + 3y = 19$

B. $x + y = 7$
$x + 5y = 19$

C. $x + y = 5$
$3x + 5y = 19$

30. TREADMILLS You exercised on a treadmill for 1.5 hours. You jogged at 4 miles per hour and then sprinted at 6 miles per hour. The treadmill monitor says that you ran for a total of 7 miles. Using the verbal model below, calculate how long you ran at each speed.

| Time spent jogging | + | Time spent sprinting | = | Total time on treadmill |

| Jogging speed | · | Time spent jogging | + | Sprinting speed | · | Time spent sprinting | = | Total distance |

31. COMMUNITY GARDENS You designate one row in your garden to broccoli and pea plants. Each broccoli plant needs 12 inches of space and each pea plant needs 6 inches of space. The row is 10 feet (120 inches) long. If you want a total of 13 plants, how many of each plant can you have?

HOUSING In Exercises 32 and 33, use the following information.
The graph below represents the need for low-income rental housing in the United States and the number of affordable rental units available.

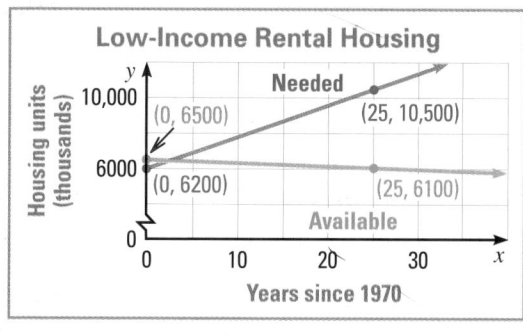

DATA UPDATE of Center on Budget and Policy Priorities data at www.mcdougallittell.com

32. Use the points (0, 6200) and (25, 10,500) to write an equation for the number of housing units needed. Then use the points (0, 6500) and (25, 6100) to write an equation for the number of affordable units available.

33. Solve the system you wrote in Exercise 32. Use the graph to check the reasonableness of your solution.

34. TREE GROWTH You plant a 14-inch spruce tree that grows 4 inches per year and an 8-inch hemlock tree that grows 6 inches per year. After how many years will the trees be the same height? How tall will each be?

COMMUNITY GARDENS allow people without yards to plant their own gardens. A 25 foot by 35 foot garden can produce enough vegetables for a family of four.

More about community gardens at www.mcdougallittell.com

35. CHALLENGE It takes you 3 hours to drive to a concert 135 miles away. You drive 55 miles per hour on highways and 40 miles per hour the rest of the time. How much time did you spend driving at each speed?

36. **Puzzler** Let the variables a, b, g, and p represent the weights of an apple, a banana, a bunch of grapes, and a pineapple, respectively. Use these variables to write three equations that model the first three diagrams below. Then use substitution to determine how many apples will balance the pineapple and two bananas in the fourth diagram.

Standardized Test Practice

37. MULTIPLE CHOICE You and your friend go to a Mexican restaurant. You order 2 tacos and 2 enchiladas and your friend orders 3 tacos and 1 enchilada. Your bill was $4.80 and your friend's bill was $4.00. Which system of linear equations represents the situation?

(A) $2t + 2e = 4.00$
$3t + e = 4.80$

(B) $2t + 2e = 4.00$
$t + 3e = 4.80$

(C) $2t + 2e = 4.80$
$3t + e = 4.00$

(D) $2t + 2e = 4.80$
$t + 3e = 4.00$

38. MULTIPLE CHOICE Solve the system of equations you chose in Exercise 37.

(F) $t = \$1.60$
$e = \$.80$

(G) $t = \$.80$
$e = \$1.60$

(H) $t = \$1.40$
$e = \$.60$

(J) $t = \$.60$
$e = \$1.40$

Mixed Review

PARALLEL LINES Determine whether the graphs of the two equations are parallel lines. Explain. *(Lesson 4.7)*

39. line *a*: $y = 4x + 3$
line *b*: $2y - 8x = -3$

40. line *a*: $4y + 5x = 1$
line *b*: $10x + 2y = 2$

41. line *a*: $3x + 9y + 2 = 0$
line *b*: $2y = -6x + 3$

42. line *a*: $4y - 1 = 5$
line *b*: $6y + 2 = 8$

GRAPHING FUNCTIONS Graph the function. *(Lesson 4.8)*

43. $f(x) = 2x + 3$

44. $h(x) = x + 5$

45. $g(x) = 5x - 4$

46. $g(x) = -x + 2$

47. $f(x) = -4x + 1$

48. $h(x) = -3x - 1$

Maintaining Skills

ADDING FRACTIONS Add. Write the answer as a fraction or a mixed number in simplest form. *(Skills Review p. 764)*

49. $\dfrac{9}{15} + \dfrac{3}{5}$

50. $\dfrac{1}{12} + \dfrac{1}{2}$

51. $\dfrac{3}{8} + \dfrac{7}{9}$

52. $\dfrac{3}{7} + \dfrac{2}{5}$

53. $\dfrac{1}{10} + \dfrac{2}{3}$

54. $\dfrac{3}{4} + \dfrac{1}{6}$

55. $\dfrac{17}{32} + \dfrac{1}{4}$

56. $\dfrac{19}{20} + \dfrac{7}{8}$

REASONING 7.5

Special Types of Systems

GOAL

Use reasoning to discover graphical and algebraic rules for finding the number of solutions of a linear system.

MATERIALS

• graph paper

Question

How can you identify the number of solutions of a linear system by graphing or by using an algebraic method?

Explore

① Graph each linear system.

    a. $\quad x + y = 0$
           $3x - 2y = 5$

    b. $2x - 4y = 6$
          $x - 2y = 3$

    c. $\quad x - y = 1$
         $-3x + 3y = 3$

② How are the three graphs different?

③ Write both equations of each system in the form $y = mx + b$.

④ How are the equations within each system alike or how are they different?

Student Help

▶ **LOOK BACK**
For help with graphing linear systems, see p. 390.

Think About It

1. Repeat **Steps 1** through **4** for the following systems.

    a. $x - 3y = 9$
        $2x + 6y = -18$

    b. $4x - y = 20$
        $20x + y = 28$

    c. $x + 2y = 3$
        $x + 2y = 6$

Write a linear system for the graphical model. If only one line is shown, write two different equations for the line.

2.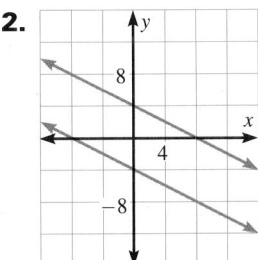

3.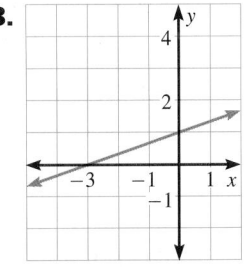

4.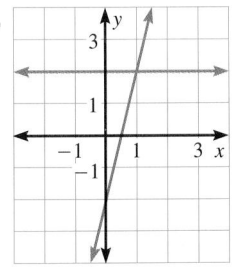

LOGICAL REASONING **The graph of a linear system is described. Determine whether the system has *no solution, exactly one solution,* or *infinitely many solutions*. Explain.**

5. The lines have the same slope and the same y-intercept.

6. The lines have the same slope but different y-intercepts.

7. The lines have different slopes.

Question

How can you solve systems that have many solutions or recognize systems that have no solution?

Explore

1 Try to solve each linear system.

a. $x + y = 0$	**b.** $2x - 4y = 6$	**c.** $x - y = 1$
$3x - 2y = 5$	$x - 2y = 3$	$-3x + 3y = 3$

2 Refer to your graph of part (a) from **Step 1** on page 415. What does the algebra of part (a) tell you about the graphs of the equation?

3 Refer to your graph of part (b) from **Step 1** on page 415. What does the algebra of part (b) tell you about the graphs of the equation?

4 Refer to your graph of part (c) from **Step 1** on page 415. What does the algebra of part (c) tell you about the graphs of the equation?

Think About It

Describe the algebraic solution of the system. Then check your answer by solving the appropriate equation you wrote for Exercises 2–4 on page 415.

1.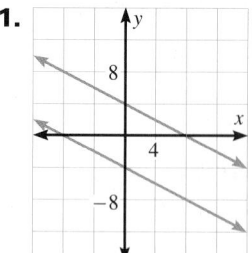

2.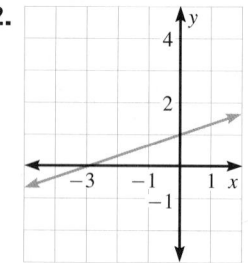

3.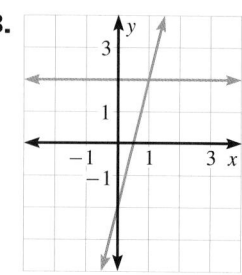

Solve the linear system using linear combinations. Then describe the graphical solution of the system.

4. $2x - y = 3$	**5.** $2x + y = 5$	**6.** $x + 3y = 2$
$-4x + 2y = 0$	$x - 3y = -1$	$2x + 6y = 4$

7. LOGICAL REASONING Summarize your results from Exercises 1–6 by writing a rule for determining algebraically whether a system of linear equations has exactly one solution, no solution, or infinitely many solutions.

7.5 Special Types of Linear Systems

Goal
Identify how many solutions a linear system has.

Key Words
- linear system

What is the weight of a bead in a necklace?

Some linear systems have no solution or infinitely many solutions. In Exercise 31 you will see why this can be a problem as you try to find the weight of a jewelry bead.

EXAMPLE 1 A Linear System with No Solution

Show that the linear system has no solution.

$2x + y = 5$ **Equation 1**
$2x + y = 1$ **Equation 2**

Solution

Method 1 **GRAPHING** Rewrite each equation in slope-intercept form. Then graph the linear system.

$y = -2x + 5$ **Revised Equation 1**
$y = -2x + 1$ **Revised Equation 2**

(graph showing $y = -2x + 5$ and $y = -2x + 1$)

Because the lines have the same slope but different y-intercepts, they are parallel. Parallel lines never intersect, so the system has no solution.

Method 2 **SUBSTITUTION** Because revised Equation 2 is $y = -2x + 1$, you can substitute $-2x + 1$ for y in Equation 1.

$2x + y = 5$ Write Equation 1.

$2x + (-2x + 1) = 5$ Substitute $-2x + 1$ for y.

$1 \neq 5$ Combine like terms.

The variables are eliminated and you are left with a statement that is false. This tells you that the system has no solution.

Student Help

▶ **LOOK BACK**
For help with equations in one variable that have no solution, see p. 153.

Checkpoint *A Linear System with No Solution*

1. Show that the linear system has no solution.

$x + 3y = 4$ **Equation 1**
$2x + 6y = 4$ **Equation 2**

EXAMPLE 2 **A Linear System with Infinitely Many Solutions**

Show that the linear system has infinitely many solutions.

$$-2x + y = 3 \quad \text{Equation 1}$$
$$-4x + 2y = 6 \quad \text{Equation 2}$$

Solution

Method 1 **GRAPHING** Rewrite each equation in slope-intercept form. Then graph the linear system.

$$y = 2x + 3 \quad \text{Revised Equation 1}$$
$$y = 2x + 3 \quad \text{Revised Equation 2}$$

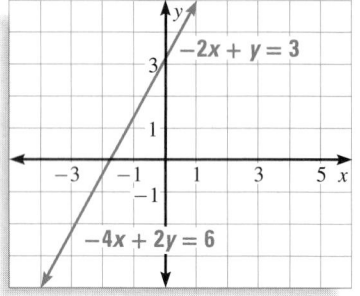

You can see that the equations represent the same line. Every point on the line is a solution of the system.

Method 2 **LINEAR COMBINATIONS** You can multiply Equation 1 by 2 to obtain an equation that is identical to Equation 2.

$$-4x + 2y = 6 \quad \text{Revised Equation 1}$$
$$-4x + 2y = 6 \quad \text{Equation 2}$$

The two equations are identical. Any solution of $-4x + 2y = 6$ is also a solution of the system. This tells you that the linear system has infinitely many solutions.

Checkpoint ✓ **A Linear System with Infinitely Many Solutions**

2. Show that the linear system has infinitely many solutions.

$$x - 2y = 4 \quad \text{Equation 1}$$
$$-x + 2y = -4 \quad \text{Equation 2}$$

SUMMARY

Number of Solutions of a Linear System

If the two equations have different slopes, then the system has one solution.	If the two equations have the same slope but different *y*-intercepts, then the system has no solution.	If the two equations have the same slope and the same *y*-intercept, then the system has infinitely many solutions
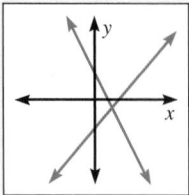	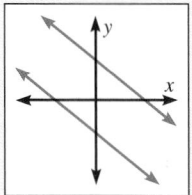	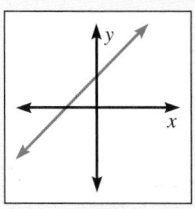
Lines intersect Exactly one solution	**Lines are parallel** No solution	**Lines coincide** Infinitely many solutions

EXAMPLE 3 Identify the Number of Solutions

a. $3x + y = -1$
$-9x - 3y = 3$

b. $x - 2y = 5$
$-2x + 4y = 2$

c. $2x + y = 4$
$4x - 2y = 0$

Solution

a. Use linear combinations.

You can multiply Equation 1 by -3 to obtain Equation 2.

$-9x - 3y = 3$ **Revised Equation 1**

$-9x - 3y = 3$ **Equation 2**

ANSWER ▶ The two equations are identical. Any solution of $-9x - 3y = 3$ is also a solution of the system. Therefore the linear system has infinitely many solutions.

b. Use linear combinations.

$x - 2y = 5$ **Multiply by 2.** $2x - 4y = 10$

$-2x + 4y = 2$ $\underline{-2x + 4y = 2}$

                                         $0 \neq 12$ Add equations.

ANSWER ▶ The resulting statement is false. The linear system has no solution.

c. Use the substitution method.

$2x + y = 4$ Write Equation 1.

$y = -2x + 4$ Solve Equation 1 for *y*. (Revised Equation 1)

$4x - 2y = 0$ Write Equation 2.

$4x - 2(-2x + 4) = 0$ Substitute $-2x + 4$ for *y*.

$4x + 4x - 8 = 0$ Use the distributive property.

$8x - 8 = 0$ Combine like terms.

$8x = 8$ Add 8 to each side.

$x = 1$ Solve for *x*.

$y = -2(1) + 4$ Substitute 1 for *x* in Revised Equation 1.

$y = -2 + 4$ Multiply.

$y = 2$ Solve for *y*.

ANSWER ▶ The linear system has exactly one solution, which is the ordered pair $(1, 2)$.

Checkpoint ✓ *Identify the Number of Solutions*

Solve the linear system and tell how many solutions the system has.

3. $x + y = 3$
$2x + 2y = 4$

4. $x + y = 3$
$2x + 2y = 6$

5. $x + y = 3$
$x + 2y = 4$

Guided Practice

Vocabulary Check

Describe the graph of a linear system that has the given number of solutions. Sketch an example.

1. No solution   **2.** Infinitely many solutions   **3.** Exactly one solution

Skill Check

Graph the system of linear equations. Does the system have *exactly one solution, no solution,* or *infinitely many solutions*? Explain.

4. $2x + y = 5$
$-6x - 3y = -15$

5. $-6x + 2y = 4$
$-9x + 3y = 12$

6. $2x + y = 7$
$3x - y = -2$

Use the substitution method or linear combinations to solve the linear system and tell how many solutions the system has.

7. $-x + y = 7$
$2x - 2y = -18$

8. $-4x + y = -8$
$-12x + 3y = -24$

9. $-4x + y = -8$
$2x - 2y = -14$

Practice and Applications

LINEAR SYSTEMS Match the linear system with its graph and tell how many solutions the system has.

10. $-2x + 4y = 1$
$3x - 6y = 9$

11. $2x - 2y = 4$
$-x + y = -2$

12. $2x + y = 4$
$-4x - 2y = -8$

13. $-x + y = 1$
$x - y = 1$

14. $5x + 3y = 17$
$x - 3y = -2$

15. $x - y = 0$
$5x - 2y = 6$

A.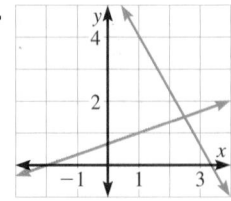

B.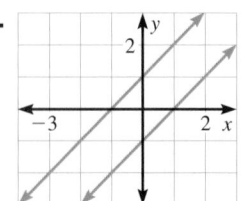

C.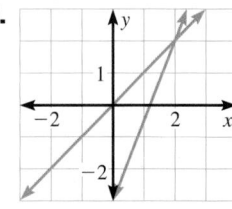

D.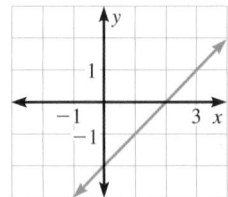

E.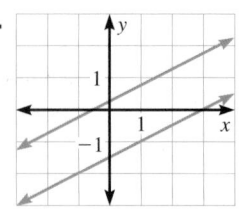

F.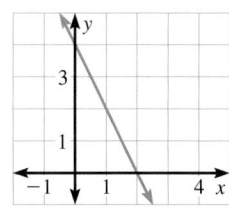

Student Help

▶ **HOMEWORK HELP**
Example 1: Exs. 10–33
Example 2: Exs. 10–33
Example 3: Exs. 10–33

16. ERROR ANALYSIS Patrick says that the graph of the linear system shown at the right has no solution. Why is he wrong?

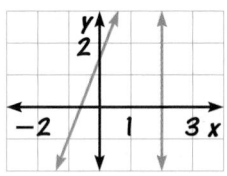

17. $x + y = 8$
$x + y = -1$

18. $3x - 2y = 3$
$-6x + 4y = -6$

19. $x - y = 2$
$-2x + 2y = 2$

20. $-x + 4y = -20$
$3x - 12y = 48$

21. $6x - 2y = 4$
$12x - 6y = 8$

22. $3x + 2y = 40$
$-3x - 2y = 8$

23. CRITICAL THINKING Explain how you can tell from the equations how
many solutions the linear system has. Then solve the system.

$x - y = 2$ **Equation 1**
$4x - 4y = 8$ **Equation 2**

INTERPRETING ALGEBRAIC RESULTS **Use the substitution method or
linear combinations to solve the linear system and tell how many
solutions the system has. Then describe the graph of the system.**

24. $-7x + 7y = 7$
$2x - 2y = -18$

25. $4x + 4y = -8$
$2x + 2y = -4$

26. $2x + y = -4$
$4x - 2y = 8$

27. $15x - 5y = -20$
$-3x + y = 4$

28. $-6x + 2y = -2$
$-4x - y = 8$

29. $2x + y = -1$
$-6x - 3y = -15$

30. BUSINESS A contracting company rents a generator for 6 hours and a
heavy-duty saw for 6 hours at a total cost of $48. For another job the
company rents the generator for 4 hours and the saw for 8 hours for a total
cost of $40. Find the hourly rates g (for the generator) and s (for the saw)
by solving the system of equations $6g + 6s = 48$ and $4g + 8s = 40$.

31. JEWELRY You have a necklace and matching bracelet with 2 types of beads.
There are 40 small beads and 6 large beads on the necklace. The bracelet has
20 small beads and 3 large beads. The necklace weighs 9.6 grams and the
bracelet weighs 4.8 grams. If the threads holding the beads have no
significant weight, can you find the weight of one large bead? Explain.

CARPENTRY **In Exercises 32 and 33, use the following information.**
A carpenter is buying supplies for the next job. The job requires 4 sheets of oak
paneling and 2 sheets of shower tileboard. The carpenter pays $99.62 for these
supplies. For the following job the carpenter buys 12 sheets of oak paneling and
6 sheets of shower tileboard and pays $298.86.

32. Can you find how much the carpenter is spending on 1 sheet of oak
paneling? Explain.

33. If the carpenter later spends a total of $139.69 for 8 sheets of oak paneling
and 1 sheet of shower tileboard, can you find how much 1 sheet of oak
paneling costs? Explain.

CHALLENGE **In Exercises 34 and 35, use the following system.**

$6x - 9y = n$ **Equation 1**
$-2x + 3y = 3$ **Equation 2**

34. Find a value of n so that the linear system has infinitely many solutions.

35. Find a value of n so that the linear system has no solution.

Student Help

▶HOMEWORK HELP

Extra help with
problem solving
in Ex. 23 is available at
www.mcdougallittell.com

Link to
Careers

CARPENTERS must be
familiar with codes that
specify what types
of materials can be used.
Carpenters also must be
able to estimate how much
material will be needed and
what the total cost will be.

More about
carpenters at
www.mcdougallittell.com

36. MULTIPLE CHOICE Which graph corresponds to a linear system that has no solution?

Ⓐ I   Ⓑ II

Ⓒ III   Ⓓ IV

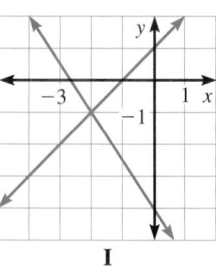

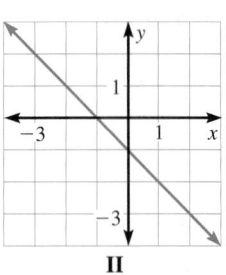

I   II

37. MULTIPLE CHOICE Which graph corresponds to a linear system that has infinitely many solutions?

Ⓕ I   Ⓖ II

Ⓗ III   Ⓙ IV

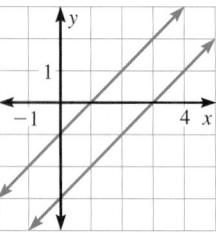

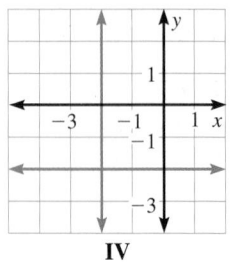

III   IV

Mixed Review

ROCK CLIMBING In Exercises 38 and 39, use the following information. You are climbing a 300 foot cliff. By 1:00 P.M. you have climbed 110 feet up the cliff. By 3:00 P.M. you have reached a height of 220 feet. *(Lesson 4.5)*

38. Find the slope of the line that passes through the points (1, 110) and (3, 220). What does it represent?

39. If you continue climbing the cliff at the same rate, at what time will you reach the top of the cliff?

GRAPHING INEQUALITIES Graph the inequality. *(Lesson 6.8)*

40. $x < 2$ **41.** $y \geq 5$ **42.** $y \leq 3x + 1$

43. $y > x + 4$ **44.** $4x + y \leq 4$ **45.** $2x - 3y < 6$

Maintaining Skills

ESTIMATING AREA Estimate the area of the figure to the nearest square unit. Then find the exact area, if possible. *(Skills Review p. 775)*

46.

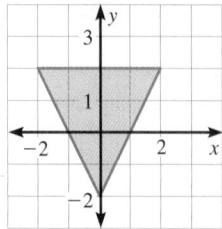

47.

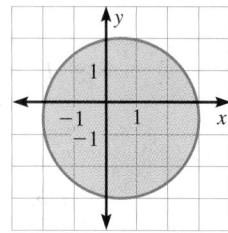

48.

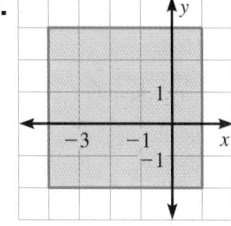

49.

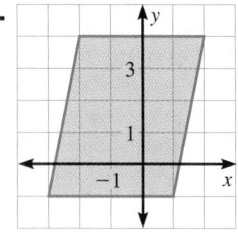

GOAL

Use graphing to describe the solution of a system of linear inequalities.

MATERIALS
• graph paper
• red and blue pencils

Question

How can you graph a system of linear inequalities?

Explore

Consider the following system of linear inequalities.

$$x + y \leq 5 \qquad \text{**Inequality 1**}$$
$$x - y \geq 1 \qquad \text{**Inequality 2**}$$

1 Graph the boundary lines $x + y = 5$ and $x - y = 1$ in the same coordinate plane.

2 Test several points with integer coordinates in the first inequality. If a point is a solution, circle the point in blue.

3 Test several points with integer coordinates in the second inequality. If a point is a solution, circle the point in red.

4 Describe the points that are solutions of both inequalities (the points that are circled with both colors).

Think About It

Follow Steps 1 through 4 to graph the system of linear inequalities. Then describe the solution.

1. $x + y \geq 4$
   $x - 2y \leq -2$

2. $x - y \leq 0$
   $x + y \leq 6$

3. $3x + 2y \geq 8$
   $-3x + y \leq 1$

4. $x \geq 3$
   $x \leq 5$

5. $y \leq 4$
   $y \geq 1$

6. $4x + y \geq 2$
   $4x + y \leq 8$

LOGICAL REASONING Use your results from Exercises 1–6 to answer the following questions.

7. When would the solution of a system of two linear inequalities be a horizontal strip? When would the solution of a system of two linear inequalities be a vertical strip?

8. When would a system of two linear inequalities have no solution?

9. When would a half-plane be the solution of a system of two linear inequalities?

10. What are the possible graphs of a general system of two linear inequalities?

7.6 Systems of Linear Inequalities

Goal
Graph a system of linear inequalities.

Key Words
- system of linear inequalities
- solution of a system of linear inequalities

How many spotlights can you afford?

In Exercises 34–36 you will graph a *system of linear inequalities* to analyze the number of spotlights that can be ordered for a theater.

From Lesson 6.8 remember that the graph of a linear inequality in two variables is a half-plane. The boundary line of the half-plane is dashed if the inequality is $<$ or $>$ and solid if the inequality is $\leq$ or $\geq$, as shown in the graphs below.

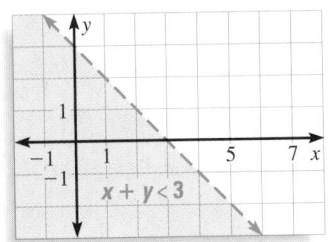
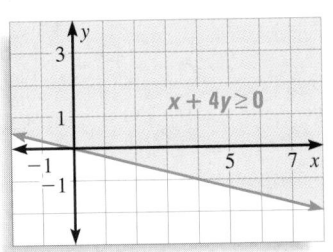

Two or more linear inequalities in the same variables form a **system of linear inequalities**, or a *system of inequalities*. A **solution of a system of linear inequalities** in two variables is an ordered pair that is a solution of each inequality in the system.

Student Help

▶ STUDY TIP
Notice how the two half-planes above can be used to find the solution in Example 1.

EXAMPLE 1 Graph a System of Two Linear Inequalities

Graph the system of linear inequalities.

$x + y < 3$	**Inequality 1**
$x + 4y \geq 0$	**Inequality 2**

Solution

Graph both inequalities in the same coordinate plane. The graph of the system is the overlap, or *intersection*, of the two half-planes shown at the right as the darker shade of blue.

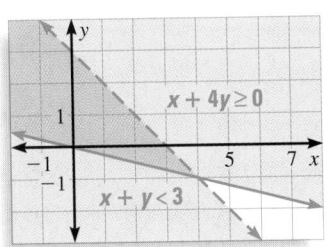

EXAMPLE **2** **Graph a System of Three Linear Inequalities**

Graph the system of linear inequalities.

$y < 2$ **Inequality 1**
$x \geq -1$ **Inequality 2**
$y > x - 2$ **Inequality 3**

Solution

The graph of $y < 2$ is the half-plane *below* the *dashed* line $y = 2$.

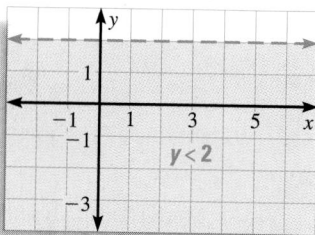

The graph of $x \geq -1$ is the half-plane *on and to the right* of the *solid* line $x = -1$.

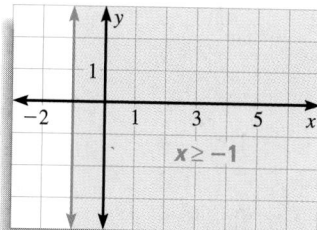

The graph of $y > x - 2$ is the half-plane *above* the *dashed* line $y = x - 2$.

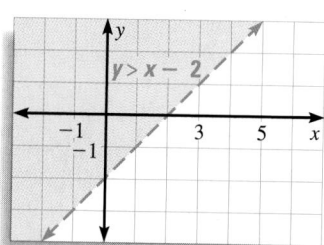

Finally, the graph of the system is the intersection of the three half-planes shown.

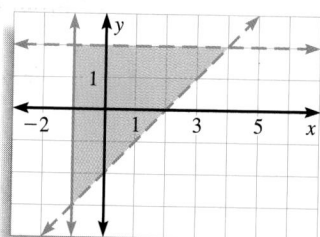

Checkpoint ✓ **Graph a System of Linear Inequalities**

Graph the system of linear inequalities.

1. $x + 2y \leq 6$
    $-x + y < 0$

2. $y < 3$
    $y > 1$

3. $x \geq 0$
    $y \geq 0$
    $2x + 3y \leq 12$

SUMMARY

Graphing a System of Linear Inequalities

STEP ❶ **Graph** the boundary lines of each inequality. Use a dashed line if the inequality is < or > and a solid line if the inequality is ≤ or ≥.

STEP ❷ **Shade** the appropriate half-plane for each inequality.

STEP ❸ **Identify** the solution of the system of inequalities as the intersection of the half-planes from Step 2.

EXAMPLE 3 Write a System of Linear Inequalities

Write a system of linear inequalities that defines the shaded region shown.

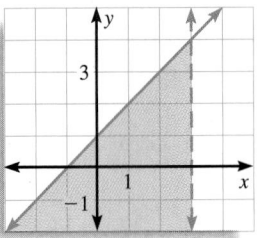

Solution

Since the shaded region is bounded by two lines, you know that the system must have two linear inequalities.

INEQUALITY 1 The first inequality is bounded by the line that passes through the points $(0, 1)$ and $(3, 4)$. The slope of this line can be found using the formula for slope.

$$m = \frac{y_2 - y_1}{x_2 - x_1} \qquad \text{Write formula for slope.}$$

$$m = \frac{4 - 1}{3 - 0} \qquad \text{Substitute coordinates into formula.}$$

$$m = 1 \qquad \text{Simplify.}$$

Since $(0, 1)$ is the point where the line crosses the y-axis, an equation for this line can be found using the slope-intercept form.

$$y = mx + b \qquad \text{Write slope-intercept form.}$$

$$y = 1x + 1 \qquad \text{Substitute 1 for } m \text{ and 1 for } b.$$

$$y = x + 1 \qquad \text{Simplify.}$$

Since the shaded region is *below* this *solid* boundary line, the inequality is $y \leq x + 1$.

INEQUALITY 2 The second inequality is bounded by the vertical line that passes through the point $(3, 0)$. An equation of this line is $x = 3$.

Since the shaded region is *to the left* of this *dashed* boundary line, the inequality is $x < 3$.

ANSWER ▶ The system of inequalities that defines the shaded region is:

$$y \leq x + 1 \qquad \text{**Inequality 1**}$$
$$x < 3 \qquad \text{**Inequality 2**}$$

Student Help

▶**LOOK BACK**
For help with writing equations in slope-intercept form, see p. 269.

Checkpoint ✔ **Write a System of Linear Inequalities**

Write a system of linear inequalities that defines the shaded region shown.

4.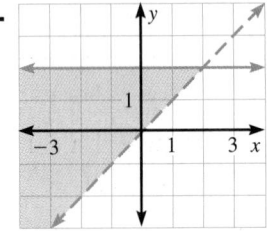

5.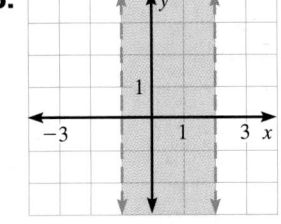

7.6 Exercises

Guided Practice

Vocabulary Check

1. Determine whether the following statement is *true* or *false*. Explain.

A solution of a system of linear inequalities is an ordered pair that is a solution of any one of the inequalities in the system.

Skill Check

Graph the system of linear inequalities.

2. $y \geq -2x + 2$
$y \leq -1$

3. $y > x$
$x < 1$

4. $x + 1 > y$
$y \geq 0$

ERROR ANALYSIS Use both the student graph shown at the right and the system of linear inequalities given below.

$y > -1$
$x \geq 2$
$y > x - 4$

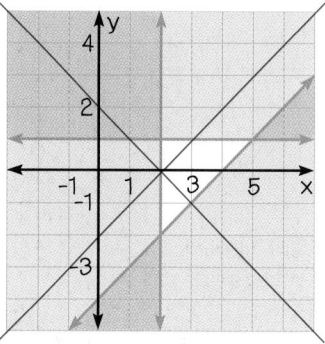

5. Find and correct the errors the student made while graphing the system.

6. Graph the system correctly.

Write a system of linear inequalities that defines the shaded region.

7.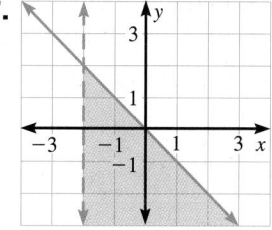

8.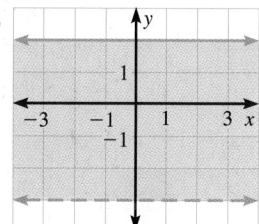

Practice and Applications

LINEAR INEQUALITIES Match the graph with the system of linear inequalities that defines it.

Student Help

▶**HOMEWORK HELP**
Example 1: Exs. 9–17,
37–39
Example 2: Exs. 18–23,
31–36
Example 3: Exs. 24–30,
40, 41

9.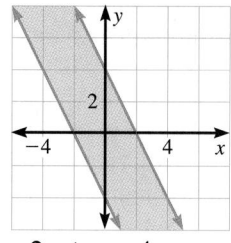

10.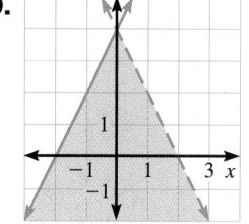

11.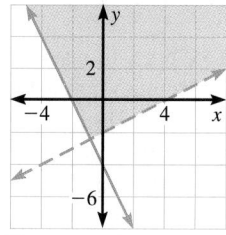

A. $2x + y < 4$
$-2x + y \leq 4$

B. $2x + y \geq -4$
$x - 2y < 4$

C. $2x + y \leq 4$
$2x + y \geq -4$

GRAPHING SYSTEMS Graph the system of linear inequalities.

12. $y \geq 0$
$x \geq -2$

13. $y > -2$
$y \leq 4 - 2x$

14. $2x + 3y < 5$
$3x + 2y > 5$

15. $y < 2x - 1$
$y > -x + 2$

16. $2x - 2y \leq 6$
$x - y \leq 9$

17. $x - 3y \geq 12$
$x - 6y < 12$

18. $x + y \leq 6$
$x \geq 1$
$y \geq 0$

19. $x < 3$
$2y < 1$
$2x + y > 2$

20. $3x - 2y \geq -6$
$x + 4y > -2$
$4x + y < 2$

21. $x \geq 0$
$y \geq 0$
$x \leq 3$

22. $x > -2$
$y \geq -2$
$y < 4$

23. $x - 2y < 3$
$3x + 2y > 9$
$x + y < 6$

WRITING SYSTEMS Write a system of linear inequalities that defines the shaded region.

24.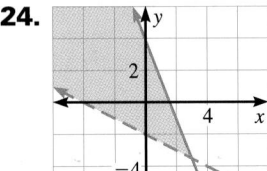

25.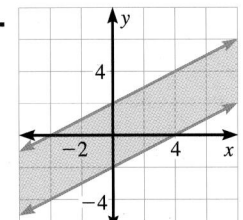

26.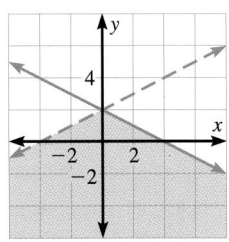

Geometry Link Plot the points and draw line segments connecting the points to create the polygon. Then write a system of linear inequalities that defines the polygonal region.

27. Triangle: $(-2, 0), (2, 0), (0, 2)$

28. Rectangle: $(1, 1), (7, 1), (7, 6), (1, 6)$

29. Triangle: $(0, 0), (-7, 0), (-3, 5)$

30. Trapezoid: $(-1, 1), (1, 3), (4, 3), (6, 1)$

FOOD BUDGET In Exercises 31–33, use the following information.
You are planning the menu for your restaurant. For Saturday night you plan to serve roast beef and teriyaki chicken. You expect to serve at least 240 pounds of meat that evening and that less beef will be ordered than chicken. The roast beef costs $5 per pound and the chicken costs $3 per pound. You have a budget of at most $1200 for meat for Saturday night.

31. Copy and complete the following system of linear inequalities that shows the pounds b of roast beef meals and the pounds c of teriyaki chicken meals that you could prepare for Saturday night.

$$b + c \geq \boxed{?}$$
$$b \ \boxed{?} \ c$$
$$\boxed{?} \cdot b + \boxed{?} \cdot c \leq 1200$$

32. Graph the system of linear inequalities.

33. **CRITICAL THINKING** What quadrant should the graph in Exercise 32 be restricted to for the solutions of the system to make sense in the real-world situation described? Explain.

LIGHTING In Exercises 34–36, use the following information.

You have $10,000 to buy spotlights for your theater. A medium-throw spotlight costs $1000 and a long-throw spotlight costs $3500. The current play needs at least 3 medium-throw spotlights and at least 1 long-throw spotlight.

34. Write a system of linear inequalities for the number m of medium-throw spotlights and the number l of long-throw spotlights that models both your budget and the needs of the current play.

35. For $0 \leq m \leq 7$ and $0 \leq l \leq 7$, plot the pairs of integers (m, l) that satisfy the inequalities you wrote in Exercise 34.

36. Which of the options plotted in Exercise 35 correspond to a cost that is less than $8000?

EARNING MONEY In Exercises 37–39, use the following information.

You can work a total of no more than 20 hours per week at your two jobs. Baby-sitting pays $5 per hour, and your job as a cashier pays $6 per hour. You need to earn at least $90 per week to cover your expenses.

37. Write a system of inequalities that shows the various numbers of hours you can work at each job.

38. Graph the system of linear inequalities.

39. Give two possible ways you could divide your hours between the two jobs.

TREE FARMING In Exercises 40–42, use the tree farm graph shown.

40. Write a system of inequalities that defines the region containing maple trees.

41. Write a system of inequalities that defines the region containing sycamore trees.

42. **CHALLENGE** Find the area of the oak tree region. Explain the method you used.

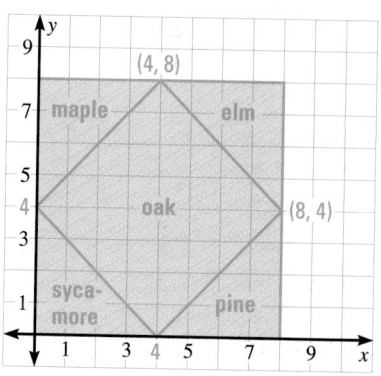

43. **MULTIPLE CHOICE** Which system of inequalities is graphed?

(A) $y < 3x - 1$
$\quad 2x + y \geq 4$

(B) $y < 3x + 1$
$\quad 2x + y \geq 4$

(C) $y < 3x - 1$
$\quad 2x - y \geq -4$

(D) $y < 3x + 1$
$\quad 2x - y \geq -4$

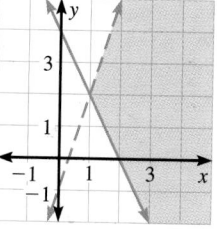

44. **MULTIPLE CHOICE** Which ordered pair is a solution of the following system of linear inequalities?

$y \leq x + 2$
$y + x > 4$

(F) $(1, 3)$ **(G)** $(2, 1)$ **(H)** $(2, 6)$ **(J)** $(4, 2)$

EVALUATING NUMERICAL EXPRESSIONS **Evaluate the expression.**
(Lessons 1.2, 1.3)

45. 3^5 **46.** $8^2 - 17$ **47.** $5^3 + 12$

48. $2(3^3 - 20)$ **49.** $2^6 - 3 + 1$ **50.** $5 \cdot 2 + 4^2$

EVALUATING EXPONENTIAL EXPRESSIONS **Evaluate the expression for the given values of the variables.** *(Lesson 1.2)*

51. $(x + y)^2$ when $x = 5$ and $y = 2$ **52.** $(b - c)^2$ when $b = 2$ and $c = 1$

53. $g - h^2$ when $g = 4$ and $h = 8$ **54.** $x^2 + z$ when $x = 8$ and $z = 12$

55. TEST QUESTIONS Your teacher is giving a test worth 250 points. There are 68 questions. Some questions are worth 5 points and the rest are worth 2 points. How many of each question are on the test? *(Lesson 7.4)*

Maintaining Skills

FRACTIONS, MIXED NUMBERS, AND DECIMALS **Write the fraction or mixed number as a decimal.** *(Skills Review pp. 763, 767)*

56. $\dfrac{22}{5}$ **57.** $\dfrac{37}{4}$ **58.** $\dfrac{51}{12}$ **59.** $\dfrac{56}{20}$

60. $1\dfrac{1}{2}$ **61.** $3\dfrac{4}{5}$ **62.** $4\dfrac{1}{4}$ **63.** $6\dfrac{7}{8}$

Quiz 2

1. **Geometry Link** The perimeter of the rectangle is 22 feet and the perimeter of the triangle is 12 feet. Find the dimensions of the rectangle. *(Lesson 7.4)*

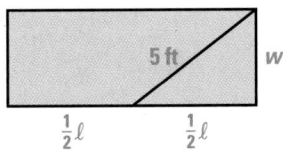

2. GASOLINE The cost of 12 gallons of regular gasoline and 18 gallons of premium gasoline is $44.46. Premium costs $.22 more per gallon than regular. What is the cost per gallon of each type of gasoline? *(Lesson 7.4)*

Use any method to solve the linear system and tell how many solutions the system has. *(Lesson 7.5)*

3. $3x + 2y = 12$
   $9x + 6y = 18$

4. $4x + 8y = 8$
   $x + y = 1$

5. $-4x + 11y = 44$
   $4x - 11y = -44$

Graph the system of linear inequalities. *(Lesson 7.6)*

6. $y < -x + 3$
   $y \geq 1$

7. $x - 2y < -6$
   $5x - 3y < -9$

8. $x + y \leq 1$
   $-x + y \leq 1$
      $y \geq 0$

9. Write a system of linear inequalities that defines the shaded region. *(Lesson 7.6)*

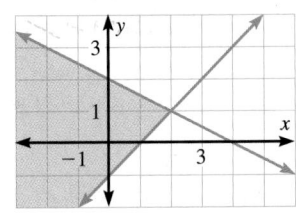

VOCABULARY

- **system of linear equations,** *p. 389*
- **solution of a linear system,** *p. 389*
- **point of intersection,** *p. 389*
- **linear combination,** *p. 402*
- **system of linear inequalities,** *p. 424*
- **solution of a system of linear inequalities,** *p. 424*

7.1 GRAPHING LINEAR SYSTEMS

Examples on pp. 389–391

EXAMPLE Estimate the solution of the linear system graphically. Then check the solution algebraically.

$$-x + y = 3 \qquad \textbf{Equation 1}$$
$$x + y = 7 \qquad \textbf{Equation 2}$$

First write each equation in slope-intercept form so that they are easy to graph.

EQUATION 1

$$-x + y = 3$$
$$y = x + 3$$

EQUATION 2

$$x + y = 7$$
$$y = -x + 7$$

Then graph both equations.

Estimate from the graph that the point of intersection is (2, 5).

Check whether (2, 5) is a solution by substituting 2 for x and 5 for y in each of the original equations.

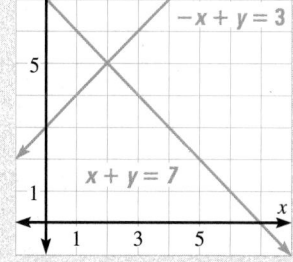

EQUATION 1

$$-x + y = 3$$
$$-(2) + 5 \stackrel{?}{=} 3$$
$$3 = 3 \checkmark$$

EQUATION 2

$$x + y = 7$$
$$2 + 5 \stackrel{?}{=} 7$$
$$7 = 7 \checkmark$$

ANSWER Because the ordered pair (2, 5) makes each equation true, (2, 5) is the solution of the linear system.

Estimate the solution of the linear system graphically. Then check the solution algebraically.

1. $x + y = 6$
$x - y = 12$

2. $4x - y = 3$
$3x + y = 4$

3. $x + 9y = 9$
$3x + 6y = 6$

4. $5x - y = -5$
$3x + 6y = -3$

5. $7x + 8y = 24$
$x - 8y = 8$

6. $2x - 3y = -3$
$x + 6y = -9$

7.2 SOLVING LINEAR SYSTEMS BY SUBSTITUTION

Examples on pp. 396–398

EXAMPLE Solve the linear system by substitution.

$2x - y = 0$ **Equation 1**
$4x - y = 8$ **Equation 2**

Solve for y in Equation 1 because it is easy to isolate y.

$2x - y = 0$	Original Equation 1
$y = 2x$	Revised Equation 1
$4x - y = 8$	Write Equation 2.
$4x - (2x) = 8$	Substitute $2x$ for y.
$x = 4$	Solve for x.
$y = 2x = 2(4) = 8$	Substitute 4 for x in Revised Equation 1 to solve for y.

ANSWER ▶ The solution is $(4, 8)$. Check the solution in the original equations.

Use the substitution method to solve the linear system.

7. $x + 3y = 9$
$4x - 2y = -6$

8. $-2x - 5y = 7$
$7x + y = -8$

9. $4x - 3y = -2$
$4x + y = 4$

10. $-x + 3y = 24$
$5x + 8y = -5$

11. $4x + 9y = 2$
$2x + 6y = 1$

12. $9x + 6y = 3$
$3x - 7y = -26$

7.3 SOLVING LINEAR SYSTEMS BY LINEAR COMBINATIONS

Examples on pp. 402–404

EXAMPLE Solve the linear system by linear combinations.

$2x - 15y = -10$ **Equation 1**
$-4x + 5y = -30$ **Equation 2**

You can get the coefficients of x to be opposites by multiplying Equation 1 by 2.

$2x - 15y = -10$	Multiply by 2. ▶	$4x - 30y = -20$
$-4x + 5y = -30$		$-4x + 5y = -30$
		$-25y = -50$ Add equations.
		$y = 2$ Solve for y.

Substitute 2 for y in Equation 2 and solve for x.

$-4x + 5y = -30$	Write Equation 2.
$-4x + 5(2) = -30$	Substitute 2 for y.
$x = 10$	Solve for x.

ANSWER ▶ The solution is $(10, 2)$. Check the solution in the original equations.

Use linear combinations to solve the linear system.

13. $-4x - 6y = 7$
   $x + 5y = 8$

14. $2x + y = 0$
   $5x - 4y = 26$

15. $3x + 5y = -16$
   $-2x + 6y = -36$

16. $9x + 6y = 3$
   $3y + 6x = 18$

17. $2 - 7x = 9y$
   $2y - 4x = 6$

18. $4x - 9y = 1$
   $25x + 6y = 4$

7.4 LINEAR SYSTEMS AND PROBLEM SOLVING

Examples on pp. 409–411

EXAMPLE Your teacher is giving a test worth 150 points. There are 46 three-point and five-point questions. How many of each are on the test?

Write an algebraic model. Let x be the number of three-point questions and let y be the number of five-point questions.

   $3x + 5y = 150$ **Equation 1**
   $x + y = 46$ **Equation 2**

Since at least one variable has a coefficient of 1, use substitution to solve the system.

   $y = -x + 46$ Solve Equation 2 for y. (Revised Equation 2)

   $3x + 5(-x + 46) = 150$ Substitute $-x + 46$ for y in Equation 1.

   $3x - 5x + 230 = 150$ Use the distributive property.

   $-2x = -80$ Combine like terms.

   $x = 40$ Divide each side by -2.

   $y = -(40) + 46 = 6$ Substitute 40 for x in Revised Equation 2.

ANSWER ▶ There are 40 three-point questions and 6 five-point questions.

19. RENTING MOVIES You spend $13 to rent five movies for the weekend. New releases rent for $3 and regular movies rent for $2. How many regular movies did you rent? How many new releases did you rent?

7.5 SPECIAL TYPES OF LINEAR SYSTEMS

Examples on pp. 417–419

EXAMPLE Tell how many solutions the following linear system has.

   $3x + 5y = 7$ **Equation 1**
   $-3x - 5y = 8$ **Equation 2**

Use linear combinations.

   $3x + 5y = 7$ Write Equation 1.
   $-3x - 5y = 8$ Write Equation 2.
   ——————————
   $0 \neq 15$ Add equations.

ANSWER ▶ The resulting statement is false. The linear system has no solution.

EXAMPLE Tell how many solutions the following linear system has.

$-x - 3y = -5$ **Equation 1**
$2x + 6y = 10$ **Equation 2**

You can multiply Equation 1 by -2 to obtain Equation 2.

$2x + 6y = 10$ **Revised Equation 1**

$2x + 6y = 10$ **Equation 2**

ANSWER ▸ The two equations are identical. Any solution of $2x + 6y = 10$ is also a solution of the system. This tells you that the linear system has infinitely many solutions.

Use the substitution method or linear combinations to solve the linear system and tell how many solutions the system has.

20. $-2x - 6y = -12$
$2x + 6y = 12$

21. $2x - 3y = 1$
$-2x + 3y = 1$

22. $-6x + 5y = 18$
$7x + 2y = 26$

7.6 SYSTEMS OF LINEAR INEQUALITIES

Examples on pp. 424–426

EXAMPLE Graph the system of linear inequalities.

$x \geq 0$ **Inequality 1**
$y < -2x + 2$ **Inequality 2**
$y \geq 3x - 7$ **Inequality 3**

Graph all three inequalities in the same coordinate plane. Use a dashed line if the inequality is $<$ or $>$ and a solid line if the inequality is $\leq$ or $\geq$.

The graph of $x \geq 0$ is the half-plane *on and to the right* of the line $x = 0$.

The graph of the $y < -2x + 2$ is the half-plane *below* the line $y = -2x + 2$.

The graph of $y \geq 3x - 7$ is the half-plane *on and above* the line $y = 3x - 7$.

The graph of the system is the intersection of the three half-planes shown.

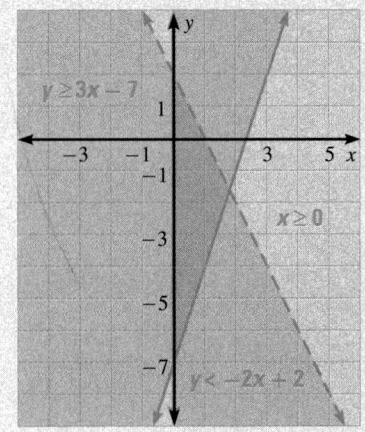

Graph the system of linear inequalities.

23. $x > -5$
$y < -2$

24. $2x - 10y > 8$
$x - 5y < 12$

25. $-x + 3y \leq 15$
$9x \geq 27$

26. $x < 5$
$y > -2$
$x + 2y > -4$

27. $x + y < 8$
$x - y < 0$
$y \geq 4$

28. $7y \geq -49$
$-7x + y \geq -14$
$x + y \leq 10$

Estimate the solution of the linear system graphically. Then check the solution algebraically.

1. $y = 2x - 3$
$-y = 2x - 1$

2. $6x + 2y = 16$
$-2x + y = -2$

3. $4x - y = 10$
$-2x + 4y = 16$

Use the substitution method to solve the linear system.

4. $-4x + 7y = -2$
$x = -y - 5$

5. $7x + 4y = 5$
$x - 6y = -19$

6. $-3x + 6y = 24$
$-2x - y = 1$

Use linear combinations to solve the linear system.

7. $6x + 7y = 5$
$4x - 2y = -10$

8. $-7x + 2y = -5$
$10x - 2y = 6$

9. $-3x + 3y = 12$
$4x + 2y = 20$

10. WILD BIRD FOOD You buy 6 bags of wild bird food to fill the feeders in your yard. Oyster shell grit, a natural calcium source, sells for $4.00 a bag. Sunflower seeds sell for $5.00 a bag. If you spend $28.00, how many bags of each type of bird food are you buying?

Use the substitution method or linear combinations to solve the linear system and tell how many solutions the system has.

11. $8x + 4y = -4$
$2x - y = -3$

12. $-6x + 3y = -6$
$2x + 6y = 30$

13. $-3x + y = -18$
$3x - y = -16$

14. $3x + y = 8$
$4x + 6y = 6$

15. $3x - 4y = 8$
$9x - 12y = 24$

16. $6x + y = 12$
$-4x - 2y = 0$

Graph the system of linear inequalities.

17. $x \le 4$
$y \ge 1$

18. $-3x + 2y > 3$
$x + 4y < -2$

19. $2x - 3y \le 12$
$-x - 3y \ge -6$

20. $x > -1$
$y < 3$
$y > -3$

21. $y \le 2$
$y \ge x - 2$
$y \ge -x - 2$

22. $x < 5$
$y \le 6$
$y > -2x + 3$

Write a system of linear inequalities that defines the shaded region.

23.

24.
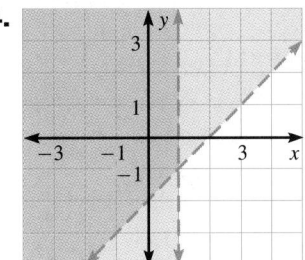

25.
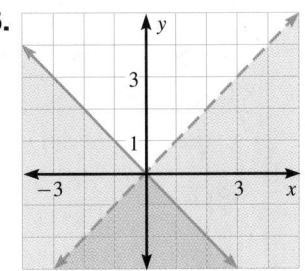

Chapter Standardized Test

Test Tip Go back and check as much of your work as you can.
Ⓐ Ⓑ Ⓒ Ⓓ

1. Which point appears to be the solution of the linear system graphed below?

Ⓐ $(-4, 0)$

Ⓑ $(-3, -1)$

Ⓒ $(-1, -3)$

Ⓓ $(0, -2)$

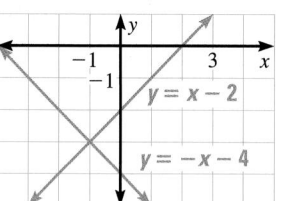

2. The ordered pair $(3, 4)$ is a solution of which linear system?

Ⓐ $x + y = 7$
$x + 2y = 11$

Ⓑ $x - y = 1$
$2x - y = 9$

Ⓒ $x - y = 1$
$2x + y = 10$

Ⓓ $x + y = 7$
$2x - 2y = 14$

3. What is the solution of the following linear system?
$$-2x + 7y = -3$$
$$x - 7y = -2$$

Ⓐ 1

Ⓑ 5

Ⓒ $(1, 5)$

Ⓓ $(5, 1)$

4. What is the solution of the following linear system?
$$5x - 6y = -10$$
$$-15x + 14y = 10$$

Ⓐ $(-5, -8)$

Ⓑ $(-2, 0)$

Ⓒ $(4, 5)$

Ⓓ $(10, 10)$

5. You have 50 ride tickets. You need 3 tickets to ride the Ferris wheel and 5 tickets to ride the roller coaster. You ride 12 times. How many times did you ride the roller coaster?

Ⓐ 5

Ⓑ 7

Ⓒ 10

Ⓓ 18

6. How many solutions does the following linear system have?
$$4x - 2y = 6$$
$$2x - y = 3$$

Ⓐ One

Ⓑ Two

Ⓒ Infinitely many

Ⓓ None

7. Which system of linear equations has no solution?

Ⓐ $y = 2x + 4$
$y = 2$

Ⓑ $3x + 4y = 10$
$3x + 2y = 8$

Ⓒ $5x + 2y = 11$
$10x + 4y = 11$

Ⓓ $2x - 4y = -5$
$3x + 6y = 15$

Ⓔ None of these

8. Which point is a solution of the following system of linear inequalities?
$$y < -x$$
$$y < x$$

Ⓐ $(6, -2)$

Ⓑ $(-2, 6)$

Ⓒ $(-1, -6)$

Ⓓ $(-6, -1)$

9. Which system of inequalities is represented by the graph below?

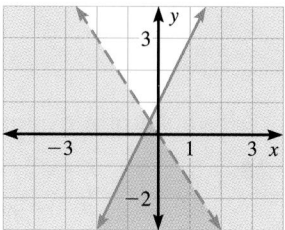

Ⓐ $y \leq 2x + 1$
$2y < -3x$

Ⓑ $y \geq 2x + 1$
$2y > -3x$

Ⓒ $y \leq 2x + 1$
$2y < 3x$

Ⓓ $y \geq 2x + 1$
$2y > 3x$

Maintaining Skills

EXAMPLE 1 Volume of a Solid

Find the volume of the figure shown.

Solution

$$\text{Volume} = \text{Area of base} \times \text{Height}$$
$$= \pi r^2 \times h$$
$$= \pi(6)^2 5$$
$$= 180\pi$$

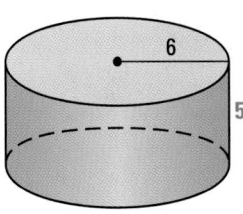

Try These

Find the volume of the geometric figure shown.

1.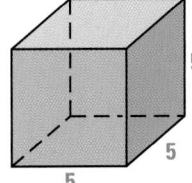

2.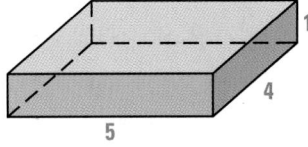

3.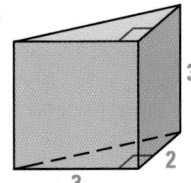

4.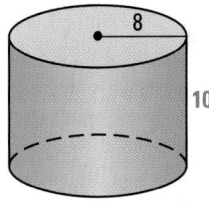

EXAMPLE 2 Decimals and Percents

a. Write 30% as a decimal.

b. Write 0.705 as a percent.

Solution

a. $30\% = \dfrac{30}{100}$

$= 0.3$

b. $0.705 = 0.705 \times 100\%$

$= 70.5\%$

Try These

Write the percent as a decimal.

5. 47%　　　**6.** 4%　　　**7.** 3.5%　　　**8.** 120%

Write the decimal as a percent.

9. 0.61　　　**10.** 0.07　　　**11.** 2　　　**12.** 0.025

CHAPTER 8

Exponents and Exponential Functions

▶ How are the speed of your bike and your air intake related?

APPLICATION: Bicycle Racing

Shifting into a higher gear helps racers increase speed but makes pedaling more difficult. When racers use more energy, their air intake increases.

The relationship between air intake and bicycle speed can be represented by a type of mathematical model that you will study in Chapter 8.

Think & Discuss

1. Construct a scatter plot of the data below. Draw a smooth curve through the points.

Bicycle speed, x (miles per hour)	Air intake, y (liters per minute)
0	6.4
5	10.7
10	18.1
15	30.5
20	51.4

2. Describe the change in the air intake after each increase of 5 miles per hour in bike speed. Does air intake increase by the same amount? Does it increase by the same percent?

Learn More About It

You will use an exponential model that relates air intake and bicycle speed in Exercises 35 and 36 on page 480.

 APPLICATION LINK More about bicycle racing is available at www.mcdougallittell.com

PREVIEW

What's the chapter about?

- **Multiplying** and **dividing** expressions with exponents
- Using **scientific notation** to solve problems
- Using **exponential growth** and **decay** models

KEY WORDS

- **exponential function,** p. 455
- **scientific notation,** p. 469
- **exponential growth,** p. 476
- **growth factor,** p. 476
- **exponential decay,** p. 482
- **decay factor,** p. 482

PREPARE

Chapter Readiness Quiz

Take this quick quiz. If you are unsure of an answer, look back at the reference pages for help.

VOCABULARY CHECK *(refer to p. 9)*

1. Complete: In the expression 7^6, 7 is the __?__.

    A base   **B** factor   **C** exponent   **D** power

2. Complete: In the expression 7^6, 6 is the __?__.

    A base   **B** factor   **C** exponent   **D** power

SKILL CHECK *(refer to pp. 11, 16, 177)*

3. Evaluate $(3x)^2$ when $x = 2$.

    A 12   **B** 18   **C** 24   **D** 36

4. Evaluate $\dfrac{x^3}{y}$ when $x = 4$ and $y = 2$.

    A 6   **B** 8   **C** 21.5   **D** 32

5. How much do you earn per hour if you earn $123.75 for working 15 hours?

    A $8.25   **B** $12.12   **C** $108.75   **D** $1856.25

STUDY TIP

Plan Your Time

A schedule or weekly planner can be a useful tool that allows you to coordinate your study time with time for other activities.

FEBRUARY

MONDAY 5
Math homework—p. 446, #13–51 odd

TUESDAY 6
Swimming Practice 3–4 p.m.

WEDNESDAY 7
History report due

DEVELOPING CONCEPTS
Investigating Powers

GOAL

Find a pattern for multiplying exponential expressions.

MATERIALS

• paper
• pencil

Question

How do you multiply powers with the same base?

Explore

❶ One way to multiply powers with the same base is to write the product in expanded form. Then count the number of factors and use this number as the exponent of the product of the powers.

	Number of factors	Product as a power
$7^3 \cdot 7^2 = \underbrace{(7 \cdot 7 \cdot 7)}_{\text{3 factors}}\underbrace{(7 \cdot 7)}_{\text{2 factors}} = \underbrace{(7)(7)(7)(7)(7)}_{\text{5 factors}}$	5	7^5

❷ Notice that the exponent for the product of powers with the same base is the sum of the exponents of the powers: $3 + 2 = 5$. See if the same pattern applies to the following products.

$7^3 \cdot 7^3$ $\qquad$ $2^3 \cdot 2^2$ $\qquad$ $x^3 \cdot x^4$

❸ What can you conclude?

Think About It

Find the product. Write your answer as a single power.

1. $6^3 \cdot 6^2$ $\qquad$ **2.** $2 \cdot 2^4$ $\qquad$ **3.** $a^4 \cdot a^6$ $\qquad$ **4.** $x^2 \cdot x^7$

5. Complete: For any nonzero number a and any positive integers m and n, $a^m \cdot a^n = \underline{\quad ? \quad}$.

Question

How do you find the power of a power?

Explore

❶ To find the power of a power, you can write the product in expanded form. Then count the number of factors and use this number as the exponent of the product of the powers.

Student Help

▶ **READING ALGEBRA**
When you read a power of a power, start with the power within the parentheses. For example, $(7^3)^2$ is read "seven cubed, squared."

		Number of factors	Product as a power
$(7^3)^2 = \overset{\text{2 times}}{\overbrace{(7^3)(7^3)}} = \underbrace{\overset{\text{3 factors}}{\overbrace{(7)(7)(7)}}\overset{\text{3 factors}}{\overbrace{(7)(7)(7)}}}_{\text{6 factors}}$		6	7^6

2 Notice that the exponent for the power of a power is the product of the exponents: $2 \cdot 3 = 6$. See if the same pattern applies to the following powers of powers.

$$(5^2)^3 \qquad (3^2)^2 \qquad (x^5)^3$$

3 What can you conclude?

Think About It

Find the power of a power. Write your answer as a single power.

1. $(4^2)^3$ **2.** $(5^4)^2$ **3.** $(d^3)^3$ **4.** $(n^3)^4$

5. Complete: For any nonzero number a and any positive integers m and n, $(a^m)^n = \underline{\ ?\ }$.

Question

How do you find the power of a product?

Explore

1 One way to find the power of a product is to write the product in expanded form and group like factors. Then count the number of each factor and write the answer as a power of each factor.

	Number of each factor	Product as a power
$(5 \cdot 4)^2 = \underbrace{(5 \cdot 4)(5 \cdot 4)}_{\text{2 times}} = \underbrace{(5 \cdot 5)}_{\text{2 factors}}\underbrace{(4 \cdot 4)}_{\text{2 factors}}$	2 and 2	$5^2 \cdot 4^2$

2 Notice that the exponent for a product of factors is distributed to each of the factors: $(5 \cdot 4)^2 = 5^2 \cdot 4^2$. See if the same pattern applies to the following powers of products.

$$(3 \cdot 2)^3 \qquad (3 \cdot 6)^4 \qquad (a \cdot b)^5$$

3 What can you conclude?

Think About It

Find the power of the product.

1. $(2 \cdot 6)^3$ **2.** $(3 \cdot 4)^5$ **3.** $(a \cdot b)^2$ **4.** $(x \cdot y)^4$

5. Complete: For any nonzero numbers a and b and any positive integer m, $(a \cdot b)^m = \underline{\ ?\ }$.

8.1 Multiplication Properties of Exponents

Goal

Use multiplication properties of exponents.

Key Words

- power
- base
- exponent

How do the areas of two irrigation circles compare?

What does it mean to say that one circle is twice as big as another? Does it mean that the radius r is twice as big or that the area is twice as big? In Example 5 you will see that these two interpretations are not the same.

PRODUCT OF POWERS As you saw in Developing Concepts 8.1, page 441, to multiply powers that have the same base, you add the exponents. This property is called the *product of powers property*. Here is an example.

$$a^2 \cdot a^3 = \underbrace{a \cdot a}_{\text{2 factors}} \cdot \overbrace{\underbrace{a \cdot a \cdot a}_{\text{3 factors}}}^{\text{5 factors}} = a^{2+3} = a^5$$

Student Help

▶ **LOOK BACK**
For help with exponential expressions, see p. 9.

EXAMPLE 1 Use the Product of Powers Property

Write the expression as a single power of the base.

a. $5^3 \cdot 5^6$ **b.** $-2(-2)^4$ **c.** $x^2 \cdot x^3 \cdot x^4$

Solution

a. $5^3 \cdot 5^6 = 5^{3+6}$ Use product of powers property.

$= 5^9$ Add the exponents.

b. $-2(-2)^4 = (-2)^1(-2)^4$ Rewrite -2 as $(-2)^1$.

$= (-2)^{1+4}$ Use product of powers property.

$= (-2)^5$ Add the exponents.

c. $x^2 \cdot x^3 \cdot x^4 = x^{2+3+4}$ Use product of powers property.

$= x^9$ Add the exponents.

Checkpoint✔ Use the Product of Powers Property

Write the expression as a single power of the base.

1. $4^2 \cdot 4^3$ **2.** $(-3)^2(-3)$ **3.** $a \cdot a^7$ **4.** $n^5 \cdot n^2 \cdot n^3$

POWER OF A POWER To find a power of a power, you multiply the exponents. This property is called the *power of a power property*. Here is an example.

$$(a^2)^3 = a^2 \cdot a^2 \cdot a^2 = a^{2+2+2} = a^6$$

Student Help

▶ **LOOK BACK**
For help with exponents and grouping symbols, see p. 11.

EXAMPLE 2 Use the Power of a Power Property

Write the expression as a single power of the base.

a. $(3^3)^2$ **b.** $(p^4)^4$

Solution

a. $(3^3)^2 = 3^{3 \cdot 2}$ Use power of a power property.

$ = 3^6$ Multiply exponents.

b. $(p^4)^4 = p^{4 \cdot 4}$ Use power of a power property.

$ = p^{16}$ Multiply exponents.

Checkpoint ✓ *Use the Power of a Power Property*

Write the expression as a single power of the base.

5. $(4^4)^3$ **6.** $[(-3)^5]^2$ **7.** $(n^4)^5$ **8.** $(x^3)^3$

POWER OF A PRODUCT To find a power of a product, find the power of each factor and multiply. This property is called the *power of a product property*. Here is an example.

$$(a \cdot b)^3 = (a \cdot b)(a \cdot b)(a \cdot b) = (a \cdot a \cdot a)(b \cdot b \cdot b) = a^3 b^3$$

EXAMPLE 3 Use the Power of a Product Property

Simplify the expression.

a. $(-6 \cdot 5)^2$ **b.** $(4yz)^3$

Student Help

▶ **STUDY TIP**
Notice that $(-6)^2 \cdot 5^2$ is equivalent to:
$(-6 \cdot 5)^2 = (-30)^2$
$ = 900$

Solution

a. $(-6 \cdot 5)^2 = (-6)^2 \cdot 5^2$ Use power of a product property.

$ = 36 \cdot 25$ Evaluate each power.

$ = 900$ Multiply.

b. $(4yz)^3 = 4^3 \cdot y^3 \cdot z^3$ Use power of a product property.

$ = 64y^3z^3$ Evaluate power.

Checkpoint ✓ *Use the Power of a Product Property*

Simplify the expression.

9. $(2 \cdot 4)^3$ **10.** $(-3 \cdot 5)^2$ **11.** $(2w)^6$ **12.** $(7a)^2$

EXAMPLE 4 Use All Three Properties

Simplify the expression $(4x^2)^3 \cdot x^5$.

Solution

$$(4x^2)^3 \cdot x^5 = 4^3 \cdot (x^2)^3 \cdot x^5 \qquad \text{Use power of a product property.}$$
$$= 64 \cdot x^6 \cdot x^5 \qquad \text{Use power of a power property.}$$
$$= 64x^{11} \qquad \text{Use product of powers property.}$$

 **Use All Three Properties**

Simplify the expression.

13. $(4x^3)^4$ **14.** $(-3a^4)^2$ **15.** $9 \cdot (9z^5)^2$ **16.** $(n^2)^3 \cdot n^7$

EXAMPLE 5 Use Multiplication Properties of Exponents

FARMING Find the ratio
of the area of the larger
irrigation circle to the
area of the smaller
irrigation circle.

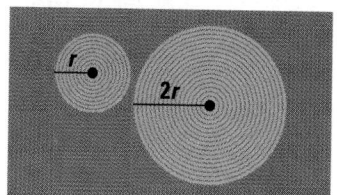

Solution

The area of a circle can be found using the formula $A = \pi r^2$.

$$\text{Ratio} = \frac{\pi(2r)^2}{\pi r^2} = \frac{\pi \cdot 2^2 \cdot r^2}{\pi \cdot r^2} = \frac{\pi \cdot 4 \cdot r^2}{\pi \cdot r^2} = \frac{4}{1}$$

ANSWER ▶ The ratio of the areas is 4 to 1.

 **Use Multiplication Properties of Exponents**

17. Find the ratio of the area of the smaller irrigation circle in Example 5 to the
area of an irrigation circle with radius $3r$.

SUMMARY

Multiplication Properties of Exponents

Let a and b be real numbers and let m and n be positive integers.

PRODUCT OF POWERS PROPERTY	POWER OF A POWER PROPERTY	POWER OF A PRODUCT PROPERTY
To multiply powers that have the same base, add the exponents.	To find a power of a power, multiply the exponents.	To find a power of a product, find the power of each factor and multiply.
$a^m \cdot a^n = a^{m+n}$	$(a^m)^n = a^{m \cdot n}$	$(a \cdot b)^m = a^m \cdot b^m$

Guided Practice

Vocabulary Check Match the multiplication property of exponents with the example that illustrates it.

1. Product of powers property

2. Power of a power property

3. Power of a product property

A. $(3 \cdot 6)^2 = 3^2 \cdot 6^2$

B. $4^3 \cdot 4^5 = 4^{3+5}$

C. $(2^4)^4 = 2^{4 \cdot 4}$

Skill Check Use the product of powers property to write the expression as a single power of the base.

4. $2^2 \cdot 2^3$

5. $(-5)^4 \cdot (-5)^2$

6. $a^4 \cdot a^6$

Use the power of a power property to write the expression as a single power of the base.

7. $(2^4)^3$

8. $(4^3)^3$

9. $(y^4)^5$

Use the power of a product property to simplify the expression.

10. $(3 \cdot 4)^3$

11. $(2n)^4$

12. $(3pq)^3$

Practice and Applications

COMPLETING EQUATIONS Copy and complete the statement.

13. $3^2 \cdot 3^? = 3^7$

14. $5^? \cdot 5^8 = 5^9$

15. $4^{10} \cdot 4^8 = 4^?$

16. $x^3 \cdot x^2 = x^?$

17. $r^? \cdot r^7 = r^{14}$

18. $a^2 \cdot a^? = a^5$

PRODUCT OF POWERS Write the expression as a single power of the base.

19. $4^3 \cdot 4^6$

20. $8^9 \cdot 8^5$

21. $(-2)^3 \cdot (-2)^3$

22. $b \cdot b^4$

23. $x^6 \cdot x^3$

24. $t^3 \cdot t^2$

COMPLETING EQUATIONS Copy and complete the statement.

25. $(5^?)^3 = 5^9$

26. $(2^2)^? = 2^8$

27. $[(-9)^4]^3 = (-9)^?$

28. $(a^2)^? = a^{10}$

29. $(x^3)^3 = x^?$

30. $(p^?)^6 = p^{12}$

Student Help

▶**HOMEWORK HELP**
Example 1: Exs. 13–24
Example 2: Exs. 25–36
Example 3: Exs. 37–51
Example 4: Exs. 52–60
Example 5: Exs. 61–68

POWER OF A POWER Write the expression as a single power of the base.

31. $(2^3)^2$

32. $(7^4)^2$

33. $[(-4)^5]^3$

34. $(t^5)^6$

35. $(c^8)^{10}$

36. $(x^3)^2$

POWER OF A PRODUCT Simplify the expression.

37. $(3 \cdot 7)^2$ **38.** $(4 \cdot 9)^3$ **39.** $(-4 \cdot 6)^2$

40. $(5x)^3$ **41.** $(-2d)^6$ **42.** $(ab)^2$

43. $(2mn)^6$ **44.** $(10xy)^2$ **45.** $(-rst)^5$

Student Help

▶HOMEWORK HELP

Extra help with problem solving in Exs. 46–51 is available at www.mcdougallittell.com

WRITING INEQUALITIES Copy and complete the statement using < or >.

46. $(5 \cdot 6)^4$ **?** $5 \cdot 6^4$ **47.** $5^2 \cdot 5^3$ **?** $(5 \cdot 5)^6$ **48.** $(3 \cdot 2)^6$ **?** $(3^2)^6$

49. $4^2 \cdot 4^8$ **?** $(4 \cdot 4)^{10}$ **50.** $7^3 \cdot 7^4$ **?** $(7 \cdot 7)^4$ **51.** $(6 \cdot 3)^3$ **?** $6 \cdot 3 \cdot 3$

SIMPLIFYING EXPRESSIONS Simplify the expression.

52. $(3b)^3 \cdot b$ **53.** $-4x \cdot (x^3)^2$ **54.** $(5a^4)^2$

55. $(r^2s^3)^4$ **56.** $(6z^4)^2 \cdot z^3$ **57.** $2x^3 \cdot (-3x)^2$

58. $4x \cdot (-x \cdot x^3)^2$ **59.** $(abc^2)^3 \cdot ab$ **60.** $(5y^2)^3 \cdot (y^3)^2$

61. **Geometry Link** The volume V of a sphere is given by the formula $V = \frac{4}{3}\pi r^3$, where r is the radius. What is the volume of the sphere in terms of a?

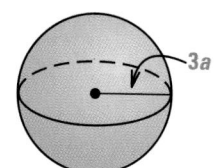

62. **Geometry Link** The volume V of a circular cone is given by the formula $V = \frac{1}{3}\pi r^2 h$, where r is the radius of the base and h is the height. What is the volume of the cone in terms of b?

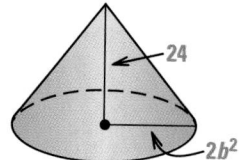

Link to Careers

ALTERNATIVE ENERGY TECHNICIANS solve technical problems in the development, maintenance, and inspection of machinery, such as windmills.

More about alternative energy technicians is at www.mcdougallittell.com

ALTERNATIVE ENERGY The power generated by a windmill can be modeled by $w = 0.015s^3$, where w is the power measured in watts and s is the wind speed in miles per hour.

63. Find the ratio of the power generated when the wind speed is 20 miles per hour to the power generated when the wind speed is 10 miles per hour.

64. Find the ratio of the power generated when the wind speed is 5 miles per hour to the power generated when the wind speed is 10 miles per hour.

PENNIES Someone offers to double the amount of money you have every day for 1 month (30 days). You have 1 penny.

65. At the end of the first day, you will have $2 \cdot 1 = 2$ pennies. On the second day, you will have $2 \cdot 2 = 4$ pennies. On the third day, you will have $2 \cdot 4 = 8$ pennies. Write each of these equations using only powers of 2.

66. Using the pattern you find in Exercise 65, write an expression for the number of pennies you will have on the nth day.

67. How many pennies will you have on the 30th day?

68. How much money (in dollars) will you have after 30 days?

69. CHALLENGE Fill in the blanks and give a reason for each step to complete a convincing argument that the power of a power property is true for this case.

$$(b^3)^2 = b^3 \cdot \underline{?}$$
$$= \underline{?} \cdot \underline{?} \cdot \underline{?} \cdot \underline{?} \cdot \underline{?} \cdot \underline{?}$$
$$= \underline{?}$$

Standardized Test Practice

70. MULTIPLE CHOICE Simplify the expression $5^2 \cdot 5^4$.

  (A) 5^6 (B) 5^8 (C) 10^6 (D) 25^8

71. MULTIPLE CHOICE Evaluate the expression $(2^3)^2$.

  (F) 18 (G) 32 (H) 36 (J) 64

72. MULTIPLE CHOICE Evaluate the expression $(4 \cdot 6)^2$.

  (A) 48 (B) 96 (C) 144 (D) 576

73. MULTIPLE CHOICE Simplify the expression $(3x^2y)^3$.

  (F) $3x^2y^3$ (G) $9x^5y^3$ (H) $9x^6y^3$ (J) $27x^6y^3$

Mixed Review

VARIABLE EXPRESSIONS **Evaluate the expression for the given value of the variable.** *(Lesson 1.3)*

74. b^2 when $b = 8$ **75.** $(5y)^4$ when $y = 2$ **76.** $\frac{1}{2}n^3$ when $n = -2$

77. $\frac{1}{y^2}$ when $y = 5$ **78.** $\frac{24}{x^3}$ when $x = 2$ **79.** $\frac{45}{a^2}$ when $a = 2$

GRAPHING EQUATIONS **Use a table of values to graph the equation.** *(Lessons 4.2, 4.3)*

80. $y = x + 2$ **81.** $y = -(x - 4)$ **82.** $y = \frac{1}{2}x - 5$

83. $y = \frac{3}{4}x + 2$ **84.** $y = 2$ **85.** $x = -3$

SOLVING INEQUALITIES **Solve the inequality.** *(Lesson 6.3)*

86. $-x - 2 < -5$ **87.** $3 - x > -4$ **88.** $7 + 3x \geq -2$

89. $6x - 10 \leq -4$ **90.** $2 < 2x + 7$ **91.** $9 - 4x \leq 2$

Maintaining Skills

LCM AND GCF **Decide whether the statement is *true* or *false*. If it is false, correct the statement to make it true.** *(Skills Review p. 761)*

92. The least common multiple of 6 and 10 is 60.

93. The greatest common factor of 6 and 10 is 2.

94. The least common multiple of 10 and 30 is 30.

95. The greatest common factor of 10 and 30 is 5.

96. The least common multiple of 45 and 82 is 105.

97. The greatest common factor of 45 and 82 is 3.

8.2 Zero and Negative Exponents

Goal

Evaluate powers that have zero or negative exponents.

Key Words

- zero exponent
- negative exponent
- reciprocal

What was the population of the U.S. in 1776?

Many real-life quantities can be modeled by functions that contain exponents. In Exercise 64 you will use such a model to estimate the population of the United States in 1776.

The definition of a^0 is determined by the product of powers property:

$$a^0 a^n = a^{0+n} = a^n$$

In order to have $a^0 a^n = a^n$, a^0 must equal 1.

The definition of a^{-n} is similarly determined:

$$a^n a^{-n} = a^{n-n} = a^0 = 1$$

In order to have $a^n a^{-n} = 1$, a^{-n} must be the reciprocal of a^n.

Student Help

▶ WRITING ALGEBRA
The definition of a negative exponent can also be written as:

$$\frac{1}{a^{-n}} = a^n$$

ZERO AND NEGATIVE EXPONENTS

Let a be a nonzero number and let n be an integer.

- A nonzero number to the zero power is 1:
$$a^0 = 1, \ a \neq 0$$

- a^{-n} is the reciprocal of a^n:
$$a^{-n} = \frac{1}{a^n}, \ a \neq 0$$

EXAMPLE 1 Powers with Zero Exponents

Evaluate the expression.

a. $5^0 = 1$ a^0 is equal to 1.

b. 0^0 (Undefined) a^0 is defined only for a *nonzero* number a.

c. $(-2)^0 = 1$ a^0 is equal to 1.

d. $\left(\frac{1}{9}\right)^0 = 1$ a^0 is equal to 1.

EXAMPLE 2 **Powers with Negative Exponents**

Evaluate the expression.

a. $2^{-2} = \dfrac{1}{2^2}$ 2^{-2} is the reciprocal of 2^2.

      $= \dfrac{1}{4}$ Evaluate power.

b. $\dfrac{1}{(-3)^{-4}} = (-3)^4$ $(-3)^4$ is the reciprocal of $(-3)^{-4}$.

        $= 81$ Evaluate power.

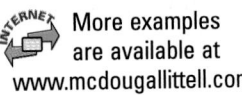 **Powers with Zero or Negative Exponents**

Evaluate the expression.

1. $\left(\dfrac{1}{8}\right)^0$ **2.** $(-9)^{-2}$ **3.** $\dfrac{1}{2^{-3}}$ **4.** $\dfrac{1}{(-5)^{-2}}$

Student Help

▶ **MORE EXAMPLES**

More examples are available at www.mcdougallittell.com

EXAMPLE 3 **Evaluate Exponential Expressions**

Evaluate the expression.

a. $6^{-4} \cdot 6^4$ **b.** $\left(2^{-3}\right)^{-2}$ **c.** $(-3 \cdot 2)^{-2}$

Solution

a. $6^{-4} \cdot 6^4 = 6^{-4+4}$ Use product of powers property.

      $= 6^0$ Add exponents.

      $= 1$ a^0 is equal to 1.

b. $\left(2^{-3}\right)^{-2} = 2^{-3 \cdot (-2)}$ Use power of a power property.

      $= 2^6$ Multiply exponents.

      $= 64$ Evaluate power.

c. $(-3 \cdot 2)^{-2} = \dfrac{1}{(-3 \cdot 2)^2}$ Use definition of negative exponent.

      $= \dfrac{1}{(-3)^2 \cdot 2^2}$ Use power of a product property.

      $= \dfrac{1}{9 \cdot 4}$ Evaluate powers.

      $= \dfrac{1}{36}$ Multiply.

Checkpoint **Evaluate Exponential Expressions**

Evaluate the expression without using a calculator.

5. $4^2 \cdot 4^{-3}$ **6.** $\left(3^{-1}\right)^{-2}$ **7.** $(2 \cdot 5)^{-2}$

Student Help

▶**KEYSTROKE HELP**
Use [y^x] or [^] to input the exponent.

EXAMPLE 4 Evaluate Expressions with a Calculator

 Use a calculator to evaluate $(2^{-2})^4$.

Solution You can simplify the expression first.

$(2^{-2})^4 = 2^{-8}$ Use power of a power property.

KEYSTROKES	DISPLAY
2 [y^x] 8 [+/-] [=]	0.00390625

ANSWER ▶ $(2^{-2})^4 \approx 0.0039$

Checkpoint ✔ *Evaluate Expressions with a Calculator*

🖩 **Use a calculator to evaluate the expression.**

8. 7^{-3} **9.** $6^{-2} \cdot 6^{-1}$ **10.** $(3^3)^{-2}$

EXAMPLE 5 Simplify Exponential Expressions

Rewrite the expression with positive exponents.

a. $2x^{-2}y^{-3}$ **b.** $\dfrac{c^{-2}}{d^{-3}}$ **c.** $(5a)^{-2}$

Solution

a. $2x^{-2}y^{-3} = 2 \cdot \dfrac{1}{x^2} \cdot \dfrac{1}{y^3}$ Use definition of negative exponents.

$\qquad\qquad = \dfrac{2}{x^2 y^3}$ Multiply.

b. $\dfrac{c^{-2}}{d^{-3}} = c^{-2} \cdot \dfrac{1}{d^{-3}}$ Multiply by reciprocal.

$\qquad\quad = \dfrac{1}{c^2} \cdot d^3$ Use definition of negative exponents.

$\qquad\quad = \dfrac{d^3}{c^2}$ Multiply.

c. $(5a)^{-2} = \dfrac{1}{(5a)^2}$ Use definition of negative exponents.

$\qquad\qquad = \dfrac{1}{5^2 \cdot a^2}$ Use power of a product property.

$\qquad\qquad = \dfrac{1}{25a^2}$ Evaluate power.

Checkpoint ✔ *Simplify Exponential Expressions*

Rewrite the expression with positive exponents.

11. $2x^{-3}y^3$ **12.** $\dfrac{3}{x^{-2}}$ **13.** $(5b)^{-3}$

Guided Practice

Vocabulary Check — **Tell whether the statement is *true* or *false*. Explain your answer.**

1. A nonzero number to the zero power is zero.

2. Let a be a nonzero number and let n be an integer. Then $a^{-n} = \dfrac{1}{a^n}$.

Skill Check — **Evaluate the expression.**

3. 6^0 **4.** 3^{-1} **5.** $\dfrac{1}{4^{-3}}$ **6.** $\dfrac{1}{(-2)^{-1}}$

Evaluate the expression without using a calculator.

7. $2^{-4} \cdot 2^5$ **8.** $(3^4)^{-1}$ **9.** $(4 \cdot 1)^{-2}$ **10.** $(9^{-1})^2$

Use a calculator to evaluate the expression. Round your answer to the nearest ten-thousandth.

11. 5^{-4} **12.** $7^{-1} \cdot 7^{-3}$ **13.** $(8^2)^{-1}$ **14.** $(3 \cdot 4)^{-3}$

Rewrite the expression with positive exponents.

15. m^{-2} **16.** $a^5 b^{-8}$ **17.** $\dfrac{3}{c^{-5}}$ **18.** $(2x)^{-3}$

Practice and Applications

RECIPROCALS **Copy and complete the table.**

19.

x	2	5	6
x^{-1}	?	?	?

20.

x	?	?	?
x^{-1}	$\dfrac{1}{3}$	$\dfrac{1}{8}$	$\dfrac{1}{7}$

ZERO AND NEGATIVE EXPONENTS **Evaluate the expression.**

21. 3^0 **22.** $(-5)^0$ **23.** 4^{-2} **24.** 9^{-1}

25. $(-7)^{-3}$ **26.** $\dfrac{1}{10^{-1}}$ **27.** $\dfrac{1}{4^{-4}}$ **28.** $\dfrac{1}{(-8)^{-2}}$

Student Help

▶**HOMEWORK HELP**
Examples 1 and 2:
        Exs. 19–28
Example 3: Exs. 29–40
Example 4: Exs. 41–48
Example 5: Exs. 49–62

EVALUATING EXPRESSIONS **Evaluate the expression without using a calculator.**

29. $2^{-3} \cdot 2^0$ **30.** $10^{-5} \cdot 10^7$ **31.** $6^2 \cdot 6^{-4}$ **32.** $4^{-1} \cdot 4^{-1}$

33. $(4^{-1})^{-3}$ **34.** $(5^{-2})^2$ **35.** $(3^2)^{-1}$ **36.** $[(-8)^{-2}]^{-1}$

37. $(10 \cdot 2)^{-2}$ **38.** $(1 \cdot 7)^{-3}$ **39.** $(-2 \cdot 2)^{-2}$ **40.** $[4 \cdot (-3)]^{-1}$

EVALUATING EXPRESSIONS Use a calculator to evaluate the expression. Round your answer to the nearest ten-thousandth.

41. 2^{-5} **42.** 11^{-2} **43.** $5^{-1} \cdot 5^{-3}$ **44.** $9^{-4} \cdot 9^2$

45. $(4^2)^{-1}$ **46.** $(3^{-3})^2$ **47.** $(2 \cdot 7)^{-1}$ **48.** $(8 \cdot 3)^{-2}$

ERROR ANALYSIS In Exercises 49 and 50, find and correct the error.

49.
$$5x^{-3} = \frac{1}{5x^3}$$

50.
$$a^{-2}b^3 = \frac{b^3}{a^{-2}}$$

SIMPLIFYING EXPRESSIONS Rewrite the expression with positive exponents.

51. x^{-5} **52.** $3x^{-4}$ **53.** $x^{-2}y^4$ **54.** $8x^{-1}y^{-6}$

55. $\dfrac{1}{x^{-2}}$ **56.** $\dfrac{2}{x^{-5}}$ **57.** $\dfrac{y^4}{x^{-10}}$ **58.** $\dfrac{9x^{-3}}{y^{-1}}$

59. $(4x)^{-3}$ **60.** $(3xy)^{-2}$ **61.** $(6x^{-3})^3$ **62.** $\dfrac{1}{(4x)^{-5}}$

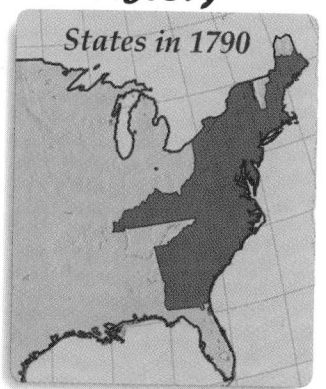

Link to
History

States in 1790

STATEHOOD After 1790, when the last of the original 13 colonies became a state, a population of at least 60,000 people was required for statehood.

EXAMPLE *Using Zero and Negative Exponents*

STATEHOOD The population P (in millions) of the United States from the late 1700s to the mid-1800s can be modeled by $P = 5.31(1.03)^y$, where y represents the number of years since 1800. Estimate the population of the United States in 1790 when the first census was taken.

Solution Since 1790 is 10 years before 1800, you want to know the value of P when $y = -10$.

$P = 5.31(1.03)^y$ Write model.

$= 5.31(1.03)^{-10}$ Substitute -10 for y.

≈ 3.95 Use a calculator to evaluate.

ANSWER ▶ The population in 1790 was about 3.95 million people.

63. Estimate the population of the United States in 1800.

64. Estimate the population of the United States in 1776.

Puzzler Refer to the squares shown.

65. What fraction of each figure is shaded?

66. Rewrite each fraction from Exercise 65 in the form 2^x.

67. Look for a pattern in your answers to Exercise 66. If this pattern continues, what fraction of Figure 10 will be shaded?

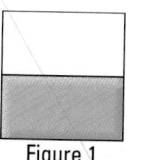
Figure 1   Figure 2

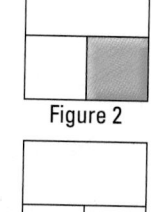
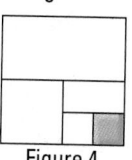
Figure 3   Figure 4

68. MULTIPLE CHOICE Which expression equals $\frac{1}{8}$?

(A) -8 (B) 4^{-2} (C) 2^{-3} (D) 1^{-8}

69. MULTIPLE CHOICE Evaluate the expression $(4^{-1})^{-2}$.

(F) $\frac{1}{64}$ (G) $\frac{1}{16}$ (H) 16 (J) 64

70. MULTIPLE CHOICE Evaluate the expression $3 \cdot 3^{-5}$.

(A) $\frac{1}{81}$ (B) $\frac{1}{5}$ (C) 45 (D) 81

71. MULTIPLE CHOICE Rewrite the expression $\dfrac{3x^{-2}}{y^3 z^{-1}}$ with positive exponents.

(F) $\dfrac{z}{3x^2 y^3}$ (G) $\dfrac{3z}{x^2 y^3}$ (H) $\dfrac{3y^3 z}{x^2}$ (J) $3x^2 y^3 z$

Mixed Review

EVALUATING EXPRESSIONS **Evaluate the expression. Then simplify the answer.** *(Lesson 1.3)*

72. $\dfrac{6 \cdot 5}{1 + 7 \cdot 2}$ **73.** $\dfrac{8 \cdot 8}{10 + 3 \cdot 2}$ **74.** $\dfrac{2 \cdot 4^2}{1 + 3^2 - 2}$

75. $\dfrac{9 + 3^3 - 4}{8 \cdot 2}$ **76.** $\dfrac{(5 - 3)^2}{2 \cdot (6 - 2)}$ **77.** $\dfrac{2 \cdot 3^4}{20 - 4^2 + 8}$

SOLVING EQUATIONS **Solve the equation.** *(Lesson 3.1)*

78. $x + 1 = 6$ **79.** $-2 = 7 + x$ **80.** $15 = x - (-4)$

81. $10 = x - 5$ **82.** $-3 + x = -8$ **83.** $x - (-6) = -9$

SOLVING INEQUALITIES **Solve the inequality. Then graph and check the solution.** *(Lesson 6.7)*

84. $|x - 3| > 4$ **85.** $|x + 9| < 4$ **86.** $|3x + 2| \geq 10$

87. $|5 + 2x| \leq 7$ **88.** $|x + 2| + 6 < 15$ **89.** $|3x + 7| - 5 > 8$

SOLVING SYSTEMS **Use substitution to solve the system.** *(Lesson 7.2)*

90. $2x - y = -2$
$\quad\ \ 4x + y = 5$ **91.** $-3x + y = 4$
$\quad\ \ -9x + 5y = 10$ **92.** $x + 4y = 30$
$\quad\ \ x - 2y = 0$

93. $2x - 3y = 10$
$\quad\ \ x + y = 5$ **94.** $x + 15y = 6$
$\quad\ \ -x - 5y = 84$ **95.** $4x - y = 5$
$\quad\ \ 2x + 4y = 16$

Maintaining Skills

EQUIVALENT FRACTIONS **Write three equivalent fractions for the given fraction.** *(Skills Review p. 764)*

96. $\dfrac{1}{4}$ **97.** $\dfrac{3}{5}$ **98.** $\dfrac{5}{6}$ **99.** $\dfrac{1}{8}$

100. $\dfrac{2}{3}$ **101.** $\dfrac{15}{16}$ **102.** $\dfrac{5}{32}$ **103.** $\dfrac{25}{32}$

8.3 Graphs of Exponential Functions

Goal
Graph an exponential function.

Key Words
• exponential function

How many shipwrecks occurred from 1680 to 1980?

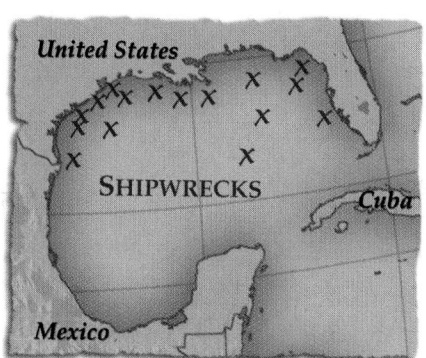

SHIPWRECKS

Many real-life relationships can be modeled by *exponential functions*. In Example 5 the number of shipwrecks that occurred in the northern part of the Gulf of Mexico from 1680 to 1980 is modeled by an *exponential function*.

In Lesson 8.2 the definition of b^n was extended to allow for zero and negative integer values of n. This lesson makes use of the expression b^x, where $b > 0$ and x is allowed to be any real number.

A function of the form $y = a \cdot b^x$ or simply $y = ab^x$, where $b > 0$ and $b \neq 1$, is an **exponential function**.

EXAMPLE 1 Evaluate an Exponential Function

Make a table of values for the exponential function $y = 2^x$. Use x-values of $-2, -1, 0, 1, 2,$ and 3.

Solution To evaluate an exponential function, use the definitions you learned in Lesson 8.2. For example, when $x = -2$ you find y as follows:

$$y = 2^{-2} = \frac{1}{2^2} = \frac{1}{4}$$

x	-2	-1	0	1	2	3
$y = 2^x$	$\frac{1}{4}$	$\frac{1}{2}$	1	2	4	8

Checkpoint ✓ Evaluate an Exponential Function

1. Make a table of values for the exponential function $y = 3^x$. Use x-values of $-2, -1, 0, 1, 2,$ and 3.

2. Make a table of values for the exponential function $y = 2\left(\frac{1}{3}\right)^x$. Use x-values of $-2, -1, 0, 1, 2,$ and 3.

EXAMPLE 2 Graph an Exponential Function when b > 1

a. Use the table of values in Example 1 to graph the function $y = 2^x$.

b. Use a calculator to evaluate $y = 2^x$ when $x = 1.5$.

Solution Begin by writing the six points given by the table on page 455:

$$\left(-2, \frac{1}{4}\right), \left(-1, \frac{1}{2}\right), (0, 1), (1, 2), (2, 4), (3, 8)$$

a. Draw a coordinate plane and plot the six points listed above. Then draw a smooth curve through the points.

Notice that the graph has a y-intercept of 1, and that it gets closer to the negative side of the x-axis as the x-values decrease.

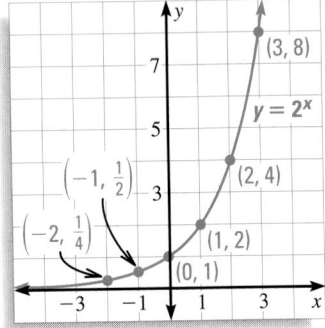

b. KEYSTROKES   **DISPLAY**

2 y^x 1 . 5 =   2.828427125

ANSWER ▶ $2^{1.5} \approx 2.83$

EXAMPLE 3 Graph an Exponential Function when 0 < b < 1

Graph the function $y = 3\left(\frac{1}{2}\right)^x$.

Solution Make a table of values that includes both positive and negative x-values. Be sure to follow the order of operations when evaluating the function. For example, when $x = -2$ you find y as follows:

$$y = 3\left(\frac{1}{2}\right)^{-2} = 3(2)^2 = 3(4) = 12$$

x	-2	-1	0	1	2	3
$y = 3\left(\frac{1}{2}\right)^x$	12	6	3	$\frac{3}{2}$	$\frac{3}{4}$	$\frac{3}{8}$

Draw a coordinate plane and plot the six points given by the table. Then draw a smooth curve through the points.

Notice that the graph has a y-intercept of 3, and that it gets closer to the positive side of the x-axis as the x-values increase.

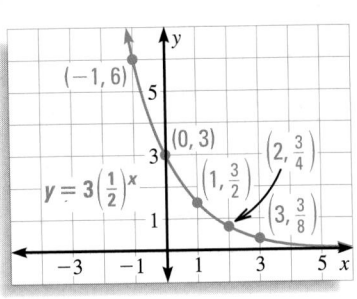

Student Help

▶ MORE EXAMPLES

More examples
are available at
www.mcdougallittell.com

EXAMPLE **4** **Find Domain and Range**

a. Describe the domain and range of the function $y = 2^x$, which is graphed in Example 2.

b. Describe the domain and range of the function $y = 3\left(\frac{1}{2}\right)^x$, which is graphed in Example 3.

Solution

a. You can see from the graph of the function that $y = 2^x$ is defined for all x-values, but only has y-values that are greater than 0. So the domain of $y = 2^x$ is all real numbers and the range is all positive real numbers.

b. You can see from the graph of the function that $y = 3\left(\frac{1}{2}\right)^x$ is defined for all x-values, but only has y-values that are greater than 0. So the domain of $y = 3\left(\frac{1}{2}\right)^x$ is all real numbers and the range is all positive real numbers.

Checkpoint ✓ **Graph an Exponential Function and Find its Domain and Range**

3. Graph the function $y = 3^x$. Then describe its domain and range.

4. Graph the function $y = 2\left(\frac{1}{3}\right)^x$. Then describe its domain and range.

Link to
History

SHIPWRECKS In 1685 La Salle claimed part of the United States for France. In 1686 his ship the *Belle* sank near Texas. This shipwreck wasn't discovered until 1995.

More about
shipwrecks at
www.mcdougallittell.com

EXAMPLE **5** **Use an Exponential Model**

SHIPWRECKS From 1680 to 1980 the number of shipwrecks per 10-year period t that occurred in the northern part of the Gulf of Mexico can be modeled by $S = 180(1.2)^t$, where S is the number of shipwrecks and $t = 0$ represents the 10-year period from 1900 to 1909. Graph the function.

Solution Make a table of values that includes positive and negative x-values.

t	-4	-2	0	2	4	6
$S = 180(1.2)^t$	87	125	180	259	373	537

Draw a coordinate plane and plot the six points given by the table. Then draw a smooth curve through the points.

Notice that the graph has a y-intercept of 180, and that it gets closer to the negative side of the x-axis as the x-values decrease.

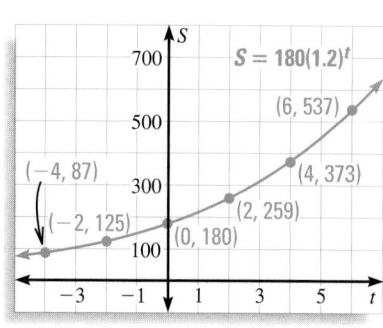

8.3 Exercises

Guided Practice

Vocabulary Check

1. Define exponential function.

Skill Check

2. Copy and complete the table of values for the exponential function.

x	-2	-1	0	1	2	3
$y = 4^x$	?	?	?	?	?	?

3. Graph $y = 4^x$. Use the points found in Exercise 2.

4. Graph the function $y = 3\left(\dfrac{1}{4}\right)^x$.

Using the graph shown, describe the domain and range of the function.

5. $y = 2^x$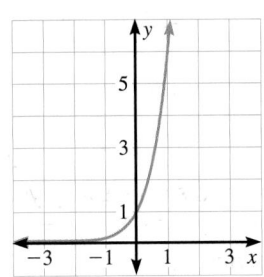

6. $y = -2^x$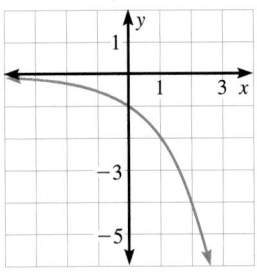

Practice and Applications

CHECKING POINTS Tell whether the graph of the function contains the point (0, 1). Explain your answer.

7. $y = 2^x$

8. $y = 5^x$

9. $y = 2(3)^x$

10. $y = 5(7)^x$

11. $y = \left(\dfrac{1}{8}\right)^x$

12. $y = \left(\dfrac{3}{4}\right)^x$

13. $y = 7\left(\dfrac{1}{5}\right)^x$

14. $y = 4\left(\dfrac{4}{9}\right)^x$

MAKING TABLES Make a table of values for the exponential function. Use x-values of -2, -1, 0, 1, 2, and 3.

15. $y = 3^x$

16. $y = 8^x$

17. $y = 5(4)^x$

18. $y = 3(5)^x$

19. $y = \left(\dfrac{1}{6}\right)^x$

20. $y = \left(\dfrac{2}{3}\right)^x$

21. $y = 2\left(\dfrac{1}{7}\right)^x$

22. $y = 5\left(\dfrac{4}{5}\right)^x$

Student Help

▶ **HOMEWORK HELP**
  Example 1: Exs. 7–22
  Example 2: Exs. 23–41
  Example 3: Exs. 31–41
  Example 4: Exs. 42–49
  Example 5: Exs. 50, 51

EVALUATING FUNCTIONS Use a calculator to evaluate the exponential function when $x = 2.5$. Round your answer to the nearest hundredth.

23. $y = 5^x$

24. $y = 9^x$

25. $y = 8(2)^x$

26. $y = 3(4)^x$

27. $y = \left(\dfrac{1}{9}\right)^x$

28. $y = \left(\dfrac{5}{8}\right)^x$

29. $y = 6\left(\dfrac{1}{2}\right)^x$

30. $y = -\left(\dfrac{3}{5}\right)^x$

EXPONENTIAL FUNCTIONS Match the equation with its graph.

31. $y = 3^x$

32. $y = 2^x$

33. $y = 9^x$

A.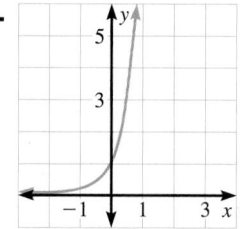

B.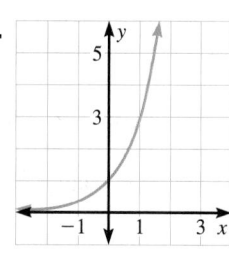

C.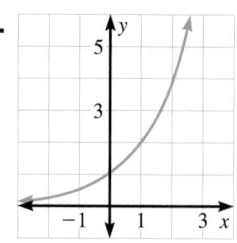

GRAPHING FUNCTIONS Graph the exponential function.

34. $y = 4^x$

35. $y = -7^x$

36. $y = 4(2)^x$

37. $y = -3(8)^x$

38. $y = \left(\dfrac{1}{2}\right)^x$

39. $y = \left(\dfrac{2}{5}\right)^x$

40. $y = -5\left(\dfrac{1}{5}\right)^x$

41. $y = 2\left(\dfrac{2}{3}\right)^x$

DOMAIN AND RANGE Using your graphs from Exercises 34–41, describe the domain and the range of the function.

42. $y = 4^x$

43. $y = -7^x$

44. $y = 4(2)^x$

45. $y = -3(8)^x$

46. $y = \left(\dfrac{1}{2}\right)^x$

47. $y = \left(\dfrac{2}{5}\right)^x$

48. $y = -5\left(\dfrac{1}{5}\right)^x$

49. $y = 2\left(\dfrac{2}{3}\right)^x$

50. SALARY INCREASE The company you work for has been giving a 5% increase in salary every year. Your salary S can be modeled by $S = 38{,}000(1.05)^t$ where $t = 0$ represents the year 2000. Make a table showing your salary in 1995, 2000, 2005, and 2010. Then graph the points given by this table and draw a smooth curve through these points.

51. WORLD WIDE WEB The number of users U (in millions) of the World Wide Web can be modeled by $U = 135(1.5)^t$ where $t = 0$ represents the year 2000. Make a table showing the number of users (in millions) in 1995, 2000, 2005, and 2010. Then graph the points given by this table and draw a smooth curve through these points. ▶ Source: *WinOpportunity*

52. CHALLENGE If $a^0 = 1$ $(a \neq 0)$, what point do all graphs of the form $y = a^x$ have in common? Is there a point that all graphs of the form $y = 2(a)^x$ have in common? If so, name the point.

53. MULTIPLE CHOICE What is the equation of the graph?

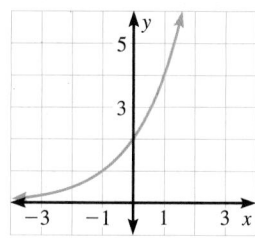

A $y = 2^x$

B $y = 2(2)^x$

C $y = \left(\dfrac{1}{2}\right)^x$

D $y = 2\left(\dfrac{1}{2}\right)^x$

54. MULTIPLE CHOICE What is the equation of the graph?

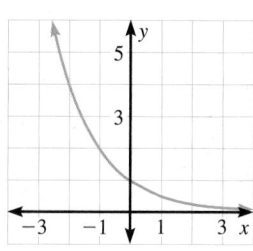

F $y = 2^x$

G $y = 2(2)^x$

H $y = \left(\dfrac{1}{2}\right)^x$

J $y = 2\left(\dfrac{1}{2}\right)^x$

SOLVING AND CHECKING Solve the equation. Round the result to the nearest hundredth. Check the rounded solution. *(Lesson 3.6)*

55. $8x + 9 = 12$ **56.** $3y - 5 = 11$ **57.** $13t + 8 = 2$

58. $14 - 6r = -17$ **59.** $11k + 12 = -9$ **60.** $-7x - 7 = -6$

STANDARD FORM Write the equation in standard form with integer coefficients. *(Lesson 5.4)*

61. $y = -8x + 4$ **62.** $y = 5x - 2$ **63.** $y = \frac{7}{8}x$

64. $y = -\frac{2}{5}x$ **65.** $y = -\frac{3}{16}x + \frac{9}{16}$ **66.** $y = \frac{1}{10}x - \frac{9}{10}$

GRAPHING SYSTEMS Use the graphing method to tell how many solutions the system has. *(Lesson 7.5)*

67. $2x - 2y = 4$
    $x + 3y = 9$

68. $-x + y = -1$
    $2x + 3y = 12$

69. $6x + 2y = 3$
    $3x + y = -2$

70. $x + y = 0$
    $x + 2y = 6$

71. $4x - y = -2$
    $-12x + 3y = 6$

72. $-x + 3y = 3$
    $2x - y = -8$

ORDERING NUMBERS Write the numbers in increasing order. *(Skills Review pp. 770, 771)*

73. $-4, -5, 6$ **74.** $\frac{3}{5}, \frac{5}{7}, \frac{4}{8}$ **75.** $-2\frac{3}{4}, -3\frac{4}{5}, -2\frac{1}{5}$

76. $-6.57, -6.9, -6.56$ **77.** $3.001, 3.25, 3.01$ **78.** $7.99, 7.09, 7.9$

Quiz 1

Evaluate the expression. *(Lessons 8.1, 8.2)*

1. $3^4 \cdot 3^6$ **2.** $(2^3)^2$ **3.** $(8 \cdot 5)^2$

4. $6^{-7} \cdot 6^9$ **5.** $(5^2)^{-1}$ **6.** $(4 \cdot 9)^0$

Simplify the expression. Use only positive exponents. *(Lessons 8.1, 8.2)*

7. $r^5 \cdot r^8$ **8.** $(k^4)^2$ **9.** $(3d)^2$

10. $2x^{-3}y^{-9}$ **11.** $\dfrac{1}{5a^{-10}b^{-12}}$ **12.** $(mn)^{-7}$

13. **SAVINGS ACCOUNT** You started a savings account in 1994. The balance A is given by $A = 1600(1.08)^t$ where $t = 0$ represents the year 2000. What is the balance in the account in 1994? in 2004? *(Lesson 8.2)*

Graph the exponential function. *(Lesson 8.3)*

14. $y = 10^x$ **15.** $y = 3(2)^x$ **16.** $y = 4\left(\dfrac{2}{3}\right)^x$

You can use a graphing calculator to graph exponential functions.

Sample

Graph $y = \left(\dfrac{1}{2}\right)^x$.

Solution

Student Help

▶ **KEYSTROKE HELP**

See keystrokes for several models of calculators at www.mcdougallittell.com

1 To enter the function in your graphing calculator, press Y=. Enter the function as

(1 ÷ 2) ^ X,T,θ .

```
Y1◼(1/2)^X
Y2=
Y3=
Y4=
Y5=
Y6=
Y7=
```

2 Adjust the *viewing window* to get the best scale for your graph.

```
WINDOW
 Xmin=-10
 Xmax=10
 Xscl=2
 Ymin=-10
 Ymax=10
 Yscl=2
```

3 Now you are ready to graph the function. Press GRAPH to see the graph.

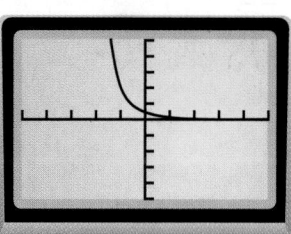

Try These

Use a graphing calculator to graph the exponential function.

1. $y = 2^x$
2. $y = 10^x$
3. $y = -3^x$

4. $y = \left(\dfrac{1}{5}\right)^x$
5. $y = \left(\dfrac{2}{7}\right)^x$
6. $y = -\left(\dfrac{2}{3}\right)^x$

LOGICAL REASONING **Use your results from Exercises 1–6 to answer the following questions.**

7. If $a > 1$, what does the graph of $y = a^x$ look like? the graph of $-a^x$?

8. If $0 < a < 1$, what does the graph of $y = a^x$ look like? the graph of $-a^x$?

8.4 Division Properties of Exponents

Goal
Use division properties of exponents.

Key Words
- power
- base
- exponent
- quotient

How much does a baseball player earn?

One way to compare numerical values is to look at their ratio. In Exercise 59 you will use division properties of exponents to compare the average salary of a baseball player in 1985 to the average salary of a baseball player in 1990.

QUOTIENT OF POWERS To divide powers that have the same base, you subtract the exponents. This is called the *quotient of powers property*. Here is an example.

$$\frac{4^5}{4^3} = \overbrace{\frac{4 \cdot 4 \cdot 4 \cdot 4 \cdot 4}{\underbrace{4 \cdot 4 \cdot 4}_{3 \text{ factors}}}}^{5 \text{ factors}} = \underbrace{4 \cdot 4}_{2 \text{ factors}} = 4^{5-3} = 4^2$$

EXAMPLE 1 Use the Quotient of Powers Property

Simplify the quotient.

a. $\dfrac{6^5}{6^4} = 6^{5-4}$ Use quotient of powers property.

$= 6^1$ Subtract exponents.

$= 6$ Evaluate power.

b. $\dfrac{y^3}{y^5} = y^{3-5}$ Use quotient of powers property.

$= y^{-2}$ Subtract exponents.

$= \dfrac{1}{y^2}$ Use definition of negative exponent.

Student Help

▶ STUDY TIP
In Example 1(b) note that the same answer would have been reached by cancelling common factors:

$$\frac{y^3}{y^5} = \frac{\cancel{y} \cdot \cancel{y} \cdot \cancel{y}}{\cancel{y} \cdot \cancel{y} \cdot \cancel{y} \cdot y \cdot y}$$

$$= \frac{1}{y^2}$$

Checkpoint ✓ **Using the Quotient of Powers Property**

Simplify the quotient.

1. $\dfrac{8^4}{8^6}$ **2.** $\dfrac{(-3)^3}{(-3)^2}$ **3.** $\dfrac{x^4}{x^4}$ **4.** $\dfrac{a^9}{a^5}$

POWER OF A QUOTIENT Recall that $\frac{a}{b} \cdot \frac{a}{b} = \frac{a^2}{b^2}$. To find a power of a quotient, first find the power of the numerator and the power of the denominator, and then divide. This is called the *power of a quotient property*. Here is an example.

$$\left(\frac{2}{3}\right)^4 = \frac{2}{3} \cdot \frac{2}{3} \cdot \frac{2}{3} \cdot \frac{2}{3} = \frac{2 \cdot 2 \cdot 2 \cdot 2}{3 \cdot 3 \cdot 3 \cdot 3} = \frac{2^4}{3^4}$$

EXAMPLE 2 **Use the Power of a Quotient Property**

Simplify the quotient.

a. $\left(\frac{2}{3}\right)^2 = \frac{2^2}{3^2}$ Use power of a quotient property.

$= \frac{4}{9}$ Evaluate powers.

b. $\left(\frac{-3}{y}\right)^3 = \frac{(-3)^3}{y^3}$ Use power of a quotient property.

$= \frac{-27}{y^3}$ Evaluate power.

c. $\left(\frac{7}{4}\right)^{-3} = \frac{7^{-3}}{4^{-3}}$ Use power of a quotient property.

▶ $= \frac{4^3}{7^3}$ Use definition of negative exponents.

$= \frac{64}{343}$ Evaluate powers.

Student Help

▶**STUDY TIP**
One step in simplifying a quotient is to make sure only positive exponents are used. ·····▶

 **Use the Power of a Quotient Property**

Simplify the quotient.

5. $\left(\frac{5}{4}\right)^3$ **6.** $\left(\frac{-x}{2}\right)^4$ **7.** $\left(\frac{3}{5}\right)^{-2}$ **8.** $\left(\frac{1}{x}\right)^{-5}$

SUMMARY

Division Properties of Exponents

Let a and b be real numbers and let m and n be integers.

QUOTIENT OF POWERS PROPERTY

To divide powers that have the same base, subtract the exponents.

$$\frac{a^m}{a^n} = a^{m-n},\ a \neq 0$$

POWER OF A QUOTIENT PROPERTY

To find a power of a quotient, find the power of the numerator and the power of the denominator and divide.

$$\left(\frac{a}{b}\right)^m = \frac{a^m}{b^m},\ b \neq 0$$

EXAMPLE **3** Simplify Expressions using Multiple Properties

Simplify the expression. Use only positive exponents.

a. $\dfrac{2x^2y}{3x} \cdot \dfrac{9xy^2}{y^4}$

b. $\left(\dfrac{2x}{y^2}\right)^4$

Solution

a. $\dfrac{2x^2y}{3x} \cdot \dfrac{9xy^2}{y^4} = \dfrac{18x^3y^3}{3xy^4}$ 　　　Use product of powers property.

$= 6x^2y^{-1}$ 　　　Use quotient of powers property.

$= \dfrac{6x^2}{y}$ 　　　Use definition of negative exponents.

b. $\left(\dfrac{2x}{y^2}\right)^4 = \dfrac{(2x)^4}{(y^2)^4}$ 　　　Use power of a quotient property.

$= \dfrac{2^4 \cdot x^4}{y^{2\cdot4}}$ 　　　Use power of a product property.
Use power of a power property.

$= \dfrac{16x^4}{y^8}$ 　　　Evaluate power.
Multiply exponents.

EXAMPLE **4** Simplify Expressions with Negative Exponents

Simplify the expression $\dfrac{x}{y^{-1}} \cdot \left(\dfrac{x^2}{y}\right)^{-3}$. Use only positive exponents.

Solution

$\dfrac{x}{y^{-1}} \cdot \left(\dfrac{x^2}{y}\right)^{-3} = \dfrac{x}{y^{-1}} \cdot \dfrac{(x^2)^{-3}}{y^{-3}}$ 　　　Use power of a quotient property.

$= x \cdot y \cdot \dfrac{y^3}{(x^2)^3}$ 　　　Use definition of negative exponents.

$= \dfrac{xy^4}{x^6}$ 　　　Use product of powers property.
Use power of a power property.

$= x^{-5}y^4$ 　　　Use quotient of powers property.

$= \dfrac{y^4}{x^5}$ 　　　Use definition of negative exponents.

Checkpoint ✓ **Simplify Expressions**

Simplify the expression. Use only positive exponents.

9. $\dfrac{3xy^4}{x^3} \cdot \dfrac{y}{xy^3}$

10. $\left(\dfrac{5x}{y^3}\right)^3$

11. $\dfrac{y^{-2}}{x^2} \cdot \left(\dfrac{x^4}{y}\right)^{-1}$

Guided Practice

Vocabulary Check Match the division property of exponents with the example that illustrates it.

1. Quotient of powers property

A. $\left(\dfrac{3}{6}\right)^2 = \dfrac{3^2}{6^2}$

2. Power of a quotient property

B. $\dfrac{4^3}{4^5} = 4^{3-5}$

Skill Check Use the quotient of powers property to simplify the expression.

3. $\dfrac{5^4}{5^1}$

4. $\dfrac{7^6}{7^9}$

5. $\dfrac{(-2)^8}{(-2)^3}$

6. $\dfrac{5^3 \cdot 5^5}{5^9}$

7. $\dfrac{x^{12}}{x^9}$

8. $\dfrac{a^5}{a^2}$

9. $\dfrac{m^5}{m^{11}}$

10. $\dfrac{x^7 \cdot x}{x^2}$

Use the power of a quotient property to simplify the expression.

11. $\left(\dfrac{1}{2}\right)^5$

12. $\left(\dfrac{3}{5}\right)^3$

13. $\left(\dfrac{-4}{3}\right)^4$

14. $\left(\dfrac{5}{4}\right)^{-3}$

15. $\left(\dfrac{-5}{m}\right)^2$

16. $\left(\dfrac{x}{y}\right)^6$

17. $\left(\dfrac{m^3}{n^5}\right)^2$

18. $\left(\dfrac{a^6}{b^9}\right)^{-5}$

Practice and Applications

COMPLETING EQUATIONS Copy and complete the statement.

19. $\dfrac{3^9}{3^5} = 3^{?}$

20. $\dfrac{7^{?}}{7^2} = 7^4$

21. $\dfrac{9^5}{9^{?}} = 9^{-6}$

22. $\dfrac{x^5}{x^{?}} = x^2$

23. $\dfrac{a^{10}}{a^4} = a^{?}$

24. $\dfrac{w^{?}}{w} = w^3$

QUOTIENT OF POWERS Simplify the quotient.

25. $\dfrac{5^6}{5^3}$

26. $\dfrac{8^2}{8^3}$

27. $\dfrac{(-3)^6}{(-3)^6}$

28. $\dfrac{6^3 \cdot 6^2}{6^5}$

29. $\dfrac{x^4}{x^5}$

30. $x^3 \cdot \dfrac{1}{x^2}$

31. $\dfrac{1}{x^8} \cdot x^5$

32. $\dfrac{x^3 \cdot x^5}{x^2}$

Student Help

▶**HOMEWORK HELP**
 Example 1: Exs. 19–32
 Example 2: Exs. 33–46
 Example 3: Exs. 47–54
 Example 4: Exs. 55–57

COMPLETING EQUATIONS Copy and complete the statement.

33. $\left(\dfrac{1}{6}\right)^4 = \dfrac{1}{?}$

34. $\left(\dfrac{-3}{5}\right)^2 = \dfrac{?}{25}$

35. $\left(\dfrac{2}{7}\right)^{?} = \dfrac{8}{343}$

36. $\left(\dfrac{x}{y}\right)^{?} = \dfrac{y^2}{x^2}$

37. $\left(\dfrac{a^2}{b}\right)^5 = \dfrac{a^{?}}{b^5}$

38. $\left(\dfrac{m^3}{n^{?}}\right)^4 = \dfrac{m^{12}}{n^8}$

POWER OF A QUOTIENT Simplify the quotient.

39. $\left(\dfrac{1}{5}\right)^4$ **40.** $\left(\dfrac{3}{4}\right)^2$ **41.** $\left(\dfrac{-2}{3}\right)^3$ **42.** $\left(\dfrac{9}{6}\right)^{-1}$

43. $\left(\dfrac{3}{x}\right)^4$ **44.** $\left(\dfrac{-x}{2}\right)^3$ **45.** $\left(\dfrac{x}{y}\right)^5$ **46.** $\left(\dfrac{8}{x}\right)^{-2}$

ERROR ANALYSIS In Exercises 47 and 48, find and correct the error.

47.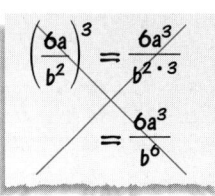

48.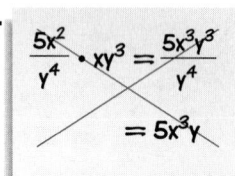

SIMPLIFYING EXPRESSIONS Simplify the expression. Use only positive exponents.

49. $\dfrac{4x^3y^3}{2xy} \cdot \dfrac{5xy^2}{2y}$ **50.** $\dfrac{16x^3y}{-4xy^3} \cdot \dfrac{-2xy}{x}$ **51.** $\dfrac{36a^8b^2}{ab} \cdot \dfrac{ab^2}{6}$

52. $\left(\dfrac{2m^3n^4}{3mn}\right)^3$ **53.** $\dfrac{6x^2y^2}{xy^3} \cdot \dfrac{(4x^2y)^2}{xy^2}$ **54.** $\dfrac{16x^5y^8}{x^7y^4} \cdot \left(\dfrac{x^3y^2}{8xy}\right)^4$

55. $\dfrac{x^2}{xy^{-4}} \cdot \dfrac{2x^{-3}y^4}{3xy^{-1}}$ **56.** $\dfrac{5x^{-3}y^2}{x^5y^{-1}} \cdot \dfrac{(2xy^3)^{-2}}{xy}$ **57.** $\dfrac{4xy}{2x^{-1}y^{-3}} \cdot \left(\dfrac{2xy^2}{3xy}\right)^{-2}$

EXAMPLE *Use Division Properties of Exponents*

STOCK EXCHANGE The number of shares n (in billions) listed on the New York Stock Exchange (NYSE) from 1977 through 1997 can be modeled by

$$n = 93.4 \cdot (1.11)^t$$

where $t = 0$ represents 1990. Find the ratio of shares listed in 1997 to the shares listed in 1977. ▶Source: New York Stock Exchange

Solution

Since 1997 is 7 years after 1990, use $t = 7$ for 1997. Since 1977 is 13 years before 1990, use $t = -13$ for 1977. Because 93.4 is a common factor to the number of shares for both years, you may omit it from the ratio below.

$$\dfrac{\text{Number listed in 1997}}{\text{Number listed in 1977}} = \dfrac{(1.11)^7}{(1.11)^{-13}}$$

$$= (1.11)^{7-(-13)}$$

$$= (1.11)^{20}$$

$$\approx 8.06 \quad \longleftarrow \text{ Use a calculator.}$$

ANSWER ▶ The ratio of shares listed in 1997 to the shares listed in 1977 is 8.06 to 1. There were about 8 times as many shares listed in 1997 as there were in 1977.

Link to
Careers

STOCKBROKERS who work on the floor of a stock exchange use hand signals that date back to the 1880s to relay information about stock trades.

More about stockbrokers at www.mcdougallittell.com

Use the example on the previous page as a model for Exercises 58–61.

58. RETAIL SALES From 1994 to 1998 the sales for a clothing store increased by about the same percent each year. The sales S (in millions of dollars) for year t can be modeled by $S = 3723\left(\dfrac{6}{5}\right)^t$, where $t = 0$ corresponds to 1994. Find the ratio of 1998 sales to 1995 sales.

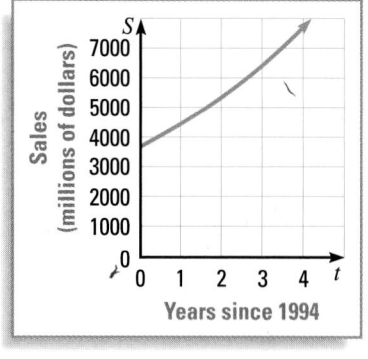

59. BASEBALL SALARIES The average salary s (in thousands) for a professional baseball player in the United States can be modeled by
$$s = 136(1.18)^t$$
where $t = 0$ represents the year 1980. Find the ratio of the average salary in 1985 to the average salary in 1990. ▶ Source: National Baseball Library and Archive

60. ATLANTIC COD The average weight w (in pounds) of an Atlantic cod can be modeled by
$$w = 1.21(1.42)^t$$
where t is the age of the fish (in years). Find the ratio of the weight of a 5-year-old cod to the weight of a 2-year-old cod.
▶ Source: National Marine Fisheries Service

61. LEARNING SPANISH You memorized a list of 200 Spanish vocabulary words. Unfortunately, each week you forget one fifth of the words you knew the previous week. The number of Spanish words S you remember after n weeks can be modeled by:
$$S = 200\left(\frac{4}{5}\right)^n$$

Copy and complete the table showing the number of words you remember after n weeks.

Weeks n	0	1	2	3	4	5	6
Words S	?	?	?	?	?	?	?

LOGICAL REASONING Give a reason for each step to show that the definitions of zero and negative exponents hold true for the properties of exponents.

62. $a^0 = a^{n-n}$
$$= \frac{a^n}{a^n}$$
$$= 1$$

63. $a^{-n} = a^{n-2n}$
$$= \frac{a^n}{a^{2n}}$$
$$= \frac{a^n}{a^n \cdot a^n}$$
$$= \frac{1}{a^n}$$

64. CHALLENGE A piece of notebook paper is about 0.0032 inch thick. If you begin with a stack consisting of a single sheet and double the stack 25 times, how thick will the stack be? *HINT:* You will need to write and solve an exponential equation.

65. MULTIPLE CHOICE Simplify the expression $\dfrac{x^{-9}}{x^{-3}}$.

(A) $\dfrac{1}{x^{-6}}$ (B) $\dfrac{1}{x^6}$ (C) x^{-3} (D) x^3

66. MULTIPLE CHOICE Simplify the expression $\left(\dfrac{2}{9}\right)^{-3}$.

(F) $-\dfrac{6}{27}$ (G) $\dfrac{27}{6}$ (H) $-\dfrac{8}{729}$ (J) $\dfrac{729}{8}$

67. MULTIPLE CHOICE Simplify the expression $\dfrac{4x^3y}{18x^2} \cdot \dfrac{9}{16x^2y}$.

(A) $\dfrac{x}{16}$ (B) $\dfrac{x}{8}$ (C) $\dfrac{x^3}{8}$ (D) $\dfrac{1}{8x}$

68. MULTIPLE CHOICE Simplify the expression $\dfrac{x^{-2}}{y^{-3}} \cdot \left(\dfrac{x}{y}\right)^{-1}$.

(F) $\dfrac{y^2}{x}$ (G) $\dfrac{y^4}{x^3}$ (H) $\dfrac{x^2}{y^3}$ (J) $\dfrac{x^3}{y^4}$

Mixed Review

POWERS OF TEN Evaluate the expression. *(Lessons 1.2, 8.2)*

69. 10^5 **70.** 10^1 **71.** 10^0 **72.** 10^{-4}

SLOPE-INTERCEPT FORM Write in slope-intercept form the equation of the line that passes through the given points. *(Lesson 5.3)*

73. $(-4, 2)$ and $(4, 6)$ **74.** $(-4, -5)$ and $(0, 3)$ **75.** $(-1, -7)$ and $(3, -11)$

76. $(3, 9)$ and $(1, -3)$ **77.** $(5, -2)$ and $(-4, 7)$ **78.** $(1, 8)$ and $(-4, -2)$

CHECKING FOR SOLUTIONS Decide whether the ordered pair is a solution of the system of linear equations. *(Lesson 7.1)*

79. $2x + 4y = 2$
$-x + 5y = 13$ $(-3, 2)$

80. $3x - 4y = 5$
$x + 6y = 8$ $(3, 1)$

81. $8x + 4y = 6$
$4x + y = 3$ $(1, -1)$

82. $x - 5y = 9$
$3x + 5y = 11$ $(4, -1)$

SOLVING LINEAR SYSTEMS Use linear combinations to solve the system. Then check your solution. *(Lesson 7.3)*

83. $x - y = 4$
$x + y = 12$

84. $-p + 2q = 12$
$p + 6q = 20$

85. $2a + 3b = 17$
$3a + 4b = 24$

86. $2m + 3n = 7$
$m + n = 1$

87. $x + 10y = -1$
$2x + 9y = 9$

88. $8r - 3t = 2$
$2r - 2t = 3$

Maintaining Skills

ESTIMATION Use front-end estimation to estimate the sum or difference. *(Skills Review p. 774)*

89. $287 + 165$ **90.** $4672 + 1807$ **91.** $46.18 + 34.42$

92. $172 - 112$ **93.** $4882 - 3117$ **94.** $3.84 - 1.68$

8.5 Scientific Notation

Goal

Read and write numbers in scientific notation.

Key Words

• scientific notation

What was the price of Alaska per square mile?

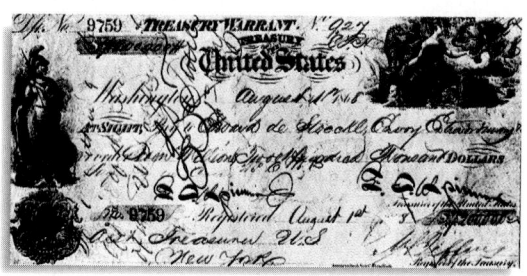

In 1867 the United States purchased Alaska by writing a check for $7.2 million. In Example 5 you will use *scientific notation* to find the price per square mile of that purchase.

Numbers such as 100, 14.2, and 0.07 are written in *decimal form*. *Scientific notation* uses powers of ten to express decimal numbers. A number is written in **scientific notation** if it is of the form $c \times 10^n$ where $1 \le c < 10$ and n is an integer. Here are three examples.

$$1.2 \times 10^3 = 1.2 \times 1000 = 1200$$

$$5.6 \times 10^0 = 5.6 \times 1 = 5.6$$

$$3.5 \times 10^{-1} = 3.5 \times 0.1 = 0.35$$

Student Help

▶ **STUDY TIP**
When multiplying by 10^n and $n > 0$, move the decimal point n places to the **right**. When $n < 0$ move the decimal point n places to the **left**.

EXAMPLE 1 Write Numbers in Decimal Form

Write the number in decimal form.

a. 2.83×10^1 **b.** 4.9×10^5 **c.** 8×10^{-1} **d.** 1.23×10^{-3}

Solution

a. $2.83 \times 10^1 = 28.3$ Move decimal point 1 place to the right.

b. $4.9 \times 10^5 = 490\,000$ Move decimal point 5 places to the right.

c. $8 \times 10^{-1} = 0.8$ Move decimal point 1 place to the left.

d. $1.23 \times 10^{-3} = 0.00123$ Move decimal point 3 places to the left.

Checkpoint ✓ Write Numbers in Decimal Form

Write the number in decimal form.

1. 2.39×10^4 **2.** 1.045×10^7 **3.** 3.7×10^8

4. 8.4×10^{-6} **5.** 1.0×10^{-2} **6.** 9.2×10^{-8}

EXAMPLE 2 Write Numbers in Scientific Notation

Write the number in scientific notation.

a. 34,000    **b.** 1.78   **c.** 0.0007

Solution

a. $34{,}000 = 3.4 \times 10^4$ Move decimal point 4 places to the left.

b. $1.78 = 1.78 \times 10^0$ Move decimal place 0 places.

c. $0.0007 = 7 \times 10^{-4}$ Move decimal point 4 places to the right.

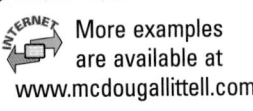 **Write Numbers in Scientific Notation**

Write the number in scientific notation.

7. 423   **8.** 2,000,000   **9.** 0.0001   **10.** 0.0098

Student Help

▶ MORE EXAMPLES

More examples are available at www.mcdougallittell.com

EXAMPLE 3 Operations with Scientific Notation

Perform the indicated operation. Write the result in scientific notation.

a. $(1.4 \times 10^4)(7.6 \times 10^3)$

$= (1.4 \cdot 7.6) \times (10^4 \cdot 10^3)$ Use properties of multiplication.

$= 10.64 \times 10^7$ Use product of powers property.

$= (1.064 \times 10^1) \times 10^7$ Write in scientific notation.

$= 1.064 \times 10^8$ Use product of powers property.

b. $\dfrac{1.2 \times 10^{-1}}{4.8 \times 10^{-4}} = \dfrac{1.2}{4.8} \times \dfrac{10^{-1}}{10^{-4}}$ Write as a product.

$= 0.25 \times 10^3$ Use quotient of powers property.

$= (2.5 \times 10^{-1}) \times 10^3$ Write in scientific notation.

$= 2.5 \times 10^2$ Use product of powers property.

c. $(4 \times 10^{-2})^3 = 4^3 \times (10^{-2})^3$ Use power of a product property.

$= 64 \times 10^{-6}$ Use power of a power property.

$= (6.4 \times 10^1) \times 10^{-6}$ Write in scientific notation.

$= 6.4 \times 10^{-5}$ Use product of powers property.

Checkpoint ✓ Operations with Scientific Notation

Perform the indicated operation. Write the result in scientific notation.

11. $(2.3 \times 10^3)(1.8 \times 10^{-5})$ **12.** $\dfrac{5.2 \times 10^3}{1.3 \times 10^1}$ **13.** $(5 \times 10^{-4})^2$

Many calculators automatically use scientific notation to display large or small numbers. Try multiplying 98,900,000 by 500 on a calculator. If the calculator follows standard procedures, it will display the product using scientific notation.

$$\boxed{4.945 \; ^{10}} \longleftarrow \text{Calculator display for } 4.945 \times 10^{10}$$

Student Help

▶**KEYSTROKE HELP**
If your calculator does not have an $\boxed{EE}$ key, you can enter a number in scientific notation as a product:

7.48 $\boxed{\times}$ 10 $\boxed{y^x}$

7 $\boxed{+/-}$

EXAMPLE 4 Use a Calculator

 Use a calculator to multiply 7.48×10^{-7} by 2.4×10^9.

Solution

KEYSTROKES	DISPLAY
7.48 $\boxed{EE}$ 7 $\boxed{+/-}$ $\boxed{\times}$ 2.4 $\boxed{EE}$ 9 $\boxed{=}$	$\boxed{1.7952 \; ^{03}}$

ANSWER ▶ The product is 1.7952×10^3, or 1795.2.

Checkpoint ✓ **Use a Calculator**

 Use a calculator to perform the indicated operation.

14. $(5.1 \times 10^2)(0.8 \times 10^{-4})$ **15.** $\dfrac{8.9 \times 10^0}{6.4 \times 10^{-5}}$ **16.** $(1.5 \times 10^6)^{-1}$

EXAMPLE 5 Scientific Notation in Real Life

ALASKA PURCHASE In 1867 the United States purchased Alaska from Russia for \$7.2 million. The total area of Alaska is about 5.9×10^5 square miles. What was the price per square mile?

Student Help

▶**LOOK BACK**
For help with unit rates, see p. 177.

Solution

The price per square mile is a unit rate.

$$\text{Price per square mile} = \frac{\text{Total price}}{\text{Number of square miles}}$$

$$= \frac{7.2 \times 10^6}{5.9 \times 10^5} \longleftarrow \text{7.2 million} = 7.2 \times 10^6$$

$$\approx 1.22 \times 10^1$$

$$= 12.2$$

ANSWER ▶ The price was about \$12.20 per square mile.

Checkpoint ✓ **Scientific Notation in Real Life**

17. In 1994 the population of California was about 3.1×10^7. In that year about 5.6×10^{10} local calls were made in California. Estimate the number of local calls made per person in California in 1994.

8.5 Exercises

Guided Practice

Vocabulary Check   **1.** Is the number 12.38×10^2 in scientific notation? Explain.

Skill Check   **Write the number in decimal form.**

2. 9×10^4 **3.** 4.3×10^2 **4.** 8.11×10^3

5. 5×10^{-2} **6.** 9.4×10^{-5} **7.** 2.45×10^{-1}

Write the number in scientific notation.

8. 15 **9.** $6,900,000$ **10.** 39.6

11. 0.99 **12.** 0.0003 **13.** 0.0205

Perform the indicated operation. Write the result in scientific notation.

14. $(5 \times 10^6)(6 \times 10^{-2})$ **15.** $\dfrac{1.4 \times 10^{-3}}{7 \times 10^7}$ **16.** $(9 \times 10^{-9})^2$

Practice and Applications

MOVING DECIMALS **Tell whether you would move the decimal *left* or *right* and how many places to write the number in decimal form.**

17. 1.5×10^2 **18.** 6.89×10^5 **19.** 9.04×10^{-7}

DECIMAL FORM **Write the number in decimal form.**

20. 5×10^5 **21.** 8×10^3 **22.** 1×10^6

23. 2.1×10^4 **24.** 7.75×10^0 **25.** 4.33×10^8

26. 3×10^{-4} **27.** 9×10^{-3} **28.** 4×10^{-5}

29. 9.8×10^{-2} **30.** 6.02×10^{-6} **31.** 1.1×10^{-10}

LOGICAL REASONING **Decide whether the number is in scientific notation. If not, write the number in scientific notation.**

32. 0.7×10^2 **33.** 2.9×10^5 **34.** 10×10^{-3}

Student Help

▶ **HOMEWORK HELP**
Example 1: Exs. 17–31
Example 2: Exs. 32–46
Example 3: Exs. 47–55
Example 4: Exs. 56–61
Example 5: Exs. 62–69

SCIENTIFIC NOTATION **Write the number in scientific notation.**

35. 900 **36.** $700,000,000$ **37.** $88,000,000$

38. 1012 **39.** 95.2 **40.** 370.2

41. 0.1 **42.** 0.05 **43.** 0.000006

44. 0.0422 **45.** 0.0085 **46.** 0.000459

EVALUATING EXPRESSIONS Perform the indicated operation without using a calculator. Write the result in scientific notation.

47. $(4.1 \times 10^2)(3 \times 10^6)$ **48.** $(9 \times 10^{-6})(2 \times 10^4)$ **49.** $(6 \times 10^5)(2.5 \times 10^{-1})$

50. $\dfrac{8 \times 10^{-3}}{4 \times 10^{-5}}$ **51.** $\dfrac{3.5 \times 10^{-4}}{5 \times 10^{-1}}$ **52.** $\dfrac{6.6 \times 10^{-1}}{1.1 \times 10^{-1}}$

53. $(3 \times 10^2)^3$ **54.** $(2 \times 10^{-3})^4$ **55.** $(0.5 \times 10)^{-2}$

 **CALCULATOR** Use a calculator to perform the indicated operation. Write the result in scientific notation and in decimal form.

56. $6{,}000{,}000 \cdot 324{,}000$ **57.** $(2.79 \times 10^{-4})(3.94 \times 10^9)$

58. $\dfrac{3{,}940{,}000}{0.0002}$ **59.** $\dfrac{6.45 \times 10^{-6}}{4.3 \times 10^5}$ **60.** $(0.000094)^3$ **61.** $(2.4 \times 10^{-4})^5$

DECIMAL FORM Write the number in decimal form.

62. The distance that light travels in one year is 9.46×10^{12} kilometers.

63. The length of a dust mite is 9.8×10^{-4} foot.

SCIENTIFIC NOTATION Write the number in scientific notation.

64. At the end of 1999 the population of the world was estimated at 6,035,000,000. **DATA UPDATE** of U.S. Census Bureau data at www.mcdougallittell.com

65. The mass of a carbon atom is 0.00000000000000000000002 gram.

66. *Science Link* Light travels at a speed of about 3×10^5 kilometers per second. It takes about 1.5×10^4 seconds for light to travel from the sun to Neptune. What is the approximate distance (in kilometers) between Neptune and the sun?

History Link In Exercises 67 and 68, use the following information.

In 1803 the Louisiana Purchase added 8.28×10^5 square miles to the United States. The price of the land was $15 million. In 1853 the Gadsden Purchase added 2.96×10^4 square miles. The price was $10 million.

67. Find the price per square mile of the Louisiana Purchase.

68. Find the price per square mile of the Gadsden Purchase.

69. *Science Link* Jupiter, the largest planet in our solar system, has a radius of about 7.15×10^4 kilometers. Use the formula for the volume of a sphere, $V = \dfrac{4}{3}\pi r^3$, to estimate Jupiter's volume.

70. MULTIPLE CHOICE Which number is *not* in scientific notation?

(A) 1×10^4 (B) 3.4×10^{-3} (C) 9.02×10^2 (D) 12.25×10^{-5}

71. MULTIPLE CHOICE Evaluate $\dfrac{1.1 \times 10^{-1}}{5.5 \times 10^{-5}}$.

(F) 0.2×10^{-6} (G) 0.2×10^{-4} (H) 2×10^3 (J) 2×10^4

Mixed Review

GRAPHING Use the graphing method to tell how many solutions the system has. *(Lesson 7.5)*

72. $4x + 2y = 12$
     $-6x + 3y = 6$

73. $3x - 2y = 0$
     $3x - 2y = -4$

74. $x - 5y = 8$
     $-x + 5y = -8$

GRAPHING Graph the system of linear inequalities. *(Lesson 7.6)*

75. $2x + y \le 1$
     $-2x + y \le 1$

76. $x + 2y < 3$
     $x - 3y > 1$

77. $2x + y \ge 2$
     $x < 2$

Maintaining Skills

FRACTIONS, DECIMALS, AND PERCENTS Write the given fraction, decimal, or percent in the indicated form. *(Skills Review pp. 767–769)*

78. Write $\frac{1}{3}$ as a decimal.

79. Write $\frac{53}{25}$ as a percent.

80. Write 1.45 as a fraction.

81. Write 0.674 as a percent.

82. Write 15% as a fraction.

83. Write 756.7% as a decimal.

Quiz 2

Simplify the quotient. *(Lesson 8.4)*

1. $\dfrac{6^7}{6^2}$ **2.** $\dfrac{x^9}{x^{11}}$ **3.** $\left(\dfrac{-7}{2}\right)^3$ **4.** $\left(\dfrac{a}{b}\right)^{-5}$

Simplify the expression. Use only positive exponents. *(Lesson 8.4)*

5. $\dfrac{3xy^5}{9x^4y^6} \cdot \dfrac{4x^4}{xy^8}$ **6.** $\dfrac{20x^3y}{4xy^2} \cdot \dfrac{-6xy}{-x}$ **7.** $\dfrac{5ab^3}{-2a^{-1}b^2} \cdot \dfrac{10a^{-3}b}{a^2b^{-4}}$

8. $\left(\dfrac{-2m^2n}{3mn^2}\right)^4$ **9.** $\dfrac{xy^{10}}{5x^3y^6} \cdot \dfrac{(2x^2y)^4}{4x^3y}$ **10.** $\dfrac{9wz^{-2}}{w^{-3}z^3} \cdot \left(\dfrac{w^2z}{3z^{-1}}\right)^{-3}$

Write the number in decimal form. *(Lesson 8.5)*

11. 5×10^9 **12.** 4.8×10^3 **13.** 3.35×10^4

14. 7×10^{-6} **15.** 1.1×10^{-2} **16.** 2.08×10^{-5}

Write the number in scientific notation. *(Lesson 8.5)*

17. 105   **18.** 99,000   **19.** 30,700,000

20. 0.25   **21.** 0.0004   **22.** 0.0000067

GOAL

Use reasoning to compare exponential and linear functions.

MATERIALS

• graph paper

Question

How are linear and exponential functions different?

Explore

1 The equation $y = 5^x$ is an *exponential function*. Copy and complete the table using this equation.

x	0	1	2	3	4	5
y	1	5	?	?	?	?

2 Use the table in Step 1 to graph $y = 5^x$.

3 The equation $y = 5x + 20$ is a *linear function*. Copy and complete the table using this equation.

x	0	1	2	3	4	5
y	20	25	?	?	?	?

4 Use the table in Step 3 to graph $y = 5x + 20$.

5 Which of the graphs below shows a *linear function*? Which shows an *exponential function*? Explain how you know.

A.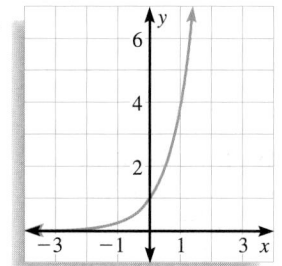

B.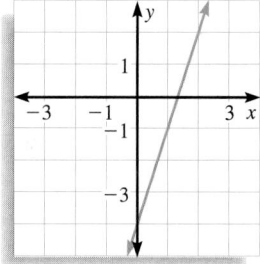

Think About It

Graph the function.

1. $y = x + 5$

2. $y = 3^x$

3. $y = 10 + 2x$

4. $y = -3(2)^x$

5. $y = 5(4x - 7)$

6. $y = 10(1.2)^x$

LOGICAL REASONING In Exercises 7–9, use the results from Exercises 1–6.

7. Complete: A linear function increases the __?__ amount for each unit on the *x*-axis.

8. Describe the rate of increase in an exponential growth model.

9. Explain one way that an equation for a linear function differs from an equation for an exponential function.

8.6 Exponential Growth Functions

Goal

Write and graph exponential growth functions.

Key Words

- exponential growth
- growth rate
- growth factor

How does a catfish's weight change as it grows?

In Lesson 8.3 you learned about exponential functions. One use of exponential functions is to model *exponential growth*. In Example 1 you will analyze the weight of a newly hatched catfish when that weight is increasing by 10% each day.

A quantity is *growing exponentially* if it increases by the same percent r in each unit of time t. This is called **exponential growth**. Exponential growth can be modeled by the equation

$$y = C(1 + r)^t$$

where C is the initial amount (the amount before any growth occurs), r is the **growth rate** (as a decimal), t represents time, and both C and r are positive. The expression $(1 + r)$ is called the **growth factor**.

Student Help

▶ STUDY TIP
To write a percent as a decimal, remove the percent sign from the number and divide the number by 100.
$$10\% = \frac{10}{100} = 0.10$$

EXAMPLE 1 Write an Exponential Growth Model

CATFISH GROWTH A newly hatched channel catfish typically weighs about 0.06 gram. During the first six weeks of life, its weight increases by about 10% each day. Write a model for the weight of the catfish during the first six weeks.

Solution

Let y be the weight of the catfish during the first six weeks and let t be the number of days. The initial weight of the catfish C is 0.06. The growth rate is r is 10%, or 0.10.

$$y = C(1 + r)^t \qquad \text{Write exponential growth model.}$$
$$= 0.06(1 + 0.10)^t \qquad \text{Substitute 0.06 for } C \text{ and 0.10 for } r.$$
$$= 0.06(1.1)^t \qquad \text{Add.}$$

Checkpoint ✓ Write an Exponential Growth Model

1. A TV station's local news program has 50,000 viewers. The managers of the station hope to increase the number of viewers by 2% per month. Write an exponential growth model to represent the number of viewers v in t months.

COMPOUND INTEREST *Compound interest* is interest paid on the *principal P*, the original amount deposited, and on the interest that has already been earned. Compound interest is a type of exponential growth, so you can use the exponential growth model to find the account balance *A*.

EXAMPLE 2 Find the Balance in an Account

COMPOUND INTEREST You deposit $500 in an account that pays 8% interest compounded yearly. What will the account balance be after 6 years?

Solution

The initial amount *P* is $500, the growth rate is 8%, and the time is 6 years.

$$A = P(1 + r)^t$$ Write yearly compound interest model.

$$= 500(1 + 0.08)^6$$ Substitute 500 for *P*, 0.08 for *r*, and 6 for *t*.

$$= 500(1.08)^6$$ Add.

$$\approx 793$$ Use a calculator.

ANSWER ▸ The balance after 6 years will be about $793.

Student Help

▸**WRITING ALGEBRA**
The model for compound interest is generally written using *A* (for the account balance) instead of *y*, and *P* (for the principal) instead of *C*.

 **Find the Balance in an Account**

2. You deposit $750 in an account that pays 6% interest compounded yearly. What is the balance in the account after 10 years?

Student Help

▸**STUDY TIP**
Growth *factors* are usually given as whole numbers and growth *rates* as percents or decimals.

EXAMPLE 3 Use an Exponential Growth Model

POPULATION GROWTH An initial population of 20 mice triples each year for 5 years. What is the mice population after 5 years?

Solution

You know that the population triples each year. This tells you the factor by which the population is growing, not the percent change in the population. Therefore the *growth factor* (not the growth rate) is 3. The initial population is 20 and the time is 5 years.

$$y = C(1 + r)^t$$ Write exponential growth model.

$$= 20(3)^5$$ Substitute for 20 for *C*, 3 for 1 + *r*, and 5 for *t*.

$$= 4860$$ Evaluate.

ANSWER ▸ There will be 4860 mice after 5 years.

 **Use an Exponential Growth Model**

3. An initial population of 30 rabbits doubles each year for 6 years. What is the rabbit population after 6 years?

EXAMPLE 4 A Model with a Large Growth Rate

Graph the exponential growth model from Example 3.

Solution

Make a table of values, plot the points in a coordinate plane, and draw a smooth curve through the points.

t	0	1	2	3	4
y	20	60	180	540	1620

Student Help

▶ STUDY TIP
A large growth rate corresponds to a rapid increase in the y-values.

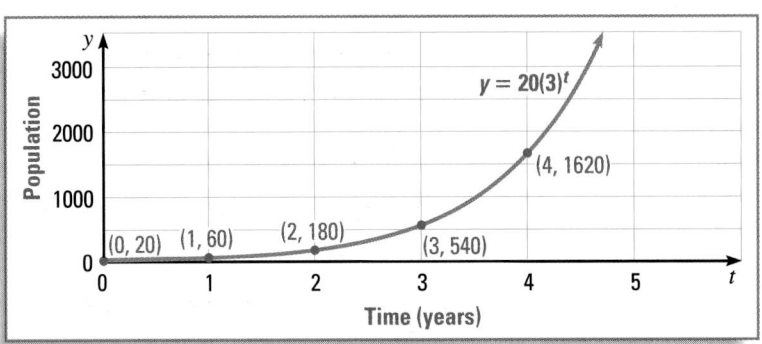

EXAMPLE 5 A Model with a Small Growth Rate

In 1980 there were only 73 peregrine falcons along the Colville River in Alaska. From 1980 to 1987 the population grew by about 9% per year. Therefore the population P of peregrine falcons can be modeled by $P = 73(1.09)^t$ where $t = 0$ represents 1980. Graph the function.

Solution

Make a table of values, plot the points in a coordinate plane, and draw a smooth curve through the points.

t	0	1	2	3	4
P	73	80	87	95	103

Student Help

▶ STUDY TIP
A small growth rate corresponds to a slow increase in the y-values.

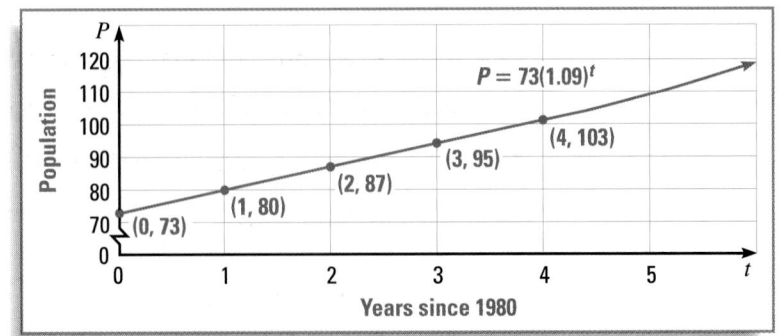

Checkpoint ✓ *Graph an Exponential Growth Model*

4. Graph the exponential growth model you found in Checkpoint 3.

Guided Practice

1. Complete: In the exponential growth model, $y = C(1 + r)^t$, C is the __?__ and $(1 + r)$ is the __?__ .

COMPOUND INTEREST **You deposit $500 in an account that pays 4% interest compounded yearly.**

2. What is the initial amount P?

3. What is the growth rate r?

4. Complete this equation to write an exponential growth model for the balance after t years: $A = $ __?__ $(1 + $ __?__ $)^t$.

5. Use the equation from Exercise 4 to find the balance after 5 years.

6. CHOOSE A MODEL Which model best represents the growth curve shown in the graph at the right?

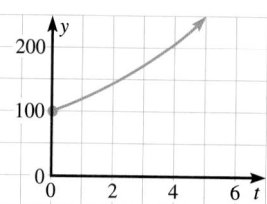

A. $y = 100(2)^t$ **B.** $y = 100(1.2)^t$

C. $y = 200(2)^t$ **D.** $y = 200(1.2)^t$

Practice and Applications

EXPONENTIAL GROWTH **Identify the initial amount and the growth rate in the exponential function.**

7. $y = 100(1 + 0.5)^t$ **8.** $y = 12(1 + 2)^t$ **9.** $y = 7.5(1.75)^t$

WRITING EXPONENTIAL FUNCTIONS **Write an exponential function to model the situation. Tell what each variable represents.**

10. Your salary of $25,000 increases 7% each year.

11. A population of 310,000 increases by 15% each year.

12. An annual benefit concert attendance of 10,000 increases by 5% each year.

BUSINESS **Write an exponential growth model for the profit.**

Student Help

▶ **HOMEWORK HELP**
Example 1: Exs. 7–15
Example 2: Exs. 16–27
Example 3: Exs. 28–35
Examples 4 and 5:
       Exs. 36–40

13. A business had a $10,000 profit in 1990. Then the profit increased by 25% per year for the next 10 years.

14. A business had a $20,000 profit in 1990. Then the profit increased by 20% per year for the next 10 years.

15. A business had a $15,000 profit in 1990. Then the profit increased by 30% per year for the next 15 years.

COMPOUND INTEREST You deposit $1400 in an account that pays 6% interest compounded yearly. Find the balance at the end of the given time period.

16. 5 years   **17.** 8 years   **18.** 12 years   **19.** 20 years

Student Help

▶ HOMEWORK HELP

INTERNET Extra help with problem solving in Exs. 33–34 is available at www.mcdougallittell.com

COMPOUND INTEREST You deposit money in an account that pays 5% interest compounded yearly. Find the balance after 5 years for the given initial amount.

20. $250   **21.** $300   **22.** $350   **23.** $400

COMPOUND INTEREST You deposit $900 in an account that compounds interest yearly. Find the balance after 10 years for the given interest rate.

24. 4%   **25.** 5%   **26.** 6%   **27.** 7%

GROWTH RATES AND FACTORS Identify the growth rate and the growth factor in the exponential function.

28. $y = 50(1 + 1)^t$ **29.** $y = 31(4)^t$ **30.** $y = 5.6(2.3)^t$

$250(1.05)^5$

POPULATION GROWTH An initial population of 1000 starfish doubles each year for 4 years.

31. What is the growth factor for the population?

32. What is the starfish population after 4 years?

SUNFISH GROWTH An ocean sunfish, the mola mola, is about 0.006 foot long when it hatches. By the time it reaches adulthood, the largest of the mola mola will have tripled its length about 7 times.

33. What is the growth factor for the length of a mola mola?

34. What is the maximum length of an adult mola mola?

BICYCLE RACING In Exercises 35 and 36, use the following information. The air intake b (in liters per minute) of a cyclist on a racing bike can be modeled by $b = 6.37(1.11)^s$, where s is the speed of the bike (in miles per hour).

35. Use a calculator to find the cyclist's air intake if the racing bike is traveling 7 miles per hour, 19 miles per hour, or 25 miles per hour.

36. GRAPHING Graph the exponential growth model.

EXPONENTIAL GROWTH MODELS Match the description with its graph.

37. $C = \$300$ $r = 6\%$ **38.** $C = \$300$ $r = 12\%$ **39.** $C = \$300$ $r = 20\%$

A. 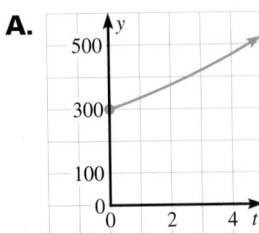   **B.** 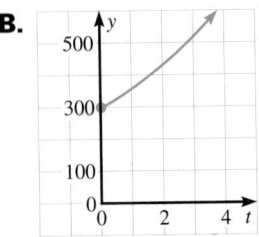   **C.**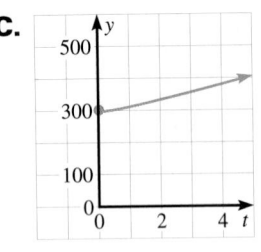

40. CRITICAL THINKING Graph the exponential growth models you found in Exercises 13–15. Which business would you rather own? Explain.

41. CHALLENGE What is the value of an $1000 investment after 5 years if it earns 6% annual interest compounded *quarterly* (four times a year).

HINT: Use the compound interest formula $A = P\left(1 + \dfrac{r}{n}\right)^{tn}$, where A is the value of the account, P is the initial investment, r is the interest rate, n is the number of times per year the interest is compounded, and t is the time period (in years).

Standardized Test Practice

42. MULTIPLE CHOICE The hourly rate of your new job is $5.00 per hour. You expect a raise of 9% at the end of each year. What will your hourly rate be at the end of your fifth year?

   Ⓐ $5.45   Ⓑ $7.25   Ⓒ $7.69   Ⓓ $9.50

43. MULTIPLE CHOICE What is the equation of the graph?

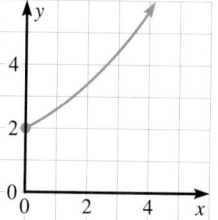

   Ⓕ $y = (2 \cdot 1.3)^x$ Ⓖ $y = 1.3(2)^x$

   Ⓗ $y = 2(1 - 0.3)^x$ Ⓙ $y = 2(1.3)^x$

Mixed Review

VARIABLE EXPRESSIONS **Evaluate the expression for the given value of the variable.** *(Lesson 1.3)*

44. $24 + m^2$ when $m = 5$ **45.** $6x - 1$ when $x = 1$

46. $3 \cdot 15y$ when $y = 2$ **47.** $1 - \dfrac{a}{3}$ when $a = 9$

SOLVING EQUATIONS **Solve the equation.** *(Lesson 3.5)*

48. $-2(4 - 3x) = 6(2x + 1) + 4$ **49.** $7x - (4x + 3) = 4(3x + 15)$

50. $\dfrac{2}{3}(6m - 3) + 10 = -8(m + 2)$ **51.** $\dfrac{1}{4}(12y - 4) - 2y = -3(y - 5)$

52. BAGELS AND DONUTS You buy 6 bagels and 8 donuts for a total of $8.60. Then you decide to buy 3 extra bagels and 3 extra donuts for a total of $3.75. How much did each bagel and donut cost? *(Lesson 7.4)*

PRODUCT OF POWERS **Write the expression as a single power of the base.** *(Lesson 8.1)*

53. $2^2 \cdot 2^2$ **54.** $7^6 \cdot 7^2$ **55.** $3^5 \cdot 3^2$

56. $y^3 \cdot y$ **57.** $r^2 \cdot r^4$ **58.** $a^9 \cdot a^4$

Maintaining Skills

SIMPLIFYING FRACTIONS **Write the fraction in simplest form.** *(Skills Review p. 763)*

59. $\dfrac{25}{100}$ **60.** $\dfrac{215}{645}$ **61.** $\dfrac{53}{424}$ **62.** $\dfrac{71}{355}$

8.7 Exponential Decay Functions

Goal
Write and graph exponential decay functions.

Key Words
- exponential decay
- decay rate
- decay factor

What will your car be worth after 8 years?

In Lesson 8.6 you used exponential functions to model values that were increasing. Exponential functions can also be used to model values that are decreasing. In Examples 1–3 you will analyze a car's value that is *decreasing exponentially* over time.

A quantity is *decreasing exponentially* if it decreases by the same percent r in each unit of time t. This is called **exponential decay**. Exponential decay can be modeled by the equation

$$y = C(1 - r)^t$$

where C is the initial amount (the amount before any decay occurs), r is the **decay rate** (as a decimal), t represents time, and where $0 < r < 1$. The expression $(1 - r)$ is called the **decay factor**.

EXAMPLE 1 Write an Exponential Decay Model

CARS You bought a car for $16,000. You expect the car to lose value, or depreciate, at a rate of 12% per year. Write an exponential decay model to represent this situation.

Solution

Let y be the value of the car and let t be the number of years of ownership. The initial value of the car C is $16,000. The decay rate r is 12%, or 0.12.

$y = C(1 - r)^t$	Write exponential decay model.
$= 16{,}000(1 - 0.12)^t$	Substitute 16,000 for C and 0.12 for r.
$= 16{,}000(0.88)^t$	Subtract.

ANSWER ▶ The exponential decay model is $y = 16{,}000(0.88)^t$.

 **Write an Exponential Decay Model**

1. Your friend bought a car for $24,000. The car depreciates at the rate of 10% per year. Write an exponential decay model to represent the car's value.

EXAMPLE 2 **Use an Exponential Decay Model**

Use the model in Example 1 to find the value of your car after 8 years.

Solution To find the value after 8 years, substitute 8 for t.

$y = 16{,}000(0.88)^t$ Write exponential decay model.

    $= 16{,}000(0.88)^8$ Substitute 8 for t.

    ≈ 5754 Use a calculator.

ANSWER ▶ Your car will be worth about $5754 after 8 years.

EXAMPLE 3 **Graph an Exponential Decay Model**

a. Graph the exponential decay model in Example 1.

b. Use the graph to estimate the value of your car after 5 years.

Solution

a. Make a table of values, plot the points in a coordinate plane, and draw a smooth curve through the points.

t	0	2	4	6	8
y	16,000	12,390	9595	7430	5754

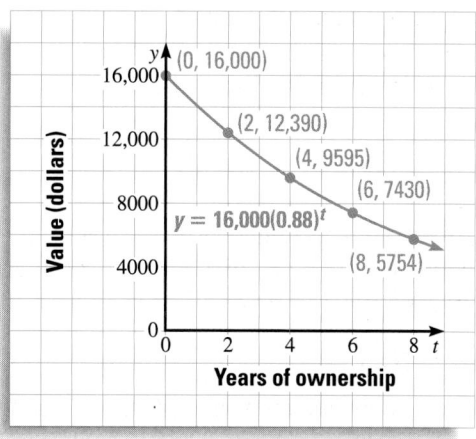

b. According to the graph, the value of your car after 5 years will be about $8400. You can check this answer by using the model in Example 1.

Checkpoint ✓ *Graph and Use an Exponential Decay Model*

Use the model in Checkpoint 1.

2. Find the value of your friend's car after 6 years.

3. Graph the exponential decay model.

4. Use the graph to estimate the value of your friend's car after 5 years.

In Lesson 8.3 you learned that for $b > 0$ a function of the form $y = ab^x$ is an exponential function. In the model for exponential growth, b is replaced by $1 + r$ where $r > 0$. In the model for exponential decay, b is replaced by $1 - r$ where $0 < r < 1$. Therefore you can conclude that an exponential model $y = Cb^t$ represents exponential growth if $b > 1$ and exponential decay if $0 < b < 1$.

EXAMPLE 4 Compare Growth and Decay Models

Classify the model as *exponential growth* or *exponential decay*. Then identify the growth or decay factor and graph the model.

a. $y = 30(1.2)^t$, where $t \geq 0$ **b.** $y = 30\left(\dfrac{3}{5}\right)^t$, where $t \geq 0$

Solution

a. Because $1.2 > 1$, the model $y = 30(1.2)^t$ is an exponential growth model. The growth factor $(1 + r)$ is 1.2. The graph is shown below.

b. Because $0 < \dfrac{3}{5} < 1$, the model $y = 30\left(\dfrac{3}{5}\right)^t$ is an exponential decay model. The decay factor $(1 - r)$ is $\dfrac{3}{5}$. The graph is shown below.

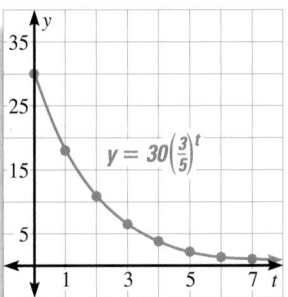

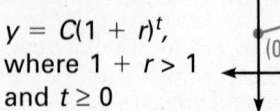 **Compare Growth and Decay Models**

Classify the model as **exponential growth** or **exponential decay**. Then identify the growth or decay factor and graph the model.

5. $y = (2)^t$ **6.** $y = (0.5)^t$ **7.** $y = 5(0.2)^t$ **8.** $y = 0.7(1.1)^t$

SUMMARY

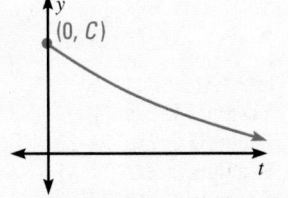

EXPONENTIAL GROWTH MODEL

$y = C(1 + r)^t$, where $1 + r > 1$ and $t \geq 0$

EXPONENTIAL DECAY MODEL

$y = C(1 - r)^t$, where $0 < 1 - r < 1$ and $t \geq 0$

Guided Practice

Vocabulary Check

1. In the exponential decay model, $y = C(1 - r)^t$, what is the decay factor?

Skill Check

2. **BUSINESS** A business earned $85,000 in 1990. Then its earnings decreased by 2% each year for 10 years. Write an exponential decay model to represent the decreasing annual earnings of the business.

CARS **You buy a used car for $7000. The car depreciates at the rate of 6% per year. Find the value of the car after the given number of years.**

3. 2 years   **4.** 5 years   **5.** 8 years   **6.** 10 years

7. **CHOOSE A MODEL** Which model best represents the decay curve shown in the graph at the right?

A. $y = 60(0.08)^t$ **B.** $y = 60(1.20)^t$

C. $y = 60(0.40)^t$ **D.** $y = 60(1.05)^t$

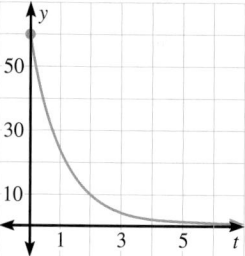

Classify the model as *exponential growth* or *exponential decay*.

8. $y = 0.55(3)^t$ **9.** $y = 3(0.55)^t$ **10.** $y = 55(3)^t$ **11.** $y = 55(0.3)^t$

Practice and Applications

EXPONENTIAL DECAY MODEL **Identify the initial amount and the decay factor in the exponential function.**

12. $y = 10(0.2)^t$ **13.** $y = 18(0.11)^t$ **14.** $y = 2\left(\frac{1}{4}\right)^t$ **15.** $y = 0.5\left(\frac{5}{8}\right)^t$

WRITING EXPONENTIAL MODELS **Write an exponential model to represent the situation. Tell what each variable represents.**

16. A $25,000 car depreciates at a rate of 9% each year. $25000(1-.09)^t$

17. A population of 100,000 decreases by 2% each year. $100,000(1-.02)^t$

18. A new sound system, valued at $800, decreases in value by 10% each year. $800(1-.1)^t$

FINANCE **Write an exponential decay model for the investment.**

19. A stock is valued at $100. Then the value decreases by 9% per year.

20. $550 is placed in a mutual fund. Then the value decreases by 4% per year.

21. A bond is purchased for $70. Then the value decreases by 1% per year.

Student Help

▶ **HOMEWORK HELP**
Example 1: Exs. 12–21
Example 2: Exs. 22–30
Example 3: Exs. 31–41
Example 4: Exs. 42–53

TRUCKS **You buy a used truck for $20,000. The truck depreciates 7% per**
year. Find the value of the truck after the given number of years.

22. 3 years   **23.** 8 years   **24.** 10 years   **25.** 12 years

PHARMACEUTICALS **In Exercises 26–28, use the following information.**
The amount of aspirin y (in milligrams) in a person's blood can be modeled by
$y = A(0.8)^t$ where A represents the dose of aspirin taken (in milligrams) and t
represents the number of hours since the aspirin was taken. Find the amount of
aspirin remaining in a person's blood for the given dosage and time.

26. Dosage: 250 mg   **27.** Dosage: 500 mg   **28.** Dosage: 750 mg
    Time: after 2 hours   Time: after 3.5 hours   Time: after 5 hours

BASKETBALL **In Exercises 29 and 30, use the following information.**
At the start of a basketball tournament consisting of six rounds, there are
64 teams. After each round, one half of the remaining teams are eliminated.

29. Write an exponential decay model showing the number of teams left in the
    tournament after each round.

30. How many teams remain after 3 rounds? after 4 rounds?

GRAPHING **Graph the exponential decay model.**

31. $y = 15(0.9)^t$ **32.** $y = 72(0.85)^t$ **33.** $y = 10\left(\dfrac{1}{2}\right)^t$ **34.** $y = 55\left(\dfrac{3}{4}\right)^t$

GRAPHING AND ESTIMATING **Write an exponential decay model for the**
situation. Then graph the model and use the graph to estimate the value
at the end of the given time period.

35. A $22,000 investment decreases in value by 9% per year for 8 years.

36. A population of 2,000,000 decreases by 2% per year for 15 years.

37. You buy a new motorcycle for $10,500. It's value depreciates by 10% each
    year for the 10 years you own it.

CABLE CARS **In Exercises 38–41, use the following information.**
From 1894 to 1903 the number of miles of cable car track in the United States
decreased by about 11% per year. There were 302 miles of track in 1894.

38. Write an exponential decay model showing the number of miles of cable car
    track left each year.

39. Copy and complete the table. You may want to use a calculator.

Year	1894	1896	1898	1900	1902
Miles of track	?	?	?	?	?

40. Graph the results.

41. Use your graph to estimate the number of miles of cable car track in 1903.

MATCHING Match the equation with its graph.

42. $y = 4 - 3t$

43. $y = 4(0.6)^t$

A.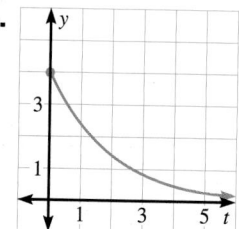

B.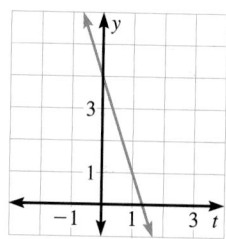

COMPARING MODELS Classify the model as *exponential growth* or *exponential decay*. Then identify the growth or decay factor and graph the model.

44. $y = 24(1.18)^t$ **45.** $y = 14(0.98)^t$ **46.** $y = 97(1.01)^t$

47. $y = 112\left(\dfrac{2}{3}\right)^t$ **48.** $y = 9\left(\dfrac{2}{5}\right)^t$ **49.** $y = 35\left(\dfrac{5}{4}\right)^t$

Student Help

▶**HOMEWORK HELP**

Extra help with problem solving in Exs. 50-52 is available at www.mcdougallittell.com

EXPONENTIAL FUNCTIONS Use a calculator to investigate the effects of *a* and *b* on the graph of $y = ab^x$.

50. In the same viewing rectangle, graph $y = 2(2)^x$, $y = 4(2)^x$, and $y = 8(2)^x$. How does an increase in the value of *a* affect the graph of $y = ab^x$?

51. In the same viewing rectangle, graph $y = 2^x$, $y = 4^x$, and $y = 8^x$. How does an increase in the value of *b* affect the graph of $y = ab^x$ when $b > 1$?

52. In the same viewing rectangle, graph $y = \left(\dfrac{1}{2}\right)^x$, $y = \left(\dfrac{1}{4}\right)^x$, and $y = \left(\dfrac{1}{8}\right)^x$. How does a decrease in the value of *b* affect the graph of $y = ab^x$ when $0 < b < 1$?

53. LOGICAL REASONING Choose a positive value for *b* and graph $y = b^x$ and $y = \left(\dfrac{1}{b}\right)^x$. What do you notice about the graphs?

54. CHALLENGE A store is having a sale on sweaters. On the first day the price of the sweaters is reduced by 20%. The price will be reduced another 20% each day until the sweaters are sold. On the fifth day of the sale will the sweaters be free? Explain.

Standardized Test Practice

55. MULTIPLE CHOICE In 1995 you purchase a parcel of land for $8000. The value of the land depreciates by 4% every year. What will the approximate value of the land be in 2002?

Ⓐ $224   Ⓑ $5760   Ⓒ $6012   Ⓓ $7999

56. MULTIPLE CHOICE Which model best represents the decay curve shown in the graph at the right?

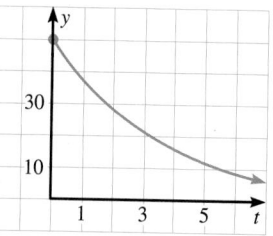

Ⓕ $y = 50(0.25)^t$ Ⓖ $y = 50(0.75)^t$

Ⓗ $y = 50(1.5)^t$ Ⓙ $y = 50(2)^t$

VARIABLE EXPRESSIONS Evaluate the expression for the given value of the variable(s). *(Lesson 1.3)*

57. $x^2 - 12$ when $x = 6$

58. $49 - 4w$ when $w = 2$

59. $100 - rs$ when $r = 4, s = 7$

60. $b^2 - 4ac$ when $a = 1, b = 5, c = 3$

SOLVING EQUATIONS Solve the equation. Round the result to the nearest hundredth. *(Lesson 3.6)*

61. $1.29x = 5.22x + 3.61$

62. $1.33x - 7.42 = 5.48x$

63. $10.52x + 1.15 = -1.12x - 6.35$

64. $8.75x + 2.16 = 18.28x - 6.59$

WRITING EQUATIONS Write in point-slope form the equation of the line that passes through the given point and has the given slope. *(Lesson 5.2)*

65. $(2, 5), m = 3$

66. $(0, -3), m = 5$

67. $(-1, -4), m = 4$

68. $(6, 3), m = -1$

69. $(-1, 7), m = -6$

70. $(-4, -5), m = -2$

Maintaining Skills

DIVIDING DECIMALS Divide. *(Skills Review p. 760)*

71. $0.5 \div 0.2$

72. $4.62 \div 0.4$

73. $0.074 \div 0.37$

74. $0.084 \div 0.007$

75. $0.451 \div 0.082$

76. $0.6064 \div 0.758$

Quiz 3

COMPOUND INTEREST You deposit $250 in an account that pays 8% interest compounded yearly. Find the balance at the end of the given time period. *(Lesson 8.6)*

1. 1 year

2. 3 years

3. 5 years

4. 8 years

5. POPULATION GROWTH An initial population of 50 raccoons doubles each year for 5 years. What is the raccoon population after 5 years? *(Lesson 8.6)*

CAR DEPRECIATION You buy a used car for $15,000. The car depreciates at a rate of 9% per year. Find the value of the car after the given number of years. *(Lesson 8.7)*

6. 2 years

7. 4 years

8. 5 years

9. 10 years

10. CAMPERS You buy a camper for $20,000. The camper depreciates at a rate of 8% per year. Write an exponential decay model to represent this situation. Then graph the model and use the graph to estimate the value of the camper after 5 years. *(Lesson 8.7)*

Classify the model as *exponential growth* or *exponential decay*. Then identify the growth or decay factor and graph the model. *(Lesson 8.7)*

11. $y = 6(0.1)^t$

12. $y = 10(1.2)^t$

13. $y = 3\left(\dfrac{9}{2}\right)^t$

14. $y = 2\left(\dfrac{1}{10}\right)^t$

Chapter 8 — Chapter Summary and Review

Chapter **8** **Chapter Summary and Review**

VOCABULARY

- **exponential function**, *p. 455*
- **scientific notation**, *p. 469*
- **exponential growth**, *p. 476*
- **growth rate**, *p. 476*
- **growth factor**, *p. 476*
- **exponential decay**, *p. 482*
- **decay rate**, *p. 482*
- **decay factor**, *p. 482*

8.1 MULTIPLICATION PROPERTIES OF EXPONENTS

Examples on pp. 443–445

EXAMPLES Use multiplication properties of exponents to simplify expressions.

a. $4^2 \cdot 4^7 = 4^{2+7} = 4^9$ Use product of powers property.

b. $(x^2)^4 = x^{2 \cdot 4} = x^8$ Use power of a power property.

c. $(6a)^3 = 6^3 \cdot a^3 = 216a^3$ Use power of a product property.

d. $w^3(v^2w)^4 = w^3 \cdot (v^2)^4 \cdot w^4$ Use power of a product property.

       $= w^3 \cdot v^8 \cdot w^4$ Use power of a power property.

       $= v^8 w^7$ Use product of powers property.

Simplify the expression.

1. $2^2 \cdot 2^5$ **2.** $x^3 \cdot x^3$ **3.** $(4^3)^2$ **4.** $(n^4)^3$

5. $(3x)^4$ **6.** $(st^2)^2$ **7.** $p(2p)^3$ **8.** $(3a)^3(2a)^2$

8.2 ZERO AND NEGATIVE EXPONENTS

Examples on pp. 449–451

EXAMPLES Use the definition of zero and negative exponents to simplify expressions.

a. $9^0 = 1$ a^0 is equal to 1.

b. $10^{-2} = \dfrac{1}{10^2}$ 10^{-2} is the reciprocal of 10^2.

       $= \dfrac{1}{100}$ Evaluate power.

c. $7x^{-3}y = 7 \cdot \dfrac{1}{x^3} \cdot y$ Use definition of negative exponents.

       $= \dfrac{7y}{x^3}$ Multiply.

Evaluate the expression.

9. 2^0
10. 5^{-3}
11. $(-7)^{-2}$
12. $\dfrac{1}{2^{-1}}$

Rewrite the expression with positive exponents.

13. $x^6 y^{-6}$
14. $\dfrac{5}{q^{-3}}$
15. $\dfrac{a^{-2}}{b^{-5}}$
16. $(2y)^{-4}$

8.3 GRAPHS OF EXPONENTIAL FUNCTIONS

Examples on pp. 455–457

EXAMPLE Graph the function $y = 3^x$.

Solution Make a table of values that includes both positive and negative x-values.

x	-2	-1	0	1	2	3
$y = 3^x$	$\dfrac{1}{9}$	$\dfrac{1}{3}$	1	3	9	27

Draw a coordinate plane and plot the points given by the table. Then draw a smooth curve through the points.

Notice that the graph has a y-intercept of 1, and that it gets closer to the negative side of the x-axis as the x-values decrease.

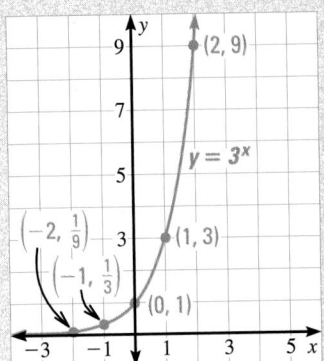

Graph the exponential function.

17. $y = 5^x$
18. $y = 2(3)^x$
19. $y = \left(\dfrac{1}{4}\right)^x$
20. $y = -\left(\dfrac{3}{2}\right)^x$

8.4 DIVISION PROPERTIES OF EXPONENTS

Examples on pp. 462–464

EXAMPLES Use division properties of exponents to simplify expressions.

a. $\dfrac{5^4}{5^2} = 5^{4-2} = 5^2 = 25$ Use quotient of powers property.

b. $\left(\dfrac{x}{3}\right)^3 = \dfrac{x^3}{3^3} = \dfrac{x^3}{27}$ Use power of a quotient property.

c. $\dfrac{2x^7 y}{x^2} \cdot \dfrac{y^3}{4xy^5} = \dfrac{2x^7 y^4}{4x^3 y^5} = \dfrac{x^4}{2y}$ Use multiplication and division properties of exponents.

Simplify the quotient.

21. $\dfrac{3^2}{3^3}$ **22.** $\dfrac{x^5}{x^2}$ **23.** $\left(\dfrac{4}{9}\right)^2$ **24.** $\left(\dfrac{r}{3}\right)^{-3}$

Simplify the expression. Use only positive exponents.

25. $\dfrac{9x^6}{y} \cdot \dfrac{y^2}{x^6}$ **26.** $\dfrac{m^7}{3n^4} \cdot \dfrac{3m^2n^2}{mn}$ **27.** $\left(\dfrac{2a^4b^5}{5a^2b}\right)^3$ **28.** $\dfrac{8s^4t^{-2}}{2s^3t^3} \cdot \dfrac{3s^2t^7}{2s^{-1}}$

8.5   SCIENTIFIC NOTATION

Examples on pp. 469–471

EXAMPLES You can write numbers in decimal form and in scientific notation. Use the properties of exponents to perform operations with numbers in scientific notation.

a. $1.24 \times 10^2 = 124$ Move decimal point 2 places to the right.

b. $1.5 \times 10^{-3} = 0.0015$ Move decimal point 3 places to the left.

c. $79\,000 = 7.9 \times 10^4$ Move decimal point 4 places to the left.

d. $0.0588 = 5.88 \times 10^{-2}$ Move decimal point 2 places to the right.

e. $(7.4 \times 10^2)(5 \times 10^3) = (7.4 \cdot 5) \times (10^2 \cdot 10^3)$ Use properties of multiplication.

$\qquad\qquad = 37 \times 10^5$ Use product of powers property.

$\qquad\qquad = (3.7 \times 10^1) \times 10^5$ Write in scientific notation.

$\qquad\qquad = 3.7 \times 10^6$ Use product of powers property.

f. $\dfrac{4.25 \times 10^{-2}}{8.5 \times 10^5} = \dfrac{4.25}{8.5} \times \dfrac{10^{-2}}{10^5}$ Write as a product.

$\qquad\qquad = 0.5 \times 10^{-7}$ Use quotient of powers property.

$\qquad\qquad = (5 \times 10^{-1}) \times 10^{-7}$ Write in scientific notation.

$\qquad\qquad = 5 \times 10^{-8}$ Use product of powers property.

Write the number in decimal form.

29. 7×10^1 **30.** 6.7×10^3 **31.** 2×10^{-4} **32.** 7.68×10^{-5}

Write the number in scientific notation.

33. $52{,}000{,}000$ **34.** 63.5 **35.** 0.009 **36.** 0.00000023

Perform the indicated operation. Write the result in scientific notation.

37. $(5 \times 10^4)(3 \times 10^2)$ **38.** $(4.1 \times 10^{-1})(6 \times 10^5)$ **39.** $(1.2 \times 10^7)(1.2 \times 10^0)$

40. $\dfrac{9 \times 10^6}{3 \times 10^3}$ **41.** $\dfrac{4.9 \times 10^1}{7 \times 10^{-8}}$ **42.** $\dfrac{3.4 \times 10^{-4}}{6.8 \times 10^{-3}}$

8.6 EXPONENTIAL GROWTH FUNCTIONS

Examples on pp. 476–478

EXAMPLE You deposit $1200 in an account that pays 9% interest compounded yearly. What is the account balance after 8 years?

Solution The initial amount P is $1200, the growth rate r is 0.09, and the time period t is 8 years. Let A be the account balance.

$A = P(1 + r)^t$ Write compound interest model.

$= 1200(1 + 0.09)^8$ Substitute 1200 for P, 0.09 for r, and 8 for t.

$= 1200(1.09)^8$ Add.

≈ 2391 Use a calculator.

ANSWER ▶ The balance after 8 years will be about $2391.

FITNESS PROGRAM **You start a walking program. You start by walking 2 miles. Then each week you increase your distance 5% per week.**

43. Write an exponential growth function to model the situation.

44. How far will you walk in the tenth week?

8.7 EXPONENTIAL DECAY FUNCTIONS

Examples on pp. 482–484

EXAMPLE You bought a 32-inch television for $600. The television is depreciating (losing value) at the rate of 8% per year. What is the value of the television after 6 years?

Solution The initial value of the television C is $600, the decay rate r is 0.08, and the time t is 6 years. Let y be the value of the television.

$y = C(1 - r)^t$ Write exponential decay model.

$= 600(1 - 0.08)^6$ Substitute 600 for C, 0.08 for r, and 6 for t.

$= 600(0.92)^6$ Subtract.

≈ 364 Use a calculator.

ANSWER ▶ The value of the television after 6 years will be about $364.

TENNIS CLUB **A tennis club had a declining enrollment from 1993 to 2000. The enrollment in 1993 was 125 people. Each year for 7 years, the enrollment decreased by 3%.**

45. Write an exponential decay model to represent the enrollment in each year.

46. Estimate the enrollment in 2000.

Simplify the expression. Use only positive exponents.

1. $x^3 \cdot x^4$

2. $(a^3)^7$

3. $(2d)^3$

4. $(mn)^2 \cdot n^4$

5. 9^0

6. $\dfrac{1}{5^{-2}}$

7. $8x^2y^{-4}$

8. $\dfrac{9p^{-3}}{q^{-4}}$

Graph the exponential function.

9. $y = 2^x$

10. $y = -5(3)^x$

11. $y = \left(\dfrac{2}{3}\right)^x$

12. $y = 10\left(\dfrac{1}{4}\right)^x$

13. RADIOACTIVE DECAY The time it takes for a radioactive substance to decay to half of its original amount is called its *half-life*. If you start with 16 grams of carbon-14, the number of grams g remaining after h half-life periods is $g = 16(0.5)^h$. Copy and complete the table and graph the function.

Half-life periods, h	0	1	2	3	4
Grams of carbon-14, g	?	?	?	?	?

Simplify the expression. Use only positive exponents.

14. $\dfrac{5^4}{5}$

15. $\left(\dfrac{3}{4}\right)^3$

16. $\dfrac{x^3}{xy^4} \cdot \dfrac{y^5}{x^5}$

17. $\dfrac{a^{-1}b^2}{ab} \cdot \dfrac{a^2b^3}{a^{-2}}$

Write the number in decimal form.

18. 4×10^5

19. 8.56×10^3

20. 5×10^{-2}

21. 6.28×10^{-4}

Write the number in scientific notation.

22. $9,000,000$

23. 6550

24. 0.012

25. 0.0000317

26. AMAZON RIVER Each second 4.2×10^6 cubic feet of water flow from the Amazon River into the Atlantic Ocean. How much water flows from the Amazon River into the Atlantic Ocean each year? *HINT:* There are about 3.2×10^7 seconds in one year.

SAVINGS In Exercises 27 and 28, use the following information.
You deposit $500 in an account that pays 7% interest compounded yearly.

27. Write an exponential growth model to represent this situation.

28. What is the account balance after 7 years?

SALES In Exercises 29 and 30, use the following information.
In 1996 you started your own business. In the first year your sales totaled $88,500. Each year for the next 5 years your sales decreased by 10%.

29. Write an exponential decay model to represent this situation.

30. Estimate your sales in 2001.

Chapter Standardized Test

1. Simplify the expression $7^4 \cdot 7^7$.

Ⓐ 7^{11} Ⓑ 7^{28}

Ⓒ 49^{11} Ⓓ 49^{28}

2. Simplify the expression $(a^3)^4$.

Ⓐ a^{-1} Ⓑ a^7

Ⓒ a^{12} Ⓓ a^{81}

3. Simplify the expression $(2x^2y^3)^2$.

Ⓐ $2x^4y^5$ Ⓑ $2x^4y^6$

Ⓒ $4x^4y^6$ Ⓓ $4x^4y^9$

4. Simplify the expression $\dfrac{2a^{-1}}{b^{-2}c^2}$.

Ⓐ $\dfrac{2b^2c^2}{a}$ Ⓑ $\dfrac{b^2c^2}{2a}$

Ⓒ $\dfrac{2b^2}{ac^2}$ Ⓓ $\dfrac{b^2}{2ac^2}$

5. What is the equation of the graph?

Ⓐ $y = 4^x$

Ⓑ $y = 5(4)^x$

Ⓒ $y = \left(\dfrac{1}{4}\right)^x$

Ⓓ $y = 5\left(\dfrac{1}{4}\right)^x$

Ⓔ none of these

6. Which expression simplifies to x^3?

Ⓐ $\dfrac{x^{-2}}{x^5}$ Ⓑ $\dfrac{x^2}{x^5}$

Ⓒ $\dfrac{x^5}{x^{-2}}$ Ⓓ $\dfrac{x^5}{x^2}$

7. Simplify the expression $\left(\dfrac{3}{5}\right)^{-2}$.

Ⓐ $\dfrac{9}{25}$ Ⓑ $\dfrac{25}{9}$

Ⓒ $\dfrac{6}{10}$ Ⓓ $\dfrac{10}{6}$

8. Simplify the expression $\dfrac{4x^2y^2}{4xy} \cdot \dfrac{8xy^3}{4y}$.

Ⓐ $2xy^2$ Ⓑ $2xy^3$

Ⓒ $2x^2y^3$ Ⓓ $2x^2y^4$

9. Which of the following numbers is *not* written in scientific notation?

Ⓐ 8.62×10^4 Ⓑ 2.12×10

Ⓒ 21.2×10^{-5} Ⓒ 9.9132×10^{-1}

10. Evaluate the expression $\dfrac{1.55 \times 10^4}{2.5 \times 10^{-3}}$. Write the result in scientific notation.

Ⓐ 0.62×10^1 Ⓑ 0.62×10^7

Ⓒ 6.2×10^0 Ⓓ 6.2×10^6

11. You deposit $450 in an account that pays 6% interest compounded yearly. What is the account balance after 6 years?

Ⓐ $471.00   Ⓑ $612.00

Ⓒ $638.33   Ⓓ $2862.00

12. A business had a profit of $42,000 in 1994. Then its profit decreased by 8% each year for 6 years. How much did the business earn in 2000?

Ⓐ $11,010   Ⓑ $20,160

Ⓒ $21,840   Ⓓ $25,467

The basic skills you'll review on this page will help prepare you for the next chapter.

Maintaining Skills

EXAMPLE 1 Write the Prime Factorization of a Number

Write the prime factorization of 1078.

Solution

Use a tree diagram to factor the number until all factors are prime numbers. To determine the factors, test the prime numbers in order.

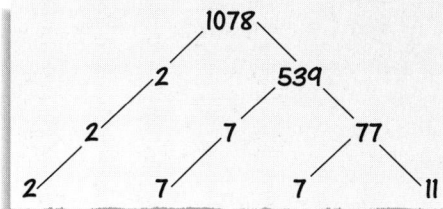

ANSWER ▶ The prime factorization of 1078 is 2 • 7 • 7 • 11. This may also be written as $2 \cdot 7^2 \cdot 11$.

Try These

Write the prime factorization of the number.

1. 8   **2.** 60   **3.** 105   **4.** 700

EXAMPLE 2 Rewrite Improper Fractions as Mixed Numbers

Rewrite the improper fraction as a mixed number.

a. $\dfrac{16}{3}$ **b.** $\dfrac{30}{4}$

Solution

a. $\dfrac{16}{3} = 16 \div 3$ Write fraction as a division problem.

   $= 5$ remainder 1 Divide 16 by 3.

   $= 5\dfrac{1}{3}$ Write remainder over divisor to form fraction.

b. $\dfrac{30}{4} = 30 \div 4$ Write fraction as a division problem.

   $= 7$ remainder 2 Divide 30 by 4.

   $= 7\dfrac{2}{4}$ Write remainder over divisor to form fraction.

   $= 7\dfrac{1}{2}$ Reduce fraction.

Student Help

▶ **EXTRA EXAMPLES**

More examples and practice exercises are available at www.mcdougallittell.com

Try These

Rewrite the improper fraction as a mixed number.

5. $\dfrac{21}{8}$ **6.** $\dfrac{42}{5}$ **7.** $\dfrac{27}{15}$ **8.** $\dfrac{75}{9}$

Quadratic Equations and Functions

▷ What is the path of a home run ball?

APPLICATION: Baseball

A baseball player usually scores a home run by hitting a ball over the outfield wall. If the ball stays in the air long enough, and drops in the outfield without being caught, a batter can score an inside-the-park home run.

The path of a baseball can be modeled with a quadratic equation. In Chapter 9 you will use mathematical models to solve different types of vertical motion problems.

Think & Discuss

1. Use the graph to approximate the maximum height the ball reaches.

2. Use the graph to approximate the maximum horizontal distance the ball travels.

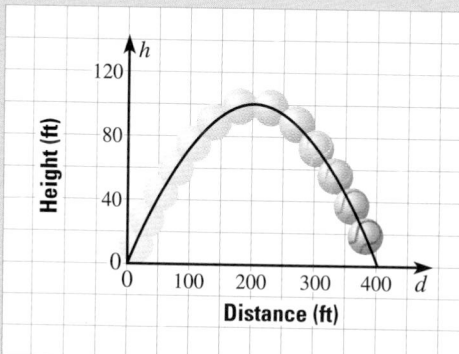

Learn More About It

You will use a vertical motion model to learn more about the path of a baseball in Exercise 79 on p. 538.

 APPLICATION LINK More about baseball is available at www.mcdougallittell.com

What's the chapter about?

- Evaluating and approximating square roots
- Simplifying radicals
- Solving quadratic equations
- Sketching graphs of quadratic functions and quadratic inequalities

---

KEY WORDS

- **square root,** *p. 499*
- **radicand,** *p. 499*
- **perfect square,** *p. 500*
- **radical expression,** *p. 501*
- **quadratic equation,** *p. 505*
- **quadratic function,** *p. 520*
- **parabola,** *p. 520*

- **vertex,** *p. 521*
- **axis of symmetry,** *p. 521*
- **roots of a quadratic equation,** *p. 527*
- **quadratic formula,** *p. 533*
- **discriminant,** *p. 540*
- **quadratic inequalities,** *p. 547*

Chapter Readiness Quiz

Take this quick quiz. If you are unsure of an answer, look back at the reference pages for help.

VOCABULARY CHECK *(refer to p. 222)*

1. Complete: The __?__ of the line shown at the right is 1.

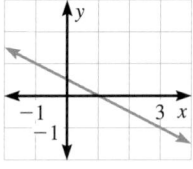

ⓐ origin   ⓑ x-intercept

ⓒ y-intercept   ⓓ slope

SKILL CHECK *(refer to pp. 15, 95, 367)*

2. Evaluate the expression $3x^2 - 108$ when $x = -4$.

ⓐ -184 ⓑ -156 ⓒ -120 ⓓ -60

3. Which ordered pair is a solution of the inequality $3x + 4y < 5$?

ⓐ $(0, 3)$ ⓑ $(-1, 2)$ ⓒ $(-2, 2)$ ⓓ $(1, 1)$

Explain Your Ideas

Talking about math and explaining your ideas to another person can help you understand a topic better.

Talking about the sign of a product

"Is the square of a nonzero number always positive? I know the square of a positive number is positive."

"In Chapter 2 we learned that a product is positive if it has an even number of negative factors. Since the square of a negative number has two negative factors, it is positive also."

9.1 Square Roots

Goal
Evaluate and approximate square roots.

Key Words
- square root
- positive square root
- negative square root
- radicand
- perfect square
- radical expression

How many squares are on each side of a chessboard?

A chessboard is a large square made up of 64 small squares. In Exercises 84 and 85, you will use *square roots* to investigate whether game boards of other sizes can be constructed.

You know how to find the square of a number. For instance, the square of 3 is $3^2 = 9$. The square of -3 is also 9. In this lesson you will learn about the inverse operation: finding a *square root* of a number.

SQUARE ROOT OF A NUMBER If $b^2 = a$, then b is a **square root** of a.

Examples: $3^2 = 9$, so 3 is a square root of 9.

$(-3)^2 = 9$, so -3 is a square root of 9.

All *positive* real numbers have two square roots: a **positive square root** (or *principal* square root) and a **negative square root**. Square roots are written with a radical symbol $\sqrt{}$. The number or expression inside a radical symbol is the **radicand**. In the following example, 9 is the radicand. As shown in part (a), the radical symbol indicates the positive square root of a positive number.

EXAMPLE 1 Read Square Root Symbols

Write the equation in words.

a. $\sqrt{9} = 3$ **b.** $-\sqrt{9} = -3$ **c.** $\pm\sqrt{9} = \pm3$

Solution

Equation	Words
a. $\sqrt{9} = 3$	The positive square root of 9 is 3.
b. $-\sqrt{9} = -3$	The negative square root of 9 is -3.
▶ **c.** $\pm\sqrt{9} = \pm3$	The positive and negative square roots of 9 are 3 and -3.

 **Checkpoint** ✓ **Read Square Root Symbols**

Write the equation in words.

   1. $\sqrt{4} = 2$ **2.** $\sqrt{25} = 5$ **3.** $-\sqrt{16} = -4$ **4.** $\pm\sqrt{36} = \pm6$

NUMBER OF SQUARE ROOTS Positive real numbers have two square roots. Zero has only one square root: zero. Negative numbers do not have real square roots because the square of every real number is either positive or zero.

Student Help

▶ READING ALGEBRA
Since negative numbers do not have real square roots, we say that $\sqrt{-64}$ is *undefined*.

EXAMPLE 2 Find Square Roots of Numbers

Evaluate the expression.

a. $\sqrt{64}$ **b.** $-\sqrt{64}$ **c.** $\pm\sqrt{64}$ **d.** $\sqrt{0}$

Solution
a. $\sqrt{64} = \sqrt{8^2} = 8$ Positive square root

b. $-\sqrt{64} = -\sqrt{8^2} = -8$ Negative square root

c. $\pm\sqrt{64} = \pm\sqrt{8^2} = \pm 8$ Two square roots

d. $\sqrt{0} = 0$ Square root of zero is zero.

 **Find Square Roots of Numbers**

Evaluate the expression.

5. $\pm\sqrt{100}$ **6.** $-\sqrt{25}$ **7.** $\sqrt{36}$ **8.** $\sqrt{16}$

The square of an integer is called a **perfect square**. Of course a square root of a perfect square is an integer. On the other hand, if n is a positive integer that is *not* a perfect square, then it can be shown that $\sqrt{n}$ is an *irrational number*. An irrational number is a number that is not the quotient of integers. In Lesson 12.9 you will use an indirect proof to prove that $\sqrt{2}$ is an irrational number.

$\sqrt{4} = 2$ 4 is a perfect square. $\sqrt{4}$ is an integer.

$\sqrt{2} \approx 1.414$ 2 is not a perfect square. $\sqrt{2}$ is neither an integer nor a rational number.

Student Help

▶ STUDY TIP
You can use a calculator or the Table of Square Roots on p. 801 to approximate an irrational square root.

EXAMPLE 3 Evaluate Square Roots of Numbers

Evaluate the expression. Give the exact value if possible. Otherwise, approximate to the nearest hundredth.

a. $-\sqrt{49}$ **b.** $\sqrt{3}$

Solution
a. $-\sqrt{49} = -\sqrt{7^2} = -7$ 49 is a perfect square.

b. $\sqrt{3} \approx 1.73$ Round to nearest hundredth.

 **Evaluate Square Roots of Numbers**

Evaluate the expression. Give the exact value if possible. Otherwise, approximate to the nearest hundredth.

9. $\sqrt{100}$ **10.** $-\sqrt{5}$ **11.** $\sqrt{23}$ **12.** $-\sqrt{81}$

RADICAL EXPRESSIONS An expression written with a radical symbol is called a **radical expression**, or sometimes just a *radical*.

EXAMPLE 4 Evaluate a Radical Expression

Evaluate $\sqrt{b^2 - 4ac}$ when $a = 1$, $b = -2$, and $c = -3$.

Solution

The radical symbol is a grouping symbol. You must evaluate the expression inside the radical symbol before you find the square root.

$$\sqrt{b^2 - 4ac} = \sqrt{(-2)^2 - 4(1)(-3)}$$ Substitute values for a, b, and c.

$$= \sqrt{4 + 12}$$ Simplify.

$$= \sqrt{16}$$ Add.

$$= 4$$ Find the positive square root.

Checkpoint ✓ **Evaluate a Radical Expression**

Evaluate $\sqrt{b^2 - 4ac}$ for the given values.

13. $a = 2$, $b = 3$, $c = -5$

14. $a = -1$, $b = 8$, $c = 20$

Student Help

▶**KEYSTROKE HELP**
To find the square root of 3 on your calculator you may need to press [√] [3] or [3] [√]. Test your calculator to find out which order it uses.

EXAMPLE 5 Use a Calculator to Evaluate an Expression

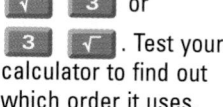 Use a calculator to evaluate $\dfrac{1 \pm 2\sqrt{3}}{4}$. Round the results to the nearest hundredth.

Solution

When the symbol $\pm$ precedes the radical, the expression represents two different numbers.

KEYSTROKES   **DISPLAY**

(1 [+] 2 [×] 3 [√]) [÷] 4 [ENTER]   1.116025404

(1 [−] 2 [×] 3 [√]) [÷] 4 [ENTER]   −0.616025403

ANSWER▶ The expression represents 1.12 and −0.62.

Checkpoint ✓ **Use a Calculator to Evaluate an Expression**

Use a calculator to evaluate the expression. Round the results to the nearest hundredth.

15. $6 \pm \sqrt{5}$ **16.** $4 \pm \sqrt{8}$ **17.** $\dfrac{2 \pm \sqrt{3}}{3}$ **18.** $\dfrac{2 \pm 3\sqrt{6}}{4}$

9.1 Exercises

Guided Practice

Vocabulary Check

1. **Complete:** Since $(-2)^2 = 4$, -2 is a __?__ of 4.

2. State the meaning of the symbols $\sqrt{}$, $-\sqrt{}$, and $\pm\sqrt{}$ when applied to a positive number n.

3. Identify the radicand in the equation $\sqrt{4} = 2$.

Skill Check

Evaluate the expression.

4. $\sqrt{81}$ 5. $\pm\sqrt{121}$ 6. $-\sqrt{36}$ 7. $-\sqrt{4}$

Determine whether each expression is *rational* or *irrational*.

8. $\sqrt{25}$ 9. $\sqrt{6}$ 10. $\sqrt{100}$ 11. $\sqrt{10}$

Use a calculator or a table of square roots to evaluate the expression. Round the results to the nearest hundredth.

12. $1 \pm \sqrt{2}$ 13. $6 \pm 5\sqrt{3}$ 14. $3 \pm \sqrt{7}$ 15. $2 \pm 4\sqrt{8}$

Practice and Applications

READING SQUARE ROOT SYMBOLS Write the equation in words.

16. $\sqrt{625} = 25$ 17. $\pm\sqrt{16} = \pm 4$ 18. $\pm\sqrt{4} = \pm 2$

19. $\sqrt{225} = 15$ 20. $-\sqrt{121} = -11$ 21. $-\sqrt{289} = -17$

22. $\sqrt{49} = 7$ 23. $\sqrt{1} = 1$ 24. $\sqrt{\dfrac{1}{9}} = \dfrac{1}{3}$

FINDING SQUARE ROOTS Evaluate the expression. Check the results by squaring each root.

25. $\sqrt{144}$ 26. $\pm\sqrt{25}$ 27. $\sqrt{196}$ 28. $\pm\sqrt{900}$

29. $\pm\sqrt{49}$ 30. $\sqrt{0}$ 31. $-\sqrt{256}$ 32. $-\sqrt{100}$

33. $\sqrt{400}$ 34. $-\sqrt{225}$ 35. $\sqrt{121}$ 36. $\sqrt{289}$

37. $-\sqrt{1}$ 38. $\pm\sqrt{81}$ 39. $\sqrt{169}$ 40. $-\sqrt{625}$

Student Help

▶ HOMEWORK HELP
Example 1: Exs. 16–24
Example 2: Exs. 25–40
Example 3: Exs. 53–64
Example 4: Exs. 65–74
Example 5: Exs. 75–83

PERFECT SQUARES Determine whether the number is a perfect square.

41. 10   42. 81   43. -5 44. 120

45. 16   46. 1   47. 111   48. 225

49. -4 50. 10,000   51. $\dfrac{9}{4}$ 52. $\dfrac{1}{2}$

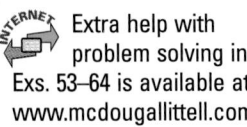

Student Help

▶ **HOMEWORK HELP**

Extra help with problem solving in Exs. 53–64 is available at www.mcdougallittell.com

EVALUATING SQUARE ROOTS Evaluate the expression. Give the exact value if possible. Otherwise, approximate to the nearest hundredth.

53. $\sqrt{5}$ **54.** $\sqrt{25}$ **55.** $\sqrt{13}$ **56.** $-\sqrt{125}$

57. $-\sqrt{49}$ **58.** $\pm\sqrt{70}$ **59.** $\pm\sqrt{1}$ **60.** $\sqrt{10}$

61. $\pm\sqrt{15}$ **62.** $-\sqrt{400}$ **63.** $-\sqrt{20}$ **64.** $\pm\sqrt{144}$

EVALUATING RADICAL EXPRESSIONS Evaluate $\sqrt{b^2 - 4ac}$ for the given values.

65. $a = 4, b = 5, c = 1$ **66.** $a = 2, b = 4, c = -6$

67. $a = -2, b = 8, c = -8$ **68.** $a = -5, b = 5, c = 10$

EVALUATING RADICAL EXPRESSIONS Evaluate the radical expression when $a = 2$ and $b = 4$.

69. $\sqrt{b^2 + 10a}$ **70.** $\sqrt{b^2 - 8a}$ **71.** $\sqrt{a^2 + 45}$

72. $\dfrac{\sqrt{b^2 + 42a}}{a}$ **73.** $\dfrac{10 + 2\sqrt{b}}{a}$ **74.** $\dfrac{36 - \sqrt{8a}}{b}$

 **EVALUATING RADICAL EXPRESSIONS** Use a calculator to evaluate the expression. Round the results to the nearest hundredth.

75. $8 \pm \sqrt{5}$ **76.** $2 \pm 5\sqrt{3}$ **77.** $-6 \pm 4\sqrt{2}$

78. $\dfrac{1 \pm 6\sqrt{8}}{6}$ **79.** $\dfrac{7 \pm 3\sqrt{2}}{-1}$ **80.** $\dfrac{4 \pm 7\sqrt{3}}{2}$

81. $\dfrac{5 \pm 6\sqrt{3}}{3}$ **82.** $\dfrac{3 \pm 4\sqrt{5}}{4}$ **83.** $\dfrac{7 \pm 3\sqrt{12}}{-6}$

CHESSBOARD A chessboard has 8 small squares on a side and therefore has a total of 64 small squares.

84. Could a similar square game board be constructed that has a total of 81 small squares?

85. If a square game board has a total of m small squares of equal size, what can you say about m?

LOGICAL REASONING In Exercises 86–88, determine whether the statement is *true* or *false*. If it is true, give an example. If it is false, give a counterexample.

86. All positive numbers have two different square roots.

87. No number has only one square root.

88. Some numbers have no real square root.

89. CHALLENGE Evaluate $3 \pm \sqrt{(-3)^2 - 4(0.5)(-8)}$.

Link to History

CHESS This illustration of Spanish women playing chess is from a thirteenth century manuscript written for the King of Spain. Historians believe the game of chess originated in India in the seventh century.

90. MULTIPLE CHOICE Evaluate $\dfrac{15 \pm 5\sqrt{225}}{3}$.

    (A) -70 and 80 (B) -20 and 30

    (C) 20 and 30 (D) 70 and 80

91. MULTIPLE CHOICE Which is an example of a perfect square?

    (F) -100 (G) 10 (H) 121 (J) 150

92. MULTIPLE CHOICE Which two consecutive integers does $\sqrt{200}$ fall between?

    (A) 10 and 11 (B) 13 and 14

    (C) 14 and 15 (D) 19 and 20

93. MULTIPLE CHOICE If $a^2 = 36$ and $b^2 = 49$, choose the greatest possible value for the expression $b - a$.

    (F) -13 (G) -1 (H) 1 (J) 13

Student Help

▶ **TEST TIP**
Square each integer to find which perfect squares 200 falls between to help you estimate $\sqrt{200}$ in Exercise 92.

Mixed Review

GRAPH AND CHECK **Graph the linear system and estimate a solution. Then check your solution algebraically.** *(Lesson 7.1)*

94. $y = -3$
    $x = 4$

95. $2x - 4y = 12$
       $y = -2$

96. $2x - y = 10$
      $x + y = 5$

97. BASKETBALL TICKETS The admission price for a high school basketball game is \$2 for students and \$3 for adults. At one game, 324 tickets were sold and \$764 was collected. How many students and adults attended the game? *(Lesson 7.2)*

98. FLOWERS You are buying a combination of irises and lilies for a flower arrangement. The irises are \$4 each and the lilies are \$3 each. You spend \$50 for an arrangement of 15 flowers. How many of each type of flower did you buy? *(Lesson 7.2)*

LINEAR COMBINATIONS **Use linear combinations to solve the system of linear equations.** *(Lesson 7.3)*

99. $10x - 3y = 17$
     $-7x + y = 9$

100. $12x - 4y = -32$
       $x + 3y = 4$

101. $8x - 5y = 70$
      $2x + y = 4$

Maintaining Skills

FRACTIONS AND DECIMALS **Write the fraction as a terminating or repeating decimal.** *(Skills Review p. 767)*

102. $\dfrac{3}{4}$ **103.** $\dfrac{8}{15}$ **104.** $\dfrac{6}{11}$ **105.** $\dfrac{7}{8}$

106. $\dfrac{2}{9}$ **107.** $\dfrac{5}{16}$ **108.** $\dfrac{5}{6}$ **109.** $\dfrac{2}{5}$

110. $\dfrac{5}{8}$ **111.** $\dfrac{8}{9}$ **112.** $\dfrac{3}{5}$ **113.** $\dfrac{9}{10}$

9.2 Solving Quadratic Equations by Finding Square Roots

Goal

Solve a quadratic equation by finding square roots.

Key Words

- quadratic equation
- leading coefficient

How long does it take for an egg to drop?

An egg is placed in a container and dropped from a height of 32 feet. Can you tell how long it will take the egg to reach the ground? In Example 5 you will use a *quadratic equation* to find the answer.

A **quadratic equation** is an equation that can be written in the standard form

$$ax^2 + bx + c = 0, \text{ where } a \neq 0; a \text{ is called the } leading \text{ } coefficient.$$

When $b = 0$, this equation becomes $ax^2 + c = 0$. One way to solve a quadratic equation of the form $ax^2 + c = 0$ is to isolate x^2 on one side of the equation. Then find the square root(s) of each side. In Example 3 you will see how to use inverse operations to isolate x^2.

Student Help

▶**STUDY TIP**
Remember that squaring a number and finding a square root of a number are inverse operations.

EXAMPLE 1 Solve Quadratic Equations

Solve the equation. Write the solutions as integers if possible. Otherwise, write them as radical expressions.

  a. $x^2 = 4$ **b.** $n^2 = 5$

Solution **a.** $x^2 = 4$ Write original equation.

               $x = \pm\sqrt{4}$ Find square roots.

               $x = \pm 2$ $2^2 = 4$ and $(-2)^2 = 4$

        ANSWER ▶ The solutions are 2 and -2.

     b. $n^2 = 5$ Write original equation.

             $n = \pm\sqrt{5}$ Find square roots.

        ANSWER ▶ The solutions are $\sqrt{5}$ and $-\sqrt{5}$.

Checkpoint ✓ **Solve Quadratic Equations**

Solve the equation. Write the solutions as integers if possible. Otherwise, write them as radical expressions. Check the results by squaring each root.

  1. $x^2 = 81$ **2.** $y^2 = 11$ **3.** $n^2 = 25$ **4.** $x^2 = 10$

EXAMPLE 2 Solve Quadratic Equations

Solve the equation.

a. $x^2 = 0$ **b.** $y^2 = -1$

Solution **a.** $x^2 = 0$ Write original equation.

$x = 0$ Find square roots.

ANSWER ▶ The only solution is zero.

b. $y^2 = -1$ has no real solution because the square of a real number is never negative.

ANSWER ▶ There is no real solution.

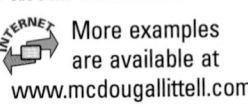
EXAMPLE 3 Rewrite Before Finding Square Roots

Solve $3x^2 - 48 = 0$.

Solution $3x^2 - 48 = 0$ Write original equation.

$3x^2 = 48$ Add 48 to each side.

$x^2 = 16$ Divide each side by 3.

$x = \pm\sqrt{16}$ Find square roots.

$x = \pm 4$ $4^2 = 16$ and $(-4)^2 = 16$

ANSWER ▶ The solutions are 4 and -4. Check both solutions in the *original* equation.

CHECK ✓ $3(4)^2 - 48 \stackrel{?}{=} 0$ $3(16) - 48 = 0$ ✓

$3(-4)^2 - 48 \stackrel{?}{=} 0$ $3(16) - 48 = 0$ ✓

Both 4 and -4 make the equation true, so $3x^2 - 48 = 0$ has two solutions.

Checkpoint ✓ *Rewrite Before Finding Square Roots*

Solve the equation.

5. $x^2 - 1 = 0$ **6.** $2x^2 - 72 = 0$ **7.** $27 - 3y^2 = 0$

As Examples 1, 2, and 3 suggest, a quadratic equation can have no real solution, one solution, or two solutions.

SUMMARY

Solving $x^2 = d$ by Finding Square Roots

- If $d > 0$, then $x^2 = d$ has two solutions: $x = \pm\sqrt{d}$. (Examples 1 and 3)
- If $d = 0$, then $x^2 = d$ has one solution: $x = 0$.   (Example 2a)
- If $d < 0$, then $x^2 = d$ has no real solution.   (Example 2b)

FALLING OBJECT MODEL When an object is dropped, the speed with which it falls continues to increase. Ignoring air resistance, its height h can be approximated by the falling object model.

> **Falling object model:** $h = -16t^2 + s$

Here h is measured in feet, t is the number of seconds the object has fallen, and s is the initial height from which the object was dropped.

EXAMPLE 4 Write a Falling Object Model

An engineering student is a contestant in an egg dropping contest. The goal is to create a container for an egg so it can be dropped from a height of 32 feet without breaking. Write a model for the egg's height. Disregard air resistance.

Solution

The initial height is $s = 32$ feet.

$h = -16t^2 + s$ Write falling object model.

$h = -16t^2 + 32$ Substitute 32 for s.

ANSWER▸ The falling object model for the egg is $h = -16t^2 + 32$.

EXAMPLE 5 Use a Falling Object Model

How long will it take the egg container in Example 4 to reach the ground? Round your solution to the nearest tenth.

Solution

Ground level is represented by $h = 0$ feet. To find the time it takes for the egg to reach the ground, substitute 0 for h in the model and solve for t.

$h = -16t^2 + 32$ Write falling egg model from Example 4.

$0 = -16t^2 + 32$ Substitute 0 for h.

$-32 = -16t^2$ Subtract 32 from each side.

$2 = t^2$ Divide each side by -16.

▸$\pm\sqrt{2} = t$ Find square roots.

$1.4 \approx t$ Use a calculator or table of square roots to approximate the positive square root of 2.

ANSWER▸ The egg container will reach the ground in about 1.4 seconds.

Student Help

▶**STUDY TIP**
The negative square root, $-\sqrt{2}$, does not make sense in this situation, so you can ignore that solution. ┈┈┈┈┈┈

 **Write and Use a Falling Object Model**

Suppose the egg dropping contest in Example 4 requires the egg to be dropped from a height of 64 feet.

8. Write a falling object model for the egg container when $s = 64$.

9. According to the model, how long will it take the egg container to reach the ground?

9.2 Exercises

Guided Practice

Vocabulary Check

1. Is $2x - 7 = 15$ a quadratic equation? Explain why or why not.

2. Write $7x^2 = 12 + 3x$ in standard form. What is the leading coefficient?

Skill Check

Determine the number of real solutions for each equation.

3. $x^2 = 6$ **4.** $x^2 = 0$ **5.** $x^2 = -17$

6. $x^2 - 8 = -8$ **7.** $x^2 - 15 = 5$ **8.** $x^2 + 2 = -2$

Solve the equation or write *no real solution*.

9. $y^2 = 49$ **10.** $x^2 = -16$ **11.** $n^2 = 7$

12. $3x^2 - 20 = -2$ **13.** $5x^2 = -25$ **14.** $2x^2 - 8 = 0$

FALLING OBJECTS Use the falling object model, $h = -16t^2 + s$. Given the initial height s, find the time it would take for the object to reach the ground, disregarding air resistance. Round the result to the nearest tenth.

15. $s = 48$ feet   **16.** $s = 160$ feet   **17.** $s = 192$ feet

Practice and Applications

QUADRATIC EQUATIONS Solve the equation or write *no real solution*. Write the solutions as integers if possible. Otherwise, write them as radical expressions.

18. $x^2 = 9$ **19.** $m^2 = 1$ **20.** $x^2 = 17$ **21.** $k^2 = -44$

22. $y^2 = 15$ **23.** $x^2 = 225$ **24.** $r^2 = -81$ **25.** $x^2 = 121$

26. $t^2 = 39$ **27.** $x^2 = 256$ **28.** $y^2 = 0$ **29.** $n^2 = 49$

30. $y^2 = 400$ **31.** $x^2 = 64$ **32.** $m^2 = -9$ **33.** $x^2 = 16$

QUADRATIC EQUATIONS Solve the equation or write *no real solution*. Write the solutions as integers if possible. Otherwise, write them as radical expressions.

34. $5x^2 = 500$ **35.** $3x^2 = 6$ **36.** $5y^2 = 25$

37. $a^2 + 3 = 12$ **38.** $x^2 - 7 = 57$ **39.** $x^2 + 36 = 0$

40. $2s^2 - 5 = 27$ **41.** $3x^2 - 75 = 0$ **42.** $7x^2 + 30 = 9$

43. $5x^2 + 5 = 20$ **44.** $5t^2 + 10 = 135$ **45.** $3x^2 - 50 = 58$

46. $m^2 - 12 = 52$ **47.** $2y^2 + 13 = 41$ **48.** $20 - x^2 = 4$

Student Help

▶ **HOMEWORK HELP**
Example 1: Exs. 18–33
Example 2: Exs. 18–33
Example 3: Exs. 34–48, 50–55
Example 4: Ex. 59
Example 5: Ex. 60

49. ERROR ANALYSIS Find and correct the error at the right.

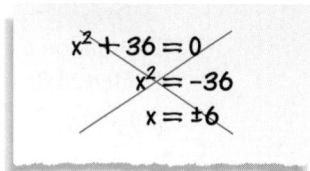

$$x^2 + 36 = 0$$
$$x^2 = -36$$
$$x = \pm 6$$

SOLVING EQUATIONS Use a calculator to solve the equation. Round the result to the nearest hundredth.

50. $4x^2 - 3 = 57$ **51.** $6y^2 + 22 = 34$ **52.** $2x^2 - 4 = 10$

53. $3x^2 + 7 = 31$ **54.** $7n^2 - 6 = 15$ **55.** $5x^2 - 12 = 5$

LOGICAL REASONING In Exercises 56–58, decide whether the statement is *true* or *false*. If it is true, give a reason. If it is false, give a counterexample.

56. $x^2 = c$ has no real solution when $c < 0$.

57. $x^2 = c$ has two solutions when $c > 0$.

58. $x^2 = c$ has no solution when $c = 0$.

FALLING ROCK In Exercises 59 and 60, a boulder falls off the top of an overhanging cliff during a storm. The cliff is 96 feet high. Find how long it will take for the boulder to hit the road below.

59. Write a falling object model when $s = 96$.

60. Solve the falling object model for $h = 0$. Round to the nearest tenth.

Science Link In Exercises 61–66, use the following information.
Mineralogists use the Vickers scale to measure the hardness of minerals. The hardness H of a mineral can be determined by hitting the mineral with a pyramid-shaped diamond and measuring the depth d of the indentation. The harder the mineral, the smaller the depth of the indentation. A model that relates mineral hardness with the indentation depth (in millimeters) is $Hd^2 = 1.89$.

Use a calculator to find the depth of the indentation for the mineral with the given value of H. Round to the nearest hundredth of a millimeter.

61. Graphite: $H = 12$ **62.** Gold: $H = 50$ **63.** Galena: $H = 80$

64. Platinum: $H = 125$ **65.** Copper: $H = 140$ **66.** Hematite: $H = 755$

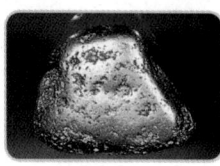  

History Link In Exercises 67 and 68, use the following information.
Population estimates for the 1800s lead a student to model the population of the United States by $P = 5,500,400 + 683,300t^2$, where $t = 0, 1, 2, 3, \ldots$ represents the years 1800, 1810, 1820, 1830, ...

67. Use this population model to estimate the United States population in 1800, 1850, and 1900.

68. Use this model to estimate the year in which the United States population reached 50 million.

Standardized Test Practice

69. MULTIPLE CHOICE Which quadratic equation is written in standard form?

    Ⓐ $8x + 5x^2 - 9 = 0$ Ⓑ $5x^2 + 8x = 9$

    Ⓒ $5x^2 + 8x - 9 = 0$ Ⓓ $9 - 8x - 5x^2 = 0$

70. MULTIPLE CHOICE Consider the equation $3x^2 - 44 = x^2 + 84$. Which statement is correct?

    Ⓕ The equation has exactly one solution.

    Ⓖ The equation has two solutions.

    Ⓗ The equation has no real solution.

    Ⓙ The number of solutions cannot be determined.

Mixed Review

EVALUATING EXPRESSIONS Evaluate the expression when $x = -2$. (Lessons 1.3, 2.3, 2.5)

71. $2x^3 + 2x + 2$ **72.** $4x^2 + 3x + 5$ **73.** $3x^2 + 4x + 8$ **74.** $x^2 + 7x + 9$

SLOPE AND Y-INTERCEPT Find the slope and y-intercept of the graph of the equation. (Lesson 4.7)

75. $y = 5x + 6$ **76.** $y = -4x + 5$ **77.** $y - 8x = 2$ **78.** $2x + 3y = 6$

SOLVING AND GRAPHING Solve the inequality. Then graph the solution. (Lesson 6.1)

79. $-9 \le x - 7$ **80.** $-15 > x - 8$ **81.** $2 + x < 4$ **82.** $6 \ge x + 1$

SCIENTIFIC NOTATION Write the number in scientific notation. (Lesson 8.5)

83. 0.0000008 **84.** 564 **85.** 8721 **86.** $23,000$

Maintaining Skills

SIMPLIFYING FRACTIONS Write the fraction in simplest form. (Skills Review p. 763)

87. $\dfrac{6}{9}$ **88.** $\dfrac{4}{8}$ **89.** $\dfrac{5}{15}$ **90.** $\dfrac{30}{48}$

91. $\dfrac{20}{24}$ **92.** $\dfrac{50}{100}$ **93.** $\dfrac{12}{16}$ **94.** $\dfrac{28}{35}$

9.3 Simplifying Radicals

Goal
Simplify radical expressions.

Key Words
- radical
- simplest form of a radical expression
- product property of radicals
- quotient property of radicals

What is the maximum speed of a sailboat?

The design of a sailboat affects its maximum speed. In Example 4 you will use a boat's water line length to estimate its maximum speed.

The **simplest form of a radical expression** is an expression that has no perfect square factors other than 1 in the radicand, no fractions in the radicand, and no radicals in the denominator of a fraction. Properties of radicals can be used to simplify expressions that contain radicals.

PRODUCT PROPERTY OF RADICALS

$\sqrt{ab} = \sqrt{a} \cdot \sqrt{b}$ where $a \geq 0$ and $b \geq 0$ **Example:** $\sqrt{4 \cdot 5} = \sqrt{4} \cdot \sqrt{5} = 2\sqrt{5}$

Student Help

▶ STUDY TIP
There can be more than one way to factor the radicand. An efficient method is to find the largest perfect square factor. For example, you can simplify $\sqrt{48}$ using $\sqrt{48} = \sqrt{16 \cdot 3} =$ $\sqrt{16} \cdot \sqrt{3} = 4\sqrt{3}$. ·····

EXAMPLE 1 Simplify with the Product Property

Simplify the expression.

a. $\sqrt{50}$ **b.** $\sqrt{48}$

Solution Look for perfect square factors to remove from the radicand.

a. $\sqrt{50} = \sqrt{25 \cdot 2}$ Factor using perfect square factor.

$\phantom{\sqrt{50}} = \sqrt{25} \cdot \sqrt{2}$ Use product property.

$\phantom{\sqrt{50}} = 5\sqrt{2}$ Simplify: $\sqrt{25} = 5$.

▶**b.** $\sqrt{48} = \sqrt{4 \cdot 12}$ Factor using perfect square factor.

$\phantom{\sqrt{48}} = \sqrt{4 \cdot 4 \cdot 3}$ Factor using perfect square factor.

$\phantom{\sqrt{48}} = \sqrt{4^2} \cdot \sqrt{3}$ Use product property.

$\phantom{\sqrt{48}} = 4\sqrt{3}$ Simplify: $\sqrt{4^2} = 4$.

 **Checkpoint** ✓ **Simplify with the Product Property**

Simplify the expression.

1. $\sqrt{12}$ **2.** $\sqrt{32}$ **3.** $\sqrt{75}$ **4.** $\sqrt{180}$

QUOTIENT PROPERTY OF RADICALS

$$\sqrt{\frac{a}{b}} = \frac{\sqrt{a}}{\sqrt{b}} \text{ where } a \geq 0 \text{ and } b > 0 \qquad \textbf{Example: } \sqrt{\frac{9}{25}} = \frac{\sqrt{9}}{\sqrt{25}} = \frac{3}{5}$$

Student Help

▶ MORE EXAMPLES

More examples are available at www.mcdougallittell.com

EXAMPLE 2 Simplify with the Quotient Property

Simplify $\sqrt{\frac{32}{50}}$.

Solution

$$\sqrt{\frac{32}{50}} = \sqrt{\frac{2 \cdot 16}{2 \cdot 25}} \qquad \text{Factor using perfect square factors.}$$

$$= \sqrt{\frac{16}{25}} \qquad \text{Divide out common factors.}$$

$$= \frac{\sqrt{16}}{\sqrt{25}} \qquad \text{Use quotient property.}$$

$$= \frac{4}{5} \qquad \text{Simplify.}$$

In Example 3 you will see how to eliminate a radical from the denominator by multiplying the radical expression by an appropriate value of 1. This process is called *rationalizing the denominator*.

Student Help

▶ STUDY TIP

$\frac{1}{\sqrt{2}}$ and $\frac{\sqrt{2}}{2}$ are equivalent radical expressions. The second expression is in simplest form with a rational denominator.

EXAMPLE 3 Rationalize the Denominator

Simplify $\sqrt{\frac{1}{18}}$.

Solution

$$\sqrt{\frac{1}{18}} = \frac{\sqrt{1}}{\sqrt{18}} \qquad \text{Use quotient property.}$$

$$= \frac{1}{\sqrt{9} \cdot \sqrt{2}} \qquad \text{Use product property.}$$

$$= \frac{1}{3\sqrt{2}} \qquad \text{Remove perfect square factor.}$$

$$= \frac{1}{3\sqrt{2}} \cdot \frac{\sqrt{2}}{\sqrt{2}} \qquad \text{Multiply by a value of 1: } \frac{\sqrt{2}}{\sqrt{2}} = 1.$$

$$= \frac{\sqrt{2}}{6} \qquad \text{Simplify: } 3\sqrt{2} \cdot \sqrt{2} = 3 \cdot 2 = 6.$$

Checkpoint ✓ **Simplify with the Quotient Property**

Simplify the expression.

5. $\sqrt{\frac{4}{9}}$ **6.** $5\sqrt{\frac{1}{25}}$ **7.** $\sqrt{\frac{1}{3}}$ **8.** $\sqrt{\frac{27}{15}}$

EXAMPLE 4 Simplify a Radical Expression

BOAT SPEED The maximum speed s (in knots, or nautical miles per hour) that certain kinds of boats can travel can be modeled by the quadratic equation $s^2 = \frac{16}{9}x$, where x is the boat's water line length (in feet).

The water line of a boat is the line on the main body of the boat that the surface of the water reaches.

32 ft water line

Use this model to express the maximum speed of a sailboat with a 32 foot water line in terms of radicals. Then find the speed to the nearest tenth.

Solution

$s^2 = \frac{16}{9}x$		Write quadratic model.
$s^2 = \frac{16}{9} \cdot 32$		Substitute 32 for x.
$\sqrt{s^2} = \sqrt{\frac{16}{9} \cdot 32}$		Find square root of each side.
$s = \frac{\sqrt{16}}{\sqrt{9}} \cdot \sqrt{32}$		Use quotient and product properties.
$= \frac{4}{3} \cdot 4\sqrt{2}$		Remove perfect square factors from radicands.
$= \frac{16\sqrt{2}}{3}$		Multiply.
≈ 7.5		Use a calculator or square root table.

ANSWER ▶ The sailboat's maximum speed is $\frac{16\sqrt{2}}{3}$ knots, or approximately 7.5 knots.

Checkpoint ✓ *Simplify a Radical Expression*

9. Use the model in Example 4 to express the maximum speed of a sailboat with a 50 foot water line in terms of radicals. Then find the speed to the nearest tenth.

SUMMARY

Simplest Form of a Radical Expression

- No perfect square factors other than 1 are in the radicand. $\sqrt{8}$ ⟹ $\sqrt{4 \cdot 2}$ ⟹ $2\sqrt{2}$

- No fractions are in the radicand. $\sqrt{\frac{5}{16}}$ ⟹ $\frac{\sqrt{5}}{\sqrt{16}}$ ⟹ $\frac{\sqrt{5}}{4}$

- No radicals are in the denominator of a fraction. $\frac{1}{\sqrt{7}}$ ⟹ $\frac{1}{\sqrt{7}} \cdot \frac{\sqrt{7}}{\sqrt{7}}$ ⟹ $\frac{\sqrt{7}}{7}$

9.3 Exercises

Guided Practice

Vocabulary Check Determine whether the radical expression is in simplest form. Explain.

1. $\frac{3}{5}\sqrt{2}$ **2.** $\sqrt{\frac{3}{16}}$ **3.** $5\sqrt{40}$ **4.** $\frac{1}{\sqrt{2}}$

Skill Check Match the radical expression with its simplest form.

5. $\sqrt{45}$ **6.** $\sqrt{98}$ **7.** $\sqrt{75}$ **8.** $\sqrt{54}$

A. $3\sqrt{6}$ **B.** $5\sqrt{3}$ **C.** $7\sqrt{2}$ **D.** $3\sqrt{5}$

Simplify the expression.

9. $\sqrt{36}$ **10.** $\sqrt{24}$ **11.** $\sqrt{60}$ **12.** $\sqrt{\frac{64}{25}}$

13. $\sqrt{\frac{15}{16}}$ **14.** $\frac{1}{2}\sqrt{20}$ **15.** $\sqrt{\frac{2}{5}}$ **16.** $9\sqrt{\frac{1}{3}}$

Practice and Applications

SIMPLEST FORM Determine whether the radical expression is in simplest form. Explain.

17. $\frac{19}{\sqrt{9}}$ **18.** $3\sqrt{20}$ **19.** $5\sqrt{31}$ **20.** $\sqrt{\frac{2}{8}}$

PRODUCT PROPERTY Simplify the expression.

21. $\sqrt{44}$ **22.** $\sqrt{54}$ **23.** $\sqrt{18}$ **24.** $\sqrt{56}$

25. $\sqrt{27}$ **26.** $\sqrt{63}$ **27.** $\sqrt{200}$ **28.** $\sqrt{90}$

29. $\sqrt{125}$ **30.** $\sqrt{132}$ **31.** $\sqrt{144}$ **32.** $\sqrt{196}$

QUOTIENT PROPERTY Simplify the expression.

33. $\sqrt{\frac{4}{16}}$ **34.** $\sqrt{\frac{9}{49}}$ **35.** $\sqrt{\frac{4}{25}}$ **36.** $\sqrt{\frac{81}{100}}$

37. $\sqrt{\frac{36}{25}}$ **38.** $\sqrt{\frac{7}{9}}$ **39.** $\sqrt{\frac{11}{81}}$ **40.** $\sqrt{\frac{5}{4}}$

41. $\sqrt{\frac{18}{32}}$ **42.** $\sqrt{\frac{27}{36}}$ **43.** $\sqrt{\frac{10}{162}}$ **44.** $\sqrt{\frac{12}{147}}$

ERROR ANALYSIS In Exercises 45 and 46, find and correct the error.

45. $\sqrt{20} = \sqrt{2 \cdot 10} = 2\sqrt{10}$

46. $\frac{\sqrt{9}}{3} = 3$

Student Help

▶ **HOMEWORK HELP**
Example 1: Exs. 21–32, 59–74
Example 2: Exs. 33–44, 59–74
Example 3: Exs. 47–58, 59–74
Example 4: Exs. 75, 76

RATIONALIZING THE DENOMINATOR Simplify the expression.

47. $\sqrt{\dfrac{1}{5}}$ **48.** $\sqrt{\dfrac{5}{6}}$ **49.** $\sqrt{\dfrac{1}{2}}$ **50.** $\sqrt{\dfrac{3}{5}}$

51. $\sqrt{\dfrac{5}{15}}$ **52.** $\sqrt{\dfrac{3}{21}}$ **53.** $\sqrt{\dfrac{4}{10}}$ **54.** $\sqrt{\dfrac{4}{3}}$

55. $\sqrt{\dfrac{1}{11}}$ **56.** $\sqrt{\dfrac{3}{2}}$ **57.** $\sqrt{\dfrac{25}{3}}$ **58.** $\sqrt{\dfrac{16}{10}}$

SIMPLIFYING Write the radical expression in simplest form.

59. $4\sqrt{25}$ **60.** $9\sqrt{100}$ **61.** $-2\sqrt{27}$ **62.** $\dfrac{1}{3}\sqrt{63}$

63. $-6\sqrt{4}$ **64.** $3\sqrt{44}$ **65.** $-\dfrac{1}{7}\sqrt{49}$ **66.** $\dfrac{1}{2}\sqrt{32}$

67. $\dfrac{3}{2}\sqrt{24}$ **68.** $\dfrac{1}{8}\sqrt{56}$ **69.** $-\dfrac{1}{2}\sqrt{360}$ **70.** $\sqrt{\dfrac{48}{81}}$

71. $\sqrt{\dfrac{21}{35}}$ **72.** $-4\sqrt{\dfrac{1}{10}}$ **73.** $6\sqrt{\dfrac{5}{9}}$ **74.** $2\sqrt{\dfrac{6}{18}}$

TSUNAMI In Exercises 75–77, use the following information. A *tsunami* is a destructive, fast-moving ocean wave that is caused by an undersea earthquake, landslide, or volcano. Scientists can predict arrival times of tsunamis by using water depth to calculate the speed of a tsunami.

A model for the speed s (in meters per second) at which a tsunami moves is $s = \sqrt{gd}$ where d is the depth (in meters) and g is 9.8 meters per second per second.

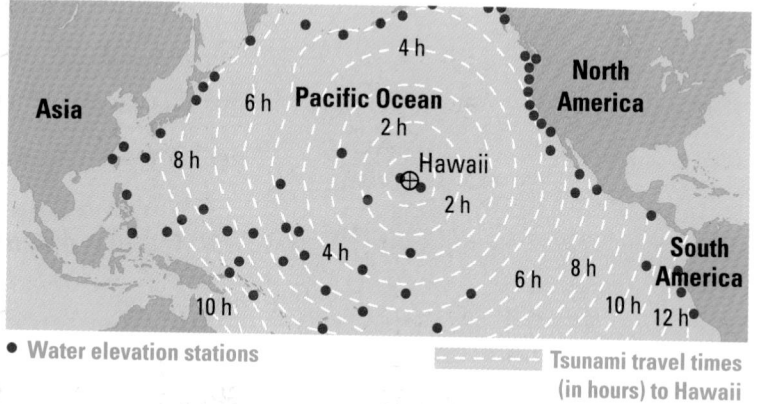

• Water elevation stations   ------ Tsunami travel times (in hours) to Hawaii

75. Find the speed of a tsunami in a region of the ocean that is 1000 meters deep. Write your solution in simplest form.

76. Find the speed of a tsunami in a region of the ocean that is 4000 meters deep. Write your solution in simplest form.

77. CRITICAL THINKING Is the speed of a tsunami in water that is 4000 meters deep four times the speed of a tsunami in water that is 1000 meters? Explain why or why not.

Geometry Link In Exercises 78 and 79, use the formula $A = \ell w$ to find
the area of the figure. Write your solution in simplest form.

78.

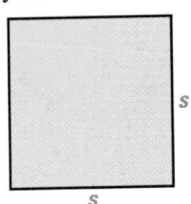

$\sqrt{10}$

$\sqrt{20}$

79.

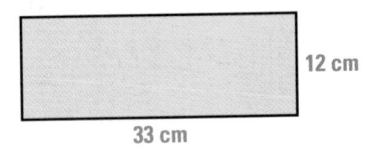

$7\sqrt{2}$

$7\sqrt{2}$

80. **Puzzler** Find the length of a side s of a square that has the same area
as a rectangle that is 12 centimeters wide and 33 centimeters long. Write
your solution in simplest form.

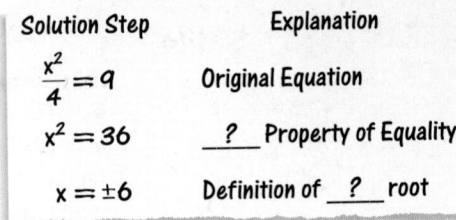

s

s

12 cm

33 cm

81. LOGICAL REASONING Copy
and complete the *proof* of the
following statement:

If $\frac{x^2}{4} = 9$, then $x = \pm 6$.

Solution Step	Explanation
$\dfrac{x^2}{4} = 9$	Original Equation
$x^2 = 36$	__?__ Property of Equality
$x = \pm 6$	Definition of __?__ root

CHALLENGE Write the radical expression in simplest form.

82. $3\sqrt{63} \cdot \sqrt{4}$

83. $-2\sqrt{27} \cdot \sqrt{3}$

84. $\sqrt{9} \cdot 4\sqrt{25}$

85. $\frac{1}{2}\sqrt{32} \cdot \sqrt{2}$

86. $-\sqrt{4} \cdot \dfrac{\sqrt{81}}{\sqrt{36}}$

87. $-5\sqrt{2} \cdot \sqrt{\dfrac{9}{50}}$

88. MULTIPLE CHOICE Which is the simplest form of $\sqrt{80}$?

(A) $2\sqrt{5}$ (B) $4\sqrt{5}$ (C) $2\sqrt{20}$ (D) 20

89. MULTIPLE CHOICE Which is the simplest form of $\dfrac{\sqrt{125}}{\sqrt{25}}$?

(F) $\sqrt{5}$ (G) $2\sqrt{5}$ (H) 5 (J) $5\sqrt{5}$

90. MULTIPLE CHOICE Which of the following does *not* equal $\sqrt{48}$?

(A) $\sqrt{2} \cdot \sqrt{24}$ (B) $2\sqrt{12}$ (C) $4\sqrt{3}$ (D) $12\sqrt{16}$

91. MULTIPLE CHOICE Which step would you use to rationalize the
denominator of $\dfrac{\sqrt{3}}{\sqrt{10}}$?

(F) Multiply by $\dfrac{\sqrt{10}}{\sqrt{10}}$.

(G) Multiply by $\dfrac{\sqrt{10}}{\sqrt{3}}$.

(H) Multiply by $\sqrt{10}$.

(J) Multiply by 10.

GRAPHING EQUATIONS Use a table to graph the equation. *(Lesson 4.2)*

92. $y = x + 5$ **93.** $x + y = -4$ **94.** $y = 3x - 1$ **95.** $2x + y = 6$

POWER OF A PRODUCT Simplify the expression. *(Lesson 8.1)*

96. $(5 \cdot 2)^5$ **97.** $(3x)^4$ **98.** $(-5x)^3$ **99.** $(-3 \cdot 4)^2$

100. $(ab)^6$ **101.** $(8xy)^2$ **102.** $(-3mn)^4$ **103.** $(-abc)^3$

DOMAIN AND RANGE Use the graph to describe the domain and the range of the function. *(Lesson 8.3)*

104. $y = 4^x$

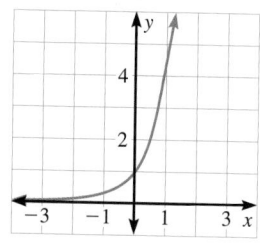

105. $y = -4^x$

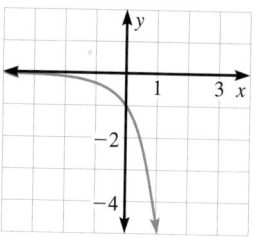

FRACTION OPERATIONS Divide. Write the answer as a fraction or as a mixed number in simplest form. *(Skills Review p. 765)*

106. $\dfrac{1}{2} \div 4$ **107.** $\dfrac{3}{4} \div 3$ **108.** $\dfrac{7}{8} \div \dfrac{3}{4}$ **109.** $\dfrac{1}{5} \div \dfrac{8}{15}$

110. $\dfrac{4}{5} \div 10$ **111.** $\dfrac{2}{3} \div 63$ **112.** $\dfrac{5}{6} \div \dfrac{1}{5}$ **113.** $\dfrac{7}{10} \div 7$

Quiz 1

Evaluate the expression. *(Lesson 9.1)*

1. $\sqrt{81}$ **2.** $-\sqrt{25}$ **3.** $\sqrt{16}$ **4.** $-\sqrt{4}$

5. $\pm\sqrt{1}$ **6.** $\sqrt{100}$ **7.** $\pm\sqrt{49}$ **8.** $\sqrt{121}$

Solve the equation or write *no real solution*. Write the solutions as integers if possible. Otherwise, write them as radical expressions. *(Lesson 9.2)*

9. $x^2 = 64$ **10.** $x^2 = 63$ **11.** $-8x^2 = -48$

12. $12x^2 = -120$ **13.** $4x^2 = 64$ **14.** $5x^2 - 44 = 81$

Write the expression in simplest form. *(Lesson 9.3)*

15. $\sqrt{18}$ **16.** $\sqrt{60}$ **17.** $\dfrac{1}{5}\sqrt{75}$ **18.** $-3\sqrt{9}$

19. $2\sqrt{120}$ **20.** $\dfrac{1}{3}\sqrt{12}$ **21.** $\dfrac{\sqrt{45}}{9}$ **22.** $\sqrt{\dfrac{5}{20}}$

23. $\sqrt{\dfrac{5}{16}}$ **24.** $\sqrt{\dfrac{32}{4}}$ **25.** $\sqrt{\dfrac{2}{3}}$ **26.** $\sqrt{\dfrac{36}{5}}$

DEVELOPING CONCEPTS
Graphing Quadratic Functions

GOAL

Use reasoning to discover how the value of a affects the graph of $y = ax^2$.

MATERIALS

• graph paper
• pencil

Question What is the shape of the graph of $y = ax^2$ and $y = -ax^2$?

In this Developing Concepts, you will explore the shape of a quadratic function and how the value of the leading coefficient a affects the shape of the graph.

Explore

❶ Complete the table of values for $y = x^2$. The value of a is 1.

x	−3	−2	−1	0	1	2	3
y	?	?	?	?	?	?	?

❷ Complete the table of values for $y = -x^2$. The value of a is −1.

x	−3	−2	−1	0	1	2	3
y	?	?	?	?	?	?	?

The graphs of $y = x^2$ and $y = -x^2$ are shown below on the same coordinate plane. Use them to help you answer the following questions.

Think About It

1. How would you describe the shape of each graph?

2. In what direction (*up or down*) does the graph of $y = x^2$ open?

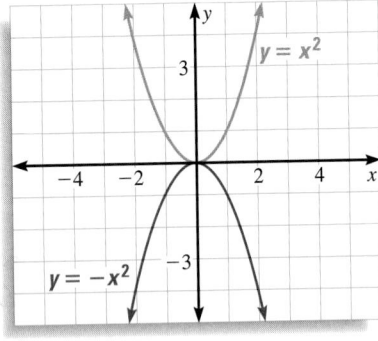

3. Does the graph of $y = x^2$ have a highest point or a lowest point?

4. In what direction (*up or down*) does the graph of $y = -x^2$ open?

5. Does the graph of $y = -x^2$ have a highest point or a lowest point?

6. Use the tables to compare the values of y for $y = x^2$ and $y = -x^2$. What is the value of y for each function when $x = 2$? when $x = 0$? when $x = -1$?

7. Generalize your results and complete the statement: For every point (k, k^2) on the graph of $y = x^2$, there is a corresponding point $(k, \underline{\quad?\quad})$ on the graph of $y = -x^2$.

8. The graph of $y = x^2$ is a *reflection*, or mirror image, of the graph of $y = -x^2$. The line of reflection is $y = \underline{\quad?\quad}$.

Question What happens to the shape of the graph of $y = ax^2$ when $|a|$ increases?

Explore

❶ Sketch the graphs of $y = \frac{1}{2}x^2$, $y = x^2$, and $y = 2x^2$ on the same coordinate plane by plotting points and connecting them with a smooth curve.

Think About It

1. Do the graphs open up or down?

2. Identify the lowest point on each graph.

3. Describe how changing the value of a from $\frac{1}{2}$ to 1 to 2 changes the shape of the graph of $y = ax^2$.

You have just explored how the graph of $y = ax^2$ changes when the value of a is positive and increases. On page 518 you explored how the graphs of $y = ax^2$ and $y = -ax^2$ are related. Use this information to help you in the next section.

Explore

❷ Predict how changing the value of a from $-\frac{1}{2}$ to -1 to -2 changes the shape of the graph of $y = ax^2$. Check your prediction by sketching the graphs of $y = -\frac{1}{2}x^2$, $y = -x^2$, and $y = -2x^2$ in the same coordinate plane that you used for the Explore at the top of the page.

Think About It

1. Do the graphs open up or down?

2. Identify the highest point on each graph.

3. Describe how changing the value of a from $-\frac{1}{2}$ to -1 to -2 changes the shape of the graph of $y = ax^2$.

4. Generalize your results and complete the statement: As $|a|$ increases, the graph of $y = ax^2$ becomes __?__ .

Determine whether the graph of the function opens *up* or *down* and whether the graph is *wider* or *narrower* than the graph of $y = x^2$.

5. $y = 5x^2$ **6.** $y = -4x^2$ **7.** $y = \frac{1}{4}x^2$

9.4 Graphing Quadratic Functions

Goal
Sketch the graph of a quadratic function.

Key Words
- quadratic function
- parabola
- vertex
- axis of symmetry

How high was the shot put?

In Exercise 48 you will find the highest point of a parabola to estimate the highest point on the path of a record-breaking shot-put throw.

A **quadratic function** is a function that can be written in the standard form

$$y = ax^2 + bx + c, \text{ where } a \neq 0.$$

Every quadratic function has a U-shaped graph called a **parabola**. As you saw in Developing Concepts 9.4, pages 518-519, the parabola opens up if the value of a is positive. The parabola opens down if the value of a is negative.

EXAMPLE 1 Describe the Graph of a Parabola

a.

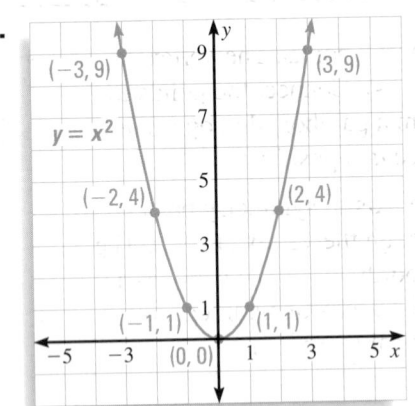

b.

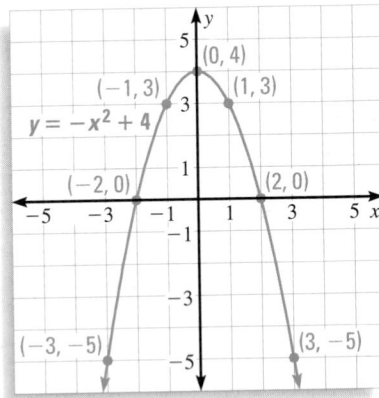

a. The graph of $y = x^2$ opens up. The lowest point is $(0, 0)$.

b. The graph of $y = -x^2 + 4$ opens down. The highest point is $(0, 4)$.

Checkpoint ✓ **Describe the Graph of a Parabola**

Decide whether the parabola opens *up* or *down*.

1. $y = -x^2$ **2.** $y = 2x^2 - 4$ **3.** $y = -3x^2 + 5x - 1$

The **vertex** is the highest or lowest point on a parabola. The vertical line passing through the vertex that divides the parabola into two symmetric parts is called the **axis of symmetry**. The two symmetric parts are mirror images of each other.

GRAPHING A QUADRATIC FUNCTION

The graph of $y = ax^2 + bx + c$, where $a \neq 0$, is a parabola.

STEP ❶ **Find** the x-coordinate of the vertex, which is $x = -\dfrac{b}{2a}$.

STEP ❷ **Make** a table of values, using x-values to the left and right of the vertex.

STEP ❸ **Plot** the points and connect them with a smooth curve to form a parabola.

EXAMPLE **2** **Graph Quadratic Function with Positive *a*-Value**

Sketch the graph of $y = x^2 - 2x - 3$.

Solution In this quadratic function, $a = 1$, $b = -2$, and $c = -3$.

❶ **Find** the x-coordinate of the vertex. $-\dfrac{b}{2a} = -\dfrac{-2}{2(1)} = 1$

❷ **Make** a table of values, using x-values to the left and right of $x = 1$.

x	−2	−1	0	1	2	3	4
y	5	0	−3	−4	−3	0	5

Student Help

▶**STUDY TIP**
If you fold the graph along the axis of symmetry, the two halves of the parabola will match up exactly.

❸ **Plot** the points. The vertex is $(1, -4)$. Connect the points to form a parabola that opens up since a is positive.

The axis of symmetry passes through the vertex $(1, -4)$. The x-coordinate of the vertex is 1, and the axis of symmetry is the vertical line $x = 1$.

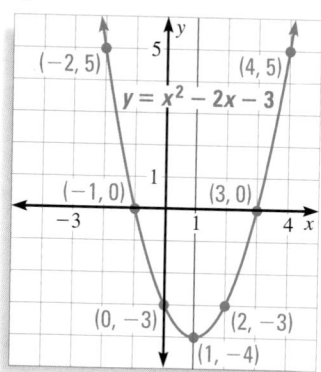

The axis of symmetry of $y = ax^2 + bx + c$ is the vertical line $x = -\dfrac{b}{2a}$.

Checkpoint ✓ **Graph a Quadratic Function with a Positive a-Value**

Sketch the graph of the function. Label the coordinates of the vertex.

4. $y = x^2 + 2$ **5.** $y = 2x^2 - 4x - 1$ **6.** $y = x^2 + 2x$

EXAMPLE 3 **Graph Quadratic Function with Negative a-Value**

Sketch the graph of $y = -x^2 - 3x + 1$.

Solution

In this quadratic function, $a = -1$, $b = -3$, and $c = 1$.

❶ **Find** the x-coordinate of the vertex: $-\dfrac{b}{2a} = -\dfrac{-3}{2(-1)} = -\dfrac{3}{2}$, or $-1\dfrac{1}{2}$.

This tells you that the axis of symmetry is the vertical line $x = -1\dfrac{1}{2}$.

Student Help

▶ **STUDY TIP**
If the x-coordinate of the vertex is a fraction, you can still choose whole numbers when you make a table.

❷ **Make** a table of values, using x-values to the left and right of $x = -1\dfrac{1}{2}$.

x	−4	−3	−2	$-1\dfrac{1}{2}$	−1	0	1
y	−3	1	3	$3\dfrac{1}{4}$	3	1	−3

❸ **Plot** the points. The vertex is $\left(-1\dfrac{1}{2}, 3\dfrac{1}{4}\right)$. Connect the points to form a parabola that opens down since a is negative.

To find the y-intercept of $y = -x^2 - 3x + 1$, let $x = 0$. The y-intercept is 1.

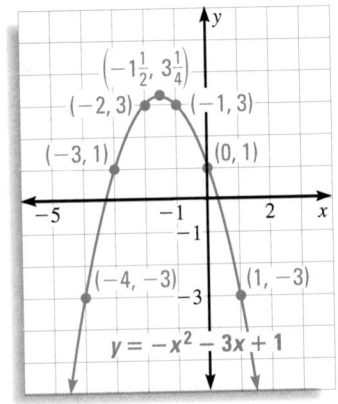

Since $y = c$ when $x = 0$ in $y = ax^2 + bx + c$, the y-intercept of the graph is c.

Checkpoint ✔ **Graph a Quadratic Function with a Negative a-Value**

Sketch the graph of the function. Label the coordinates of the vertex.

7. $y = -x^2 + 1$ **8.** $y = -x^2 + 3x$ **9.** $y = -2x^2 + 4x + 1$

SUMMARY

Graph of a Quadratic Function

The graph of $y = ax^2 + bx + c$ is a parabola.

- If a is positive, the parabola opens up.
- If a is negative, the parabola opens down.
- The vertex has an x-coordinate of $-\dfrac{b}{2a}$.
- The axis of symmetry is the vertical line $x = -\dfrac{b}{2a}$.
- The y-intercept is c.

9.4 Exercises

Guided Practice

Vocabulary Check

1. Identify the values of a, b, and c for the quadratic function in standard form $y = -5x^2 + 7x - 4$.

2. What is the U-shaped graph of a quadratic function called?

Skill Check

Decide whether the graph of the quadratic function opens *up* or *down*.

3. $y = x^2 + 4x - 1$ **4.** $y = 3x^2 + 8x + 6$ **5.** $y = -x^2 + 7x - 3$

6. $y = -x^2 - 4x + 2$ **7.** $y = 5x^2 - 2x + 4$ **8.** $y = -8x^2 - 4$

Sketch the graph of the function. Label the coordinates of the vertex. Write an equation for the axis of symmetry.

9. $y = -3x^2$ **10.** $y = -5x^2 + 10$ **11.** $y = x^2 + 4$

12. $y = x^2 - 6x + 8$ **13.** $y = -3x^2 + 6x + 2$ **14.** $y = 2x^2 - 8x + 3$

Practice and Applications

DESCRIBING GRAPHS **Decide whether the parabola opens *up* or *down*.**

15. $y = 2x^2$ **16.** $y = -5x^2$ **17.** $y = -7x^2 + 5$

18. $y = 5x + 6x^2 - 1$ **19.** $y = -8x^2 - 9$ **20.** $y = 3x^2 - 2x + 7$

21. $y = -3x^2 + 24x$ **22.** $y = -6x^2 - 15x$ **23.** $y = 8x - x^2$

PREPARING TO GRAPH **Find the coordinates of the vertex. Make a table of values, using *x*-values to the left and to the right of the vertex.**

24. $y = 3x^2$ **25.** $y = 6x^2$ **26.** $y = -12x^2$

27. $y = 2x^2 - 10x$ **28.** $y = -7x^2 + 2x$ **29.** $y = 6x^2 + 2x + 4$

30. $y = 5x^2 + 10x + 7$ **31.** $y = -4x^2 - 4x + 8$ **32.** $y = -x^2 + 8x + 32$

GRAPHS OF FUNCTIONS **Match the quadratic function with its graph.**

33. $y = -x^2 - 3$ **34.** $y = x^2 - 3$ **35.** $y = x^2 - 3x$

Student Help

▶ HOMEWORK HELP
Example 1: Exs. 15–23
Example 2: Exs. 24–32,
    36–44
Example 3: Exs. 24–32,
    36–44

A. 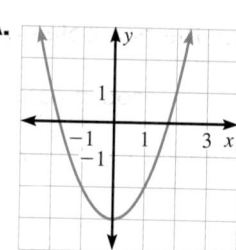   **B.** 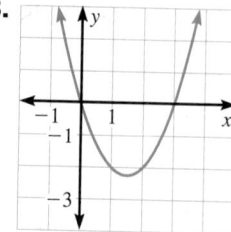   **C.**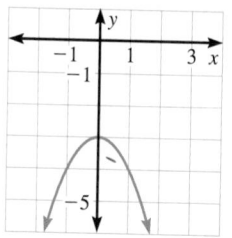

SKETCHING GRAPHS Sketch the graph of the function. Label the coordinates of the vertex.

36. $y = -2x^2$ **37.** $y = 4x^2$ **38.** $y = x^2 + 4x - 1$

39. $y = 4x^2 + 8x - 3$ **40.** $y = x^2 + x + 4$ **41.** $y = 3x^2 - 2x - 1$

42. $y = 2x^2 + 5x - 3$ **43.** $y = -4x^2 + 4x + 7$ **44.** $y = -3x^2 - 3x + 4$

EXAMPLE *Use a Quadratic Model*

TABLE TENNIS The path of a table-tennis ball that bounces over the net can be modeled by $h = -4.9x^2 + 2.07x$, where h is the height above the table (in meters) and x is the time (in seconds). Estimate the maximum height reached by the table-tennis ball. Round to the nearest tenth.

Solution The maximum height of the table-tennis ball occurs at the vertex of the parabolic path. Use $a = -4.9$ and $b = 2.07$ to find the x-coordinate of the vertex. Round your solution to the nearest tenth.

$$-\frac{b}{2a} = -\frac{2.07}{2(-4.9)} \approx 0.2$$

Substitute 0.2 for x in the model and use a calculator to find the maximum height.

$$h = -4.9(0.2)^2 + 2.07(0.2) = 0.218 \approx 0.2$$

ANSWER ▶ The maximum height of the table-tennis ball is about 0.2 meters.

45. **BASKETBALL** You throw a basketball. The height of the ball can be modeled by $h = -16t^2 + 15t + 6$, where h represents the height of the basketball (in feet) and t represents time (in seconds). Find the vertex of the graph of the function. Interpret the result to find the maximum height that the basketball reaches.

Link to
Nature

DOLPHINS follow the path of a parabola when they jump out of the water.

More about dolphins is available at www.mcdougallittell.com

DOLPHINS In Exercises 46 and 47, use the following information.
A bottle-nosed dolphin jumps out of the water. The path the dolphin travels can be modeled by $h = -0.2d^2 + 2d$, where h represents the height of the dolphin and d represents horizontal distance.

46. What is the vertex of the parabola? Interpret the result.

47. What horizontal distance did the dolphin travel?

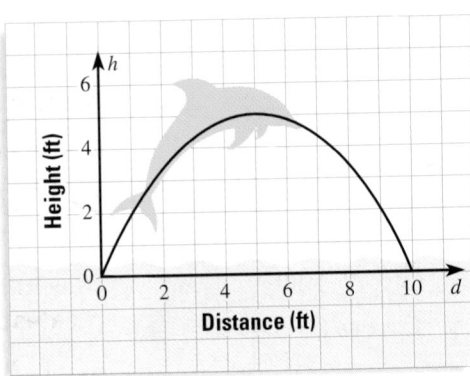

Student Help

▶ **HOMEWORK HELP**

Extra help with problem solving in Exercise 48 is available at www.mcdougallittell.com

48. TRACK AND FIELD Natalya Lisovskaya holds the world record for the women's shot put. The path of her record-breaking throw can be modeled by $h = -0.0137x^2 + 0.9325x + 5.5$, where h is the height (in feet) and x is the horizontal distance (in feet). Use a calculator to find the maximum height of the throw by Lisovskaya. Round to the nearest tenth.

CHALLENGE In Exercises 49–51, sketch the graphs of the three functions in the same coordinate plane. Then describe how the three parabolas are similar to each other and how they are different.

49. $y = -\frac{1}{2}x^2 + x + 1$ **50.** $y = x^2 + x + 1$ **51.** $y = x^2 - x + 1$

$y = -x^2 + x + 1$ $\qquad$ $y = x^2 + 2x + 1$ $\qquad$ $y = x^2 - x + 3$

$y = -2x^2 + x + 1$ $\qquad$ $y = x^2 + 3x + 1$ $\qquad$ $y = x^2 - x - 2$

Standardized Test Practice

52. MULTIPLE CHOICE Which equation is represented by the graph below?

Ⓐ $y = x^2 - 2x + 1$

Ⓑ $y = -x^2 - 2x + 1$

Ⓒ $y = x^2 + 2x + 1$

Ⓓ $y = -x^2 + 2x - 1$

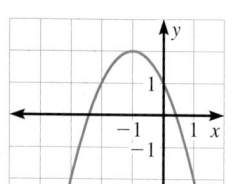

53. MULTIPLE CHOICE What are the coordinates of the vertex of the graph of $y = -2x^2 + 8x - 5$?

Ⓕ $(-2, -29)$ $\qquad$ Ⓖ $(2, 3)$ $\qquad$ Ⓗ $(2, 7)$ $\qquad$ Ⓙ $(4, -5)$

54. MULTIPLE CHOICE What is the axis of symmetry of the graph of $y = x^2 + 3x - 2$?

Ⓐ $x = -\frac{17}{4}$ $\qquad$ Ⓑ $x = -\frac{3}{2}$ $\qquad$ Ⓒ $x = \frac{3}{2}$ $\qquad$ Ⓓ $x = \frac{19}{4}$

Mixed Review

GRAPHING A SYSTEM Graph the system of linear inequalities. (Lesson 7.6)

55. $x - 3y \geq 3$ $\qquad$ **56.** $x + y \leq 5$ $\qquad$ **57.** $x + y < 10$

$x - 3y < 12$ $\qquad\qquad$ $x \geq 2$ $\qquad\qquad$ $2x + y > 10$

$\qquad\qquad\qquad$ $y \geq 0$ $\qquad\qquad$ $x - y < 2$

PRODUCT OF POWERS Write the expression as a single power of the base. (Lesson 8.1)

58. $4^2 \cdot 4^5$ **59.** $(-5) \cdot (-5)^8$ **60.** $x^2 \cdot x^4 \cdot x^6$ **61.** $x^3 \cdot x^5$

62. $t \cdot (t^3)$ **63.** $m \cdot m^4 \cdot m^3$ **64.** $5 \cdot 5^2 \cdot 5^3$ **65.** $2(2)^4$

Maintaining Skills

ORDERING FRACTIONS Write the numbers in order from least to greatest. (Skills Review p. 770)

66. $\frac{1}{2}, \frac{2}{3}, \frac{5}{12}$ **67.** $\frac{1}{3}, \frac{4}{15}, \frac{2}{5}$ **68.** $\frac{3}{5}, \frac{4}{10}, \frac{5}{15}$ **69.** $\frac{9}{10}, \frac{7}{8}, \frac{3}{4}$

9.5 Solving Quadratic Equations by Graphing

Goal
Use a graph to find or check a solution of a quadratic equation.

Key Words
• x-intercept
• roots of a quadratic equation

How far apart are the Golden Gate Bridge towers?

The Golden Gate Bridge in California hangs from steel cables that are supported by two towers. In Example 3 you will use the graph of a parabola to estimate the distance between the towers.

The x-intercepts of the graph of $y = ax^2 + bx + c$ are the solutions of the related equation $ax^2 + bx + c = 0$. Recall that an x-intercept is the x-coordinate of a point where a graph crosses the x-axis. At this point, $y = 0$.

EXAMPLE 1 Use a Graph to Solve an Equation

The graph of $y = \frac{1}{2}x^2 - 8$ is shown at the right. Use the graph to estimate the solutions of $\frac{1}{2}x^2 - 8 = 0$.

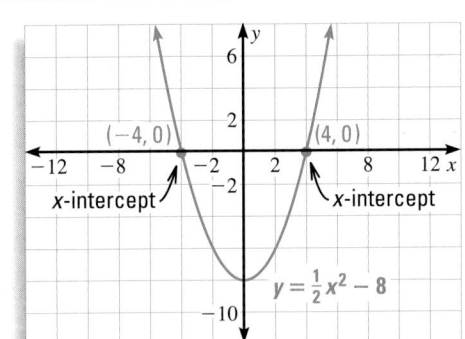

Solution

The graph appears to intersect the x-axis at $(-4, 0)$ and $(4, 0)$. By substituting $x = -4$ and $x = 4$ in $\frac{1}{2}x^2 - 8 = 0$, you can check that -4 and 4 are solutions of the given equation.

Checkpoint ✔ Use a Graph to Solve an Equation

1. The graph of $y = 2x^2 - 4x$ is shown at the right. Use the graph to estimate the solutions of $2x^2 - 4x = 0$. Check your solutions algebraically by substituting each one for x in the given equation.

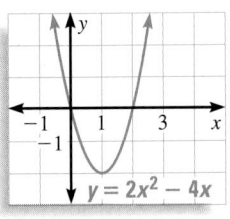

The solutions of a quadratic equation in one variable x can be estimated by graphing. Use the following steps:

STEP ① **Write** the equation in the standard form $ax^2 + bx + c = 0$.

STEP ② **Sketch** the graph of the related quadratic function $y = ax^2 + bx + c$.

STEP ③ **Estimate** the values of the x-intercepts, if any.

The solutions, or **roots**, of $ax^2 + bx + c = 0$ are the x-intercepts of the graph.

Student Help

▶**MORE EXAMPLES**

More examples are available at www.mcdougallittell.com

EXAMPLE 2 Solve an Equation by Graphing

Use a graph to estimate the solutions of $x^2 - x = 2$. Check your solutions algebraically.

Solution

① **Write** the equation in the standard form $ax^2 + bx + c = 0$.

$$x^2 - x = 2 \qquad \text{Write original equation.}$$

$$x^2 - x - 2 = 0 \qquad \text{Subtract 2 from each side.}$$

② **Sketch** the graph of the related quadratic function $y = x^2 - x - 2$.

③ **Estimate** the values of the x-intercepts. From the graph, the x-intercepts appear to be -1 and 2.

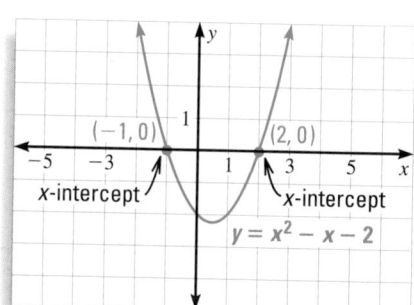

CHECK ✓

You can check your solutions algebraically using substitution.

CHECK $x = -1$:

$$x^2 - x = 2$$

$$(-1)^2 - (-1) \overset{?}{=} 2$$

$$1 + 1 = 2 \checkmark$$

CHECK $x = 2$:

$$x^2 - x = 2$$

$$2^2 - 2 \overset{?}{=} 2$$

$$4 - 2 = 2 \checkmark$$

ANSWER▶ The solutions are -1 and 2.

Checkpoint ✓ Solve an Equation by Graphing

2. Use a graph to estimate the solutions of $x^2 - x = 6$.

3. Check your solutions algebraically.

Student Help

EXAMPLE 3 Points on a Parabola

The main suspension cables of the Golden Gate Bridge form a parabola that can be modeled by the quadratic function

$$y = 0.000112x^2 + 8$$

where x is the horizontal distance from the middle of the bridge (in feet) and y is the vertical distance from the road (in feet).

The cables are connected to the towers at points that are 500 feet above the road. How far apart are the towers?

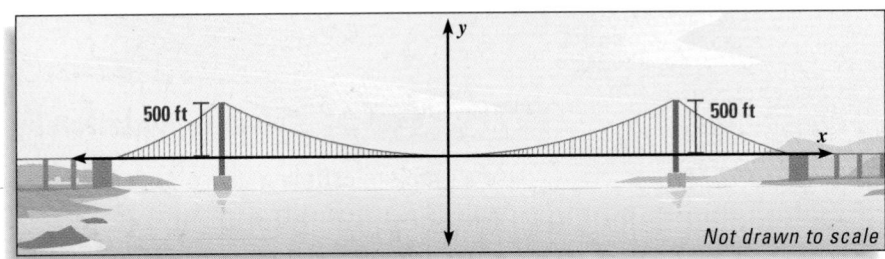

500 ft   500 ft

Not drawn to scale

Solution

You can find the distance between the towers by finding the x-values for which $y = 500$, or $0.000112x^2 + 8 = 500$. Use a graphing calculator to find the solutions of the equation.

Write the equation in the standard form $ax^2 + bx + c = 0$.

$0.000112x^2 + 8 = 500$	Write original equation.
$0.000112x^2 - 492 = 0$	Subtract 500 from each side.

Sketch the graph of the related quadratic function $y = 0.000112x^2 - 492$ using a graphing calculator.

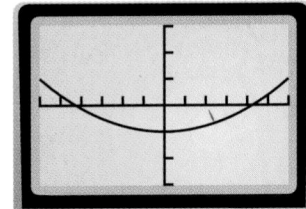

Estimate the values of the x-intercepts. From the graphing calculator screen, you can see that the x-intercepts are approximately -2100 and 2100.

Each tower is approximately 2100 feet from the midpoint. Because the towers are on opposite sides of the midpoint, the distance between the towers is $2100 + 2100 = 4200$.

ANSWER ▶ The towers are approximately 4200 feet apart.

Checkpoint ✔ Points on a Parabola

4. The main suspension cables of the Royal Gorge Bridge can be modeled by the quadratic function $y = 0.0007748x^2$. In the equation, x is the horizontal distance from the middle of the bridge (in feet) and y is the vertical distance from the road (in feet). The cables are connected to the towers at points that are 150 feet above the road. Approximately how far apart are the towers?

9.5 Exercises

Guided Practice

Vocabulary Check

1. What are the roots of a quadratic equation?

2. Explain how you can use a graph to check the solutions of a quadratic equation.

Skill Check

Match the quadratic function with its graph.

3. $y = x^2 - 3$

4. $y = x^2 + x - 4$

5. $y = x^2 - 2x - 1$

A.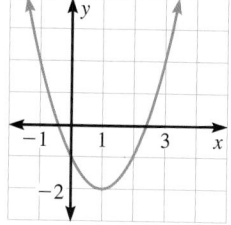

B.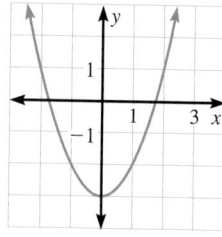

C.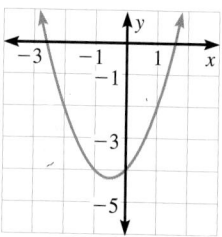

Solve the equation algebraically. Check your solutions by graphing.

6. $3x^2 - 12 = 0$

7. $5x^2 - 5 = 0$

8. $-2x^2 = -18$

Estimate the solutions of the equation by graphing. Check your solutions algebraically.

9. $3x^2 = 48$

10. $x^2 - 4 = 5$

11. $-x^2 + 7x - 10 = 0$

Practice and Applications

WRITING IN STANDARD FORM Write the quadratic equation in standard form.

12. $4x^2 = 12$

13. $x^2 - 6x = -6$

14. $-x^2 = 15$

15. $5 + x = 3x^2$

16. $2x - x^2 = 1$

17. $6x^2 = 12x$

IDENTIFYING THE ROOTS Use the graph to identify the roots of the quadratic equation.

18. $-x^2 + 3x - 2 = 0$

19. $-x^2 - 2x + 3 = 0$

20. $x^2 - 2x - 8 = 0$

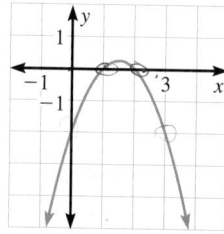

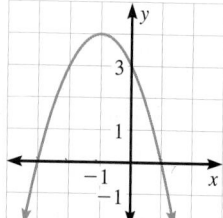

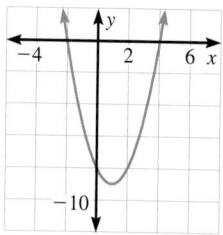

Student Help

▶ **HOMEWORK HELP**
Example 1: Exs. 18–21
Example 2: Exs. 22–45
Example 3: Exs. 47–50, 52

21. CHECKING SOLUTIONS Use substitution to check the solutions of the quadratic equations in Exercises 18–20.

SOLVING GRAPHICALLY Use a graph to estimate the solutions of the equation. Check your solutions algebraically.

22. $x^2 + 2x = 3$

23. $-4x^2 - 8x = -12$

24. $-x^2 + 3x = -4$

25. $2x^2 + 4x = 6$

26. $3x^2 + 3x = 6$

27. $x^2 - 4x - 5 = 0$

28. $x^2 - x = 12$

29. $-x^2 - 4x = -5$

30. $x^2 + x = 2$

31. $-x^2 - x + 6 = 0$

32. $2x^2 - 8x = 10$

33. $-x^2 + x = -2$

CHECKING GRAPHICALLY Solve the equation algebraically. Check your solutions by graphing.

34. $2x^2 = 32$

35. $4x^2 = 100$

36. $4x^2 = 16$

37. $x^2 - 11 = 14$

38. $x^2 - 13 = 36$

39. $x^2 - 4 = 12$

40. $x^2 - 53 = 11$

41. $x^2 + 37 = 118$

42. $2x^2 - 89 = 9$

43. $2x^2 + 8 = 16$

44. $3x^2 + 5 = 32$

45. $2x^2 - 7 = 11$

46. SWISS CHEESE The consumption of Swiss cheese in the United States from 1970 to 1996 can be modeled by $P = -0.002t^2 + 0.056t + 0.889$. P is the number of pounds consumed per person and t is the number of years since 1970.

According to the graph of the model, in what year would the consumption of Swiss cheese drop to 0? Is this a realistic prediction?

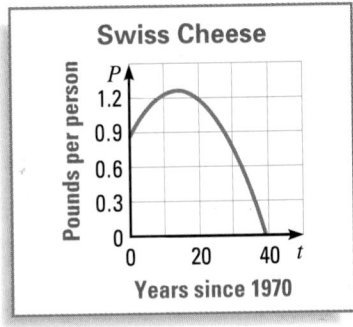

Swiss Cheese

▶ Source: U.S. Department of Agriculture

MICROGRAVITY
Researchers can investigate the effects of microgravity aboard an airplane. A plane can attain low gravity conditions for 15-second periods by repeatedly flying in a parabolic path.

APPROXIMATING SOLUTIONS Use a graphing calculator to approximate the solutions of the equation.

47. $-x^2 - 3x + 4 = 0$

48. $x^2 + 6x - 7 = 0$

49. $-\frac{1}{2}x^2 + 2x + 16 = 0$

50. $\frac{5}{4}x^2 + 15x + 40 = 0$

Science Link In Exercises 51 and 52, use the following information.
Scientists use a state of free fall to simulate a gravity-free environment called *microgravity*. In microgravity conditions, the distance d (in meters) that an object that is dropped falls in t seconds can be modeled by the equation $d = 4.9t^2$.

In Japan a 490-meter-deep mine shaft has been converted into a free-fall facility. This creates the longest period of free fall currently available on Earth. How long is a period of free fall in this facility?

51. Solve the problem algebraically.

52. Use a graphing calculator to check your answer by graphing the related function $y = 4.9x^2 - 490$.

53. MULTIPLE CHOICE What are the x-intercepts of $y = x^2 - 2x - 3$?

   Ⓐ 1 and -3 Ⓑ 2 and -3 Ⓒ 6 and -1 Ⓓ 3 and -1

54. MULTIPLE CHOICE Choose the equation whose roots are shown in the graph.

   Ⓕ $5x^2 - 1 = 0$

   Ⓖ $\frac{1}{5}x^2 - 5 = 0$

   Ⓗ $x^2 - 5 = 0$

   Ⓙ $\frac{1}{5}x^2 - 1 = 0$

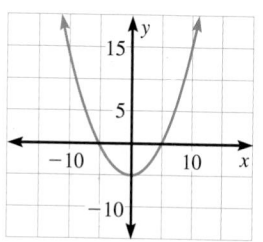

Mixed Review

55. LUNCH TIME At lunch, you order 1 pasta dish and 1 type of salad. Your friend orders 1 pasta dish and 2 types of salads. The restaurant charges the same price for each pasta dish and the same price for each salad. Your bill is $7.90 and your friend's bill is $9.85. How much did each pasta dish and each salad cost? *(Lesson 7.4)*

SOLVING LINEAR SYSTEMS Use the substitution method or linear combinations to solve the linear system and tell how many solutions the system has. *(Lesson 7.5)*

56. $-2x + 8y = 11$
$x + 6y = 2$

57. $-2x + 8y = 10$
$x + 6y = 15$

58. $-2x + 2y = 4$
$x - y = -2$

59. $8x + 4y = -4$
$4x - y = -20$

60. $6x + 4y = -4$
$2x - y = -6$

61. $5x + 4y = -3$
$15x + 12y = 9$

EVALUATING RADICAL EXPRESSIONS Evaluate the radical expression when $a = -1$ and $b = 5$. *(Lesson 9.1)*

62. $\sqrt{b^2 - 11a}$ **63.** $\sqrt{b^2 + 9a}$ **64.** $\sqrt{a^2 + 8}$ **65.** $\sqrt{a^2 - 1}$

66. $\dfrac{\sqrt{b^2 + 24a}}{a}$ **67.** $\dfrac{\sqrt{b^2 - 75a}}{b}$ **68.** $\dfrac{\sqrt{65 - a^2}}{-a}$ **69.** $\dfrac{\sqrt{86 + ab}}{a}$

SIMPLIFYING RADICAL EXPRESSIONS Simplify the radical expression. *(Lesson 9.3)*

70. $\sqrt{40}$ **71.** $\sqrt{24}$ **72.** $\sqrt{60}$ **73.** $\sqrt{200}$

74. $\frac{1}{2}\sqrt{80}$ **75.** $\frac{1}{3}\sqrt{27}$ **76.** $\frac{1}{8}\sqrt{32}$ **77.** $\frac{2}{3}\sqrt{300}$

Maintaining Skills

COMPARING FRACTIONS AND MIXED NUMBERS Complete the statement using <, >, or =. *(Skills Review pp. 763, 770, 771)*

78. $\frac{8}{7}$? $1\frac{1}{7}$ **79.** $\frac{8}{3}$? $2\frac{1}{3}$ **80.** $\frac{17}{5}$? $3\frac{4}{5}$ **81.** $\frac{13}{6}$? $1\frac{1}{6}$

82. $\frac{23}{10}$? $2\frac{3}{10}$ **83.** $\frac{100}{9}$? $11\frac{2}{9}$ **84.** $1\frac{7}{17}$? $1\frac{22}{17}$ **85.** $\frac{9}{4}$? $2\frac{3}{4}$

USING A GRAPHING CALCULATOR
Approximating Solutions

For use with Lesson 9.5

You can use the *root* or *zero* feature of a graphing calculator to approximate the solutions, or roots, of a quadratic equation.

Sample

Approximate the roots of $2x^2 + 3x - 4 = 0$.

Solution

1 Enter the related function $y = 2x^2 + 3x - 4$ into the graphing calculator.

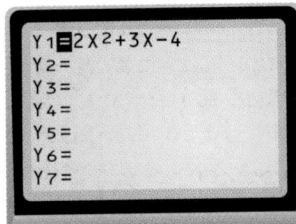

2 Adjust the viewing window so you can see the graph cross the x-axis twice. Graph the function.

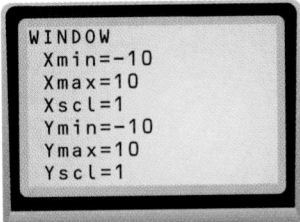

3 Choose the *Root* or *Zero* feature.

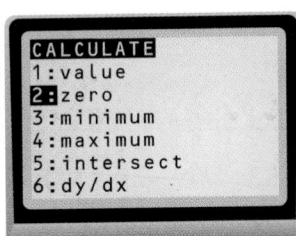

4 Follow your graphing calculator's procedure to find one root.

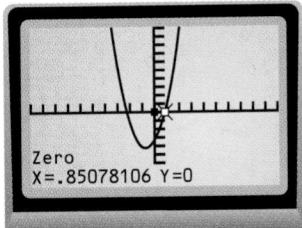

The positive root is approximately 0.85. Follow similar steps to find the negative root, -2.35.

Try These

APPROXIMATING ROOTS In Exercises 1–4, use a graphing calculator to approximate the roots of the quadratic equation to the nearest hundredth.

1. $x^2 - x - 2 = 0$

2. $6x^2 + 4x - 12 = 0$

3. $-4x^2 + 6x + 7 = 0$

4. $-2x^2 + 3x + 6 = 0$

5. Each equation in Exercises 1–4 has two solutions, or roots. How many x-intercepts does each related function have?

6. If a quadratic equation has one solution, how many times do you think the graph of its related function will cross the x-axis? No real solution?

9.6 Solving Quadratic Equations by the Quadratic Formula

Goal
Use the quadratic formula to solve a quadratic equation.

Key Words
• quadratic formula
• vertical motion model

When will a baseball hit the ground?

In Exercise 79 you will use the *quadratic formula* to find how long it takes a baseball to reach the ground after being hit by a batter.

The **quadratic formula** gives the solutions of $ax^2 + bx + c = 0$ in terms of the coefficients a, b, and c. In Lesson 12.5 you will see how the quadratic formula is developed from the standard form of a quadratic equation.

Student Help

▶ READING ALGEBRA
The quadratic formula is read as "x equals the opposite of b, plus or minus the square root of b squared minus $4ac$, all divided by $2a$."

THE QUADRATIC FORMULA

The solutions of the quadratic equation $ax^2 + bx + c = 0$ are

$$x = \frac{-b \pm \sqrt{b^2 - 4ac}}{2a}$$ when $a \neq 0$ and $b^2 - 4ac \geq 0$.

EXAMPLE 1 Use the Quadratic Formula

Solve $x^2 + 9x + 14 = 0$.

Solution $1x^2 + 9x + 14 = 0$ Identify $a = 1$, $b = 9$, and $c = 14$.

$$x = \frac{-9 \pm \sqrt{9^2 - 4(1)(14)}}{2(1)}$$ Substitute values in the quadratic formula: $a = 1$, $b = 9$, and $c = 14$.

$$x = \frac{-9 \pm \sqrt{25}}{2}$$ Simplify.

$$x = \frac{-9 \pm 5}{2}$$ Solutions.

ANSWER ▶ The two solutions are $x = \dfrac{-9 + 5}{2} = -2$ and $x = \dfrac{-9 - 5}{2} = -7$.

Checkpoint ✓ Use the Quadratic Formula

Use the quadratic formula to solve the equation.

1. $x^2 - 4x + 3 = 0$ **2.** $2x^2 + x - 10 = 0$ **3.** $-x^2 + 3x + 4 = 0$

Student Help

▶**MORE EXAMPLES**

More examples
are available at
www.mcdougallittell.com

EXAMPLE 2 Write in Standard Form

Solve $2x^2 - 3x = 8$. Round the results to the nearest hundredth.

Solution

$2x^2 - 3x = 8$	Write original equation.
$2x^2 - 3x - 8 = 0$	Rewrite equation in standard form.
$x = \dfrac{-(-3) \pm \sqrt{(-3)^2 - 4(2)(-8)}}{2(2)}$	Substitute values in the quadratic formula: $a = 2$, $b = -3$, $c = -8$.
$x = \dfrac{3 \pm \sqrt{9 + 64}}{4}$	Simplify.
$x = \dfrac{3 \pm \sqrt{73}}{4}$	Solutions.

ANSWER ▶ The two solutions are $x = \dfrac{3 + \sqrt{73}}{4} \approx 2.89$ and $x = \dfrac{3 - \sqrt{73}}{4} \approx -1.39$.

Checkpoint ✓ **Write in Standard Form**

Use the quadratic formula to solve the equation. If the solution involves radicals, round to the nearest hundredth.

4. $x^2 + x = 1$ **5.** $-x^2 = 2x - 3$ **6.** $7x^2 - 1 = -2x$

Student Help

▶**STUDY TIP**
Recall from Lesson 9.5
that the x-intercepts of
the graph of a quadratic
equation in one variable
are also called the
roots of the equation.

EXAMPLE 3 Find the x-Intercepts of a Graph

Find the x-intercepts, or roots, of the graph of $y = x^2 + 4x - 5$.

Solution The x-intercepts occur when $y = 0$.

$y = x^2 + 4x - 5$	Write original equation.
$0 = 1x^2 + 4x - 5$	Substitute 0 for y.
$x = \dfrac{-4 \pm \sqrt{(4)^2 - 4(1)(-5)}}{2(1)}$	Substitute values in the quadratic formula: $a = 1$, $b = 4$, $c = -5$.
$x = \dfrac{-4 \pm \sqrt{16 + 20}}{2}$	Simplify.
$x = \dfrac{-4 \pm 6}{2}$	Solutions

ANSWER ▶ The two solutions are $x = 1$ and $x = -5$.

CHECK ✓ Use a graph to check your solutions. You can see from the graph that the x-intercepts of $y = x^2 + 4x - 5$ are -5 and 1.

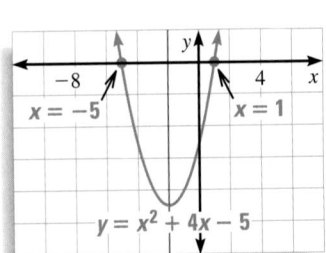

VERTICAL MOTION MODELS In Lesson 9.2 you studied the model for the height of a falling object that is *dropped*. For an object that is *thrown* up or down, the model has an extra term *v*. It is called the initial velocity.

VERTICAL MOTION MODELS

Object is dropped: $h = -16t^2 + s$ **Object is thrown:** $h = -16t^2 + vt + s$

h = height (feet) t = time in motion (seconds)

s = initial height (feet) v = initial velocity (feet per second)

EXAMPLE 4 Model Vertical Motion

HOT-AIR BALLOONS You are competing in the field target event at a hot-air balloon festival. From a hot-air balloon directly over a target, you throw a marker with an initial downward velocity of −30 feet per second from a height of 200 feet. How long does it take the marker to reach the target?

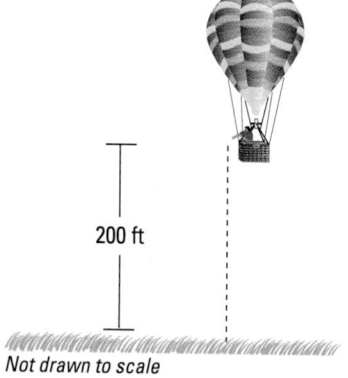

200 ft

Not drawn to scale

Solution The marker is thrown *down*, so the initial velocity *v* is −30 feet per second. The initial height *s* is 200 feet. The marker will hit the target when its height is 0.

$h = -16t^2 + vt + s$ Choose the vertical motion model for a thrown object.

$h = -16t^2 + (-30)t + 200$ Substitute values for *v* and *s* in the vertical motion model.

$0 = -16t^2 - 30t + 200$ Substitute 0 for *h*. Write in standard form.

$t = \dfrac{-(-30) \pm \sqrt{(-30)^2 - 4(-16)(200)}}{2(-16)}$ Substitute values for *a*, *b*, and *c* in the quadratic formula.

$t = \dfrac{30 \pm \sqrt{13{,}700}}{-32}$ Simplify.

$t \approx 2.72$ or -4.60 Evaluate the radical expressions.

ANSWER ▶ The weighted marker will reach the ground about 2.72 seconds after it was thrown. The solution −4.60 doesn't make sense in this problem.

Checkpoint ✓ *Model Vertical Motion*

7. In Example 4, suppose you throw a marker with an initial downward velocity of −60 feet per second. Do you think it would hit the ground in half the time? Check your prediction using the quadratic formula.

Guided Practice

Vocabulary Check

1. Write the formula that you can use to solve any quadratic equation when $a \neq 0$ and $b^2 - 4ac \geq 0$.

2. Describe how you can check the solutions of a quadratic equation by looking at the graph of the related function.

3. What new feature was introduced in the vertical motion model used in Example 4?

Skill Check

Write the equation in standard form. Identify the values of *a*, *b*, and *c* that you would use to solve the equation using the quadratic formula.

4. $x^2 = 1$

5. $16x - 32 = 2x^2$

6. $x^2 - 7x + 42 = 6x$

Use the quadratic formula to solve the equation. Write your solutions in simplest form.

7. $x^2 + 6x - 7 = 0$

8. $x^2 - 2x - 15 = 0$

9. $x^2 + 12x + 36 = 0$

10. $4x^2 - 8x + 3 = 0$

11. $3x^2 + x - 1 = 0$

12. $x^2 + 6x - 3 = 0$

Write the equation in standard form. Then use the quadratic formula to solve the equation.

13. $2x^2 = -x + 6$

14. $-3x = 2x^2 + 1$

15. $2 = x^2 - x$

16. $-14x = -2x^2 + 36$

17. $-x^2 + 4x = 3$

18. $4x^2 + 4x = -1$

Practice and Applications

STANDARD FORM Write the equation in standard form. Identify the values of *a*, *b*, and *c*.

19. $3x^2 = 3x + 6$

20. $-2t^2 = -8$

21. $-x^2 = -5x + 6$

22. $3x^2 = 27x$

23. $-24x + 45 = -3x^2$

24. $32 - 4m^2 = 28m$

25. $k^2 = \dfrac{1}{4}$

26. $2x^2 - \dfrac{1}{5} = -\dfrac{2}{5}x$

27. $\dfrac{1}{3} - 2x = \dfrac{2}{3}x^2$

FINDING VALUES Find the value of $b^2 - 4ac$ for the equation.

28. $x^2 - 3x - 4 = 0$

29. $4x^2 + 5x + 1 = 0$

30. $-5w^2 - 3w + 2 = 0$

31. $r^2 - 11r + 30 = 0$

32. $s^2 - 13s + 42 = 0$

33. $3x^2 - 5x - 12 = 0$

34. $2x^2 + 4x - 1 = 0$

35. $3t^2 - 8t - 7 = 0$

36. $-8m^2 - 6m + 3 = 0$

37. $5x^2 + 5x + \dfrac{1}{5} = 0$

38. $\dfrac{1}{2}t^2 + 5t - 8 = 0$

39. $\dfrac{1}{4}v^2 - 6v - 3 = 0$

Student Help

▶ **HOMEWORK HELP**
Example 1: Exs. 40–48
Example 2: Exs. 49–57
Example 3: Exs. 58–66
Example 4: Exs. 67–80

SOLVING EQUATIONS Use the quadratic formula to solve the equation. If the solution involves radicals, round to the nearest hundredth.

40. $4x^2 - 13x + 3 = 0$ **41.** $y^2 + 11y + 10 = 0$ **42.** $7x^2 + 8x + 1 = 0$

43. $-3y^2 + 2y + 8 = 0$ **44.** $6n^2 - 10n + 3 = 0$ **45.** $9x^2 + 14x + 3 = 0$

46. $8m^2 + 6m - 1 = 0$ **47.** $-\frac{1}{2}x^2 + 6x + 13 = 0$ **48.** $2x^2 - 3x + 1 = 0$

STANDARD FORM Write the quadratic equation in standard form. Then solve using the quadratic formula.

49. $2x^2 = 4x + 30$ **50.** $x^2 + 3x = -2$ **51.** $5 = x^2 + 6x$

52. $5x + 2 = 2x^2$ **53.** $5x - 2x^2 + 15 = 8$ **54.** $-2 + x^2 = -x$

55. $x^2 - 2x = 3$ **56.** $2x^2 + 4 = 6x$ **57.** $12 = 2x^2 - 2x$

FINDING INTERCEPTS Find the *x*-intercepts of the graph of the function.

58. $y = -x^2 + x + 6$ **59.** $y = x^2 + 5x + 6$ **60.** $y = x^2 - 11x + 24$

61. $y = x^2 + 10x + 16$ **62.** $y = -x^2 - 4x + 2$ **63.** $y = 2x^2 - 6x - 8$

64. $y = x^2 - 2x - 2$ **65.** $y = 2x^2 + 4x - 6$ **66.** $y = -3x^2 + 17x - 20$

Link to
Ecology

FIELD TARGET EVENT In Exercises 67–72, six balloonists compete in a field target event at a hot-air balloon festival. Calculate the amount of time it takes for the marker to reach the target when thrown down from the given initial height (in feet) with the given initial downward velocity (in feet per second). Round to the nearest hundredth of a second.

67. $s = 200; v = -50$ **68.** $s = 150; v = -25$ **69.** $s = 100; v = -10$

70. $s = 150; v = -33$ **71.** $s = 50; v = -40$ **72.** $s = 50; v = -20$

URBAN BIRDS Cities provide a habitat for many species of wildlife including birds of prey such as peregrine falcons and red-tailed hawks.

More about urban birds is available at www.mcdougallittell.com

73. PEREGRINE FALCON A falcon dives toward a pigeon on the ground. When the falcon is at a height of 100 feet, the pigeon sees the falcon, which is diving at 220 feet per second. Estimate the time the pigeon has to escape. Round your solution to the nearest tenth of a second.

74. RED-TAILED HAWK A hawk dives toward a snake. When the hawk is at a height of 200 feet, the snake sees the hawk, which is diving at 105 feet per second. Estimate the time the snake has to escape. Round your solution to the nearest tenth of a second.

▶ HOMEWORK HELP

INTERNET Extra help with
problem solving in
Exs. 75–78 is available at
www.mcdougallittell.com

VERTICAL MOTION In Exercises 75–78, use a vertical motion model to find how long it will take for the object to reach the ground. Round your solution to the nearest tenth.

75. You drop your keys from a window 30 feet above ground to your friend below. Your friend does not catch them.

76. An acorn falls 45 feet from the top of a tree.

77. A lacrosse player throws a ball upward from her playing stick from an initial height of 7 feet, with an initial velocity of 90 feet per second.

78. You throw a ball downward with an initial velocity of -10 feet per second out of a window to a friend 20 feet below. Your friend does not catch the ball.

79. **BASEBALL** A batter hits a pitched baseball when it is 3 feet off the ground. After it is hit, the height h (in feet) of the ball is modeled by $h = -16t^2 + 80t + 3$, where t is the time (in seconds). How long will it take for the ball to hit the ground? Round to the nearest hundredth.

80. **Science Link** An astronaut standing on the moon's surface throws a rock upward with an initial velocity of 50 feet per second. The height of the rock can be modeled by $m = -2.7t^2 + 50t + 6$, where m is the height of the rock (in feet) and t is the time (in seconds). If the astronaut throws the same rock upward with the same initial velocity on Earth, the height of the rock is modeled by $e = -16t^2 + 50t + 6$. Would the rock hit the ground in less time on the moon or on Earth? Explain your answer.

Standardized Test Practice

81. **MULTIPLE CHOICE** Which expression gives the solutions of $2x^2 - 10 = x$?

Ⓐ $\dfrac{1 \pm \sqrt{1 - (4)(2)(-10)}}{4}$

Ⓑ $\dfrac{-1 \pm \sqrt{1 - (4)(2)(10)}}{4}$

Ⓒ $\dfrac{10 \pm \sqrt{100 - (4)(2)(1)}}{4}$

Ⓓ $\dfrac{10 \pm \sqrt{100 - (4)(2)(-1)}}{4}$

82. **MULTIPLE CHOICE** What are the roots of the quadratic equation in Exercise 81?

Ⓕ $\dfrac{-5 \pm 3\sqrt{3}}{2}$ Ⓖ $\dfrac{1 \pm 9}{4}$ Ⓗ $\dfrac{5 \pm \sqrt{23}}{2}$ Ⓙ None of these

83. **MULTIPLE CHOICE** Which quadratic equation has the solutions $x = \dfrac{-9 \pm \sqrt{81 - 56}}{4}$?

Ⓐ $2x^2 + 9x - 7 = 0$ Ⓑ $2x^2 - 9x + 7 = 0$

Ⓒ $4x^2 + 9x + 14 = 0$ Ⓓ $2x^2 + 9x + 7 = 0$

84. **MULTIPLE CHOICE** Which equation would you use to model the height of an object that is thrown down with an initial velocity of -10 feet per second from a height of 100 feet?

Ⓕ $h = -16t^2 + 100$ Ⓖ $h = -16t^2 + 10t + 100$

Ⓗ $h = -16t^2 - 10t + 100$ Ⓙ $h = -16t^2 - 10t - 100$

EVALUATING EXPRESSIONS Evaluate the expression for the given value of the variable. *(Lesson 2.5)*

85. $-3(x)$ when $x = 9$

86. $-5(-n)(-n)$ when $n = 2$

87. $4(-6)(m)$ when $m = -2$

88. $2(-1)(-x)^3$ when $x = -3$

GRAPHING LINES Write the equation in slope-intercept form. Then graph the equation. *(Lesson 4.7)*

89. $-3x + y + 6 = 0$

90. $-x + y - 7 = 0$

91. $4x + 2y - 12 = 0$

SOLVING INEQUALITIES Solve the inequality. Then graph the solution. *(Lesson 6.2)*

92. $6x \leq -2$

93. $-3x \geq 15$

94. $\frac{3}{4}x > 12$

95. RECREATION There were about 1.4×10^7 people who visited Golden Gate Recreation Area in California in 1996. Find the average number of visitors per month. ▶ Source: National Park Service *(Lesson 8.5)*

COMPARING FRACTIONS Complete the statement using <, >, or =. *(Skills Review pp. 770, 771)*

96. $\frac{8}{15}$ **?** $\frac{2}{15}$

97. $\frac{2}{3}$ **?** $\frac{5}{6}$

98. $\frac{1}{4}$ **?** $\frac{1}{5}$

99. $\frac{7}{8}$ **?** $\frac{11}{12}$

100. $4\frac{1}{8}$ **?** $4\frac{1}{5}$

101. $2\frac{2}{3}$ **?** $3\frac{1}{2}$

Quiz 2

Decide whether the graph of the function opens *up* or *down*. *(Lesson 9.4)*

1. $y = x^2 + 2x - 11$

2. $y = 2x^2 - 8x - 6$

3. $y = -3x^2 + 6x - 10$

4. $y = \frac{1}{2}x^2 + 5x - 3$

5. $y = -7x^2 - 7x + 7$

6. $y = -x^2 + 9x$

Sketch the graph of the function. Label the coordinates of the vertex. *(Lesson 9.4)*

7. $y = -x^2 + 2x - 3$

8. $y = -3x^2 + 12x - 10$

9. $y = 2x^2 - 6x + 7$

Use a graph to estimate the solutions of the equation. Check your solutions algebraically. *(Lesson 9.5)*

10. $x^2 - 3x = 10$

11. $x^2 - 12x = -36$

12. $3x^2 + 12x = -9$

Use the quadratic formula to solve the equation. If your solution involves radicals, round to the nearest hundredth. *(Lesson 9.6)*

13. $x^2 + 6x + 9 = 0$

14. $2x^2 + 13x + 6 = 0$

15. $-x^2 + 6x + 16 = 0$

16. $-2x^2 + 7x - 6 = 0$

17. $-3x^2 - 5x + 10 = 0$

18. $3x^2 - 4x - 1 = 0$

9.7 Using the Discriminant

In the example on page 545, you will determine

Goal

Use the discriminant to determine the number of solutions of a quadratic equation.

Key Words

• discriminant

Can you throw a stick high enough?

One way that campers protect food from bears is to hang it from a high tree branch. In the example on page 545, you will determine whether a stick and a rope were thrown fast enough to go over a tree branch.

In the quadratic formula, the expression inside the radical is the **discriminant**.

$$x = \frac{-b \pm \sqrt{b^2 - 4ac}}{2a} \longleftarrow \text{Discriminant}$$

The discriminant $b^2 - 4ac$ of a quadratic equation can be used to find the number of solutions of the quadratic equation.

Student Help

▶ **STUDY TIP**
Recall that positive real numbers have two square roots, zero has only one square root, negative numbers have no real square roots.

THE NUMBER OF SOLUTIONS OF A QUADRATIC EQUATION

Consider the quadratic equation $ax^2 + bx + c = 0$.

• If the value of $b^2 - 4ac$ is positive, then the equation has two solutions.

• If the value of $b^2 - 4ac$ is zero, then the equation has one solution.

• If the value of $b^2 - 4ac$ is negative, then the equation has no real solution.

EXAMPLE 1 Find the Number of Solutions

Find the value of the discriminant. Then use the value to determine whether $x^2 - 3x - 4 = 0$ has *two solutions*, *one solution*, or *no real solution*.

Solution Use the standard form of a quadratic equation, $ax^2 + bx + c = 0$, to identify the coefficients.

$$x^2 - 3x - 4 = 0 \qquad \text{Identify } a = 1, b = -3, c = -4.$$

$$b^2 - 4ac = (-3)^2 - 4(1)(-4) \qquad \text{Substitute values for } a, b, \text{ and } c.$$

$$= 9 + 16 \qquad \text{Simplify.}$$

$$= 25 \qquad \text{Discriminant is positive.}$$

ANSWER ▶ The discriminant is positive, so the equation has two solutions.

EXAMPLE 2 Find the Number of Solutions

Find the value of the discriminant. Then use the value to determine whether the equation has *two solutions*, *one solution*, or *no real solution*.

a. $-x^2 + 2x - 1 = 0$ **b.** $2x^2 - 2x + 3 = 0$

Solution

a. $-x^2 + 2x - 1 = 0$ Identify $a = -1$, $b = 2$, $c = -1$.

$b^2 - 4ac = (2)^2 - 4(-1)(-1)$ Substitute values for a, b, and c.

$= 4 - 4$ Simplify.

$= 0$ Discriminant is zero.

ANSWER ▶ The discriminant is zero, so the equation has one solution.

b. $2x^2 - 2x + 3 = 0$ Identify $a = 2$, $b = -2$, $c = 3$.

$b^2 - 4ac = (-2)^2 - 4(2)(3)$ Substitute values for a, b, and c.

$= 4 - 24$ Simplify.

$= -20$ Discriminant is negative.

ANSWER ▶ The discriminant is negative, so the equation has no real solution.

Checkpoint ✓ *Find the Number of Solutions*

Find the value of the discriminant. Then use the value to determine whether the equation has *two solutions*, *one solution*, or *no real solution*.

1. $x^2 - 3x + 4 = 0$ **2.** $x^2 - 4x + 4 = 0$ **3.** $x^2 - 5x + 4 = 0$

Because each solution of $ax^2 + bx + c = 0$ represents an x-intercept of $y = ax^2 + bx + c$, you can use the discriminant to determine the number of times the graph of a quadratic function intersects the x-axis.

EXAMPLE 3 Find the Number of x-Intercepts

Determine whether the graph of $y = x^2 + 2x - 2$ will intersect the x-axis in *zero*, *one*, or *two* points.

Solution

Let $y = 0$. Then find the value of the discriminant of $x^2 + 2x - 2 = 0$.

$x^2 + 2x - 2 = 0$ Identify $a = 1$, $b = 2$, $c = -2$.

$b^2 - 4ac = (2)^2 - 4(1)(-2)$ Substitute values for a, b, and c.

$= 4 + 8$ Simplify.

$= 12$ Discriminant is positive.

ANSWER ▶ The discriminant is positive, so the equation has two solutions and the graph will intersect the x-axis in two points.

Student Help

▶MORE EXAMPLES

More examples are available at www.mcdougallittell.com

EXAMPLE **4** **Find the Number of x-Intercepts**

Determine whether the graph of the function will intersect the x-axis in *zero*, *one*, or *two* points.

a. $y = x^2 + 2x + 1$ **b.** $y = x^2 + 2x + 3$

Solution

a. Let $y = 0$. Then find the value of the discriminant of $x^2 + 2x + 1 = 0$.

$x^2 + 2x + 1 = 0$	Identify $a = 1$, $b = 2$, $c = 1$.
$b^2 - 4ac = (2)^2 - 4(1)(1)$	Substitute values for a, b, and c.
$= 4 - 4$	Simplify.
$= 0$	Discriminant is zero.

ANSWER▶ The discriminant is zero, so the equation has one solution *and* the graph will intersect the x-axis in one point.

b. Let $y = 0$. Then find the value of the discriminant of $x^2 + 2x + 3 = 0$.

$x^2 + 2x + 3 = 0$	Identify $a = 1$, $b = 2$, $c = 3$.
$b^2 - 4ac = (2)^2 - 4(1)(3)$	Substitute values for a, b, and c.
$= 4 - 12$	Simplify.
$= -8$	Discriminant is negative.

ANSWER▶ The discriminant is negative, so the equation has no real solution *and* the graph will intersect the x-axis in zero points.

Student Help

▶LOOK BACK
For help with sketching the graph of a quadratic function, see p. 521.

EXAMPLE **5** **Change the Value of c**

Sketch the graphs of the functions in Examples 3 and 4 to check the number of x-intercepts of $y = x^2 + 2x + c$. What effect does changing the value of c have on the graph?

Solution By changing the value of c, you can move the graph of $y = x^2 + 2x + c$ up or down in the coordinate plane.

a. $y = x^2 + 2x - 2$

b. $y = x^2 + 2x + 1$

c. $y = x^2 + 2x + 3$

If the graph is moved high enough, it will not have an x-intercept and the equation $x^2 + 2x + c = 0$ will have no real solution.

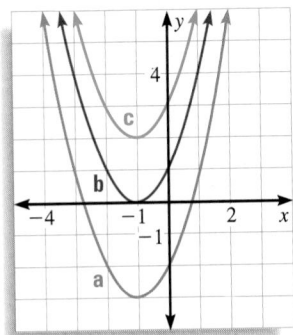

Checkpoint ✓ **Find the Number of x-Intercepts**

Find the number of x-intercepts of the graph of the function.

4. $y = x^2 - 4x + 3$ **5.** $y = x^2 - 4x + 4$ **6.** $y = x^2 - 4x + 5$

Guided Practice

Vocabulary Check

1. Write the quadratic formula and circle the part that is the discriminant.

2. What can the discriminant tell you about a quadratic equation?

3. Describe how the graphs of $y = 4x^2$, $y = 4x^2 + 3$, and $y = 4x^2 - 6$ are alike and how they are different.

Skill Check

Use the discriminant to determine whether the quadratic equation has *two solutions, one solution,* or *no real solution.*

4. $3x^2 - 3x + 5 = 0$ **5.** $-3x^2 + 6x - 3 = 0$ **6.** $x^2 - 5x - 10 = 0$

Give the letter of the graph that matches the value of the discriminant.

7. $b^2 - 4ac = 2$ **8.** $b^2 - 4ac = 0$ **9.** $b^2 - 4ac = -3$

A. 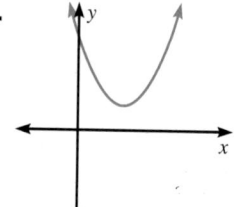   **B.** 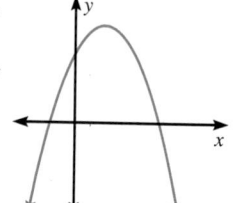   **C.**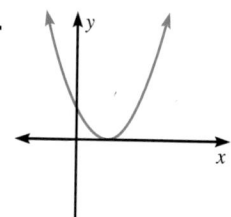

Determine whether the graph of the function will intersect the *x*-axis in *zero, one,* or *two* points.

10. $y = x^2 + 2x + 4$ **11.** $y = -x^2 - 3x + 5$ **12.** $y = 6x - 3 - 3x^2$

Practice and Applications

WRITING THE DISCRIMINANT Find the discriminant of the quadratic equation.

$b^2 - 4ac$

13. $-2x^2 - 5x + 3 = 0$ **14.** $3x^2 + 6x - 8 = 0$ **15.** $x^2 + 10 = 0$

16. $5x^2 + 3x = 12$ **17.** $2x^2 + 8x = -8$ **18.** $7 - 5x^2 + 9x = x$

19. $-x = 7x^2 + 4$ **20.** $2x = x^2 - x$ **21.** $-2 - x^2 = 4x^2$

USING THE DISCRIMINANT Determine whether the equation has *two solutions, one solution,* or *no real solution.*

22. $x^2 - 3x + 2 = 0$ **23.** $2x^2 - 4x + 3 = 0$ **24.** $-3x^2 + 5x - 1 = 0$

25. $2x^2 + 3x - 2 = 0$ **26.** $x^2 - 2x + 4 = 0$ **27.** $6x^2 - 2x + 4 = 0$

28. $3x^2 - 6x + 3 = 0$ **29.** $4x^2 - 5x + 1 = 0$ **30.** $-5x^2 + 6x - 6 = 0$

31. $-\frac{1}{2}x^2 + x + 3 = 0$ **32.** $\frac{1}{4}x^2 - 2x + 4 = 0$ **33.** $5x^2 + 4x + \frac{4}{5} = 0$

Student Help

▶ HOMEWORK HELP
Example 1: Exs. 13–33
Example 2: Exs. 13–33
Example 3: Exs. 38–43
Example 4: Exs. 38–43
Example 5: Exs. 44–46

34. ERROR ANALYSIS For the equation $3x^2 + 4x - 2 = 0$, find and correct the error.

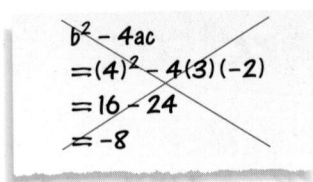

$$b^2 - 4ac$$
$$= (4)^2 - 4(3)(-2)$$
$$= 16 - 24$$
$$= -8$$

INTERPRETING THE DISCRIMINANT In Exercises 35–37, consider the quadratic equation $y = 2x^2 + 6x - 3$.

35. Evaluate the discriminant.

36. How many solutions does the equation have?

37. What does the discriminant tell you about the graph of $y = 2x^2 + 6x - 3$?

NUMBER OF X-INTERCEPTS Determine whether the graph of the function will intersect the x-axis in *zero*, *one*, or *two* points.

38. $y = 2x^2 + 3x - 2$ **39.** $y = x^2 - 2x + 4$ **40.** $y = -2x^2 + 4x - 2$

41. $y = 2x^2 + 2x + 6$ **42.** $y = 5x^2 + 2x - 3$ **43.** $y = 3x^2 - 6x + 3$

CHANGING THE VALUE OF C Match the function with its graph.

44. $y = -x^2 - 2x - 1$ **45.** $y = -x^2 - 2x - 3$ **46.** $y = -x^2 - 2x + 3$

A.

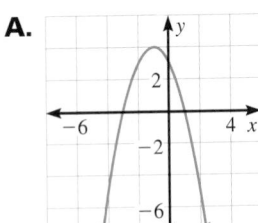

B.

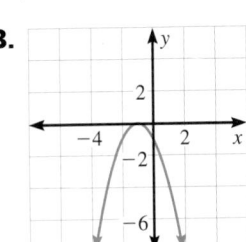

C.

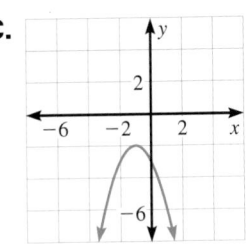

FINANCIAL ANALYSIS In Exercises 47–49, use a graphing calculator and the following information.

A software company's net profit for each year from 1993 to 1998 lead a financial analyst to model the company's net profit by
$$P = 6.84t^2 - 3.76t + 9.29,$$
where P is the profit in millions of dollars and t is the number of years since 1993. In 1993 the net profit was approximately 9.29 million dollars ($t = 0$).

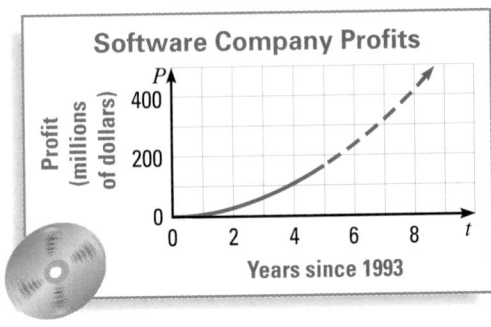

47. Give the domain and range of the function for 1993 through 1998.

48. Use the graph to predict whether the net profit will reach 650 million dollars.

49. Use a graphing calculator to estimate how many years it will take for the company's net profit to reach 475 million dollars according to the model.

CAMPING Bears have an excellent sense of smell that often leads them to campsites in search of food. Campers can hang a food sack from a high tree branch to keep it away from bears.

EXAMPLE *Using the Discriminant*

CAMPING You and a friend want to get a rope over a tree branch that is 20 feet high. Your friend attaches a stick to the rope and throws the stick upward with an initial velocity of 29 feet per second. You then throw it with an initial velocity of 32 feet per second. Both throws have an initial height of 6 feet. Will the stick reach the branch each time it is thrown?

Solution

Use a vertical motion model for an object that is thrown: $h = -16t^2 + vt + s$, where h is the height you want to reach, t is the time in motion, v is the initial velocity, and s is the initial height.

$$h = -16t^2 + vt + s$$
$$20 = -16t^2 + 29t + 6$$
$$0 = -16t^2 + 29t - 14$$
$$b^2 - 4ac = (29)^2 - 4(-16)(-14)$$

The discriminant is -55.

ANSWER ▶ The discriminant is negative. The stick thrown by your friend *will not* reach the branch.

$$h = -16t^2 + vt + s$$
$$20 = -16t^2 + 32t + 6$$
$$0 = -16t^2 + 32t - 14$$
$$b^2 - 4ac = (32)^2 - 4(-16)(-14)$$

The discriminant is 128.

ANSWER ▶ The discriminant is positive. The stick thrown by you *will* reach the branch.

50. BASKETBALL You can jump with an initial velocity of 12 feet per second. You need to jump 2.2 feet to dunk a basketball. Use the vertical motion model $h = -16t^2 + vt + s$ to find if you can dunk the ball. Justify your answer.

Standardized Test Practice

51. MULTIPLE CHOICE For which value of c will $-3x^2 + 6x + c = 0$ *not* have a real solution?

Ⓐ $c < -3$ Ⓑ $c = -3$ Ⓒ $c > -3$ Ⓓ $c = 3$

52. MULTIPLE CHOICE How many real solutions does $x^2 - 10x + 25 = 0$ have?

Ⓕ No solutions Ⓖ One solution Ⓗ Two solutions Ⓙ Many solutions

Mixed Review

SOLVING AND GRAPHING INEQUALITIES Solve the inequality. Then graph the solution. *(Lesson 6.4)*

53. $2 \le x + 1 < 5$ **54.** $8 > 2x > -4$ **55.** $-12 < 2x - 6 < 4$

GRAPHING LINEAR INEQUALITIES Graph the inequality. *(Lesson 6.8)*

56. $3x + y \le 9$ **57.** $y - 4x < 0$ **58.** $-2x - y \ge 4$

Maintaining Skills

MULTIPLYING DECIMALS Find the product. *(Skills Review p. 759)*

59. 3×0.02 **60.** 0.7×0.8 **61.** 0.1×0.1

62. 0.05×0.003 **63.** 0.09×0.02 **64.** 0.06×0.0004

DEVELOPING CONCEPTS
Graphing Quadratic Inequalities

For use with Lesson 9.8

GOAL

Use reasoning to discover a strategy for sketching the graph of a quadratic inequality.

MATERIALS

• graph paper
• pencil

Question How do you determine which portion of the graph of a quadratic inequality to shade?

In Lesson 6.8 you learned how to graph a *linear* inequality in two variables. You can use similar strategies to graph a *quadratic* inequality in two variables.

Explore

① Consider the graphs of the following two quadratic inequalities.

a. $y < x^2 - 2x - 3$ **b.** $y \ge x^2 - 2x - 3$

Graph $y = x^2 - 2x - 3$. Use a *dashed line* for < and a *solid line* for ≥.

Student Help

▶ **LOOK BACK**
  To review strategies for graphing a linear inequality, see pp. 367–369.

② Use substitution to test points inside and outside the parabola. An ordered pair (x, y) is a solution of a quadratic inequality if the inequality is true when the values of x and y are substituted into the inequality. Try testing $(0, 0)$.

a.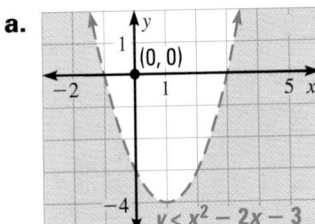

b.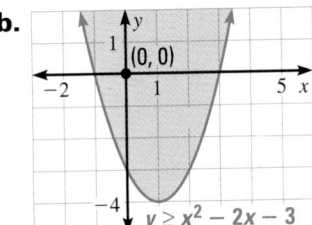

The point $(0, 0)$ __?__ a solution. The solutions appear to be the set of all points that lie *outside* the graph of $y = x^2 - 2x - 3$.

The point $(0, 0)$ __?__ a solution. The solutions appear to be the set of all points that lie *inside or on* the graph of $y = x^2 - 2x - 3$.

③ Can the inequality $y < x^2 - 2x - 3$ be interpreted as "all points (x, y) that lie below the parabola $y = x^2 - 2x - 3$"? Explain.

Think About It

Match the quadratic inequality with its graph. Explain your reasoning.

1. $y \le x^2 - 4$ **2.** $y > x^2 - 4x$ **3.** $y < (x - 4)^2$

A.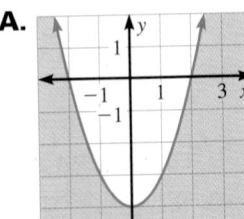

B.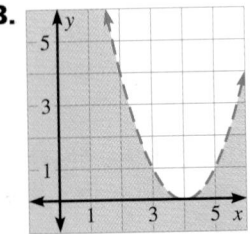

C.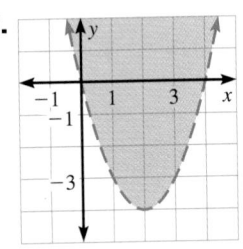

9.8 Graphing Quadratic Inequalities

Goal

Sketch the graph of a quadratic inequality in two variables.

Key Words

- quadratic inequalities
- graph of a quadratic inequality

How does a flashlight work?

A flashlight has a *parabolic* reflector that helps to focus the light into a beam. In Exercise 38 you will use a *quadratic inequality* to learn more about how a flashlight works.

In this lesson you will study the following types of **quadratic inequalities**.

$$y < ax^2 + bx + c \qquad y \le ax^2 + bx + c$$

$$y > ax^2 + bx + c \qquad y \ge ax^2 + bx + c$$

The **graph of a quadratic inequality** consists of the graph of all ordered pairs (x, y) that are solutions of the inequality.

EXAMPLE 1 Check Points

Sketch the graph of $y = x^2 - 3x - 3$. Plot and label the points $A(3, 2)$, $B(1, 4)$, and $C(4, -3)$. Determine whether each point lies inside or outside the parabola.

Solution

❶ **Sketch** the graph of $y = x^2 - 3x - 3$.

❷ **Plot** and label the points $A(3, 2)$, $B(1, 4)$, and $C(4, -3)$.

ANSWER ▸ Points A and B lie inside the parabola. Point C lies outside the parabola.

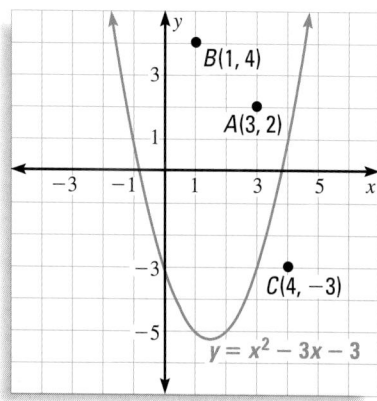

Checkpoint ✓ **Check Points**

Sketch the graph of $y = x^2 - 4x + 3$. Plot the point and determine whether it lies *inside* or *outside* the parabola.

1. $A(-1, 2)$ **2.** $B(0, 0)$ **3.** $C(2, 1)$

The shaded part of the graph of a quadratic inequality contains all of the ordered pairs that are solutions of the inequality. Checking points tells you which region to shade. You can use the following steps to graph any quadratic inequality.

METHOD I: GRAPHING A QUADRATIC INEQUALITY

STEP ❶ Sketch the graph of $y = ax^2 + bx + c$ that corresponds to the inequality.

Sketch a dashed parabola for inequalities with < or > to show that the points on the parabola are *not* solutions.

Sketch a solid parabola for inequalities with ≤ or ≥ to show that the points on the parabola are solutions.

STEP ❷ The parabola separates the coordinate plane into two regions. Test a point that is *not* on the parabola to determine whether the point is a solution of the inequality.

STEP ❸ If the test point is a solution, shade its region. If not, shade the other region.

EXAMPLE 2 Graph a Quadratic Inequality

Sketch the graph of $y < 2x^2 - 3x$.

Solution

❶ **Sketch** the graph of the equation $y = 2x^2 - 3x$ that corresponds to the inequality $y < 2x^2 - 3x$. Use a dashed line since the inequality contains the symbol <.

The parabola opens up since a is positive.

The vertex is $\left(\dfrac{3}{4}, -1\dfrac{1}{8}\right)$.

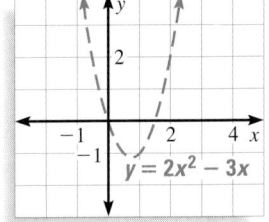

Student Help

▶**STUDY TIP**
If the point (0, 0) is not on the parabola, then (0, 0) is usually good to use as a test point. For help with checking ordered pairs as solutions, see p. 367.

❷ **Test** a point, such as (1, 2), that is *not* on the parabola. The point (1, 2) lies inside the parabola.

$y < 2x^2 - 3x$	Write original inequality.
$2 \overset{?}{<} 2(1)^2 - 3(1)$	Substitute 1 for x and 2 for y.
$2 \not< -1$	2 is not less than -1.

Because 2 is *not* less than -1, the ordered pair (1, 2) is *not* a solution.

❸ **Shade** the region outside the parabola. The point (1, 2) is inside the parabola and it is not a solution, so the graph of $y < 2x^2 - 3x$ is all the points that are outside, but not on, the parabola.

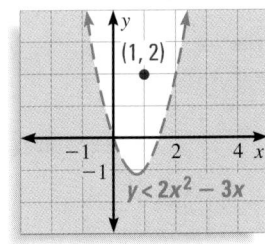

Until now you have used the fact that a parabola divides the plane into two regions, one of which is inside the parabola and one of which is outside. For parabolas given by $y = ax^2 + bx + c$, these regions can also be described as lying *above* and *below* the parabola and can be graphed using the following steps.

METHOD II: GRAPHING A QUADRATIC INEQUALITY

STEP ❶ Sketch the graph of $y = ax^2 + bx + c$, using a dashed or a solid curve as in Method I.

STEP ❷ If the inequality is $y > ax^2 + bx + c$ or $y \geq ax^2 + bx + c$, shade the region above the parabola.

If the inequality is $y < ax^2 + bx + c$ or $y \leq ax^2 + bx + c$, shade the region below the parabola.

Student Help

▶ **MORE EXAMPLES**

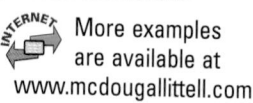 More examples are available at www.mcdougallittell.com

EXAMPLE 3 Graph a Quadratic Inequality

Sketch the graph of $y \leq -x^2 - 5x + 4$.

Solution

❶ **Sketch** the graph of the equation $y = -x^2 - 5x + 4$ that corresponds to the inequality $y \leq -x^2 - 5x + 4$. The x-coordinate of the vertex is $-\frac{b}{2a}$, or $-2\frac{1}{2}$. Make a table of values, using x-values to the left and right of $x = -2\frac{1}{2}$.

x	−5	−4	−3	$-2\frac{1}{2}$	−2	−1	0
y	4	8	10	$10\frac{1}{4}$	10	8	4

Plot the points and connect them with a smooth curve to form a parabola. Use a solid line since the inequality contains the symbol $\leq$.

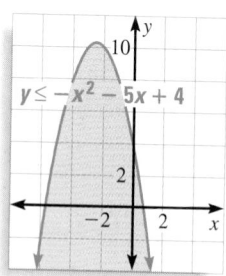

$y \leq -x^2 - 5x + 4$

❷ **Shade** the region *below* the parabola because the inequality states that y is *less* than or equal to $-x^2 - 5x + 4$.

Checkpoint ✔ *Graph a Quadratic Inequality*

Sketch the graph of the inequality.

4. $y < x^2 + 2x + 2$ **5.** $y > -x^2 - 2x + 3$ **6.** $y \geq 2x^2 - 4x + 2$

Guided Practice

Vocabulary Check

1. Give an example of each of the four types of quadratic inequalities.

2. *True* or *False*? For inequalities with < or >, you sketch a solid parabola to show that the points on the parabola are not solutions.

Skill Check

Sketch the graph of the equation $y = x^2 + 2x - 4$. **Plot the point and determine whether it lies *inside* or *outside* the parabola.**

3. $A(0, 0)$ **4.** $B(-1, 3)$ **5.** $C(2, -2)$

Decide whether each labeled ordered pair is a solution of the inequality.

6. $y < -x^2$ **7.** $y \geq x^2 - 2$ **8.** $y \leq 2x^2 + 5x$

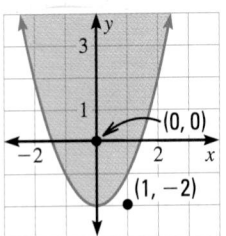
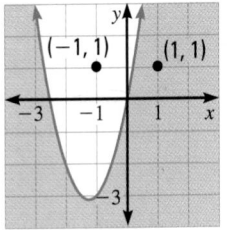

Sketch the graph of the inequality.

9. $y \leq x^2$ **10.** $y > -x^2 + 3$ **11.** $y < -x^2 + 2x$

12. $y \geq x^2 - 2x$ **13.** $y < -2x^2 + 6x$ **14.** $y \leq 2x^2 - 4x + 3$

Practice and Applications

SOLUTIONS **Determine whether the ordered pair is a solution of the inequality.**

15. $y \geq 2x^2 - x, (-2, 10)$ **16.** $y \leq 3x^2 + 7, (4, 31)$

17. $y < x^2 + 9x, (-3, 18)$ **18.** $y < 5x^2 + 8, (3, 45)$

19. $y > 4x^2 - 7x, (2, 0)$ **20.** $y \geq x^2 - 13x, (-1, 14)$

CHECKING POINTS **Sketch the graph of the function. Plot the given point and determine whether the point lies *inside* or *outside* the parabola.**

21. $y = x^2 - 2x + 5$ **22.** $y = -x^2 + 4x - 2$
  $A(0, 4)$ $B(3, -2)$

Student Help

▶ HOMEWORK HELP
 Example 1: Exs. 21–24
 Example 2: Exs. 29–38
 Example 3: Exs. 29–38

23. $y = \frac{1}{2}x^2 + x - 4$ **24.** $y = 4x^2 - x + 1$
  $C(1, 0)$ $D(-2, 5)$

LOGICAL REASONING Complete the statement with *always, sometimes,* or *never.*

25. If $a > b$, then a^2 is __?__ greater than b^2.

26. If $a > b$ and $b > 0$, then a^2 is __?__ greater than b^2.

27. If $a^2 = 4$, then a is __?__ equal to 2.

28. If a is a real number, then $\sqrt{a^2}$ is __?__ equal to $|a|$.

MATCHING INEQUALITIES Match the inequality with its graph.

29. $y \geq -2x^2 - 2x + 1$ **30.** $y > -2x^2 + 4x + 3$ **31.** $y \leq 2x^2 + x + 1$

A.
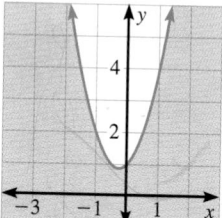

B.
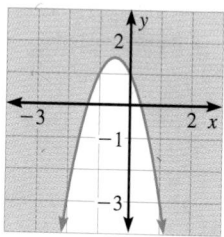

C.
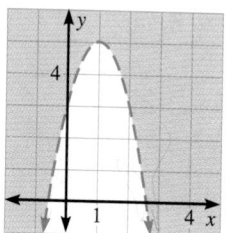

SKETCHING GRAPHS Sketch the graph of the inequality.

32. $y < -x^2 + x$ **33.** $y < x^2 - 4$ **34.** $y \geq x^2 - 5x$

35. $y > -x^2 - 3x - 2$ **36.** $y \leq -x^2 + 3x + 4$ **37.** $y > -3x^2 - 5x - 1$

38. FLASHLIGHT Light rays from a flashlight bulb bounce off a parabolic reflector inside a flashlight. The reflected rays are parallel to the axis of the flashlight. In this way, flashlights produce narrow beams of light.

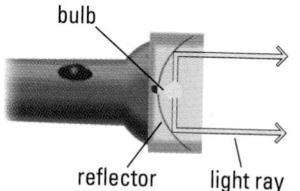

A cross section of a flashlight's parabolic reflector is shown in the graph at the right. An equation for the parabola is $y = \frac{1}{24}x^2 + 1$. Choose the region of the graph where the bulb is located.

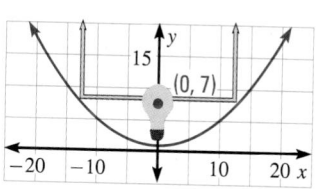

A. $y < \frac{1}{24}x^2 + 1$ **B.** $y > \frac{1}{24}x^2 + 1$ **C.** $y \leq \frac{1}{24}x^2 + 1$

Standardized Test Practice

39. MULTIPLE CHOICE Which ordered pair is *not* a solution of the inequality $y \geq 2x^2 - 7x - 10$?

Ⓐ $(0, -4)$ Ⓑ $(-1, -1)$ Ⓒ $(4, -13)$ Ⓓ $(5, 15)$

40. MULTIPLE CHOICE Choose the statement that is *true* about the graph of the quadratic inequality $y < 5x^2 + 6x + 2$.

Ⓐ Points on the parabola are solutions.

Ⓑ The vertex is $\left(-\frac{3}{5}, \frac{1}{5}\right)$.

Ⓒ The parabola opens down.

Ⓓ $(0, 0)$ is not a solution.

FINDING EQUATIONS The variables *x* and *y* vary directly. Use the given values to write an equation that relates *x* and *y*. *(Lesson 4.6)*

41. $x = 6, y = 42$ **42.** $x = -9, y = 54$ **43.** $x = 14, y = 7$

44. $x = -13, y = -52$ **45.** $x = 3, y = -6$ **46.** $x = -5, y = 60$

GRAPHING FUNCTIONS Graph the exponential function. *(Lesson 8.3)*

47. $y = 3^x$ **48.** $y = 5^x$ **49.** $y = 3(2)^x$

50. $y = \left(\frac{1}{3}\right)^x$ **51.** $y = 2\left(\frac{1}{4}\right)^x$ **52.** $y = \left(\frac{2}{3}\right)^x$

PERCENTS AND FRACTIONS Write the percent as a fraction or as a mixed number in simplest form. *(Skills Review p. 768)*

53. 4% **54.** 392% **55.** 45% **56.** 500%

57. 3% **58.** 6% **59.** 24% **60.** 10%

61. 390% **62.** 225% **63.** 175% **64.** 8%

65. 91% **66.** 2% **67.** 25% **68.** 16%

Quiz 3

Determine whether the equation has *two solutions, one solution,* or *no real solution.* *(Lesson 9.7)*

1. $x^2 - 15x + 56 = 0$ **2.** $x^2 + 8x + 16 = 0$ **3.** $x^2 - 3x + 4 = 0$

4. THROWING A BASEBALL Your friend is standing on a balcony that is 45 feet above the ground. You throw a baseball to her with an initial upward velocity of 50 feet per second. If you released the baseball 5 feet above the ground, did it reach your friend? Explain. *HINT:* Use a vertical motion model for an object that is thrown: $h = -16t^2 + vt + s$. *(Lesson 9.7)*

Match the inequality with its graph. *(Lesson 9.8)*

5. $y < -2x^2 + 4x - 2$ **6.** $y \leq -2x^2 + 3x + 2$ **7.** $y \geq -2x^2 - 3x + 2$

A. 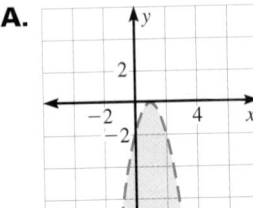   **B.** 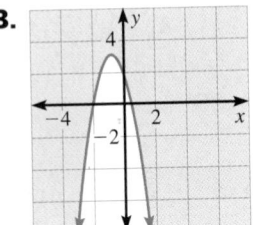   **C.**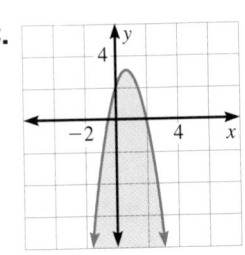

Sketch the graph of the inequality. *(Lesson 9.8)*

8. $y \geq 2x^2 + 5$ **9.** $y < x^2 + 3x$ **10.** $y > -x^2 - 2$

11. $y \leq x^2 + 3x - 2$ **12.** $y > x^2 + 2x + 1$ **13.** $y \leq -x^2 + 2x - 3$

VOCABULARY

- **square root**, *p. 499*
- **positive square root**, *p. 499*
- **negative square root**, *p. 499*
- **radicand**, *p. 499*
- **perfect square**, *p. 500*
- **radical expression**, *p. 501*

- **quadratic equation**, *p. 505*
- **simplest form of a radical expression**, *p. 511*
- **quadratic function**, *p. 520*
- **parabola**, *p. 520*
- **vertex**, *p. 521*
- **axis of symmetry**, *p. 521*

- **roots of a quadratic equation**, *p. 527*
- **quadratic formula**, *p. 533*
- **discriminant**, *p. 540*
- **quadratic inequalities**, *p. 547*
- **graph of a quadratic inequality**, *p. 547*

9.1 SQUARE ROOTS

Examples on pp. 499–501

EXAMPLES Positive real numbers have a positive square root and a negative square root. The radical symbol $\sqrt{}$ indicates the positive square root of a positive number.

a. $\sqrt{36} = 6$ 36 is a perfect square: $6^2 = 36$.

b. $-\sqrt{81} = -9$ 81 is a perfect square: $9^2 = 81$, so $\sqrt{81} = 9$ and $-\sqrt{81} = -9$.

Evaluate the expression.

1. $-\sqrt{4}$ **2.** $\sqrt{144}$ **3.** $\sqrt{100}$ **4.** $-\sqrt{25}$

9.2 SOLVING QUADRATIC EQUATIONS BY FINDING SQUARE ROOTS

Examples on pp. 505–507

EXAMPLE To find the real solutions of a quadratic equation in the form $ax^2 + c = 0$, isolate x^2 on one side of the equation. Then find the square root(s) of each side.

$2x^2 - 98 = 0$	Write original equation.
$2x^2 = 98$	Add 98 to each side.
$x^2 = 49$	Divide each side by 2.
$x = \pm\sqrt{49}$	Find square roots.
$x = \pm 7$	$7^2 = 49$ and $(-7)^2 = 49$

Solve the equation.

5. $x^2 = 144$ **6.** $8y^2 = 968$ **7.** $5y^2 - 80 = 0$ **8.** $3x^2 - 4 = 8$

9.3   SIMPLIFYING RADICALS

*Examples on
pp. 511–513*

EXAMPLES You can use properties of radicals to simplify radical expressions.

a. $\sqrt{28} = \sqrt{4 \cdot 7}$ Factor using perfect square factor.

$= \sqrt{4} \cdot \sqrt{7}$ Use product property.

$= 2\sqrt{7}$ Remove perfect square factor from radicand.

b. $\sqrt{\dfrac{16}{3}} = \dfrac{\sqrt{16}}{\sqrt{3}}$ Use quotient property.

$= \dfrac{4}{\sqrt{3}}$ Remove perfect square factor from radicand.

$= \dfrac{4}{\sqrt{3}} \cdot \dfrac{\sqrt{3}}{\sqrt{3}}$ Multiply by a value of 1: $\dfrac{\sqrt{3}}{\sqrt{3}} = 1$.

$= \dfrac{4\sqrt{3}}{3}$ Simplify.

Simplify the expression.

9. $\sqrt{45}$ **10.** $\sqrt{28}$ **11.** $\sqrt{\dfrac{36}{24}}$ **12.** $\sqrt{\dfrac{8}{6}}$

9.4   GRAPHING QUADRATIC FUNCTIONS

*Examples on
pp. 520–522*

EXAMPLE Sketch the graph of $y = x^2 - 4x - 3$.
In this quadratic function, $a = 1$, $b = -4$, and $c = -3$.

❶ **Find** the x-coordinate of the vertex.

$$-\dfrac{b}{2a} = -\dfrac{-4}{2(1)} = 2$$

❷ **Make** a table of values, using x-values
to the left and right of $x = 2$.

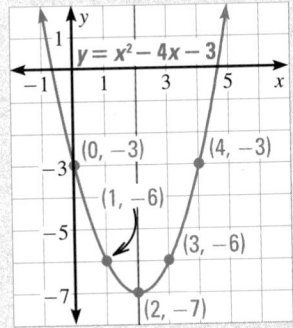

x	−1	0	1	2	3	4	5
y	2	−3	−6	−7	−6	−3	2

❸ **Plot** the points. The vertex is $(2, -7)$. Connect the points to form a parabola that
opens up since a is positive. The axis of symmetry is the vertical line $x = 2$. The
y-intercept is -3.

Sketch the graph of the function. Label the coordinates of the vertex.

13. $y = x^2 - 5x + 4$ **14.** $y = -x^2 + 2x - 1$ **15.** $y = 2x^2 - 3x - 2$

9.5 SOLVING QUADRATIC EQUATIONS BY GRAPHING

Examples on pp. 526–528

EXAMPLE Use a graph to estimate the solutions of $-x^2 + 3x = 2$.

❶ **Write** the equation in the standard form $ax^2 + bx + c = 0$.

$-x^2 + 3x = 2$ Write original equation.

$-x^2 + 3x - 2 = 0$ Subtract 2 from each side.

❷ **Sketch** the graph of the related quadratic function $y = -x^2 + 3x - 2$. The *x*-intercepts of the graph are the solutions of the quadratic equation.

❸ **Estimate** the values of the *x*-intercepts.

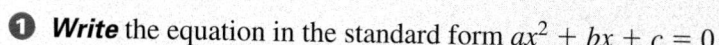

ANSWER ▶ From the graph, the *x*-intercepts appear to be 1 and 2. Check your solutions algebraically by substituting each one in the original equation.

Use a graph to estimate the solutions of the equation. Check your solutions algebraically.

16. $x^2 - 3x = -2$ **17.** $-x^2 + 6x = 5$ **18.** $x^2 - 2x = 3$

9.6 SOLVING QUADRATIC EQUATIONS BY THE QUADRATIC FORMULA

Examples on pp. 533–535

EXAMPLE You can solve equations of the form $ax^2 + bx + c = 0$ by substituting the values of *a*, *b*, and *c* into the quadratic formula. Solve $x^2 + 6x - 16 = 0$.

Quadratic Formula: $x = \dfrac{-b \pm \sqrt{b^2 - 4ac}}{2a}$ when a ≠ 0 and $b^2 - 4ac \geq 0$.

The equation $1x^2 + 6x - 16 = 0$ is in standard form. Identify $a = 1$, $b = 6$, and $c = -16$.

$$x = \frac{-6 \pm \sqrt{6^2 - 4(1)(-16)}}{2(1)}$$

$$x = \frac{-6 \pm \sqrt{36 + 64}}{2}$$

$$x = \frac{-6 \pm \sqrt{100}}{2}$$

$$x = \frac{-6 \pm 10}{2}$$

ANSWER ▶ The two solutions are $x = \dfrac{-6 + 10}{2} = 2$ and $x = \dfrac{-6 - 10}{2} = -8$.

Use the quadratic formula to solve the equation.

19. $3x^2 - 4x + 1 = 0$ **20.** $-2x^2 + x + 6 = 0$ **21.** $10x^2 - 11x + 3 = 0$

9.7 USING THE DISCRIMINANT

Examples on pp. 540–542

EXAMPLE You can use the discriminant, $b^2 - 4ac$, to find the number of solutions of a quadratic equation in the standard form $ax^2 + bx + c = 0$. A positive value indicates two solutions, zero indicates one solution, and a negative value indicates no real solution. The value of the discriminant can also be used to find the number of x-intercepts of the graph of $y = ax^2 + bx + c$.

EQUATION	DISCRIMINANT	NUMBER OF SOLUTIONS
$3x^2 - 6x + 2 = 0$	$(-6)^2 - 4(3)(2) = 12$	2
$2x^2 + 8x + 8 = 0$	$8^2 - 4(2)(8) = 0$	1
$x^2 + 7x + 15 = 0$	$7^2 - 4(1)(15) = -11$	0

Determine whether the equation has *two solutions, one solution,* or *no real solution.*

22. $3x^2 - 12x + 12 = 0$ **23.** $2x^2 + 10x + 6 = 0$ **24.** $-x^2 + 3x - 5 = 0$

Find the number of x-intercepts of the graph of the function.

25. $y = 2x^2 - 3x - 1$ **26.** $y = -x^2 - 3x + 3$ **27.** $y = x^2 + 2x + 1$

9.8 GRAPHING QUADRATIC INEQUALITIES

Examples on pp. 547–549

EXAMPLE Sketch the graph of $y < x^2 - 9$.

❶ **Sketch** the graph of $y = x^2 - 9$ that corresponds to $y < x^2 - 9$.

The x-coordinate of the vertex is $-\dfrac{b}{2a}$, or 0. Make a table of values, using x-values to the left and right of $x = 0$

x	−3	−2	−1	0	1	2	3
y	0	−5	−8	−9	−8	−5	0

❷ **Plot** the points and connect them with a smooth curve to form a parabola. Use a dashed line since the inequality contains the symbol $<$.

❸ **Shade** the region *below* the parabola because the inequality states that y is *less* than $x^2 - 9$.

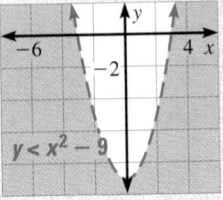

$y < x^2 - 9$

Sketch the graph of the inequality.

28. $y \le x^2 - 4$ **29.** $y \ge -x^2 - 2x + 3$ **30.** $y > 2x^2 - 4x - 6$

Evaluate the expression.

1. $\sqrt{64}$

2. $-\sqrt{25}$

3. $\pm\sqrt{169}$

4. $-\sqrt{100}$

Solve the equation or write *no real solution*.

5. $x^2 = 1$

6. $n^2 = 36$

7. $4y^2 = 16$

8. $8x^2 = 800$

9. $t^2 - 64 = 0$

10. $5x^2 + 125 = 0$

11. $2x^2 + 1 = 19$

12. $x^2 + 6 = -10$

Simplify the expression.

13. $\sqrt{150}$

14. $5\sqrt{\dfrac{4}{25}}$

15. $\sqrt{\dfrac{27}{45}}$

16. $\sqrt{\dfrac{9}{7}}$

Give the letter of the graph that matches the function.

17. $y = -x^2 - 2x + 3$

18. $y = -3x^2 - x + 2$

19. $y = 2x^2 + x - 3$

A.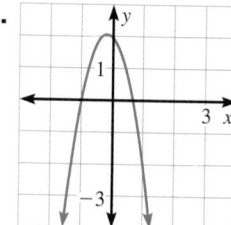

B.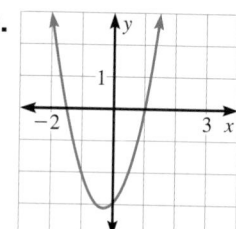

C.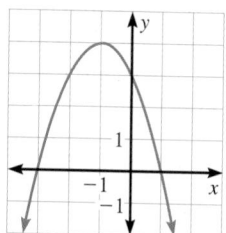

Use a graph to estimate the solutions of the equation. Check your solutions algebraically.

20. $x^2 - 4 = 5$

21. $-x^2 + 7x - 10 = 0$

22. $-2x^2 + 4x + 6 = 0$

Use the quadratic formula to solve the equation.

23. $x^2 - 6x - 27 = 0$

24. $-x^2 + 3x + 10 = 0$

25. $3x^2 + 4x - 7 = 0$

Find the value of the discriminant. Then determine whether the equation has *two solutions, one solution,* **or** *no real solution*.

26. $-3x^2 + x - 2 = 0$

27. $x^2 - 4x + 4 = 0$

28. $5x^2 - 2x - 6 = 0$

Sketch the graph of the inequality.

29. $y < x^2 + 2x - 3$

30. $y \le -x^2 + 5x - 4$

31. $y \ge x^2 + 7x + 6$

VERTICAL MOTION **In Exercises 32 and 33, suppose you are standing on a bridge over a creek, holding a stone 20 feet above the water.**

32. You release the stone. How long will it take the stone to reach the water? Use a vertical motion model for an object that is dropped: $h = -16t^2 + s$.

33. You take another stone and toss it straight up with an initial velocity of 30 feet per second. How long will it take the stone to reach the water? Use a vertical motion model for an object that is thrown: $h = -16t^2 + vt + s$.

Chapter Standardized Test

Test Tip If you are unsure of an answer, try to eliminate some of the choices so you can make an educated guess.

Ⓐ Ⓑ Ⓒ Ⓓ

---

1. Which number is a perfect square?

Ⓐ -25 Ⓑ $\sqrt{100}$

Ⓒ 55 Ⓓ 100

2. Which one of the following is *not* a quadratic equation?

Ⓐ $x^2 - 4 = 0$ Ⓑ $-9 + x^2 = 0$

Ⓒ $-7x + 12 = 0$ Ⓓ $-2 + 9x + x^2 = 0$

3. Which value of t is a solution of $2t^2 - 21 = 51$?

Ⓐ -6 Ⓑ -4

Ⓒ $\sqrt{15}$ Ⓓ 4

4. What are the values of x when $3x^2 - 78 = 114$?

Ⓐ $\pm 2\sqrt{3}$ Ⓑ ± 6

Ⓒ $\pm 4\sqrt{3}$ Ⓓ ± 8

5. Which radical expression is in simplest form?

Ⓐ $\sqrt{\dfrac{8}{5}}$ Ⓑ $\sqrt{\dfrac{5}{6}}$

Ⓒ $\dfrac{2}{\sqrt{3}}$ Ⓓ $\sqrt{12}$

Ⓔ None of these

6. Find the area of the rectangle.

Ⓐ $4\sqrt{15}$

Ⓑ $12\sqrt{5}$

Ⓒ 60

Ⓓ 240

$\sqrt{12}$

$\sqrt{20}$

7. What is the x-coordinate of the vertex of the graph of $y = -2x^2 - x + 8$?

Ⓐ -1 Ⓑ $-\dfrac{1}{4}$

Ⓒ $\dfrac{1}{4}$ Ⓓ $\dfrac{1}{2}$

8. What are the x-intercepts of the graph of $y = -x^2 - 6x + 40$?

Ⓐ -10 and 4 Ⓑ -4 and 10

Ⓒ 0 and 4 Ⓓ 4 and 10

9. Which function has a y-intercept of 6?

Ⓐ $y = 6x^2 + 2$ Ⓑ $y = 2x^2 + 6x$

Ⓒ $y = 2x^2 + 6$ Ⓓ $y = 2x^2 - 6$

10. What is the value of the discriminant of the equation $5x^2 + 2x - 7 = 0$?

Ⓐ -136 Ⓑ 2

Ⓒ 12 Ⓓ 144

11. Which inequality is represented by the graph?

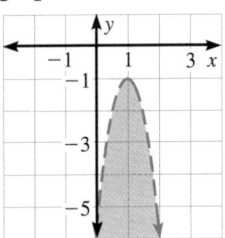

Ⓐ $y < -4x^2 + 8x - 5$

Ⓑ $y > -4x^2 + 8x - 5$

Ⓒ $y \le -4x^2 + 8x - 5$

Ⓓ $y \ge -4x^2 + 8x - 5$

Maintaining Skills

EXAMPLE 1 Use the Distributive Property

Use the distributive property to rewrite the expression without parentheses.

a. $6(14x + 9)$ **b.** $-3(5x - 2)$

Solution

a. $6(14x + 9) = 6(14x) + 6(9)$ Distribute 6 to each term of $(14x + 9)$.

$\qquad = 84x + 54$ Multiply.

b. $-3(5x - 2) = -3(5x) - (-3)(2)$ Distribute -3 to each term of $(5x - 2)$.

$\qquad = -15x + 6$ Multiply.

Try These

Use the distributive property to rewrite the expression without parentheses.

1. $8(2x - 12)$ **2.** $4(3x + 2)$ **3.** $-5(13 - m)$

4. $8(-5 + 6c)$ **5.** $10(8 + 3a)$ **6.** $-12(5 + 6t)$

EXAMPLE 2 Combine Like Terms

Simplify the expression.

a. $5x - 9y + 6x - 8y$ **b.** $6 + 3(x - 1)$

Solution

a. $5x - 9y + 6x - 8y = 5x + 6x - 9y - 8y$ Group like terms.

$\qquad = (5 + 6)x + (-9 - 8)y$ Use distributive property.

$\qquad = 11x - 17y$ Add coefficients.

b. $6 + 3(x - 1) = 6 + 3(x) - 3(1)$ Use distributive property.

$\qquad = 6 + 3x - 3$ Multiply.

$\qquad = 3x + 6 - 3$ Group like terms.

$\qquad = 3x + 3$ Combine like terms.

Student Help

▶ **EXTRA EXAMPLES**

More examples and practice exercises are available at www.mcdougallittell.com

Try These

Simplify the expression.

7. $8n - 2n + 18m + 3m$ **8.** $25c - 7d - 10d + 5c$

9. $4 + 2(x + 3)$ **10.** $2x + 4(2x - 5)$

Does the table represent a function? Explain. (Lesson 1.7)

1.

Input x	5	3	5	2
Output y	8	7	4	3

2.

Input x	3	6	9	12
Output y	5	8	5	8

Simplify the expression. (Lesson 2.8)

3. $\dfrac{27x - 54}{9}$

4. $\dfrac{66r + 39}{-3}$

5. $\dfrac{-72 + 16h}{-8}$

6. $\dfrac{-28 - 10t}{-2}$

7. PRETZELS You sell pretzels at a baseball game for \$1.25 each. Write and solve an equation to find how many pretzels you need to sell to earn \$60. (Lesson 3.2)

Solve the percent problem. (Lesson 3.9)

8. What number is 75% of 48?

9. 54 is 15% of what number?

10. 64 is what percent of 80?

11. 20 is what percent of 5?

Find the x-intercept and the y-intercept of the line. (Lesson 4.4)

12. $x + 2y = 8$

13. $x - 6y = -3$

14. $y = 12x - 2$

15. $y = -5x + 14$

16. $-2x - 7y = 20$

17. $-14x - y = 28$

Determine whether the graphs of the two equations are parallel lines. Explain your answer. (Lesson 4.7)

18. line a: $y = 2x + 3$
line b: $y - 3x = 2$

19. line a: $y - 4x + 1 = 0$
line b: $2y = 8x + 6$

20. line a: $2x - 5y = -30$
line b: $-4x + 10y = -10$

Write in slope-intercept form the equation of the line that passes through the given points. (Lesson 5.3)

21. (7, 3) and (6, 4)

22. (2, 5) and (11, 8)

23. (−4, 6) and (3, −8)

24. (0, −12) and (3, 3)

25. (5, 2) and (−5, 7)

26. (5, −10) and (8, 2)

Write the equation in standard form with integer coefficients. (Lesson 5.4)

27. $3x - 5y + 6 = 0$

28. $6y = 2x + 4$

29. $-2x + 7y - 15 = 0$

30. $y = \dfrac{2}{3}x - 1$

31. $y = -\dfrac{1}{4}x + 6$

32. $y = \dfrac{4}{5}x + 5$

Solve the inequality. (Lessons 6.1–6.3)

33. $m + 5 \le -4$

34. $8 > c - 3$

35. $-5t \ge 40$

36. $\dfrac{2}{3}x < 9$

37. $-\dfrac{1}{2}y \le -7$

38. $-\dfrac{x}{5} \ge 2$

39. $5y + 6 > -14$

40. $4(a - 1) < 8$

41. $6 + 2k \le 3k - 1$

Solve the linear system. (Lessons 7.1–7.3)

42. $x + 4y = 0$
$\quad\quad x = 12$

43. $x + y = 8$
$\quad\quad 2x + y = 10$

44. $10x - 3y = -1$
$\quad\quad -5x + 3y = 2$

45. $3x + y = -19$
$\quad\quad -32x + 4y = 144$

46. $-2x + 20y = 10$
$\quad\quad x - 5y = -5$

47. $4x + 2y = 3$
$\quad\quad 3x - 4y = 5$

48. VEGETABLES You buy 13 bell peppers to use in a vegetable platter. Green peppers cost $1.20 each and red peppers cost $1.50 each. If you spend a total of $18, how many of each kind are you buying? (Lesson 7.4)

Graph the system of linear inequalities. (Lesson 7.6)

49. $x \geq 0$
$\quad y \geq 0$
$\quad x < 5$
$\quad y < 2$

50. $x > 2$
$\quad x - y \leq 2$
$\quad x + 2y \leq 6$

51. $3x + 5y \geq 15$
$\quad x - 2y < 10$
$\quad x > 1$

52. $-x + 4y \leq 8$
$\quad -4x + y \geq -4$
$\quad 2x + y \geq -4$

Simplify the expression. Use only positive exponents. (Lessons 8.1, 8.2, 8.4)

53. $x^3 \cdot x^6$

54. $(c^5)^4$

55. $(8t)^2$

56. $-3(-5)^2$

57. $3^2 \cdot 3^3$

58. $3x^5y^{-3}$

59. $4^{-2} \cdot 4^0$

60. $\left(\dfrac{2}{3}\right)^{-4}$

61. $\dfrac{1}{4x^{-4}y^{-8}}$

62. $\dfrac{x^8}{x^3}$

63. $\dfrac{3x^2y}{y^3} \cdot \dfrac{6xy^2}{2y}$

64. $\dfrac{2x^4}{y^{-3}} \cdot \left(\dfrac{x^3}{y^2}\right)^{-2}$

Perform the indicated operation without using a calculator. Write the result in scientific notation. (Lesson 8.5)

65. $(5 \times 10^{-2})(3 \times 10^4)$

66. $(6 \times 10^{-8})(7 \times 10^5)$

67. $(20 \times 10^6)(3 \times 10^3)$

68. $(7 \times 10^3)^{-3}$

69. $\dfrac{8.8 \times 10^{-1}}{1.1 \times 10^{-1}}$

70. $(2.8 \times 10^{-2})^3$

Simplify the radical expression. (Lesson 9.3)

71. $\sqrt{40}$

72. $\sqrt{52}$

73. $\sqrt{72}$

74. $\sqrt{96}$

75. $\dfrac{1}{4}\sqrt{84}$

76. $\sqrt{\dfrac{28}{36}}$

77. $3\sqrt{\dfrac{18}{9}}$

78. $\sqrt{\dfrac{12}{75}}$

79. $\dfrac{1}{\sqrt{10}}$

80. $-2\sqrt{\dfrac{1}{6}}$

81. $\sqrt{\dfrac{14}{21}}$

82. $\sqrt{\dfrac{1}{27}}$

Sketch the graph of the quadratic function or the quadratic inequality. (Lessons 9.4, 9.8)

83. $y = -3x^2 + 6x - 1$

84. $y \geq 5x^2 + 20x + 15$

85. $y < 2x^2 - 5x + 2$

SENDING UP FLARES In Exercises 86 and 87, a flare is fired straight up from ground level with an initial velocity of 100 feet per second. (Lesson 9.7)

86. How long will it take the flare to reach a height of 150 feet? Use the vertical motion model $h = -16t^2 + vt + s$.

87. Will the flare reach a height of 180 feet? Explain.

Designing a Stairway

Materials
- graph paper
- pencil
- ruler
- calculator

OBJECTIVE Compare step measurements to see how they affect stairway design.

INVESTIGATING THE DATA

The horizontal part of a step is the *tread*, and the vertical part is the *riser*. The table gives the tread and riser measurements of four different stairways.

Stairway	Tread (in.)	Riser (in.)
A	10	7
B	11	7
C	9	8
D	12	6

1. Use the measurements in the table to draw three steps for each Stairway A–D on a piece of graph paper.

2. Analyze your drawings. Which stairway is the steepest? Which stairway gives the most foot space on a step?

3. For each Stairway A–D, find the ratio of riser size to tread size $\left(\dfrac{\text{riser}}{\text{tread}}\right)$.

Then write each ratio as a decimal rounded to the nearest tenth. What characteristic of a stairway do these ratios describe?

> Two generally accepted rules for designing stairways are listed below.
>
> **Rule 1: The sum of one tread and one riser is from 17 inches to 18 inches.**
>
> **Rule 2: The sum of one tread and two risers is from 24 inches to 25 inches.**

4. You can use the following linear inequalities to represent Rule 1.

$$t + r \geq 17 \text{ and } t + r \leq 18$$

Write linear inequalities to represent Rule 2. Then use the inequalities to show that each Stairway A–D follows one of the rules.

5. Graph the system of four inequalities on the same coordinate plane. Use the horizontal axis for t and the vertical axis for r. Then use the values in the table to label the point (t, r) for each Stairway A–D. What does each solution of the system represent?

6. Name any other point E that is a solution of the system. Give tread and riser measurements for a Stairway E that the point represents.

PRESENTING YOUR RESULTS

Write a report about tread and riser measurements for stairways.

- Include a discussion of how various tread and riser measurements create stairways that are different.

- Compare Stairways A–E in terms of steepness and foot space. Use diagrams or numbers to support your comparison.

tread
riser

A step is one unit of a stairway.

Step measurements can affect the comfort and safety of stairways.

- Include your answers to Exercises 1–6.

- Explain how the two rules for designing stairways limit the possible measurements for treads and risers. Use the graph of the linear system to give the range of possible measurements for treads and the range of possible measurement for risers. *HINT:* You can use inequalities to represent these ranges.

- Give some examples of tread and riser measurements that do *not* follow one of the given rules for designing stairways. Explain how these measurements might create stairways that are hard to use or unsafe. Draw diagrams to support your explanation.

EXTENDING THE PROJECT

Design a stairway by determining its tread and riser measurements. Suppose the vertical distance from one floor to the next is 105 inches.

1. Decide on a riser measurement that will give you a whole number of steps on your stairway. *HINT:* You can choose fractional measurements for your treads and risers.

2. Decide on a tread measurement which, along with your riser measurement, follows one of the generally accepted rules for designing stairways.

3. Find the slope of your stairway.

4. On graph paper, make a scale drawing of your whole stairway. Number the steps.

Polynomials and Factoring

▷ How wide and how deep are each of the dishes of the VLA radio telescope?

APPLICATION: Radio Telescopes

The Very Large Array (VLA) radio telescope in New Mexico is the most powerful radio telescope in the world. It consists of 27 mobile parabolic dishes that are combined electronically to provide images that would result from a single dish that is 22 miles (116,160 feet) across.

A cross section of one of the VLA dishes is shown below, where x and y are measured in feet. This cross section of a dish can be modeled by a polynomial equation.

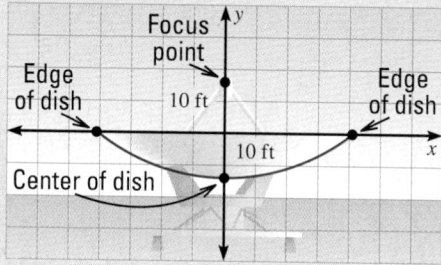

Think & Discuss

Use the graph above to answer the following questions.

1. Find the x-intercepts. How can you use this information to find the diameter of the dish?

2. Estimate the depth of the dish.

Learn More About It

You will use an algebraic model of the VLA radio telescope dishes in Exercises 46 and 47 on p. 592.

APPLICATION LINK More information about the VLA radio telescope is available at www.mcdougallittell.com

PREVIEW

What's the chapter about?

- Adding, subtracting, and multiplying **polynomials**
- **Factoring** polynomials
- Solving **quadratic** and **cubic equations** by factoring

> **KEY WORDS**
>
> - **monomial**, *p. 568*
> - **degree of a monomial**, *p. 568*
> - **polynomial**, *p. 569*
> - **binomial**, *p. 569*
> - **trinomial**, *p. 569*
> - **standard form**, *p. 569*
> - **degree of a polynomial**, *p. 569*
>
> - **FOIL pattern**, *p. 576*
> - **factored form**, *p. 588*
> - **zero-product property**, *p. 588*
> - **factor a trinomial**, *p. 595*
> - **perfect square trinomial**, *p. 609*
> - **prime polynomial**, *p. 617*
> - **factor completely**, *p. 617*

PREPARE

Chapter Readiness Quiz

Take this quick quiz. If you are unsure of an answer, look back at the reference pages for help.

VOCABULARY CHECK *(refer to p. 100)*

1. Which equation uses the distributive property correctly?

- **(A)** $3x(x + 6) = 3x^2 + 6$
- **(B)** $3x(x + 6) = 3x^2 + 18x$
- **(C)** $3x(x + 6) = x + 18x = 19x$
- **(D)** $3x(x + 6) = 3x + 18x = 21x$

SKILL CHECK *(refer to pp. 444, 540)*

2. Simplify the expression $(x^6)^2$.

- **(A)** x^8
- **(B)** x^4
- **(C)** x^{12}
- **(D)** x^3

3. How many real solutions does the equation $3x^2 - 4x + 6 = 0$ have?

- **(A)** Three solutions
- **(B)** Two solutions
- **(C)** One solution
- **(D)** No solution

STUDY TIP

Make Property Cards

Be sure to express the property in words and in symbols.

> *Zero-product property*
>
> If the product of two factors is zero, then at least one of the factors must be zero.
>
> If $ab = 0$, then $a = 0$ or $b = 0$.

DEVELOPING CONCEPTS
Addition of Polynomials

For use with Lesson 10.1

GOAL

Use algebra tiles to model the addition of polynomials.

MATERIALS

• algebra tiles

Question

How can you model the addition of polynomials with algebra tiles?

Explore

Algebra tiles can be used to model polynomials.

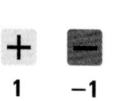  

1   −1 x $-x$ x^2 $-x^2$

Each of these 1-by-1 square tiles has an area of 1 square unit.

Each of these 1-by-x rectangular tiles has an area of x square units.

Each of these x-by-x square tiles has an area of x^2 square units.

1 You can use algebra tiles to add the polynomials $x^2 + 4x + 2$ and $2x^2 - 3x - 1$.

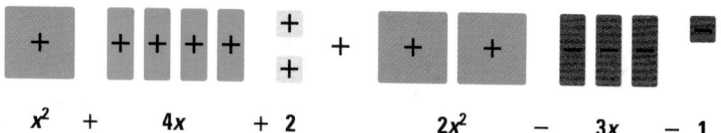

x^2 + $4x$ + 2 $2x^2$ − $3x$ − 1

Student Help

▶ **LOOK BACK**
For help with zero pairs, see p. 77.

2 To add the polynomials, combine like terms. Group the x^2-tiles, the x-tiles, and the 1-tiles.

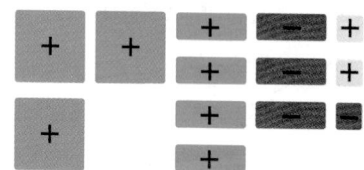

3 Rearrange the tiles to form zero pairs. Remove the zero pairs. The sum is $3x^2 + x + 1$.

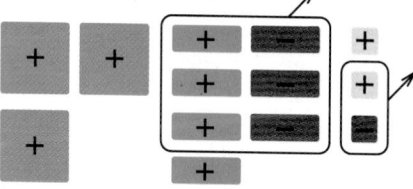

Think About It

In Exercises 1–6, use algebra tiles to find the sum. Sketch your solution.

1. $(-x^2 + x - 1) + (4x^2 + 2x - 3)$ **2.** $(3x^2 + 5x - 6) + (-2x^2 - 3x - 6)$

3. $(5x^2 - 3x + 4) + (-x^2 + 3x - 2)$ **4.** $(2x^2 - x - 1) + (-2x^2 + x + 1)$

5. $(4x^2 - 3x - 1) + (-2x^2 + x + 1)$ **6.** $(4x^2 + 5) + (4x^2 + 5x)$

7. Describe how to use algebra tiles to model *subtraction* of polynomials.

Use algebra tiles to find the difference. Sketch your solution.

8. $(x^2 + 3x + 4) - (x^2 + 3)$ **9.** $(x^2 - 2x + 5) - (3 - 2x)$

10.1 Adding and Subtracting Polynomials

Goal
Add and subtract polynomials.

Key Words
- monomial
- degree of a monomial in one variable
- polynomial
- binomial
- trinomial
- standard form
- degree of a polynomial in one variable

How large is the walkway around a pool?

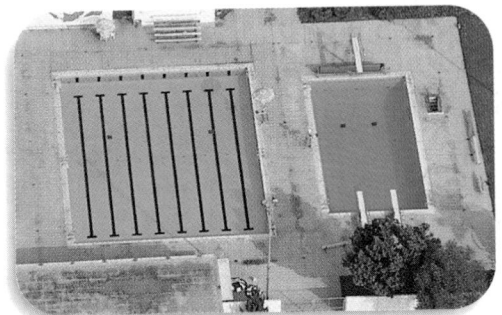

In Example 5 you will use subtraction of polynomials to find the area of a walkway around a pool.

A **monomial** is a number, a variable, or the product of a number and one or more variables with whole number exponents. The following expressions are monomials.

$$8 \qquad -2x \qquad 3x^2y \qquad \frac{1}{2}x^2$$

The **degree of a monomial** is the sum of the exponents of the variables in the monomial. The degree of $3x^2$ is 2. The degree of $-6z^4$ is 4. The degree of $3x^2y$ is $2 + 1$, or 3.

Student Help

▶ **READING ALGEBRA**
The monomial $-5x^4$ is read as "negative five times x to the fourth power." The coefficient is -5. · · · · · · · · · ·

EXAMPLE 1 Find the Degree of a Monomial

State the degree of the monomial.

a. $-5x^4$ **b.** $\frac{1}{2}b^3$ **c.** 12

Solution

a. The exponent of x is 4.
ANSWER ▶ The degree of the monomial is 4.

b. The exponent of b is 3.
ANSWER ▶ The degree of the monomial is 3.

c. Recall $12 = 12x^0$, so the exponent is 0.
ANSWER ▶ The degree of the monomial is 0.

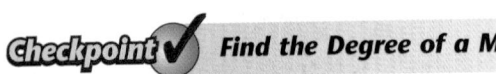 **Checkpoint** ✓ **Find the Degree of a Monomial**

State the degree of the monomial.

1. $6x^3$ **2.** $4p$ **3.** -10 **4.** $-3a^5$

POLYNOMIALS A **polynomial** is a monomial or a sum of monomials. A polynomial such as $x^2 + (-4x) + (-5)$ is usually written as $x^2 - 4x - 5$. Each of the following expressions is a polynomial.

$$4x^3 \qquad x^3 - 8 \qquad 7x^2 - 4x + 6$$

A polynomial of *two* terms is a **binomial**. A polynomial of *three* terms is a **trinomial**. Polynomials are usually written in **standard form**, which means that the terms are arranged in decreasing order, from largest exponent to smallest exponent. The **degree of a polynomial in one variable** is the largest exponent of that variable.

EXAMPLE 2 Identify Polynomials

POLYNOMIAL	DEGREE	IDENTIFIED BY DEGREE	IDENTIFIED BY NUMBER OF TERMS
a. 6	0	constant	monomial
b. $3x + 1$	1	linear	binomial
c. $-x^2 + 2x - 5$	2	quadratic	trinomial
d. $4x^3 - 8x$	3	cubic	binomial

 **Identify Polynomials**

Identify the polynomial by degree and by the number of terms.

5. $8x$ **6.** $10x - 5$ **7.** $x^2 - 4x + 4$ **8.** $-24 - x^3$

To add polynomials, you can use either a vertical format or a horizontal format, as shown in Example 3.

EXAMPLE 3 Add Polynomials

Find the sum. Write the answer in standard form.

a. $(5x^3 - 2x + x^2 + 7) + (3x^2 + 7 - 4x)$ **b.** $(2x^2 + x - 5) + (x + x^2 + 6)$

Solution

a. **Vertical format:** Write each expression in standard form. Line up like terms vertically.

$$\begin{array}{r} 5x^3 + x^2 - 2x + 7 \\ 3x^2 - 4x + 7 \\ \hline 5x^3 + 4x^2 - 6x + 14 \end{array}$$

b. **Horizontal format:** Group like terms.

$$(2x^2 + x - 5) + (x + x^2 + 6) = (2x^2 + x^2) + (x + x) + (-5 + 6)$$
$$= 3x^2 + 2x + 1$$

 **Add Polynomials**

Find the sum. Write the answer in standard form.

9. $(x^2 + 3x + 2) + (2x^2 - 4x + 2)$ **10.** $(2x^2 - 4x + 3) + (x^2 - 4x - 4)$

EXAMPLE 4 Subtract Polynomials

Find the difference. Write the answer in standard form.

a. $(-2x^3 + 5x^2 - 4x + 8) - (-2x^3 + 3x - 4)$

b. $(3x^2 - 5x + 3) - (2x^2 - x - 4)$

Solution

a. Use a vertical format. To subtract one polynomial from another, you *add the opposite*. One way to do this is to multiply each term in the subtracted polynomial by -1 and line up like terms vertically. Then add.

$$(-2x^3 + 5x^2 - 4x + 8)$$
$$-(-2x^3 \qquad + 3x - 4) \quad \text{Add the opposite.}$$

$$\begin{array}{r} -2x^3 + 5x^2 - 4x + 8 \\ +\quad 2x^3 \qquad - 3x + 4 \\ \hline 5x^2 - 7x + 12 \end{array}$$

b. Use a horizontal format. Group like terms and simplify.

$$(3x^2 - 5x + 3) - (2x^2 - x - 4) = 3x^2 - 5x + 3 - 2x^2 + x + 4$$
$$= (3x^2 - 2x^2) + (-5x + x) + (3 + 4)$$
$$= x^2 - 4x + 7$$

EXAMPLE 5 Subtracting Polynomials

You are installing a swimming pool. Write a model for the area of the walkway.

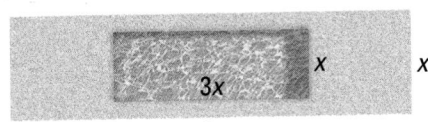

Solution

VERBAL MODEL	$\boxed{\text{Area of walkway}}$ = Total area − Area of pool

LABELS	Area of walkway = A	(square inches)
	Total area = $(6x)(x + 6)$	(square inches)
	Area of pool = $(3x)(x)$	(square inches)

ALGEBRAIC MODEL

$$A = (6x)(x + 6) - (3x)(x)$$
$$= 6x^2 + 36x - 3x^2$$
$$= 3x^2 + 36x$$

ANSWER ▶ A model for the area of the walkway is $A = 3x^2 + 36x$.

Checkpoint ✓ Subtract Polynomials

Find the difference. Write the answer in standard form.

11. $(2x^2 + 3x - 5) - (2x + 8 + x^2)$ **12.** $(4x^3 + 4x^2 - x - 2) - (3x^3 - 2x^2 + 1)$

Guided Practice

Vocabulary Check

1. Is $-4x^2 + 5x - 3x^3 + 6$ written in standard form? Explain.

2. Is $9x^2 + 8x - 4x^3 + 3$ a polynomial with a degree of 2? Explain.

Skill Check

Identify the polynomial by degree and by the number of terms.

3. $-9y + 5$ **4.** $6x^3$ **5.** $12x^2 + 7x$

6. $4w^3 - 8w + 9$ **7.** $7y + 2y^3 - y^2$ **8.** -15

ERROR ANALYSIS In Exercises 9 and 10, find and correct the error.

9.
$$7x^3 - 3x^2 + 5$$
$$+ \; 2x^3 - 5x - 7$$
$$\overline{9x^3 - 8x^2 - 2}$$

10.
$$(4x^2 - 9x) - (-8x^2 + 3x - 7)$$
$$= (4x^2 + 8x^2) + (-9x + 3x) - 7$$
$$= 12x^2 - 6x - 7$$

Find the sum or the difference of the polynomials.

11. $(2x - 9) + (x - 7)$ **12.** $(7x - 3) - (9x - 2)$

13. $(x^2 - 4x + 3) + (3x^2 - 3x - 5)$ **14.** $(3x^2 + 2x - 4) - (2x^2 + x - 1)$

Practice and Applications

LOGICAL REASONING Complete the statement with *always*, *sometimes*, or *never*.

15. The terms of a polynomial are __?__ monomials.

16. Like terms __?__ have the same coefficient and same variable part.

17. The sum of two trinomials is __?__ a trinomial.

18. A binomial is __?__ a polynomial of degree 2.

19. Subtraction is __?__ addition of the opposite.

FINDING THE DEGREE State the degree of the monomial.

20. $8n$ **21.** $12b^4$ **22.** $-c^3$ **23.** $-100w^4$

CLASSIFYING POLYNOMIALS Write the polynomial in standard form. Then identify the polynomial by degree and by the number of terms.

24. $2x$ **25.** $20m^3$ **26.** $7 - 3w$

27. -16 **28.** $8 + 5y^2 - 3y$ **29.** $-14 + 11y^3$

30. $-2x + 5x^3 - 6$ **31.** $-4b^2 + 7b^3$ **32.** $14w^2 + 9w^3$

Student Help

▶ **HOMEWORK HELP**
Example 1: Exs. 20–23
Example 2: Exs. 24–32
Example 3: Exs. 33–50
Example 4: Exs. 33–50
Example 5: Exs. 51, 52

VERTICAL FORMAT Use a vertical format to add or subtract.

33. $(12x^3 + x^2) - (18x^3 - 3x^2 + 6)$ **34.** $(a + 3a^2 + 2a^3) - (a^2 - a^3)$

35. $(2m - 8m^2 - 3) + (m^2 + 5m)$ **36.** $(8y^2 + 2) + (5 - 3y^2)$

37. $(3x^2 + 7x - 6) - (3x^2 + 7x)$ **38.** $(4x^2 - 7x + 2) + (-x^2 + x - 2)$

HORIZONTAL FORMAT Use a horizontal format to add or subtract.

39. $(x^2 - 7) + (2x^2 + 2)$ **40.** $(-3a^2 + 5) + (-a^2 + 4a - 6)$

41. $(z^3 + z^2 + 1) - z^2$ **42.** $12 - (y^3 + 10y + 16)$

43. $(3n^2 + 2n - 7) - (n^3 - n - 2)$ **44.** $(3a^3 - 4a^2 + 3) - (a^3 + 3a^2 - a - 4)$

POLYNOMIAL ADDITION AND SUBTRACTION Use a vertical format or a horizontal format to add or subtract.

45. $(9x^3 + 12x) + (16x^3 - 4x + 2)$ **46.** $(-2t^4 + 6t^2 + 5) - (-2t^4 + 5t^2 + 1)$

47. $(3x + 2x^2 - 4) - (x^2 + x - 6)$ **48.** $(u^3 - u) - (u^2 + 5)$

49. $(-7x^2 + 12) - (6 - 4x^2)$ **50.** $(10x^3 + 2x^2 - 11) + (9x^2 + 2x - 1)$

Link to
Careers

CONSTRUCTION MANAGERS are responsible for coordinating and managing people, materials, and equipment; budgets, schedules, and contracts; and the safety of employees and the general public.

BUILDING A HOUSE In Exercises 51 and 52, use the following information. You plan to build a house that is 1.5 times as long as it is wide. You want the land around the house to be 20 feet wider than the width of the house, and twice as long as the length of the house, as shown in the figure below.

51. Write an expression for the area of the land surrounding the house.

52. If $x = 30$ feet, what is the area of each floor of the house? What is the area of the entire property?

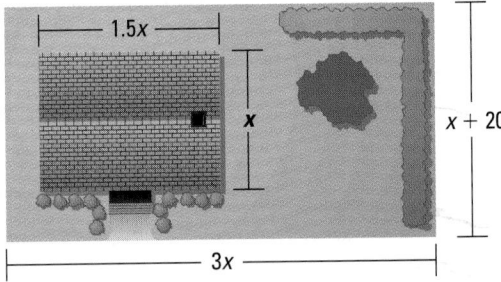

ENERGY USE In Exercises 53 and 54, use the following information. From 1989 through 1993, the amounts (in billions of dollars) spent on natural gas N and electricity E by United States residents can be modeled by the following equations, where t is the number of years since 1989.
▶ Source: U.S. Energy Information Administration

Gas spending model: $N = 1.488t^2 - 3.403t + 65.590$
Electricity spending model: $E = -0.107t^2 + 6.897t + 169.735$

53. Find a model for the total amount A (in billions of dollars) spent on natural gas and electricity by United States residents from 1989 through 1993.

54. CRITICAL THINKING According to the models, will more money be spent on natural gas or on electricity in 2020. *HINT:* It may be helpful to graph the equations on a graphing calculator to answer this question.

55. MULTIPLE CHOICE Which of the following polynomials is *not* written in standard form?

   (A) $8n^2 - 16n + 144$ (B) $3y^3 - y^2 - 15 + 4y$

   (C) $3w^4 + 4w^2 - w - 9$ (D) $3p^4 - 6p^3 + 2p + 16$

56. MULTIPLE CHOICE What is the degree of $-6x^4$?

   (F) 4   (G) -6 (H) -4 (J) 6

57. MULTIPLE CHOICE Which of the following is classified as a monomial?

   (A) $x + 1$ (B) $5 - y^2$ (C) $a^3 - a - 1$ (D) $2y$

DISTRIBUTIVE PROPERTY **Simplify the expression.** *(Lesson 2.6)*

58. $-3(x + 1) - 2$ **59.** $(2x - 1)(2) + x$

60. $11x + 3(8 - x)$ **61.** $(5x - 1)(-3) + 6$

62. $-4(1 - x) + 7$ **63.** $-12x - 5(11 - x)$

64. GAS MILEAGE The table below shows mileage and gasoline used for 6 months. For each of these months, find the mileage rate in miles per gallon. Round to the nearest tenth. *(Lesson 3.8)*

Mileage (miles)	295	320	340	280	310	355
Gas Used (gallons)	12.3	13.3	14.2	11.6	12.9	14.8

 EXPONENTIAL EXPRESSIONS **In Exercises 65–70, simplify. Then use a calculator to evaluate the expression.** *(Lesson 8.1)*

65. $2^2 \cdot 2^3$ **66.** $(3^2 \cdot 1^3)^2$ **67.** $[(-1)^8 \cdot 2^4]^2$

68. $(-1 \cdot 3^2)^3$ **69.** $(2^2 \cdot 2^2)^2$ **70.** $(3^2 \cdot 2^3)^3$

71. ALABAMA The population P of Alabama (in thousands) for 1995 projected through 2025 can be modeled by $P = 4227(1.0104)^t$, where t is the number of years since 1995. Find the ratio of the population in 2025 to the population in 2000. *(Lesson 8.6)* ▶ Source: U.S. Bureau of the Census

ADDING FRACTIONS **Add. Write the answer as a mixed number in simplest form.** *(Skills Review p. 764)*

72. $\frac{12}{11} + 1\frac{3}{11}$ **73.** $\frac{2}{5} + 3\frac{3}{5}$ **74.** $1\frac{2}{3} + \frac{1}{6}$ **75.** $\frac{1}{8} + 1\frac{1}{2}$

76. $\frac{11}{3} + 5\frac{5}{6}$ **77.** $2\frac{3}{4} + \frac{19}{20}$ **78.** $5\frac{1}{2} + 4\frac{5}{16}$ **79.** $9\frac{2}{7} + 3\frac{11}{28}$

80. $2\frac{1}{2} + \frac{4}{3}$ **81.** $2\frac{1}{2} + \frac{5}{7}$ **82.** $12\frac{7}{12} + 8\frac{9}{32}$ **83.** $9\frac{7}{24} + 6\frac{5}{36}$

REASONING 10.2

DEVELOPING CONCEPTS
Multiplying Polynomials

For use with Lesson 10.2

GOAL

Multiply two polynomials using the distributive property.

MATERIALS

- paper
- pencil

Question

How can you multiply two polynomials using the distributive property?

The arithmetic operations for polynomials are very much like the corresponding operations for integers. For example, you can multiply $(x + 3)(2x + 1)$ by using the distributive property.

$$\begin{array}{r l}
2x + 1 & \\
\times \quad x + 3 & \\
\hline
6x + 3 & \longleftarrow \text{Multiply } 2x + 1 \text{ by } 3. \\
2x^2 + x & \longleftarrow \text{Multiply } 2x + 1 \text{ by } x. \\
\hline
2x^2 + 7x + 3 &
\end{array}$$

So $(x + 3)(2x + 1) = 2x^2 + 7x + 3$.

Explore

1 To multiply $(3x + 2)(x + 4)$, write the multiplication vertically.

$$\begin{array}{r}
3x + 2 \\
\times \quad x + 4 \\
\hline
\underline{\ ?\ } + \underline{\ ?\ } \\
\underline{\ ?\ } + \underline{\ ?\ } \\
\hline
\underline{\ ?\ } + \underline{\ ?\ } + \underline{\ ?\ }
\end{array}$$

2 Multiply $4 \times (3x + 2)$.

3 Multiply $x \times (3x + 2)$.

4 Add the terms by using a vertical format. Align like terms. Then add.

Try These

In Exercises 1–10, multiply the polynomials using the method shown above.

1. $(x + 3)(x + 7)$

2. $(2x + 5)(3x + 4)$

3. $(x - 5)(x + 7)$

4. $(4x + 1)(5x + 2)$

5. $(3x - 1)(5x - 2)$

6. $(3x + 7)(2x + 9)$

7. $(x + 4)(x^2 + 2x + 3)$

8. $(x - 2)(x^2 - 4x + 6)$

9. $(3x + 1)(x^2 + 3x + 5)$

10. $(4x - 1)(x^2 + 5x - 7)$

11. Explain how you can use the distributive property to multiply $(3x + 2)(x + 4)$ *horizontally.*
HINT: Use $(3x + 2)(x + 4) = (3x + 2)x + (3x + 2)4$ to do so.

EXAMPLE 4 Multiply Polynomials Horizontally

Find the product $(4x^2 - 3x - 1)(2x - 5)$.

Solution Multiply $2x - 5$ by each term of $4x^2 - 3x - 1$.

$(4x^2 - 3x - 1)(2x - 5)$

$4x^2(2x - 5) - 3x(2x - 5) - 1(2x - 5)$ Use distributive property.

$8x^3 - 20x^2 - 6x^2 + 15x - 2x + 5$ Use distributive property.

$8x^3 + (-20x^2 - 6x^2) + (15x - 2x) + 5$ Group like terms.

$8x^3 - 26x^2 + 13x + 5$ Combine like terms.

EXAMPLE 5 **Multiply Binomials to Find an Area**

The glass has a height-to-width ratio of 3 : 2. The frame adds 6 inches to the width and 10 inches to the height. Write a polynomial expression that represents the total area of the window, including the frame.

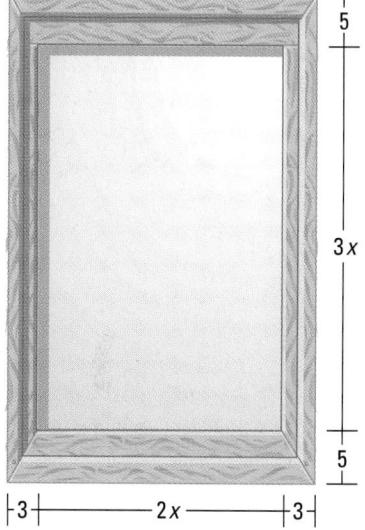

Solution

The window has a total height of $3x + 10$ and a total width of $2x + 6$. The area of the window is represented by the product of the height and width.

$A = $ **height** $\cdot$ **width**   Write area model for a rectangle.

$A = (3x + 10)(2x + 6)$ Substitute $(3x + 10)$ for height and $(2x + 6)$ for width.

$= 6x^2 + 18x + 20x + 60$ Use FOIL pattern.

$= 6x^2 + 38x + 60$ Combine like terms.

ANSWER ▶ The area of the window can be represented by the model $A = 6x^2 + 38x + 60$.

Checkpoint ✓ **Multiply Polynomials**

In Exercises 10–12, use a horizontal format to find the product.

10. $(x - 4)(x^2 + x + 1)$ **11.** $(x + 5)(x^2 - x - 3)$ **12.** $(2x + 1)(3x^2 + x - 1)$

13. Suppose the height-to-width ratio of the glass portion of the window in Example 5 above were 5 : 3. Write a model to represent the total area.

10.2 Exercises

Guided Practice

Vocabulary Check

1. How do the letters in "FOIL" help you remember how to multiply two binomials?

2. Give an example of a monomial, a binomial, and a trinomial.

Skill Check

Copy the equation and fill in the blanks.

3. $(x - 2)(x + 3) = x(\underline{\,?\,}) + (-2)(\underline{\,?\,})$ **4.** $(3x + 4)(2x - 1) = 3x(\underline{\,?\,}) + 4(\underline{\,?\,})$

5. $(x - 3)(x + 1) = x^2 - 2x - \underline{\,?\,}$ **6.** $(x + 2)(x + 6) = x^2 + \underline{\,?\,} + 12$

7. $(x - 4)(x - 5) = x^2 - 9x + \underline{\,?\,}$ **8.** $(x + 2)(2x + 1) = \underline{\,?\,} + 5x + 2$

Use the distributive property to find the product.

9. $(4x + 7)(-2x)$ **10.** $2x(x^2 + x - 5)$ **11.** $-4x^2(3x^2 + 2x - 6)$

12. $(a + 4)(a + 5)$ **13.** $(y - 2)(y + 8)$ **14.** $(2x + 3)(4x + 1)$

Use the FOIL pattern to find the product.

15. $(w - 3)(w + 5)$ **16.** $(x + 6)(x + 9)$ **17.** $(x - 4)(8x + 3)$

18. $(x - 3)(x + 4)$ **19.** $(x + 8)(x - 7)$ **20.** $(3x - 4)(2x - 1)$

Practice and Applications

MULTIPLYING EXPRESSIONS **Find the product.**

21. $(2x - 5)(-4x)$ **22.** $3t^2(7t - t^3 - 3)$ **23.** $2x(x^2 - 8x + 1)$

24. $(-y)(6y^2 + 5y)$ **25.** $4w^2(3w^3 - 2w^2 - w)$ **26.** $-b^2(6b^3 - 16b + 11)$

DISTRIBUTIVE PROPERTY **Use the distributive property to find the product.**

27. $(t + 8)(t + 5)$ **28.** $(x + 6)(x - 2)$ **29.** $(d - 5)(d + 3)$

30. $(a + 8)(a - 3)$ **31.** $(y + 2)(2y + 1)$ **32.** $(m - 2)(4m + 3)$

33. $(3s - 1)(s + 2)$ **34.** $(2d + 3)(3d + 1)$ **35.** $(4y - 7)(2y - 1)$

Student Help

▶ **HOMEWORK HELP**
Example 1: Exs. 21–35
Example 2: Exs. 36–47
Example 3: Exs. 48–51
Example 4: Exs. 52–55
Example 5: Exs. 56–60

USING THE FOIL PATTERN **Use the FOIL pattern to find the product.**

36. $(a + 6)(a + 7)$ **37.** $(y + 5)(y - 8)$ **38.** $(x + 6)(x - 6)$

39. $(2w - 5)(w + 5)$ **40.** $(4b - 1)(b - 6)$ **41.** $(x - 9)(2x + 15)$

42. $(3a - 1)(a - 9)$ **43.** $(2z + 7)(3z + 2)$ **44.** $(4q - 1)(3q + 8)$

45. $(5t - 3)(2t + 3)$ **46.** $(4x + 5)(4x - 3)$ **47.** $(9w - 5)(7w - 12)$

MULTIPLYING EXPRESSIONS Use a vertical format to find the product.

48. $(x + 2)(x^2 + 3x + 5)$

49. $(d - 5)(d^2 - 2d - 6)$

50. $(a - 3)(a^2 - 4a - 6)$

51. $(2x + 3)(3x^2 - 4x + 2)$

MULTIPLYING EXPRESSIONS Use a horizontal format to find the product.

52. $(x + 4)(x^2 - 2x + 3)$

53. $(a - 2)(a^2 + 6a - 7)$

54. $(m^2 + 2m - 9)(m - 4)$

55. $(4y^2 - 3y - 2)(y + 12)$

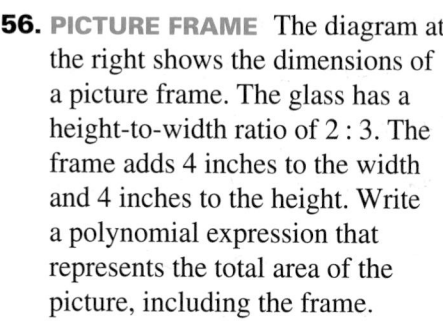

Link to Careers

PICTURE FRAMERS use math when deciding on the dimensions of the frame, the matting, and the glass.

56. PICTURE FRAME The diagram at the right shows the dimensions of a picture frame. The glass has a height-to-width ratio of 2 : 3. The frame adds 4 inches to the width and 4 inches to the height. Write a polynomial expression that represents the total area of the picture, including the frame.

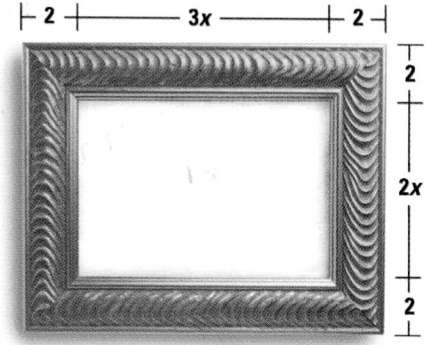

FOOTBALL In Exercises 57 and 58, a football field's dimensions are represented by a width of $(3x + 10)$ feet and a length of $(7x + 10)$ feet.

57. Find an expression for the area A of the football field. Give your answer as a quadratic trinomial.

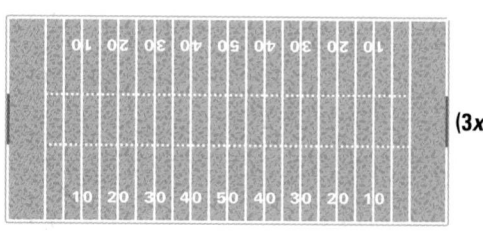

$(7x + 10)$ ft

58. An actual football field is 160 feet wide and 360 feet long. For what value of x do the expressions $3x + 10$ and $7x + 10$ give these dimensions?

VIDEOCASSETTES In Exercises 59 and 60, use the following information about videocassette sales from 1987 to 1996, where t is the number of years since 1987. The number of blank videocassettes B sold annually in the United States can be modeled by $B = 15t + 281$, where B is measured in millions. The wholesale price P for a videocassette can be modeled by $P = -0.21t + 3.52$, where P is measured in dollars.

▶ Source: EIA Market Research Department

Student Help

▶**HOMEWORK HELP**

Help with problem solving in Exs. 59 and 60 is available at www.mcdougallittell.com

59. Find a model for the revenue R from sales of blank videocassettes. Give the model as a quadratic trinomial.

60. What conclusions can you make from your model about the revenue over time?

61. LOGICAL REASONING Find the product $(2x + 1)(x + 3)$ using the distributive property and explain how this leads to the FOIL pattern.

62. MULTIPLE CHOICE Find the product $2a^2(a^2 - 3a + 1)$.

(A) $2a^2 - 6a + 2$ (B) $2a^4 - 6a^3 + 2a$

(C) $2a^2 - 3a^3 + 2a^2$ (D) $2a^4 - 6a^3 + 2a^2$

63. MULTIPLE CHOICE Find the product $(x + 9)(x - 2)$.

(F) $x^2 + 7x - 18$ (G) $x^2 - 11x - 18$

(H) $x^2 - 18$ (J) $x^2 - 7x$

64. MULTIPLE CHOICE Find the product $(x - 1)(2x^2 + x + 1)$.

(A) $2x^3 - 3x^2 - 1$ (B) $2x^3 - x^2 - 2x - 1$

(C) $2x^3 - x^2 - 1$ (D) $2x^3 + 3x^2 + 2x + 1$

Mixed Review

SIMPLIFYING EXPRESSIONS **Simplify the expression. Write your answer as a power.** *(Lesson 8.1)*

65. $(7x)^2$ **66.** $\left(\frac{1}{3}m\right)^2$ **67.** $\left(\frac{2}{5}y\right)^2$ **68.** $(0.5w)^2$

69. $9^3 \cdot 9^5$ **70.** $(4^2)^4$ **71.** $b^2 \cdot b^5$ **72.** $(4c^2)^4$

73. $(2t)^4 \cdot 3^3$ **74.** $(-w^4)^3$ **75.** $(-3xy)^3(2y)^2$ **76.** $(8x^2y^8)^3$

USING THE DISCRIMINANT **Tell whether the equation has *two solutions*, *one solution*, or *no real solution*.** *(Lesson 9.7)*

77. $x^2 - 5x + 6 = 0$ **78** $x^2 + 7x + 12 = 0$ **79.** $x^2 - 2x - 24 = 0$

80. $2x^2 - 3x - 1 = 0$ **81.** $4x^2 + 4x + 1 = 0$ **82.** $3x^2 - 7x + 5 = 0$

83. $7x^2 - 8x - 6 = 0$ **84.** $10x^2 - 13x - 9 = 0$ **85.** $6x^2 - 12x - 6 = 0$

SKETCHING GRAPHS **In Exercises 86–88, sketch the graph of the inequality.** *(Lesson 9.8)*

86. $y \geq 4x^2 - 7x$ **87.** $y < x^2 - 3x - 10$ **88.** $y > -2x^2 + 4x + 16$

89. ASTRONOMY The distance from the sun to Earth is approximately 1.5×10^8 km. The distance from the sun to the planet Neptune is approximately 4.5×10^9 km. What is the ratio of Earth's distance from the sun to Neptune's distance from the sun? *(Lesson 8.4)*

Maintaining Skills

DIVIDING FRACTIONS **Divide. Write the answer in simplest form.** *(Skills Review p. 765)*

90. $\frac{1}{6} \div \frac{2}{3}$ **91.** $\frac{3}{4} \div \frac{9}{24}$ **92.** $\frac{7}{8} \div \frac{5}{2}$

93. $\frac{3}{4} \div \frac{2}{9}$ **94.** $\frac{13}{15} \div \frac{7}{10}$ **95.** $\frac{29}{32} \div \frac{23}{24}$

96. $\frac{11}{16} \div \frac{11}{12}$ **97.** $1\frac{1}{2} \div \frac{3}{4}$ **98.** $2\frac{1}{3} \div \frac{7}{27}$

Special Products of Polynomials

Goal

Use special product patterns to multiply polynomials.

Key Words

- special product
- area model

What color will the offspring of two tigers be?

In Checkpoint Exercise 14 you will use the square of a binomial pattern to determine the possible coat colors of the offspring of two tigers.

Some pairs of binomials have *special products*. If you learn to recognize such pairs, finding the product of two binomials will sometimes be quicker and easier.

For example, to find the product of $(y + 3)(y - 3)$, you could multiply the two binomials using the FOIL pattern.

$$(y + 3)(y - 3) = y^2 + (-3y) + 3y - 9 \qquad \text{Use FOIL pattern.}$$
$$= y^2 - 9 \qquad \text{Combine like terms.}$$

Notice that the middle term is zero. This suggests a simple pattern for finding the product of the sum and difference of two terms:

$$(a + b)(a - b) = a^2 - b^2$$

Also, to find the product of $(x + 4)^2$, you could multiply $(x + 4)(x + 4)$.

$$(x + 4)(x + 4) = x^2 + 4x + 4x + 16 \qquad \text{Use FOIL pattern.}$$
$$= x^2 + 8x + 16 \qquad \text{Combine like terms.}$$

Notice that the middle term is twice the product of the terms of the binomial. This suggests a simple pattern for finding the product of the square of a binomial:

$$(a + b)^2 = a^2 + 2ab + b^2 \quad \text{or} \quad (a - b)^2 = a^2 - 2ab + b^2$$

SPECIAL PRODUCT PATTERNS

Sum and Difference Pattern

$(a + b)(a - b) = a^2 - b^2$ **Example:** $(3x - 4)(3x + 4) = 9x^2 - 16$

Square of a Binomial Pattern

$(a + b)^2 = a^2 + 2ab + b^2$ **Example:** $(x + 5)^2 = x^2 + 10x + 25$

$(a - b)^2 = a^2 - 2ab + b^2$ **Example:** $(2x - 3)^2 = 4x^2 - 12x + 9$

EXAMPLE 1 Use the Sum and Difference Pattern

Find the product $(5t - 2)(5t + 2)$.

Solution

$$(a - b)(a + b) = a^2 - b^2 \qquad \text{Write pattern.}$$

$$(5t - 2)(5t + 2) = (5t)^2 - 2^2 \qquad \text{Apply pattern.}$$

$$= 25t^2 - 4 \qquad \text{Simplify.}$$

CHECK ✓ You can use the FOIL pattern to check your answer.

$$(5t - 2)(5t + 2) = (5t)(5t) + (5t)(2) + (-2)(5t) + (-2)(2) \qquad \text{Use FOIL.}$$

$$= 25t^2 + 10t + (-10t) + (-4) \qquad \text{Simplify.}$$

$$= 25t^2 - 4 \qquad \text{Combine like terms.}$$

Checkpoint ✓ Use the Sum and Difference Pattern

Use the sum and difference pattern to find the product.

1. $(x + 2)(x - 2)$　　　**2.** $(n - 3)(n + 3)$　　　**3.** $(p + 8)(p - 8)$

4. $(2x - 1)(2x + 1)$　　**5.** $(3x + 2)(3x - 2)$　　**6.** $(2x + 5)(2x - 5)$

EXAMPLE 2 Use the Square of a Binomial Pattern

Find the product.

a. $(3n + 4)^2$ 　　　　　　　　　　**b.** $(2x - 7y)^2$

Solution

a. $(a + b)^2 = a^2 + 2ab + b^2 \qquad \text{Write pattern.}$

$\quad (3n + 4)^2 = (3n)^2 + 2(3n)(4) + 4^2 \qquad \text{Apply pattern.}$

$\quad\quad\quad\quad = 9n^2 + 24n + 16 \qquad \text{Simplify.}$

b. $(a - b)^2 = a^2 - 2ab + b^2 \qquad \text{Write pattern.}$

$\quad (2x - 7y)^2 = (2x)^2 - 2(2x)(7y) + (7y)^2 \qquad \text{Apply pattern.}$

$\quad\quad\quad\quad = 4x^2 - 28xy + 49y^2 \qquad \text{Simplify.}$

Checkpoint ✓ Use the Square of a Binomial Pattern

Use the square of a binomial pattern to find the product.

7. $(x + 1)^2$　　　　　　　**8.** $(t - 3)^2$　　　　　　　**9.** $(a - 7)^2$

10. $(2x + 1)^2$　　　　　　**11.** $(4x - 1)^2$　　　　　　**12.** $(3a - 4)^2$

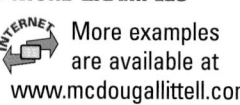
AREA MODELS Area models may be helpful when multiplying two binomials or using any of the special patterns.

The square of a binomial pattern $(a + b)^2 = a^2 + 2ab + b^2$ can be modeled as shown below.

The area of the large square is $(a + b)^2$, which is equal to the sum of the areas of the two small squares and two rectangles. Note that the two rectangles with area ab produce the middle term $2ab$.

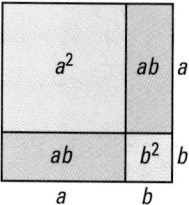

EXAMPLE 3 Find the Area of a Figure

GEOMETRY LINK Write an expression for the area of the blue region.

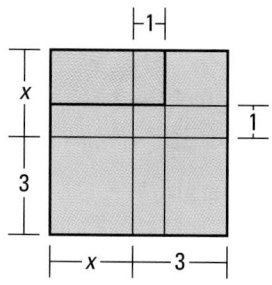

Solution

VERBAL MODEL		Area of blue region	=	Area of entire square	−	Area of red region

LABELS
Area of blue region = A (square units)

Area of entire region = $(x + 3)^2$ (square units)

Area of red region = $(x + 1)(x - 1)$ (square units)

ALGEBRAIC MODEL

$A = (x + 3)^2 - (x + 1)(x - 1)$ Write algebraic model.

$= (x^2 + 6x + 9) - (x^2 - 1)$ Apply patterns.

$= x^2 + 6x + 9 - x^2 + 1$ Use distributive property.

$= 6x + 10$ Simplify.

ANSWER ▶ The area of the blue region is $6x + 10$ square units.

Checkpoint ✓ *Find the Area of a Figure*

13. Write an expression for the area of the figure at the right. Name the special product pattern that is represented.

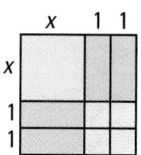

EXAMPLE 4 **Use a Punnett Square**

PUNNETT SQUARES The Punnett square at the right shows the possible results of crossing two pink snapdragons, each with one red gene R and one white gene W. Each parent snapdragon passes along only one gene for color to its offspring. Show how the square of a binomial can be used to model the Punnett square.

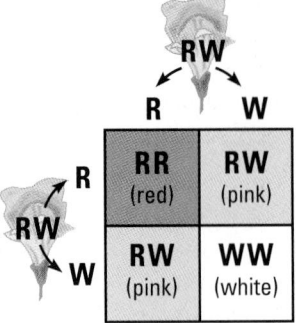

Solution

Each parent snapdragon has half red genes and half white genes. You can model the genetic makeup of each parent as follows:

$$0.5R + 0.5W$$

The genetic makeup of the offspring can be modeled by the product

$$(0.5R + 0.5W)^2$$

Expand the product to find the possible colors of the offspring.

$$(a + b)^2 = a^2 + 2ab + b^2 \qquad \text{Write pattern.}$$
$$(0.5R + 0.5W)^2 = (0.5R)^2 + 2(0.5R)(0.5W) + (0.5W)^2 \qquad \text{Apply pattern.}$$
$$= 0.25R^2 + 0.5RW + 0.25W^2 \qquad \text{Simplify.}$$

      ↑   ↑   ↑
   Red   Pink   White

ANSWER ▶ Given a sufficiently large number of offspring, 25% will be red, 50% will be pink, and 25% will be white.

Checkpoint ✓ **Use a Punnett Square**

14. SCIENCE LINK In tigers, the normal color gene C is dominant and the gene for white coat color c is recessive. This means that a tiger whose color genes are CC or Cc will have normal coloring. A tiger whose color genes are cc will be white. *Note:* The recessive gene c that results in a white tiger is extremely rare.

a. The Punnett square at the right shows the possible results of crossing two tigers, each with one dominant gene C and one recessive gene c. Find a model that can be used to represent the Punnett square. Write the model as a polynomial.

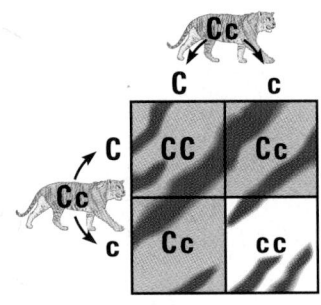

b. What percent of the offspring are likely to have normal coloring? What percent are likely to be white?

Guided Practice

Vocabulary Check

1. What is the sum and difference pattern for the product of two binomials?

2. Complete: $(x + 3)^2 = x^2 + 6x + 9$ is an example of the __?__ pattern.

Skill Check

Use a special product pattern to find the product.

3. $(x - 6)^2$ **4.** $(w + 11)(w - 11)$ **5.** $(6 + p)^2$

6. $(3y - 1)^2$ **7.** $(t - 6)(t + 6)$ **8.** $(a - 2)(a + 2)$

LOGICAL REASONING **Tell whether the statement is *true* or *false*. If the statement is false, rewrite the right-hand side to make the statement true.**

9. $(3x + 4)^2 = 9x^2 + 12x + 16$

10. $(3 + 2y)^2 = 9 + 12y + 4y^2$

11. $(5x - 1)^2 = 25x^2 - 10x + 1$

12. $(2x - 6)(2x + 6) = 4x^2 - 12$

Practice and Applications

DIFFERENCE PATTERN **Tell whether the expression is a difference of two squares.**

13. $x^2 - 9$ **14.** $b^2 - 36$ **15.** $a^2 + 16$ **16.** $n^2 - 50$

SQUARE OF A BINOMIAL **Tell whether the expression is the square of a binomial.**

17. $a^2 + 8a + 16$ **18.** $m^2 - 12m - 36$ **19.** $y^2 - 10y + 25$

20. $x^2 - 3x + 9$ **21.** $n^2 - 18n + 81$ **22.** $b^2 + 22b + 121$

SUM AND DIFFERENCE PATTERN **Write the product of the sum and difference.**

23. $(x + 5)(x - 5)$ **24.** $(y - 1)(y + 1)$ **25.** $(2m + 2)(2m - 2)$

26. $(3b - 1)(3b + 1)$ **27.** $(3 + 2x)(3 - 2x)$ **28.** $(6 - 5n)(6 + 5n)$

SQUARE OF A BINOMIAL **Write the square of the binomial as a trinomial.**

29. $(x + 5)^2$ **30.** $(a + 8)^2$ **31.** $(3x + 1)^2$

32. $(2y - 4)^2$ **33.** $(4b - 3)^2$ **34.** $(x - 7)^2$

Student Help

▶**HOMEWORK HELP**
Example 1: Exs. 13–16,
      23–28, 35–46
Example 2: Exs. 17–22,
      29–46
Example 3: Exs. 51–53
Example 4: Exs. 56, 57

SPECIAL PRODUCT PATTERNS Find the product.

35. $(x + 4)(x - 4)$ **36.** $(x - 3)(x + 3)$ **37.** $(3x - 1)^2$

38. $(4 - n)^2$ **39.** $(2y + 5)(2y - 5)$ **40.** $(4n - 3)^2$

41. $(a + 2b)(a - 2b)$ **42.** $(4x + 5)^2$ **43.** $(3x - 4y)(3x + 4y)$

44. $(3y + 8)^2$ **45.** $(9 - 4t)(9 + 4t)$ **46.** $(a - 2b)^2$

CHECKING PRODUCTS Tell whether the statement is *true* or *false*. If the statement is false, rewrite the right-hand side to make the statement true.

47. $(a + 2b)^2 = a^2 + 2ab + 4b^2$ **48.** $(3s + 2t)(3s - 2t) = 9s^2 + 4t^2$

49. $(9x + 8)(9x - 8) = 81x^2 - 64$ **50.** $(6y - 7w)^2 = 36y^2 - 49w^2$

AREA MODELS Write two expressions for the area of the figure. Describe the special product pattern that is represented.

51.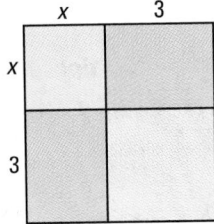

52.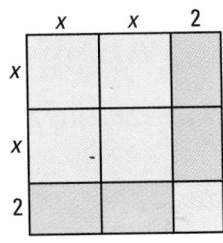

53.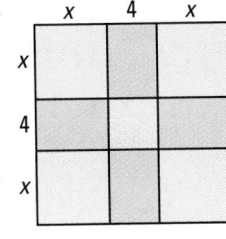

54. *Geometry Link* The area of a square is given by $4x^2 - 20x + 25$. Express its perimeter as a function of x.

55. *Geometry Link* The side of a square is $(3x - 4)$ inches. What is its area?

Science Link **In Exercises 56 and 57, use the following information.**
In chickens, neither the normal-feathered gene N nor the extremely rare frizzle-feathered gene F is dominant. So chickens whose feather genes are NN will have normal feathers. Chickens with NF will have mildly frizzled feathers. Chickens with FF will have extremely frizzled feathers.

56. The Punnett square at the right shows the possible results of crossing two chickens with mildly frizzled feathers. Find a model that can be used to represent the results shown in the Punnett square. Write the model as a polynomial.

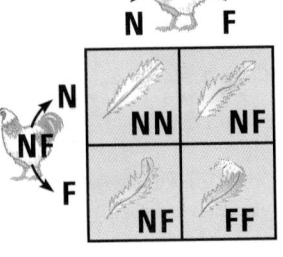

57. What percent of the offspring are likely to have normal feathers? What percent are likely to have mildly frizzled feathers? What percent are likely to have extremely frizzled feathers?

58. MULTIPLE CHOICE Find the product $(2x + 3)(2x - 3)$.

    Ⓐ $2x^2 - 6x - 9$ Ⓑ $4x^2 - 9$

    Ⓒ $2x^2 - 9$ Ⓓ $4x^2 + 12x + 9$

59. MULTIPLE CHOICE Find the product of $(3x + 5)^2$.

    Ⓕ $3x^2 + 15x + 5$ Ⓖ $9x^2 + 25$

    Ⓗ $3x^2 + 25$ Ⓙ $9x^2 + 30x + 25$

Mixed Review

SIMPLIFYING EXPRESSIONS Simplify the expression. Use only positive exponents. *(Lesson 8.4)*

60. $\left(\dfrac{6}{x}\right)^2$ **61.** $\dfrac{x^3}{x^2}$ **62.** $x^7 \cdot \dfrac{1}{x^4}$ **63.** $\dfrac{5x^4y}{3xy^2} \cdot \dfrac{9xy}{x^2y}$

SKETCHING GRAPHS Sketch the graph of the function. Label the vertex. *(Lesson 9.4)*

64. $y = 2x^2 + 3x + 6$ **65.** $y = 3x^2 - 9x - 12$ **66.** $y = -x^2 + 4x + 16$

Maintaining Skills

MULTIPLYING FRACTIONS Multiply the fractions. *(Skills Review p. 765)*

67. $\dfrac{1}{2} \cdot \dfrac{1}{2}$ **68.** $\dfrac{1}{4} \cdot \dfrac{1}{4}$ **69.** $\dfrac{2}{3} \cdot \dfrac{2}{3}$ **70.** $\dfrac{4}{9} \cdot \dfrac{4}{9}$

71. $\dfrac{1}{3} \cdot \dfrac{1}{3} \cdot \dfrac{1}{3}$ **72.** $\dfrac{2}{5} \cdot \dfrac{2}{5} \cdot \dfrac{2}{5}$ **73.** $\dfrac{3}{4} \cdot \dfrac{3}{4} \cdot \dfrac{3}{4}$ **74.** $\dfrac{5}{8} \cdot \dfrac{5}{8} \cdot \dfrac{5}{8}$

Quiz 1

State the degree of the monomial. *(Lesson 10.1)*

1. $6x^2$ **2.** -8 **3.** $-a^3$ **4.** $25m^5$

Use a vertical or a horizontal format to add or subtract. *(Lesson 10.1)*

5. $(2x^2 + 7x + 1) + (x^2 - 2x + 8)$

6. $(-4x^3 - 5x^2 + 2x) - (2x^3 + 9x^2 + 2)$

7. $(7t^2 - 3t + 5) - (4t^2 + 10t - 9)$

8. $(5x^3 - x^2 + 3x + 3) + (x^3 + 4x^2 + x)$

Find the product. *(Lesson 10.2)*

9. $(x + 8)(x - 1)$ **10.** $(y + 2)(y + 9)$ **11.** $-x^2(12x^3 - 11x^2 + 3)$

12. $(3x - y)(2x + 5y)$ **13.** $(4n + 7)(4n - 7)$ **14.** $(2x^2 + x - 4)(x - 2)$

Use a special product pattern to find the product. *(Lesson 10.3)*

15. $(x - 6)(x + 6)$ **16.** $(4x + 3)(4x - 3)$ **17.** $(5 + 3b)(5 - 3b)$

18. $(2x - 7y)(2x + 7y)$ **19.** $(3x + 6)^2$ **20.** $(-6 - 8x)^2$

10.4 Solving Quadratic Equations in Factored Form

Goal
Solve quadratic equations in factored form.

Key Words
- factored form
- zero-product property

How deep is a crater?

In Exercises 50 and 51 you will solve a quadratic equation to find the depth of the Barringer Meteor Crater.

A polynomial is in **factored form** if it is written as the product of two or more factors. The polynomials in the following equations are written in factored form.

$$x(x - 7) = 0 \qquad (x + 2)(x + 5) = 0 \qquad (x + 1)(x - 3)(x + 8) = 0$$

A value of x that makes any of the factors zero is a solution of the polynomial equation. That these are the *only* solutions follows from the **zero-product property**, stated below.

ZERO-PRODUCT PROPERTY

Let a and b be real numbers. If $ab = 0$, then $a = 0$ or $b = 0$.

If the product of two factors is zero, then at least one of the factors must be zero.

EXAMPLE 1 Using the Zero-Product Property

Solve the equation $(x - 2)(x + 3) = 0$.

Solution

$(x - 2)(x + 3) = 0$	Write original equation.
$x - 2 = 0 \quad or \quad x + 3 = 0$	Set each factor equal to 0.
$x = 2 \quad \mid \quad x = -3$	Solve for x.

ANSWER ▶ The solutions are 2 and −3. Check these in the original equation.

Checkpoint ✓ *Solution by Factoring*

Solve the equation and check the solutions.

1. $(x + 1)(x - 3) = 0$ **2.** $x(x - 2) = 0$ **3.** $(x - 5)(x + 7) = 0$

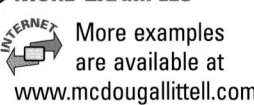
EXAMPLE **2** Solve a Repeated-Factor Equation

Solve $(x + 5)^2 = 0$.

Solution

This equation is a square of a binomial, so the factor $(x + 5)$ is a *repeated* factor. Repeated factors are used twice or more in an equation. To solve this equation you set $(x + 5)$ equal to zero.

$(x + 5)^2 = 0$	Write original equation.
$x + 5 = 0$	Set factor equal to 0.
$x = -5$	Solve for x.

ANSWER ▶ The solution is -5.

CHECK ✓ Substitute the solution into the original equation to check.

$(x + 5)^2 = 0$	Write original equation.
$(-5 + 5)^2 = 0$	Substitute -5 for x.
$0 = 0$ ✓	Simplify. Solution is correct.

Checkpoint ✓ *Solve a Repeated-Factor Equation*

Solve the equation and check the solutions.

4. $(x - 4)^2 = 0$ **5.** $(x + 6)^2 = 0$ **6.** $(2x - 5)^2 = 0$

EXAMPLE **3** Solve a Factored Cubic Equation

Solve $(2x + 1)(3x - 2)(x - 1) = 0$.

Solution

$(2x + 1)(3x - 2)(x - 1) = 0$ — Write original equation.

$2x + 1 = 0$ *or* $3x - 2 = 0$ *or* $x - 1 = 0$ — Set factors equal to 0.

$2x = -1$ | $3x = 2$ | $x = 1$ — Solve for x.

$x = -\dfrac{1}{2}$ | $x = \dfrac{2}{3}$ |

ANSWER ▶ The solutions are $-\dfrac{1}{2}, \dfrac{2}{3}$, and 1. Check these in the original equation.

Checkpoint ✓ *Solve a Factored Cubic Equation*

Solve the equation and check the solutions.

7. $(x - 4)(x + 6)(4x + 3) = 0$ **8.** $(x - 3)(x + 6)(3x + 2) = 0$

9. $(2x + 1)(x - 8)^2 = 0$ **10.** $(y - 3)^2(3y - 2) = 0$

EXAMPLE 4 Graph a Factored Equation

Sketch the graph of $y = (x - 3)(x + 2)$.

❶ Find the x-intercepts. Solve $(x - 3)(x + 2) = 0$ to find the x-intercepts: 3 and -2.

❷ Use the x-intercepts to find the coordinates of the vertex.

- The x-coordinate of the vertex is the average of the x-intercepts.

$$x = \frac{3 + (-2)}{2} = \frac{1}{2}$$

- Substitute the x-coordinate into the original equation to find the y-coordinate.

$$y = \left(\frac{1}{2} - 3\right)\left(\frac{1}{2} + 2\right) = -\frac{25}{4}$$

- The vertex is at $\left(\frac{1}{2}, -\frac{25}{4}\right)$.

❸ Sketch the graph using the vertex and the x-intercepts.

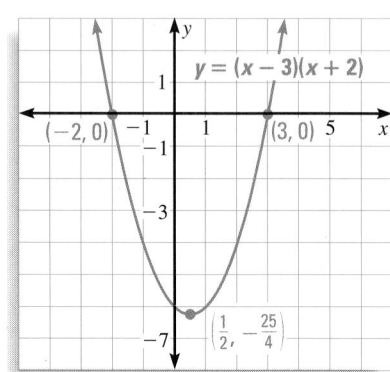

Checkpoint ✓ **Graph a Factored Equation**

Find the *x*-intercepts and the vertex of the graph of the function. Then sketch a graph of the function.

11. $y = x(x + 2)$ **12.** $y = (x + 4)(x - 5)$ **13.** $y = (x - 1)(x - 6)$

EXAMPLE 5 Use a Quadratic Model

An arch is modeled by $y = -0.15(x - 8)(x + 8)$, with x and y measured in feet. How wide is the arch at the base? How high is the arch?

❶ Find the x-intercepts: 8 and -8.

- The width of the arch at the base is $8 + 8 = 16$.

❷ Use the x-intercepts to find the coordinates of the vertex.

- $x = \frac{8 + (-8)}{2} = 0$

- Substitute 0 into the original equation:
  $y = -0.15(0 - 8)(0 + 8) = 9.6$

- The vertex is at $(0, 9.6)$.

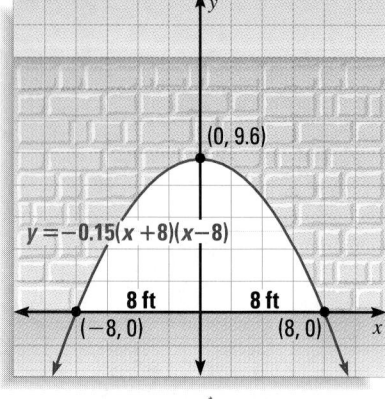

ANSWER ▶ The arch is 16 feet wide at the base and 9.6 feet high.

Student Help

▶ **SKILLS REVIEW**
For help with multiplying decimals, see p. 759.

10.4 Exercises

Guided Practice

Vocabulary Check

1. What is the zero-product property?

2. Is $(x - 2)(x^2 - 9) = 0$ in factored form? Explain.

Skill Check

3. Are $-5, 2,$ and 3 the solutions of $3(x - 2)(x + 5) = 0$? Explain.

4. ERROR ANALYSIS Find and correct the error at the right.

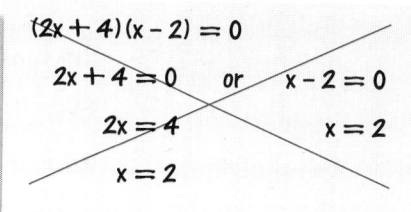

Does the graph of the function have *x*-intercepts of 4 and −5?

5. $y = 2(x + 4)(x - 5)$ **6.** $y = 4(x - 4)(x - 5)$

7. $y = -(x - 4)(x + 5)$ **8.** $y = 3(x + 5)(x - 4)$

Use the zero-product property to solve the equation.

9. $(b + 1)(b + 3) = 0$ **10.** $(t - 3)(t - 5) = 0$

11. $(x - 7)^2 = 0$ **12.** $(y + 9)(y - 2)(y - 5) = 0$

13. Sketch the graph of $y = (x + 2)(x - 2)$. Label the vertex and the *x*-intercepts.

Practice and Applications

ZERO-PRODUCT PROPERTY Use the zero-product property to solve the equation.

14. $(x + 4)(x + 1) = 0$ **15.** $(t + 8)(t - 6) = 0$ **16.** $x(x + 8) = 0$

17. $(y + 3)^2 = 0$ **18.** $(b - 9)(b + 8) = 0$ **19.** $(d + 7)^2 = 0$

20. $(y - 2)(y + 1) = 0$ **21.** $(z + 2)(z + 3) = 0$ **22.** $(v - 7)(v - 5) = 0$

23. $(w - 17)^2 = 0$ **24.** $p(2p + 1) = 0$ **25.** $4(c + 9)^2 = 0$

26. $(z + 9)(z - 11) = 0$ **27.** $(a - 20)(a + 15) = 0$ **28.** $(d + 6)(3d - 4) = 0$

Student Help

▶ **HOMEWORK HELP**
Example 1: Exs. 14–36
Example 2: Exs. 14–36
Example 3: Exs. 29–36
Example 4: Exs. 37–45
Example 5: Exs. 46–51

SOLVING FACTORED CUBIC EQUATIONS Solve the equation.

29. $(x + 1)(x + 2)(x - 4) = 0$ **30.** $y(y - 4)(y - 8) = 0$

31. $(a + 5)(a - 6)^2 = 0$ **32.** $r(r - 12)^2 = 0$

33. $5(d + 8)(d - 12)(d + 9) = 0$ **34.** $8(n + 9)(n - 9)(n + 12) = 0$

35. $(b - 8)(2b + 1)(b + 2) = 0$ **36.** $(y - 5)(y - 6)(3y - 2) = 0$

37. $y = (x + 2)(x - 4)$ **38.** $y = (x - 2)(x + 4)$ **39.** $y = (x + 4)(x + 2)$

A. 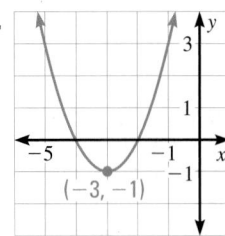   **B.** 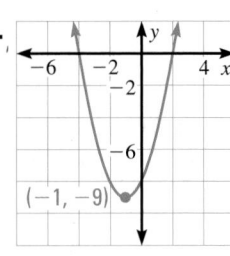   **C.**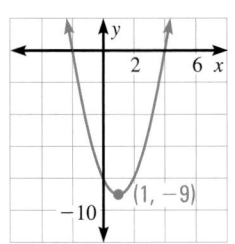

SKETCHING GRAPHS Find the *x*-intercepts and the vertex of the graph of the function. Then sketch the graph of the function.

40. $y = (x - 4)(x + 2)$ **41.** $y = (x + 5)(x + 3)$ **42.** $y = (x - 3)(x + 3)$

43. $y = (x - 1)(x + 7)$ **44.** $y = (x - 2)(x - 6)$ **45.** $y = (x + 4)(x + 3)$

VLA TELESCOPE In Exercises 46 and 47, use the cross section of one of the Very Large Array's telescope dishes shown below.

The cross section of the telescope's dish can be modeled by the polynomial function

$$y = \frac{14}{41^2}(x + 41)(x - 41)$$

where *x* and *y* are measured in feet, and the center of the dish is at $x = 0$.

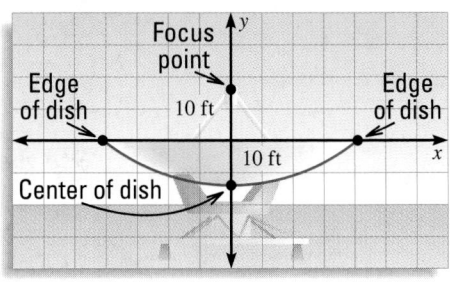

46. Find the width of the dish. Explain your reasoning.

47. Use the model to find the coordinates of the center of the dish.

GATEWAY ARCH In Exercises 48 and 49, use the following information.
The Gateway Arch in St. Louis, Missouri, has the shape of a catenary (a U-shaped curve similar to a parabola). It can be approximated by the following model, where *x* and *y* are measured in feet. ▶ Source: National Park Service

Gateway Arch model: $y = -\dfrac{7}{1000}(x + 300)(x - 300)$

48. How far apart are the legs of the arch at the base?

49. How high is the arch?

THE BARRINGER METEOR CRATER was formed about 49,000 years ago when a nickel and iron meteorite struck the desert at about 25,000 miles per hour.

BARRINGER METEOR CRATER In Exercises 50 and 51, use the following equation which models a cross section of the Barringer Meteor Crater, near Winslow, Arizona. Note that *x* and *y* are measured in meters and the center of the crater is at $x = 0$. ▶ Source: Jet Propulsion Laboratory

Barringer Meteor model: $y = \dfrac{1}{1800}(x - 600)(x + 600)$

50. Assuming the lip of the crater is at $y = 0$, how wide is the crater?

51. What is the depth of the crater?

52. MULTIPLE CHOICE Solve $6(x - 3)(x + 5)(x - 9) = 0$.

Ⓐ 6, 3, 5, and 9

Ⓑ 3, −5, and 9

Ⓒ 6, 3, −5, and 9

Ⓓ 6, 3, 5, and −9

53. MULTIPLE CHOICE Which function represents the graph at the right?

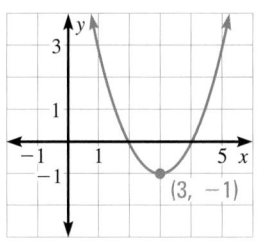

Ⓕ $y = (x + 2)(x + 4)$

Ⓖ $y = (x + 2)(x - 4)$

Ⓗ $y = (x - 2)(x - 4)$

Ⓙ $y = (x - 2)(x + 4)$

Mixed Review

DECIMAL FORM Write the number in decimal form. *(Lesson 8.5)*

54. 2.1×10^5 **55.** 4.443×10^{-2} **56.** 8.57×10^8 **57.** 1.25×10^6

58. 3.71×10^{-3} **59.** 9.96×10^6 **60.** 7.22×10^{-4} **61.** 8.17×10^7

MULTIPLYING EXPRESSIONS Find the product. *(Lesson 10.2)*

62. $(x - 2)(x - 7)$ **63.** $(x + 8)(x - 8)$ **64.** $(x - 4)(x + 5)$

65. $(2x + 7)(3x - 1)$ **66.** $(5x - 1)(5x + 2)$ **67.** $(3x + 1)(8x - 3)$

68. $(2x - 4)(4x - 2)$ **69.** $(x + 10)(x + 10)$ **70.** $(3x + 5)(2x - 3)$

EXPONENTIAL MODELS Tell whether the situation can be represented by a model of *exponential growth* or *exponential decay*. Then write a model that represents the situation. *(Lessons 8.6, 8.7)*

71. COMPUTER PRICES From 1996 to 2000, the average price of a computer company's least expensive home computer system decreased by 16% per year.

72. MUSIC SALES From 1995 to 1999, the number of CDs a band sold increased by 23% per year.

73. COOKING CLUB From 1996 to 2000, the number of members in the cooking club decreased by 3% per year.

74. INTERNET SERVICE From 1993 to 1998, the total revenues for a company that provides Internet service increased by about 137% per year.

Maintaining Skills

FINDING FACTORS List all the factors of the number. *(Skills Review p. 761)*

75. 12 **76.** 20 **77.** 18 **78.** 35

79. 51 **80.** 24 **81.** 36 **82.** 48

83. 64 **84.** 90 **85.** 84 **86.** 112

DEVELOPING CONCEPTS

10.5 Factoring $x^2 + bx + c$

For use with Lesson 10.5

GOAL

Use algebra tiles to model the factorization of a trinomial of the form $x^2 + bx + c$.

MATERIALS

• algebra tiles

Question

How can you use algebra tiles to factor $x^2 + 5x + 6$?

Explore

Factor the trinomial $x^2 + 5x + 6$.

1 Use algebra tiles to model $x^2 + 5x + 6$.

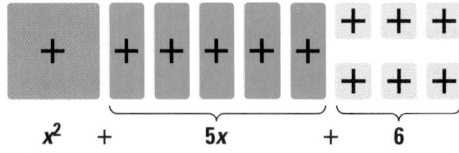

$x^2 \quad + \qquad 5x \qquad + \quad 6$

2 With the x^2-tile at the upper left, arrange the x-tiles and 1-tiles around the x^2-tile to form a rectangle.

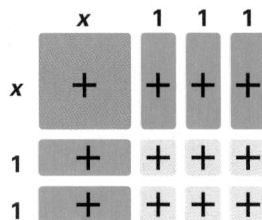

3 The width of the rectangle is (? + ?), and the length of the rectangle is (? + ?). Complete the statement: $x^2 + 5x + 6 = (? + ?) \cdot (? + ?)$.

Think About It

Write the factors of the trinomial represented by the algebra tiles.

1.

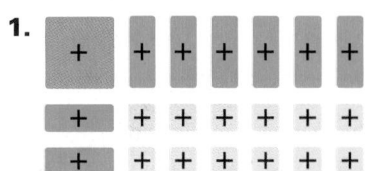

2.

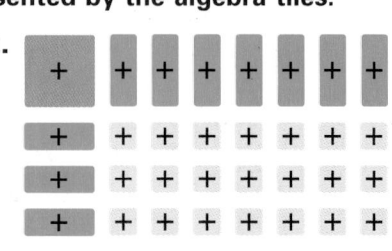

In Exercises 3–8, use algebra tiles to factor the trinomial. Sketch your model.

3. $x^2 + 7x + 6$ **4.** $x^2 + 6x + 8$ **5.** $x^2 + 8x + 15$

6. $x^2 + 6x + 9$ **7.** $x^2 + 4x + 4$ **8.** $x^2 + 7x + 10$

9. Use algebra tiles to show why the trinomial $x^2 + 3x + 4$ cannot be factored.

Factoring $x^2 + bx + c$

Goal

Factor trinomials of the form $x^2 + bx + c$.

Key Words

- factor a trinomial
- factored form

How wide should the border of a garden be?

In Example 7 you will factor a quadratic equation to find the width of a border around a garden.

A trinomial of the form $x^2 + bx + c$, where b and c are integers is shown below.

$$x^2 + 9x + 14, \qquad b = 9, \qquad c = 14$$

To **factor a trinomial** of this form means to write the trinomial as the product of two binomials (factored form).

Trinomial		Factored Form
$x^2 + 9x + 14$	$=$	$(x + 2)(x + 7)$
$x^2 - x - 12$	$=$	$(x + 3)(x - 4)$
$x^2 - 2x - 15$	$=$	$(x + 3)(x - 5)$

In order to write $x^2 + bx + c$ in the form $(x + p)(x + q)$, note that

$$(x + p)(x + q) = x^2 + (p + q)x + pq$$

This leads you to seek numbers p and q such that $p + q = b$ and $pq = c$.

EXAMPLE 1 Factor when b and c Are Positive

Factor $x^2 + 6x + 8$.

Solution

The first term of each binomial factor is x. For this trinomial, $b = 6$ and $c = 8$. You need to find numbers p and q whose product is 8 and whose sum is 6.

p and q	$p + q$	
1, 8	9	
2, 4	6	The numbers you need are 2 and 4.

ANSWER $x^2 + 6x + 8 = (x + 2)(x + 4)$. Check your answer by multiplying.

Checkpoint ✓ *Factor when b and c Are Positive*

Factor the trinomial.

1. $x^2 + 4x + 3$ **2.** $x^2 + 5x + 6$ **3.** $x^2 + 8x + 7$ **4.** $x^2 + 7x + 6$

EXAMPLE 2 Factor when b Is Negative and c Is Positive

Factor $x^2 - 5x + 6$.

Solution

The first term of each binomial factor is x.

$$(x \ \_\_)(x \ \_\_)$$

For this trinomial, $b = -5$ and $c = 6$. Because c is positive, you need to find numbers p and q with the same sign. Find numbers p and q whose sum is -5 and whose product is 6.

p and q	$p + q$	
$-1, -6$	-7	
$-2, -3$	-5	The numbers you need are -2 and -3.

ANSWER ▶ $x^2 - 5x + 6 = (x - 2)(x - 3)$. Check your answer by multiplying.

 **Factor when b Is Negative and c Is Positive**

Factor the trinomial.

5. $x^2 - 5x + 4$ **6.** $x^2 - 4x + 4$ **7.** $x^2 - 8x + 7$ **8.** $x^2 - 7x + 12$

EXAMPLE 3 Factor when b and c Are Negative

Factor $x^2 - 11x - 12$.

Solution

The first term of each binomial factor is x.

$$(x \ \_\_)(x \ \_\_)$$

For this trinomial, $b = -11$ and $c = -12$. Because c is negative, you need to find numbers p and q with different signs. Find numbers p and q whose sum is -11 and whose product is -12.

p and q	$p + q$	
$-1, \quad 12$	11	
$1, -12$	-11	The numbers you need are 1 and -12.

ANSWER ▶ $x^2 - 11x - 12 = (x + 1)(x - 12)$. Check your answer by multiplying.

 **Factor when b and c Are Negative**

Factor the trinomial.

9. $x^2 - 5x - 6$ **10.** $x^2 - 3x - 10$ **11.** $x^2 - 13x - 14$ **12.** $x^2 - 6x - 7$

EXAMPLE 4 Factor when _b_ Is Positive and _c_ Is Negative

Factor $x^2 + 17x - 18$.

Solution

The first term of each binomial factor is x.

$$(x \ \_\_)(x \ \_\_)$$

For this trinomial, $b = 17$ and $c = -18$. Because c is negative, you need to find numbers p and q with different signs. Find numbers p and q whose sum is 17 and whose product is -18.

p and q	$p + q$	
$1, -18$	-17	
$-1, \ \ 18$	17	The numbers you need are -1 and 18.

ANSWER ▶ $x^2 + 17x - 18 = (x - 1)(x + 18)$.

Checkpoint ✓ Factor when _b_ Is Positive and _c_ Is Negative

Factor the trinomial.

13. $x^2 + x - 6$ **14.** $x^2 + 2x - 8$ **15.** $x^2 + 8x - 20$ **16.** $x^2 + 3x - 10$

EXAMPLE 5 Check Using a Graphing Calculator

Factor $x^2 - 2x - 8$.

Solution

The first term of each binomial factor is x.

$$(x \ \_\_)(x \ \_\_)$$

For this trinomial, $b = -2$ and $c = -8$. Because c is negative, you need to find numbers p and q with different signs. Find numbers p and q whose sum is -2 and whose product is -8.

p and q	$p + q$	
$-1, \ \ 8$	7	
$1, -8$	-7	
$-2, \ \ 4$	2	
$2, -4$	-2	The numbers you need are 2 and -4.

ANSWER ▶ $x^2 - 2x - 8 = (x + 2)(x - 4)$.

CHECK ✓ Use a graphing calculator. Graph $y = x^2 - 2x - 8$ and $y = (x + 2)(x - 4)$ on the same screen. The graphs are the same, so your answer is correct.

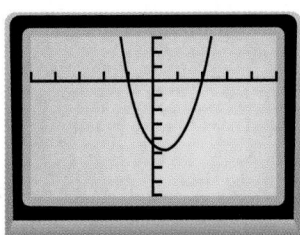

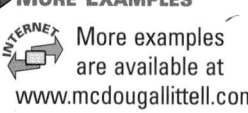
EXAMPLE 6 Solve a Quadratic Equation

Solve $x^2 - 3x = 10$ by factoring.

Solution

$x^2 - 3x = 10$	Write equation.
$x^2 - 3x - 10 = 0$	Write in standard form.
$(x - 5)(x + 2) = 0$	Factor left side.
$x - 5 = 0 \quad or \quad x + 2 = 0$	Use zero-product property.
$x = 5 \qquad\qquad x = -2$	Solve for x.

ANSWER ▶ The solutions are 5 and -2. Check these in the original equation.

Link to Careers

LANDSCAPE DESIGNERS plan and map out the appearance of outdoor spaces like parks, gardens, golf courses, and other recreational areas.

More about landscape designers available at www.mcdougallittell.com

EXAMPLE 7 Write a Quadratic Model

LANDSCAPE DESIGN You are putting a stone border along two sides of a rectangular Japanese garden that measures 6 yards by 15 yards. Your budget limits you to only enough stone to cover 46 square yards. How wide should the border be?

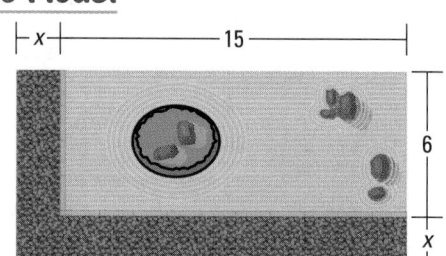

Solution

Area of border	=	Total area	−	Garden area

$46 = (x + 15)(x + 6) - (15)(6)$	Write quadratic model.
$46 = x^2 + 6x + 15x + 90 - 90$	Multiply.
$46 = x^2 + 21x$	Combine like terms.
$0 = x^2 + 21x - 46$	Write in standard form.
$0 = (x + 23)(x - 2)$	Factor.
$x + 23 = 0 \quad or \quad x - 2 = 0$	Use zero-product property.
$x = -23 \qquad\qquad x = 2$	Solve for x.

The solutions are -23 and 2. Only $x = 2$ is a reasonable solution, because negative values for dimension do not make sense.

ANSWER ▶ The border should be 2 yards wide.

Checkpoint ✔ *Solve a Quadratic Equation*

Solve the equation by factoring.

17. $0 = x^2 + 4x + 3$ **18.** $0 = x^2 - 5x + 4$ **19.** $0 = x^2 - 5x - 6$

20. Suppose the garden in Example 7 above measured 7 yards by 12 yards and the budget lets you cover 66 square yards. How wide should the border be?

Guided Practice

Vocabulary Check   **1.** What does it mean to factor a trinomial of the form $x^2 + bx + c$?

Skill Check   **Match the trinomial with a correct factorization.**

2. $x^2 - x - 20$ **A.** $(x + 5)(x - 4)$

3. $x^2 + x - 20$ **B.** $(x + 4)(x + 5)$

4. $x^2 + 9x + 20$ **C.** $(x - 4)(x - 5)$

5. $x^2 - 9x + 20$ **D.** $(x + 4)(x - 5)$

Solve the equation by factoring.

6. $0 = x^2 - 4x + 4$ **7.** $0 = x^2 - 4x - 5$ **8.** $0 = x^2 + x - 6$

LOGICAL REASONING **Complete the statement with *always, sometimes,* or *never*.**

9. Factoring ___?___ reverses the effects of multiplication.

10. In the factoring of a trinomial, if the constant term is positive, then the signs in both binomial factors will ___?___ be the same.

11. In the factoring of a trinomial, if the constant term is negative, then the signs in both binomial factors will ___?___ be negative.

Practice and Applications

FACTORED FORM **Choose the correct factorization.**

12. $x^2 + 7x + 12$ **13.** $x^2 - 10x + 16$ **14.** $x^2 + 11x - 26$

    A. $(x + 6)(x + 2)$ **A.** $(x - 4)(x - 4)$ **A.** $(x - 13)(x + 2)$

    B. $(x + 4)(x + 3)$ **B.** $(x - 8)(x - 2)$ **B.** $(x + 13)(x - 2)$

FACTORING TRINOMIALS **Factor the trinomial.**

15. $z^2 + 6z + 5$ **16.** $x^2 + 8x - 9$ **17.** $b^2 + 5b - 24$

18. $a^2 - a - 20$ **19.** $r^2 + 8r + 16$ **20.** $y^2 - 3y - 18$

21. $m^2 - 7m - 30$ **22.** $w^2 + 13w + 36$ **23.** $b^2 + 3b - 40$

Student Help

▶ **HOMEWORK HELP**
 Example 1: Exs. 12–23
 Example 2: Exs. 12–23
 Example 3: Exs. 12–23
 Example 4: Exs. 12–23
 Example 5: Exs. 39–41
 Example 6: Exs. 24–35
 Example 7: Exs. 42–45

SOLVING QUADRATIC EQUATIONS **Solve the equation by factoring.**

24. $x^2 + 7x + 10 = 0$ **25.** $x^2 + 5x - 14 = 0$ **26.** $x^2 + 6x + 9 = 0$

27. $x^2 + 16x + 15 = 0$ **28.** $x^2 - 9x = -14$ **29.** $x^2 + 3x = 54$

30. $x^2 + 100 = 20x$ **31.** $x^2 - 15x + 44 = 0$ **32.** $x^2 - 20x = -51$

33. $x^2 + 8x = 65$ **34.** $x^2 + 42 = 13x$ **35.** $-x + x^2 = 56$

Solve $x^2 - 9x + 18 = 2x$.

Solution

$x^2 - 9x + 18 = 2x$	Write original equation.
$x^2 - 9x + 18 - 2x = 0$	Add $-2x$ to each side.
$x^2 - 11x + 18 = 0$	Combine like terms.
$(x - 2)(x - 9) = 0$	Factor.
$x - 2 = 0$ *or* $x - 9 = 0$	Use zero-product property.
$x = 2$ | $x = 9$	Solve for x.

ANSWER ▶ The solutions are 2 and 9. Check your answers.

Solve the equation by factoring.

36. $x^2 - x - 8 = 82$ **37.** $n^2 + 8n + 32 = -4n$ **38.** $c^2 + 10c - 48 = 12c$

CHECKING GRAPHICALLY Solve the equation by factoring. Then use a graphing calculator to check your answer.

39. $x^2 - 17x + 30 = 0$ **40.** $x^2 - 20x + 19 = 0$ **41.** $x^2 + 3x - 18 = 0$

MAKING A SIGN In Exercises 42 and 43, a triangular sign has a base that is 2 feet less than twice its height. A local zoning ordinance restricts the surface area of street signs to be no more than 20 square feet.

42. Write an inequality involving the height that represents the largest triangular sign allowed.

43. Find the base and height of the largest triangular sign that meets the zoning ordinance.

THE TAJ MAHAL In Exercises 44 and 45, refer to the illustration of the Taj Mahal below.

44. The platform is about 38 meters wider than the main building. The total area of the platform is about 9025 square meters. Using the fact that the platform and the base of the building are squares, find their dimensions.

45. The entire complex of the Taj Mahal is about 245 meters longer than it is wide. The area of the entire complex is about 167,750 square meters. What are the dimensions of the entire complex? Explain your steps in finding the solution.

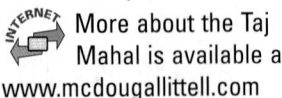
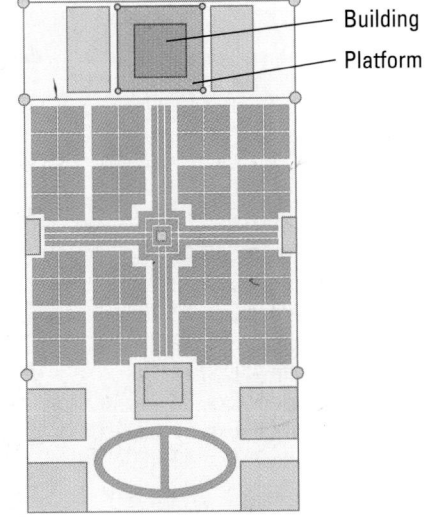

Building
Platform

46. MULTIPLE CHOICE Factor $x^2 - 10x - 24$.

   A $(x - 4)(x - 6)$ **B** $(x + 4)(x + 6)$

   C $(x + 2)(x - 12)$ **D** $(x - 2)(x + 12)$

47. MULTIPLE CHOICE Solve $x^2 - 9x = 36$ by factoring.

   F 12 and -3 **G** -12 and 3

   H 4 and -9 **J** 9 and -4

48. MULTIPLE CHOICE The length of a rectangular plot of land is 24 meters more than its width. A paved area measuring 8 meters by 12 meters is placed on the plot. The area of the unpaved part of the land is then 880 square meters. If w represents the width of the plot of land in meters, which of the following equations can be factored to find the possible values of w? *HINT:* Begin by drawing and labeling a diagram.

   A $w^2 + 24w = 880$ **B** $w^2 + 24w + 96 = 880$

   C $w^2 + 24w - 96 = 880$ **D** $w^2 + 24w = 96$

49. MULTIPLE CHOICE A triangle's base is 16 feet less than 2 times its height. If h represents the height in feet, and the total area of the triangle is 48 square feet, which of the following equations can be used to determine the height?

   F $2h + 2(h + 4) = 48$ **G** $h^2 - 8h = 48$

   H $h^2 + 8h = 48$ **J** $2h^2 - 16h = 48$

Mixed Review

FINDING THE GCF **Find the greatest common factor.** *(Skills Review p. 761)*

50. 12, 36   **51.** 30, 45   **52.** 24, 72

53. 49, 64   **54.** 20, 32, 40   **55.** 36, 54, 90

MULTIPLYING EXPRESSIONS **Find the product.** *(Lessons 10.2 and 10.3)*

56. $3q(q^3 - 5q^2 + 6)$ **57.** $(y + 9)(y - 4)$ **58.** $(7x - 11)^2$

59. $(5 - w)(12 + 3w)$ **60.** $(3a - 2)(4a + 6)$ **61.** $(5t - 3)(4t - 10)$

SOLVING FACTORED EQUATIONS **Solve the equation.** *(Lesson 10.4)*

62. $(x + 12)(x + 7) = 0$ **63.** $(z + 2)(z + 3) = 0$

64. $(t - 19)^2 = 0$ **65.** $5(x - 9)(x - 6) = 0$

66. $(y + 47)(y - 27) = 0$ **67.** $(z - 1)(4z + 2) = 0$

68. $(a - 3)(a + 5)^2 = 0$ **69.** $(b + 4)(b - 3)(2b - 1) = 0$

Maintaining Skills

ADDING DECIMALS **Add.** *(Skills Review p. 759)*

70. $3.7 + 1.04 + 5.2$ **71.** $6.7 + 0.356 + 4$

72. $7.421 + 5 + 8.09$ **73.** $8.1 + 0.2 + 3.56$

74. $6.012 + 2.9 + 5.6314$ **75.** $7.9 + 3.0204 + 10$

76. $3.2 + 5.013 + 0.0021$ **77.** $100 + 9.81 + 5.0006$

DEVELOPING CONCEPTS
Factoring $ax^2 + bx + c$

GOAL

Use algebra tiles to model the factorization of a trinomial of the form $ax^2 + bx + c$.

MATERIALS

• algebra tiles

Question

How can you use algebra tiles to factor $2x^2 + 5x + 3$?

Explore

Factor the trinomial $2x^2 + 5x + 3$.

① Use algebra tiles to model $2x^2 + 5x + 3$.

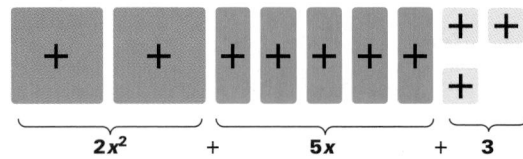

② With the x^2-tiles at the upper left, arrange the x-tiles and the 1-tiles around the x^2-tiles to form a rectangle.

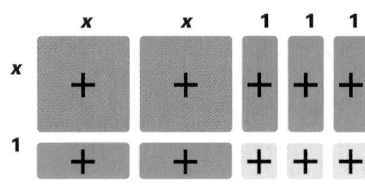

③ The width of the rectangle is (? + ?), and the length of the rectangle is (? + ?).

Complete the statement: $2x^2 + 5x + 3 = ($? $+$? $) \cdot ($? $+$? $)$.

Think About It

Use algebra tiles to factor the trinomial. Sketch your model.

1. $2x^2 + 9x + 9$ **2.** $2x^2 + 7x + 3$ **3.** $3x^2 + 4x + 1$

4. $3x^2 + 10x + 3$ **5.** $3x^2 + 10x + 8$ **6.** $4x^2 + 5x + 1$

ERROR ANALYSIS **The algebra tile model shown below is incorrect. Sketch the correct model, and use the model to factor the trinomial.**

7. $2x^2 + 3x + 1$ **8.** $2x^2 + 4x + 2$ **9.** $4x^2 + 4x + 1$

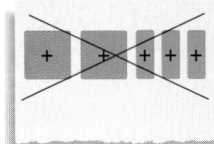 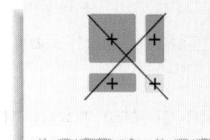 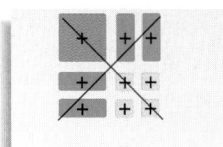

10.6 Factoring $ax^2 + bx + c$

How long will it take a cliff diver to enter the water?

Goal

Factor trinomials of the form $ax^2 + bx + c$.

Key Words

- factor a trinomial
- FOIL pattern
- quadratic

In Example 5 you will use a vertical motion model to find the time it takes a cliff diver to enter the water.

To factor a trinomial of the form $ax^2 + bx + c$, write the trinomial as the product of two binomials (factored form).

factors of 6

Example: $6x^2 + 22x + 20 = (3x + 5)(2x + 4)$ $b = 12 + 10 = 22$

factors of 20

One way to factor $ax^2 + bx + c$ is to find numbers m and n whose product is a and numbers p and q whose product is c so that the middle term is the sum of the **O**uter and **I**nner products of **FOIL**.

$m \times n = a$

$$ax^2 + bx + c = (mx + p)(nx + q) \qquad b = mq + np$$

$p \times q = c$

EXAMPLE ① Factor when a and c Are Prime Numbers

Factor $2x^2 + 11x + 5$.

		m and n	p and q
①	**Write** the numbers m and n whose product is 2 and the numbers p and q whose product is 5.	1, 2	1, 5

		Trial Factors	**Middle Term**
②	**Use** these numbers to write trial factors. Then use the **O**uter and **I**nner products of **FOIL** to check the middle term.	$(x + 1)(2x + 5)$ $(2x + 1)(x + 5)$	$5x + 2x = 7x$ $10x + x = 11x$

ANSWER ▶ $2x^2 + 11x + 5 = (2x + 1)(x + 5)$.

 **Factor when a and c Are Prime Numbers**

Factor the trinomial.

1. $2x^2 + 7x + 3$ **2.** $2x^2 + 5x + 3$ **3.** $3x^2 + 10x + 3$

EXAMPLE **2** **Factor when *a* and *c* Are not Prime Numbers**

Factor $6x^2 - 33x + 15$.

Solution

For this trinomial, $a = 6$, $b = -33$, and $c = 15$. Because c is positive, you need to find numbers p and q with the same sign. Because b is negative, only negative numbers p and q need to be tried.

Student Help

▶**STUDY TIP**
Once you find the correct binomial factors, it is not necessary to continue checking the remaining trial factors.

❶ *Write* the numbers m and n whose product is 6 and the numbers p and q whose product is 15.

m and *n*	*p* and *q*
1, 6	−1, −15
2, 3	−3, −5

❷ *Use* these numbers to write trial factors. Then use the **O**uter and **I**nner products of **FOIL** to check the middle term.

Trial Factors	Middle Term
$(x - 1)(6x - 15)$	$-15x - 6x = -21x$
$(x - 15)(6x - 1)$	$-x - 90x = -91x$
$(2x - 1)(3x - 15)$	$-30x - 3x = -33x$

ANSWER ▶ $6x^2 - 33x + 15 = (2x - 1)(3x - 15)$.

EXAMPLE **3** **Factor with a Common Factor for *a*, *b*, and *c***

Factor $6x^2 + 2x - 4$.

Solution

The coefficients of this trinomial have a common factor 2.

$2(3x^2 + x - 2)$ Factor out the common factor.

It remains to factor a trinomial with $a = 3$, $b = 1$, and $c = -2$. Because c is negative, you need to find numbers p and q with different signs.

❶ *Write* the numbers m and n whose product is 3 and the numbers p and q whose product is -2.

m and *n*	*p* and *q*
1, 3	−1, 2
	1, −2

❷ *Use* these numbers to write trial factors. Then use the **O**uter and **I**nner products of **FOIL** to check the middle term.

Trial Factors	Middle Term
$(x - 1)(3x + 2)$	$2x - 3x = -x$
$(x + 2)(3x - 1)$	$-x + 6x = 5x$
$(x + 1)(3x - 2)$	$-2x + 3x = x$

Remember to include the common factor 2 in the complete factorization.

ANSWER ▶ $6x^2 + 2x - 4 = 2(x + 1)(3x - 2)$.

Checkpoint ✔ *Factor Trinomials*

Factor the trinomial.

4. $2x^2 + 5x + 2$ **5.** $5x^2 - 7x + 2$ **6.** $4x^2 + 8x + 3$

7. $8r^2 - 6r - 9$ **8.** $6x^2 - 14x + 4$ **9.** $20x^2 + 5x - 15$

Student Help

▶ MORE EXAMPLES

 More examples are available at www.mcdougallittell.com

EXAMPLE 4 Solve a Quadratic Equation

$21n^2 + 14n + 7 = 6n + 11$	Write original equation.
$21n^2 + 8n - 4 = 0$	Write in standard form.
$(3n + 2)(7n - 2) = 0$	Factor left side.
$3n + 2 = 0$ or $7n - 2 = 0$	Use zero-product property.
$n = -\dfrac{2}{3}$ $n = \dfrac{2}{7}$	Solve for n.

ANSWER ▶ The solutions are $-\dfrac{2}{3}$ and $\dfrac{2}{7}$. Check these in the original equation.

Checkpoint ✓ *Solve a Quadratic Equation*

Solve the equation.

10. $2x^2 + 7x + 3 = 0$ **11.** $2x^2 - x - 3 = 0$ **12.** $4x^2 - 16x + 15 = 0$

EXAMPLE 5 Write a Quadratic Model

Student Help

▶ LOOK BACK
For help with using a vertical motion model see p. 535.

When a diver jumps from a ledge, the vertical component of his motion can be modeled by the vertical motion model. Suppose the ledge is 48 feet above the ocean and the initial upward velocity is 8 feet per second. How long will it take until the diver enters the water?

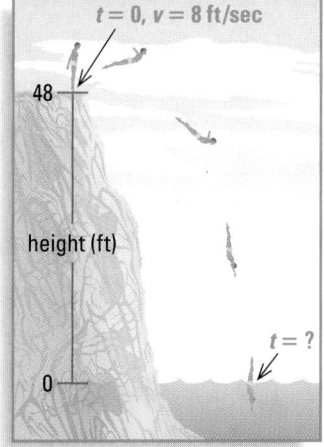

Not drawn to scale

Use a vertical motion model.
Let $v = 8$ and $s = 48$.

$h = -16t^2 + vt + s$	Vertical motion model
$= -16t^2 + 8t + 48$	Substitute values.

Solve the resulting equation for t to find the time when the diver enters the water.
Let $h = 0$.

$0 = -16t^2 + 8t + 48$	Write quadratic model.
$0 = (-8)(2t^2 - t - 6)$	Factor out common factor -8.
$0 = (-8)(t - 2)(2t + 3)$	Factor.
$t - 2 = 0$ or $2t + 3 = 0$	Use zero-product property.
$t = 2$ $t = -\dfrac{3}{2}$	Solve for t.

The solutions are 2 and $-\dfrac{3}{2}$. Negative values of time do not make sense for this problem, so the only reasonable solution is $t = 2$.

ANSWER ▶ It will take 2 seconds until the diver enters the water.

Guided Practice

Vocabulary Check

1. What is the difference between factoring quadratic polynomials of the form $x^2 + bx + c$ and $ax^2 + bx + c$?

Skill Check

Copy and complete the statement.

2. $(2x + 1)(x + 1) = 2x^2 \underline{\ ?\ } + 1$ **3.** $(3x + 2)(x - 3) = 3x^2 - 7x \underline{\ ?\ }$

4. $(3x - 4)(x - 5) = 3x^2 \underline{\ ?\ } + 20$ **5.** $(5x + 2)(2x + 1) = \underline{\ ?\ } + 9x + 2$

Match the trinomial with a correct factorization.

6. $3x^2 - 17x - 6$ **A.** $(3x + 2)(x + 3)$

7. $3x^2 + 7x - 6$ **B.** $(3x + 1)(x - 6)$

8. $3x^2 + 11x + 6$ **C.** $(3x - 1)(x + 6)$

9. $3x^2 + 17x - 6$ **D.** $(3x - 2)(x + 3)$

Factor the trinomial.

10. $2x^2 + 17x + 21$ **11.** $2x^2 - 3x - 2$ **12.** $6t^2 - t - 5$

13. $12x^2 - 19x + 4$ **14.** $6x^2 + 7x - 20$ **15.** $3x^2 + 2x - 8$

Solve the equation.

16. $3b^2 + 26b + 35 = 0$ **17.** $2z^2 + 15z = 8$ **18.** $-7n^2 - 40n = -12$

Practice and Applications

FACTORIZATIONS **Choose the correct factorization. If neither choice is correct, find the correct factorization.**

19. $3x^2 + 2x - 8$ **20.** $6y^2 - 29y - 5$ **21.** $4w^2 - 14w - 30$

    A. $(3x - 4)(x + 2)$ **A.** $(2y + 1)(3y - 5)$ **A.** $(2w + 3)(2w - 10)$

    B. $(3x - 4)(x - 2)$ **B.** $(6y - 1)(y + 5)$ **B.** $(4w + 15)(w - 2)$

FACTORING TRINOMIALS **Factor the trinomial.**

22. $2x^2 - x - 3$ **23.** $3t^2 + 16t + 5$ **24.** $5x^2 + 2x - 3$

Student Help

▶**HOMEWORK HELP**
Example 1: Exs. 19–39
Example 2: Exs. 19–39
Example 3: Exs. 19–39
Example 4: Exs. 42–54
Example 5: Exs. 55–57

25. $6a^2 + 5a + 1$ **26.** $5w^2 - 9w - 2$ **27.** $6b^2 - 11b - 2$

28. $8b^2 + 2b - 3$ **29.** $6x^2 - 9x - 15$ **30.** $12y^2 - 20y + 8$

31. $2z^2 + 19z - 10$ **32.** $6y^2 - 11y - 10$ **33.** $4x^2 + 27x + 35$

34. $4n^2 - 22n - 42$ **35.** $3c^2 - 37c + 44$ **36.** $24r^2 - 6r - 45$

37. $6t^2 + t - 70$ **38.** $14y^2 - 15y + 4$ **39.** $8y^2 - 26y + 15$

ERROR ANALYSIS Find and correct the error.

40.
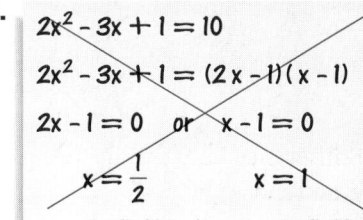
$2x^2 - 3x + 1 = 10$
$2x^2 - 3x + 1 = (2x - 1)(x - 1)$
$2x - 1 = 0$ or $x - 1 = 0$
$x = \frac{1}{2}$ $x = 1$

41.
$3y^2 - 16y - 35 = 0$
$3y^2 - 16y - 35 = (3y + 7)(y - 5)$
$3y + 7 = 0$ or $y - 5 = 0$
$y = -\frac{7}{3}$ $y = 5$

SOLVING EQUATIONS Solve the equation by factoring.

42. $2x^2 - 9x - 35 = 0$ **43.** $7x^2 - 10x + 3 = 0$ **44.** $3x^2 + 34x + 11 = 0$

45. $4x^2 - 21x + 5 = 0$ **46.** $2x^2 - 17x - 19 = 0$ **47.** $5x^2 - 3x - 26 = 0$

48. $2x^2 + 19x = -24$ **49.** $4x^2 - 8x = -3$ **50.** $6x^2 - 23x = 18$

51. $8x^2 - 34x + 24 = -11$ **52.** $6x^2 + 19x - 10 = -20$

53. $28x^2 - 9x - 1 = -4x + 2$ **54.** $10x^2 + x - 10 = -2x + 8$

VERTICAL COMPONENT OF MOTION In Exercises 55–57, use the vertical motion model $h = -16t^2 + vt + s$ where h is the height (in feet), t is the time in motion (in seconds), v is the initial velocity (in feet per second), and s is the initial height (in feet). Solve by factoring.

55. GYMNASTICS A gymnast dismounts the uneven parallel bars at a height of 8 feet with an initial upward velocity of 8 feet per second.

a. Write a quadratic equation that models her height above the ground.

b. Use the model to find the time t (in seconds) it takes for the gymnast to reach the ground. Is your answer reasonable?

56. CIRCUS ACROBATS An acrobat is shot out of a cannon and lands in a safety net that is 10 feet above the ground. Before being shot out of the cannon, she was 4 feet above the ground. She left the cannon with an initial upward velocity of 50 feet per second.

a. Write a quadratic model to represent this situation.

b. Use the model to find the time t (in seconds) it takes for her to reach the net. Explain why only one of the two solutions is reasonable.

57. T-SHIRT CANNON At a basketball game, T-shirts are rolled-up into a ball and shot from a "T-shirt cannon" into the crowd. The T-shirts are released from a height of 6 feet with an initial upward velocity of 44 feet per second. If you catch a T-shirt at your seat 30 feet above the court, how long was it in the air before you caught it? Is your answer reasonable?

58. MULTIPLE CHOICE Factor $9x^2 - 6x - 35$.

    Ⓐ $(9x - 5)(x + 7)$ Ⓑ $(3x + 5)(3x - 7)$

    Ⓒ $(9x + 5)(x - 7)$ Ⓓ $(3x - 5)(3x + 7)$

59. MULTIPLE CHOICE Solve $2x^2 + 5x + 3 = 0$.

    Ⓕ -1 and $-\dfrac{3}{2}$ Ⓖ $-\dfrac{2}{3}$ and $\dfrac{5}{3}$ Ⓗ $\dfrac{3}{2}$ and $-\dfrac{3}{2}$ Ⓙ 1 and $\dfrac{3}{2}$

Mixed Review

SOLVING SYSTEMS Use linear combinations to solve the linear system. Then check your solution. *(Lesson 7.3)*

60. $4x + 5y = 7$
$6x - 2y = -18$

61. $6x - 5y = 3$
$-12x + 8y = 5$

62. $2x + y = 120$
$x + 2y = 120$

SPECIAL PRODUCT PATTERNS Find the product. *(Lesson 10.3)*

63. $(4t - 1)^2$ **64.** $(b + 9)(b - 9)$ **65.** $(3x + 5)(3x + 5)$

66. $(2a - 7)(2a + 7)$ **67.** $(11 - 6x)^2$ **68.** $(100 + 27x)^2$

Maintaining Skills

OPERATIONS WITH FRACTIONS Simplify. *(Skills Review p. 765)*

69. $\dfrac{2}{3} \cdot \dfrac{6}{9} \div \dfrac{11}{3}$ **70.** $\dfrac{1}{2} \div \dfrac{1}{9} \cdot \dfrac{2}{3}$ **71.** $\dfrac{1}{2} \cdot \dfrac{4}{9} \cdot \dfrac{5}{6}$ **72.** $\dfrac{8}{9} \div \dfrac{9}{8} \cdot \dfrac{8}{9}$

73. $\dfrac{2}{3} \cdot \dfrac{4}{5} \cdot \dfrac{6}{7}$ **74.** $\dfrac{12}{15} \cdot \dfrac{3}{4} \div \dfrac{1}{7}$ **75.** $\dfrac{5}{6} \cdot \dfrac{9}{4} \cdot \dfrac{1}{3} \div \dfrac{1}{2}$ **76.** $\dfrac{1}{2} \cdot \dfrac{1}{3} \div \dfrac{1}{4} \cdot \dfrac{1}{5}$

Quiz 2

Solve the equation. *(Lesson 10.4)*

1. $(x + 5)(2x + 10) = 0$ **2.** $(2x + 8)^2 = 0$ **3.** $(2x + 7)(3x - 12) = 0$

4. $x(5x - 2) = 0$ **5.** $3(x - 5)(2x + 1) = 0$ **6.** $x(x + 4)(x - 7)^2 = 0$

Find the *x*-intercepts and the vertex of the graph of the function. Then sketch the graph of the function. *(Lesson 10.4)*

7. $y = (x - 2)(x + 2)$ **8.** $y = (x + 3)(x + 5)$ **9.** $y = (x - 1)(x + 3)$

Factor the trinomial. *(Lesson 10.5)*

10. $y^2 + 3y - 4$ **11.** $w^2 + 13w + 22$ **12.** $n^2 + 16n - 57$

13. $x^2 + 7x + 24$ **14.** $b^2 - 6b - 16$ **15.** $r^2 - 3r - 28$

16. $m^2 - 4m - 45$ **17.** $x^2 + 17x + 66$ **18.** $r^2 - 41r - 86$

Solve the equation by factoring. *(Lesson 10.6)*

19. $y^2 + 5y - 6 = 0$ **20.** $n^2 + 26n + 25 = 0$ **21.** $z^2 - 14z + 45 = 0$

22. $t^2 + 11t = -18$ **23.** $2a^2 + 11a + 5 = 0$ **24.** $3p^2 - 4p + 1 = 0$

25. $3b^2 - 10b - 8 = 0$ **26.** $4c^2 + 12c + 9 = 0$ **27.** $15b^2 + 41b = -14$

Factoring Special Products

Goal

Factor special products.

Key Words

• perfect square trinomial

What height can a pole-vaulter reach?

In Exercise 65 you will factor a quadratic polynomial to find the height a pole-vaulter can vault.

In Lesson 10.5 you learned to factor trinomials of the form $x^2 + bx + c$, where b and c are integers. For example, to factor $x^2 + 3x + 2$, you looked for two numbers whose product was 2 and whose sum was 3. The two numbers are 1 and 2, so you wrote $x^2 + 3x + 2 = (x + 1)(x + 2)$.

You can factor $x^2 - 9$ using the same reasoning. Since there is no middle term, its coefficient must be *zero*. So you will need two numbers whose product is -9 and whose sum is 0. The two numbers are 3 and -3. Thus, you can write

$$x^2 - 9 = (x + 3)(x - 3).$$

This suggests a simple pattern for factoring the difference of two squares.

$$a^2 - b^2 = (a + b)(a - b)$$

If we rewrite the square of a binomial pattern (from page 581) as shown below, two useful factoring patterns are created.

$$a^2 + 2ab + b^2 = (a + b)^2 \qquad \text{or} \qquad a^2 - 2ab + b^2 = (a - b)^2$$

Consider factoring $x^2 - 10x + 25$, for example. You can try the second pattern because the middle term is negative. Let $a = x$ and $b = 5$. The pattern requires that $-2ab$ be the constant term, which is true here because $-2(x)(5) = -10x$. Therefore, $x^2 - 10x + 25 = (x - 5)^2$.

Trinomials of the form $a^2 + 2ab + b^2$ and $a^2 - 2ab + b^2$ are called **perfect square trinomials** because they can be factored as the squares of binomials.

FACTORING SPECIAL PRODUCTS

Difference of Two Squares Patterns

$a^2 - b^2 = (a + b)(a - b)$ **Example:** $9x^2 - 25 = (3x + 5)(3x - 5)$

Perfect Square Trinomial Pattern

$a^2 + 2ab + b^2 = (a + b)^2$ **Example:** $x^2 + 14x + 49 = (x + 7)^2$

$a^2 - 2ab + b^2 = (a - b)^2$ **Example:** $x^2 - 12x + 36 = (x - 6)^2$

EXAMPLE 1 Factor the Difference of Two Squares

Factor the expression.

a. $m^2 - 4$ **b.** $4p^2 - 25$ **c.** $9q^2 - 64$ **d.** $a^2 - 8$

Solution

a. $m^2 - 4 = m^2 - 2^2$ Write as $a^2 - b^2$.

        $= (m + 2)(m - 2)$ Factor using pattern.

b. $4p^2 - 25 = (2p)^2 - 5^2$ Write as $a^2 - b^2$.

           $= (2p + 5)(2p - 5)$ Factor using pattern.

c. $9q^2 - 64 = (3q)^2 - 8^2$ Write as $a^2 - b^2$.

          $= (3q + 8)(3q - 8)$ Factor using pattern.

d. $a^2 - 8$ cannot be factored using integers because it does not fit the difference of two squares pattern; 8 is not the square of an integer.

Checkpoint ✓ *Factor the Difference of Two Squares*

Factor the expression.

1. $x^2 - 16$ **2.** $n^2 - 36$ **3.** $r^2 - 20$ **4.** $m^2 - 100$

5. $8y^2 - 1$ **6.** $4y^2 - 49$ **7.** $9x^2 - 25$ **8.** $16q^2 - 45$

EXAMPLE 2 Factor Perfect Square Trinomials

Factor the expression.

a. $x^2 - 4x + 4$ **b.** $a^2 - 18a + 81$ **c.** $16y^2 + 24y + 9$

Solution

a. $x^2 - 4x + 4 = x^2 - 2(x)(2) + 2^2$ Write as $a^2 - 2ab + b^2$.

          $= (x - 2)^2$ Factor using pattern.

b. $a^2 - 18a + 81 = a^2 - 2(a)(9) + 9^2$ Write as $a^2 - 2ab + b^2$.

          $= (a - 9)^2$ Factor using pattern.

c. $16y^2 + 24y + 9 = (4y)^2 + 2(4y)(3) + 3^2$ Write as $a^2 + 2ab + b^2$.

          $= (4y + 3)^2$ Factor using pattern.

Checkpoint ✓ *Factor Perfect Square Trinomials*

Factor the expression.

9. $x^2 + 6x + 9$ **10.** $n^2 - 8n + 16$ **11.** $a^2 + 18a + 81$

12. $4b^2 - 4b + 1$ **13.** $25m^2 + 10m + 1$ **14.** $9a^2 - 30a + 25$

EXAMPLE 3 **Factor Out a Constant First**

a. $50 - 98x^2 = 2(25 - 49x^2)$ Factor out common factor.

$\qquad\qquad = 2\left[5^2 - (7x)^2\right]$ Write as $a^2 - b^2$.

$\qquad\qquad = 2(5 + 7x)(5 - 7x)$ Factor using pattern.

b. $3x^2 - 30x + 75 = 3(x^2 - 10x + 25)$ Factor out common factor.

$\qquad\qquad\qquad = 3\left[x^2 - 2(x)(5) + 5^2\right]$ Write as $a^2 - 2ab + b^2$.

$\qquad\qquad\qquad = 3(x - 5)^2$ Factor using pattern.

c. $4x^2 + 24x + 44 = 4(x^2 + 6x + 11)$ Factor out common factor.

Since 11 is not the square of any integer, you cannot factor $4(x^2 + 6x + 11)$ with integers using the perfect square trinomial pattern.

Checkpoint ✓ **Factor Out a Constant First**

Factor the expression.

15. $2x^2 - 32$ **16.** $3p^2 + 36p + 108$ **17.** $3b^2 - 48$

18. $8n^2 - 24n + 18$ **19.** $1000 - 10m^2$ **20.** $2a^2 + 28a + 98$

EXAMPLE 4 **Graphical and Analytical Reasoning**

Solve the equation $-2x^2 + 12x - 18 = 0$.

$-2x^2 + 12x - 18 = 0$ Write original equation.

$-2(x^2 - 6x + 9) = 0$ Factor out common factor.

$-2\left[x^2 - 2(x)(3) + 3^2\right] = 0$ Write as $a^2 - 2ab + b^2$.

$-2(x - 3)^2 = 0$ Factor using pattern.

$x - 3 = 0$ Set repeated factor equal to 0.

$x = 3$ Solve for x.

ANSWER ▶ The solution is 3.

CHECK ✓ You can check your answer by substitution or by graphing. Also, a graphing calculator will provide a graphical representation of the solution $x = 3$.

Graph $y = -2x^2 + 12x - 18$.

Graph the x-axis, $y = 0$.

🖩 Use your graphing calculator's *Intersect* feature to find the x-intercept, where $-2x^2 + 12x - 18 = 0$.

When $x = 3$, $-2x^2 + 12x - 18 = 0$, so your answer is correct.

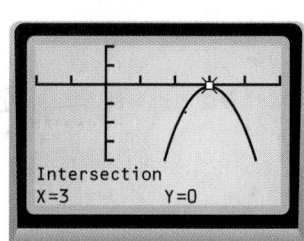

Intersection
X=3   Y=0

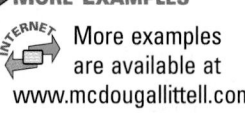
EXAMPLE 5 **Solve a Quadratic Equation**

Solve $4x^2 + 4x + 1 = 0$.

Solution

$$4x^2 + 4x + 1 = 0 \qquad \text{Write original equation.}$$

$$(2x)^2 + 2(2x) + 1^2 = 0 \qquad \text{Write as } a^2 + 2ab + b^2.$$

$$(2x + 1)^2 = 0 \qquad \text{Factor using pattern.}$$

$$2x + 1 = 0 \qquad \text{Set repeated factor equal to 0.}$$

$$x = -\frac{1}{2} \qquad \text{Solve for } x.$$

ANSWER ▶ The solution is $-\frac{1}{2}$. Check this in the original equation.

Checkpoint ✓ **Solve a Quadratic Equation**

Solve the equation by factoring. Then use a graphing calculator to check your solutions.

21. $x^2 - 81 = 0$ **22.** $m^2 - 4m + 4 = 0$ **23.** $2n^2 - 288 = 0$

EXAMPLE 6 **Write and Use a Quadratic Model**

BLOCK AND TACKLE An object lifted with a rope or wire should not weigh more than the safe working load for the rope or wire. The safe working load S (in pounds) for a natural fiber rope is a function of C, the circumference of the rope in inches.

Safe working load model: $150 \cdot C^2 = S$

You are setting up a block and tackle to lift a 1350-pound safe. What size natural fiber rope do you need to have a safe working load?

Solution

$$150C^2 = S \qquad \text{Write model.}$$

$$150C^2 = 1350 \qquad \text{Substitute 1350 for } S.$$

$$150C^2 - 1350 = 0 \qquad \text{Subtract 1350 from each side.}$$

$$150(C^2 - 9) = 0 \qquad \text{Factor out common factor.}$$

$$150(C + 3)(C - 3) = 0 \qquad \text{Factor.}$$

$$C + 3 = 0 \quad or \quad C - 3 = 0 \qquad \text{Use zero-product property.}$$

$$C = -3 \qquad \qquad C = 3 \qquad \text{Solve for } C.$$

ANSWER ▶ Negative values for circumference do not make sense, so you will need a rope with a circumference of at least 3 inches.

Link to
Science

BLOCK AND TACKLE A block and tackle makes it easier to lift a heavy object. For instance, using a block and tackle with 4 pulleys, you can lift 1000 pounds with only 250 pounds of applied force.

Guided Practice

Vocabulary Check

1. Write the three special product factoring patterns. Give an example of each pattern.

Skill Check

Factor the expression.

2. $x^2 - 9$ **3.** $b^2 + 10b + 25$ **4.** $p^2 + 25$

5. $w^2 - 16w + 64$ **6.** $16 - c^2$ **7.** $6y^2 - 24$

8. $18 - 2b^2$ **9.** $4x^2 - 4x + 1$ **10.** $4a^2 - b^2$

Solve the equation by factoring.

11. $x^2 + 6x + 9 = 0$ **12.** $144 - y^2 = 0$ **13.** $s^2 - 14s + 49 = 0$

14. $-25 + x^2 = 0$ **15.** $4y^2 - 24y + 36 = 0$ **16.** $7x^2 + 28x + 28 = 0$

17. VERTICAL COMPONENT OF MOTION You throw a ball upward from the ground with an initial velocity of 96 feet per second. How long will it take the ball to reach a height of 144 feet? *HINT:* Use the vertical motion model on page 607.

Practice and Applications

DIFFERENCE OF TWO SQUARES **Factor the expression.**

18. $n^2 - 16$ **19.** $q^2 - 64$ **20.** $b^2 - 48$

21. $9c^2 - 1$ **22.** $49 - a^2$ **23.** $81 - x^2$

24. $36x^2 + 25$ **25.** $w^2 - 9y^2$ **26.** $25s^2 - 16t^2$

PERFECT SQUARES **Factor the expression.**

27. $x^2 + 8x + 16$ **28.** $x^2 - 20x + 100$ **29.** $b^2 - 14b + 49$

30. $y^2 + 30y + 225$ **31.** $9x^2 + 6x + 1$ **32.** $4r^2 + 12r + 9$

33. $25n^2 - 20n + 4$ **34.** $18x^2 + 12x + 2$ **35.** $16w^2 - 80w + 100$

36. $36m^2 - 84m + 49$ **37.** $a^2 - 4ab + 4b^2$ **38.** $x^2 + 12xy + 36y^2$

Student Help

▶HOMEWORK HELP
Example 1: Exs. 18–26
Example 2: Exs. 27–38
Example 3: Exs. 39–50
Example 4: Exs. 51–58
Example 5: Exs. 51–58
Example 6: Exs. 60–65

COMMON FACTOR **Factor the expression.**

39. $4n^2 - 36$ **40.** $-32 + 18x^2$ **41.** $5c^2 + 20c + 20$

42. $6b^2 - 54$ **43.** $27t^2 + 18t + 9$ **44.** $28y^2 - 7$

45. $3k^2 - 39k + 90$ **46.** $24a^2 - 54$ **47.** $4b^2 - 40b + 100$

48. $32x^2 - 48x + 18$ **49.** $16w^2 + 80w + 100$ **50.** $2x^2 + 28xy + 98y^2$

SOLVING EQUATIONS Solve the equation by factoring. Use a graphing calculator to check your solution if you wish.

51. $4x^2 + 4x + 1 = 0$

52. $25x^2 - 4 = 0$

53. $3x^2 - 24x + 48 = 0$

54. $-27 + 3x^2 = 0$

55. $6b^2 - 72b + 216 = 0$

56. $90x^2 - 120x + 40 = 0$

57. $16x^2 - 56x + 49 = 0$

58. $50x^2 + 60x + 18 = 0$

59. VERTICAL COMPONENT OF MOTION A model rocket is fired upward with an initial velocity of 160 feet per second. How long will it take the rocket to reach a height of 400 feet? *Hint:* Use the vertical motion model on p. 607.

SAFE WORKING LOAD In Exercises 60 and 61, the safe working load *S* (in tons) for a wire rope is a function of *D*, the diameter of the rope (in inches).

Safe working load model for wire rope: $4 \cdot D^2 = S$

60. What diameter of wire rope do you need to lift a 9-ton load and have a safe working load?

61. When determining the safe working load *S* of a rope that is old or worn, decrease *S* by 50%. Write a model for *S* when using an old wire rope. What diameter of old wire rope do you need to safely lift a 9-ton load?

HANG TIME In Exercises 62 and 63, use the following information about a basketball player's hang time, the length of time spent in the air after jumping.

The maximum height *h* jumped (in feet) is a function of *t*, where *t* is the hang time (in seconds).

Hang time model: $h = 4t^2$

62. If you jump 1 foot into the air, what is your hang time?

63. If a professional player jumps 4 feet into the air, what is the hang time?

POLE-VAULTING In Exercises 64 and 65, use the following information. In the sport of pole-vaulting, the height *h* (in feet) reached by a pole-vaulter can be approximated by a function of *v*, the velocity of the pole-vaulter, as shown in the model below. The constant *g* is approximately 32 feet per second per second.

Pole-vaulter height model: $h = \dfrac{v^2}{2g}$

64. To reach a height of 9 feet, what is the pole-vaulter's velocity?

65. What height will a pole-vaulter reach if the pole-vaulter's velocity is 32 feet per second?

66. MULTIPLE CHOICE Which of the following is a correct factorization of $-12x^2 + 147$?

   Ⓐ $-3(2x + 7)^2$ Ⓑ $3(2x - 7)(2x + 7)$

   Ⓒ $-2(2x - 7)(2x + 7)$ Ⓓ $-3(2x - 7)(2x + 7)$

67. MULTIPLE CHOICE Which of the following is a correct factorization of $72x^2 - 24x + 2$?

   Ⓕ $-9(3x - 1)^2$ Ⓖ $2(6x - 1)^2$

   Ⓗ $8(3x - 1)^2$ Ⓙ $9(3x - 1)^2$

68. MULTIPLE CHOICE Solve $9x^2 - 12x + 4 = 0$.

   Ⓐ -3 Ⓑ $-\dfrac{2}{3}$ Ⓒ $\dfrac{2}{3}$ Ⓓ 3

CHECKING FOR SOLUTIONS Determine whether the ordered pair is a solution of the system of linear equations. *(Lesson 7.1)*

69. $x + 9y = -11$
   $-4x + y = -30$ $(7, -2)$

70. $2x + 6y = 22$
   $-x - 4y = -13$ $(-5, -2)$

71. $-2x + 7y = -41$
   $3x + 5y = 15$ $(-10, 3)$

72. $-5x - 8y = 28$
   $9x - 2y = 48$ $(4, -6)$

SOLVING LINEAR SYSTEMS Use the substitution method to solve the linear system. *(Lesson 7.2)*

73. $x - y = 2$
   $2x + y = 1$

74. $x - 2y = 10$
   $3x - y = 0$

75. $-x + y = 0$
   $2x + y = 0$

76. $x - 2y = 4$
   $2x + y = 3$

77. $x - y = 0$
   $3x + 4y = 14$

78. $2x + 3y = -5$
   $x - 2y = -6$

SIMPLIFYING RADICAL EXPRESSIONS Simplify the expression. *(Lesson 9.3)*

79. $\sqrt{216}$ **80.** $\sqrt{5} \cdot \sqrt{15}$ **81.** $\sqrt{10} \cdot \sqrt{20}$ **82.** $\sqrt{4} \cdot 3\sqrt{9}$

83. $\sqrt{\dfrac{28}{49}}$ **84.** $\dfrac{10\sqrt{8}}{\sqrt{25}}$ **85.** $\dfrac{12\sqrt{4}}{\sqrt{9}}$ **86.** $\dfrac{-6\sqrt{12}}{\sqrt{4}}$

SOLVING EQUATIONS Use the quadratic formula to solve the equation. *(Lesson 9.6)*

87. $9x^2 - 14x - 7 = 0$ **88.** $9d^2 - 58d + 24 = 0$ **89.** $7y^2 - 9y - 17 = 0$

PRIME FACTORIZATION Write the prime factorization of the number if it is not a prime number. If a number is prime, write *prime*. *(Skills Review p. 761)*

90. 8   **91.** 20   **92.** 45   **93.** 57

94. 96   **95.** 80   **96.** 101   **97.** 120

98. 244   **99.** 345   **100.** 250   **101.** 600

Factoring Cubic Polynomials

What are the dimensions of a terrarium?

In Example 6 you will factor a cubic polynomial to determine the dimensions of a terrarium, which is an enclosed space for keeping small animals indoors.

Goal
Factor cubic polynomials.

Key Words
• prime polynomial
• factor a polynomial completely

You have already been using the distributive property to factor out constants that are common to the terms of a polynomial.

$$9x^2 - 15 = 3(3x^2 - 5)$$ Factor out common factor.

You can also use the distributive property to factor out *variable* factors that are common to the terms of a polynomial. When factoring a cubic polynomial, you should factor out the *greatest common factor* (GCF) first and then look for other patterns.

EXAMPLE 1 **Find the Greatest Common Factor**

Factor the greatest common factor out of $14x^3 - 21x^2$.

Solution

First find the greatest common factor of $14x^3$ and $21x^2$.

$$14x^3 = 2 \cdot 7 \cdot x \cdot x \cdot x$$
$$21x^2 = 3 \cdot 7 \cdot x \cdot x$$
$$\text{GCF} = 7 \cdot x \cdot x = 7x^2$$

Then use the distributive property to factor out the greatest common factor from each term.

ANSWER $14x^3 - 21x^2 = 7x^2(2x - 3)$.

Student Help

▶ SKILLS REVIEW
For help with finding the GCF, see p. 761.

 **Find the Greatest Common Factor**

Factor out the greatest common factor.

1. $11x - 22$

2. $6x^2 + 12x + 18$

3. $8x^3 - 16x$

4. $3n^3 - 36n^2 + 12n$

5. $4y^3 - 10y^2$

6. $9x^3 + 6x^2 + 18x$

PRIME FACTORS A polynomial is **prime** if it cannot be factored using integer coefficients. To **factor a polynomial completely**, write it as the product of monomial and prime factors.

EXAMPLE 2 **Factor Completely**

Factor $4x^3 + 20x^2 + 24x$ completely.

Solution

$$4x^3 + 20x^2 + 24x = 4x(x^2 + 5x + 6) \qquad \text{Factor out GCF.}$$
$$= 4x\underbrace{(x + 2)(x + 3)}_{} \qquad \text{Factor trinomial.}$$

Monomial factor ——→   ←—— Prime factors

Checkpoint ✓ **Factor Completely**

Factor the expression completely.

7. $2n^3 + 4n^2 + 2n$ **8.** $3x^3 - 12x$ **9.** $5m^3 - 45m$

10. $x^3 + 4x^2 + 4x$ **11.** $2x^3 - 10x^2 + 8x$ **12.** $6p^3 + 21p^2 + 9p$

FACTORING BY GROUPING Another use of the distributive property is in factoring polynomials that have four terms. Sometimes you can factor the polynomial by grouping the terms into two groups and factoring the greatest common factor out of each term.

EXAMPLE 3 **Factor by Grouping**

Factor $x^3 - 2x^2 - 9x + 18$ completely.

Solution

$$x^3 - 2x^2 - 9x + 18 = (x^3 - 2x^2) + (-9x + 18) \qquad \text{Group terms.}$$
$$= x^2(x - 2) + (-9)(x - 2) \qquad \text{Factor each group.}$$
$$= (x - 2)(x^2 - 9) \qquad \text{Use distributive property.}$$
$$= (x - 2)(x - 3)(x + 3) \qquad \text{Factor difference of two squares.}$$

Checkpoint ✓ **Factor by Grouping**

Use grouping to factor the expression completely.

13. $2x^3 - 8x^2 + 3x - 12$ **14.** $x^3 + 5x^2 - 4x - 20$ **15.** $x^3 - 4x^2 - 9x + 36$

Student Help

▶**MORE EXAMPLES**

More examples are available at www.mcdougallittell.com

SUM OR DIFFERENCE OF TWO CUBES In Lessons 10.3 and 10.7, you used the difference property to study the special product pattern of the difference of two squares. You can also use the distributive property to confirm the following special product patterns for the sum or difference of two cubes.

FACTORING MORE SPECIAL PRODUCTS

Sum of Two Cubes Pattern

$a^3 + b^3 = (a + b)(a^2 - ab + b^2)$ **Example:** $(x^3 + 1) = (x + 1)(x^2 - x + 1)$

Difference of Two Cubes Pattern

$a^3 - b^3 = (a - b)(a^2 + ab + b^2)$ **Example:** $(x^3 - 8) = (x - 2)(x^2 + 2x + 4)$

EXAMPLE 4 Factor the Sum of Two Cubes

Factor $x^3 + 27$.

Solution

$x^3 + 27 = x^3 + 3^3$	Write as sum of cubes.
$\quad\quad = (x + 3)(x^2 - 3x + 9)$	Use special product pattern. Notice that $x^2 - 3x + 9$ is prime and does not factor.

Checkpoint ✓ **Factor the Sum of Two Cubes**

Factor the expression.

16. $x^3 + 125$ **17.** $n^3 + 8$ **18.** $2m^3 + 2$ **19.** $4x^3 + 32$

EXAMPLE 5 Factor the Difference of Two Cubes

Factor $n^3 - 64$.

Solution

$n^3 - 64 = n^3 - 4^3$	Write as difference of cubes.
$\quad\quad = (n - 4)(n^2 + 4n + 16)$	Use special product pattern. Notice that $n^2 + 4n + 16$ is prime and does not factor.

Checkpoint ✓ **Factor the Difference of Two Cubes**

Factor the expression.

20. $x^3 - 27$ **21.** $p^3 - 216$ **22.** $2n^3 - 250$ **23.** $4z^3 - 32$

EXAMPLE 6 *Write and Use a Polynomial Model*

SPACE REQUIREMENTS A terrarium has a volume of 12 cubic feet. Find the dimensions of the terrarium. Do the dimensions meet the space requirements of an adult bearded dragon lizard?

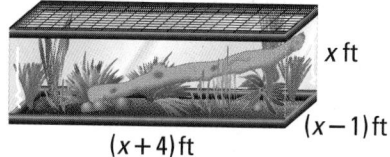

x ft
$(x-1)$ ft
$(x+4)$ ft

Solution

$V = \text{height} \cdot \text{width} \cdot \textbf{length}$	Write volume model for a prism.
$12 = x(x-1)(x+4)$	Substitute for height, width and length.
$12 = x^3 + 3x^2 - 4x$	Multiply.
$0 = (x^3 + 3x^2) + (-4x - 12)$	Write in standard form and group terms.
$0 = x^2(x+3) + (-4)(x+3)$	Factor each group of terms.
$0 = (x+3)(x^2-4)$	Use distributive property.
$0 = (x+3)(x-2)(x+2)$	Factor difference of two squares.

By setting each factor equal to zero, you can see that the solutions are -3, 2, and -2. The only positive solution is $x = 2$.

ANSWER ▶ The dimensions of the terrarium are 2 feet by 1 foot by 6 feet. Because the height must be between 2 and 3.5 feet, the dimensions do *not* meet the space requirements of an adult bearded dragon lizard.

SUMMARY

Patterns Used to Solve Polynomial Equations

GRAPHING: Can be used to solve any equation, but gives only approximate solutions. Examples 2 and 3, pp. 527–528

THE QUADRATIC FORMULA: Can be used to solve any *quadratic* equation. Examples 1–3, pp. 533–534

FACTORING: Can be used with the zero-product property to solve an equation that is in standard form and whose polynomial is factorable.

- Factoring $x^2 + bx + c$: Examples 1–7, pp. 595–598
- Factoring $ax^2 + bx + c$: Examples 1–5, pp. 603–605
- Special Products: Examples 1–6, pp. 610–612 and Examples 4 and 5, p. 618

$$a^2 - b^2 = (a+b)(a-b)$$
$$a^2 + 2ab + b^2 = (a+b)^2$$
$$a^2 - 2ab + b^2 = (a-b)^2$$
$$a^3 + b^3 = (a+b)(a^2 - ab + b^2)$$
$$a^3 - b^3 = (a-b)(a^2 + ab + b^2)$$

- Factoring Completely: Examples 1–3, pp. 616–617

10.8 Exercises

Guided Practice

Vocabulary Check

1. What does it mean to say that a polynomial is prime?

Skill Check

ERROR ANALYSIS Find and correct the error.

2.

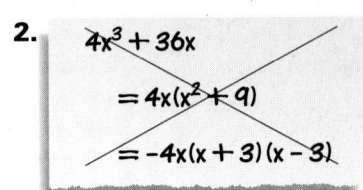

$$4x^3 + 36x$$
$$= 4x(x^2 + 9)$$
$$= -4x(x + 3)(x - 3)$$

3.

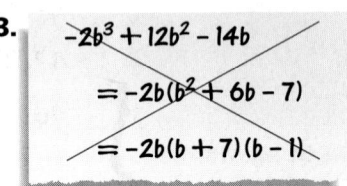

$$-2b^3 + 12b^2 - 14b$$
$$= -2b(b^2 + 6b - 7)$$
$$= -2b(b + 7)(b - 1)$$

Find the greatest common factor of the terms and factor it out of the expression.

4. $5n^3 - 20n$ **5.** $6x^2 + 3x^4$ **6.** $6y^4 + 14y^3 - 10y^2$

Factor the expression.

7. $x^3 - 1$ **8.** $x^3 + 64$ **9.** $27x^3 + 1$ **10.** $125x^3 - 1$

Factor the expression completely.

11. $2b^3 - 18b$ **12.** $7a^3 - 14a^2 - 21a$ **13.** $3t^3 + 18t^2 + 27t$

14. $y^3 - 6y^2 + 5y$ **15.** $x^3 - 16x$ **16.** $5b^3 - 25b^2 - 70b$

Practice and Applications

FACTORING THE GCF Find the greatest common factor of the terms and factor it out of the expression.

17. $6v^3 - 18v$ **18.** $4q^4 + 12q$ **19.** $3x - 9x^2$

20. $10x^2 + 15x^3$ **21.** $4a^2 - 8a^5$ **22.** $24t^5 + 6t^3$

23. $15x^3 - 5x^2 - 10x$ **24.** $4a^5 + 8a^3 - 2a^2$ **25.** $18d^6 - 6d^2 + 3d$

FACTOR BY GROUPING Factor the expression.

26. $x^2 + 2x + xy + 2y$ **27.** $a^2 + 3a + ab + 3b$

28. $2x^3 - 3x^2 - 4x + 6$ **29.** $10x^2 - 15x + 2x - 3$

30. $8x^2 - 3x - 8x + 3$ **31.** $10x^2 - 7x - 10x + 7$

SUM AND DIFFERENCE OF TWO CUBES Factor the expression.

32. $m^3 + 1$ **33.** $c^3 - 8$ **34.** $r^3 + 64$ **35.** $m^3 - 125$

Student Help

▶ **HOMEWORK HELP**
Example 1: Exs. 17–25
Example 2: Exs. 36–44
Example 3: Exs. 26–31
Example 4: Exs. 32–35
Example 5: Exs. 32–35
Example 6: Exs. 59–61

FACTORING COMPLETELY Factor the expression completely.

36. $24x^3 + 18x^2$ **37.** $2y^3 - 10y^2 - 12y$ **38.** $5s^3 + 30s^2 + 40s$

39. $4t^3 - 144t$ **40.** $-12z^3 + 3z^2$ **41.** $c^4 + c^3 - 12c - 12$

42. $x^3 - 3x^2 + x - 3$ **43.** $3x^3 + 3000$ **44.** $2x^3 - 6750$

SOLVING EQUATIONS Solve the equation. Tell which method you used.

45. $y^2 + 7y + 12 = 0$ **46.** $x^2 - 3x - 4 = 0$

47. $27 + 6w - w^2 = 0$ **48.** $5x^4 - 80x^2 = 0$

49. $-16x^3 + 4x = 0$ **50.** $10x^3 - 290x^2 - 620x = 0$

Student Help

▶ LOOK BACK
For help with finding roots, see p. 534.

FINDING ROOTS OF POLYNOMIALS Use the quadratic formula or factoring to find the roots of the polynomial. Write your solutions in simplest form.

51. $4x^2 - 9x - 9$ **52.** $5x^2 + 2x - 3$ **53.** $2x^2 + 5x + 1$

54. $3x^2 - 4x + 1$ **55.** $6x^2 - 2x - 7$ **56.** $3x^2 + 8x - 2$

Science Link In Exercises 57 and 58, use the vertical motion models, where *h* is the height (in feet), *v* is the initial upward velocity (in feet per second), *s* is the initial height (in feet), and *t* is the time (in seconds) the object spends aloft.

Vertical motion model for Earth: $h = -16t^2 + vt + s$

Vertical motion model for the moon: $h = -\dfrac{16}{6}t^2 + vt + s$

Note: the two equations are different because the acceleration due to gravity on the moon's surface is about one-sixth that of Earth.

57. EARTH On Earth, you toss a tennis ball from a height of 96 feet with an initial upward velocity of 16 feet per second. How long will it take the tennis ball to reach the ground?

58. MOON On the moon, you toss a tennis ball from a height of 96 feet with an initial upward velocity of 16 feet per second. How long will it take the tennis ball to reach the surface of the moon?

PACKAGE DESIGNERS consider the function of a package to determine the appropriate size, shape, weight, color and materials to use.

PACKAGING In Exercises 59–61, use the following information. Refer to the diagram of the box.

The length ℓ of a box is 3 inches less than the height *h*. The width *w* is 9 inches less than the height. The box has a volume of 324 cubic inches.

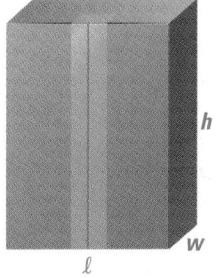

59. Copy and complete the diagram by labeling the dimensions.

60. Write a model that you can solve to find the length, height, and width of the box.

61. What are the dimensions of the box?

62. MULTIPLE CHOICE Which of the following is the complete factorization of $x^3 - 5x^2 + 4x - 20$?

A $(x + 2)(x + 2)(x - 5)$ **B** $(x + 2)(x - 2)(x - 5)$

C $(x^2 + 4)(x - 5)$ **D** $(x - 4)(x - 1)(x - 20)$

63. MULTIPLE CHOICE Solve $x^3 - 4x = 0$.

F 0 and 2   **G** 0, 2, and -2 **H** 2 and -2 **J** -2 and 0

Mixed Review

SOLVING INEQUALITIES Solve the inequality. *(Lesson 6.3)*

64. $7 + x \le -9$ **65.** $-3 > 2x - 5$ **66.** $-x + 6 \le 12$

SOLVING ABSOLUTE-VALUE EQUATIONS Solve the equation. *(Lesson 6.6)*

67. $|x| = 3$ **68.** $|x - 5| = 7$ **69.** $|x + 6| = 13$ **70.** $|4x + 3| = 9$

GRAPHING INEQUALITIES Graph the inequality. *(Lesson 6.8)*

71. $x + y < 9$ **72.** $y - 3x \ge 2$ **73.** $y - 4x \le 10$

Maintaining Skills

RECIPROCALS Find the reciprocal. *(Skills Review p. 763)*

74. 18 **75.** -7 **76.** $\dfrac{2}{9}$ **77.** $1\dfrac{3}{4}$

78. $\dfrac{5}{6}$ **79.** $-2\dfrac{5}{8}$ **80.** $9\dfrac{7}{10}$ **81.** $-8\dfrac{3}{4}$

Quiz 3

Factor the expression. Tell which special product factoring pattern you used. *(Lesson 10.7)*

   1. $49x^2 - 64$ **2.** $121 - 9x^2$ **3.** $4t^2 + 20t + 25$

   4. $72 - 50y^2$ **5.** $9y^2 + 42y + 49$ **6.** $3n^2 - 36n + 108$

Solve the equation by factoring. *(Lesson 10.7)*

   7. $x^2 - 8x + 16 = 0$ **8.** $4x^2 + 32x + 64 = 0$ **9.** $x^3 + 9x^2 - 36x = 0$

Find the greatest common factor and factor it out of the expression. *(Lesson 10.8)*

   10. $3x^3 + 12x^2$ **11.** $6x^2 + 3x$ **12.** $18x^4 - 9x^3$ **13.** $8x^5 + 4x^2 - 2x$

Factor the expression completely. *(Lesson 10.8)*

   14. $2x^3 - 6x^2 + 4x$ **15.** $x^3 + 3x^2 + 4x + 12$ **16.** $4x^3 - 500$

Solve the equation by factoring. *(Lesson 10.8)*

   17. $108y^3 - 75y = 0$ **18.** $3x^3 - 6x^2 + 5x = 10$

VOCABULARY

- **monomial,** *p. 568*
- **degree of a monomial,** *p. 568*
- **polynomial,** *p. 569*
- **binomial,** *p. 569*
- **trinomial,** *p. 569*

- **standard form,** *p. 569*
- **degree of a polynomial in one variable,** *p. 569*
- **FOIL pattern,** *p. 576*
- **factored form,** *p. 588*
- **zero-product property,** *p. 588*

- **factor a trinomial,** *p. 595*
- **perfect square trinomial,** *p. 609*
- **prime polynomial,** *p. 617*
- **factor a polynomial completely,** *p. 617*

10.1 ADDING AND SUBTRACTING POLYNOMIALS

Examples on pp. 568–570

EXAMPLES To add or subtract polynomials, add or subtract like terms.

HORIZONTAL FORMAT

$(4x^3 + 6x - 8) - (-x^2 + 7x - 2)$

$= 4x^3 + 6x - 8 + x^2 - 7x + 2$

$= 4x^3 + x^2 - x - 6$

VERTICAL FORMAT

$$-2x^3 - 4x^2 - x + 5$$
$$3x^3 + 2x^2 - 4x + 9$$
$$+ \quad -x^3 + 5x^2 - x - 1$$
$$\overline{ 3x^2 - 6x + 13}$$

Use a vertical format or a horizontal format to add or subtract.

1. $(5x - 12) - (2x - 7)$

2. $(24m - 13) - (18m + 7) + (6m - 4)$

3. $(-x^2 + x + 2) + (3x^2 + 4x + 5)$

4. $(x^2 + 3x - 1) - (4x^2 - 5x + 6)$

5. $(x^3 + 5x^2 - 4x) - (3x^2 - 6x + 2)$

6. $(4x^3 + x^2 - 1) + (2 - x - x^2)$

10.2 MULTIPLYING POLYNOMIALS

Examples on pp. 575–577

EXAMPLES To multiply polynomials, use the distributive property or FOIL pattern.

a. $(3x + 2)(5x^2 - 4x + 1) = 5x^2(3x + 2) + (-4x)(3x + 2) + 1(3x + 2)$

$$= 15x^3 + 10x^2 - 12x^2 - 8x + 3x + 2$$

$$= 15x^3 - 2x^2 - 5x + 2$$

First　　Outer　　Inner　　Last

b. $(4x + 5)(-3x - 6) = -12x^2 - 24x - 15x - 30$

$$= -12x^2 - 39x - 30 \qquad \text{Combine like terms.}$$

Find the product.

7. $3a(2a^2 - 5a + 1)$

8. $-4x^3(x^2 + 2x - 7)$

9. $(a - 5)(a + 8)$

10. $(4x - 1)(5x + 2)$

11. $(d + 2)(d^2 - 3d - 10)$

12. $(2b - 1)(3b^2 + 5b + 4)$

10.3   SPECIAL PRODUCTS OF POLYNOMIALS

Examples on
pp. 581–584

> **EXAMPLES** Use special product patterns to multiply some polynomials.
>
> $(a + b)(a - b) = a^2 - b^2$ $(a + b)^2 = a^2 + 2ab + b^2$
>
> $(3x + 7)(3x - 7) = (3x)^2 - 7^2$ $(5t + 4)^2 = (5t)^2 + 2(5t)(4) + 4^2$
>
> $\qquad\qquad\quad = 9x^2 - 49$ $\qquad\qquad = 25t^2 + 40t + 16$

In Exercises 13–16, find the product.

13. $(x + 15)(x - 15)$ **14.** $(5x - 2)(5x + 2)$ **15.** $(x + 2)^2$ **16.** $(7m - 6)^2$

17. Write two expressions for the area of the figure at the right. Describe the special product pattern that is represented.

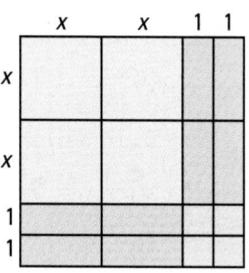

10.4   SOLVING QUADRATIC EQUATIONS IN FACTORED FORM

Examples on
pp. 588–590

> **EXAMPLE** Solve the equation $(x + 1)(x - 5) = 0$.
>
> **Solution**
>
> $(x + 1)(x - 5) = 0$ $\qquad\qquad$ Write original equation.
>
> $x + 1 = 0 \quad or \quad x - 5 = 0$ $\qquad$ Use the zero product property.
>
> $\qquad x = -1 \quad\ \bigg|\qquad x = 5$ $\qquad$ Solve for x.
>
> *ANSWER* ▶ The solutions are -1 and 5. Check these in the original equation.

Solve the equation.

18. $(x + 1)(x + 10) = 0$

19. $(x - 3)(x - 2) = 0$

20. $(y - 7)^2 = 0$

21. $b(5b - 3) = 0$

22. $6(5a - 1)(3a + 1) = 0$

23. $n(n + 9)(n - 12) = 0$

24. $(c + 5)(2c - 1)(3c + 2) = 0$

25. $(3x + 1)(x - 4)^2 = 0$

26. $2c(4c + 3)^2 = 0$

10.5 FACTORING $x^2 + bx + c$

Examples on pp. 595–598

EXAMPLE Factor $x^2 - 6x + 8$.

The first term of each binomial factor is x. For this trinomial, $b = -6$ and $c = 8$.
Because c is positive, you need to find numbers p and q with the same sign. Find
numbers p and q whose sum is -6 and whose product is 8.

p and q	$p + q$	
$-1, -8$	-9	
$-2, -4$	-6	The numbers you need are -2 and -4.

ANSWER ▸ $x^2 - 6x + 8 = (x - 2)(x - 4)$. Check your answer by multiplying.

Factor the trinomial.

27. $x^2 + 10x + 24$ **28.** $a^2 - 6a - 16$ **29.** $m^2 - 8m - 20$

Solve the equation by factoring.

30. $b^2 - 11b + 28 = 0$ **31.** $y^2 + 4y - 32 = 0$ **32.** $a^2 - 6a - 40 = 0$

10.6 FACTORING $ax^2 + bx + c$

Examples on pp. 603–605

EXAMPLE Factor $3x^2 + 5x - 2$.

For this trinomial, $a = 3$, $b = 5$ and $c = -2$. Because c is negative, you need to
find numbers p and q with different signs.

❶ **Write** the numbers m and n whose
product is 3 and the numbers p
and q whose product is -2.

	m and n	p and q
	$1, 3$	$-1, 2$
		$1, -2$

❷ **Use** these numbers to write trial
factors. Then use the **O**uter and
Inner products of **FOIL** to
check the middle term.

Trial Factors	Middle Term
$(x - 1)(3x + 2)$	$2x - 3x = -x$
$(x + 1)(3x - 2)$	$-2x + 3x = x$
$(x + 2)(3x - 1)$	$-x + 6x = 5x$

ANSWER ▸ $3x^2 + 5x - 2 = (x + 2)(3x - 1)$.

Factor the trinomial.

33. $12x^2 + 7x + 1$ **34.** $3x^2 - 8x + 4$ **35.** $4r^2 + 5r - 6$ **36.** $5c^2 - 33c - 14$

Solve the equation by factoring.

37. $2p^2 - p - 1 = 0$ **38.** $4x^2 - 3x - 1 = 0$ **39.** $2a^2 + 7a = 4$

10.7   FACTORING SPECIAL PRODUCTS

Examples on pp. 609–612

EXAMPLES Factor using the special product patterns to solve the equations.

$$a^2 - b^2 = (a + b)(a - b)$$

$$x^2 - 64 = 0$$

$$x^2 - 8^2 = 0$$

$$(x + 8)(x - 8) = 0$$

$$x + 8 = 0 \quad or \quad x - 8 = 0$$

$$x = -8 \quad | \quad x = 8$$

ANSWER The solutions are −8 and 8.

$$a^2 - 2ab + b^2 = (a - b)^2$$

$$x^2 - 4x + 4 = 0$$

$$x^2 - 2(x)(2) + 2^2 = 0$$

$$(x - 2)^2 = 0$$

$$x - 2 = 0$$

$$x = 2$$

ANSWER The solution is 2.

Use factoring to solve the equation.

40. $b^2 - 49 = 0$

41. $16a^2 - 1 = 0$

42. $9d^2 - 6d + 1 = 0$

43. $m^2 - 100 = 0$

44. $4b^2 - 12b + 9 = 0$

45. $25x^2 + 20x + 4 = 0$

10.8   FACTORING CUBIC POLYNOMIALS

Examples on pp. 616–619

EXAMPLES Factor using the distributive property or the special product patterns.

$$a^3 + b^3 = (a + b)(a^2 - ab + a^2)$$

$$x^3 + 125 = x^3 + 5^3$$

$$= (x + 5)(x^2 - 5x + 25)$$

$$a^3 - b^3 = (a - b)(a^2 + ab + b^2)$$

$$c^3 - 216 = c^3 - 6^3$$

$$= (c - 6)(c^2 + 6c + 36)$$

Factor by Grouping

$$x^3 - 4x^2 - 4x + 16$$

$$= (x^3 - 4x^2) + (-4x + 16)$$

$$= x^2(x - 4) + (-4)(x - 4)$$

$$= (x - 4)(x^2 - 4)$$

$$= (x - 4)(x + 2)(x - 2)$$

Factor the expression completely.

46. $-2x^3 + 6x^2 - 14x$

47. $5y^4 - 20y^3 + 10y^2$

48. $x^3 + 3x^2 - 4x - 12$

49. $3y^3 - 4y^2 - 6y + 8$

50. $x^3 - 64$

51. $27b^3 + 1$

Solve the equation.

52. $x^2 - 6x + 5 = 0$

53. $2x^2 - 50 = 0$

54. $8x^3 + 25x = 30x^2$

Use a vertical format or a horizontal format to add or subtract.

1. $(x^2 + 4x - 1) + (5x^2 + 2)$ **2.** $(5t^2 - 9t + 1) - (8t + 13)$

3. $(7n^3 + 2n^2 - n - 4) - (4n^3 - 3n^2 + 8)$ **4.** $(x^4 + 6x^2 + 7) + (2x^4 - 3x^2 + 1)$

Find the product.

5. $(x + 3)(2x + 3)$ **6.** $(3x - 1)(5x + 1)$ **7.** $(w - 6)(4w^2 + w - 7)$

8. $(5t + 2)(4t^2 + 8t - 7)$ **9.** $(3z^3 - 5z^2 + 8)(z + 2)$ **10.** $(4x + 1)(4x - 3)$

11. $(x - 12)^2$ **12.** $(7x + 2)^2$ **13.** $(8x + 3)(8x - 3)$

Use the zero-product property to solve the equation.

14. $(6x - 5)(x + 2) = 0$ **15.** $(x + 8)^2 = 0$ **16.** $(x + 3)(x - 1)(3x + 2) = 0$

Find the x-intercepts and the vertex of the graph of the function. Then sketch the graph.

17. $y = (x + 1)(x - 5)$ **18.** $y = (x - 4)(x + 4)$ **19.** $y = (x + 2)(x + 6)$

Solve the equation by factoring.

20. $x^2 + 13x + 30 = 0$ **21.** $x^2 - 19x + 84 = 0$ **22.** $x^2 - 34x - 240 = 0$

23. $2x^2 + 15x - 108 = 0$ **24.** $9x^2 - 9x = 28$ **25.** $18x^2 - 57x = -35$

Factor the expression.

26. $x^2 - 196$ **27.** $16x^2 - 36$ **28.** $128 - 50x^2$

29. $x^2 - 6x + 9$ **30.** $4x^2 + 44x + 121$ **31.** $-6x^3 - 3x^2 + 45x$

32. $9t^2 - 54$ **33.** $x^3 + 2x^2 - 16x - 32$ **34.** $2x^3 - 162x$

Solve the equation by a method of your choice.

35. $x^2 - 60 = -11$ **36.** $2x^2 + 15x - 8 = 0$ **37.** $x^2 - 13x = -40$

38. $x(x - 16) = 0$ **39.** $12x^2 + 3x = 0$ **40.** $x^4 + 7x^3 - 8x - 56 = 0$

41. $5x^3 - 605x = 0$ **42.** $4x^3 + 24x^2 + 36x = 0$ **43.** $16x^2 - 34x - 15 = 0$

44. ROOM DIMENSIONS   A room's length is 3 feet less than twice its width. The area of the room is 135 square feet. What are the room's dimensions?

45. RUG SIZE   A rug 4 meters by 5 meters covers $\frac{2}{3}$ of the floor area in a room. The rug touches two walls, leaving a strip of uniform width around the other two walls. How wide is the strip?

Chapter Standardized Test

---

1. Classify $3x^2 - 7 + 4x^3 - 5x$ by degree and by the number of terms.

    Ⓐ quadratic trinomial

    Ⓑ cubic polynomial

    Ⓒ quartic polynomial

    Ⓓ quadratic polynomial

    Ⓔ None of these

2. Which of the following is equal to $(-x^2 - 5x + 7) + (-7x^2 + 5x - 2)$?

    Ⓐ $-8x^2 + 5$

    Ⓑ $-8x^2 + 10x + 5$

    Ⓒ $6x^2 + 5$

    Ⓓ $-8x^2 - 10x + 5$

3. Which of the following is equal to $(5x^3 + 3x^2 - x + 1) - (2x^3 + x - 5)$?

    Ⓐ $7x^3 + 3x^2 - 2x + 6$

    Ⓑ $3x^3 + 3x^2 - 2x - 4$

    Ⓒ $3x^3 + 3x^2 - 2x - 6$

    Ⓓ $3x^3 + 3x^2 - 2x + 6$

4. Which of the following is equal to $(4x - 1)(5x - 2)$?

    Ⓐ $20x^2 - 5x + 2$

    Ⓑ $20x^2 - 13x + 2$

    Ⓒ $20x^2 - 3x - 2$

    Ⓓ $20x^2 - 8x - 2$

5. Which of the following is equal to $(2x - 9)^2$?

    Ⓐ $4x^2 + 81$

    Ⓑ $4x^2 - 18x + 81$

    Ⓒ $4x^2 + 36x + 81$

    Ⓓ $4x^2 - 36x + 81$

6. Which of the following is one of the solutions of the equation $x^2 - 2x = 120$?

    Ⓐ -12 **Ⓑ** -10

    Ⓒ 20 **Ⓓ** 60

7. Which of the following is a correct factorization of $-45x^2 + 150x - 125$?

    Ⓐ $-5(3x + 5)^2$

    Ⓑ $-5(3x + 5)(3x - 5)$

    Ⓒ $-5(3x - 5)^2$

    Ⓓ $-5(9x + 25)$

8. Which of the following is equal to the expression $x^3 - 2x^2 - 11x + 22$?

    Ⓐ $(x - 2)(x - 11)$ **Ⓑ** $(x - 2)(x^2 + 11)$

    Ⓒ $(x - 2)(x + 11)$ **Ⓓ** $(x - 2)(x^2 - 11)$

9. Which of the following is equal to $x^3 + 64$?

    Ⓐ $x(x + 4)(x - 4)$

    Ⓑ $(x + 4)(x^2 - 4x + 16)$

    Ⓒ $(x - 4)(x^2 + 4x + 16)$

    Ⓓ $(x + 8)(x^2 - 8x + 16)$

Maintaining Skills

EXAMPLE 1 The Least Common Denominator

Write the numbers $\frac{3}{4}$, $\frac{2}{3}$, and $\frac{5}{8}$ in order from least to greatest.

Solution The LCD of the fractions is 24.

$$\frac{3}{4} = \frac{3 \cdot 6}{4 \cdot 6} = \frac{18}{24} \qquad \frac{2}{3} = \frac{2 \cdot 8}{3 \cdot 8} = \frac{16}{24} \qquad \frac{5}{8} = \frac{5 \cdot 3}{8 \cdot 3} = \frac{15}{24}$$

Compare the numerators: $15 < 16 < 18$, so $\frac{5}{8} < \frac{2}{3} < \frac{3}{4}$.

ANSWER ▶ In order from least to greatest, the fractions are $\frac{5}{8}$, $\frac{2}{3}$, and $\frac{3}{4}$.

Try These

Write the numbers in order from least to greatest.

1. $\frac{1}{4}, \frac{2}{5}$

2. $\frac{4}{7}, \frac{3}{8}$

3. $\frac{1}{3}, \frac{5}{6}, \frac{1}{2}$

4. $\frac{3}{4}, \frac{1}{6}, \frac{1}{2}$

5. $\frac{3}{10}, \frac{3}{4}, \frac{13}{20}$

6. $\frac{7}{8}, \frac{5}{4}, \frac{7}{24}$

7. $1\frac{1}{3}, \frac{5}{4}, \frac{5}{6}$

8. $2\frac{1}{4}, 1\frac{2}{3}, \frac{5}{6}$

EXAMPLE 2 Operations with Fractions

Add $\frac{5}{6} + \frac{3}{8}$.

Solution

$$\frac{5}{6} + \frac{3}{8} = \frac{20}{24} + \frac{9}{24} \qquad \text{Rewrite fractions using the LCD.}$$

$$= \frac{20 + 9}{24} \qquad \text{Add numerators.}$$

$$= \frac{29}{24}, \text{ or } 1\frac{5}{24} \qquad \text{Simplify.}$$

Try These

Add or subtract. Write the answer as a fraction or mixed number in simplest form.

9. $\frac{2}{3} + \frac{5}{12}$

10. $\frac{1}{6} - \frac{3}{4}$

11. $\frac{2}{5} + \frac{3}{7}$

12. $\frac{7}{8} - \frac{5}{12}$

13. $\frac{7}{10} - \frac{1}{3}$

14. $\frac{5}{9} + \frac{11}{12}$

15. $1\frac{1}{2} + 3\frac{5}{6}$

16. $2\frac{3}{4} - \frac{17}{20}$

Student Help

▶ **EXTRA EXAMPLES**

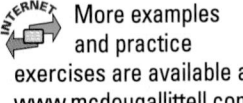 More examples and practice exercises are available at www.mcdougallittell.com

Rational Expressions and Equations

▶ How do scale models fit into the design process?

Application: Scale Models

A floor plan is a smaller diagram of a room or a building drawn as if seen from above. Two- and three-dimensional scale models are used by architects, builders, and city planners in the design process.

Think & Discuss

In the floor plan below, 1 inch represents 14 feet.

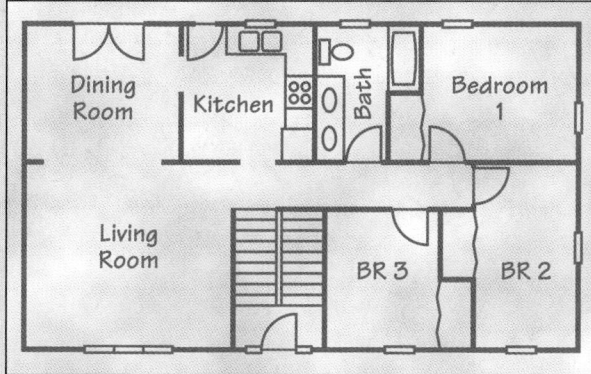

In the floor plan, Bedroom 2 is 1 inch by $\frac{1}{2}$ inch.

1. What is the actual length of Bedroom 2?

2. What is the actual width of Bedroom 2?

3. Solve the equation $\frac{3}{1} = \frac{x}{14}$ to find the actual length x of the whole floor of the house.

Learn More About It

You will write and use a proportion for a problem about a scale model in Exercise 37 on page 637.

 APPLICATION LINK More about scale models is available at www.mcdougallittell.com

What's the chapter about?

- Recognizing direct variation and **inverse variation** models
- Simplifying, adding, subtracting, multiplying, and dividing **rational expressions**
- Solving **proportions** and **rational equations**

KEY WORDS

- **proportion,** *p. 633*
- **extremes,** *p. 633*
- **means,** *p. 633*
- **inverse variation,** *p. 639*
- **rational number,** *p. 646*
- **rational expression,** *p. 646*
- **least common denominator (LCD),** *p. 663*
- **rational equation,** *p. 670*

Chapter Readiness Quiz

Take this quick quiz. If you are unsure of an answer, look back at the reference pages for help.

VOCABULARY CHECK *(refer to p. 132)*

1. Which of the following are equivalent equations?

Ⓐ $y = x^2 + 3$
$x^2 + y = 3$

Ⓑ $y = (x - 5)(x + 1)$
$y - x^2 = -4x - 5$

Ⓒ $y = (2x + 1)(x + 4)$
$y = 2x^2 + 8x + 4$

Ⓓ $y = (x - 5)^2$
$y = x^2 - 25$

SKILL CHECK *(refer to pp. 462, 605)*

2. Simplify the expression $49x^2 \div \dfrac{-7x}{3}$.

Ⓐ $\dfrac{343x^3}{3}$ Ⓑ $-21x$ Ⓒ $-21x^2$ Ⓓ $21x$

3. Solve the equation $4x^2 - 10x + 6 = 0$ by factoring.

Ⓐ $x = -\dfrac{3}{2}, -1$ Ⓑ $x = \dfrac{1}{2}, 3$ Ⓒ $x = -\dfrac{1}{2}, -3$ Ⓓ $x = \dfrac{3}{2}, 1$

Preview and Review

Before studying the chapter, list what you know about each topic. After studying the chapter, go back to each topic and list what you know about each topic. Compare the two sets of notes and see what you have learned.

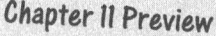

Chapter 11 Preview

Proportions: deal with fractions, ratios

Direct and Inverse Variation:
direct variation equation, y = kx
graph of direct variation is linear

11.1 Proportions

Goal

Solve proportions.

Key Words

- ratio
- proportion
- extremes
- means
- reciprocal property
- cross product property
- cross multiplying

How many clay warriors were buried in the tomb?

Many real-life quantities are *proportional* to each other. In Example 5 you will use a proportion to estimate the number of clay warriors buried in Emperor Qin Shi Huang's tomb.

An equation that states that two ratios are equal is a **proportion**,

$$\frac{a}{b} = \frac{c}{d}, \quad \text{where } a, b, c, d \neq 0.$$

When the ratios are written in this order, a and d are the **extremes** of the proportion and b and c are the **means** of the proportion. If two nonzero numbers are equal, then their reciprocals are equal. This property carries over to ratios.

RECIPROCAL PROPERTY OF PROPORTIONS

If two ratios are equal, then their reciprocals are also equal.

If $\frac{a}{b} = \frac{c}{d}$, then $\frac{b}{a} = \frac{d}{c}$.   **Example:** $\frac{2}{3} = \frac{4}{6}$ ➡ $\frac{3}{2} = \frac{6}{4}$

EXAMPLE 1 Use the Reciprocal Property

Solve the proportion $\frac{5}{2} = \frac{60}{x}$ using the reciprocal property.

❶ **Write** the original proportion. $\frac{5}{2} = \frac{60}{x}$

❷ **Use** the reciprocal property. $\frac{2}{5} = \frac{x}{60}$

❸ **Multiply** each side of the equation by 60 $24 = x$
    to clear the equation of fractions.

ANSWER▶ The solution is $x = 24$. Check this in the original equation.

CROSS PRODUCT PROPERTY By writing both fractions in the proportion $\frac{a}{b} = \frac{c}{d}$ over a common denominator bd, the proportion becomes $\frac{ad}{bd} = \frac{bc}{bd}$. This observation is the basis for the cross product property, shown on the next page.

> ## CROSS PRODUCT PROPERTY OF PROPORTIONS
>
> The product of the extremes equals the product of the means.
>
> If $\dfrac{a}{b} = \dfrac{c}{d}$, then $ad = bc$.   **Example:** $\dfrac{2}{3} = \dfrac{4}{6}$ ⟹ $2 \cdot 6 = 3 \cdot 4$

EXAMPLE 2 Use the Cross Product Property

Solve the proportion $\dfrac{3}{y} = \dfrac{5}{8}$ using the cross product property.

❶ **Write** the original proportion. $\dfrac{3}{y} = \dfrac{5}{8}$

❷ **Use** the cross product property. $3 \cdot 8 = y \cdot 5$

❸ **Simplify** the equation. $24 = 5y$

❹ **Solve** by dividing each side by 5. $\dfrac{24}{5} = y$

CHECK ✓ Substituting $\dfrac{24}{5}$ for y, $\dfrac{3}{\frac{24}{5}}$ becomes $3 \cdot \dfrac{5}{24}$, which simplifies to $\dfrac{5}{8}$.

Student Help

▶ **STUDY TIP**
Remember to check your solution in the *original* proportion. Since Example 3 has two solutions, you need to check both of them.

EXAMPLE 3 Use the Cross Product Property

Solve the proportion $\dfrac{3}{x} = \dfrac{x+1}{4}$.

❶ **Write** the original proportion. $\dfrac{3}{x} = \dfrac{x+1}{4}$

❷ **Use** the cross product property. $(3)(4) = (x)(x+1)$

❸ **Multiply.** $12 = x^2 + x$

❹ **Collect** terms on one side. $0 = x^2 + x - 12$

❺ **Factor** the right-hand side. $0 = (x-3)(x+4)$

❻ **Solve** the equation. $x = 3$ or -4

ANSWER ▶ The solutions are $x = 3$ and $x = -4$. Check both solutions.

Checkpoint ✓ **Use the Cross Product Property**

Solve the proportion. Check your solutions.

1. $\dfrac{2}{b} = \dfrac{5}{2}$ **2.** $\dfrac{25}{n} = \dfrac{n}{4}$ **3.** $\dfrac{-3}{x} = \dfrac{x+6}{3}$ **4.** $\dfrac{x}{4} = \dfrac{x-1}{x}$

Consider the equation $\dfrac{p}{q} = \dfrac{r}{s}$ where p, q, r and s are polynomials and q and s are restricted so that they do not equal zero. Writing both fractions with a common denominator leads to $\dfrac{ps}{qs} = \dfrac{qr}{qs}$, and then to $ps = qr$. This reasoning is the basis for *cross multiplying*, a method of solving equations used in Example 4.

EXAMPLE 4 Cross Multiply and Check Solutions

Solve the equation $\dfrac{y^2 - 9}{y + 3} = \dfrac{y - 3}{2}$.

Solution

1 **Write** the original equation.

$$\dfrac{y^2 - 9}{y + 3} = \dfrac{y - 3}{2}$$

2 **Cross multiply.**

$$(y^2 - 9)2 = (y + 3)(y - 3)$$

3 **Multiply.**

$$2y^2 - 18 = y^2 - 9$$

4 **Isolate** the variable term.

$$y^2 = 9$$

5 **Solve** by taking the square root of each side.

$$y = \pm 3$$

The solutions appear to be $y = 3$ and $y = -3$. However, you must discard $y = -3$, since the denominator of the left-hand side would become zero.

ANSWER ▶ The solution is $y = 3$. Check this in the original equation.

EXCLUDE ZERO DENOMINATORS Because division by zero is undefined, when dealing with proportions, you must check your answer to make sure that any values of a variable that result in a zero denominator are excluded from the final answer, as shown in Example 4.

Link to
Archaeology

CLAY WARRIORS In 1974, archaeologists excavated the tomb of Emperor Qin Shi Huang (259–210 B.C.) in China. Buried close to the tomb was an entire army of life-sized clay warriors.

More about this excavation at www.mcdougallittell.com

EXAMPLE 5 Write and Use a Proportion

CLAY WARRIORS Pit 1 of the tomb of Emperor Qin Shi Huang, shown below, consists of two end sites, containing a total of 450 warriors, and a central region. The site (shown in red) in the central region contains 282 warriors. This 10-meter-wide site is thought to be representative of the 200-meter central region. Estimate the total number of warriors in Pit 1.

Not drawn to scale

240 warriors   282 warriors   210 warriors   62 m

5 m   10 m   5 m

central region
200 m

Solution Let n represent the number of warriors in the 200-meter central region. You can find the value of n by solving a proportion.

$$\dfrac{\text{Number of warriors found}}{\text{Total number of warriors}} = \dfrac{\text{Number of meters excavated}}{\text{Total number of meters}}$$

$$\dfrac{282}{n} = \dfrac{10}{200}$$

ANSWER ▶ The solution is $n = 5640$, indicating that there are about 5640 warriors in the central region. With the 450 warriors at the ends, that makes a total of about 6090 warriors in Pit 1.

Guided Practice

Vocabulary Check

1. Identify the extremes and the means of the proportion.

a. $\dfrac{3}{4} = \dfrac{9}{12}$

b. $\dfrac{9}{12} = \dfrac{3}{4}.$

Skill Check

Solve the proportion. Check your solution.

2. $\dfrac{2}{x} = \dfrac{16}{40}$

3. $\dfrac{72}{96} = \dfrac{x}{4}$

4. $\dfrac{x}{3} = \dfrac{2}{7}$

5. $\dfrac{4}{x+1} = \dfrac{7}{2}$

6. $\dfrac{2}{2x+1} = \dfrac{1}{5}$

7. $\dfrac{x-2}{x} = \dfrac{2}{3}$

Determine whether the equation follows from $\dfrac{a}{b} = \dfrac{c}{d}$.

8. $ad = bc$

9. $ba = dc$

10. $\dfrac{a}{d} = \dfrac{b}{c}$

11. $\dfrac{b}{a} = \dfrac{d}{c}$

Practice and Applications

RECIPROCAL PROPERTY Solve the proportion using the reciprocal property. Check your solution.

12. $\dfrac{3}{x} = \dfrac{1}{2}$

13. $\dfrac{3}{4} = \dfrac{8}{3c}$

14. $\dfrac{13}{z} = \dfrac{1}{3}$

CROSS PRODUCT PROPERTY Solve the proportion using the cross product property. Check your solution.

15. $\dfrac{5}{8} = \dfrac{c}{56}$

16. $\dfrac{x}{3} = \dfrac{7}{3}$

17. $\dfrac{16}{4} = \dfrac{12}{z}$

18. $\dfrac{42}{28} = \dfrac{3}{x}$

19. $\dfrac{5}{y} = \dfrac{8}{9}$

20. $\dfrac{4}{2w} = \dfrac{7}{3}$

21. $\dfrac{5}{3d} = \dfrac{2}{3}$

22. $\dfrac{14}{3} = \dfrac{7b}{2}$

23. $\dfrac{3}{10} = \dfrac{1}{10a}$

CHECKING SOLUTIONS Solve the equation. Check your solutions.

24. $\dfrac{z}{9} = \dfrac{4}{z}$

25. $\dfrac{4}{p} = \dfrac{p}{16}$

26. $\dfrac{x+6}{3} = \dfrac{x-5}{2}$

27. $\dfrac{x-2}{4} = \dfrac{x+10}{10}$

28. $\dfrac{r+4}{3} = \dfrac{r}{5}$

29. $\dfrac{5}{2y} = \dfrac{7}{y-3}$

30. $\dfrac{2}{3t} = \dfrac{t-1}{t}$

31. $\dfrac{x}{2} = \dfrac{5}{x+3}$

32. $\dfrac{x-3}{18} = \dfrac{3}{x}$

33. $\dfrac{-2}{a-7} = \dfrac{a}{5}$

34. $\dfrac{x-3}{x} = \dfrac{x}{x+6}$

35. $\dfrac{9-x}{x+4} = \dfrac{5}{2x}$

Student Help

▶ **HOMEWORK HELP**
Example 1: Exs. 12–14
Example 2: Exs. 15–23
Example 3: Exs. 24–35
Example 4: Exs. 24–35
Example 5: Ex. 36

36. CLAY POTS Assume that a 15-meter-wide site is representative of a larger 60-meter-wide site. If an archaeologist excavates the 15-meter-wide site and finds 30 clay pots, estimate the number of clay pots in the larger 60-meter-wide site. Assume that both sites are the same length.

> **EXAMPLE** **Scale Models**
>
> You want to make a scale model of one of the clay horses found in Emperor Qin Shi Huang's tomb. The clay horse is 1.5 meters tall and 2 meters long. Your scale model will be 18 inches long. How tall should it be?
>
> **Solution** Let h represent the height of the model.
>
> $$\frac{\text{Height of actual statue}}{\text{Length of actual statue}} = \frac{\textbf{Height of model}}{\text{Length of model}}$$ Write verbal model.
>
> $$\frac{1.5}{2} = \frac{h}{18}$$ Write proportion.
>
> $(1.5)(18) = 2h$ Use cross product property.
>
> $27 = 2h$ Multiply.
>
> $13.5 = h$ Divide by 2.
>
> **ANSWER** ▶ Your scale model should be $13\frac{1}{2}$ inches tall.

37. **History Link** The ratio of the sculpture of John Wesley Dobbs' head to actual size is about 10 to 1. Suppose that his head was 9 inches high and $6\frac{1}{2}$ inches wide. Estimate the height and width of the sculpture. Write the answer in feet.

MURAL PROJECT **In Exercises 38 and 39, use the following information. Refer to the example above if necessary.**

Art is the Heart of the City is a fence mural project in Charlotte, North Carolina. Artists Cordelia Williams and Paul Rousso along with 22 high school students created drawings of the mural. Then slides of the drawings were made and projected to fit onto 4-foot-wide by 8-foot-long sheets of plywood used for the fence panels. Students traced and later painted the enlarged images.

38. If the paper used for the original drawings was 11 inches wide, how long did it need to be?

39. Suppose the height of a flower on the panel shown is $2\frac{1}{2}$ feet. Use Exercise 38 to find the height of the flower in the student's drawing.

40. CHALLENGE A scale model uses a scale of $\frac{1}{16}$ inch to represent 1 foot. Explain how you can use a proportion and the cross product property to show that a scale of $\frac{1}{16}$ in. to 1 ft is the same as a scale of 1 in. to 192 in.

41. MULTIPLE CHOICE What are the extremes of the proportion $\frac{1}{3} = \frac{x}{18}$? What are the extremes of $\frac{x}{18} = \frac{1}{3}$?

    A 1, 3; x, 18   **B** x, 18; 1, 3   **C** x, 3; 1, 18   **D** 1, 18; x, 3

42. MULTIPLE CHOICE Solve $\frac{x-2}{x+5} = \frac{x-5}{x+2}$.

    F 1   **G** -2 and -5 **H** 2 and 5   **J** No solution

43. MULTIPLE CHOICE Solve $\frac{c}{c-4} = \frac{8}{c-10}$.

    A 0   **B** 2 and 16   **C** -18 and 32   **D** No solution

POINT-SLOPE FORM **Write in point-slope form the equation of the line that passes through the given point and has the given slope.** *(Lesson 5.2)*

44. $(-1, -2)$, $m = 2$ **45.** $(5, -3)$, $m = -4$ **46.** $(-8, 8)$, $m = -1$

STANDARD FORM **Write in standard form the equation of the line that passes through the given point and has the given slope.** *(Lesson 5.4)*

47. $(10, 6)$, $m = -2$ **48.** $(-7, -7)$, $m = \frac{1}{2}$ **49.** $(1, 8)$, $m = \frac{3}{4}$

50. $(0, 5)$, $m = 3$ **51.** $(6, 12)$, $m = -12$ **52.** $(6, -1)$, $m = 0$

FINDING SQUARE ROOTS **Evaluate the expression. Check the results by squaring the answer.** *(Lesson 9.1)*

53. $\sqrt{64}$ **54.** $-\sqrt{9}$ **55.** $\sqrt{10{,}000}$ **56.** $\pm\sqrt{169}$

SIMPLIFYING RADICALS **Simplify the radical expression.** *(Lesson 9.3)*

57. $\sqrt{18}$ **58.** $\sqrt{20}$ **59.** $\sqrt{80}$ **60.** $\sqrt{162}$

61. $9\sqrt{36}$ **62.** $\sqrt{\frac{11}{9}}$ **63.** $\frac{1}{2}\sqrt{28}$ **64.** $\sqrt{\frac{5}{8}}$

65. FRACTIONS, DECIMALS, AND PERCENTS **Copy and complete the table. Write the fractions in simplest form.** *(Skills Review pp. 767–769)*

Decimal	?	0.2	?	0.073	?	?
Percent	78%	?	?	?	3%	?
Fraction	?	?	$\frac{2}{3}$	?	?	$\frac{12}{25}$

11.2 Direct and Inverse Variation

Goal
Use direct and inverse variation.

Key Words
• direct variation
• inverse variation
• constant of variation

How are banking angle and turning radius related?

In Lesson 4.6 you studied direct variation. In Example 4 you will use a different kind of variation to relate the banking angle of a bicycle to its turning radius.

In this lesson you will review direct variation and learn about **inverse variation**, where the product of two variables is a constant.

Student Help

▶ **STUDY TIP**
Direct and inverse variation are sometimes called *direct* and *inverse proportions*.

MODELS FOR DIRECT AND INVERSE VARIATION

Direct Variation

The variables x and y *vary directly* if for a constant k

$$\frac{y}{x} = k, \text{ or } y = kx, \text{ where } k \neq 0.$$

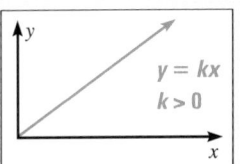

Inverse Variation

The variables x and y *vary inversely* if for a constant k

$$xy = k, \text{ or } y = \frac{k}{x}, \text{ where } k \neq 0$$

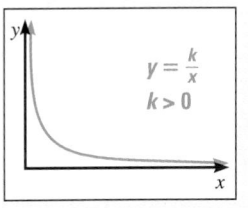

The number k is the constant of variation.

EXAMPLE 1 Use Direct Variation

Find an equation that relates x and y such that x and y vary directly, and $y = 4$ when $x = 2$.

Solution

❶ **Write** the direct variation model. $\dfrac{y}{x} = k$

❷ **Substitute** 2 for x and 4 for y. $\dfrac{4}{2} = k$

❸ **Simplify** the left-hand side. $2 = k$

ANSWER ▶ The direct variation that relates x and y is $\dfrac{y}{x} = 2$, or $y = 2x$.

EXAMPLE 2 Use Inverse Variation

Find an equation that relates x and y such that x and y vary inversely, and $y = 4$ when $x = 2$.

❶ *Write* the inverse variation model. $xy = k$

❷ *Substitute* 2 for x and 4 for y. $(2)(4) = k$

❸ *Simplify* the left-hand side. $8 = k$

ANSWER ▶ The inverse variation that relates x and y is $xy = 8$, or $y = \dfrac{8}{x}$.

Student Help

▶**STUDY TIP**
Direct and inverse variation models represent functions because for each value of *x* there is exactly one value of *y*. For inverse variation, the domain excludes 0.

EXAMPLE 3 Compare Direct and Inverse Variation

Compare the direct variation model and the inverse variation model you found in Examples 1 and 2 using $x = -4, -3, -2, -1, 1, 2, 3,$ and 4.

a. numerically **b.** graphically

Solution

a. Use the models $y = 2x$ and $y = \dfrac{8}{x}$ to make a table.

x-value	-4	-3	-2	-1	1	2	3	4
Direct, $y = 2x$	-8	-6	-4	-2	2	4	6	8
Inverse, $y = \dfrac{8}{x}$	-2	$-\dfrac{8}{3}$	-4	-8	8	4	$\dfrac{8}{3}$	2

DIRECT VARIATION: Because k is positive, y increases as x increases. As x increases by 1, y increases by 2.

INVERSE VARIATION: Because k is positive, y decreases as x increases.

b. Use the table of values to graph each model.

DIRECT VARIATION: The graph for this model is a line passing through the origin.

INVERSE VARIATION: The graph for this model is a *hyperbola*. Since neither x nor y can equal 0, the graph does not intersect either axis.

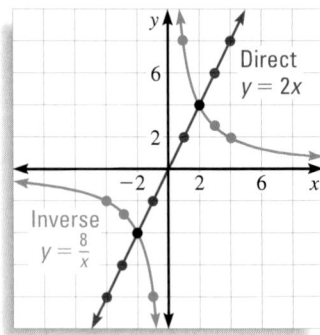

Student Help

▶**VOCABULARY TIP**
A *hyperbola* is a curve with two branches. You will learn more about hyperbolas in later math courses.

Checkpoint ✓ *Compare Direct and Inverse Variation*

1. Suppose $y = 6$ when $x = 2$. Find an equation that relates x and y such that:

a. x and y vary directly. **b.** x and y vary inversely.

2. Compare the direct and inverse variation models in Checkpoint 1 numerically and graphically using $x = -4, -3, -2, -1, 1, 2, 3,$ and 4.

EXAMPLE 4 **Write and Use a Model**

BICYCLE BANKING ANGLE Assume that the graph below shows an inverse relationship between the banking angle B and the turning radius r for a bicycle traveling at a particular speed.

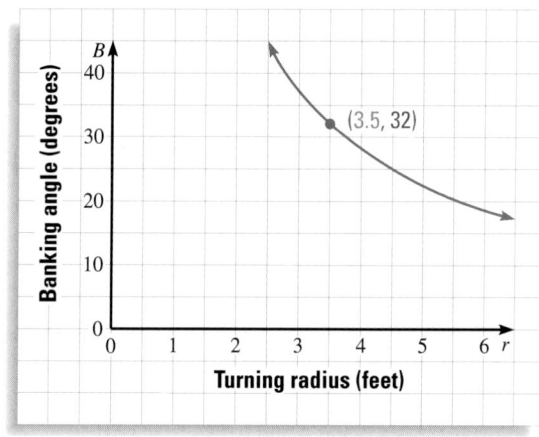

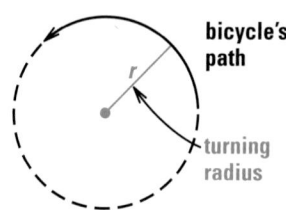

bicycle's path

turning radius

a. Find an inverse variation model that relates B and r.

b. Use the model to find the banking angle for a turning radius of 5 feet.

c. How does the banking angle change as the turning radius gets smaller?

Solution

a. From the graph, you can see that $B = 32°$ when $r = 3.5$ feet.

① **Write** the inverse variation model. $B = \dfrac{k}{r}$

② **Substitute** 32 for B and 3.5 for r. $32 = \dfrac{k}{3.5}$

③ **Multiply** each side by 3.5. $112 = k$

ANSWER ▶ The model is $B = \dfrac{112}{r}$, where B is in degrees and r is in feet.

b. Substitute 5 for r in the model found in part (a). $B = \dfrac{112}{5} = 22.4°$

c. As the turning radius gets smaller, the banking angle becomes greater. From the graph, you can see that the increase in the banking angle is about 10° for a 1-foot decrease in banking angle from 4 to 3 feet, but the increase in banking angle is only about 4° for a 1-foot decrease from 6 feet to 5 feet.

Checkpoint ✓ **Write and Use a Model**

Use the inverse variation model $B = \dfrac{112}{r}$.

3. What is the bicycle banking angle when the turning radius is 8 feet?

4. Does this model apply when $r = 1$? Explain.

Guided Practice

Vocabulary Check

1. What does it mean for two quantities to vary directly?

2. What does it mean for two quantities to vary inversely?

Skill Check

Does the graph model *direct variation*, *inverse variation*, or *neither*? Explain.

3. 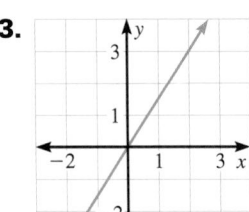 **4.** 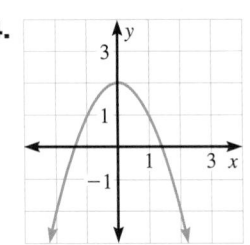 **5.**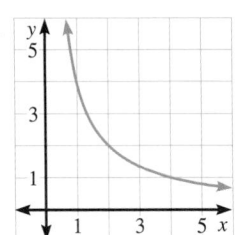

Does the equation model *direct variation*, *inverse variation*, or *neither*?

6. $x = \dfrac{4}{y}$ **7.** $y = 7x - 2$ **8.** $x = 12y$ **9.** $xy = 9$

Suppose $y = 6$ when $x = 4$. For the given type of variation, find an equation that relates x and y.

10. x and y vary directly. **11.** x and y vary inversely.

Practice and Applications

DIRECT VARIATION EQUATIONS The variables x and y vary directly. Use the given values to write an equation that relates x and y.

12. $x = 3, y = 9$ **13.** $x = 2, y = 8$ **14.** $x = 18, y = 6$

15. $x = 8, y = 24$ **16.** $x = 36, y = 12$ **17.** $x = 27, y = 3$

INVERSE VARIATION EQUATIONS The variables x and y vary inversely. Use the given values to write an equation that relates x and y.

18. $x = 2, y = 5$ **19.** $x = 3, y = 7$ **20.** $x = 16, y = 1$

21. $x = 11, y = 2$ **22.** $x = \dfrac{1}{2}, y = 8$ **23.** $x = 5, y = \dfrac{13}{5}$

24. $x = 1.5, y = 50$ **25.** $x = 45, y = 0.6$ **26.** $x = 10.5, y = 7$

Student Help

▶ HOMEWORK HELP
  Exs. 12–17
  Exs. 18–26
  Exs. 27–34
  Exs. 35–42

641

DIRECT OR INVERSE VARIATION Make a table of values for $x = -4, -3, -2, -1, 1, 2, 3,$ and 4. Use the table to sketch the graph. State whether x and y vary *directly* or *inversely*.

27. $y = \dfrac{4}{x}$ **28.** $y = \dfrac{3x}{2}$ **29.** $y = 3x$ **30.** $y = \dfrac{6}{x}$

Student Help

▶**HOMEWORK HELP**

Extra help with problem solving in Exs. 31–33 is available at www.mcdougallittell.com

VARIATION MODELS IN CONTEXT In Exercises 31–33, state whether the variables model *direct variation*, *inverse variation*, or *neither*.

31. BASE AND HEIGHT The area B of the base and the height h of a prism with a volume of 10 cubic units are related by the equation $Bh = 10$.

32. MASS AND VOLUME The mass m and the volume V of a substance are related by the equation $2V = m$, where 2 is the density of the substance.

33. HOURS AND PAY RATE The number of hours h that you must work to earn $480 and your hourly rate of pay p are related by the equation $ph = 480$.

34. MODELING WITH GRAPHS Which graph models direct variation where the constant of variation is 3?

A.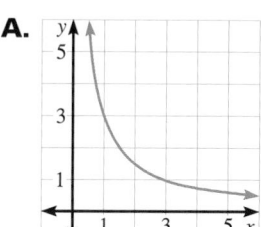
B.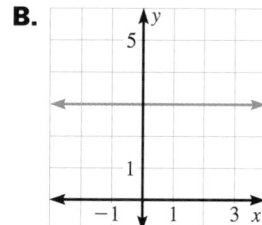
C.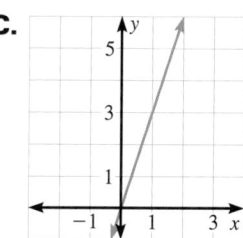

Link to
Snowshoes

SNOWSHOES distribute a person's weight over a large area, allowing a person to walk over deep snow without sinking. Native Americans were among the first people to use snowshoes.

SNOWSHOES In Exercises 35–37, use the following information.

When a person walks, the pressure on each boot sole varies inversely with the area of the sole. Denise is walking through deep snow, wearing boots that have a sole area of 29 square inches each. The pressure on the sole is 4 pounds per square inch when she stands on one foot.

35. Use unit analysis to explain why the constant of variation is Denise's weight. How much does she weigh?

36. Using the constant of variation from Exercise 35, write an equation that relates area of the sole A and pressure P.

37. If Denise wears snowshoes, each with an area of 319 square inches, what is the pressure on the snowshoe when she stands on one foot?

OCEAN TEMPERATURES In Exercises 38 and 39, use the graph and the following information.

The graph at the right shows water temperatures for part of the Pacific Ocean. At depths greater than 900 meters, the temperature of ocean water (in degrees Celsius) varies inversely with depth (in meters).

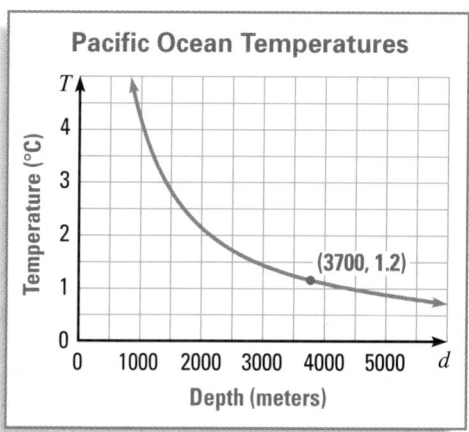

Pacific Ocean Temperatures
(3700, 1.2)

38. Find a model that relates the temperature T and the depth d.

39. Find the temperature at a depth of 2000 meters. Round to the nearest tenth.

CHALLENGE You are taking a trip on a highway in a car that gets a gas mileage of 26 miles per gallon for highway driving. You start with a full tank of 12 gallons of gasoline.

40. Find your rate of gas consumption (gallons of gas used to drive 1 mile).

41. Use your results from Exercise 40 to write an equation relating the number of gallons of gas g in your tank and the number of miles m you have driven.

42. Do the variables g and m vary *directly*, *inversely*, or *neither*? Explain.

Standardized Test Practice

43. MULTIPLE CHOICE Assuming $y = 14$ when $x = 6$, find an equation that relates x and y such that x and y vary directly.

(A) $xy = 84$ (B) $y = \frac{7}{3}x$ (C) $y = \frac{3}{7}x$ (D) $xy = \frac{7}{3}$

44. MULTIPLE CHOICE Assuming $y = 9$ when $x = 10$, find an equation that relates x and y such that x and y vary inversely.

(F) $xy = 90$ (G) $y = \frac{9}{10}x$ (H) $y = \frac{10}{9}x$ (J) $xy = \frac{9}{10}$

Mixed Review

USING PERCENTS Evaluate. *(Lesson 3.9)*

45. 45% of 10

46. 30% of 42

47. $\frac{1}{2}$% of 200

48. 150% of 300

49. 11% of 50

50. 99% of 10,000

CHECKING SOLUTIONS Decide whether the ordered pair is a solution of the inequality. *(Lesson 9.8)*

51. $y < x^2 + 6x + 12$; $(-1, 4)$

52. $y \le x^2 - 7x + 9$; $(-1, 2)$

53. $y \ge x^2 - 25$; $(5, 5)$

54. $y > x^2 - 2x + 5$; $(1, -7)$

FACTORING EXPRESSIONS Completely factor the expression. *(Lesson 10.6)*

55. $x^2 + 5x - 14$

56. $7x^2 + 8x + 1$

57. $5x^2 - 51x + 54$

58. $36x^3 - 9x$

59. $15x^4 - 50x^3 - 40x^2$

60. $6x^2 + 16x$

61. POPULATION The population P of Texas (in thousands), as projected through 2025, is modeled by $P = 18{,}870(1.0124)^t$, where $t = 0$ represents 1995. Find the ratio of the population in 2025 to the population in 2000.
▶ Source: U.S. Bureau of the Census *(Lesson 8.3)*

Maintaining Skills

SUBTRACTING FRACTIONS Subtract. Write the answer as a whole number, fraction, or mixed number in simplest form. *(Skills Review p. 765)*

62. $2\frac{7}{8} - \frac{7}{8}$

63. $\frac{16}{9} - 1\frac{1}{9}$

64. $4\frac{1}{2} - \frac{20}{8}$

65. $3\frac{1}{3} - \frac{4}{3}$

66. $\frac{10}{4} - \frac{1}{2}$

67. $\frac{41}{3} - 4\frac{1}{5}$

68. $12\frac{5}{6} - \frac{50}{7}$

69. $\frac{43}{11} - 2\frac{2}{5}$

USING A GRAPHING CALCULATOR
Modeling Inverse Variation

For use with Lesson 11.2

Use a graphing calculator to develop an inverse or direct variation model.

Sample

x	y
20	1.06771
19	1.11276
18	1.17583
17	1.24341
16	1.32450
15	1.40559
14	1.51371
13	1.62183
12	1.74347
11	1.90566

During a chemistry experiment, the volume of a fixed mass of air was decreased and the pressure at different volumes was recorded. The data are shown at the left, where x is the volume (in cubic centimeters) and y is the pressure (in atmospheres). Use a graphing calculator to determine if a direct or an inverse variation model is appropriate. Then make a scatter plot to check your model.

Solution

Since y increases as x decreases, direct variation can be ruled out.

1 Let L_1 represent the volume x and L_2 represent the pressure y. Use the *Stat Edit* feature to enter the ordered pairs from the table. Then create lists L_3 and L_4 using ⬛L₂ ⬛÷ ⬛L₁ ⬛STO▶ ⬛L₃ and ⬛L₁ ⬛× ⬛L₂ ⬛STO▶ ⬛L₄ .

2 Notice that the values in L_3 are all different. However, the values in L_4 are all about 21.1. Thus, x and y can be modeled using inverse variation.

```
L2      L3      L4
1.0677 .05339  21.354
1.1128 .05857  21.142
1.1758 .06532  21.165
1.2434 .07314  21.138
1.3245 .08278  21.192
L4=(21.3542,21. ...
```

3 Choose the constant of variation k using the *List Math* feature to calculate `mean(L₄)`. Use the rounded value, 21.12, to write an inverse variation model in the form $y = \dfrac{k}{x}$.

4 Set the viewing rectangle so that $11 \le x \le 20$ and $1 \le y \le 2$. Use the *Stat Plot* feature to make a scatter plot of L_1 and L_2. Then graph $y = \dfrac{21.12}{x}$ on the same screen.

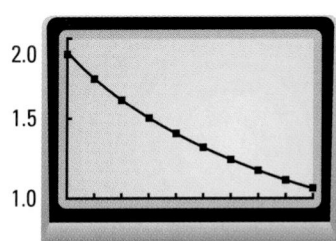

Student Help

▶ KEYSTROKE HELP

See keystrokes for several models of graphing calculators at www.mcdougallittell.com

Try These

Decide whether the data might vary directly or inversely. Then choose the constant of variation and write a model for the data.

1. (10, 8.25), (9, 7.425), (8, 6.6), (7, 5.775), (6, 4.95), (5, 4.125), (4, 3.3)

2. (18, 1.389), (17, 1.471), (16, 1.563), (15, 1.667), (14, 1.786), (13, 1.923)

11.3 Simplifying Rational Expressions

Goal
Simplify rational expressions.

Key Words
- rational number
- rational expression
- simplest form of a rational expression

What is the air pressure at 36,000 feet?

In Exercise 47 you will simplify an expression that models the relationship between air pressure and altitude. Then you will use the simplified expression to determine the air pressure on *Breitling Orbiter 3*, the first manned balloon to circle Earth.

A **rational number** is a number that can be written as the quotient of two integers, such as $\frac{1}{2}$, $\frac{4}{3}$, and $\frac{7}{1}$. A fraction whose numerator and denominator are nonzero polynomials is a **rational expression**. Here are some examples.

$$\frac{3}{x+4} \qquad \frac{2x}{x^2-9} \qquad \frac{3x+1}{x^2+1} \qquad \frac{2x^2+x-2}{3x}$$

Simplifying rational expressions is similar to simplifying fractions because the variables in a rational expression represent real numbers. To simplify a rational expression, we factor the numerator and denominator and then divide out any common factors. (Exercise 48, page 650, shows the reasoning used.) A rational expression is in *simplest form* if its numerator and denominator have no factors in common other than ± 1.

SIMPLIFYING RATIONAL EXPRESSIONS

Let *a*, *b*, and *c* be nonzero polynomials.

$$\frac{ac}{bc} = \frac{a \cdot \cancel{c}}{b \cdot \cancel{c}} = \frac{a}{b}$$

EXAMPLE 1 Simplify Rational Expressions

Simplify the rational expression if possible.

a. $\dfrac{14x}{7} = \dfrac{2 \cdot \cancel{7} \cdot x}{\cancel{7}} = 2x$

b. $\dfrac{6x}{9x^2} = \dfrac{2 \cdot \cancel{3} \cdot \cancel{x}}{\cancel{3} \cdot 3 \cdot \cancel{x} \cdot x} = \dfrac{2}{3x}$

▶ STUDY TIP
When you simplify
rational expressions,
you can divide out only
factors, not *terms*.

For example,
$\dfrac{\cancel{x} \cdot 4}{\cancel{x}} = 4$, but $\dfrac{x + 4}{x}$
cannot be simplified.

EXAMPLE 2 Write in Simplest Form

Simplify the expression if possible.

a. $\dfrac{2x}{2(x + 5)}$ **b.** $\dfrac{x(x^2 + 6)}{x^2}$ **c.** $\dfrac{x + 4}{x}$

Solution

a. $\dfrac{2x}{2(x + 5)} = \dfrac{\cancel{2} \cdot x}{\cancel{2} \cdot (x + 5)}$ Divide out the common factor 2.

$\quad = \dfrac{x}{x + 5}$ Simplify.

b. $\dfrac{x(x^2 + 6)}{x^2} = \dfrac{\cancel{x} \cdot (x^2 + 6)}{\cancel{x} \cdot x}$ Divide out the common factor x.

$\quad = \dfrac{x^2 + 6}{x}$ Simplify.

c. $\dfrac{x + 4}{x}$ Already in simplest form.

Checkpoint ✓ Write in Simplest Form

Simplify the expression. If not possible, write *already in simplest form*.

1. $\dfrac{3x^3}{6x^2}$ **2.** $\dfrac{3m}{3(m - 4)}$ **3.** $\dfrac{x^2(x + 3)}{x}$ **4.** $\dfrac{5}{n + 5}$

Student Help

▶ MORE EXAMPLES

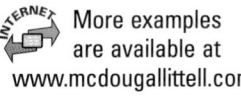
More examples
are available at
www.mcdougallittell.com

EXAMPLE 3 Factor Numerator and Denominator

Simplify $\dfrac{2x^2 - 6x}{6x^2}$.

Solution

❶ Write the original expression. $\quad \dfrac{2x^2 - 6x}{6x^2}$

❷ Factor the numerator and denominator. $\quad \dfrac{2x(x - 3)}{2 \cdot 3 \cdot x \cdot x}$

❸ Divide out the common factors 2 and x. $\quad \dfrac{\cancel{2}\cancel{x}(x - 3)}{\cancel{2} \cdot 3 \cdot \cancel{x} \cdot x}$

❹ Simplify the expression. $\quad \dfrac{x - 3}{3x}$

Checkpoint ✓ Factor Numerator and Denominator

Simplify the expression.

5. $\dfrac{2x - 6}{4}$ **6.** $\dfrac{5x}{10x^2 - 5x}$ **7.** $\dfrac{4m^3}{2m^3 + 8m^2}$ **8.** $\dfrac{p^3 - p^2}{p^2}$

▶ STUDY TIP
Rational expressions in

the form $\dfrac{a-b}{b-a}$ are

equal to −1 because
of the following.

$\dfrac{a-b}{b-a} = \dfrac{-(-a+b)}{b-a} =$

$\dfrac{-(b-a)}{b-a} = -1$

EXAMPLE 4 **Recognize Opposite Factors**

Simplify $\dfrac{4-x^2}{x^2-x-2}$.

Solution

❶ **Write** the original expression. $\dfrac{4-x^2}{x^2-x-2}$

❷ **Factor** the numerator and denominator. $\dfrac{(2-x)(2+x)}{(x-2)(x+1)}$

❸ **Factor** −1 from $(2-x)$. $\dfrac{-(x-2)(2+x)}{(x-2)(x+1)}$

❹ **Divide** out the common factor $(x-2)$. $\dfrac{-(x-2)(x+2)}{(x-2)(x+1)}$

❺ **Simplify** the expression. $-\dfrac{x+2}{x+1}$

Checkpoint ✔ *Recognize Opposite Factors*

Simplify the expression.

9. $\dfrac{3(4-m)}{3(m-4)}$

10. $\dfrac{3-x}{x^2-9}$

11. $\dfrac{4(1-m)}{m^2-2m+1}$

12. $\dfrac{2x-5}{20-8x}$

13. $\dfrac{y^2+3y-28}{16-y^2}$

14. $\dfrac{10x-5}{1-2x}$

EXAMPLE 5 **Divide a Polynomial by a Binomial**

Divide (x^2-2x-3) by $(x-3)$.

Solution

❶ **Rewrite** the problem as a rational expression. $\dfrac{x^2-2x-3}{x-3}$

❷ **Factor** the numerator. $\dfrac{(x-3)(x+1)}{x-3}$

❸ **Divide** out the common factor $(x-3)$. $\dfrac{(x-3)(x+1)}{x-3}$

❹ **Simplify** the expression. $x+1$

Checkpoint ✔ *Divide a Polynomial by a Binomial*

Find the quotient.

15. Divide (x^2-4) by $(x+2)$.

16. Divide $(2n^2-8n+8)$ by $(n-2)$.

17. $(m^2-4m+3) \div (m-1)$

18. $(x^2-2x-8) \div (x-4)$

Guided Practice

Vocabulary Check

1. Define *rational number*. Which of the following are rational numbers?

$$5, \quad \frac{2}{3}, \quad \frac{-17}{2}, \quad \sqrt{3}, \quad 1.45, \quad 0, \quad \pi$$

2. Define *rational expression*. Give an example of a rational expression.

3. Define the *simplest form* of a rational expression. Give an example of a rational expression in simplest form.

Skill Check

Simplify the expression. If not possible, write *already in simplest form*.

4. $\dfrac{28y}{4}$

5. $\dfrac{16}{128c}$

6. $\dfrac{12x^2}{6x}$

7. $\dfrac{a - 8}{4}$

8. $\dfrac{t^4}{t^2(t + 2)}$

9. $\dfrac{8n^3}{12n^4 + 40n^2}$

10. $\dfrac{18}{2x + 4}$

11. $\dfrac{y^7 - y^3}{y^3}$

12. $\dfrac{7 - m}{m^2 - 49}$

Find the quotient.

13. Divide $(3y^2 + 22y + 7)$ by $(y + 7)$.

14. Divide $(x^2 + 5x + 6)$ by $(x + 3)$.

15. Divide $(2x^2 - 5x - 7)$ by $(2x - 7)$.

Practice and Applications

SIMPLIFYING EXPRESSIONS Simplify the expression. If not possible, write *already in simplest form*.

16. $\dfrac{4x}{20}$

17. $\dfrac{45x}{15}$

18. $\dfrac{-18x^2}{12x}$

19. $\dfrac{14x^2}{50x^4}$

20. $\dfrac{10x^5}{16x^3}$

21. $\dfrac{36x}{27x}$

22. $\dfrac{x - 14}{x}$

23. $\dfrac{t^4}{t^2(t + 2)}$

24. $\dfrac{10(r - 6)}{10r}$

FACTORING AND SIMPLIFYING Simplify the expression. If not possible, write *already in simplest form*.

Student Help

▶ **HOMEWORK HELP**
Example 1: Exs. 16–21
Example 2: Exs. 22–24
Example 3: Exs. 25–42
Example 4: Exs. 25–42
Example 5: Exs. 43–46

25. $\dfrac{7x}{12x + x^2}$

26. $\dfrac{3x^2 - 18x}{-9x^2}$

27. $\dfrac{42x - 6x^3}{36x}$

28. $\dfrac{x^2 + 25}{2x + 10}$

29. $\dfrac{2(5 - d)}{2(d - 5)}$

30. $\dfrac{x^2 + 8x + 16}{3x + 12}$

31. $\dfrac{x^2 + x - 20}{x^2 + 2x - 15}$

32. $\dfrac{x^3 + 9x^2 + 14x}{x^2 - 4}$

33. $\dfrac{x^3 - x}{x^3 + 5x^2 - 6x}$

BALLOONING On March 20, 1999, Dr. Bertrand Piccard (pictured above) and Brian Jones became the first balloonists to circle the globe nonstop. The 29,000 mile trip at an altitude of 36,000 feet took them 19 days, 21 hours, and 55 minutes.

SIMPLIFYING EXPRESSIONS Simplify the expression if possible.

34. $\dfrac{x^2 - 9}{x^2 - 5x - 6}$

35. $\dfrac{2x^2 + 11x - 6}{x + 6}$

36. $\dfrac{121 - x^2}{x^2 + 15x + 44}$

37. $\dfrac{1 - x}{x^2 - x}$

38. $\dfrac{12 - 5x}{10x^2 - 24x}$

39. $\dfrac{8y^2 - 7y}{14y^2 - 16y^3}$

40. $\dfrac{5 - x}{x^2 - 8x + 15}$

41. $\dfrac{9 - 2y}{2y^2 - 3y - 27}$

42. $\dfrac{3x - 5}{25 - 30x + 9x^2}$

DIVIDING POLYNOMIALS Find the quotient.

43. Divide $(a^2 - 3a + 2)$ by $(a - 1)$.   **44.** Divide $(5g^2 + 13g - 6)$ by $(g + 3)$.

45. Divide $(x^2 - 6x - 16)$ by $(x + 2)$.   **46.** Divide $(-5m^2 + 25m)$ by $5m$.

47. **Science Link** The air pressure at sea level is about 14.7 pounds per square inch. As the altitude increases, the air pressure decreases. For altitudes between 0 and 60,000 feet, a model that relates air pressure to altitude is

$$P = \dfrac{2952x - 44x^2}{200x + 5x^2}, \text{ where } P \text{ is}$$

measured in pounds per square inch and x is measured in thousands of feet. Simplify this rational expression. Suppose you are in *Breitling Orbiter 3* at 36,000 feet. What is the pressure at that altitude?

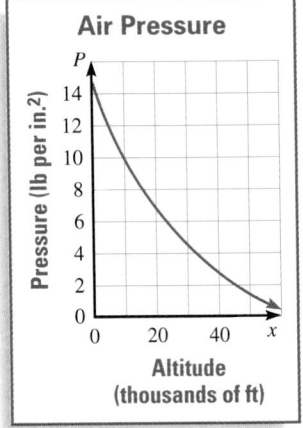

Air Pressure

Pressure (lb per in.²) vs. Altitude (thousands of ft)

48. **LOGICAL REASONING** Copy and complete the *proof* to show why you can divide out common factors.

Statement	Explanation
$\dfrac{ac}{bc} = \dfrac{a}{b} \cdot \dfrac{?}{?}$	Apply the rule for multiplying rational expressions.
$\dfrac{?}{\underline{\quad}} = \dfrac{a}{b} \cdot \underline{\ ?\ }$	Any nonzero number divided by itself is 1.
$\dfrac{?}{\underline{\quad}} = \dfrac{a}{b}$	Any nonzero number multiplied by 1 is itself.

49. **MULTIPLE CHOICE** Simplify the expression $\dfrac{6 + 2x}{x^2 + 5x + 6}$.

Ⓐ $\dfrac{2}{x + 2}$ Ⓑ $\dfrac{2}{x + 3}$ Ⓒ $\dfrac{2}{x + 5}$ Ⓓ $\dfrac{2x}{x^2 + 5x}$

50. **MULTIPLE CHOICE** Simplify the expression $\dfrac{3 - x}{x^2 - 5x + 6}$.

Ⓕ $\dfrac{1}{x + 2}$ Ⓖ $\dfrac{1}{x - 2}$ Ⓗ $\dfrac{-1}{x + 2}$ Ⓙ $\dfrac{-1}{x - 2}$

PRODUCTS AND QUOTIENTS Simplify. *(Lessons 2.5, 2.8)*

51. $\left(-\dfrac{1}{2}\right)\left(\dfrac{2}{3}\right)$

52. $(-15)\left(-\dfrac{5}{6}\right)$

53. $\dfrac{2}{7} \div \dfrac{14}{24}$

54. $\dfrac{4}{9} \div (-36)$

55. $\left(-\dfrac{3}{4}\right)\left(\dfrac{3y}{-5}\right)$

56. $-(-5)^2(2j)$

57. $\dfrac{2m}{3} \cdot 6m^2$

58. $\dfrac{36}{45a} \div \dfrac{-9a}{5}$

59. $18c^3 \div \dfrac{-27c}{-4}$

60. *Geometry Link* The area of the triangle is 192 square meters. What is the value of x? What is the perimeter? *(Lesson 9.2)*

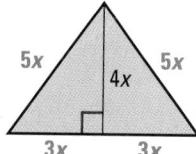

SKETCHING GRAPHS Sketch the graph of the function. *(Lesson 9.4)*

61. $y = x^2$

62. $y = 4 - x^2$

63. $y = \dfrac{1}{2}x^2$

64. $y = 5x^2 + 4x - 5$

65. $y = 4x^2 - x + 6$

66. $y = -3x^2 - x + 7$

ADDING DECIMALS Find the sum. *(Skills Review p. 759)*

67. $0.987 + 1.4$

68. $0.009 + 9$

69. $75.6 + 35.8$

70. $1.23 + 0.45$

71. $0.01 + 0.01$

72. $100.02 + 10$

Quiz 1

Solve the proportion. Check your solutions. *(Lesson 11.1)*

1. $\dfrac{x}{10} = \dfrac{4}{5}$

2. $\dfrac{3}{x} = \dfrac{7}{9}$

3. $\dfrac{x}{4x - 8} = \dfrac{2}{x}$

4. $\dfrac{6x + 4}{5} = \dfrac{2}{x}$

The variables x and y vary directly. Use the given values to write an equation that relates x and y. *(Lesson 11.2)*

5. $x = 8, y = 32$

6. $x = 5, y = 3$

7. $x = 10, y = 15$

The variables x and y vary inversely. Use the given values to write an equation that relates x and y. *(Lesson 11.2)*

8. $x = 12, y = 2$

9. $x = 4, y = 4$

10. $x = 3, y = 2.5$

Simplify the expression if possible. *(Lesson 11.3)*

11. $\dfrac{15x^2}{10x}$

12. $\dfrac{x^2 - 7x + 12}{x^2 + 3x - 18}$

13. $\dfrac{3 - x}{x^2 + x - 12}$

14. $\dfrac{5x}{11x + x^2}$

Find the quotient. *(Lesson 11.3)*

15. Divide $(x^2 - 3x - 28)$ by $(x - 7)$.

16. Divide $(6x^2 + 11x + 3)$ by $(3x + 1)$.

11.4 Multiplying and Dividing Rational Expressions

Goal
Multiply and divide rational expressions.

Key Words
- rational expression
- reciprocal
- divisor

What is the ratio of two prairie dog populations?

In Exercise 47 you will use the rules for dividing rational expressions to compare the growth of two prairie dog populations.

Because the variables in a rational expression represent real numbers, the rules for multiplying and dividing rational expressions are the same as the rules for multiplying and dividing fractions that you learned in previous courses.

MULTIPLYING AND DIVIDING RATIONAL EXPRESSIONS

Let a, b, c, and d be nonzero polynomials.

TO MULTIPLY, multiply numerators and denominators. $\dfrac{a}{b} \cdot \dfrac{c}{d} = \dfrac{ac}{bd}$

TO DIVIDE, multiply by the reciprocal of the divisor. $\dfrac{a}{b} \div \dfrac{c}{d} = \dfrac{a}{b} \cdot \dfrac{d}{c}$

Student Help

▶ STUDY TIP
In Step 3, you do not need to write the prime factorizations of 24 and 60 if you recognize 12 as their greatest common factor.

EXAMPLE 1 Multiply Rational Expressions

Simplify $\dfrac{3x^3}{4x} \cdot \dfrac{8x}{15x^4}$.

① Write the original expression.

$$\dfrac{3x^3}{4x} \cdot \dfrac{8x}{15x^4}$$

② Multiply the numerators and denominators.

$$\dfrac{24x^4}{60x^5}$$

③ Factor and divide out the common factors.

$$\dfrac{2 \cdot 2 \cdot 2 \cdot 3 \cdot \cancel{x} \cdot \cancel{x} \cdot \cancel{x} \cdot \cancel{x}}{2 \cdot 2 \cdot 3 \cdot 5 \cdot \cancel{x} \cdot \cancel{x} \cdot \cancel{x} \cdot \cancel{x} \cdot x}$$

④ Simplify the expression.

$$\dfrac{2}{5x}$$

EXAMPLE **2** **Multiply Rational Expressions**

Simplify $\dfrac{x}{3x^2 - 9x} \cdot \dfrac{x - 3}{2x^2 + x - 3}$.

❶ **Write** the original expression.

$$\frac{x}{3x^2 - 9x} \cdot \frac{x - 3}{2x^2 + x - 3}$$

❷ **Factor** the numerators and denominators.

$$\frac{x}{3x(x - 3)} \cdot \frac{x - 3}{(x - 1)(2x + 3)}$$

❸ **Multiply** the numerators and denominators.

$$\frac{x(x - 3)}{3x(x - 3)(x - 1)(2x + 3)}$$

❹ **Divide** out the common factors.

$$\frac{x(x - 3)}{3x(x - 3)(x - 1)(2x + 3)}$$

❺ **Simplify** the expression.

$$\frac{1}{3(x - 1)(2x + 3)}$$

Checkpoint ✓ **Multiply Rational Expressions**

Write the product in simplest form.

1. $\dfrac{y^3}{2y^2} \cdot \dfrac{4y^2}{6}$

2. $\dfrac{5x + 10}{x - 3} \cdot \dfrac{x^2 - 9}{5}$

3. $\dfrac{4x^2}{(x + 2)^2} \cdot \dfrac{x^2 + 3x + 2}{x^2 + 1}$

EXAMPLE **3** **Multiply by a Polynomial**

Simplify $\dfrac{7x}{x^2 + 5x + 4} \cdot (x + 4)$.

Solution

$$\frac{7x}{x^2 + 5x + 4} \cdot (x + 4) = \frac{7x}{x^2 + 5x + 4} \cdot \frac{x + 4}{1} \qquad \text{Write } x + 4 \text{ as } \tfrac{x + 4}{1}.$$

$$= \frac{7x}{(x + 1)(x + 4)} \cdot \frac{x + 4}{1} \qquad \text{Factor.}$$

$$= \frac{7x(x + 4)}{(x + 1)(x + 4)} \qquad \text{Multiply numerators and denominators.}$$

$$= \frac{7x(x + 4)}{(x + 1)(x + 4)} \qquad \text{Divide out common factor.}$$

$$= \frac{7x}{x + 1} \qquad \text{Write in simplest form.}$$

Checkpoint ✓ **Multiply by a Polynomial**

Write the product in simplest form.

4. $\dfrac{3}{x + 1} \cdot (2x + 2)$

5. $\dfrac{x}{2x + 4} \cdot (x^2 + 2x)$

6. $(x - 3) \cdot \dfrac{x + 3}{x^2 - 9}$

11.4 *Multiplying and Dividing Rational Expressions* **653**

EXAMPLE **4** **Divide Rational Expressions**

Simplify $\dfrac{4n}{n+5} \div \dfrac{n-9}{n+5}$.

❶ **Write** the original problem.

$$\dfrac{4n}{n+5} \div \dfrac{n-9}{n+5}$$

❷ **Multiply** by the reciprocal.

$$\dfrac{4n}{n+5} \cdot \dfrac{n+5}{n-9}$$

❸ **Multiply** the numerators and denominators.

$$\dfrac{4n(n+5)}{(n+5)(n-9)}$$

❹ **Divide** out the common factor $(n+5)$.

$$\dfrac{4n(n+\cancel{5})}{(n+\cancel{5})(n-9)}$$

❺ **Simplify** the expression.

$$\dfrac{4n}{n-9}$$

Checkpoint ✔ *Divide Rational Expressions*

Write the quotient in simplest form.

7. $\dfrac{4}{x+2} \div \dfrac{3}{x+2}$

8. $\dfrac{x+3}{4} \div \dfrac{2x+6}{3}$

9. $\dfrac{3x}{2x-4} \div \dfrac{6x^2}{x-2}$

EXAMPLE **5** **Divide by a Polynomial**

Simplify $\dfrac{x^2-9}{4x^2} \div (x-3)$.

Solution

$$\dfrac{x^2-9}{4x^2} \div (x-3) = \dfrac{x^2-9}{4x^2} \cdot \dfrac{1}{x-3} \qquad \text{Multiply by reciprocal.}$$

$$= \dfrac{(x+3)(x-3)}{4x^2} \cdot \dfrac{1}{x-3} \qquad \text{Factor.}$$

$$= \dfrac{(x+3)(x-3)}{4x^2(x-3)} \qquad \begin{array}{l}\text{Multiply numerators and}\\ \text{denominators.}\end{array}$$

$$= \dfrac{(x+3)(x\cancel{-3})}{4x^2(x\cancel{-3})} \qquad \text{Divide out common factor.}$$

$$= \dfrac{x+3}{4x^2} \qquad \text{Write in simplest form.}$$

Checkpoint ✔ *Divide by a Polynomial*

Write the quotient in simplest form.

10. $\dfrac{x+1}{x+2} \div (2x+2)$

11. $\dfrac{x+2}{x-1} \div (x^2+2x)$

12. $\dfrac{x^2-4}{x+2} \div (4x-8)$

Guided Practice

Vocabulary Check   **In Exercises 1 and 2, complete the sentence.**

1. To multiply rational expressions, multiply the __?__ and __?__ .

2. To divide rational expressions, multiply by the __?__ of the __?__ .

Skill Check   **Simplify the expression.**

3. $\dfrac{3x}{8x^2} \cdot \dfrac{4x^3}{3x^4}$

4. $\dfrac{x^2 - 1}{x} \cdot \dfrac{2x}{3x - 3}$

5. $\dfrac{x}{x^2 - 25} \cdot \dfrac{x - 5}{x + 5}$

6. $\dfrac{3x}{x^2 - 2x - 15} \cdot (x + 3)$ **7.** $\dfrac{x}{8 - 2x} \div \dfrac{2x}{4 - x}$

8. $\dfrac{4x^2 - 25}{4x} \div (2x - 5)$

9. ERROR ANALYSIS   Find and correct the error.

$$\dfrac{x+3}{x-3} \div \dfrac{4x}{x^2-9} = \dfrac{x+3}{x-3} \cdot \dfrac{4x}{(x+3)(x-3)} = \dfrac{4x}{(x-3)^2}$$

Practice and Applications

MULTIPLYING RATIONAL EXPRESSIONS   **Write the product in simplest form.**

10. $\dfrac{4x}{3} \cdot \dfrac{1}{x}$

11. $\dfrac{9x^2}{4} \cdot \dfrac{8}{18x}$

12. $\dfrac{7d^2}{6d} \cdot \dfrac{12d^2}{2d}$

13. $\dfrac{6x}{14} \cdot \dfrac{2x^3}{5x^5}$

14. $\dfrac{y}{16} \cdot \dfrac{4y^4}{y^2}$

15. $\dfrac{-3}{x - 4} \cdot \dfrac{x - 4}{12(x - 7)}$

16. $\dfrac{3x}{x^2 - 2x - 24} \cdot \dfrac{x - 6}{6x^2}$

17. $\dfrac{z^2 + 8z + 7}{10z} \cdot \dfrac{z^2}{z^2 - 49}$

18. $\dfrac{5 - 2x}{6} \cdot \dfrac{24}{10 - 4x}$

19. $\dfrac{3a}{a + 4} \cdot \dfrac{a^2 + 5a + 4}{a^2 + a}$

20. $\dfrac{3x^2 - 6x}{2x + 1} \cdot \dfrac{4x + 2}{x - 2}$

21. $\dfrac{x}{x - 2} \cdot \dfrac{x^2 - 3x + 2}{x - 1}$

22. $\dfrac{45x^3 - 9x^2}{x} \cdot \dfrac{2}{6(x - 5)}$

23. $\dfrac{c^2 - 64}{4c^3} \cdot \dfrac{c}{c^2 + 9c + 8}$

24. $\dfrac{3}{x^2 - 5x + 6} \cdot \dfrac{x - 3}{x - 2}$

MULTIPLYING BY POLYNOMIALS   **Write the product in simplest form.**

25. $\dfrac{3x}{x + 4} \cdot (3x + 12)$

26. $\dfrac{7x - 15}{11x + 121} \cdot (x + 11)$

27. $(y - 3)^2 \cdot \dfrac{2y - 2}{y^2 - 4y + 3}$

28. $(x^2 + 2x + 1) \cdot \dfrac{x + 2}{x^2 + 3x + 2}$

29. $\dfrac{2x + 3}{2x^2 - 3x - 9} \cdot (x^2 - 9)$

30. $3z^2 + 10z + 3 \cdot \dfrac{z + 3}{3z^2 + 4z + 1}$

DIVIDING RATIONAL EXPRESSIONS Write the quotient in simplest form.

31. $\dfrac{25x^2}{10x} \div \dfrac{5x}{10x}$

32. $\dfrac{16x^2}{8x} \div \dfrac{4x^2}{16x}$

33. $\dfrac{3x^2}{10} \div \dfrac{9x^3}{25}$

34. $\dfrac{x}{x+2} \div \dfrac{x+5}{x+2}$

35. $\dfrac{2(x+2)}{5(x-3)} \div \dfrac{4(x-2)}{5x-15}$

36. $\dfrac{x}{x-2} \div \dfrac{2x-2}{x^2-3x+2}$

37. $\dfrac{x}{x+6} \div \dfrac{x+3}{x^2-36}$

38. $\dfrac{3x+12}{4x} \div \dfrac{x+4}{2x}$

39. $\dfrac{2x^2+3x+1}{12x-12} \div \dfrac{x^2-1}{6x}$

DIVIDING BY POLYNOMIALS Write the quotient in simplest form.

40. $\dfrac{x+5}{2+3x} \div (x^2-25)$

41. $\dfrac{x^2-36}{-5x^2} \div (x-6)$

42. $\dfrac{x^2+19x-20}{x^2} \div (x^2-1)$

43. $\dfrac{y-12}{2y+3} \div (y^2-14y+24)$

44. $\dfrac{3x^2+2x-8}{3x} \div (3x-4)$

45. $\dfrac{4x+3}{x-1} \div (4x^2+x-3)$

PRAIRIE DOGS In Exercises 46–49, use the following information.
Scientists are monitoring two distinct prairie dog populations, P_1 and P_2, modeled as follows.

$$P_1 = \frac{100x^2}{x+1} \text{ and } P_2 = \frac{100x^2}{x+3} \text{ where } x \text{ is time in years.}$$

46. Copy and complete the table below. Round to the nearest whole number.

x	1	2	3	4	5	6	7	8	9	10
P_1	?	?	?	?	?	?	?	?	?	?
P_2	?	?	?	?	?	?	?	?	?	?

47. Find the ratio in simplest form of Population 1 to Population 2, that is $\dfrac{P_1}{P_2}$.

48. Add another row to your table labeled $\dfrac{P_1}{P_2}$ and evaluate for each value of x.

49. Describe the pattern in the ratios you found in Exercise 48. If the value of x gets very large, what value does $\dfrac{P_1}{P_2}$ approach? Explain.

50. *Geometry Link* Write the ratio in simplest form comparing the area of the smaller rectangle to the area of the larger rectangle.

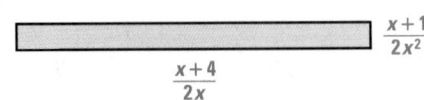

$\dfrac{x-3}{x^2-3x-4}$

$\dfrac{x^2-16}{x^2-x-6}$

$\dfrac{x+1}{2x^2}$

$\dfrac{x+4}{2x}$

51. CHALLENGE Write the expression in simplest form.

$$\frac{x^2 + 11x + 18}{x^2 - 25} \div \frac{14x^3}{x^2 - x - 20} \cdot \frac{x}{x + 4} \div \frac{2x - 1}{6x} \cdot \frac{2x^2 + 9x - 5}{x^2 + 3x + 2}$$

52. MULTIPLE CHOICE Which of the following represents the expression $\frac{x^2 - 3x}{x^2 - 5x + 6} \cdot \frac{(x - 2)^2}{2x}$ in simplest form?

(A) $\frac{x(x - 3)}{2}$ (B) $\frac{x^2 - 4x + 4}{x - 2}$ (C) $\frac{x - 2}{2}$ (D) $\frac{x}{2}$

53. MULTIPLE CHOICE Which product represents $(2x + 2) \div \frac{x^2 + x}{4}$?

(F) $\frac{2x + 2}{2x + 2} \cdot \frac{4}{x^2 + x}$ (G) $\frac{2x + 2}{1} \cdot \frac{x^2 + x}{4}$

(H) $\frac{1}{2x + 2} \cdot \frac{4}{x^2 + x}$ (J) $\frac{2x + 2}{1} \cdot \frac{4}{x^2 + x}$

FUNCTIONS In Exercises 54–56, use the function $y = x + 9$, where $2 \le x \le 6$. *(Lesson 1.8)*

54. Calculate the output y for several inputs x.

55. Make an input-output table.

56. State the domain and range of the function.

ABSOLUTE-VALUE INEQUALITIES Solve the absolute-value inequality. *(Lesson 6.7)*

57. $|x + 7| < 12$ **58.** $|2x - 15| \le 15$ **59.** $|x + 13| \ge 33$

60. $|3x - 10| < 4$ **61.** $|x + 5| > 17$ **62.** $|5x - 1| \le 0$

QUADRATIC EQUATIONS Solve the quadratic equation. *(Lesson 9.6)*

63. $2x^2 + 12x - 6 = 0$ **64.** $x^2 - 6x + 7 = 0$ **65.** $3x^2 + 11x + 10 = 0$

66. $6x^2 = 130$ **67.** $5 = 6x^2 + 7x$ **68.** $2x^2 + 4x = 7$

POLYNOMIALS Add or subtract the polynomials. *(Lesson 10.1)*

69. $(-5x^2 + 2x - 12) - (6 - 9x - 7x^2)$ **70.** $(a^4 - 12a) + (4a^3 + 11a - 1)$

71. $(16p^3 - p^2 + 24) + (12p^2 - 8p - 16)$ **72.** $(4t^2 + 5t + 2) - (t^2 - 3t - 8)$

ADDING FRACTIONS AND DECIMALS Add. Write the answer as a decimal. *(Skills Review pp. 759, 767)*

73. $0.35 + \frac{1}{2}$ **74.** $0.58 + \frac{2}{5}$ **75.** $0.99 + \frac{3}{4}$ **76.** $0.06 + \frac{1}{8}$

77. $\frac{7}{8} + 0.25$ **78.** $\frac{3}{5} + 0.4$ **79.** $\frac{12}{12} + 0.12$ **80.** $\frac{3}{10} + 0.45$

11.5 Adding and Subtracting with Like Denominators

Goal
Add and subtract rational expressions with like denominators.

Key Words
- rational expression
- common denominator

What happens when you hit a tennis ball?

In Exercises 42–45 you will subtract rational expressions with like denominators to analyze the effects of hitting a tennis ball with a racket.

As with fractions, to add or subtract rational expressions with *like*, or the same, denominators, combine their numerators and write the result over the common denominator.

ADDING OR SUBTRACTING WITH LIKE DENOMINATORS

Let a, b, and c be polynomials, with $c \neq 0$.

TO ADD, add the numerators. $\qquad \dfrac{a}{c} + \dfrac{b}{c} = \dfrac{a+b}{c}$

TO SUBTRACT, subtract the numerators. $\qquad \dfrac{a}{c} - \dfrac{b}{c} = \dfrac{a-b}{c}$

EXAMPLE 1 Add Rational Expressions

Simplify $\dfrac{5}{2x} + \dfrac{x-5}{2x}$.

Solution

❶ **Write** the original expression. $\qquad \dfrac{5}{2x} + \dfrac{x-5}{2x}$

❷ **Add** the numerators. $\qquad \dfrac{5+(x-5)}{2x}$

❸ **Combine** like terms. $\qquad \dfrac{x}{2x}$

❹ **Simplify** the expression. $\qquad \dfrac{1}{2}$

EXAMPLE **2** Subtract Rational Expressions

Simplify $\dfrac{4}{x+2} - \dfrac{x+4}{x+2}$.

Solution

❶ **Write** the original expression. $\dfrac{4}{x+2} - \dfrac{x+4}{x+2}$

❷ **Subtract** the numerators. $\dfrac{4-(x+4)}{x+2}$

❸ **Distribute** the negative. $\dfrac{4-x-4}{x+2}$

❹ **Simplify** the numerator. $-\dfrac{x}{x+2}$

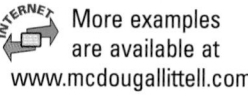 **Add and Subtract Rational Expressions**

Simplify the expression.

1. $\dfrac{x+2}{x} + \dfrac{3x-2}{x}$

2. $\dfrac{x+2}{x^2+5} - \dfrac{3x+2}{x^2+5}$

3. $\dfrac{3x-4}{x-4} - \dfrac{2x}{x-4}$

EXAMPLE **3** Simplify after Subtracting

Simplify $\dfrac{4x}{3x^2-x-2} - \dfrac{x-2}{3x^2-x-2}$.

Solution

$\dfrac{4x}{3x^2-x-2} - \dfrac{x-2}{3x^2-x-2} = \dfrac{4x-(x-2)}{3x^2-x-2}$ Subtract numerators.

$= \dfrac{3x+2}{3x^2-x-2}$ Simplify.

$= \dfrac{3x+2}{(3x+2)(x-1)}$ Factor.

$= \dfrac{\cancel{3x+2}}{\cancel{(3x+2)}(x-1)}$ Divide out common factor.

$= \dfrac{1}{x-1}$ Write simplest form.

Checkpoint ✓ **Simplify after Adding or Subtracting**

Write the sum or difference in simplest form.

4. $\dfrac{2x}{x^2+2x+1} + \dfrac{2}{x^2+2x+1}$

5. $\dfrac{2x-4}{x^2+3x} - \dfrac{x-7}{x^2+3x}$

Guided Practice

Vocabulary Check

1. Complete: To add or subtract rational expressions with like denominators, add or subtract their numerators, and write the result over the __?__.

Skill Check

Add. Simplify your answer.

2. $\dfrac{1}{3x} + \dfrac{5}{3x}$

3. $\dfrac{8y}{y+3} + \dfrac{10-3y}{y+3}$

4. $\dfrac{x}{x^2-9} + \dfrac{3x+1}{x^2-9}$

Subtract. Simplify your answer.

5. $\dfrac{8}{3r} - \dfrac{1}{3r}$

6. $\dfrac{12k}{k^2} - \dfrac{3k+7}{k^2}$

7. $\dfrac{c+1}{c^2-4} - \dfrac{c+6}{c^2-4}$

Add or subtract, then factor and simplify.

8. $\dfrac{5x}{x+4} + \dfrac{20}{4+x}$

9. $\dfrac{-12y}{y^2-9y+14} + \dfrac{84}{y^2-9y+14}$

10. $\dfrac{2y+3}{y^2-4y} - \dfrac{-y+15}{y^2-4y}$

11. $\dfrac{10}{r^2+9r+20} - \dfrac{-2r}{r^2+9r+20}$

Practice and Applications

ADDING RATIONAL EXPRESSIONS **Simplify the expression.**

12. $\dfrac{7}{2x} + \dfrac{x+2}{2x}$

13. $\dfrac{2}{x+7} + \dfrac{5}{x+7}$

14. $\dfrac{4t-1}{1-4t} + \dfrac{2t+3}{1-4t}$

15. $\dfrac{4}{x+1} + \dfrac{2x-2}{x+1}$

16. $\dfrac{a+1}{15a} + \dfrac{2a-1}{15a}$

17. $\dfrac{2x}{4x+6} + \dfrac{3}{4x+6}$

SUBTRACTING RATIONAL EXPRESSIONS **Simplify the expression.**

18. $\dfrac{7x}{x^3} - \dfrac{6x}{x^3}$

19. $\dfrac{8+6t}{3t} - \dfrac{5t-6}{3t}$

20. $\dfrac{2x}{x+2} - \dfrac{2x+1}{x+2}$

21. $\dfrac{2}{3x-1} - \dfrac{5x}{3x-1}$

22. $\dfrac{4x}{2x+6} - \dfrac{16}{2x+6}$

23. $\dfrac{4m}{m-2} - \dfrac{2m+4}{m-2}$

FACTORING AFTER ADDING OR SUBTRACTING **Simplify the expression.**

24. $\dfrac{x}{x^2+5x-24} + \dfrac{8}{x^2+5x-24}$

25. $\dfrac{a^2-2}{a^2-25} + \dfrac{4a-3}{a^2-25}$

26. $\dfrac{2x}{x^2+5x+4} + \dfrac{8}{x^2+5x+4}$

27. $\dfrac{x^2-10}{x^2-4} + \dfrac{3x}{x^2-4}$

28. $\dfrac{2x}{x^2+5x} - \dfrac{x}{x^2+5x}$

29. $\dfrac{2x(x+4)}{(x+1)^2} - \dfrac{3x-3}{(x+1)^2}$

30. $\dfrac{y^2-2y}{y^2-7y-18} - \dfrac{9(y-2)}{y^2-7y-18}$

31. $\dfrac{y^2}{y^2-3y-28} - \dfrac{12-y}{y^2-3y-28}$

Student Help

▶ **HOMEWORK HELP**
Example 1: Exs. 12–17
Example 2: Exs. 18–23
Example 3: Exs. 24–31

ERROR ANALYSIS In Exercises 32 and 33, find and correct the error.

32.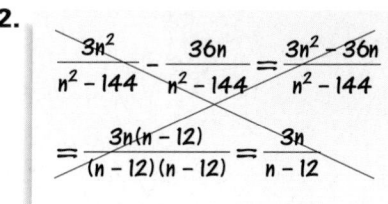

$$\frac{3n^2}{n^2 - 144} - \frac{36n}{n^2 - 144} = \frac{3n^2 - 36n}{n^2 - 144}$$

$$= \frac{3n(n-12)}{(n-12)(n-12)} = \frac{3n}{n-12}$$

33.

$$\frac{y+2}{y+3} + \frac{y-4}{y+3} = \frac{(y+2)(y-4)}{(y+3)^2}$$

$$= \frac{y^2 - 2y - 8}{y^2 + 6y + 9}$$

Student Help

▶**HOMEWORK HELP**

INTERNET Extra help with problem solving in Exs. 34–39 is available at www.mcdougallittell.com

COMBINING OPERATIONS In Exercises 34–39, simplify the expression.

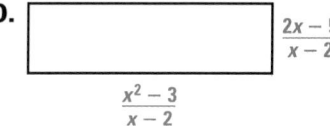

34. $\dfrac{11x - 5}{2x + 5} + \dfrac{11x + 12}{2x + 5} + \dfrac{3x - 100}{2x + 5}$

35. $\dfrac{4 + x}{x - 9} + \dfrac{6 + x}{x - 9} - \dfrac{1 - x}{x - 9}$

36. $\dfrac{c - 15}{2c + 6} - \dfrac{2c}{2c + 6} + \dfrac{12}{2c + 6}$

37. $\dfrac{2x}{x^2 - 9} - \dfrac{4x + 2}{x^2 - 9} - \dfrac{4}{x^2 - 9}$

38. $\left(\dfrac{3x^2}{56}\right)\left(\dfrac{3}{x} + \dfrac{5}{x}\right)$

39. $\left(\dfrac{3x - 5}{x} + \dfrac{1}{x}\right) \div \left(\dfrac{x}{6x - 8}\right)$

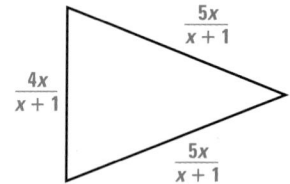

Geometry Link Find expressions for the perimeter of the rectangle and triangle. Simplify your answer.

40. [rectangle with side $\dfrac{2x - 5}{x - 2}$ and side $\dfrac{x^2 - 3}{x - 2}$]

41. [triangle with sides $\dfrac{5x}{x + 1}$, $\dfrac{4x}{x + 1}$, $\dfrac{5x}{x + 1}$]

Link to Science

Science Link In Exercises 42–45, use the following information.

When a tennis player hits a ball that is already moving, the work done by the racket is the change in the ball's kinetic energy. The total work done on an object is given by the formula

$$W = K_2 - K_1$$

where W represents work, K_1 represents the initial kinetic energy of an object, and K_2 represents the final kinetic energy of an object. Work and energy are measured in joules. (A joule is the amount of work done when a force of 1 newton acts on an object that moves 1 meter.)

Copy and complete the table, by computing the work done on the tennis ball.

KINETIC ENERGY Every moving object has kinetic energy. The tennis player and tennis racket have kinetic energy as he swings the racket at the ball. The ball has kinetic energy as it flies through the air.

	K_2	K_1	Work
42.	$\dfrac{9}{x}$	$\dfrac{7}{x}$	?
43.	$\dfrac{5}{a}$	$\dfrac{5 - a}{a}$	?
44.	$\dfrac{2t}{t - 1}$	$\dfrac{t + 4}{t - 1}$	?
45.	$\dfrac{x^2 - 7}{x^2 - 100}$	$\dfrac{-10x - 7}{x^2 - 100}$	?

46. MULTIPLE CHOICE Which of the following expressions can be simplified to $x + 3$?

(A) $\dfrac{x^2}{x+3} - \dfrac{9}{x+3}$

(B) $\dfrac{x^2}{x-7} - \dfrac{4x+21}{x-7}$

(C) $\dfrac{x-6}{x-3} - \dfrac{x+9}{x-3}$

(D) None of these

47. MULTIPLE CHOICE Simplify $\dfrac{x^2}{x+5} - \dfrac{25}{x+5}$.

(F) $\dfrac{1}{x-5}$

(G) $\dfrac{x^2-25}{x+5}$

(H) $x - 5$

(J) $\dfrac{x-5}{x+5}$

48. MULTIPLE CHOICE Simplify $\dfrac{24y^2+24}{8y-3} - \dfrac{73y}{8y-3}$.

(A) $\dfrac{(8y+3)(3y+8)}{8y-3}$

(B) $\dfrac{3y-8}{(8y-3)^2}$

(C) $\dfrac{3y-8}{8y-3}$

(D) $3y - 8$

SIMPLIFYING EXPRESSIONS Rewrite the expression with positive exponents. *(Lesson 8.2)*

49. $x^5 y^{-6}$

50. $8x^{-1}y^{-3}$

51. $\dfrac{1}{2x^8 y^{-5}}$

52. $\dfrac{3}{10t^{-3}r^{-1}}$

53. $(-6c)^{-4}$

54. $(-y)^0 n$

55. $\dfrac{d}{c^{-2}}$

56. $\dfrac{1}{(-7m)^{-3}}$

SIMPLIFYING EXPRESSIONS Simplify the expression. The simplified expression should have no negative exponents. *(Lesson 8.4)*

57. $\dfrac{p^6}{p^8}$

58. $x^5 \cdot \dfrac{1}{x^4}$

59. $\left(\dfrac{a^8}{a^3}\right)^{-1}$

60. $\left(\dfrac{y^5}{y^7}\right)^{-2}$

61. $\dfrac{m^8 \cdot m^{10}}{m^2}$

62. $\dfrac{(a^3)^4}{(a^3)^8}$

63. $\left(\dfrac{-2u^2 v}{uv^4}\right)^{-3}$

64. $\left(\dfrac{42a^3 b^{-4}}{6ab}\right)^3$

EVALUATING EXPRESSIONS Perform the indicated operation. Write the result in scientific notation. *(Lesson 8.5)*

65. $\dfrac{8 \times 10^{-3}}{5 \times 10^{-5}}$

66. $\dfrac{1.4 \times 10^{-1}}{3.5 \times 10^{-4}}$

67. $(3 \times 10^{-2})^4$

68. $2 \times 10^3 + 3 \times 10^2$

69. $(2.5 \times 10)^{-2}$

70. $3.2 \times 10 + 5.8 \times 10$

PATTERNS List the next three numbers suggested by the sequence. *(Skills Review pp. 781)*

71. 1, 3, 5, 7, ?, ?, ?

72. 1, 3, 6, 10, ?, ?, ?

73. 60, 57, 53, 48, ?, ?, ?

74. $\dfrac{1}{2}, \dfrac{2}{3}, \dfrac{3}{4}, \dfrac{4}{5}$, ?, ?, ?

75. $2, \dfrac{7}{2}, 5, \dfrac{13}{2}$, ?, ?, ?

76. 100, 81, 64, 49, ?, ?, ?

11.6 Adding and Subtracting with Unlike Denominators

Goal

Add and subtract rational expressions with unlike denominators.

Key Words

- least common denominator (LCD)

How should you plan a 300-mile car trip?

In Example 6 you will add rational expressions with *unlike* denominators to analyze the total time needed for a 300-mile car trip.

As with fractions, to add or subtract rational expressions with *unlike* denominators, you first rewrite the expressions so that they have *like* denominators. The like denominator that you usually use is the least common multiple of the original denominators, called the **least common denominator** or **LCD**.

Student Help

▶ **SKILLS REVIEW**
For practice on finding the LCD of numerical fractions, see p. 762.

EXAMPLE 1 Find the LCD of Rational Expressions

Find the least common denominator of $\dfrac{1}{12x}$ and $\dfrac{2+x}{40x^4}$.

Solution

❶ **Factor** the denominators.

$$12x = 2^2 \cdot 3 \cdot x$$
$$40x^4 = 2^3 \cdot 5 \cdot x^4$$

❷ **Find** the highest power of each factor that appears in either denominator.

$$2^3, 3, 5, x^4$$

❸ **Multiply** these to find the LCD.

$$2^3 \cdot 3 \cdot 5 \cdot x^4 = 120x^4$$

ANSWER ▶ The LCD is $120x^4$.

Checkpoint ✓ Find the LCD of Rational Expressions

Find the least common denominator.

1. $\dfrac{x+1}{5}, \dfrac{2x}{6}$

2. $\dfrac{1}{36x}, \dfrac{3x+1}{9x^5}$

3. $\dfrac{5x+9}{16x^3}, \dfrac{7}{24x^2}$

4. $\dfrac{x}{x-5}, \dfrac{2x^3}{x+7}$

5. $\dfrac{12}{x+1}, \dfrac{x}{x-1}$

6. $\dfrac{2x+3}{30x^5}, \dfrac{1}{8x}$

EXAMPLE 2 Rewrite Rational Expressions

Find the missing numerator.

a. $\dfrac{2}{3y} = \dfrac{?}{15y}$

b. $\dfrac{3x - 7}{4x^2} = \dfrac{?}{36x^5}$

Solution

a. $\dfrac{2}{3y} = \dfrac{?}{15y}$ Multiply $3y$ by 5 to get $15y$.

$\dfrac{2}{3y} = \dfrac{10}{15y}$ Therefore, multiply 2 by 5 to get 10.

b. $\dfrac{3x - 7}{4x^2} = \dfrac{?}{36x^5}$ Multiply $4x^2$ by $9x^3$ to get $36x^5$.

$\dfrac{3x - 7}{4x^2} = \dfrac{(3x - 7) \cdot 9x^3}{36x^5}$ Therefore, multiply $(3x - 7)$ by $9x^3$ to get $(3x - 7) \cdot 9x^3$.

$\dfrac{3x - 7}{4x^2} = \dfrac{27x^4 - 63x^3}{36x^5}$ Simplify.

Checkpoint ✓ **Rewrite Rational Expressions**

Find the missing numerator.

7. $\dfrac{9}{5x} = \dfrac{?}{30x^5}$

8. $\dfrac{y - 1}{y} = \dfrac{?}{13y^2}$

9. $\dfrac{c}{c + 1} = \dfrac{?}{(c + 1)(c - 3)}$

EXAMPLE 3 Add with Unlike Denominators

Simplify $\dfrac{2}{x} + \dfrac{1 - 2x}{x^2}$.

Student Help

▶ **STUDY TIP**

To rewrite $\dfrac{2}{x}$ with a denominator of x^2, multiply the numerator and denominator by x.

$\dfrac{2}{x} \cdot \dfrac{x}{x} = \dfrac{2x}{x^2}$

Solution

❶ **Find** the LCD.   The LCD is x^2.

❷ **Write** the original expression. $\dfrac{2}{x} + \dfrac{1 - 2x}{x^2}$

❸ **Rewrite** the expression using the LCD. $\dfrac{2x}{x^2} + \dfrac{1 - 2x}{x^2}$

❹ **Add.** $\dfrac{2x + (1 - 2x)}{x^2}$

❺ **Simplify** the expression. $\dfrac{1}{x^2}$

Checkpoint ✓ **Add with Unlike Denominators**

Write the sum in simplest form.

10. $\dfrac{1}{x^2} + \dfrac{2}{x}$

11. $\dfrac{2}{3m} + \dfrac{3 - 2m}{m^2}$

12. $\dfrac{3}{15x^2} + \dfrac{1}{9x^3}$

EXAMPLE 4 Subtract with Unlike Denominators

Simplify $\dfrac{7}{6x} - \dfrac{x+1}{8x^2}$.

Solution

The LCD is $24x^2$.

$$\dfrac{7}{6x} - \dfrac{x+1}{8x^2} = \dfrac{7}{6x} \cdot \dfrac{4x}{4x} - \dfrac{(x+1)}{8x^2} \cdot \dfrac{3}{3} \qquad \text{Rewrite using LCD.}$$

$$= \dfrac{28x}{24x^2} - \dfrac{3x+3}{24x^2} \qquad \text{Simplify numerators and denominators.}$$

$$= \dfrac{28x - (3x+3)}{24x^2} \qquad \text{Subtract.}$$

$$= \dfrac{25x - 3}{24x^2} \qquad \text{Simplify.}$$

EXAMPLE 5 Add with Unlike Binomial Denominators

Simplify $\dfrac{x+2}{x-1} + \dfrac{12}{x+6}$.

Solution

Neither denominator can be factored. The least common denominator is the product $(x-1)(x+6)$ because it must contain both of these factors.

$$\dfrac{x+2}{x-1} + \dfrac{12}{x+6} \qquad \text{Write original expression.}$$

$$\dfrac{(x+2)(x+6)}{(x-1)(x+6)} + \dfrac{12(x-1)}{(x-1)(x+6)} \qquad \text{Rewrite using LCD.}$$

$$\dfrac{x^2 + 8x + 12}{(x-1)(x+6)} + \dfrac{12x - 12}{(x-1)(x+6)} \qquad \text{Simplify numerators.}$$

$$\dfrac{x^2 + 8x + 12 + (12x - 12)}{(x-1)(x+6)} \qquad \text{Add.}$$

$$\dfrac{x^2 + 20x}{(x-1)(x+6)} \qquad \text{Combine like terms.}$$

$$\dfrac{x(x+20)}{(x-1)(x+6)} \qquad \text{Factor.}$$

Checkpoint ✓ Add or Subtract with Unlike Denominators

Simplify the expression.

13. $\dfrac{3}{x^2} - \dfrac{2}{3x}$

14. $\dfrac{2}{p} - \dfrac{3 - 10p}{5p^2}$

15. $\dfrac{3 + 4x}{4x^3} - \dfrac{1}{10x^2}$

16. $\dfrac{1}{x+1} + \dfrac{1}{x-1}$

17. $\dfrac{3}{x-6} + \dfrac{1}{x}$

18. $\dfrac{x-5}{x+5} - \dfrac{x+2}{x-2}$

EXAMPLE **6** **Write and Use a Model**

PLANNING A TRIP You are planning a 300-mile car trip. You can make the trip using a combination of two roads: a highway on which you can drive 60 mi/h and a country road on which you can drive 40 mi/h. Write an expression for the total time the trip will take driving on both roads.

SPEED LIMIT 40
SPEED LIMIT 60

Country road

Highway

Solution

VERBAL MODEL

$$\text{Total time} = \frac{\text{Distance on country road}}{\text{Speed on country road}} + \frac{\text{Distance on highway}}{\text{Speed on highway}}$$

Student Help

▶**STUDY TIP**
Since the distance on the country road is *x* and the total distance is 300 miles, the distance left to go on the highway is
300 − *x*. ••••••••••

LABELS

Total time = **T**   (hours)

Distance on country road = **x**   (miles)

Speed on country road = **40**   (miles/hour)

Distance on highway = **300 − x**   (miles)

Speed on highway = **60**   (miles/hour)

ALGEBRAIC MODEL

$T = \dfrac{x}{40} + \dfrac{300 - x}{60}$ Write algebraic model.

$= \dfrac{3x}{120} + \dfrac{2(300 - x)}{120}$ Rewrite using LCD.

$= \dfrac{3x + 600 - 2x}{120}$ Add.

$= \dfrac{x + 600}{120}$ Simplify.

Checkpoint ✓ **Write and Use a Model**

19. Evaluate the expression for the total time at 60 mile intervals by completing the table. The table can help you decide how many miles to drive on each road.

Distance (country), *x*	0	60	120	180	240	300
Total time, *T*	?	?	?	?	?	?

Guided Practice

Vocabulary Check

1. Explain what is meant by the *least common denominator* of two rational expressions.

Skill Check

2. ERROR ANALYSIS Find and correct the error.

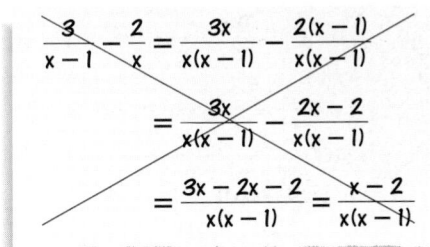

$$\frac{3}{x-1} - \frac{2}{x} = \frac{3x}{x(x-1)} - \frac{2(x-1)}{x(x-1)}$$

$$= \frac{3x}{x(x-1)} - \frac{2x-2}{x(x-1)}$$

$$= \frac{3x - 2x - 2}{x(x-1)} = \frac{x-2}{x(x-1)}$$

In Exercises 3–6, simplify the expression.

3. $\dfrac{x}{12} + \dfrac{x}{4}$ **4.** $\dfrac{3}{10x} - \dfrac{1}{4x^2}$ **5.** $\dfrac{x+6}{x+1} - \dfrac{4}{2x+3}$ **6.** $\dfrac{x-2}{2x-10} + \dfrac{x+3}{x-5}$

7. You can use $x - 3$ as the LCD when finding the sum $\dfrac{5}{x-3} + \dfrac{2}{3-x}$. What number can you multiply the numerator and the denominator of the second fraction by to get an equivalent fraction with $x - 3$ as the new denominator?

Practice and Applications

FINDING THE LCD **Find the least common denominator of the pair of rational expressions.**

8. $\dfrac{1}{3x}, \dfrac{1}{9x^3}$ **9.** $\dfrac{4x}{15}, \dfrac{3x^2}{5}$ **10.** $\dfrac{17y^4}{z^2}, \dfrac{8z}{3y}$ **11.** $\dfrac{3}{c^3}, \dfrac{-5}{7c^5}$

12. $\dfrac{10}{13v^7}, \dfrac{10}{3v^5}$ **13.** $\dfrac{6b}{5}, \dfrac{-5}{b}$ **14.** $\dfrac{x-1}{x-2}, \dfrac{x-3}{x-4}$ **15.** $\dfrac{x+1}{15x}, \dfrac{25}{18x^3}$

REWRITING RATIONAL EXPRESSIONS **Find the missing numerator.**

16. $\dfrac{11}{3x} = \dfrac{?}{12x^3}$ **17.** $\dfrac{8}{5} = \dfrac{?}{15y^2}$ **18.** $\dfrac{x-3}{2} = \dfrac{?}{28x}$

19. $\dfrac{3a+1}{9a^5} = \dfrac{?}{63a^{11}}$ **20.** $\dfrac{x-9}{2x+3} = \dfrac{?}{x(2x+3)}$ **21.** $\dfrac{2a-3}{35a^2} = \dfrac{?}{140a^5}$

ADDING **Write the sum in simplest form.**

22. $\dfrac{3}{2z} + \dfrac{1}{z}$ **23.** $\dfrac{11}{6x} + \dfrac{2}{13x}$ **24.** $\dfrac{9}{4x} + \dfrac{7}{-5x}$

25. $\dfrac{2x+3}{4} + \dfrac{x+1}{2}$ **26.** $\dfrac{3}{12m^3} + \dfrac{m+1}{4m^3}$ **27.** $\dfrac{3n}{15} + \dfrac{n^2+1}{30n}$

Student Help

▶**HOMEWORK HELP**
Example 1: Exs. 8–15
Example 2: Exs. 16–21
Example 3: Exs. 22–27
Example 4: Exs. 28–33
Example 5: Exs. 34–42
Example 6: Exs. 43–48

SUBTRACTING Write the difference in simplest form.

28. $\dfrac{2x}{5} - \dfrac{x+1}{4}$

29. $\dfrac{9}{2x} - \dfrac{2}{7x^2}$

30. $\dfrac{3}{6b^2} - \dfrac{1}{4b}$

31. $\dfrac{x-1}{6x^2} - \dfrac{2}{3x}$

32. $\dfrac{5c}{15} - \dfrac{2+c}{25c}$

33. $\dfrac{2x-1}{3x} - \dfrac{1}{11}$

ADDING OR SUBTRACTING Simplify the expression.

34. $\dfrac{2}{x+1} + \dfrac{3}{x-2}$

35. $\dfrac{x}{x-10} + \dfrac{x+4}{x+6}$

36. $\dfrac{x-3}{x+3} + \dfrac{x+9}{x-3}$

37. $\dfrac{x+8}{3x-1} + \dfrac{x+3}{x+1}$

38. $\dfrac{4}{x+4} - \dfrac{7}{5x}$

39. $\dfrac{2x+1}{3x-1} - \dfrac{x+4}{x-2}$

40. $\dfrac{4x}{5x-2} - \dfrac{2x}{5x+1}$

41. $\dfrac{2x}{x-1} - \dfrac{7x}{x+4}$

42. $\dfrac{3x+10}{7x-4} - \dfrac{x}{4x+3}$

TRAVEL BY BIKE In Exercises 43–45, use the following information.
You are riding your bike to a pond that is 8 miles away. You have a choice to ride in the woods, on the road, or both. In the woods, you can ride at a speed of 10 mi/h. On the road, you can ride at a speed of 20 mi/h.

43. Write an expression for your total time.

44. Write your answer to Exercise 43 in simplest form.

45. Evaluate the expression for total time at 2 mile intervals.

TRAVEL BY BOAT In Exercises 46–48, use the following information.
A boat moves through still water at x kilometers per hour (km/h). It travels 24 km upstream against a current of 2 km/h and then returns to the starting point with the current. The rate upstream is $x - 2$ because the boat moves against the current, and the rate downstream is $x + 2$ because the boat moves with the current.

46. Write an algebraic model for the total time for the round trip.

47. Write your answer to Exercise 46 as a single rational expression.

48. Use your answer to Exercise 47 to find how long the round trip will take if the boat travels 10 km/h through still water.

Geometry Link In Exercises 49–51, use the diagram of the rectangle.

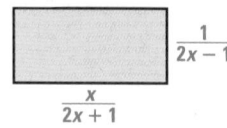

49. Find an expression for the perimeter of the rectangle.

50. What is the perimeter of the rectangle when $x = 3$?

51. What is the area of the rectangle when $x = 3$?

52. MULTIPLE CHOICE Find the LCD of $\dfrac{15}{3t^6}$ and $\dfrac{9}{2t^4}$.

(A) $\dfrac{1}{6t^6}$ (B) $6t^2$ (C) $6t^6$ (D) $6t^{10}$

53. MULTIPLE CHOICE Find the missing numerator $\dfrac{5x + 6}{8x^2} = \dfrac{?}{48x^3}$.

(F) $6x$ (G) $41x$ (H) $30x^2 + 36x$ (J) $11x + 6$

54. MULTIPLE CHOICE What is the difference of $\dfrac{x}{x - 1}$ and $\dfrac{1}{2x + 1}$ in simplest form?

(A) $\dfrac{x - 1}{(x - 1)(2x + 1)}$ (B) $-\dfrac{x}{x - 1}$

(C) $\dfrac{2x^2 + 1}{(x - 1)(2x + 1)}$ (D) $\dfrac{2x^2 - 1}{(x - 1)(2x + 1)}$

Mixed Review

POINT-SLOPE FORM Write in point-slope form the equation of the line that passes through the given point and has the given slope. *(Lesson 5.2)*

55. $(-3, -2)$, $m = 2$ **56.** $(0, 5)$, $m = -1$ **57.** $(-3, 6)$, $m = \dfrac{1}{2}$

58. $(5, 5)$, $m = 5$ **59.** $(7, 0)$, $m = \dfrac{3}{7}$ **60.** $(14, -3)$, $m = \dfrac{1}{3}$

SIMPLIFYING EXPRESSIONS Simplify the expression. *(Lesson 8.4)*

61. $\dfrac{5}{10x}$ **62.** $\dfrac{4m^2}{6m}$ **63.** $\dfrac{16x^4}{32x^8}$ **64.** $\dfrac{42x^4y^3}{6x^3y^9}$

65. $\dfrac{12x}{144x^2}$ **66.** $\dfrac{2x^2y^3z^4}{5x^4y^3z^2}$ **67.** $\dfrac{33p^4}{44p^2q}$ **68.** $\dfrac{15w^2}{9w^5}$

STANDARD FORM Write the equation in standard form. *(Lesson 9.6)*

69. $6x^2 = 5x - 7$ **70.** $9 - 6x = 2x^2$ **71.** $-4 + 3y^2 = y$

72. $12x = x^2 + 25$ **73.** $7 - 12x^2 = 5x$ **74.** $8 = 5x^2 - 4x$

75. GAME SHOW A contestant on a television game show must guess the price of a trip within $1000 of the actual price in order to win. The actual price of the trip is $8500. Write an absolute-value inequality that shows the range of possible guesses that will win the trip. *(Lesson 6.7)*

Maintaining Skills

FRACTIONS AND DECIMALS Write the fraction as a decimal rounded to the nearest thousandth. *(Skills Review p. 767)*

76. $\dfrac{47}{99}$ **77.** $\dfrac{63}{200}$ **78.** $\dfrac{32}{155}$ **79.** $\dfrac{59}{199}$

80. $-\dfrac{115}{144}$ **81.** $-\dfrac{63}{89}$ **82.** $-\dfrac{12}{43}$ **83.** $-\dfrac{79}{145}$

84. $-\dfrac{23}{25}$ **85.** $\dfrac{8}{77}$ **86.** $\dfrac{12}{7}$ **87.** $-\dfrac{18}{35}$

11.7 Rational Equations

Goal
Solve rational equations.

Key Words
- rational equation
- cross product property
- least common denominator (LCD)

How long does it take to shovel a driveway?

If you can shovel a snowy driveway in 3 hours and your friend can do it in 2 hours, how long would it take to shovel it together? In Example 4 you will write and solve a rational equation to answer this question.

A **rational equation** is an equation that contains rational expressions. Example 1 and Example 2 show the two basic strategies for solving a rational equation.

Student Help

▶ **STUDY TIP**
When you solve rational equations, be sure to check your answers. Remember, values of the variable that make any denominator equal to 0 are excluded.

EXAMPLE 1 Cross Multiply

Solve $\dfrac{5}{y+2} = \dfrac{y}{3}$.

❶ **Write** the original equation. $\qquad\qquad \dfrac{5}{y+2} = \dfrac{y}{3}$

❷ **Cross multiply.** $\qquad\qquad\qquad 5(3) = y(y+2)$

❸ **Simplify** each side of the equation. $\qquad 15 = y^2 + 2y$

❹ **Write** the equation in standard form. $\qquad 0 = y^2 + 2y - 15$

❺ **Factor** the right-hand side. $\qquad\qquad 0 = (y+5)(y-3)$

ANSWER ▶ The solutions are $y = -5$ and $y = 3$.

CHECK ✓ Neither -5 nor 3 results in a zero denominator. Substitute $y = -5$ and $y = 3$ into the original equation.

y = −5: $\dfrac{5}{(-5)+2} \overset{?}{=} \dfrac{-5}{3}$ $\qquad$ Since $\dfrac{5}{-3} = \dfrac{-5}{3}$, $y = -5$ is a solution. ✓

y = 3: $\dfrac{5}{3+2} \overset{?}{=} \dfrac{3}{3}$ $\qquad$ Since $\dfrac{5}{5} = \dfrac{3}{3}$, $y = 3$ is a solution. ✓

Checkpoint ✓ Cross Multiply

Solve the equation. Check your solutions.

1. $\dfrac{x}{2} = \dfrac{x+2}{6}$ $\qquad\qquad$ **2.** $\dfrac{3}{2m} = \dfrac{m+1}{4m}$ $\qquad\qquad$ **3.** $\dfrac{y}{5} = \dfrac{6}{y+7}$

TWO METHODS Cross multiplying is appropriate for solving equations in which each side is a single rational expression. A second method, multiplying by the LCD, works for any rational equation.

| EXAMPLE | 2 | **Multiply by the LCD** |

Solve $\dfrac{2}{x} + \dfrac{1}{3} = \dfrac{4}{x}$.

❶ **Find** the LCD.   The LCD is $3x$.

❷ **Write** the original equation. $\dfrac{2}{x} + \dfrac{1}{3} = \dfrac{4}{x}$

❸ **Multiply** each side by the LCD $3x$. $3x \cdot \dfrac{2}{x} + 3x \cdot \dfrac{1}{3} = 3x \cdot \dfrac{4}{x}$

❹ **Simplify** each side of the equation. $6 + x = 12$

❺ **Solve** by subtracting 6 from each side. $x = 6$

| EXAMPLE | 3 | **Factor First, then Multiply by the LCD** |

Solve $\dfrac{3}{x + 3} + \dfrac{4}{x^2 + 6x + 9} = 1$.

Solution

$$\dfrac{3}{x + 3} + \dfrac{4}{x^2 + 6x + 9} = 1 \qquad \text{Write original equation.}$$

$$\dfrac{3}{x + 3} + \dfrac{4}{(x + 3)^2} = 1 \qquad \text{Factor denominator.}$$

$$\dfrac{3}{x + 3} \cdot (x + 3)^2 + \dfrac{4}{(x + 3)^2} \cdot (x + 3)^2 = 1 \cdot (x + 3)^2 \qquad \begin{array}{l}\text{Multiply by}\\ \text{LCD } (x + 3)^2.\end{array}$$

$$3(x + 3) + 4 = (x + 3)^2 \qquad \text{Simplify.}$$

$$3x + 13 = x^2 + 6x + 9 \qquad \text{Simplify each side.}$$

$$0 = x^2 + 3x - 4 \qquad \begin{array}{l}\text{Write in standard}\\ \text{form.}\end{array}$$

$$0 = (x + 4)(x - 1) \qquad \text{Factor.}$$

$$x = -4 \text{ and } x = 1 \qquad \text{Solve.}$$

ANSWER ▶ The solutions are $x = -4$ and $x = 1$. Check both values.

Checkpoint ✓ **Multiply by the LCD**

Solve the equation. Check your solutions.

4. $\dfrac{3}{x} + \dfrac{1}{4} = \dfrac{4}{x}$ **5.** $\dfrac{1}{n + 1} + \dfrac{1}{n} = \dfrac{11}{n^2 + n}$ **6.** $\dfrac{4}{x - 3} + \dfrac{x}{x + 3} = 1$

WORK PROBLEMS Writing and solving rational equations can help to solve problems such as finding out how long it would take you and a friend to clear snow off of a driveway.

Student Help

▶MORE EXAMPLES

More examples are available at www.mcdougallittell.com

EXAMPLE **4** **Solve a Work Problem**

SHOVELING SNOW Alone, you can shovel your driveway in 3 hours. Your friend Amy can shovel the driveway in 2 hours. How long will it take you and Amy to shovel your driveway, working together?

Solution

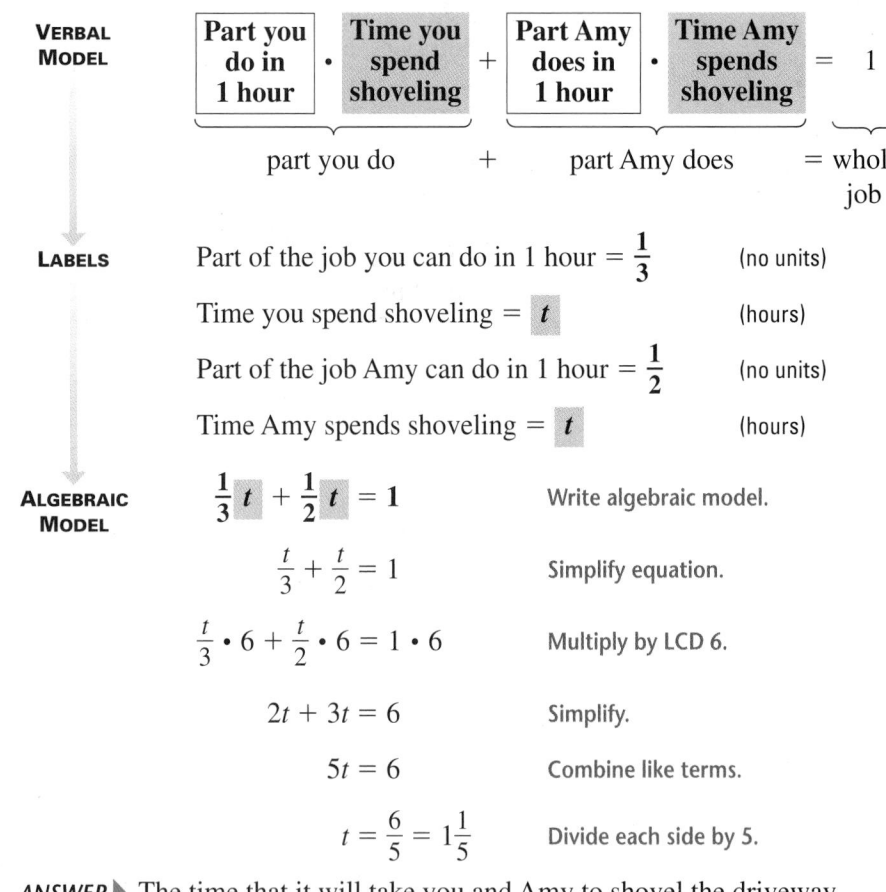

VERBAL MODEL

$$\underbrace{\boxed{\begin{array}{c}\textbf{Part you}\\\textbf{do in}\\\textbf{1 hour}\end{array}} \cdot \boxed{\begin{array}{c}\textbf{Time you}\\\textbf{spend}\\\textbf{shoveling}\end{array}}}_{\text{part you do}} + \underbrace{\boxed{\begin{array}{c}\textbf{Part Amy}\\\textbf{does in}\\\textbf{1 hour}\end{array}} \cdot \boxed{\begin{array}{c}\textbf{Time Amy}\\\textbf{spends}\\\textbf{shoveling}\end{array}}}_{\text{part Amy does}} = \underbrace{1}_{\substack{\text{whole}\\\text{job}}}$$

LABELS

Part of the job you can do in 1 hour $= \dfrac{1}{3}$ (no units)

Time you spend shoveling $= t$ (hours)

Part of the job Amy can do in 1 hour $= \dfrac{1}{2}$ (no units)

Time Amy spends shoveling $= t$ (hours)

ALGEBRAIC MODEL

$\dfrac{1}{3}t + \dfrac{1}{2}t = 1$	Write algebraic model.
$\dfrac{t}{3} + \dfrac{t}{2} = 1$	Simplify equation.
$\dfrac{t}{3} \cdot 6 + \dfrac{t}{2} \cdot 6 = 1 \cdot 6$	Multiply by LCD 6.
$2t + 3t = 6$	Simplify.
$5t = 6$	Combine like terms.
$t = \dfrac{6}{5} = 1\dfrac{1}{5}$	Divide each side by 5.

ANSWER ▶ The time that it will take you and Amy to shovel the driveway is $1\dfrac{1}{5}$ hours, or 1 hour 12 minutes.

Student Help

▶STUDY TIP
To find how many minutes are in $\dfrac{1}{5}$ hour, do the following calculation.
$\dfrac{1}{5} \cdot 60$ minutes $=$ 12 minutes. Therefore $1\dfrac{1}{5}$ hours equals 1 hour 12 minutes.

Checkpoint ✓ **Solve a Work Problem**

7. You can clean your house in 4 hours. Your sister can clean it in 6 hours. How long will it take you to clean the house, working together?

8. A roofing contractor estimates that he can shingle a house in 20 hours and that his assistant can do it in 30 hours. How long will it take them to shingle the house, working together?

MIXTURE PROBLEMS *Mixture problems*—problems that involve combining two or more items—occur in many different settings. Example 5 discusses mixing roasted nuts and raisins. The exercise set presents mixture problems from other fields, such as chemistry.

EXAMPLE 5 **Solve a Mixture Problem**

RAISINS AND NUTS A store sells a mixture of raisins and roasted nuts. Raisins cost $3.50 per kilogram and nuts cost $4.75 per kilogram. How many kilograms of each should be mixed to make 20 kilograms of this snack worth $4.00 per kilogram?

Solution

When you solve a mixture problem, it is helpful to make a chart.

Let x = Number of kilograms of raisins.

Then $20 - x$ = Number of kilograms of nuts.

Use the information from the problem to complete the chart below. Then write and solve an equation that relates the cost of the raisins, the cost of nuts, and the cost of mixture.

	Number of kg $\times$	Price per kg $=$	Cost
Raisins	x	3.50	$3.5x$
Nuts	$20 - x$	4.75	$4.75(20 - x)$
Mixture	20	4.00	80

Cost of raisins + Cost of nuts = Cost of mixture	Write verbal model.
$3.5x + 4.75(20 - x) = 80$	Write algebraic model.
$350x + 475(20 - x) = 8000$	Multiply each side by 100 to clear equation of decimals.
$350x + 9500 - 475x = 8000$	Use distributive property.
$9500 - 125x = 8000$	Combine like terms.
$-125x = -1500$	Subtract 9500 from each side.
$x = 12$	Divide each side by -125.

Therefore, $20 - x = 8$

ANSWER ▶ 12 kilograms of raisins and 8 kilograms of nuts are needed.

Student Help

▶**STUDY TIP**
Because the number of kilograms of the mixture is 20 and the number of kilograms of raisins is x, the number of kilograms of nuts is $20 - x$.

Checkpoint ✓ **Solve a Mixture Problem**

9. You make a mixture of dried apples costing $6.00 per kilogram and dried apricots costing $8.00 per kilogram. How many kilograms of each do you need to make 10 kilograms of a mixture worth $7.20 per kilogram? Make a chart to help you solve the problem.

11.7 Exercises

Guided Practice

Vocabulary Check

1. What are two methods of solving rational equations?

2. Which method is limited to solving equations in which each side is a single rational expression?

Skill Check

Find the least common denominator.

3. $\dfrac{1}{x}, \dfrac{x}{3}, \dfrac{2}{3x}$

4. $\dfrac{3}{4x}, \dfrac{1}{6x^2}, \dfrac{1}{8x^2}$

5. $\dfrac{5}{x}, \dfrac{2}{3x^2}, \dfrac{1}{x^3}$

Solve the equation using the cross product property. Remember to check your solutions.

6. $\dfrac{3}{x} = \dfrac{x}{12}$

7. $\dfrac{x}{x+2} = \dfrac{3}{x-2}$

8. $\dfrac{3}{u+2} = \dfrac{1}{u-2}$

Solve the equation by multiplying by the least common denominator. Check your solutions.

9. $\dfrac{1}{5} - \dfrac{2}{5x} = \dfrac{1}{x}$

10. $\dfrac{2}{x} + \dfrac{1}{4} = \dfrac{1}{x}$

11. $\dfrac{1}{x} + \dfrac{x}{x+2} = 1$

Practice and Applications

CROSS MULTIPLYING Solve the equation by cross multiplying. Check your solutions.

12. $\dfrac{x}{5} = \dfrac{7}{3}$

13. $\dfrac{x}{10} = \dfrac{14}{5}$

14. $\dfrac{4}{x} = \dfrac{12}{5(x+2)}$

15. $\dfrac{7}{x+1} = \dfrac{5}{x-3}$

16. $\dfrac{6}{x+2} = \dfrac{x}{4}$

17. $\dfrac{5}{x+4} = \dfrac{5}{3(x+1)}$

18. $\dfrac{1}{y} = \dfrac{2}{y-3}$

19. $\dfrac{3(t^2+1)}{6t^2-t-1} = \dfrac{1}{2}$

20. $\dfrac{(x+1)^2}{(x-3)^2} = 1$

MULTIPLYING BY THE LCD Solve the equation by multiplying each side by the least common denominator. Check your solutions.

21. $\dfrac{5}{x} + 2 = \dfrac{x}{4}$

22. $\dfrac{x}{x+9} = \dfrac{9}{x+9} + 4$

23. $\dfrac{3x}{x-1} = \dfrac{x}{5}$

24. $\dfrac{3}{t} - \dfrac{1}{3t} = \dfrac{2}{3}$

25. $\dfrac{4}{x(x+1)} = \dfrac{3}{x}$

26. $\dfrac{x}{x+3} + \dfrac{1}{x-3} = 1$

27. $\dfrac{1}{s} + \dfrac{s}{s+2} = 1$

28. $\dfrac{2}{3x+1} + 2 = \dfrac{2}{3}$

29. $\dfrac{5}{2r+1} - \dfrac{3}{2r-1} = 0$

30. $u = \dfrac{2}{5} - \dfrac{u}{2}$

31. $\dfrac{5}{x+1} - \dfrac{7}{x+1} = \dfrac{12}{x}$

32. $\dfrac{5}{3} + \dfrac{250}{9r} = \dfrac{r}{9}$

Student Help

▶ HOMEWORK HELP
Example 1: Exs. 12–20
Example 2: Exs. 21–32
Example 3: Exs. 33–38
Example 4: Exs. 48–50
Example 5: Exs. 51–53

Student Help

▶ **HOMEWORK HELP**

Extra help with problem solving in Exs. 33–38 is available at www.mcdougallittell.com

FACTOR FIRST Factor first, then solve the equation. Check your solutions.

33. $\dfrac{2}{y-2} + \dfrac{1}{y+2} = \dfrac{4}{y^2-4}$

34. $\dfrac{3}{x+1} - \dfrac{1}{x-2} = \dfrac{1}{x^2-x-2}$

35. $\dfrac{3}{x-1} + \dfrac{10}{x^2-2x+1} = 4$

36. $\dfrac{x}{x+3} + \dfrac{1}{x-1} = \dfrac{4}{x^2+2x-3}$

37. $\dfrac{2}{x-1} - \dfrac{x}{x+3} = \dfrac{6}{x^2+2x-3}$

38. $\dfrac{1}{y^2-16} - \dfrac{2}{y+4} = \dfrac{2}{y-4}$

CHOOSING A METHOD Solve the equation. Check your solutions.

39. $\dfrac{1}{4} + \dfrac{4}{x} = \dfrac{1}{x}$

40. $\dfrac{-3x}{x+1} = \dfrac{-2}{x-1}$

41. $\dfrac{x}{6} - \dfrac{1}{x} = \dfrac{1}{6}$

42. $\dfrac{x}{9} - \dfrac{8}{x} = \dfrac{1}{9}$

43. $\dfrac{x+42}{x} = x$

44. $\dfrac{2}{x} - \dfrac{x}{8} = \dfrac{3}{4}$

45. $\dfrac{-3}{x+7} = \dfrac{2}{x+2}$

46. $\dfrac{2}{x+3} + \dfrac{1}{x} = \dfrac{4}{3x}$

47. $\dfrac{1}{x} - \dfrac{2}{x^2} = \dfrac{1}{9}$

48. MOWING THE LAWN With your new lawn mower, you can mow a lawn in 4 hours. With an older mower, your friend can mow the same lawn in 5 hours. How long will it take you to mow the lawn, working together?

49. HIGHWAY PAVING The county's new asphalt paving machine can surface one mile of highway in 10 hours. A much older machine can surface one mile in 18 hours. How long will it take them to surface 1 mile of highway, working together? How long will it take them to surface 20 miles?

Link to
Careers

SPORTS REPORTER
Sports reporters gather statistics, such as a baseball player's batting average, and prepare stories that cover all aspects of sports from local sporting events to international competitions.

 More about sports reporters is available at www.mcdougallittell.com

50. CAR WASHING Arthur can wash a car in 30 minutes, Bonnie can wash a car in 40 minutes, and Claire can wash a car in 60 minutes. How will it take them to wash a car, working together?

51. NOODLE MIXTURE A grocer mixes 5 pounds of egg noodles costing $.80 per pound with 2 pounds of spinach noodles costing $1.50 per pound. What is the cost per pound of the mixture?

52. JUICE MIXTURE A farm stand owner mixes apple juice and cranberry juice. How much should he charge if he mixes 8 liters of apple juice selling for $0.45 per liter with 10 liters of cranberry juice selling for $1.08 per liter?

53. COINS You have 12 coins worth $1.95. If you only have dimes and quarters, how many of each do you have?

54. BATTING AVERAGE You have 35 hits in 140 times at bat. Your batting average is $\dfrac{35}{140} = 0.250$. How many consecutive hits must you get to increase your batting average to 0.300? Use the following verbal model to answer the question.

$$\text{Desired Batting average} = \frac{\text{Past hits} + \text{Future hits}}{\text{Past times at bat} + \text{Future times at bat}}$$

55. CHALLENGE How many liters of water must be added to 50 liters of a 30% acid solution in order to produce a 20% acid solution? Copy and complete the chart to help you solve the problem.

	Number of liters × % acid = Liters of acid		
Original Solution	?	?	?
Water Added	x	?	?
New Solution	?	?	?

56. MULTIPLE CHOICE What is the LCD of $\frac{1}{2x}$, $\frac{3x}{7x^2}$, and $\frac{3+x}{4x}$?

(A) $56x^4$ (B) $28x^2$ (C) $28x$ (D) $7x^2$

57. MULTIPLE CHOICE What is the solution of the equation $\frac{10r}{r+1} + \frac{1}{r+1} = 2$?

(F) 8 (G) $\frac{1}{8}$ (H) 10 (J) $\frac{1}{2}$

58. MULTIPLE CHOICE What is the solution of the equation $\frac{x}{6} - \frac{6}{x} = 0$?

(A) $6, -6$ (B) 6 (C) 36 (D) None of these

59. MULTIPLE CHOICE Solve the equation $\frac{5}{x+1} + \frac{x}{x^2-1} = \frac{1}{x-1}$.

(F) 1 (G) 0 (H) $\frac{5}{6}$ (J) $\frac{6}{5}$

FUNCTION VALUES Evaluate the function when $x = 0, 1, 2, 3,$ and 4.
(Lesson 4.8)

60. $f(x) = 4x$ **61.** $f(x) = -x + 9$ **62.** $f(x) = 3x + 1$

63. $f(x) = -x^2$ **64.** $f(x) = x^2 - 1$ **65.** $f(x) = \frac{x^2}{2}$

EVALUATING EXPRESSIONS Evaluate the expression.
(Lessons 8.1, 8.2)

66. $2^4 \cdot 2^3$ **67.** $6^3 \cdot 6^{-1}$ **68.** $(3^3)^2$

69. $(4^5)^0$ **70.** $12^{-5} \cdot 12^3$ **71.** $5^2 \cdot 5^1$

RADICAL EXPRESSIONS Simplify the radical expression. *(Lesson 9.3)*

72. $\sqrt{50}$ **73.** $\sqrt{72}$ **74.** $\frac{1}{4}\sqrt{112}$ **75.** $\frac{1}{2}\sqrt{52}$

76. $\sqrt{128}$ **77.** $\frac{1}{4}\sqrt{90}$ **78.** $3\sqrt{63}$ **79.** $\frac{7}{8}\sqrt{153}$

80. $\frac{2}{3}\sqrt{18}$ **81.** $\sqrt{27}$ **82.** $\frac{1}{5}\sqrt{500}$ **83.** $\frac{3}{7}\sqrt{147}$

OPERATIONS WITH FRACTIONS Evaluate the expression. Write the answer as a fraction or mixed number in simplest form. *(Skills Review p. 764)*

84. $\dfrac{2}{3} + \dfrac{1}{6} - \dfrac{1}{3}$

85. $\dfrac{3}{4} + \dfrac{5}{8} - \dfrac{1}{2}$

86. $\dfrac{2}{5} + \dfrac{3}{8} - \dfrac{1}{4}$

87. $\dfrac{2}{9} - \dfrac{1}{3} + \dfrac{4}{5}$

88. $\dfrac{1}{10} + \dfrac{1}{5} - \dfrac{3}{10} + \dfrac{2}{5}$

89. $\dfrac{1}{4} + \dfrac{2}{4} - \dfrac{3}{4} + \dfrac{4}{4}$

90. $\dfrac{3}{17} - \dfrac{3}{34} + \dfrac{1}{2}$

91. $\dfrac{1}{2} - \dfrac{3}{4} + \dfrac{5}{6} - \dfrac{7}{8}$

92. $\dfrac{12}{13} + \dfrac{7}{26} - \dfrac{1}{2}$

93. $\dfrac{103}{202} + \dfrac{1}{2} - \dfrac{1}{101}$

94. $\dfrac{7}{3} + \dfrac{1}{5} - \dfrac{2}{15}$

95. $\dfrac{5}{11} - \dfrac{4}{5} + \dfrac{3}{4}$

Quiz 2

Multiply or divide. Simplify the expression. *(Lesson 11.4)*

1. $\dfrac{5x^2}{2x} \cdot \dfrac{14x^2}{10x}$

2. $\dfrac{5}{10 + 4x} \cdot (20 + 8x)$

3. $\dfrac{3x + 12}{4x} \div \dfrac{x + 4}{2x}$

4. $\dfrac{5x^2 - 30x + 45}{x + 2} \div (5x - 15)$

Add or subtract. Simplify the expression. *(Lessons 11.5, 11.6)*

5. $\dfrac{x}{x^2 - 2x - 35} + \dfrac{5}{x^2 - 2x - 35}$

6. $\dfrac{4x - 1}{3x^2 + 8x + 5} - \dfrac{x - 6}{3x^2 + 8x + 5}$

7. $\dfrac{6}{x^2 - 1} + \dfrac{7x}{x + 1}$

8. $\dfrac{3x^2}{3x - 9} - \dfrac{2x}{x^2 - x - 6}$

Solve the equation. Check your solution. *(Lesson 11.7)*

9. $\dfrac{3}{x} = \dfrac{9}{2(x + 2)}$

10. $\dfrac{1}{2} + \dfrac{2}{t} = \dfrac{1}{t}$

11. $\dfrac{1}{x - 5} + \dfrac{1}{x + 5} = \dfrac{x + 3}{x^2 - 25}$

12. $\dfrac{7}{8} - \dfrac{16}{x - 2} = \dfrac{3}{4}$

CANOEING In Exercises 13–15, use the following information.
You are on a canoe trip. You can paddle your canoe at a rate of $x + 2$ miles per hour downstream and $x - 2$ miles per hour upstream. You travel 15 miles downstream and 15 miles back upstream. *(Lesson 11.6)*

13. Write an expression for the travel time downstream and an expression for the travel time upstream.

14. Write and simplify an expression for the total travel time.

15. Find the total travel time if $x = 3$.

16. RAKING LEAVES You can rake your neighbor's yard in 3 hours. Your neighbor can rake his yard in 4 hours. How long will it take you if you rake the yard together? *(Lesson 11.7)*

Rational Functions

Goal

Perform operations on rational functions.

Key Words

• rational function

The inverse variation models you graphed in Lesson 11.2 are a type of *rational function*. A **rational function** is a function that can be written as a quotient of polynomials.

$$f(x) = \frac{\text{polynomial}}{\text{polynomial}}$$

In this lesson you will perform arithmetic operations on rational functions using properties to combine and simplify functions.

OPERATIONS ON FUNCTIONS

Let f and g be two functions. Each function listed below is defined for all values of x in the domain of both f and g.

Sum of functions f and g	$(f + g)(x) = f(x) + g(x)$
Difference of functions f and g	$(f - g)(x) = f(x) - g(x)$
Product of functions f and g	$(f \cdot g)(x) = f(x) \cdot g(x)$
Quotient of functions f and g, if $g(x) = 0$	$(f \div g)(x) = f(x) \div g(x)$

Student Help

▶ **READING ALGEBRA**
The function notation $f(x)$ is read "f of x."

EXAMPLE 1 Add Rational Functions

Let $f(x) = \dfrac{1}{2x + 2}$ and $g(x) = \dfrac{x}{2x + 2}$. Find a rule for the function $(f + g)(x)$.

Solution

❶ **Write** the rule for the sum of functions. $(f + g)(x) = f(x) + g(x)$

❷ **Substitute** $\dfrac{1}{2x + 2}$ for $f(x)$ and $\dfrac{x}{2x + 2}$ for $g(x)$. $= \dfrac{1}{2x + 2} + \dfrac{x}{2x + 2}$

❸ **Add.** $= \dfrac{1 + x}{2x + 2}$

❹ **Factor** the denominator. $= \dfrac{(1 + x)}{2(x + 1)}$

❺ **Divide** out common factors and simplify. $= \dfrac{1(1 + x)}{2(1 + x)} = \dfrac{1}{2}$

ANSWER ▶ $(f + g)(x) = \dfrac{1}{2}$

Checkpoint ✓ **Add Rational Functions**

Find a rule for the function $(f + g)(x)$.

1. $f(x) = \dfrac{x + 1}{x}$, $g(x) = \dfrac{1}{x}$

2. $f(x) = \dfrac{1}{x - 3}$, $g(x) = \dfrac{1}{x + 3}$

EXAMPLE 2 Subtract Rational Functions

Let $f(x) = \dfrac{x}{x+2}$ and $g(x) = \dfrac{1}{x}$. Find a rule for the function $(f - g)(x)$.

① **Write** the rule for the difference of functions.

$$(f - g)(x) = f(x) - g(x)$$

② **Substitute** $\dfrac{x}{x+2}$ for $f(x)$ and $\dfrac{1}{x}$ for $g(x)$.

$$= \dfrac{x}{x+2} - \dfrac{1}{x}$$

③ **Rewrite** the expressions using the LCD $x(x + 2)$.

$$= \dfrac{x(x)}{x(x+2)} - \dfrac{1(x+2)}{x(x+2)}$$

④ **Simplify** the numerators.

$$= \dfrac{x^2}{x(x+2)} - \dfrac{x+2}{x(x+2)}$$

⑤ **Subtract.**

$$= \dfrac{x^2 - x - 2}{x(x+2)}$$

⑥ **Factor** the numerator.

$$= \dfrac{(x-2)(x+1)}{x(x+2)}$$

ANSWER ▶ $(f - g)(x) = \dfrac{(x-2)(x+1)}{x(x+2)}$

▶ **STUDY TIP**
In Step 6, you must factor the numerator to determine whether the numerator and denominator have any common factors.

Checkpoint ✓ *Subtract Rational Functions*

Find a rule for the function $(f - g)(x)$.

3. $f(x) = \dfrac{x+1}{x}$, $g(x) = \dfrac{1}{x}$

4. $f(x) = \dfrac{1}{x-3}$, $g(x) = \dfrac{1}{x+3}$

EXAMPLE 3 Multiply and Divide Rational Functions

Let $f(x) = \dfrac{x-4}{x}$ and $g(x) = \dfrac{x+4}{x-4}$. Find a rule for the function.

a. $(f \cdot g)(x) = f(x) \cdot g(x)$

$$= \dfrac{x-4}{x} \cdot \dfrac{x+4}{x-4}$$

$$= \dfrac{(x-4)(x+4)}{x(x-4)}$$

$$= \dfrac{x+4}{x}$$

b. $(f \div g)(x) = f(x) \div g(x)$

$$= \dfrac{x-4}{x} \div \dfrac{x+4}{x-4}$$

$$= \dfrac{x-4}{x} \cdot \dfrac{x-4}{x+4}$$

$$= \dfrac{(x-4)^2}{x(x+4)}$$

Checkpoint ✓ *Multiply and Divide Rational Functions*

5. Let $f(x) = \dfrac{x}{x+7}$ and $g(x) = \dfrac{2x+14}{8}$. Find a rule for the function $(f \cdot g)(x)$.

6. Let $f(x) = \dfrac{1-x}{x}$ and $g(x) = \dfrac{x-1}{x^2}$. Find a rule for the function $(f \div g)(x)$.

Exercises

SUMS Find a rule for the function $(f + g)(x)$.

1. $f(x) = \dfrac{1}{x - 9}$, $g(x) = \dfrac{9}{x - 9}$

2. $f(x) = \dfrac{x}{x^2 - 25}$, $g(x) = \dfrac{5}{x^2 - 25}$

3. $f(x) = \dfrac{x - 1}{x^2}$, $g(x) = \dfrac{1}{x}$

4. $f(x) = \dfrac{2}{x - 3}$, $g(x) = \dfrac{7}{3 - x}$

5. $f(x) = \dfrac{6x}{x - 7}$, $g(x) = \dfrac{5x}{x + 7}$

6. $f(x) = \dfrac{x - 3}{20x}$, $g(x) = \dfrac{x + 4}{15x}$

DIFFERENCES Find a rule for the function $(f - g)(x)$.

7. $f(x) = \dfrac{4x}{3x + 7}$, $g(x) = \dfrac{x - 5}{3x + 7}$

8. $f(x) = \dfrac{x}{x^2 - 36}$, $g(x) = \dfrac{6}{x^2 - 36}$

9. $f(x) = \dfrac{1}{x}$, $g(x) = \dfrac{2x + 3}{x^2}$

10. $f(x) = \dfrac{3}{x + 4}$, $g(x) = \dfrac{4}{x - 2}$

11. $f(x) = \dfrac{1}{x + 9}$, $g(x) = \dfrac{1}{x - 9}$

12. $f(x) = \dfrac{2x}{x - 3}$, $g(x) = \dfrac{3}{2x - 6}$

PRODUCTS Find a rule for the function $(f \cdot g)(x)$.

13. $f(x) = \dfrac{1}{2x}$, $g(x) = \dfrac{6}{x + 15}$

14. $f(x) = \dfrac{4}{3x + 6}$, $g(x) = \dfrac{x + 2}{x}$

15. $f(x) = \dfrac{x^2 - 5x + 6}{2x}$, $g(x) = \dfrac{3x - 6}{x - 3}$

16. $f(x) = \dfrac{x + 2}{x^2}$, $g(x) = \dfrac{8x}{4x^2 - 16}$

17. $f(x) = \dfrac{x^2 + 3x - 10}{x + 2}$, $g(x) = \dfrac{x^2 - 4}{x + 5}$

18. $f(x) = \dfrac{x^2 - 3x + 2}{x^2 + 3x + 2}$, $g(x) = \dfrac{8x + 8}{4x + 8}$

QUOTIENTS Find a rule for the function $(f \div g)(x)$.

19. $f(x) = \dfrac{x + 3}{x^2}$, $g(x) = \dfrac{x + 1}{x^3}$

20. $f(x) = \dfrac{2}{3x}$, $g(x) = \dfrac{1}{4x}$

21. $f(x) = \dfrac{x}{2x + 1}$, $g(x) = \dfrac{2x + 1}{x}$

22. $f(x) = \dfrac{2x}{x^3 - 5x^2}$, $g(x) = \dfrac{10}{x^2 - 5x}$

23. $f(x) = \dfrac{x^2 + 3x - 10}{x + 2}$, $g(x) = \dfrac{x^2 - 4}{x + 5}$

24. $f(x) = \dfrac{x^2 - x - 20}{5x - 25}$, $g(x) = \dfrac{x - 1}{x^2 - 25}$

GRAPHING Graph the function by making a table of values, plotting the points, and then connecting them with two smooth curves.

25. $f(x) = \dfrac{1}{x - 9}$

26. $f(x) = \dfrac{1}{2x} - 3$

27. $g(x) = \dfrac{x}{2x + 3}$

28. $g(x) = \dfrac{-1}{x + 2} + 1$

Student Help

▶ HOMEWORK HELP
Example 1: Exs. 1–6
Example 2: Exs. 7–12
Example 3: Exs. 13–24

- **proportion**, *p. 633*
- **extremes**, *p. 633*
- **means**, *p. 633*
- **inverse variation**, *p. 639*
- **rational number**, *p. 646*
- **rational expression**, *p. 646*
- **least common denominator (LCD)**, *p. 663*
- **rational equation**, *p. 670*

11.1 PROPORTIONS

Examples on pp. 633–635

EXAMPLE Solve the proportion $\dfrac{12}{7} = \dfrac{5}{x}$ using the cross product property.

❶ **Write** the original proportion. $\qquad \dfrac{12}{7} = \dfrac{5}{x}$

❷ **Use** the cross product property. $\qquad 12 \cdot x = 7 \cdot 5$

❸ **Divide** each side by 12. $\qquad\qquad x = \dfrac{35}{12}$

Solve the proportion. Check your solutions.

1. $\dfrac{x}{2} = \dfrac{4}{7}$
2. $\dfrac{7}{10} = \dfrac{9+x}{x}$
3. $\dfrac{x^2 - 16}{x + 4} = \dfrac{x - 4}{3}$
4. $\dfrac{5}{x + 6} = \dfrac{x - 6}{x}$

11.2 DIRECT AND INVERSE VARIATION

Examples on pp. 639–641

EXAMPLES Assuming $y = 4$ when $x = 8$, find an equation that relates x and y in each case.

a. x and y vary directly.

b. x and y vary inversely.

Solution

a. $\dfrac{y}{x} = k \qquad$ Write direct variation model.

$\dfrac{4}{8} = k \qquad$ Substitute 8 for x and 4 for y.

$\dfrac{1}{2} = k \qquad$ Simplify.

ANSWER ▶ $\dfrac{y}{x} = \dfrac{1}{2}$ or $y = \dfrac{1}{2}x$.

b. $xy = k \qquad$ Write inverse variation model.

$(8)(4) = k \qquad$ Substitute 8 for x and 4 for y.

$32 = k \qquad$ Simplify.

ANSWER ▶ $xy = 32$ or $y = \dfrac{32}{x}$.

Find an equation such that x and y vary directly.

5. $y = 50$ when $x = 10$ **6.** $y = 6$ when $x = 24$ **7.** $y = 36$ when $x = 45$

8. $y = 20$ when $x = 2$ **9.** $y = 7$ when $x = \frac{1}{2}$ **10.** $y = 132$ when $x = 66$

Find an equation such that x and y vary inversely.

11. $y = 3$ when $x = 12$ **12.** $y = 10$ when $x = 20$ **13.** $y = 5$ when $x = 90$

14. $y = 3$ when $x = \frac{2}{3}$ **15.** $y = \frac{11}{2}$ when $x = 4$ **16.** $y = \frac{1}{4}$ when $x = 24$

11.3 SIMPLIFYING RATIONAL EXPRESSIONS

Examples on pp. 646–648

> **EXAMPLE** Simplify $\dfrac{2x^2 + 3x - 2}{2x^2 + 5x + 2}$.
>
> To simplify a rational expression, look for common factors.
>
> **Solution**
>
> **1** **Write** the original expression. $\qquad \dfrac{2x^2 + 3x - 2}{2x^2 + 5x + 2}$
>
> **2** **Factor** the numerator and denominator. $\qquad \dfrac{(2x - 1)(x + 2)}{(2x + 1)(x + 2)}$
>
> **3** **Divide** out the common factor $(x + 2)$. $\qquad \dfrac{(2x - 1)\cancel{(x + 2)}}{(2x + 1)\cancel{(x + 2)}}$
>
> **4** **Simplify** the expression. $\qquad \dfrac{2x - 1}{2x + 1}$

In Exercises 17–25, simplify the expression.

17. $\dfrac{3x}{9x^2 + 3}$ **18.** $\dfrac{6x^2}{12x^4 + 18x^2}$ **19.** $\dfrac{7x^3 - 28x}{3x^2 + 8x + 4}$

20. $\dfrac{5x^2 + 21x + 4}{25x + 100}$ **21.** $\dfrac{x^2 + 4x + 4}{x^2 + 9x + 14}$ **22.** $\dfrac{6x^2 - 19x + 10}{2x^2 - 5x}$

23. $\dfrac{2x^2 + 17x + 21}{2x^2 + x - 3}$ **24.** $\dfrac{13x^2 - 39x}{3x^2 - 8x - 3}$ **25.** $\dfrac{y^2 - 2y - 48}{2y^2 + 9y - 18}$

26. Find the ratio of the area of the smaller rectangle to the area of the larger rectangle. Simplify the expression.

$4(x + 3)$

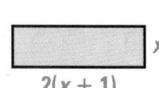

$2(x + 1)$

11.4 **MULTIPLYING AND DIVIDING RATIONAL EXPRESSIONS**   *Examples on pp. 652–654*

EXAMPLE Simplify $\dfrac{6x^2 + x - 1}{2x + 1} \div \dfrac{9x - 3}{x + 1}$.

To divide rational expressions, multiply by the reciprocal.

$$\frac{6x^2 + x - 1}{2x + 1} \div \frac{9x - 3}{x + 1} = \frac{6x^2 + x - 1}{2x + 1} \cdot \frac{x + 1}{9x - 3}$$ Multiply by reciprocal.

$$= \frac{(2x + 1)(3x - 1)}{2x + 1} \cdot \frac{x + 1}{3(3x - 1)}$$ Factor numerators and denominators.

$$= \frac{\cancel{(2x + 1)}\cancel{(3x - 1)}(x + 1)}{\cancel{(2x + 1)} \cdot 3\cancel{(3x - 1)}}$$ Multiply and divide out common factors.

$$= \frac{x + 1}{3}$$ Write in simplest form.

Simplify the expression.

27. $\dfrac{12x^2}{5x^3} \cdot \dfrac{25x^4}{3x}$

28. $\dfrac{a^2 - 7a - 18}{4a^2 + 8a} \cdot \dfrac{12}{a^2 - 81}$

29. $\dfrac{2x^2 + 9x + 7}{2x} \cdot \dfrac{16x^2}{x^3 - x}$

30. $\dfrac{6y^2}{y + 3} \div \dfrac{9y}{(y + 3)^2}$

31. $\dfrac{9x^3}{x^3 - x^2} \div \dfrac{x - 8}{x^2 - 9x + 8}$

32. $\dfrac{x^2 + 3x + 2}{x^2 + 7x + 12} \div \dfrac{x^2 + 5x + 4}{x^2 + 5x + 6}$

11.5 **ADDING AND SUBTRACTING WITH LIKE DENOMINATORS**   *Examples on pp. 658–659*

EXAMPLE Simplify $\dfrac{5x}{x^2 + 2x - 8} - \dfrac{2x + 6}{x^2 + 2x - 8}$.

$$\frac{5x}{x^2 + 2x - 8} - \frac{2x + 6}{x^2 + 2x - 8} = \frac{5x - (2x + 6)}{x^2 + 2x - 8}$$ Subtract numerators.

$$= \frac{3x - 6}{x^2 + 2x - 8}$$ Simplify numerator.

$$= \frac{3\cancel{(x - 2)}}{\cancel{(x - 2)}(x + 4)}$$ Factor and divide out common factor $(x - 2)$.

$$= \frac{3}{x + 4}$$ Write in simplest form.

In Exercises 33–36, simplify the expression.

33. $\dfrac{2x + 1}{3x} + \dfrac{x + 5}{3x}$

34. $\dfrac{-2b - 5}{b^2} + \dfrac{5}{b^2}$

35. $\dfrac{6x}{x + 4} - \dfrac{5x - 4}{x + 4}$

36. $\dfrac{x(x + 1)}{(x - 3)^2} - \dfrac{12}{(x - 3)^2}$

37. Find an expression in simplest form for the perimeter of a rectangle whose side lengths are $\dfrac{x + 1}{16}$ and $\dfrac{x + 3}{16}$.

Examples on
pp. 663–666

11.6 ADDING AND SUBTRACTING WITH UNLIKE DENOMINATORS

EXAMPLE Simplify $\dfrac{x}{x-5} - \dfrac{2}{x+2}$.

The LCD is $(x-5)(x+2)$.

$$\frac{x}{x-5} - \frac{2}{x+2} = \frac{x(x+2)}{(x-5)(x+2)} - \frac{2(x-5)}{(x-5)(x+2)}$$ Rewrite fractions using LCD.

$$= \frac{x^2+2x}{(x-5)(x+2)} - \frac{2x-10}{(x-5)(x+2)}$$ Simplify numerators.

$$= \frac{(x^2+2x)-(2x-10)}{(x-5)(x+2)}$$ Subtract fractions.

$$= \frac{x^2+10}{(x-5)(x+2)}$$ Simplify.

In Exercises 38–41, simplify the expression.

38. $\dfrac{x+3}{3x-1} + \dfrac{4}{x-3}$ **39.** $\dfrac{-5x-10}{x^2-4} + \dfrac{4x}{x-2}$ **40.** $\dfrac{p}{p-1} - \dfrac{p}{p+1}$ **41.** $\dfrac{x-4}{2x} - \dfrac{x-6}{3x}$

42. Find an expression in simplest form for the perimeter of a rectangle whose side lengths are $\dfrac{x+3}{x-2}$ and $\dfrac{6}{x+4}$.

11.7 RATIONAL EQUATIONS

Examples on
pp. 670–673

EXAMPLE Solve the equation $\dfrac{2x}{9} - \dfrac{1}{x} = \dfrac{1}{3}$.

The LCD is $9x$.

$$9x \cdot \frac{2x}{9} - 9x \cdot \frac{1}{x} = 9x \cdot \frac{1}{3}$$ Multiply each side of original equation by LCD $9x$.

$$2x^2 - 9 = 3x$$ Simplify equation.

$$2x^2 - 3x - 9 = 0$$ Write equation in standard form.

$$(2x+3)(x-3) = 0$$ Factor left side of equation.

ANSWER When you set each factor equal to 0, you find that the solutions are $x = -\dfrac{3}{2}$ and 3. Check your solutions back into the original equation.

Solve the equation. Check your solutions.

43. $\dfrac{x+2}{2} = \dfrac{4}{x}$ **44.** $\dfrac{1}{s} + \dfrac{s}{s+2} = 1$ **45.** $\dfrac{1}{x-1} + \dfrac{1}{x+2} = \dfrac{3}{x^2+x-2}$

Solve the proportion. Check your solutions.

1. $\dfrac{6}{x} = \dfrac{17}{5}$

2. $\dfrac{x}{4} = \dfrac{x+8}{x}$

3. $\dfrac{x}{-3} = \dfrac{7}{x-10}$

4. $\dfrac{x}{x^2+4} = \dfrac{4}{5x}$

Make a table of values for $x = 1, 2, 3,$ and 4. Use the table to sketch the graph. State whether x and y vary *directly* or *inversely*.

5. $y = 4x$

6. $y = \dfrac{50}{x}$

7. $y = \dfrac{9}{2}x$

8. $y = \dfrac{15}{2x}$

Simplify the expression.

9. $\dfrac{56x^6}{4x^4}$

10. $\dfrac{5x^2 - 15x}{15x^4}$

11. $\dfrac{x^2 - x - 6}{x^2 - 4}$

12. $\dfrac{2x - 14}{3x^2 - 21x}$

13. $\dfrac{x^2 - 1}{2x^2 + x - 1}$

14. $\dfrac{2x^2 + 12x + 18}{x^2 - x - 12}$

Write the product or quotient in simplest form.

15. $\dfrac{6x^2}{8x} \cdot \dfrac{-4x^3}{2x^2}$

16. $\dfrac{x^3 + x^2}{x^2 - 16} \cdot \dfrac{x + 4}{3x^4 + x^3 - 2x^2}$

17. $\dfrac{3x^2 - 6x}{x^2 - 6x + 9} \cdot \dfrac{x^2 - x - 6}{x^2 - 4}$

18. $\dfrac{3x^2 + 6x}{4x} \div \dfrac{15}{8x^2}$

19. $\dfrac{x + 3}{x^3 - x^2 - 6x} \div \dfrac{x^2 - 9}{x}$

20. $\dfrac{x^2}{x - 1} \div \dfrac{x}{x^2 + x - 2}$

Write the sum or difference in simplest form.

21. $\dfrac{12x - 4}{x - 1} + \dfrac{4x}{x - 1}$

22. $\dfrac{6(2y + 1)}{y^2 - 100} - \dfrac{2(5y - 7)}{y^2 - 100}$

23. $\dfrac{5}{2x^2} + \dfrac{4}{3x}$

24. $\dfrac{4}{x + 3} + \dfrac{3x}{x - 2}$

25. $\dfrac{8}{5x} - \dfrac{4}{x^2}$

26. $\dfrac{5x + 1}{x - 3} - \dfrac{2x}{x - 1}$

Solve the equation. Check your solutions.

27. $\dfrac{3}{4x - 9} = \dfrac{x}{3}$

28. $\dfrac{5}{9} + \dfrac{2}{9x} = \dfrac{3}{x}$

29. $\dfrac{x}{7} - \dfrac{6}{x} = \dfrac{1}{7}$

30. $\dfrac{3}{u + 2} = \dfrac{1}{u - 2}$

31. $\dfrac{1}{4} - \dfrac{6}{x} = \dfrac{3}{x}$

32. $\dfrac{x}{x + 1} + \dfrac{x}{x - 2} = 2$

33. LENGTH AND WIDTH The length ℓ and width w of a rectangle with an area of 60 square units are related by the equation $\ell w = 60$. Does this model represent *direct variation*, *inverse variation*, or *neither*?

34. STREET SWEEPERS A town's old street sweeper can clean the streets in 60 hours. The new street sweeper can clean the streets in 20 hours. How long would it take the old sweeper and the new sweeper to clean the streets together?

Chapter Standardized Test

1. Which of the following is the solution of the proportion $\dfrac{4}{y+9} = \dfrac{6}{y-7}$?

  A -82 **B** -41

  C 7 **D** 41

2. The variables x and y vary inversely. When x is 9, y is 36. If x is 3, what is y?

  A 12 **B** 36

  C 108 **D** 324

3. What is the simplest form of the expression $\dfrac{x^3 - 10x^2 + 9x}{x^2 + 5x - 6}$?

  A $\dfrac{x-9}{x+6}$ **B** $\dfrac{x}{x+6}$

  C $\dfrac{x}{(x-1)(x+6)}$ **D** $\dfrac{x(x-9)}{x+6}$

4. What is the simplest form of the product $\dfrac{9x^2}{4x} \cdot \dfrac{16x^3}{x^5}$?

  A $36x$ **B** $\dfrac{64}{9x^3}$

  C $\dfrac{36}{x}$ **D** $36x^3$

5. Divide $\dfrac{x^2 - 64}{3x^2}$ by $(x - 8)$.

  A $\dfrac{x+8}{3x^2}$ **B** $\dfrac{x-8}{3x^2}$

  C $\dfrac{x+8}{3x^2(x-8)}$ **D** $\dfrac{x^3 - 512}{3x}$

6. What is the simplest form of the sum $\dfrac{x+2}{x^2 - 25} + \dfrac{3}{x^2 - 25}$?

  A $\dfrac{x+5}{x^2 - 25}$ **B** $\dfrac{x+5}{(x^2 - 25)^2}$

  C $\dfrac{3x+6}{x-5}$ **D** $\dfrac{1}{x-5}$

7. What is the simplest form of the difference $\dfrac{2x+9}{x+5} - \dfrac{x-4}{x-2}$?

  A $\dfrac{x^2 + 6x + 2}{(x+5)(x-2)}$ **B** $\dfrac{x^2 + 6x - 38}{(x+5)(x-2)}$

  C $\dfrac{x^2 + 4x - 38}{(x+5)(x-2)}$ **D** $\dfrac{x^2 + 4x + 2}{(x+5)(x-2)}$

8. Solve the equation $\dfrac{4}{x+2} + \dfrac{3}{x} = 1$.

  A -1 **B** -2

  C $1, -6$ **D** $-1, 6$

  E None of these

9. What is the ratio in simplest form of the area of the red rectangle to the area of the blue rectangle?

  A $\dfrac{1}{2}$ **B** $\dfrac{1}{6}$

  C $\dfrac{x+7}{3x+21}$ **D** $\dfrac{x(x+7)}{6x(x+7)}$

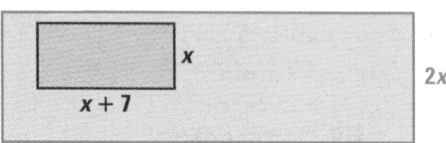

Maintaining Skills

EXAMPLE 1 Simplify Radicals

Simplify the expression $\sqrt{\dfrac{63}{100}}$ using the quotient property.

Solution

$\sqrt{\dfrac{63}{100}}$ Write original expression.

$\dfrac{\sqrt{63}}{\sqrt{100}}$ Use quotient property.

$\dfrac{\sqrt{9 \cdot 7}}{\sqrt{100}}$ Factor using perfect square factors.

$\dfrac{\sqrt{9} \cdot \sqrt{7}}{\sqrt{100}}$ Use product property.

$\dfrac{3\sqrt{7}}{10}$ Simplify.

Try These

Simplify the expression using the quotient property.

1. $\sqrt{\dfrac{32}{49}}$ **2.** $\sqrt{\dfrac{32}{64}}$ **3.** $\sqrt{\dfrac{125}{225}}$ **4.** $\sqrt{\dfrac{162}{4}}$

5. $\sqrt{\dfrac{363}{144}}$ **6.** $\sqrt{\dfrac{288}{400}}$ **7.** $\sqrt{\dfrac{72}{9}}$ **8.** $\sqrt{\dfrac{14}{200}}$

EXAMPLE 2 Factor Perfect Squares

Factor $x^2 + 16x + 64$.

Solution Recall from Chapter 10 the pattern for factoring a perfect square trinomial: $a^2 + 2ab + b^2 = (a + b)^2$ or $a^2 - 2ab - b^2 = (a - b)^2$.

$x^2 + 16x + 64 = x^2 + 2(x)(8) + 8^2$ Write as $a^2 + 2ab + b^2$.

$= (x + 8)^2$ Factor using pattern.

Student Help

▶ **EXTRA EXAMPLES**

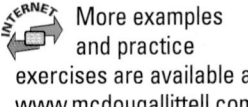 More examples and practice exercises are available at www.mcdougallittell.com

Try These

Factor the trinomial.

9. $a^2 - 18a + 81$ **10.** $x^2 + 6x + 9$ **11.** $y^2 - 22y + 121$

12. $169 + 26m + m^2$ **13.** $225 + 30r + r^2$ **14.** $100 - 20t + t^2$

15. $4x^2 + 20x + 25$ **16.** $9b^2 - 6a + 1$ **17.** $16 - 56x + 49x^2$

CHAPTER 12

Radicals and More Connections to Geometry

▷ How are passengers kept in place on a spinning amusement ride?

APPLICATION: Spinning Rides

Some amusement park rides spin so fast that the riders "stick" to the walls of the ride. The force exerted by the wall on the rider is called *centripetal force.* You'll learn more about calculating centripetal force in Chapter 12.

Think & Discuss

When designing spinning rides, engineers must calculate the dimensions of the ride as well as how many times per minute it will spin. The table shows the height and revolutions per minute for four spinning rides.

Ride name	Height (feet)	Revolutions per minute
Football Ride	34.4	15
Chaos	36	12
Centrox	44.3	17.5
Galactica	44.3	17

1. Based on the numbers in the table, is revolutions per minute a function of height? Explain.

2. You are designing a spinning ride that is 40 feet high. Use the information in the table to decide on a reasonable range for how many revolutions per minute the ride would make.

Learn More About It

You will calculate the centripetal force exerted on a rider in Example 5 on p. 706.

 APPLICATION LINK More about amusement park rides is available at www.mcdougallittell.com

PREVIEW

What's the chapter about?

- Solving **radical equations** and graphing **radical functions**
- Applying the **Pythagorean theorem**
- **Proving theorems** by using algebraic properties and logical reasoning

KEY WORDS

- **square root function,**
  p. 692
- **extraneous solution,**
  p. 705
- **rational exponent,**
  p. 711
- **completing the square,**
  p. 716

- **theorem,** p. 724
- **Pythagorean theorem,**
  p. 724
- **hypotenuse,** p. 724
- **legs of a right triangle,**
  p. 724
- **converse,** p. 726
- **distance formula,** p. 730

- **midpoint,** p. 736
- **midpoint formula,**
  p. 736
- **postulate,** p. 740
- **axiom,** p. 740
- **conjecture,** p. 741
- **indirect proof,** p. 742

PREPARE

Chapter Readiness Quiz

Take this quick quiz. If you are unsure of an answer, look back at the reference pages for help.

VOCABULARY CHECK *(refer to p. 512)*

1. Which is the simplest form of the radical expression $\dfrac{\sqrt{36}}{\sqrt{9}}$?

  A $\dfrac{\sqrt{6}}{3}$ **B** $\sqrt{2}$ **C** $\dfrac{\sqrt{36}}{3}$ **D** 2

SKILL CHECK *(refer to pp. 511, 596)*

2. Which is the simplest form of $\sqrt{140}$?

  A $2\sqrt{35}$ **B** $4\sqrt{35}$ **C** $10\sqrt{7}$ **D** $14\sqrt{5}$

3. Which of the following is the correct factorization of the trinomial $x^2 - 3x - 18$?

  A $(x + 3)(x + 6)$ **B** $(x + 3)(x - 6)$
  C $(x - 3)(x - 6)$ **D** $(x - 3)(x + 6)$

STUDY TIP

Draw Diagrams

Including a diagram or another visual aid when you take notes can be helpful.

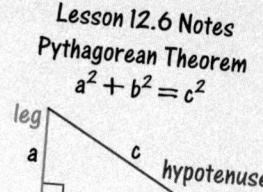

Lesson 12.6 Notes
Pythagorean Theorem
$a^2 + b^2 = c^2$

DEVELOPING CONCEPTS
Functions with Radicals

GOAL

Use a function's graph to determine its domain and range.

MATERIALS

- graph paper
- pencil

Question **How do you determine the domain and range of functions with radicals?**

A function's graph can provide a representation of the domain and range. Recall that when a function is given by a formula, its domain is all possible input values. The range of a function is the set of output values.

Explore

1 Copy and complete the table of values for the function $y = \sqrt{x}$. Round to the nearest tenth.

x	−2	−1	0	1	2	3	4	5
y	?	?	?	?	?	?	?	?

For what values of x is $\sqrt{x}$ *not* defined?

2 For those values of x for which $\sqrt{x}$ *is* defined, plot the points from the table on a piece of graph paper and connect them with a smooth curve.

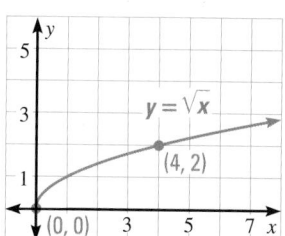

3 The table of values suggests that the domain of the function is the set of all nonnegative real numbers. You can verify this observation as follows: (1) The square root of a negative number is not defined. (2) The square root of any nonnegative real number is defined. The range is the set of all nonnegative real numbers because every nonnegative real number is the square root of its square.

Think About It

Use the formula for *y* to identify the domain and range of the function. Explain your reasoning.

1. $y = \sqrt{x + 1}$

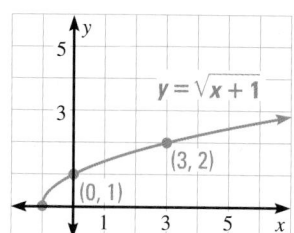

2. $y = 2 + \sqrt{x}$

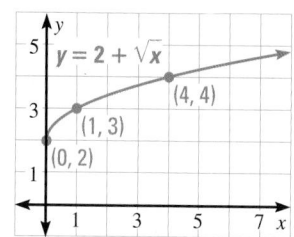

12.1 Functions Involving Square Roots

Goal

Evaluate and graph a function involving square roots.

Key Words

- square root function
- domain
- range

How fast can a dinosaur walk?

The maximum walking speed of a dinosaur is a function of the length of its leg. In Exercise 57 you will use a function involving a square root to compare the maximum walking speeds for two species of dinosaurs.

The **square root function** is defined by the equation

$$y = \sqrt{x}.$$

Its domain is all nonnegative numbers, and its range is all nonnegative numbers. Understanding the square root function will help you work with other functions involving square roots.

Student Help

▶ STUDY TIP
Recall that the square root of a negative number is undefined. $\sqrt{x}$ can be evaluated only when $x \geq 0$.

EXAMPLE 1 Evaluate Functions Involving Square Roots

Find the domain of $y = 2\sqrt{x}$. Use several values in the domain to make a table of values for the function.

Solution

A square root is defined only when the radicand is nonnegative. Therefore the domain of $y = 2\sqrt{x}$ consists of all nonnegative numbers. A table of values for $x = 0, 1, 2, 3, 4,$ and 5 is shown at the right.

x	y
0	$y = 2\sqrt{0} = 0$
1	$y = 2\sqrt{1} = 2$
2	$y = 2\sqrt{2} \approx 2.8$
3	$y = 2\sqrt{3} \approx 3.5$
4	$y = 2\sqrt{4} = 4$
5	$y = 2\sqrt{5} \approx 4.5$

Checkpoint ✓ Evaluate Functions Involving Square Roots

Find the domain of the function. Then use several values in the domain to make a table of values for the function.

1. $y = \sqrt{x}$ **2.** $y = 3\sqrt{x}$ **3.** $y = \sqrt{2x}$ **4.** $y = \sqrt{x} - 1$

It is a good idea to find the domain of a function before you make a table of values. This will help you choose appropriate values of x for the table.

Student Help

▶MORE EXAMPLES

More examples are available at www.mcdougallittell.com

EXAMPLE 2 Graph $y = 2\sqrt{x}$

Sketch the graph of $y = 2\sqrt{x}$. Then find its range.

Solution

From Example 1, you know the domain is all nonnegative real numbers. Use the table of values from Example 1. Then plot the points and connect them with a smooth curve. The range is all nonnegative real numbers.

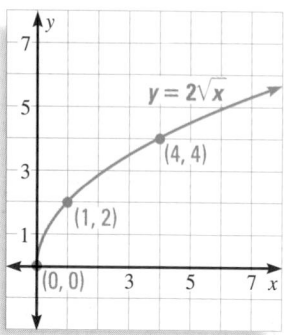

Student Help

▶STUDY TIP
When you make a table of values to sketch the graph of a function, choose several values to see the shape of the curve.

EXAMPLE 3 Graph $y = \sqrt{x} + 1$

Find the domain of $y = \sqrt{x} + 1$. Then sketch its graph and find the range.

Solution

The domain is the values of x for which the radicand is nonnegative, so the domain consists of all nonnegative real numbers. Make a table of values, plot the points, and connect them with a smooth curve.

x	y
0	$y = \sqrt{0} + 1 = 1$
1	$y = \sqrt{1} + 1 = 2$
2	$y = \sqrt{2} + 1 \approx 2.4$
3	$y = \sqrt{3} + 1 \approx 2.7$
4	$y = \sqrt{4} + 1 = 3$
5	$y = \sqrt{5} + 1 \approx 3.2$

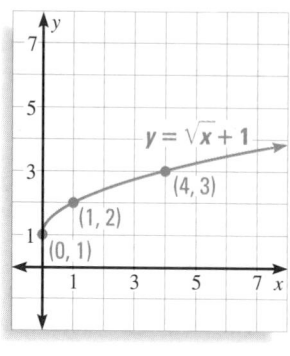

The range is all real numbers that are greater than or equal to 1.

Checkpoint ✔ **Graph Functions Involving Square Roots**

Find the domain of the function. Then sketch its graph and find the range.

5. $y = -3\sqrt{x}$ **6.** $y = -2\sqrt{x}$ **7.** $y = \sqrt{x} + 2$

8. $y = \sqrt{x} - 2$ **9.** $y = 3 - \sqrt{x}$ **10.** $y = 2\sqrt{x} + 1$

EXAMPLE **4** **Graph** $y = \sqrt{x - 3}$

Find the domain of $y = \sqrt{x - 3}$. Then sketch its graph.

Solution

To find the domain, find the values of x for which the radicand is nonnegative.

$x - 3 \geq 0$ Write an inequality for the domain.

$x \geq 3$ Add 3 to each side.

The domain is all numbers that are greater than or equal to 3. Make a table of values, plot the points, and connect them with a smooth curve.

x	y
3	$y = \sqrt{3 - 3} = 0$
4	$y = \sqrt{4 - 3} = 1$
5	$y = \sqrt{5 - 3} \approx 1.4$
6	$y = \sqrt{6 - 3} \approx 1.7$
7	$y = \sqrt{7 - 3} = 2$
8	$y = \sqrt{8 - 3} \approx 2.2$

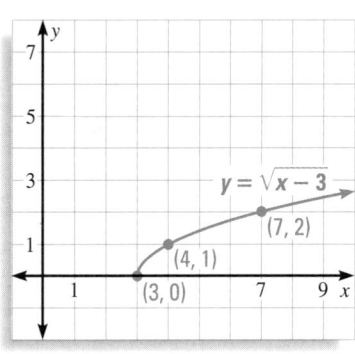

Link to
Science

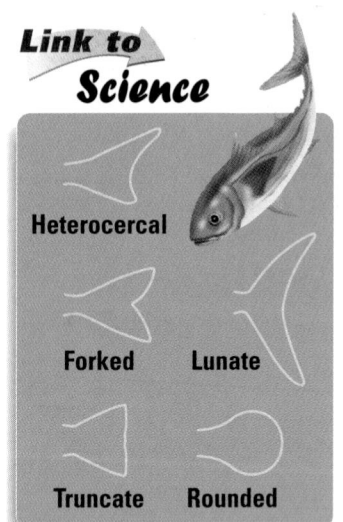

Heterocercal

Forked   Lunate

Truncate   Rounded

FISH TAILFINS, also called caudal fins, help fish swim and steer. The speed at which a fish moves through the water is affected by the size of the fish tailfin.

EXAMPLE **5** **Use a Square Root Model**

FISH TAILFINS The tailfin height h of a tuna can be modeled by $h = \sqrt{7.5A}$ where A is the surface area of the tailfin. Sketch the graph of the model.

Solution

The domain is all nonnegative numbers. Make a table of values, plot the points, and connect them with a smooth curve.

A	h
0	$h = \sqrt{7.5 \cdot 0} = 0$
1	$h = \sqrt{7.5 \cdot 1} \approx 2.7$
2	$h = \sqrt{7.5 \cdot 2} \approx 3.9$
3	$h = \sqrt{7.5 \cdot 3} \approx 4.7$
4	$h = \sqrt{7.5 \cdot 4} \approx 5.5$

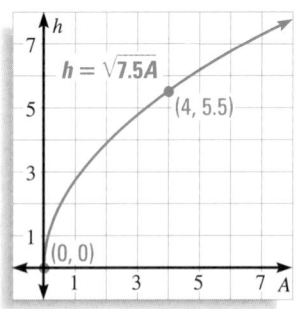

Checkpoint ✓ *Graph Functions Involving Square Roots*

11. The tailfin height h of a bottom-dwelling fish can be modeled by $h = \sqrt{0.6A}$, where A is the surface area of the tailfin. Sketch the graph of the model.

Guided Practice

Vocabulary Check

1. Describe the square root function.

2. Complete: Finding the __?__ of a square root function helps you choose appropriate input values of x for a table of values.

Skill Check

Evaluate the function for $x = 0, 1, 2, 3,$ and 4. Round your answers to the nearest tenth.

3. $y = 4\sqrt{x}$ **4.** $y = -\sqrt{x}$ **5.** $y = 3\sqrt{x} + 4$

6. $y = 6\sqrt{x} - 3$ **7.** $y = \sqrt{x + 2}$ **8.** $y = \sqrt{4x - 1}$

Find the domain and the range of the function.

9. $y = 5\sqrt{x}$ **10.** $y = \sqrt{x}$ **11.** $y = \sqrt{x} - 10$

12. $y = \sqrt{x} + 6$ **13.** $y = \sqrt{x + 5}$ **14.** $y = \sqrt{x - 10}$

Find the domain of the function. Then sketch its graph.

15. $y = 4\sqrt{x}$ **16.** $y = \sqrt{x} + 5$ **17.** $y = 3\sqrt{x + 1}$

FIRE HOSES **In Exercises 18 and 19, use the following information.** For a particular fire hose, the flow rate f (in gallons per minute) can be modeled by $f = 120\sqrt{p}$, where p is the nozzle pressure in pounds per square inch.

18. Find the domain of the flow rate model. Then sketch its graph.

19. If the nozzle pressure is 100 pounds per square inch, what is the flow rate?

Practice and Applications

EVALUATING FUNCTIONS **Evaluate the function for the given value of x.**

20. $y = 2\sqrt{x};\ 9$ **21.** $y = -2\sqrt{x};\ 25$ **22.** $y = \sqrt{32x};\ 2$

23. $y = \sqrt{3x};\ 12$ **24.** $y = \sqrt{x} + 4;\ 4$ **25.** $y = 10 - \sqrt{x};\ 16$

26. $y = \sqrt{x - 7};\ 56$ **27.** $y = \sqrt{3x - 5};\ 7$ **28.** $y = \sqrt{21 - 2x}\ ;\ -2$

Student Help

▶**HOMEWORK HELP**
  Example 1: Exs. 20–39
  Example 2: Exs. 40–55
  Example 3: Exs. 40–55
  Example 4: Exs. 40–55
  Example 5: Exs. 56–59

FINDING THE DOMAIN **Find the domain of the function. Then use several values in the domain to make a table of values for the function.**

29. $y = 6\sqrt{x}$ **30.** $y = \sqrt{x - 17}$ **31.** $y = \sqrt{3x - 10}$

32. $y = \sqrt{x + 1}$ **33.** $y = 4 + \sqrt{x}$ **34.** $y = \sqrt{x} - 3$

35. $y = \sqrt{x + 9}$ **36.** $y = 2\sqrt{4x}$ **37.** $y = x\sqrt{x}$

INVESTIGATING ACCIDENTS In Exercises 38 and 39, use the following information. When a car skids to a stop, its speed S (in miles per hour) before the skid can be modeled by the equation $S = \sqrt{30df}$, where d is the length of the tires' skid marks (in feet) and f is the coefficient of friction for the road.

38. In an accident, a car makes skid marks that are 120 feet long. The coefficient of friction is 1.0. What can you say about the speed the car was traveling before the accident?

39. In an accident, a car makes skid marks that are 147 feet long. The coefficient of friction is 0.4. A witness says that the driver was traveling under the speed limit of 35 miles per hour. Can the witness's statement be correct? Explain your reasoning.

GRAPHING FUNCTIONS Find the domain of the function. Then sketch its graph and find the range.

40. $y = 7\sqrt{x}$ **41.** $y = 4\sqrt{x}$ **42.** $y = 5\sqrt{x}$ **43.** $y = 6\sqrt{x}$

44. $y = \sqrt{3x}$ **45.** $y = -\sqrt{2x}$ **46.** $y = \sqrt{x} + 4$ **47.** $y = \sqrt{x} - 3$

48. $y = 5 - \sqrt{x}$ **49.** $y = 6 - \sqrt{x}$ **50.** $y = 2\sqrt{x} + 3$ **51.** $y = 5\sqrt{x} - 2$

52. $y = \sqrt{x - 4}$ **53.** $y = \sqrt{x + 1}$ **54.** $y = \sqrt{3x + 1}$ **55.** $y = 2\sqrt{4x + 10}$

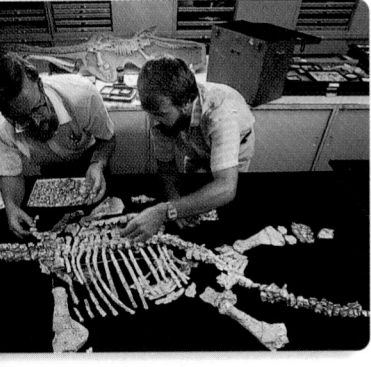

PALEONTOLOGISTS study fossils of animals and plants to better understand the history of life on Earth.

More about paleontologists at www.mcdougallittell.com

DINOSAURS In Exercises 56 and 57, use the following information. In a natural history museum you see leg bones for two species of dinosaurs and want to know how fast they walked. The maximum walking speed S (in feet per second) of a dinosaur can be modeled by the equation below, where L is the length (in feet) of the dinosaur's leg. ▶ Source: *Discover*

Walking speed model: $S = \sqrt{32L}$

56. Find the domain of the walking speed model. Then sketch its graph.

57. For one dinosaur the length of the leg is 1 foot. For the other dinosaur the length of the leg is 4 feet. How much faster does the taller dinosaur walk than the shorter dinosaur?

CHALLENGE In Exercises 58 and 59, use the following information. The lateral surface area S of a cone whose base has radius r can be found using the formula

$$S = \pi \cdot r\sqrt{r^2 + h^2}$$

where h is the height of the cone.

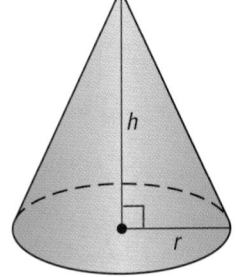

58. For $r = 14$ and $h \geq 0$, sketch the graph of the function.

59. Find the lateral surface area of a cone that has a height of 30 centimeters and whose base has a radius of 14 centimeters.

60. CRITICAL THINKING Find the domain of $y = \dfrac{3}{\sqrt{x} - 2}$.

Standardized Test
Practice

61. MULTIPLE CHOICE Which function best represents the graph?

(A) $y = 2\sqrt{x} - 3$

(B) $y = \sqrt{2x - 3}$

(C) $y = \sqrt{2x} - 3$

(D) $y = 2\sqrt{x} - 3$

(E) None of these

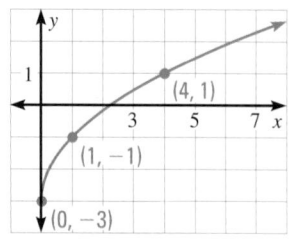

Mixed Review

SIMPLIFYING Simplify the radical expression. *(Lesson 9.3)*

62. $\sqrt{24}$　　**63.** $\sqrt{60}$　　**64.** $\sqrt{175}$　　**65.** $\sqrt{360}$

66. $\sqrt{\dfrac{20}{25}}$　　**67.** $\dfrac{1}{2}\sqrt{80}$　　**68.** $\dfrac{3\sqrt{7}}{\sqrt{9}}$　　**69.** $4\sqrt{\dfrac{11}{16}}$

SOLVING EQUATIONS Use the quadratic formula to solve the equation. If the solution involves radicals, round to the nearest hundredth. *(Lesson 9.6)*

70. $x^2 + 4x - 8 = 0$　　**71.** $x^2 - 2x - 4 = 0$　　**72.** $x^2 - 6x + 1 = 0$

73. $x^2 + 3x - 1 = 0$　　**74.** $2x^2 + x - 3 = 0$　　**75.** $4x^2 - 6x + 1 = 0$

MULTIPLYING EXPRESSIONS Find the product. *(Lesson 10.2)*

76. $(x - 2)(x + 11)$　　**77.** $(x + 4)(3x - 7)$　　**78.** $(x - 5)(x - 4)$

79. $(2x - 3)(5x - 9)$　　**80.** $(6x + 2)(x^2 - x - 1)$　　**81.** $(2x - 1)(x^2 + x + 1)$

82. MOUNT RUSHMORE Carved on Mount Rushmore are the faces of four Presidents of the United States: Washington, Jefferson, Roosevelt, and Lincoln. The ratio of each face on the cliff to a scale model is 12 to 1. How tall is Washington's face on Mount Rushmore if the scale model is 5 feet tall? *(Lesson 11.1)*

MULTIPLYING RATIONAL EXPRESSIONS Write the product in simplest form. *(Lesson 11.4)*

83. $\dfrac{8x}{3} \cdot \dfrac{1}{x}$　　**84.** $\dfrac{8x^2}{3} \cdot \dfrac{9}{16x}$　　**85.** $\dfrac{x}{x + 6} \cdot \dfrac{x + 6}{x + 1}$

Maintaining Skills

AREA Find the area of a triangle with the given base and height. *(Skills Review p. 774)*

86. $b = 4, h = 9$　　**87.** $b = 1, h = 1$　　**88.** $b = 12, h = 9$

89. $b = 6, h = 8$　　**90.** $b = 8, h = 3$　　**91.** $b = 10, h = 7$

92. $b = 0.75, h = 4$　　**93.** $b = 0.85, h = 0.62$　　**94.** $b = 0.25, h = 1.75$

12.2 Operations with Radical Expressions

Goal
Add, subtract, multiply, and divide radical expressions.

Key Words
• simplest form of a radical expression

How far can you see to the horizon?

The distance you can see to Earth's horizon depends on your eye-level height. In Example 4 you will compare the distance you can see to the distance a friend can see when you are at different heights on a schooner's mast.

You can use the distributive property to simplify sums and differences of radical expressions when the expressions have the same radicand.

SUM: $\sqrt{2} + 3\sqrt{2} = (1 + 3)\sqrt{2} = 4\sqrt{2}$

DIFFERENCE: $\sqrt{2} - 3\sqrt{2} = (1 - 3)\sqrt{2} = -2\sqrt{2}$

In part (b) of Example 1, the first step is to identify a perfect square factor in the radicand, as you learned on page 511.

Student Help

▶ LOOK BACK
For help simplifying radical expressions, see pp. 511–512.

EXAMPLE 1 Add and Subtract Radicals

Simplify the radical expression.

a. $2\sqrt{2} + \sqrt{5} - 6\sqrt{2} = (2\sqrt{2} - 6\sqrt{2}) + \sqrt{5}$ Group radicals having the same radicand.

$\qquad\qquad\qquad\quad = -4\sqrt{2} + \sqrt{5}$ Subtract.

b. $4\sqrt{3} - \sqrt{27} = 4\sqrt{3} - \sqrt{9 \cdot 3}$ Factor using perfect square factor.

$\qquad\qquad\quad = 4\sqrt{3} - \sqrt{9} \cdot \sqrt{3}$ Use product property.

$\qquad\qquad\quad = 4\sqrt{3} - 3\sqrt{3}$ Simplify.

$\qquad\qquad\quad = \sqrt{3}$ Subtract.

Checkpoint✓ Add and Subtract Radicals

Simplify the radical expression.

1. $\sqrt{3} + 2\sqrt{3}$ **2.** $3\sqrt{5} - 2\sqrt{5}$ **3.** $\sqrt{7} + \sqrt{2} + 3\sqrt{7}$

4. $\sqrt{8} - \sqrt{2}$ **5.** $\sqrt{18} + \sqrt{2}$ **6.** $5\sqrt{3} - \sqrt{12}$

Student Help

▶ **STUDY TIP**
As you can see in part (c) of Example 2, the product of two radical expressions having the sum and difference pattern has no radical. In general,
$(a + \sqrt{b})(a - \sqrt{b}) = a^2 - b$.

EXAMPLE **2** **Multiply Radicals**

Simplify the radical expression.

a. $\sqrt{2} \cdot \sqrt{8} = \sqrt{16} = 4$ Use product property and simplify.

b. $\sqrt{2}(5 - \sqrt{3}) = \sqrt{2} \cdot 5 - \sqrt{2} \cdot \sqrt{3}$ Use distributive property.

            $= 5\sqrt{2} - \sqrt{6}$ Use product property.

c. $(2 + \sqrt{3})(2 - \sqrt{3}) = 2^2 - (\sqrt{3})^2$ Use sum and difference pattern.

            $= 4 - 3 = 1$ Evaluate powers and simplify.

Checkpoint✔ *Multiply Radicals*

Simplify the radical expression.

7. $\sqrt{3} \cdot \sqrt{12}$ **8.** $\sqrt{5}(\sqrt{2} + 1)$ **9.** $(\sqrt{2} + 1)(\sqrt{2} - 1)$

To simplify expressions with radicals in the denominator, you may be able to rewrite the denominator as a rational number without changing the value of the expression, as you learned on page 512.

Student Help

▶ **STUDY TIP**
Multiplying the fractions in Example 3 by $\frac{\sqrt{5}}{\sqrt{5}}$ and $\frac{2 + \sqrt{3}}{2 + \sqrt{3}}$ is justified since both are equivalent to 1.

EXAMPLE **3** **Simplify Radicals**

Simplify the radical expression.

a. $\dfrac{3}{\sqrt{5}} = \dfrac{3}{\sqrt{5}} \cdot \dfrac{\sqrt{5}}{\sqrt{5}}$ Multiply by $\frac{\sqrt{5}}{\sqrt{5}}$.

     $= \dfrac{3\sqrt{5}}{\sqrt{5} \cdot \sqrt{5}}$ Multiply fractions.

     $= \dfrac{3\sqrt{5}}{5}$ Simplify perfect square.

b. $\dfrac{1}{2 - \sqrt{3}} = \dfrac{1}{2 - \sqrt{3}} \cdot \dfrac{2 + \sqrt{3}}{2 + \sqrt{3}}$ Use the fact that the product $(a + \sqrt{b})(a - \sqrt{b})$ does not involve radicals: multiply by $\frac{2 + \sqrt{3}}{2 + \sqrt{3}}$.

     $= \dfrac{2 + \sqrt{3}}{(2 - \sqrt{3})(2 + \sqrt{3})}$ Multiply fractions.

     $= \dfrac{2 + \sqrt{3}}{2^2 - (\sqrt{3})^2}$ Use sum and difference pattern.

     $= 2 + \sqrt{3}$ Evaluate powers and simplify.

Checkpoint✔ *Simplify Radicals*

Simplify the radical expression.

10. $\dfrac{1}{\sqrt{2}}$ **11.** $\dfrac{\sqrt{18}}{\sqrt{2}}$ **12.** $\dfrac{7}{3 - \sqrt{2}}$ **13.** $\dfrac{11}{5 + \sqrt{3}}$

EXAMPLE 4 Use a Radical Model

SAILING You and a friend are working on a schooner. The distance d (in miles) you can see to the horizon can be modeled by the equation

$$d = \sqrt{\frac{3h}{2}}$$

where h is your eye-level height (in feet) above the water. Your eye-level height is 32 feet and your friend's eye-level height is 18 feet. Write an expression that shows how much farther you can see than your friend. Simplify the expression.

32 ft
18 ft

Not drawn to scale

Solution

| VERBAL MODEL | $\boxed{\begin{array}{c}\textbf{Difference}\\\textbf{in distances}\end{array}} = \boxed{\begin{array}{c}\textbf{Your}\\\textbf{distance}\end{array}} - \boxed{\begin{array}{c}\textbf{Your friend's}\\\textbf{distance}\end{array}}$ |

LABELS   Difference in distances $= \boxed{D}$ (miles)

Your distance $= \sqrt{\dfrac{3(32)}{2}}$ (miles)

Your friend's distance $= \sqrt{\dfrac{3(18)}{2}}$ (miles)

ALGEBRAIC MODEL

$\boxed{D} = \sqrt{\dfrac{3(32)}{2}} - \sqrt{\dfrac{3(18)}{2}}$ Write algebraic model.

$D = \sqrt{48} - \sqrt{27}$ Simplify.

$D = \sqrt{16 \cdot 3} - \sqrt{9 \cdot 3}$ Factor using perfect square factors.

$D = 4\sqrt{3} - 3\sqrt{3}$ Use product property and simplify.

$D = \sqrt{3} \approx 1.7$ Subtract like radicals.

ANSWER ▶ You can see about 1.7 miles farther than your friend.

Checkpoint ✓ *Use a Radical Model*

14. Your eye-level height is 16 feet and your friend's eye-level height is 20 feet. Write an expression showing how much farther your friend can see than you.

12.2 Exercises

Guided Practice

Vocabulary Check

1. **Complete:** In the expression "$3\sqrt{2}$", 2 is called the __?__.

2. Which of the following is the simplest form of the radical expression $\dfrac{4}{\sqrt{3}}$?

    A. $\dfrac{4\sqrt{3}}{9}$ **B.** $\dfrac{4\sqrt{3}}{3}$ **C.** $\dfrac{4}{\sqrt{3}}$ **D.** $\dfrac{\sqrt{12}}{3}$

Skill Check

Simplify the expression.

3. $4 + \sqrt{5} + 5\sqrt{5}$ 4. $3\sqrt{7} - 2\sqrt{7}$ 5. $3\sqrt{6} + \sqrt{24}$

6. $\sqrt{3} \cdot \sqrt{8}$ 7. $(3 + \sqrt{7})^2$ 8. $\sqrt{3}(5\sqrt{3} - 2\sqrt{6})$

9. $\dfrac{4}{\sqrt{13}}$ 10. $\dfrac{3}{8 - \sqrt{10}}$ 11. $\dfrac{6}{\sqrt{10}}$

12. **SAILING** In Example 4 on page 700, suppose your eye-level height is 24 feet and your friend's is 12 feet. Write an expression that shows how much farther you can see than your friend. Simplify the expression.

Practice and Applications

ADDING AND SUBTRACTING RADICALS **Simplify the expression.**

13. $5\sqrt{7} + 2\sqrt{7}$ 14. $\sqrt{3} + 5\sqrt{3}$ 15. $11\sqrt{3} - 12\sqrt{3}$

16. $2\sqrt{6} - \sqrt{6}$ 17. $4\sqrt{5} + \sqrt{3} + \sqrt{5}$ 18. $3\sqrt{11} - \sqrt{5} + \sqrt{11}$

19. $\sqrt{32} + \sqrt{2}$ 20. $\sqrt{75} + \sqrt{3}$ 21. $\sqrt{80} - \sqrt{45}$

22. $\sqrt{72} - \sqrt{18}$ 23. $4\sqrt{5} + \sqrt{125} + \sqrt{45}$ 24. $\sqrt{24} - \sqrt{96} + \sqrt{6}$

MULTIPLYING RADICALS **Simplify the expression.**

25. $\sqrt{3} \cdot \sqrt{75}$ 26. $\sqrt{16} \cdot \sqrt{4}$ 27. $\sqrt{18} \cdot \sqrt{5}$

28. $\sqrt{5} \cdot \sqrt{8}$ 29. $\sqrt{6}(\sqrt{6} - 1)$ 30. $\sqrt{6}(7\sqrt{3} + 6)$

31. $\sqrt{5}(4 + \sqrt{5})$ 32. $\sqrt{2}(\sqrt{8} - 4)$ 33. $\sqrt{3}(5\sqrt{2} + \sqrt{3})$

MULTIPLYING RADICALS **Simplify the expression using the sum and difference pattern.**

34. $(\sqrt{2} + 6)(\sqrt{2} - 6)$ 35. $(1 + \sqrt{13})(1 - \sqrt{13})$

36. $(\sqrt{2} + \sqrt{3})(\sqrt{2} - \sqrt{3})$ 37. $(\sqrt{7} + \sqrt{2})(\sqrt{7} - \sqrt{2})$

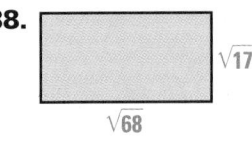 **Geometry Link** Find the area. (See the Table of Formulas on page 798.)

38.

$\sqrt{17}$

$\sqrt{68}$

39.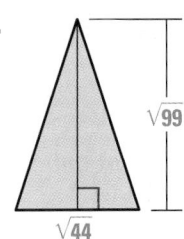

$\sqrt{99}$

$\sqrt{44}$

40.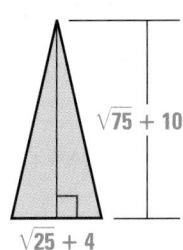

$\sqrt{75} + 10$

$\sqrt{25} + 4$

Student Help

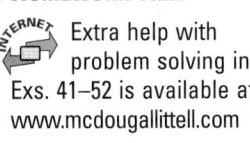

▶ HOMEWORK HELP

Extra help with problem solving in Exs. 41–52 is available at www.mcdougallittell.com

SIMPLEST FORM Simplify the radical expression.

41. $\dfrac{5}{\sqrt{7}}$

42. $\dfrac{2}{\sqrt{2}}$

43. $\dfrac{3}{\sqrt{48}}$

44. $\dfrac{5}{\sqrt{13}}$

45. $\dfrac{\sqrt{10}}{\sqrt{3}}$

46. $\dfrac{\sqrt{3}}{\sqrt{7}}$

47. $\dfrac{6}{6 + \sqrt{3}}$

48. $\dfrac{9}{5 - \sqrt{7}}$

49. $\dfrac{1}{2 + \sqrt{2}}$

50. $\dfrac{6}{10 + \sqrt{2}}$

51. $\dfrac{\sqrt{5}}{3 - \sqrt{5}}$

52. $\dfrac{\sqrt{3}}{\sqrt{3} - 1}$

ERROR ANALYSIS In Exercises 53 and 54, find and correct the error.

53. ~~$\sqrt{12} + \sqrt{13} = \sqrt{25} = 5$~~

54. ~~$\dfrac{5}{1 + \sqrt{3}} = \dfrac{5(1 - \sqrt{3})}{(1 + \sqrt{3})(1 - \sqrt{3})} = \dfrac{5 - 5\sqrt{3}}{1 + 3} = \dfrac{5 - 5\sqrt{3}}{4}$~~

55. POLE-VAULTING A pole-vaulter's approach velocity v (in feet per second) and height reached h (in feet) are related by the following equation.

Pole-vaulter model: $v = 8\sqrt{h}$

Suppose you are a pole-vaulter and reach a height of 20 feet and your opponent reaches a height of 16 feet. Write an expression that shows how much faster you ran than your opponent. Simplify the expression and round your answer to the nearest hundredth.

56. Science Link Many birds drop clams or other shellfish in order to break the shell and get the food inside. The time t (in seconds) it takes such an object to fall a certain distance d (in feet) is given by the following equation.

$$t = \dfrac{\sqrt{d}}{4}$$

A gull drops a clam from a height of 50 feet. A second gull drops a clam from a height of 32 feet. Write an expression that shows the difference in the time that it takes for the two clams to reach the ground. Simplify the expression.

57. MULTIPLE CHOICE Simplify $\sqrt{5}(6 + \sqrt{5})$.

Ⓐ $\sqrt{30} + 5$ Ⓑ $5\sqrt{6} + 5$ Ⓒ $6\sqrt{5} + 5$ Ⓓ $11\sqrt{5}$

58. MULTIPLE CHOICE Which of the following is equal to the difference $\sqrt{3} - 5\sqrt{9}$?

Ⓕ $\sqrt{3} - 15$ Ⓖ $-4\sqrt{3}$ Ⓗ $\sqrt{3} - 3$ Ⓙ $3 + 2\sqrt{5}$

59. MULTIPLE CHOICE Simplify $\dfrac{3}{5 - \sqrt{2}}$.

Ⓐ $\dfrac{15 + 3\sqrt{2}}{23}$ Ⓑ $\dfrac{15 + 3\sqrt{2}}{25}$ Ⓒ $\dfrac{15 + \sqrt{6}}{23}$ Ⓓ $\dfrac{15 + \sqrt{6}}{25}$

Mixed Review

PERCENTS Solve the percent problem. *(Lesson 3.9)*

60. What is 30% of 160?

61. 105 is what percent of 240?

62. 203 is what percent of 406?

63. What is 70% of 210?

SOLVING QUADRATIC EQUATIONS Solve the equation by factoring. *(Lesson 10.5)*

64. $x^2 - 25 = 0$ **65.** $x^2 + 2x - 15 = 0$ **66.** $x^2 - 13x = -42$

67. $x^2 - 26 = 11x$ **68.** $-9x + 4 = -2x^2$ **69.** $2 + 3x^2 = -5x$

CROSS PRODUCT PROPERTY Solve the equation using the cross product property. Check your solutions. *(Lesson 11.7)*

70. $\dfrac{2}{x + 3} = \dfrac{1}{x - 6}$ **71.** $\dfrac{6}{x} = \dfrac{7}{x - 5}$ **72.** $\dfrac{7}{x + 4} = \dfrac{2}{x - 6}$

FINDING THE DOMAIN Find the domain of the function. Then use several values in the domain to make a table of values for the function. *(Lesson 12.1)*

73. $y = \sqrt{x} - 3$ **74.** $y = \sqrt{x} + 4$ **75.** $y = 6\sqrt{x}$

76. $y = 11\sqrt{x}$ **77.** $y = \sqrt{x + 3}$ **78.** $y = \sqrt{x - 8}$

Maintaining Skills

COMPARING PERCENTS AND DECIMALS Complete the statement using <, >, or =. *(Skills Review pp. 768, 770)*

79. 40% ? 0.35   **80.** 110% ? 110   **81.** 1.8 ? 180%

82. 0.22 ? 20%   **83.** 200% ? 1.0   **84.** 12% ? 1

85. 0.3 ? 33%   **86.** 0.75 ? 85%   **87.** 1% ? 0.1

88. 5% ? 0.5   **89.** 1.5 ? 150%   **90.** 0.9 ? 89%

91. 101% ? 1.1   **92.** 20% ? 0.25   **93.** 0.66 ? 60%

94. 2.25 ? 250%   **95.** 80% ? 1.8   **96.** 100% ? 1.0

12.3 Solving Radical Equations

Goal

Solve a radical equation.

Key Words

• radical
• extraneous solution

What is the nozzle pressure of a de-icing hose?

The nozzle pressure of a hose is a function of the flow rate of the hose and the diameter of the nozzle. In Exercises 37 and 38 you will use an equation involving radicals to find the nozzle pressure of a hose used to de-ice an airplane.

In solving an equation involving radicals, the following property can be useful.

SQUARING BOTH SIDES OF AN EQUATION

If $a = b$, then $a^2 = b^2$, where a and b are algebraic expressions.

Example: $\sqrt{x + 1} = 5$, so $x + 1 = 25$.

EXAMPLE 1 Solve a Radical Equation

a. Solve $\sqrt{x} - 7 = 0$. **b.** Solve $3\sqrt{x + 4} = 15$.

Solution

a.
$\sqrt{x} - 7 = 0$	Write original equation.
$\sqrt{x} = 7$	Isolate the radical expression on one side of the equation.
$\left(\sqrt{x}\right)^2 = 7^2$	Square each side.
$x = 49$	Simplify.

ANSWER ▶ The solution is 49. Check the solution in the original equation.

b.
$3\sqrt{x + 4} = 15$	Write original equation.
$\sqrt{x + 4} = 5$	Divide each side by 3.
$\left(\sqrt{x + 4}\right)^2 = 5^2$	Square each side.
$x + 4 = 25$	Simplify.
$x = 21$	Subtract 4 from each side.

ANSWER ▶ The solution is 21. Check the solution in the original equation.

EXAMPLE 2 Solve a Radical Equation

To solve the equation $\sqrt{2x - 3} + 4 = 5$, you need to isolate the radical expression first.

1 **Write** the original equation. $\qquad\qquad\qquad\qquad \sqrt{2x - 3} + 4 = 5$

2 **Subtract** 4 from each side of the equation. $\qquad\qquad \sqrt{2x - 3} = 1$

3 **Square** each side of the equation. $\qquad\qquad\quad (\sqrt{2x - 3})^2 = 1^2$

4 **Simplify** the equation. $\qquad\qquad\qquad\qquad\qquad 2x - 3 = 1$

5 **Add** 3 to each side of the equation. $\qquad\qquad\qquad 2x = 4$

6 **Divide** each side of the equation by 2. $\qquad\qquad\quad x = 2$

ANSWER ▸ The solution is 2. Check the solution in the original equation.

Checkpoint ✓ *Solve a Radical Equation*

Solve the equation.

1. $\sqrt{x} = 3$ **2.** $\sqrt{m} - 4 = 0$ **3.** $\sqrt{x - 6} = 4$

4. $\sqrt{n + 1} = 1$ **5.** $\sqrt{x - 4} + 5 = 11$ **6.** $\sqrt{3n + 1} - 3 = 1$

EXTRANEOUS SOLUTIONS Squaring both sides of an equation can introduce a solution to the squared equation that does *not* satisfy the original equation. Such a solution is called an **extraneous solution**. When you solve by squaring both sides of an equation, check each solution in the original equation.

Student Help

▸**MORE EXAMPLES**

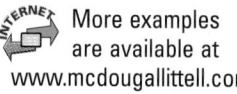 More examples are available at www.mcdougallittell.com

EXAMPLE 3 Check for Extraneous Solutions

Solve $\sqrt{x + 2} = x$ and check for extraneous solutions.

Solution

1 **Write** the original equation. $\qquad\qquad\qquad\qquad \sqrt{x + 2} = x$

2 **Square** each side of the equation. $\qquad\qquad (\sqrt{x + 2})^2 = x^2$

3 **Simplify** the equation. $\qquad\qquad\qquad\qquad\quad x + 2 = x^2$

4 **Write** the equation in standard form. $\qquad x^2 - x - 2 = 0$

5 **Factor** the equation. $\qquad\qquad\qquad\quad (x - 2)(x + 1) = 0$

6 **Use** the zero-product property to solve for x. $\quad x = 2 \ or \ x = -1$

CHECK ✓ Substitute 2 and -1 in the *original* equation.

$$\sqrt{2 + 2} \stackrel{?}{=} 2 \qquad\qquad \sqrt{-1 + 2} \stackrel{?}{=} -1$$

$$2 = 2 \ ✓ \qquad\qquad\qquad 1 \neq -1$$

ANSWER ▸ The only solution is 2, because $x = -1$ does not satisfy the original equation.

EXAMPLE 4 Check for Extraneous Solutions

Solve $\sqrt{x} + 13 = 0$ and check for extraneous solutions.

Solution

$\sqrt{x} + 13 = 0$	Write original equation.
$\sqrt{x} = -13$	Subtract 13 from each side.
$(\sqrt{x})^2 = (-13)^2$	Square each side.
$x = 169$	Simplify.

ANSWER ▶ $\sqrt{169} + 13 \neq 0$, so $x = 169$ is not a solution. The equation has no solution because $\sqrt{x} \geq 0$ for all values of x.

Checkpoint ✓ **Check for Extraneous Solutions**

Solve the equation. Check for extraneous solutions.

7. $\sqrt{x + 6} = x$ **8.** $x = \sqrt{8 - 2x}$ **9.** $\sqrt{n} + 4 = 0$

Link to
Science

CENTRIPETAL FORCE
keeps you spinning in a circle on an amusement park ride. Forces can be measured in newtons. A force of one newton will accelerate a mass of one kilogram at one meter per second per second.

EXAMPLE 5 **Use a Radical Model**

CENTRIPETAL FORCE The centripetal force F exerted on a passenger by a spinning amusement park ride and the number of seconds t the ride takes to complete one revolution are related by the following equation.

$$t = \sqrt{\frac{1620\pi^2}{F}}$$

Find the centripetal force experienced by this person if $t = 10$.

Solution

$t = \sqrt{\dfrac{1620\pi^2}{F}}$	Write model for centripetal force.
$10^2 = \left(\sqrt{\dfrac{1620\pi^2}{F}}\right)^2$	Substitute 10 for t and square each side.
$100 = \dfrac{1620\pi^2}{F}$	Simplify.
$F = \dfrac{1620\pi^2}{100} \approx 160$	Solve for F.

ANSWER ▶ The person experiences a centripetal force of about 160 newtons.

Checkpoint ✓ **Use a Radical Model**

10. Find the centripetal force exerted on the passenger in Example 5 if the amusement park ride takes 11 seconds to complete one revolution.

Guided Practice

Vocabulary Check

1. Explain what a *radical equation* is.

2. Explain what an *extraneous solution* is.

Skill Check

Solve the equation. Check for extraneous solutions.

3. $8 = \sqrt{x}$

4. $\sqrt{x} = 11$

5. $14 = \sqrt{x}$

6. $\sqrt{x} = -7$

7. $6 = \sqrt{x}$

8. $\sqrt{x} = 1$

9. $\sqrt{x} + 6 = 0$

10. $\sqrt{x} - 20 = 0$

11. $\sqrt{4x} - 1 = 3$

12. $x = \sqrt{x + 12}$

13. $-5 + \sqrt{x} = 0$

14. $x = \sqrt{5x + 24}$

15. $\sqrt{5x + 1} + 8 = 12$

16. $\sqrt{4x + 5} = x$

17. $\sqrt{x + 6} = x$

Practice and Applications

SOLVING RADICAL EQUATIONS Solve the equation.

18. $\sqrt{x} - 9 = 0$

19. $\sqrt{x} - 1 = 0$

20. $\sqrt{x} - 5 = 0$

21. $\sqrt{x} - 10 = 0$

22. $\sqrt{x} - 15 = 0$

23. $\sqrt{x} - 16 = 0$

24. $\sqrt{6x} - 13 = 23$

25. $\sqrt{4x + 1} + 5 = 10$

26. $\sqrt{9 - x} - 10 = 14$

27. $\sqrt{5x + 1} + 2 = 6$

28. $\sqrt{6x - 2} - 3 = 7$

29. $4 = 7 - \sqrt{33x - 2}$

30. $4\sqrt{3x + 3} = 24$

31. $\sqrt{2x + 4} + 1 = 11$

32. $8\sqrt{x + 3} = 64$

ERROR ANALYSIS In Exercises 33 and 34, find and correct the error.

33.
$$\sqrt{x} = 7$$
$$(\sqrt{x})^2 = (\sqrt{7})^2$$
$$x^2 = 7$$
$$x = \sqrt{7}$$

34.
$$\sqrt{x} - 15 = 0$$
$$\sqrt{x} = 15$$
$$(\sqrt{x})^2 = (15)^2$$
$$x = 225 \text{ and } -225$$

Student Help

▶**HOMEWORK HELP**
Example 1: Exs. 18–36
Example 2: Exs. 18–36
Example 3: Exs. 40–54
Example 4: Exs. 40–54
Example 5: Exs. 37, 38, 55, 56

Geometry Link Find the value of *x*.

35. Perimeter = 30

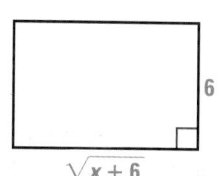

36. Area = 88

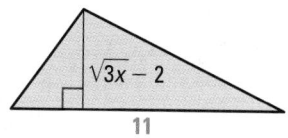

PLANE DE-ICING In Exercises 37 and 38, use the following information.
You work for a commercial airline and remove ice from planes. The relationship among the flow rate r (in gallons per minute) of the antifreeze for de-icing, the nozzle diameter d (in inches), and the nozzle pressure P (in pounds per square inch) is shown in the diagram. You want a flow rate of 250 gallons per minute.

37. Find the nozzle pressure P for a nozzle whose diameter is 1.25 inches.

38. Find the nozzle pressure P for a nozzle whose diameter is 1.75 inches.

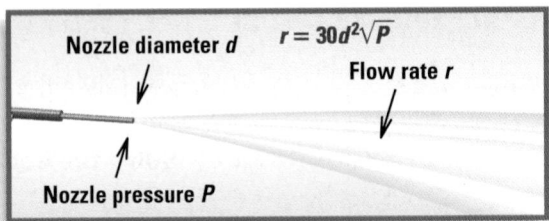

Nozzle diameter d

$r = 30d^2\sqrt{P}$

Flow rate r

Nozzle pressure P

39. MATHEMATICAL REASONING Write a radical equation that has a solution of 18.

CHECKING SOLUTIONS Solve the equation. Check for extraneous solutions.

40. $\sqrt{x} - 3 = 4$

41. $\sqrt{x} - 6 = 0$

42. $\sqrt{x} + 5 = 1$

43. $6 + \sqrt{3x} = -3$

44. $\sqrt{x + 5} = 7$

45. $\sqrt{5x + 10} = -5$

46. $\sqrt{x + 11} = 1$

47. $x = \sqrt{x + 42}$

48. $\sqrt{x} - 5 = 20$

49. $\sqrt{x - 10} = -1$

50. $3\sqrt{x} = -21$

51. $x = \sqrt{2x + 3}$

52. $2\sqrt{x} = -18$

53. $x = \sqrt{-x + 12}$

54. $2\sqrt{x} + 7 = 19$

SPORTS In Exercises 55 and 56, use the following information.
During the hammer throw event, a hammer is swung around in a circle several times until the thrower releases it. As the hammer travels in the path of the circle, it accelerates toward the center. This acceleration is known as *centripetal acceleration*. The speed s that the hammer is thrown can be modeled by the formula $s = \sqrt{1.2a}$, where a is the centripetal acceleration of the hammer prior to being released.

55. Find the approximate centripetal acceleration (in meters per second per second) when the ball is thrown with a speed of 18 meters per second.

56. Find the approximate centripetal acceleration (in meters per second per second) when the ball is thrown with a speed of 24 meters per second.

57. LOGICAL REASONING Determine whether the statement is *true* or *false*. Explain your reasoning.

36 is a solution of $\sqrt{x} = -6$.

58. MULTIPLE CHOICE Which of the following is a solution of $x = \sqrt{30 - x}$?

    (A) -6 **(B)** 0 **(C)** 5 **(D)** 30

59. MULTIPLE CHOICE Which of the following is a solution of $x = \sqrt{x + 20}$?

    (F) -5 **(G)** -4 **(H)** 4 **(J)** 5

Mixed Review

QUADRATIC EQUATIONS Solve the equation. Write the solutions as integers if possible. Otherwise, write them as radical expressions. *(Lesson 9.2)*

60. $x^2 = 36$ **61.** $x^2 = 11$ **62.** $7x^2 = 700$

63. $25x^2 - 9 = 91$ **64.** $x^2 - 16 = -7$ **65.** $-16x^2 + 48 = 0$

SPECIAL PRODUCT PATTERNS Find the product. *(Lesson 10.3)*

66. $(x + 5)^2$ **67.** $(2x - 3)^2$ **68.** $(6y - 4)(6y + 4)$

69. $(3x + 5y)(3x - 5y)$ **70.** $(x + 7y)^2$ **71.** $(2a - 9b)^2$

PERFECT SQUARES Factor the expression. *(Lesson 10.7)*

72. $x^2 + 18x + 81$ **73.** $x^2 - 12x + 36$ **74.** $4x^2 + 28x + 49$

Maintaining Skills

RECIPROCALS Find the reciprocal of the mixed number. Write your answer in lowest terms. *(Skills Review p. 763)*

75. $2\frac{1}{9}$ **76.** $4\frac{2}{5}$ **77.** $1\frac{3}{10}$ **78.** $6\frac{1}{2}$

79. $1\frac{7}{50}$ **80.** $8\frac{1}{6}$ **81.** $3\frac{7}{9}$ **82.** $5\frac{8}{25}$

Quiz 1

Find the domain of the function. Then sketch its graph and find the range. *(Lesson 12.1)*

  1. $y = 10\sqrt{x}$ **2.** $y = \sqrt{x - 9}$ **3.** $y = \sqrt{2x - 1}$ **4.** $y = \sqrt{x} - 2$

Simplify the expression. *(Lesson 12.2)*

  5. $7\sqrt{10} + 11\sqrt{10}$ **6.** $\sqrt{3}(3\sqrt{2} + \sqrt{3})$ **7.** $4\sqrt{7} + \sqrt{125} - \sqrt{80}$

Solve the equation. Check for extraneous solutions. *(Lesson 12.3)*

  8. $\sqrt{x} - 2 = 0$ **9.** $\sqrt{x} - 8 = 0$ **10.** $\sqrt{3x + 2} + 2 = 3$

  11. $\sqrt{3x - 2} + 3 = 7$ **12.** $\sqrt{77 - 4x} = x$ **13.** $x = \sqrt{2x + 3}$

14. NOZZLE PRESSURE Using the flow rate equation $r = 30d^2\sqrt{P}$ given in Exercises 37 and 38 on page 708, find the nozzle pressure for a hose that has a flow rate of 250 gallons per minute and a diameter of 2.5 inches. *(Lesson 12.3)*

12.4 Rational Exponents

Goal
Evaluate expressions involving rational exponents.

Key Words
• cube root of a
• radical notation
• rational exponent
• rational exponent notation

How large is the sphere used in women's shot put?

The metal sphere used in women's shot put is called a shot. In Exercise 46 you will find the size of this shot.

CUBE ROOT OF A NUMBER In Chapter 1 you learned how to cube a number. Now we define a *cube root*.

> If $b^3 = a$, then b is called a **cube root of** a.

For instance, 2 is a cube root of 8 because $2^3 = 8$. In radical notation, a cube root of a is written as $\sqrt[3]{a}$. In general, for any integer n greater than 1,

> if $b^n = a$, then b is an nth root of a.

In radical notation, the nth root of a is written as $\sqrt[n]{a}$.

Student Help

▶READING ALGEBRA
When the *cube root of a* is written in rational exponent notation, $a^{1/3}$, it is read "a raised to the one-third power."

RATIONAL EXPONENT NOTATION Because $\sqrt[3]{a} \cdot \sqrt[3]{a} \cdot \sqrt[3]{a} = a$, it is natural to define $\sqrt[3]{a} = a^{1/3}$. With this definition the product of powers property for exponents holds for fractional exponents:

$$\sqrt[3]{a} \cdot \sqrt[3]{a} \cdot \sqrt[3]{a} = a^{1/3} \cdot a^{1/3} \cdot a^{1/3} = a^{(1/3 + 1/3 + 1/3)} = a^1 = a$$

More generally, $\sqrt[n]{a} = a^{1/n}$ for any $a > 0$ and integer n greater than 1. The value of $a^{1/n}$ is restricted to nonnegative numbers.

EXAMPLE 1 Find Cube and Square Roots

Find the cube root or square root.

a. $27^{1/3}$ **b.** $\sqrt[3]{1000}$ **c.** $64^{1/2}$

Solution

a. Because $3^3 = 27$, you know that $27^{1/3} = 3$.

b. Because $10^3 = 1000$, you know that $\sqrt[3]{1000} = 10$.

c. Because $8^2 = 64$ and 8 is a nonnegative number, you know that $64^{1/2} = 8$.

RATIONAL EXPONENTS A rational exponent does not have to be of the form $\frac{1}{n}$. Other rational numbers, such as $\frac{3}{2}$ and $\frac{4}{3}$, may also be used as exponents. For integers m and n we have the rule $(a^m)^n = a^{mn}$. This produces a basis for the following definition of powers written with **rational exponents**.

RATIONAL EXPONENTS

Let a be a nonnegative number, and let m and n be positive integers.
$$a^{m/n} = (a^{1/n})^m = (\sqrt[n]{a})^m$$

EXAMPLE 2 Evaluate Expressions with Rational Exponents

Rewrite the expressions using rational exponent notation *and* radical notation.

a. $16^{3/2}$ **b.** $8^{4/3}$

Solution

a. Use rational exponent notation. $16^{3/2} = (16^{1/2})^3 = 4^3 = 64$

Use radical notation. $16^{3/2} = (\sqrt{16})^3 = 4^3 = 64$

b. Use rational exponent notation. $8^{4/3} = (8^{1/3})^4 = 2^4 = 16$

Use radical notation. $8^{4/3} = (\sqrt[3]{8})^4 = 2^4 = 16$

 **Evaluate Expressions with Rational Exponents**

Evaluate the expression without using a calculator.

1. $\sqrt[3]{64}$ **2.** $625^{1/2}$ **3.** $225^{1/2}$ **4.** $216^{1/3}$

5. $64^{3/2}$ **6.** $(\sqrt[3]{27})^2$ **7.** $(\sqrt{4})^5$ **8.** $1000^{2/3}$

The multiplication properties of exponents presented in Lesson 8.1 can also be applied to rational exponents.

SUMMARY

Properties of Rational Exponents

Let a and b be nonnegative real numbers and let m and n be rational numbers.

PROPERTY	EXAMPLE
$a^m \cdot a^n = a^{m+n}$	$3^{1/2} \cdot 3^{3/2} = 3^{(1/2 + 3/2)} = 3^2 = 9$
$(a^m)^n = a^{mn}$	$(4^{3/2})^2 = 4^{(3/2 \cdot 2)} = 4^3 = 64$
$(ab)^m = a^m b^m$	$(9 \cdot 4)^{1/2} = 9^{1/2} \cdot 4^{1/2} = 3 \cdot 2 = 6$

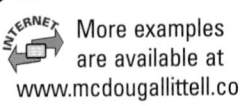
EXAMPLE 3 Use Properties of Rational Exponents

Evaluate the expression using the properties of rational exponents.

a. $5^{1/3} \cdot 5^{2/3}$ **b.** $\left(7^{1/3}\right)^6$ **c.** $(4 \cdot 25)^{1/2}$

Solution

a. Use the product of powers property.

$$5^{1/3} \cdot 5^{2/3} = 5^{(1/3 + 2/3)} = 5^{3/3} = 5^1 = 5$$

b. Use the power of a power property.

$$\left(7^{1/3}\right)^6 = 7^{(1/3 \cdot 6)} = 7^2 = 49$$

c. Use the power of a product property.

$$(4 \cdot 25)^{1/2} = 4^{1/2} \cdot 25^{1/2} = 2 \cdot 5 = 10$$

Checkpoint ✓ Use Properties of Rational Exponents

Evaluate the expression using the properties of rational exponents.

9. $\left(8^{1/3}\right)^2$ **10.** $(4 \cdot 16)^{1/2}$ **11.** $4^{1/2} \cdot 4^{3/2}$ **12.** $\left(3^{1/2}\right)^2$

13. $(27 \cdot 64)^{1/3}$ **14.** $2^{5/2} \cdot 2^{1/2}$ **15.** $\left(6^{2/3}\right)^{3/2}$ **16.** $(64 \cdot 81)^{1/2}$

EXAMPLE 4 Use Properties of Rational Exponents

Simplify the variable expression $(x \cdot y^{1/2})^2 \sqrt{x}$ using the properties of rational exponents.

Solution

❶ **Use** the power of a product property. $(x \cdot y^{1/2})^2 \sqrt{x} = \left(x^2 \cdot y^{1/2 \cdot 2}\right)\sqrt{x}$

❷ **Write** $\sqrt{x}$ in rational exponent notation. $= x^2 \cdot y^1 \cdot x^{1/2}$

❸ **Use** the product of powers property. $= x^{2 + 1/2} \cdot y^1$

❹ **Add** the exponents. $= x^{5/2}y$

Checkpoint ✓ Use Properties of Rational Exponents

Simplify the expression.

17. $(x \cdot y^{1/2})^4 x$ **18.** $(x^{3/2} \cdot y)^2$ **19.** $\left(y^3\right)^{1/6}$

20. $\left(x^{1/3} \cdot x^{5/3}\right)^{1/2}$ **21.** $\left(x^{1/2} \cdot y^{1/3}\right)^6$ **22.** $\sqrt[3]{x}(x^3 \cdot y^2)^{1/3}$

Guided Practice

Vocabulary Check

1. Write "the cube root of 27" in both radical notation and rational exponent notation.

Skill Check

Evaluate the expression without using a calculator.

2. $\sqrt[3]{125}$ **3.** $49^{1/2}$ **4.** $(\sqrt[3]{8})^5$ **5.** $25^{3/2}$

6. $121^{1/2}$ **7.** $9^{3/2}$ **8.** $\sqrt[3]{343}$ **9.** $(\sqrt{81})^3$

Practice and Applications

RATIONAL EXPONENTS **Rewrite the expression using rational exponent notation.**

10. $\sqrt{14}$ **11.** $\sqrt[3]{11}$ **12.** $(\sqrt[3]{5})^2$ **13.** $(\sqrt{16})^5$

RADICALS **Rewrite the expression using radical notation.**

14. $6^{1/3}$ **15.** $7^{1/2}$ **16.** $10^{3/2}$ **17.** $8^{7/3}$

EVALUATING EXPRESSIONS **Evaluate the expression without using a calculator.**

18. $\sqrt[3]{8}$ **19.** $\sqrt{10,000}$ **20.** $512^{1/3}$ **21.** $4^{1/2}$

22. $1^{1/3}$ **23.** $256^{1/2}$ **24.** $(\sqrt{16})^4$ **25.** $(\sqrt[3]{27})^4$

26. $4^{3/2}$ **27.** $125^{2/3}$ **28.** $(\sqrt{100})^3$ **29.** $(\sqrt[3]{64})^4$

PROPERTIES OF RATIONAL EXPONENTS **Evaluate the expression.**

30. $3^{5/3} \cdot 3^{1/3}$ **31.** $4^{3/2} \cdot 4^{1/2}$ **32.** $(8^{2/3})^{1/2}$

33. $(6^{1/3})^6$ **34.** $(8 \cdot 27)^{1/3}$ **35.** $(16 \cdot 25)^{1/2}$

36. $(2^3 \cdot 3^3)^{1/3}$ **37.** $(2^{2/3} \cdot 2^{1/3})^6$ **38.** $(4^2 \cdot 5^2)^{1/2}$

PROPERTIES OF RATIONAL EXPONENTS **Simplify the variable expression.**

39. $x^{1/3} \cdot x^{1/2}$ **40.** $x \cdot \sqrt[3]{y^6} + y^2 \cdot \sqrt[3]{x^3}$ **41.** $(y^{1/6})^3 \cdot \sqrt{x}$

42. $(36x^3)^{1/2}$ **43.** $(y \cdot y^{1/3})^{3/2}$ **44.** $(x^{1/3} \cdot y^{1/2})^6 \cdot \sqrt{x}$

45. LOGICAL REASONING Complete the statement with *always*, *sometimes*, or *never*.

If a and b are whole numbers, then $\sqrt{a^2 + b^2}$ is __?__ equal to $a + b$.

Student Help

▶ HOMEWORK HELP
Example 1: Exs. 10–29
Example 2: Exs. 18–29
Example 3: Exs. 30–38
Example 4: Exs. 39–44

EXAMPLE *Volume of a Sphere*

The formula for the volume of a sphere is $V = \frac{4}{3}\pi r^3$, where r is the radius of the sphere. Find the radius of a sphere that has a volume of 33.5 cubic centimeters.

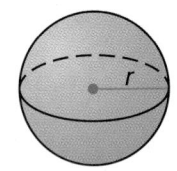

Solution

To find the radius of the sphere, first solve the equation $V = \frac{4}{3}\pi r^3$ for r.

❶ **Write** the formula for the volume of a sphere.

$$V = \frac{4}{3}\pi r^3$$

❷ **Multiply** each side by $\frac{3}{4}$ and divide each side by π.

$$\frac{\frac{3}{4}V}{\pi} = r^3$$

❸ **Take** the cube root of each side.

$$r = \sqrt[3]{\frac{\frac{3}{4}V}{\pi}}$$

❹ **Substitute** 33.5 for V.

$$r = \sqrt[3]{\frac{\frac{3}{4}(33.5)}{\pi}}$$

❺ **Evaluate** the radicand.

$$r \approx \sqrt[3]{8.0}$$

❻ **Solve** for r.

$$r \approx 2$$

ANSWER ▶ The radius of the sphere is about 2 centimeters.

46. SHOT PUT The shot (a metal sphere) used in the women's shot put has a volume of about 524 cubic centimeters. Find the radius of the shot.

Standardized Test Practice

47. MULTIPLE CHOICE Evaluate the expression $100^{3/2}$.

Ⓐ 10　　　　Ⓑ 100　　　　Ⓒ 1000　　　　Ⓓ 10,000

Mixed Review

QUADRATIC EQUATIONS Solve the equation. Write the solutions as integers if possible. Otherwise, write them as radical expressions. *(Lesson 9.2)*

48. $16 + x^2 = 64$　　　**49.** $x^2 + 25 = 81$　　　**50.** $x^2 + 81 = 144$

51. $4x^2 - 144 = 0$　　　**52.** $x^2 - 30 = -3$　　　**53.** $x^2 = \frac{20}{25}$

SOLVING EQUATIONS Solve the equation. *(Lesson 10.4)*

54. $(x + 4)^2 = 0$　　　**55.** $(x + 4)(x - 8) = 0$　　　**56.** $x(x - 14)^2 = 0$

Maintaining Skills

FACTORS Determine whether the number is prime or composite. If it is composite, give its prime factorization. *(Skills Review p. 761)*

57. 13　　　**58.** 28　　　**59.** 75　　　**60.** 99

61. 18　　　**62.** 33　　　**63.** 69　　　**64.** 80

714　**Chapter 12**　*Radicals and More Connections to Geometry*

DEVELOPING CONCEPTS
Completing the Square

For use with Lesson 12.5

GOAL

Use algebra tiles to complete the square.

MATERIALS

• pencil
• algebra tiles

Question How can you use algebra tiles to complete the square?

Explore

1 You can use algebra tiles to model the expression $x^2 + 6x$.

> You will need one x^2-tile and six x-tiles.

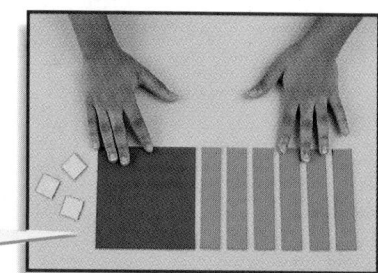

2 Arrange the x^2-tile and the x-tiles to form part of a square. Your arrangement will be incomplete in one corner.

> You want the length and width of your "square" to be equal.

3 To complete the square, you need to add nine 1-tiles.

> By adding nine 1-tiles, you can see that $x^2 + 6x + 9 = (x + 3)^2$.

Student Help

▶ **LOOK BACK**
For help with algebra tiles, see p. 567.

Think About It

1. Copy and complete the table by following the steps above.

Expression	Number of tiles to complete the square	Number of tiles as a perfect square
$x^2 + 6x$	9	3^2
$x^2 + 4x$	?	?
$x^2 + 2x$	?	?

2. How is the number in the third column related to the coefficient of x?

3. Use the pattern you found in Exercise 2 to predict how many tiles you would need to add to complete the square for the expression $x^2 + 8x$.

12.5 Completing the Square

Goal

Solve a quadratic equation by completing the square.

Key Words

- completing the square
- quadratic formula
- perfect square trinomial

How far does a penguin leap?

Penguins leap out of the water every few feet when swimming. The distance a penguin leaps can be modeled by a quadratic equation, as you will see in Example 4.

In Developing Concepts 12.5, page 715, you **completed the square** for expressions of the form $x^2 + bx$ when $b = 2, 4, 6,$ and 8. In each case,

$x^2 + bx + \left(\dfrac{b}{2} \cdot \dfrac{b}{2}\right)$ was modeled by a square with sides of length $x + \dfrac{b}{2}$.

By using FOIL to expand $\left(x + \dfrac{b}{2}\right)\left(x + \dfrac{b}{2}\right)$, you can show that this pattern holds for any real number b.

COMPLETING THE SQUARE

To complete the square of the expression $x^2 + bx$, add the square of half the coefficient of x, that is, add $\left(\dfrac{b}{2}\right)^2$.

$$x^2 + bx + \left(\dfrac{b}{2}\right)^2 = \left(x + \dfrac{b}{2}\right)^2$$

EXAMPLE 1 Complete the Square

What term should you add to $x^2 - 8x$ to create a perfect square trinomial?

The coefficient of x is -8, so you should add $\left(\dfrac{-8}{2}\right)^2$, or 16, to the expression.

$$x^2 - 8x + \left(\dfrac{-8}{2}\right)^2 = x^2 - 8x + 16$$
$$= (x - 4)^2$$

Checkpoint ✓ *Complete the Square*

Find the term that should be added to the expression to create a perfect square trinomial.

1. $x^2 + 2x$ **2.** $x^2 - 4x$ **3.** $x^2 + 6x$ **4.** $x^2 - 10x$

Student Help

▶ **STUDY TIP**
When completing the square to solve an equation, remember that you must always add the term $\left(\dfrac{b}{2}\right)^2$ to both sides of the equation.

EXAMPLE **2** **Solve a Quadratic Equation**

Solve $x^2 + 10x = 24$ by completing the square.

Solution

$x^2 + 10x = 24$	Write original equation.
$x^2 + 10x + 5^2 = 24 + 5^2$	Add $\left(\dfrac{10}{2}\right)^2$, or 5^2, to each side.
$(x + 5)^2 = 49$	Write left side as perfect square.
$x + 5 = \pm 7$	Find square root of each side.
$x = -5 \pm 7$	Subtract 5 from each side.
$x = 2 \quad or \quad x = -12$	Simplify.

ANSWER ▶ The solutions are 2 and -12. Check these in the original equation to confirm that both are solutions.

 **Checkpoint** ✓ **Solve a Quadratic Equation**

Solve the equation by completing the square.

5. $x^2 - 2x - 3 = 0$ **6.** $x^2 - 12x + 4 = 0$ **7.** $x^2 + 16x + 4 = 0$

EXAMPLE **3** **Develop the Quadratic Formula**

The quadratic formula can be established by completing the square for the general quadratic equation $ax^2 + bx + c = 0$, where $a \neq 0$.

❶ **Write** the original equation. $\qquad ax^2 + bx + c = 0$

❷ **Subtract** c from each side. $\qquad ax^2 + bx = -c$

❸ **Divide** each side by a. $\qquad x^2 + \dfrac{b}{a}x = -\dfrac{c}{a}$

❹ **Add** $\left(\dfrac{b}{2a}\right)^2 = \dfrac{b^2}{4a^2}$ to each side. $\qquad x^2 + \dfrac{b}{a}x + \dfrac{b^2}{4a^2} = \dfrac{b^2}{4a^2} - \dfrac{c}{a}$

❺ **Write** the left side of the equation as a perfect square. $\qquad \left(x + \dfrac{b}{2a}\right)^2 = \dfrac{b^2 - 4ac}{4a^2}$

❻ **Find** the square root of each side. $\qquad x + \dfrac{b}{2a} = \pm\sqrt{\dfrac{b^2 - 4ac}{4a^2}}$

❼ **Subtract** $\dfrac{b}{2a}$ from each side. $\qquad x = -\dfrac{b}{2a} \pm \dfrac{\sqrt{b^2 - 4ac}}{2a}$

❽ **Write** the right side of the equation as a single fraction. $\qquad x = \dfrac{-b \pm \sqrt{b^2 - 4ac}}{2a}$

This result is the quadratic formula.

EXAMPLE 4 **Choose a Solution Method**

PENGUINS The path followed by a penguin leaping out of the water is given by $h = -0.05x^2 + 1.178x$, where h is the vertical height (in feet) of the penguin above the water and x is the horizontal distance (in feet) traveled over the water. Find the horizontal distance traveled by this penguin when it reaches a vertical height of 6 feet.

Solution

To find the horizontal distance when $h = 6$, solve the quadratic equation $6 = -0.05x^2 + 1.178x$. This equation cannot be factored easily and cannot be solved easily by completing the square. The quadratic formula is a good choice.

$$x = \frac{-b \pm \sqrt{b^2 - 4ac}}{2a}$$ Write quadratic formula.

$$x = \frac{-1.178 \pm \sqrt{1.178^2 - 4(-0.05)(-6)}}{2(-0.05)}$$ Substitute values for a, b, and c.

$$x \approx 7.4 \quad or \quad x \approx 16.1$$ Use a calculator.

ANSWER ▶ The penguin reaches a vertical height of 6 feet at horizontal distances of about 7.4 feet and about 16.1 feet. Check these solutions in the original equation.

 **Choose a Solution Method**

Choose a method and solve the quadratic equation. Explain your choice.

8. $x^2 - 3 = 0$ **9.** $2x^2 = 8$ **10.** $x^2 + 3x + 4 = 6$

You have learned the following five methods for solving quadratic equations.

SUMMARY

Methods for Solving Quadratic Equations

Method	Comments
FINDING SQUARE ROOTS (Lesson 9.2)	Efficient way to solve $ax^2 + c = 0$.
GRAPHING (Lesson 9.5)	Can be used for *any* quadratic equation. Enables you to approximate solutions.
USING THE QUADRATIC FORMULA (Lesson 9.6)	Can be used for *any* quadratic equation.
FACTORING (Lesson 10.5–10.8)	Efficient way to solve a quadratic equation if the quadratic expression can be factored easily.
COMPLETING THE SQUARE (Lesson 12.5)	Can be used for *any* quadratic equation, but is best suited for quadratic equations where $a = 1$ and b is an even number.

12.5 Exercises

Guided Practice

Vocabulary Check

1. Explain how to complete the square of the expression $x^2 + bx$.

2. **LOGICAL REASONING** Determine whether the statement is *true* or *false*. Explain your reasoning.

   To solve $x^2 + 6x = 12$ by completing the square, add 6 to both sides.

Skill Check

Find the term that should be added to the expression to create a perfect square trinomial.

3. $x^2 + 20x$ **4.** $x^2 + 30x$ **5.** $x^2 - 10x$

6. $x^2 - 14x$ **7.** $x^2 - 22x$ **8.** $x^2 + 24x$

9. Solve $x^2 - 3x = 8$ by completing the square. Solve the equation by using the quadratic formula. Which method did you find easier?

Solve the quadratic equation by completing the square.

10. $x^2 - 2x - 18 = 0$ **11.** $x^2 + 10x - 10 = 0$

12. $x^2 + 8x = -3$ **13.** $x^2 + 14x = -13$

Choose a method and solve the quadratic equation. Explain your choice.

14. $x^2 - x - 2 = 0$ **15.** $3x^2 + 17x + 10 = 0$ **16.** $x^2 - 9 = 0$

17. $-3x^2 + 5x + 5 = 0$ **18.** $x^2 + 2x - 14 = 0$ **19.** $3x^2 - 2 = 0$

Practice and Applications

PERFECT SQUARES Find the term that should be added to the expression to create a perfect square trinomial.

20. $x^2 - 12x$ **21.** $x^2 + 8x$ **22.** $x^2 + 10x$

23. $x^2 + 22x$ **24.** $x^2 + 14x$ **25.** $x^2 - 40x$

26. $x^2 + 4x$ **27.** $x^2 - 6x$ **28.** $x^2 + 16x$

COMPLETING THE SQUARE Solve by completing the square.

29. $x^2 - 8x + 12 = 0$ **30.** $x^2 - 2x = 3$ **31.** $x^2 + 6x - 16 = 0$

32. $x^2 + 4x = 12$ **33.** $x^2 + 10x = 12$ **34.** $x^2 + 8x = 15$

35. $x^2 + 10x = 39$ **36.** $x^2 + 16x = 17$ **37.** $x^2 - 24x = -44$

38. $x^2 - 6x - 11 = 0$ **39.** $x^2 - 2x = 5$ **40.** $x^2 + 30x - 7 = 0$

41. $x^2 - 4x - 1 = 0$ **42.** $x^2 + 20x + 3 = 0$ **43.** $x^2 + 14x - 2 = 0$

Student Help

▶ **HOMEWORK HELP**
Example 1: Exs. 20–28
Example 2: Exs. 29–55
Example 3: Exs. 29–56
Example 4: Exs. 57–76

SOLVING EQUATIONS Solve the quadratic equation.

44. $x^2 + 4x + 5 = 0$ **45.** $x^2 + 10x - 3 = 0$ **46.** $x^2 + 16x + 9 = 0$

47. $x^2 + 22x + 1 = 0$ **48.** $x^2 + 2x - 11 = 0$ **49.** $x^2 + 8x - 6 = 0$

50. $x^2 + 14x - 7 = 0$ **51.** $x^2 + 20x + 2 = 0$ **52.** $x^2 - 6x - 10 = 0$

53. $x^2 - 12x - 3 = 0$ **54.** $x^2 - 18x + 5 = 0$ **55.** $x^2 - 2x - 4 = 0$

56. LOGICAL REASONING Explain why the quadratic formula gives real solutions only if $a \neq 0$ and $b^2 - 4ac \geq 0$.

Student Help

▶ **HOMEWORK HELP**

Extra help with problem solving in Exs. 57–59 is available at www.mcdougallittell.com

Geometry Link In Exercises 57–59, make a sketch and write a quadratic equation to model the situation. Then solve the equation.

57. In art class you are designing the floor plan of a house. The kitchen is supposed to have 150 square feet of space. What should the dimensions of the kitchen floor be if you want it to be square?

58. A rectangle is $2x$ feet long and $x + 5$ feet wide. The area is 600 square feet. What are the dimensions of the rectangle?

59. The base of a triangle is x feet and the height is $(4 + 2x)$ feet. The area of the triangle is 60 square feet. What are the dimensions of the triangle?

CHOOSING A METHOD Choose a method and solve the quadratic equation. Explain your choice.

60. $x^2 - x - 12 = 0$ **61.** $x^2 - 9 = 0$ **62.** $x^2 - 4x = 8$

63. $x^2 + 5x - 14 = 0$ **64.** $x^2 - 2x = 2$ **65.** $3x^2 + 5x - 12 = 0$

66. $x^2 + 5x - 6 = 0$ **67.** $x^2 - 6x + 7 = 0$ **68.** $x^2 + 2 = 6$

69. $2x^2 + 7x + 3 = 0$ **70.** $2x^2 - 200 = 0$ **71.** $x^2 - 24x = 6$

72. $3x^2 - 48 = 0$ **73.** $x^2 + 3x + 4 = 1$ **74.** $3x^2 + 7x + 2 = 0$

75. DIVING The path of a diver diving from a 10-foot high diving board is

$$h = -0.44x^2 + 2.61x + 10$$

where h is the height (in feet) of the diver above water and x is the horizontal distance from the end of the board. How far from the end of the board will the diver enter the water?

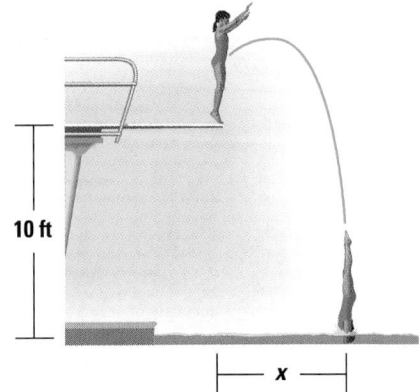

10 ft

x

76. VERTICAL MOTION Suppose you throw a ball upward from a height of 5 feet and with an initial velocity of 15 feet per second. The vertical motion model $h = -16t^2 + 15t + 5$ gives the height h (in feet) of the ball, where t is the number of seconds that the ball is in the air. Find the time that it takes for the ball to reach the ground ($h = 0$) after it has been thrown.

77. MULTIPLE CHOICE Which of the following is a solution of the equation $2x^2 + 8x - 25 = 5$?

   Ⓐ $-\sqrt{19} - 2$ Ⓑ $\sqrt{17} - 2$ Ⓒ $\sqrt{21} - 2$ Ⓓ $\sqrt{17} + 1$

78. MULTIPLE CHOICE What term should you add to $x^2 - \frac{1}{2}x$ to create a perfect square trinomial?

   Ⓕ $\frac{1}{2}$ Ⓖ $\frac{1}{4}$ Ⓗ $\frac{1}{16}$ Ⓙ $\frac{1}{32}$

79. MULTIPLE CHOICE Solve $x^2 + 8x - 2 = 0$.

   Ⓐ $-4 \pm 3\sqrt{2}$ Ⓑ $-4 \pm 2\sqrt{2}$ Ⓒ $4 \pm 3\sqrt{2}$ Ⓓ $4 \pm \sqrt{16}$

Mixed Review

SOLVING LINEAR SYSTEMS Solve the linear system. *(Lessons 7.2, 7.3)*

80. $y = 4x$ **81.** $3x + y = 12$ **82.** $2x - y = 8$
       $x + y = 10$ $9x - y = 36$ $2x + 2y = 2$

QUADRATIC EQUATIONS Solve the equation. Write the solutions as integers if possible. Otherwise, write them as radical expressions. *(Lesson 9.2)*

83. $3x^2 - 147 = 0$ **84.** $x^2 - 5 = 20$ **85.** $x^2 + 2 = 83$

86. $9 + x^2 = 49$ **87.** $x^2 - 16 = 144$ **88.** $x^2 + 64 = 169$

SOLVING GRAPHICALLY Use a graph to estimate the solutions of the equation. Check your solutions algebraically. *(Lesson 9.5)*

89. $x^2 + x + 2 = 0$ **90.** $-3x^2 - x - 4 = 0$ **91.** $2x^2 - 3x + 4 = 0$

92. $x^2 - x - 12 = 0$ **93.** $x^2 - 2x - 3 = 0$ **94.** $2x^2 + 10x + 12 = 0$

ZERO-PRODUCT PROPERTY Use the zero-product property to solve the equation. *(Lesson 10.4)*

95. $(x + 4)(x - 8) = 0$ **96.** $(x - 3)(x - 2) = 0$ **97.** $(x + 5)(x + 6) = 0$

98. $(x + 4)^2 = 0$ **99.** $(x - 3)^2 = 0$ **100.** $6(x - 14)^2 = 0$

FACTORING TRINOMIALS Factor the trinomial. *(Lessons 10.5, 10.6)*

101. $x^2 + x - 20$ **102.** $x^2 - 10x + 24$ **103.** $x^2 + 4x + 4$

104. $3x^2 - 15x + 18$ **105.** $2x^2 - x - 3$ **106.** $14x^2 - 19x - 3$

Maintaining Skills

PERCENTS AND FRACTIONS Subtract. Write the answer as a fraction in simplest form. *(Skills Review p. 768)*

107. $\frac{3}{4} - 15\%$ **108.** $\frac{7}{8} - 80\%$ **109.** $\frac{1}{2} - 39\%$

110. $\frac{4}{5} - 45\%$ **111.** $26\% - \frac{1}{4}$ **112.** $75\% - \frac{3}{4}$

113. $8\% - \frac{1}{20}$ **114.** $100\% - \frac{2}{5}$ **115.** $50\% - \frac{1}{8}$

DEVELOPING CONCEPTS
The Pythagorean Theorem

For use with Lesson 12.6

GOAL

Work in groups to investigate the Pythagorean theorem and its converse.

MATERIALS

• graph paper
• scissors
• glue or tape

Student Help

▶ **VOCABULARY TIP**
An obtuse triangle has one angle measuring between 90° and 180°. An acute triangle has three angles that each measure between 0° and 90°.

Question If you are able to classify a triangle as acute, right, or obtuse, what conclusions can you draw about the lengths of its sides?

Explore

1 Cut graph paper into squares with the following side lengths: 3, 4, 5, 6, 7, 8, 10, 12, and 13.

2 Create a triangle with side lengths $a = 3$, $b = 4$, and $c = 6$, as shown. Label the vertices A, B, and C, placing C opposite the longest side.

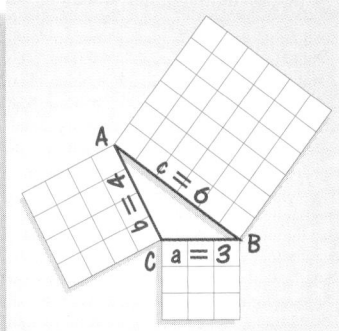

3 Using a protractor, classify the triangle as acute, right, or obtuse.

4 Repeat Steps 2 and 3 using the remaining squares. Create one triangle with side lengths $a = 5$, $b = 12$, $c = 13$ and one triangle with side lengths $a = 7$, $b = 8$, $c = 10$.

5 Compare the values of $a^2 + b^2$ with the values of c^2 for each of the three triangles. Then copy and complete the table below.

Type of triangle	Side lengths	$a^2 + b^2$	$<$, $>$, or $=$	c^2
obtuse	3, 4, 6	25	?	36
?	5, 12, 13	?	?	?
?	7, 8, 10	?	?	?

Think About It

In Exercises 1 and 2, *a*, *b*, and *c* are the lengths of the sides of a triangle, and *c* is the length of the longest side.

1. Repeat Steps 1–4 above with a number of different triangles. Be sure to include acute triangles, right triangles, and obtuse triangles.

2. Complete the following statements using $<$, $>$, or $=$ as conjectures based on your observations.

In an obtuse triangle, $a^2 + b^2$ **?** c^2.

In a right triangle, $a^2 + b^2$ **?** c^2. (Pythagorean theorem)

In an acute triangle, $a^2 + b^2$ **?** c^2.

Question Does the converse of the Pythagorean theorem hold true?

Explore

1 Select three of the graph paper squares and form a triangle. Label the vertices A, B, and C, placing C opposite the longest side. Two triangles are shown.

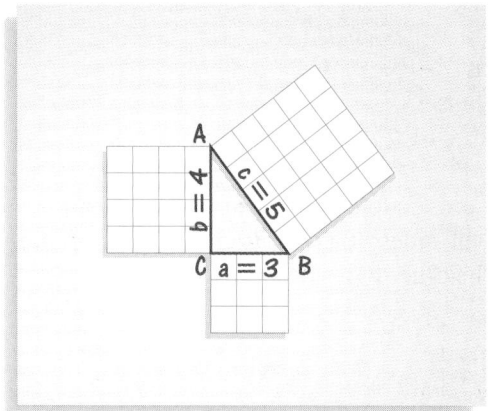
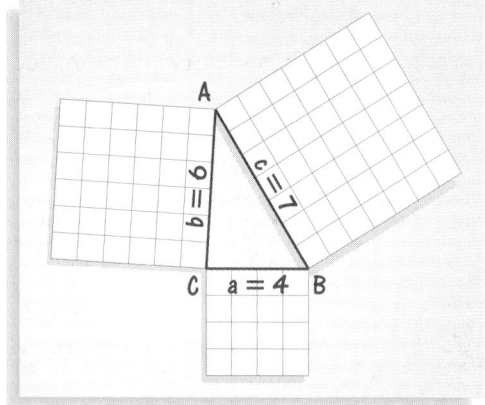

2 Compare the values of $a^2 + b^2$ with the values of c^2 for each triangle. Based on your answers in Exercise 2 on page 722, classify the triangle as acute, right, or obtuse. Then copy and complete the table below.

Side lengths	$a^2 + b^2$	<, >, or =	c^2	Type of triangle
3, 4, 5	25	=	25	?
4, 6, 7	52	>	49	?

Think About It

Let a, b, and c be the side lengths of a triangle with c the longest side.

1. Repeat Steps 1 and 2 above with a number of different triangles. Choose a variety of lengths so $a^2 + b^2 = c^2$ is sometimes true, and sometimes not.

2. Complete the following conjectures based on your observations.

If the sides of a triangle satisfy $a^2 + b^2 = c^2$, then the triangle is a __?__ triangle. (Converse of the Pythagorean theorem)

If the sides of a triangle satisfy $a^2 + b^2 < c^2$, then the triangle is a __?__ triangle.

If the sides of a triangle satisfy $a^2 + b^2 > c^2$, then the triangle is a __?__ triangle.

12.6 The Pythagorean Theorem and Its Converse

Goal

Use the Pythagorean theorem and its converse

Key Words

• theorem
• Pythagorean theorem
• hypotenuse
• legs of a right triangle
• converse

What is the distance from home plate to second base?

You will use the *Pythagorean theorem* in Exercise 31 to find the distance from home plate to second base of a standard baseball diamond.

A **theorem** is a statement that can be proven to be true. The **Pythagorean theorem** states a relationship among the sides of a right triangle. The **hypotenuse** is the side opposite the right angle. The other two sides are the **legs.**

THE PYTHAGOREAN THEOREM

If a triangle is a right triangle, then the sum of the squares of the lengths of the legs a and b equals the square of the length of the hypotenuse c.

$$a^2 + b^2 = c^2$$

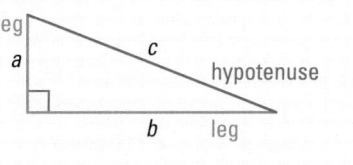

In Exercise 23 in Lesson 12.9, you will outline a proof of the Pythagorean theorem.

Student Help

▶ **STUDY TIP**
When you use the Pythagorean theorem to find the length of a side of a right triangle, you need only the positive square root because the length of a side cannot be negative.

EXAMPLE 1 Use the Pythagorean Theorem

a. Given $a = 6$ and $b = 8$, find c. Use the Pythagorean theorem: $a^2 + b^2 = c^2$.

$$6^2 + 8^2 = c^2$$
$$100 = c^2$$
$$\sqrt{100} = \sqrt{c^2}$$
$$10 = c$$

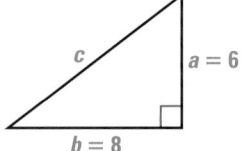

b. Given $a = 5$ and $c = 6$, find b. Use the Pythagorean theorem: $a^2 + b^2 = c^2$.

$$5^2 + b^2 = 6^2$$
$$b^2 = 6^2 - 5^2$$
$$b^2 = 11$$
$$b = \sqrt{11} \approx 3.32$$

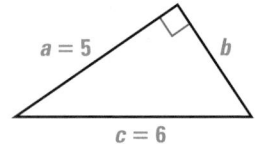

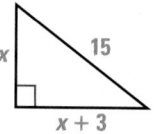
EXAMPLE 2 Use the Pythagorean Theorem

A right triangle has one leg that is 3 inches longer than the other leg. The hypotenuse is 15 inches. Find the unknown lengths.

Solution

Sketch a right triangle and label the sides. Let x be the length of the shorter leg. Use the Pythagorean theorem to solve for x.

$$a^2 + b^2 = c^2$$ Write Pythagorean theorem.

$$x^2 + (x + 3)^2 = 15^2$$ Substitute for a, b, and c.

$$x^2 + x^2 + 6x + 9 = 225$$ Simplify.

$$2x^2 + 6x - 216 = 0$$ Write in standard form.

$$2(x - 9)(x + 12) = 0$$ Factor.

$$x = 9 \quad or \quad x = -12$$ Zero-product property

ANSWER ▶ Length is positive, so the solution $x = -12$ is extraneous. The sides have lengths 9 inches and $9 + 3 = 12$ inches.

EXAMPLE 3 Use the Pythagorean Theorem

A board game is a square 2 feet by 2 feet. What is the length of the diagonal from one corner of the board game to the opposite corner?

Solution

The diagonal is the hypotenuse c of a right triangle. Each leg is 2 feet in length.

$$c^2 = a^2 + b^2$$ Write Pythagorean theorem.

$$c^2 = 2^2 + 2^2$$ Substitute 2 for a and 2 for b.

$$c^2 = 8$$ Simplify right side of the equation.

$$c = \sqrt{8} \approx 2.8$$ Find square root of each side.

ANSWER ▶ The length from one corner of the board game to the opposite corner is about 2.8 feet.

Checkpoint ✓ Use the Pythagorean Theorem

Find the hypotenuse of the right triangle with the given legs.

1. $a = 12, b = 5$ **2.** $a = 3, b = 4$ **3.** $a = 12, b = 16$

Solve for x to find the missing lengths of the right triangle.

4.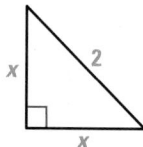

5.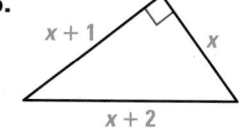

6.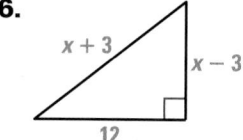

Student Help

▶**LOOK BACK**
For help with if-then
statements, see p. 120.

LOGICAL REASONING In mathematics an *if-then statement* is a statement of the form "If *p*, then *q*," where *p* is the *hypothesis* and *q* is the *conclusion*. The **converse** of the statement "If *p*, then *q*" is the related statement "If *q*, then *p*," in which the hypothesis and conclusion are interchanged.

In many cases, a theorem is true, but its converse is false. For example, the statement "If $a = b$, then $a^2 = b^2$" is true, while the converse "If $a^2 = b^2$, then $a = b$" is false. In the case of the Pythagorean theorem, however, both the theorem and its converse are true.

CONVERSE OF THE PYTHAGOREAN THEOREM

If a triangle has side lengths *a*, *b*, and *c* such that $a^2 + b^2 = c^2$, then the triangle is a right triangle.

Student Help

▶**STUDY TIP**
In a right triangle the
hypotenuse is always
the longest side.

EXAMPLE 4 **Determine Right Triangles**

Determine whether the given lengths are sides of a right triangle: 15, 20, 25.

Solution Use the converse of the Pythagorean theorem. The lengths are sides of a right triangle because

$$15^2 + 20^2 = 225 + 400 = 625 = 25^2.$$

EXAMPLE 5 **Use the Pythagorean Converse**

You can take a rope and tie 12 equally spaced knots in it. You can then use the rope to check that a corner is a right angle. Why does this method work?

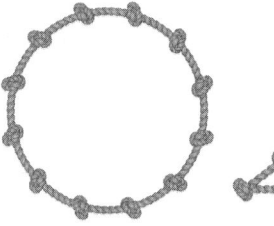 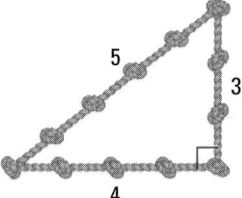

Solution

You can use the rope to form a triangle with longest side of length 5 and other sides of lengths 3 and 4. Check that

$$3^2 + 4^2 = 9 + 16 = 25 = 5^2.$$

Therefore, by the converse of the Pythagorean theorem, the triangle is a right triangle.

ANSWER ▶ Because you can use the knots to form the sides of a right triangle, one angle of the triangle must measure 90°. This is why you can check with a rope that a corner is a right angle.

 **Use the Pythagorean Converse**

Determine whether the given lengths are sides of a right triangle.

7. 5, 11, 12   **8.** 5, 12, 13   **9.** 11.9, 12, 16.9

12.6 Exercises

Guided Practice

Vocabulary Check

1. Complete: Sides of a right triangle that are not the hypotenuse are the __?__ .

2. State the hypothesis and the conclusion of the statement "If x is an even number, then x^2 is an even number."

Skill Check

Find the missing length of the right triangle if a and b are the lengths of the legs and c is the length of the hypotenuse.

3. $a = 7, b = 24$　　**4.** $a = 5, c = 13$　　**5.** $b = 15, c = 17$

6. $a = 9, c = 41$　　**7.** $b = 11, c = 61$　　**8.** $a = 12, b = 35$

Find each unknown length of the right triangle.

9.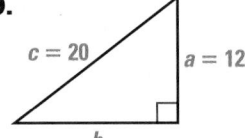

10.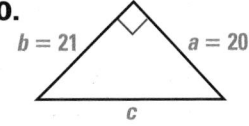

11.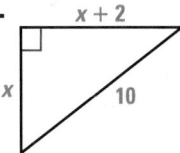

12. Explain how you can use the converse of the Pythagorean theorem to tell whether three given lengths can be sides of a right triangle.

Practice and Applications

USING THE PYTHAGOREAN THEOREM Find the missing length of the right triangle if a and b are the lengths of the legs and c is the length of the hypotenuse.

13. $a = 3, c = 4$　　**14.** $a = 10, b = 24$　　**15.** $b = 3, c = 7$

16. $b = 9, c = 16$　　**17.** $a = 5, c = 10$　　**18.** $a = 14, c = 21$

19. $a = 2, b = 8$　　**20.** $a = 11, b = 15$　　**21.** $b = 3, c = 10$

22. $b = 1, c = 3$　　**23.** $a = 4, c = 7$　　**24.** $a = 8, c = 10$

MISSING LENGTH Find the unknown lengths of the right triangle.

25.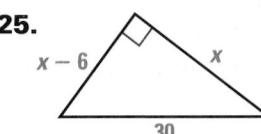

26.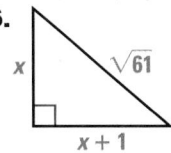

27.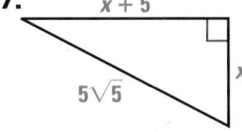

Student Help

▶ **HOMEWORK HELP**
Example 1: Exs. 13–24
Example 2: Exs. 25–30
Example 3: Exs. 31–35
Example 4: Exs. 36–41
Example 5: Exs. 42–44

28.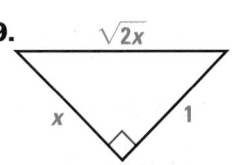

29.

30.

31. BASEBALL The length of each side of a baseball diamond is 90 feet. What is the diagonal distance c from home plate to second base?

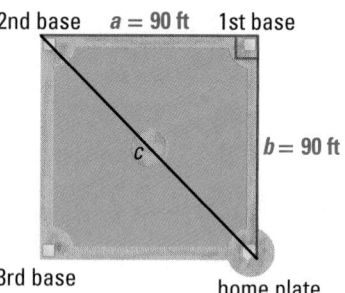

2nd base $a = 90$ ft   1st base

c

$b = 90$ ft

3rd base   home plate

32. DIAGONAL OF A FIELD A field hockey field is a rectangle 60 yards by 100 yards. What is the length of the diagonal from one corner of the field to the opposite corner?

Student Help

▶ **HOMEWORK HELP**

Extra help with problem solving in Exs. 33–34 is available at www.mcdougallittell.com

DESIGNING A STAIRCASE
You are building the staircase shown at the right.

33. Find the distance d between the edges of each step.

34. The staircase will also have a handrail that is as long as the distance between the edge of the first step and the edge of the top step. How long is the handrail?

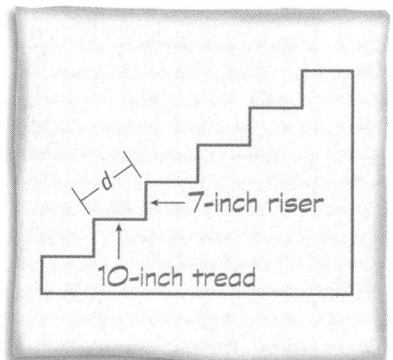

7-inch riser

d

10-inch tread

35. PLANTING A NEW TREE. You have just planted a new tree. To support the tree, you attach four guy wires from the trunk of the tree to stakes in the ground. Each guy wire has a length of 7 feet.

Suppose you put the stakes in the ground 5 feet from the base of the trunk. Approximately how far up the trunk should you attach the guy wires?

guy wire 7 ft

5 ft

DETERMINING RIGHT TRIANGLES Determine whether the given lengths are sides of a right triangle. Explain your reasoning.

36. 2, 10, 11   **37.** 5, 12, 13   **38.** 12, 16, 20

39. 11, 60, 61   **40.** 7, 24, 26   **41.** 3, 9, 10

DETERMINING RIGHT TRIANGLES Determine whether the given lengths are sides of a right triangle. Explain your reasoning.

42.
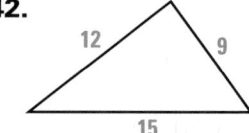
12   9
15

43.
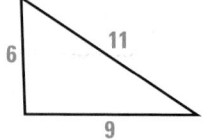
6   11
9

44.
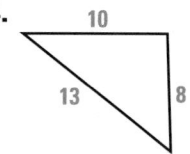
10
13   8

45. CHALLENGE You have a rope with 24 equally spaced knots in it. Form a triangle with the rope and give the length of each side. How can you use this rope to check that a corner is a right angle?

46. MULTIPLE CHOICE Given the lengths of the three sides of a triangle, determine which triangle is *not* a right triangle.

  (A) $a = 9, b = 40, c = 41$ (B) $a = 3, b = 4, c = 5$

  (C) $a = 7, b = 24, c = 25$ (D) $a = 10, b = 49, c = 50$

Mixed Review

PLOTTING POINTS **Plot and label the ordered pairs in a coordinate plane.** *(Lesson 4.1)*

47. $A(2, 5), B(0, -1), C(3, 1)$ **48.** $A(2, -5), B(2, 4), C(-3, 0)$

49. $A(-1, -2), B(-4, 5), C(0, 2)$ **50.** $A(1, 4), B(-2, -1), C(3, -1)$

NUMBER OF X-INTERCEPTS **Determine whether the graph of the function intersects the x-axis in *zero*, *one*, or *two* points.** *(Lesson 9.7)*

51. $y = x^2 + 2x + 15$ **52.** $y = x^2 + 8x + 12$ **53.** $y = x^2 + x - 10$

54. $y = x^2 + 8x + 16$ **55.** $y = x^2 + 3x + 1$ **56.** $y = x^2 - 8x - 11$

Maintaining Skills

ESTIMATING AREA **Estimate the area of a rectangle whose sides are given. First round each side length to the nearest whole number. Then multiply to find the area.** *(Skills Review p. 775)*

57. 5.1 by 7.2   **58.** 10.6 by 17.3   **59.** 5.1 by 9.9

60. 100.4 by 7.0   **61.** 17.3 by 2.8   **62.** 20.5 by 1.5

Quiz 2

Evaluate the radical expression using the properties of rational exponents. *(Lesson 12.4)*

  1. $2^{1/3} \cdot 2^{2/3}$ **2.** $(36 \cdot 49)^{1/2}$ **3.** $\left(3^{1/2}\right)^4$

Solve the quadratic equation by completing the square. *(Lesson 12.5)*

  4. $x^2 - 6x + 7 = 0$ **5.** $x^2 + 4x - 1 = 0$ **6.** $x^2 + 2x = 2$

Determine whether the given lengths are sides of a right triangle. Explain your reasoning. *(Lesson 12.6)*

  7. $6, 9, 11$ **8.** $12, 35, 37$ **9.** $1, 1, \sqrt{2}$

10. DEPTH OF A SUBMARINE
The sonar of a Navy cruiser detects a submarine that is 2500 feet away. The point on the water directly above the submarine is 1500 feet away from the front of the cruiser. What is the depth of the submarine? *(Lesson 12.6)*

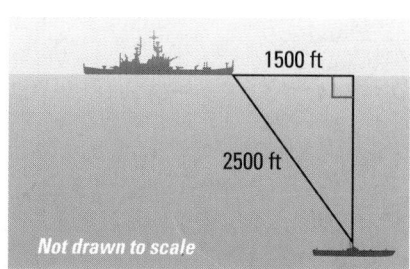

1500 ft

2500 ft

Not drawn to scale

12.7 The Distance Formula

Goal
Find the distance between two points in a coordinate plane.

Key Words
• distance formula

How far was the soccer ball kicked?

You can use the *distance formula* to find the distance between two points in a coordinate plane. In Example 3 you will find the distance that a soccer ball was kicked.

To find a general formula for the distance between two points $A(x_1, y_1)$ and $B(x_2, y_2)$, draw a right triangle as shown at the right. Using the Pythagorean theorem, you can write the equation

$$(x_2 - x_1)^2 + (y_2 - y_1)^2 = d^2.$$

Solving the equation for d leads to the following **distance formula**.

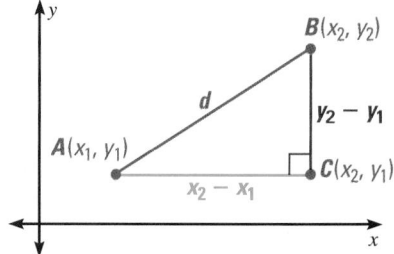

THE DISTANCE FORMULA

The distance d between the points (x_1, y_1) and (x_2, y_2) is

$$d = \sqrt{(x_2 - x_1)^2 + (y_2 - y_1)^2}.$$

EXAMPLE 1 Find the Distance Between Two Points

Use the distance formula to find the distance between $(1, 4)$ and $(-2, 3)$.

$$d = \sqrt{(x_2 - x_1)^2 + (y_2 - y_1)^2} \qquad \text{Write distance formula.}$$

$$= \sqrt{(-2 - 1)^2 + (3 - 4)^2} \qquad \text{Substitute.}$$

$$= \sqrt{(-3)^2 + (-1)^2} \qquad \text{Simplify.}$$

$$= \sqrt{9 + 1} \qquad \text{Evaluate powers.}$$

$$= \sqrt{10} \qquad \text{Add.}$$

$$\approx 3.16 \qquad \text{Use a calculator.}$$

Find the distance between the points. Round your solution to the nearest hundredth if necessary.

1. $(2, 5), (0, 4)$ **2.** $(-3, 2), (2, -2)$

3. $(8, 0), (0, 6)$ **4.** $(-4, 2), (-1, 3)$

Student Help

▶ **VOCABULARY TIP**
Vertices is the plural of *vertex*. A triangle has three vertices.

EXAMPLE **2** **Check a Right Triangle**

Determine whether the points $(3, 2), (2, 0),$ and $(-1, 4)$ are vertices of a right triangle.

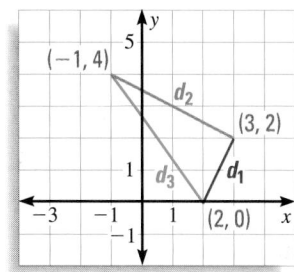

Solution

Use the distance formula to find the lengths of the three sides.

$$d_1 = \sqrt{(3 - 2)^2 + (2 - 0)^2} = \sqrt{1^2 + 2^2} = \sqrt{1 + 4} = \sqrt{5}$$

$$d_2 = \sqrt{[3 - (-1)]^2 + (2 - 4)^2} = \sqrt{4^2 + (-2)^2} = \sqrt{16 + 4} = \sqrt{20}$$

$$d_3 = \sqrt{[2 - (-1)]^2 + (0 - 4)^2} = \sqrt{3^2 + (-4)^2} = \sqrt{9 + 16} = \sqrt{25}$$

Next find the sum of the squares of the lengths of the two shorter sides.

$$d_1^2 + d_2^2 = (\sqrt{5})^2 + (\sqrt{20})^2 \qquad \text{Substitute for } d_1 \text{ and } d_2.$$

$$= 5 + 20 \qquad\qquad\qquad \text{Simplify.}$$

$$= 25 \qquad\qquad\qquad\qquad \text{Add.}$$

The sum of the squares of the lengths of the two shorter sides is 25, which is equal to the square of the length of the longest side, $(\sqrt{25})^2$.

ANSWER ▶ By the converse of the Pythagorean theorem, the given points are vertices of a right triangle.

Determine whether the points are the vertices of a right triangle.

5.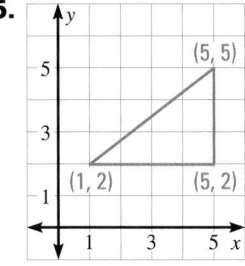

6.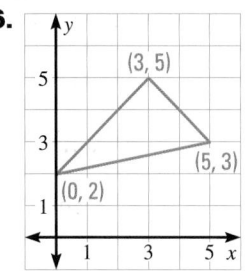

7.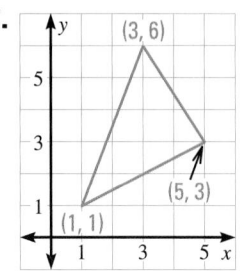

DRAW A DIAGRAM To use the distance formula to find a distance in a real-life problem, the first step is to draw a diagram with coordinate axes and assign coordinates to the points. This process is called *superimposing* a coordinate system on the diagram.

EXAMPLE **3** **Apply the Distance Formula**

SOCCER A player kicks a soccer ball from a position that is 10 yards from a sideline and 5 yards from a goal line. The ball lands 45 yards from the same goal line and 40 yards from the same sideline. How far was the ball kicked?

Solution

Begin by superimposing a coordinate system on the soccer field as below. Assuming the kicker is left of the goalie, the ball is kicked from the point (10, 5) and lands at the point (40, 45). Use the distance formula.

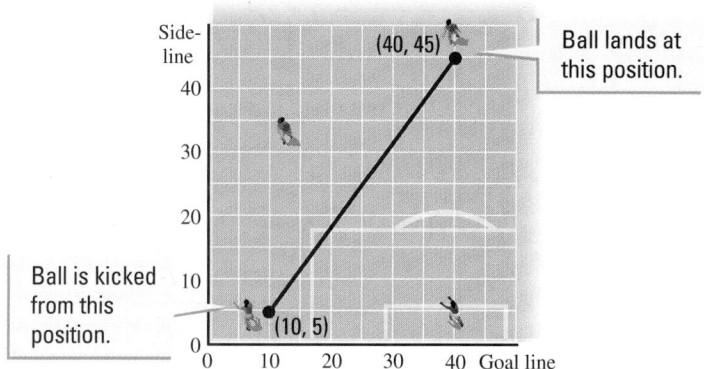

$$d = \sqrt{(x_2 - x_1)^2 + (y_2 - y_1)^2}$$ Write the distance formula.

$$= \sqrt{(40 - 10)^2 + (45 - 5)^2}$$ Substitute.

$$= \sqrt{30^2 + 40^2}$$ Simplify.

$$= \sqrt{900 + 1600}$$ Evaluate powers.

$$= \sqrt{2500}$$ Add.

$$= 50$$ Find the square root.

ANSWER ▶ The ball was kicked 50 yards.

Checkpoint ✓ **Apply the Distance Formula**

8. A player kicks a football from a position that is 15 yards from a sideline and 25 yards from a goal line. The ball lands at a position that is 30 yards from the same sideline and 65 yards from the same goal line. Find the distance that the ball was kicked.

12.7 Exercises

Guided Practice

Vocabulary Check

1. The distance formula is related to which theorem?

Skill Check

Use the coordinate plane to estimate the distance between the two points. Then use the distance formula to find the distance between the points. Round your solution to the nearest hundredth.

2. (1, 5), (−3, 1)   **3.** (−3, −2), (4, 1)   **4.** (5, −2), (−1,1)

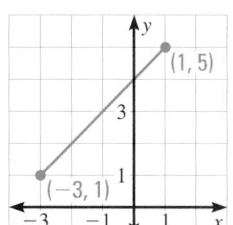   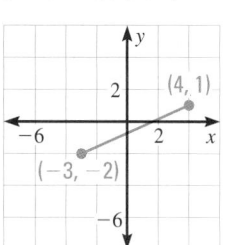   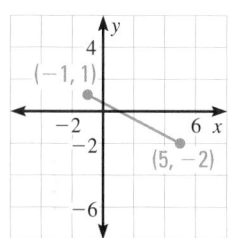

Determine whether the points are vertices of a right triangle.

5. (0, 0), (20, 0), (20, 21)   **6.** (4, 0), (4, −4), (10, −4)

7. (−2, 0), (−1, 0), (1, 7)   **8.** (2, 0), (−2, 2), (−3, −5)

9. SOCCER Suppose the soccer ball in Example 3 on page 732 lands in a position that is 25 yards from the same goal line and 25 yards from the same sideline. How far was the ball kicked?

Practice and Applications

FINDING DISTANCE **Find the distance between the two points. Round your solution to the nearest hundredth if necessary.**

10. (2, 0), (8, −3)   **11.** (2, −8), (−3, 3)   **12.** (3, −2), (0, 3)

13. (5, 8), (−2, 3)   **14.** (−3, 1), (2, 6)   **15.** (−6, −2), (−3, −5)

16. (4, 5), (−1, 3)   **17.** (−6, 1), (3, 1)   **18.** (−2, −1), (3, −3)

19. (7, 12), (−7, −4)   **20.** (2, 1), (8, 4)   **21.** (2, 1), (−4, 16)

22. (−1, 9), (0, 7)   **23.** (4, 11), (−5, 2)   **24.** (−10, −2), (1, 7)

RIGHT TRIANGLES **Graph the points. Determine whether they are vertices of a right triangle.**

25. (4, 0), (2, 1), (−1, −5)   **26.** (5, 4), (2, 1), (−3, 2)

27. (1, −5), (2, 3), (−3, 4)   **28.** (−1, 1), (−3, 3), (−7, −1)

29. (−3, 2), (−3, 5), (0, 2)   **30.** (3, −1), (2, 4), (−3, 0)

Student Help

▶**HOMEWORK HELP**
  Example 1: Exs. 10–24
  Example 2: Exs. 25–30
  Example 3: Exs. 31–37

In Exercises 31 and 32, use the diagram at the right.

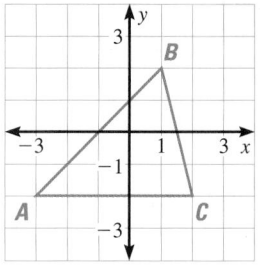

31. Copy the diagram of triangle *ABC* on graph paper. Find the length of each side of the triangle.

32. Find the perimeter of triangle *ABC* to the nearest hundredth.

Puzzler **In Exercises 33 and 34, use the following information.**

You are planning a family vacation. Each side of a square in the coordinate plane that is superimposed on the map represents 50 miles.

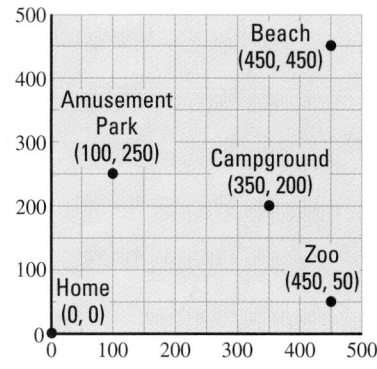

33. How far is it from your home to the amusement park?

34. You leave your home and go to the amusement park. After visiting the amusement park, you go to the beach. You return home. How far did you travel?

Link to
Careers

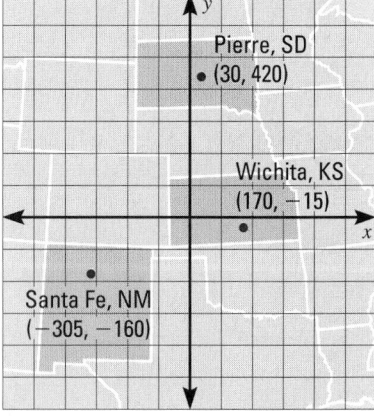

MAPS **In Exercises 35–37, use the map. Each side of a square in the coordinate plane that is superimposed on the map represents 95 miles. The points represent city locations.**

35. Use the distance formula to estimate the distance between Pierre, South Dakota, and Santa Fe, New Mexico.

36. Use the distance formula to estimate the distance between Wichita, Kansas, and Santa Fe, New Mexico.

37. Use the distance formula to estimate the distance between Pierre, South Dakota, and Wichita, Kansas.

CARTOGRAPHERS prepare maps using information from surveys, aerial photographs, and satellite data.

More about cartographers at www.mcdougallittell.com

CHALLENGE **In Exercises 38 and 39, use the distance formula to find the perimeter of the geometric figure.**

38.

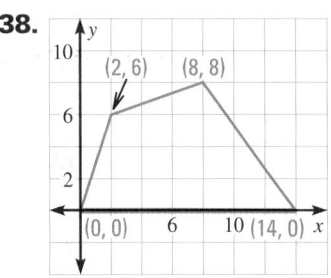

39.

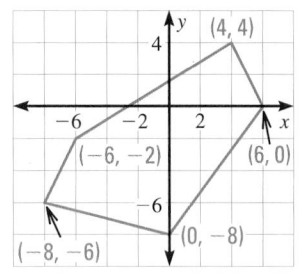

40. MULTIPLE CHOICE What is the distance between $(-6, -2)$ and $(2, 4)$?

    Ⓐ $2\sqrt{5}$ Ⓑ $2\sqrt{7}$ Ⓒ 10 Ⓓ 28

41. MULTIPLE CHOICE The vertices of a right triangle are $(0, 0)$, $(0, 6)$, and $(6, 0)$. What is the length of the hypotenuse?

    Ⓕ 6 Ⓖ $6\sqrt{2}$ Ⓗ 36 Ⓙ 72

Mixed Review

FACTORING Factor the expression. *(Lesson 10.7)*

42. $m^2 - 25$ **43.** $81x^2 - 144$ **44.** $16t^2 - 49$

45. $x^2 + 12x + 36$ **46.** $c^2 - 22c + 121$ **47.** $9s^2 + 6s + 1$

48. $4n^2 - 64$ **49.** $72 - 50p^2$ **50.** $60y^2 - 240$

FACTORING COMPLETELY Factor the expression completely. *(Lesson 10.8)*

51. $3y^3 + 15y^2 - 18y$ **52.** $2t^3 - 98t$

53. $2x^4 - 8x^2$ **54.** $c^3 + 2c^2 - 8c - 16$

SIMPLIFYING EXPRESSIONS Simplify the expression. *(Lesson 11.3)*

55. $\dfrac{4x}{28}$ **56.** $\dfrac{15x}{75}$ **57.** $\dfrac{-48x^3}{-12x^2}$

58. $\dfrac{18x^3}{56x^7}$ **59.** $\dfrac{-3x^2 + 21x}{12x^2}$ **60.** $\dfrac{35x - 7x^3}{49x}$

DIVIDING POLYNOMIALS Find the quotient. *(Lesson 11.3)*

61. Divide $(-4x^2 - 24x)$ by $-4x$.   **62.** Divide $(7p^5 + 18p^4)$ by p^4.

63. Divide $(9a^2 - 27a - 36)$ by $(a + 1)$.   **64.** Divide $(4n^2 - 41n + 45)$ by $(4n - 5)$.

ADDING RATIONAL EXPRESSIONS Simplify the expression. *(Lessons 11.5, 11.6)*

65. $\dfrac{3}{x} + \dfrac{x + 9}{x}$ **66.** $\dfrac{8}{4a + 1} + \dfrac{5}{4a + 1}$ **67.** $\dfrac{2}{2x} + \dfrac{12}{x}$

68. $\dfrac{2x}{x + 1} + \dfrac{5}{x + 3}$ **69.** $\dfrac{5}{4x} + \dfrac{7}{3x}$ **70.** $\dfrac{6x}{x + 1} + \dfrac{2x + 4}{x + 1}$

Maintaining Skills

FRACTIONS AND PERCENTS Write the fraction as a percent. *(Skills Review p. 769)*

71. $\dfrac{2}{5}$ **72.** $\dfrac{4}{5}$ **73.** $\dfrac{1}{3}$ **74.** $\dfrac{9}{10}$

75. $\dfrac{5}{8}$ **76.** $\dfrac{11}{20}$ **77.** $\dfrac{4}{100}$ **78.** $\dfrac{9}{25}$

12.8 The Midpoint Formula

Goal
Find the midpoint of a line segment in a coordinate plane.

Key Words
• midpoint
• midpoint formula

How are computer games designed?

You can use the *midpoint formula* to find the midpoint of a line segment in a coordinate plane. In Example 3 you will locate the midpoint as part of designing a computer game.

The **midpoint** of a line segment is the point on the segment that is equidistant from its endpoints.

Student Help

▶**STUDY TIP**
Midpoint can be thought of as an average.

THE MIDPOINT FORMULA

The midpoint between (x_1, y_1) and (x_2, y_2) is $\left(\dfrac{x_1 + x_2}{2}, \dfrac{y_1 + y_2}{2} \right)$.

EXAMPLE 1 Find the Midpoint

Find the midpoint of the line segment connecting the points $(-2, 3)$ and $(4, 2)$. Use a graph to explain the result.

Solution
Let $(-2, 3) = (x_1, y_1)$ and $(4, 2) = (x_2, y_2)$.

$$\left(\frac{x_1 + x_2}{2}, \frac{y_1 + y_2}{2} \right) = \left(\frac{-2 + 4}{2}, \frac{3 + 2}{2} \right) = \left(\frac{2}{2}, \frac{5}{2} \right) = \left(1, \frac{5}{2} \right)$$

ANSWER ▶ The midpoint is $\left(1, \dfrac{5}{2} \right)$.

From the graph, you can see that the point $\left(1, \dfrac{5}{2} \right)$ appears to be halfway between $(-2, 3)$ and $(4, 2)$. In Example 2 you will use the distance formula to check a midpoint.

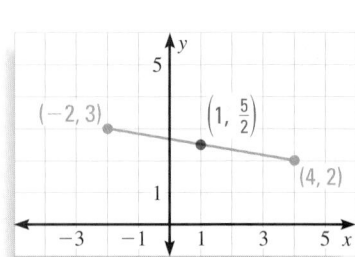

Checkpoint ✓ Find the Midpoint

Find the midpoint of the line segment connecting the given points.

1. $(-2, 3), (4, 1)$ **2.** $(2, 5), (2, -1)$ **3.** $(0, 0), (4, 6)$ **4.** $(1, 2), (2, -2)$

You can use the distance formula to check that the distances from the midpoint to each given point are equal.

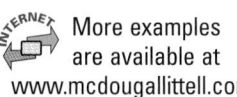
EXAMPLE 2 Check a Midpoint

Use the distance formula to check the midpoint in Example 1.

Solution

The distance between $\left(1, \frac{5}{2}\right)$ and $(-2, 3)$ is

$$d_1 = \sqrt{(-2-1)^2 + \left(3 - \frac{5}{2}\right)^2} = \sqrt{(-3)^2 + \left(\frac{1}{2}\right)^2} = \sqrt{9 + \frac{1}{4}} = \sqrt{\frac{37}{4}} = \frac{\sqrt{37}}{2}.$$

The distance between $\left(1, \frac{5}{2}\right)$ and $(4, 2)$ is

$$d_2 = \sqrt{(4-1)^2 + \left(2 - \frac{5}{2}\right)^2} = \sqrt{(3)^2 + \left(-\frac{1}{2}\right)^2} = \sqrt{9 + \frac{1}{4}} = \sqrt{\frac{37}{4}} = \frac{\sqrt{37}}{2}.$$

ANSWER ▶ The distances from $\left(1, \frac{5}{2}\right)$ to the ends of the segment are equal.

Link to
Careers

SOFTWARE ENGINEERS design and develop computer programs that are used to perform desired tasks. These programs are referred to as computer software.

EXAMPLE 3 Apply the Midpoint Formula

COMPUTERS You are using software to design a computer game. You want to place a buried treasure chest halfway between the points corresponding to a palm tree and a boulder. Where should you place the treasure chest?

Solution

The palm tree is located at (200, 75). The boulder is at (25, 175). Use the midpoint formula to find the halfway point between the two landmarks.

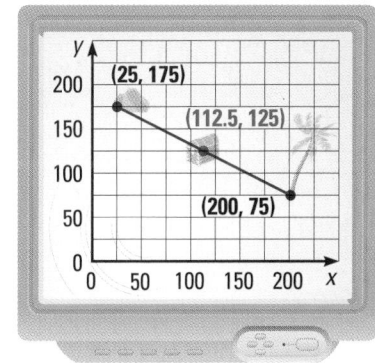

$$\left(\frac{x_1 + x_2}{2}, \frac{y_1 + y_2}{2}\right) = \left(\frac{25 + 200}{2}, \frac{175 + 75}{2}\right)$$

$$= \left(\frac{225}{2}, \frac{250}{2}\right)$$

$$= (112.5, 125)$$

ANSWER ▶ You should place the treasure chest at (112.5, 125).

Checkpoint ✓ Apply the Midpoint Formula

5. In the computer video game in Example 3, you want to place another buried treasure halfway between the boulder and the treasure chest. What are the coordinates of the point?

12.8 Exercises

Guided Practice

Vocabulary Check

1. What is meant by the *midpoint* of a line segment?

2. Give two methods for checking the midpoint of a line segment.

Skill Check

Find the midpoint of the line segment with the given endpoints.

3. $(4, 4), (-1, 2)$ **4.** $(6, 2), (2, -3)$ **5.** $(-5, 3), (-3, -3)$

6. $(-4, 4), (2, 0)$ **7.** $(0, 0), (0, 10)$ **8.** $(2, 1), (14, 6)$

Find the midpoint of the line segment with the given endpoints. Then show that the midpoint is the same distance from each given point.

9. $(-2, 0), (6, 2)$ **10.** $(-2, 2) (2, -10)$ **11.** $(2, 6), (4, 2)$

12. $(-6, 0), (-10, -2)$ **13.** $(-3, 6), (1, 8)$ **14.** $(0, 0), (-8, 12)$

Practice and Applications

FINDING THE MIDPOINT **Find the midpoint of the line segment connecting the given points.**

15. $(1, 2), (5, 4)$ **16.** $(0, 0), (0, 8)$ **17.** $(-1, 2), (7, 4)$

18. $(0, -3), (-4, 2)$ **19.** $(-3, 3), (2, -2)$ **20.** $(5, -5), (-5, 1)$

21. $(-1, 1), (-4, -4)$ **22.** $(-4, 0), (-1, -5)$ **23.** $(-4, -3), (-1, -5)$

CHECKING A MIDPOINT **Find the midpoint of the line segment connecting the given points. Then show that the midpoint is the same distance from each point.**

24. $(7, -3), (-1, -9)$ **25.** $(1, 2), (0, 0)$ **26.** $(3, 0), (-5, 4)$

27. $(5, 1), (1, -5)$ **28.** $(2, 7), (4, 3)$ **29.** $(-3, -2), (1, 7)$

30. $(-3, -3), (6, 7)$ **31.** $(-9, 17), (5, -7)$ **32.** $(-4, -2), (10, -6)$

Geometry Link **In Exercises 33 and 34, use the diagram below.**

33. Find the midpoint of each side of the triangle.

34. Join the midpoints to form a new triangle. Find the length of each of its sides.

Student Help

▶ **HOMEWORK HELP**
Example 1: Exs. 15–23
Example 2: Exs. 24–32
Example 3: Exs. 33–37

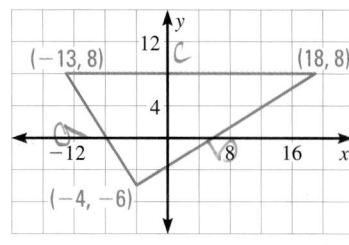

35. **History Link** Pony Express stations were 10 to 15 miles apart. The latitude-longitude coordinates of 2 former stations in Nevada are (40.0° N, 115.5° W) and (39.9° N, 115.2° W). These stations were about 22 miles apart. Find the coordinates of the station halfway between them.

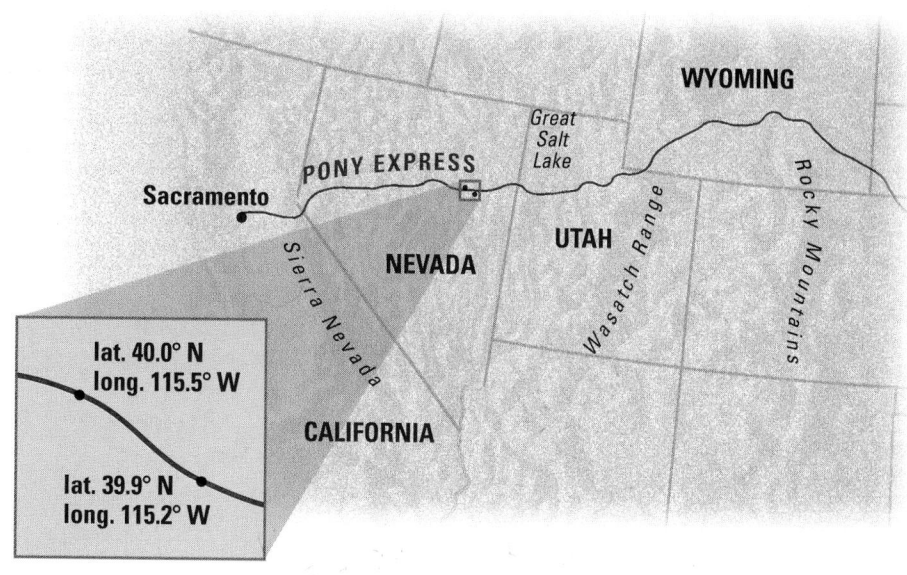

HIKING TRIP **In Exercises 36 and 37, use the following information.**
You and a friend go hiking. You hike 3 miles north and 2 miles west. Starting from the same point, your friend hikes 4 miles east and 1 mile south.

36. At the end of the hike how far apart are you and your friend? *HINT:* Draw a diagram on a grid.

37. If you and your friend want to meet for lunch, where could you meet so that both of you hike the same distance? How far do you have to hike?

38. MULTIPLE CHOICE What is the midpoint between $(-2, -3)$ and $(1, 7)$?

Ⓒ $\left(\frac{1}{2}, -2\right)$ Ⓑ $\left(-\frac{1}{2}, 2\right)$ Ⓔ $\left(\frac{1}{2}, 2\right)$ Ⓕ $\left(-\frac{1}{2}, 5\right)$

ARRANGING LIKE TERMS **Use linear combinations to solve the linear system. Then check your solution.** *(Lesson 7.3)*

39. $4x + 3y = 1$
$2x - 3y = 1$

40. $3x + 5y = 6$
$-4x + 2y = 5$

41. $2x + 3y = 1$
$5x - 4y = 14$

INTERPRETING ALGEBRAIC RESULTS **Use the substitution method or linear combinations to solve the linear system and tell how many solutions the system has.** *(Lesson 7.5)*

42. $2x + y = 3$
$4x + 2y = 8$

43. $2x + 2y = 3$
$4x + 2y = 6$

44. $2x + y = -4$
$y + 2x = 8$

COMPARING FRACTIONS, DECIMALS, AND PERCENTS **Complete the statement using <, >, or =.** *(Skills Review pp. 768–771)*

45. 54% ? 0.54 **46.** $\frac{2}{3}$? $6\frac{2}{3}\%$ **47.** $\frac{3}{1000}$? 0.03 **48.** 0.23 ? $\frac{23}{100}$

 # Logical Reasoning: Proof

Goal
Use logical reasoning and proof to prove that a statement is true or false.

Key Words
- postulate
- axiom
- theorem
- indirect proof
- counterexample

How can a lawyer prove that a client is not guilty?

Often lawyers use logical reasoning to defend a client in court. In Example 4 you will use logical reasoning to prove your client's innocence.

LOGICAL REASONING Mathematics is believed to have begun with practical "rules of thumb" that were developed to deal with real-life problems. Then, about 2500 years ago, Greek geometers (specialists in geometry) developed a different approach to mathematics. Starting with a handful of properties that they believed to be true, they insisted on logical reasoning as the basis for developing more elaborate mathematical tools, or *theorems*.

AXIOMS The properties that mathematicians accept without proof are called **postulates** or **axioms**. Many of the rules discussed in Chapter 2 fall in this category. The following is a summary of the rules that underlie algebra.

THE BASIC AXIOMS OF ALGEBRA

Let a, b, and c be real numbers.

Axioms of Addition and Multiplication

CLOSURE:	$a + b$ is a real number	ab is a real number
COMMUTATIVE:	$a + b = b + a$	$ab = ba$
ASSOCIATIVE:	$(a + b) + c = a + (b + c)$	$(ab)c = a(bc)$
IDENTITY:	$a + 0 = a, 0 + a = a$	$a(1) = a, 1(a) = a$
INVERSE:	$a + (-a) = 0$	$a\left(\dfrac{1}{a}\right) = 1, a \neq 0$

Axiom Relating Addition and Multiplication

DISTRIBUTIVE:	$a(b + c) = ab + ac$	$(a + b)c = ac + bc$

Axioms of Equality

ADDITION:	If $a = b$, then $a + c = b + c$.
MULTIPLICATION:	If $a = b$, then $ac = bc$.
SUBSTITUTION:	If $a = b$, then a can be substituted for b.

DEFINITIONS In order to formulate the axioms and postulates of mathematics, one needs a vocabulary of terms such as *number*, *equal*, *addition*, *point*, and *line*. Aside from their role in formulating axioms, these terms can also be used to define other terms. For example, *whole number* and *addition* are used to define *integer* and *subtraction*. Definitions do not need to be proved.

THEOREMS Recall that a theorem is a statement that can be proven to be true. All proposed theorems have to be proved. For instance, you can use the basic axioms to prove the theorem that for all real numbers b and c, $c(-b) = -cb$. Once a theorem is proved, it can be used as a reason in proofs of other theorems.

Student Help

▶ STUDY TIP
When you are proving a theorem, every step must be justified by an axiom, a definition, given information, or a previously proved theorem.

EXAMPLE 1 **Prove a Theorem**

Use the subtraction property, $a - b = a + (-b)$, to prove the following theorem: $c(a - b) = ca - cb$.

Solution

$c(a - b) = c[a + (-b)]$	Subtraction property
$= ca + c(-b)$	Distributive property
$= ca + (-cb)$	Theorem stated above
$= ca - cb$	Subtraction property

Checkpoint ✓ **Prove a Theorem**

1. Use the associative and commutative properties to prove the following theorem.

If a, b, *and* c *are real numbers, then* (a + b) + c = (b + c) + a.

CONJECTURES A **conjecture** is a statement that is thought to be true but has not yet been proved. Conjectures are often based on observations.

EXAMPLE 2 **Goldbach's Conjecture**

Christian Goldbach (1690–1764) thought the following statement might be true. It is now referred to as *Goldbach's Conjecture*.

Every even integer, except 2, is equal to the sum of two prime numbers.

The following list shows that every even number between 4 and 26 is equal to the sum of two prime numbers. Does this list prove Goldbach's Conjecture?

$4 = 2 + 2$	$6 = 3 + 3$	$8 = 3 + 5$	$10 = 3 + 7$
$12 = 5 + 7$	$14 = 3 + 11$	$16 = 3 + 13$	$18 = 5 + 13$
$20 = 3 + 17$	$22 = 3 + 19$	$24 = 5 + 19$	$26 = 3 + 23$

Solution

This list of examples *does not* prove the conjecture. No number of examples can prove that the rule is true for *every* even integer greater than 2. (At the time this book was published, no one had been able to prove or disprove Goldbach's Conjecture.)

COUNTEREXAMPLES Sometimes a person makes a general statement they suppose to be true. To show that a general statement is false, you need only one *counterexample*.

EXAMPLE 3 Find a Counterexample

Show that the statement below is false by finding a counterexample.

For all numbers a and b, a + (−b) = (−a) + b.

Solution The statement claims that $a + (-b) = (-a) + b$ for all values of a and b. If we let $a = 1$ and $b = 2$, we find $a + (-b) = 1 + (-2) = -1$, but $(-a) + b = (-1) + 2 = 1$. Since $-1 \neq 1$, the counterexample $a = 1$ and $b = 2$ shows that the general statement proposed above is false.

INDIRECT PROOF In this lesson you have used direct proofs to prove that statements are true and counterexamples to prove that statements are false.

Another type of proof is **indirect proof**. To prove a statement indirectly, assume that the statement is false. If this assumption leads to an impossibility, then you have proved that the original statement is true. An indirect proof is also called a *proof by contradiction*.

Link to
Careers

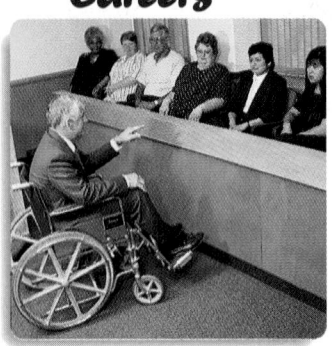

LAWYERS represent people in criminal and civil trials by presenting evidence supporting their client's case. They also give advice on legal matters.

INTERNET More about lawyers is available at www.mcdougallittell.com

EXAMPLE 4 Use of Contradiction in Real Life

LAWYERS You are a lawyer defending a client accused of violating a law on the north side of town at 10:00 A.M. on March 22. You argue that if guilty, your client must have been there at that time. You have a video of your client being interviewed by a TV reporter on the south side of town at the same time.

You argue that it would be impossible for your client to be in two different places at the same time on March 22. Therefore your client cannot be guilty.

EXAMPLE 5 Use an Indirect Proof

Use an indirect proof to prove the following statement.

If a is a positive integer and a² is divisible by 2, then a is divisible by 2.

Solution Suppose the statement is false. Then there exists a positive integer a such that a^2 is divisible by 2, but a is not divisible by 2. If so, a is odd and can be written as $a = 2n + 1$.

$a = 2n + 1$	Definition of odd integer
$a^2 = 4n^2 + 4n + 1$	Apply FOIL to $(2n + 1)(2n + 1)$.
$a^2 = 2(2n^2 + 2n) + 1$	Distributive property
a^2 is odd	Definition of odd integer

The proof contradicts the assumption, thereby showing a is divisible by 2.

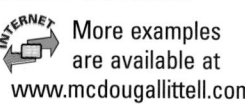
EXAMPLE 6 **Use an Indirect Proof**

Use an indirect proof to prove that $\sqrt{2}$ is an irrational number.

Solution

If you assume that $\sqrt{2}$ is *not* an irrational number, then $\sqrt{2}$ is rational and can be written as the quotient of two integers a and b that have no common factors other than 1.

$$\sqrt{2} = \frac{a}{b} \qquad \text{Assume } \sqrt{2} \text{ is a rational number.}$$

$$2 = \frac{a^2}{b^2} \qquad \text{Square each side.}$$

$$2b^2 = a^2 \qquad \text{Multiply each side by } b^2.$$

This implies that 2 is a factor of a^2. Therefore 2 is also a factor of a. Thus a can be written as $2c$.

$$2b^2 = (2c)^2 \qquad \text{Substitute } 2c \text{ for } a.$$

$$2b^2 = 4c^2 \qquad \text{Simplify.}$$

$$b^2 = 2c^2 \qquad \text{Divide each side by 2.}$$

This implies that 2 is a factor of b^2 and also a factor of b. So 2 is a factor of both a and b. But this is impossible because a and b have no common factors other than 1. Therefore it is impossible that $\sqrt{2}$ is a rational number. So you can conclude that $\sqrt{2}$ must be an irrational number.

 **Use of Contradiction in Real Life**

2. You are defending a client who is accused of violating a law near her home at 9:00 A.M. on June 5. Your client's boss and coworkers testify that she arrived at work at 9:15 A.M. on June 5. It takes your client 45 minutes to commute from her house to work. Construct an argument to prove that your client is *not* guilty.

12.9 Exercises

Guided Practice

Vocabulary Check

1. Explain the difference between an *axiom* and a *theorem*.

2. What is the first step in an indirect proof?

Skill Check

In Exercises 3–8, state the basic axiom of algebra that is represented.

3. $y(1) = y$

4. $2x + 3 = 3 + 2x$

5. $5(x + y) = 5x + 5y$

6. $(4x)y = 4(xy)$

7. $y + 0 = y$

8. $x + (-x) = 0$

Practice and Applications

9. STATING REASONS Copy and complete the proof of the statement:

For all real numbers a *and* b, $(a + b) - b = a$.

$$(a + b) - b = (a + b) + (-b) \qquad \text{Definition of subtraction}$$
$$= a + [b + (-b)] \qquad \text{Associative property of addition}$$
$$= a + 0 \qquad\qquad\qquad \underline{\quad ? \quad}$$
$$= a \qquad\qquad\qquad\quad \underline{\quad ? \quad}$$

PROVING THEOREMS **In Exercises 10 and 11, prove the theorem. Use the basic axioms of algebra and the definition of subtraction given in Example 1.**

10. If a and b are real numbers, then $a - b = -b + a$.

11. If a, b, and c are real numbers, then $(a - b)c = ac - bc$.

12. MAKING A CONJECTURE A student proposes the following conjecture:

The sum of the first n *odd integers is* n^2.

She gives four examples: $1 = 1^2$, $1 + 3 = 4 = 2^2$, $1 + 3 + 5 = 9 = 3^2$, and $1 + 3 + 5 + 7 = 16 = 4^2$. Do the examples prove her conjecture? Explain. Do you think the conjecture is true?

FINDING A COUNTEREXAMPLE **In Exercises 13–16, find a counterexample to show that the statement is *not* true.**

13. If a and b are real numbers, then $(a + b)^2 = a^2 + b^2$.

14. If a, b, and c are nonzero real numbers, then $(a \div b) \div c = a \div (b \div c)$. (*Note*: The counterexample shows that the associative property does not hold for division.)

15. If a and b are integers, then $a \div b$ is an integer.

16. If $a > 4$, then $\sqrt{a}$ is not rational.

17. THE FOUR-COLOR PROBLEM

A famous theorem states that any map can be colored with four different colors so that no two countries that share a border have the same color. No matter how the map shown at the right is colored with three different colors, at least two countries having a common border will have the same color. Does this map serve as a counterexample to the following statement? Explain.

Any map can be colored with three different colors so that no two countries that share a border have the same color.

18. **Geometry Link** Explain how the diagrams below can be used to give a geometrical argument to support the conjecture in Exercise 12 on page 744.

INDIRECT PROOF In Exercises 19–21, use an indirect proof to prove that the conclusion is true.

19. Your bus leaves a track meet at 4:30 P.M. and does not travel faster than 60 miles per hour. The meet is 45 miles from home. Your bus will not get you home in time for dinner at 5:00 P.M.

20. If $a < b$, then $a + c < b + c$.

21. If $ac > bc$ and $c > 0$, then $a > b$.

22. **PROOF USING THE MIDPOINT** Let D represent the midpoint between B and C, as shown at the right. Prove that for any right triangle, the midpoint of its hypotenuse is equidistant from the three vertices of the triangle. In order to prove this, you must first find the distance between B and C. Using the distance formula, you get $BC = \sqrt{x^2 + y^2}$, so BD and CD must be $\frac{1}{2}\sqrt{x^2 + y^2}$.

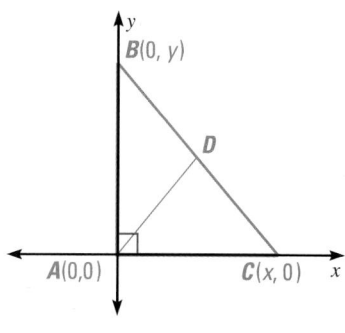

HINT: Use the distance formula to find the distance between A and D.

23. **CHALLENGE** Explain how the following diagrams could be used to give a geometrical proof of the Pythagorean theorem.

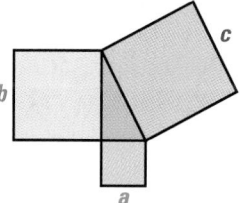 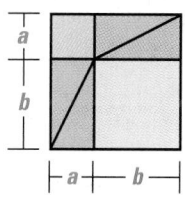 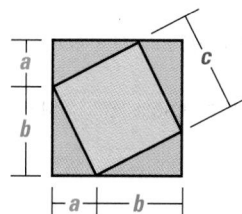

Standardized Test Practice

24. **MULTIPLE CHOICE** What is the first step to prove the following theorem: *If* a *and* b *are real numbers and* $(x + a) = b$, *then* $x = b - a$.

(A) $x + (a - a) = b - a$

(B) $x = b - a$

(C) $(x + a) - a = b - a$

(D) $x + 0 = b - a$

25. **MULTIPLE CHOICE** Which represents the distributive property?

(F) $(4x)y = 4(xy)$

(G) $z(1) = z$

(H) $4(x + 1) = 4x + 4$

(J) $y + 0 = y$

PERCENTS **Solve the percent problem.** *(Lesson 3.9)*

26. How much is 15% of $15?   **27.** 100 is 1% of what number?

28. 6 is what percent of 3?   **29.** 5 is 25% of what number?

USING THE DISCRIMINANT Determine whether the equation has *two solutions, one solution,* or *no real solution.* *(Lesson 9.7)*

30. $x^2 - 2x + 4 = 0$ **31.** $2x^2 + 4x - 2 = 0$ **32.** $8x^2 - 8x + 2 = 0$

33. $x^2 - 14x + 49 = 0$ **34.** $3x^2 - 5x + 1 = 0$ **35.** $6x^2 - x + 5 = 0$

SOLUTIONS Determine whether the ordered pair is a solution of the inequality. *(Lesson 9.8)*

36. $y > x^2 - 2x - 5$, $(1, 1)$ **37.** $y \geq 2x^2 - 8x + 8$, $(3, -2)$

38. $y \leq 2x^2 - 3x + 10$, $(-2, 20)$ **39.** $y \geq 4x^2 - 48x + 61$, $(1, 17)$

OPERATIONS WITH FRACTIONS Evaluate the expression. Write the answer as a fraction or as a mixed number in simplest form. *(Skills Review pp. 764–765)*

40. $\frac{2}{3} \cdot \frac{2}{5} + \frac{1}{5}$ **41.** $\frac{2}{7} \div \frac{1}{14} - \frac{5}{4}$ **42.** $\frac{11}{2}\left(\frac{1}{10} - \frac{1}{4}\right)$

43. $\frac{5}{3} - \left(\frac{2}{9} \cdot \frac{3}{4} + \frac{7}{12}\right)$ **44.** $\frac{1}{2} + \frac{2}{3} - \frac{3}{4} \cdot \frac{4}{5}$ **45.** $\left(\frac{3}{8} - \frac{2}{3}\right) \div \frac{1}{3}$

Quiz 3

Use the distance formula to determine whether the points are the vertices of a right triangle. *(Lesson 12.7)*

1. 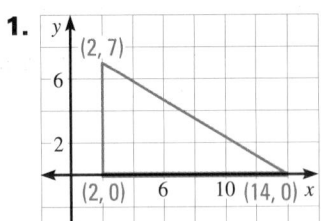   **2.**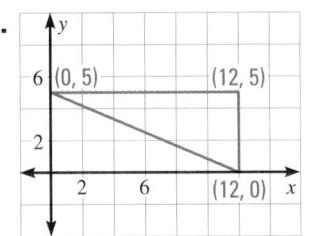

Find the distance between the two points. Round your solution to the nearest hundredth if necessary. Then find the midpoint of the line segment connecting the two given points. *(Lessons 12.7, 12.8)*

3. $(1, 3), (7, -9)$ **4.** $(2, -5), (6, -11)$ **5.** $(0, 0), (8, -14)$

6. $(-8, -8), (-8, 8)$ **7.** $(3, 4), (-3, 4)$ **8.** $(1, 7), (-4, -2)$

Find a counterexample to show that the statement is *not* true. *(Lesson 12.9)*

9. If a, b, and c are real numbers and $a < b$, then $ac < bc$.

10. If a and b are real numbers, then $-(a + b) = (-a) - (-b)$.

Chapter Summary and Review

12.1   FUNCTIONS INVOLVING SQUARE ROOTS

Examples on pp. 692–694

EXAMPLE   To sketch the graph of $y = \sqrt{x} - 1$, note that the rule is defined for all nonnegative numbers. Make a table of values, plot the points, and connect them with a smooth curve. The range is all numbers greater than or equal to -1.

x	y
0	$y = \sqrt{0} - 1 = -1$
1	$y = \sqrt{1} - 1 = 0$
2	$y = \sqrt{2} - 1 \approx .41$
3	$y = \sqrt{3} - 1 \approx .73$
4	$y = \sqrt{4} - 1 = 1$

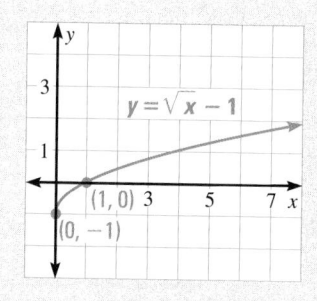

Find the domain of the function. Then sketch its graph and find the range.

1. $y = 11\sqrt{x}$

2. $y = 2\sqrt{x} - 5$

3. $y = \sqrt{x} + 3$

12.2   OPERATIONS WITH RADICAL EXPRESSIONS

Examples on pp. 698–700

EXAMPLE   You can use radical operations and the distributive property to simplify radical expressions.

$$4\sqrt{20} - 3\sqrt{5} = 4\sqrt{\mathbf{4 \cdot 5}} - 3\sqrt{5} \qquad \text{Perfect square factor}$$

$$= 4\sqrt{\mathbf{2 \cdot 2}} \cdot \sqrt{5} - 3\sqrt{5} \qquad \text{Product property}$$

$$= 8\sqrt{5} - 3\sqrt{5} \qquad \text{Simplify.}$$

$$= 5\sqrt{5} \qquad \text{Subtract like radicals.}$$

Simplify the expression.

4. $6\sqrt{2} - \sqrt{2}$

5. $\sqrt{5} + \sqrt{20} - \sqrt{3}$

6. $(3 - \sqrt{10})(3 + \sqrt{10})$

7. $\sqrt{6}(2\sqrt{3} - 4\sqrt{2})$

8. $\dfrac{21}{\sqrt{3}}$

9. $\dfrac{8}{6 - \sqrt{7}}$

12.3 SOLVING RADICAL EQUATIONS

Examples on pp. 704–706

EXAMPLE Solve $\sqrt{3x - 2} = x$.

❶ **Square** both sides of the equation. $\qquad (\sqrt{3x - 2})^2 = x^2$

❷ **Simplify** the left side of the equation. $\qquad 3x - 2 = x^2$

❸ **Write** in standard form. $\qquad 0 = x^2 - 3x + 2$

❹ **Factor** the quadratic equation. $\qquad 0 = (x - 2)(x - 1)$

❺ **Solve** for x. $\qquad x = 2 \quad or \quad x = 1$

CHECK ✓ Substitute 2 and 1 in the original equation.

$\sqrt{3(2) - 2} \stackrel{?}{=} 2 \qquad\qquad \sqrt{3(1) - 2} \stackrel{?}{=} 1$

$2 = 2 \checkmark \qquad\qquad\qquad 1 = 1 \checkmark$

ANSWER ▶ The solutions are 2 *and* 1.

Solve the equation. Check for extraneous solutions.

10. $2\sqrt{x} - 4 = 0$

11. $\sqrt{-4x - 4} = x$

12. $\sqrt{x - 3} + 2 = 8$

13. $\sqrt{x - 1} = 5$

14. $8\sqrt{x} - 16 = 0$

15. $\sqrt{5x + 36} = x$

12.4 RATIONAL EXPONENTS

Examples on pp. 710–712

EXAMPLE Simplify the expression $(x^2 \cdot x^{1/2} \cdot y)^2$.

❶ **Use** the product of powers property. $\qquad (x^2 \cdot x^{1/2} \cdot y)^2 = (x^{5/2} \cdot y)^2$

❷ **Use** the power of a product property. $\qquad = x^{(5/2 \cdot 2)} \cdot y^2$

❸ **Simplify** by multiplying exponents. $\qquad = x^5 y^2$

Evaluate the expression without using a calculator.

16. $27^{2/3}$

17. $(\sqrt[3]{64})^2$

18. $121^{3/2}$

19. $(\sqrt{4})^4$

Simplify the expression.

20. $5^{1/3} \cdot 5^{5/3}$

21. $(4 \cdot 121)^{1/2}$

22. $(125^{2/3})^{1/2}$

12.5 COMPLETING THE SQUARE

Examples on pp. 716–718

> **EXAMPLE** Solve $x^2 - 6x - 1 = 6$ by completing the square.
>
> $x^2 - 6x = 7$ Isolate x^2-term and x-term.
>
> $x^2 - 6x + 9 = 7 + 9$ Add $\left(\dfrac{-6}{2}\right)^2 = 9$ to each side.
>
> $(x - 3)^2 = 16$ Write left side as perfect square.
>
> $x - 3 = \pm 4$ Find square root of each side.
>
> $x = 7$ *or* $x = -1$ Solve for x.

Solve the equation by completing the square.

23. $x^2 - 4x - 1 = 7$ **24.** $x^2 + 20x + 19 = 0$ **25.** $x^2 - 16x + 8 = 0$

Choose a method and solve the quadratic equation. Explain your choice.

26. $4x^2 + 8x + 8 = 0$ **27.** $x^2 - x - 3 = 0$ **28.** $3x^2 - x + 2 = 0$

12.6 PYTHAGOREAN THEOREM AND ITS CONVERSE

Examples on pp. 724–726

> **EXAMPLE** Given $a = 6$ and $c = 12$, find b.
>
> ❶ **Write** the Pythagorean theorem. $a^2 + b^2 = c^2$
>
> ❷ **Substitute** 6 for a and 12 for c. $6^2 + b^2 = 12^2$
>
> ❸ **Subtract** 6^2 from each side and simplify. $b^2 = 108$
>
> ❹ **Find** square root of each side. $b = 6\sqrt{3}$
>
>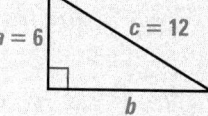

Find the missing length of the right triangle.

29. 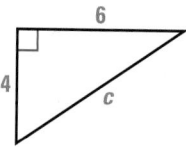   **30.** 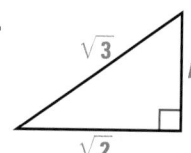   **31.**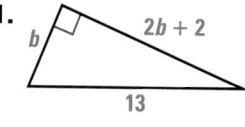

Determine whether the given lengths are sides of a right triangle. Explain your reasoning.

32. 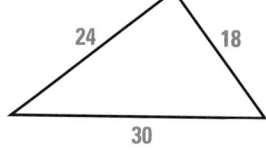   **33.** 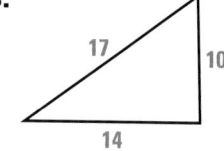   **34.**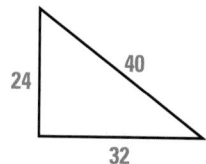

12.7–12.8 THE DISTANCE AND MIDPOINT FORMULAS

Examples on pp. 730–732, 736–737

EXAMPLE Find the distance d and the midpoint m between $(-6, -2)$ and $(4, 3)$.

$$d = \sqrt{(x_2 - x_1)^2 + (y_2 - y_1)^2}$$

$$= \sqrt{[4 - (-6)]^2 + [3 - (-2)]^2}$$

$$= \sqrt{10^2 + 5^2}$$

$$= \sqrt{125}$$

$$= 5\sqrt{5}$$

$$m = \left(\frac{x_1 + x_2}{2}, \frac{y_1 + y_2}{2}\right)$$

$$= \left(\frac{-6 + 4}{2}, \frac{-2 + 3}{2}\right)$$

$$= \left(-1, \frac{1}{2}\right)$$

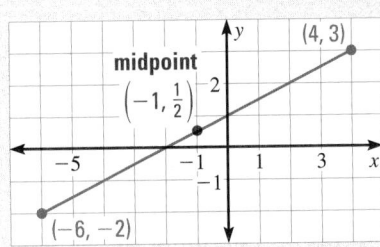

Find the distance between the two points. Round to the nearest hundredth.

35. $(8, 5)$ and $(11, -4)$
36. $(-3, 6)$ and $(1, 7)$
37. $(-2, -2)$ and $(2, 8)$

38. Use the distance formula to decide whether the points $(-4, 1)$, $(0, -2)$, and $(-4, -2)$ are the vertices of a right triangle.

Find the midpoint of the line segment connecting the given points. Use a graph to check the result.

39. $(-1, -3)$ and $(5, 1)$
40. $(0, 4)$ and $(-2, 4)$
41. $(9, -5)$ and $(-10, -8)$

12.9 LOGICAL REASONING: PROOF

Examples on pp. 740–743

EXAMPLE Prove that for all numbers a and b, $(a + b) - b = a$.

$(a + b) - b = (a + b) + (-b)$	Definition of subtraction
$= a + [b + (-b)]$	Associative property of addition
$= a + 0$	Inverse property of addition
$= a$	Identity property of addition

42. Which basic axiom of algebra is represented by $\left(\frac{2}{3}\right)\left(\frac{4}{5}\right) = \left(\frac{4}{5}\right)\left(\frac{2}{3}\right)$?

43. Prove that $(c)(-b) = -cb$ for all real numbers c and b.

Find the domain of the function. Then sketch its graph and find the range of the function.

1. $y = 12\sqrt{x}$ **2.** $y = \sqrt{2x + 7}$ **3.** $y = \sqrt{3x} - 3$ **4.** $y = \sqrt{x - 5}$

Simplify the expression.

5. $3\sqrt{2} - \sqrt{2}$ **6.** $(4 + \sqrt{7})(4 - \sqrt{7})$ **7.** $\dfrac{4}{\sqrt{10}}$ **8.** $\dfrac{8}{3 - \sqrt{5}}$

9. $\dfrac{1}{\sqrt{6}}$ **10.** $\dfrac{\sqrt{11}}{2 - \sqrt{11}}$ **11.** $(8 - \sqrt{5})(8 + \sqrt{5})$ **12.** $\sqrt{3}(\sqrt{12} + 4)$

Solve the equation. Check for extraneous solutions.

13. $\sqrt{y} + 6 = 10$ **14.** $\sqrt{2m + 3} - 6 = 4$ **15.** $n = \sqrt{9n - 18}$ **16.** $p = \sqrt{-3p + 18}$

Simplify the variable expression using the rules for rational exponents.

17. $x^{1/2} \cdot x^{3/2}$ **18.** $\sqrt{25x^3}$ **19.** $\left(x^{1/3}\right)^2 \cdot \sqrt{y}$ **20.** $\left(x^2 \cdot x^{1/3}\right)^{3/2}$

Solve the equation by completing the square.

21. $x^2 - 6x = -5$ **22.** $x^2 - 2x = 2$ **23.** $x^2 + 16x - 1 = 0$

Find the missing length of the right triangle if a and b are the lengths of the legs and c is the length of the hypotenuse.

24. $a = 7, b = 24$ **25.** $a = 5, c = 13$ **26.** $b = 15, c = 17$

27. $a = 30, b = 40$ **28.** $a = 6, c = 10$ **29.** $b = 12, c = 15$

Determine whether the given lengths are sides of a right triangle. Explain your reasoning.

30.
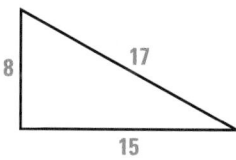

31.
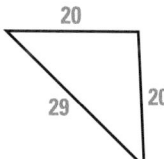

32.
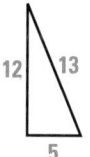

In Exercises 33–35, use the diagram shown at the right.

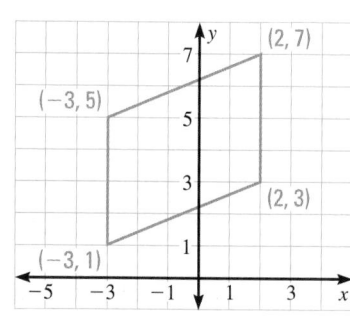

33. Use the distance formula to find the length of each side of the parallelogram.

34. Use your answers from Exercise 33 to find the perimeter of the parallelogram.

35. Find the coordinates of the midpoint of each side of the parallelogram.

36. Prove that if a, b, and c are real numbers and $a + c = b + c$, then $a = b$.

 **Test Tip** Learn as much as you can about a test ahead of time, such as the types of questions and the topics that the test will cover.

1. What is the value of $y = \dfrac{x\sqrt{x^2 - 1}}{x^2 + 8}$ when $x = 8$?

ⓐ $\dfrac{3\sqrt{7}}{16}$ ⓑ $\dfrac{7}{8}$

ⓒ $\dfrac{\sqrt{7}}{3}$ ⓓ $\dfrac{8}{9}$

2. What is the range of the function $y = \sqrt{x} + 7$?

ⓐ All positive real numbers

ⓑ All real numbers

ⓒ All real numbers greater than or equal to 7

ⓓ All real numbers less than 7

3. Which of the following is the value of the expression $5\sqrt{7} + \sqrt{448} + \sqrt{175} - \sqrt{63}$?

ⓐ $15\sqrt{7}$ ⓑ $16\sqrt{7}$

ⓒ $18\sqrt{7}$ ⓓ $20\sqrt{7}$

4. Which of the following is the simplest form of $\dfrac{2}{3 - \sqrt{6}}$?

ⓐ $\dfrac{6 + \sqrt{12}}{3}$ ⓑ $\dfrac{6 + 2\sqrt{6}}{3}$

ⓒ $\dfrac{6 + 2\sqrt{6}}{15}$ ⓓ $\dfrac{6 + \sqrt{12}}{15}$

5. Which of the following is a solution of the equation $x = \sqrt{880 - 18x}$?

ⓐ -22 ⓑ 0

ⓒ 22 ⓓ 40

6. Which of the following is the simplest form of $(xy^{1/3}x^{2/3})^3$?

ⓐ x^6y ⓑ $x^6y^{1/9}$

ⓒ x^5y ⓓ $x^5y^{10/3}$

7. What term should you add to $x^2 - 18x$ to create a perfect square trinomial?

ⓐ -36 ⓑ -9

ⓒ 9 ⓓ 81

8. What is the length of the missing side of the triangle?

ⓐ 10 ⓑ 11

ⓒ 12 ⓓ 13

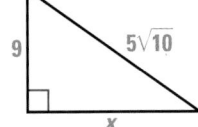

9. What is the distance between points P and Q?

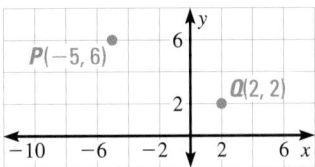

ⓐ $\sqrt{33}$ ⓑ $\sqrt{65}$

ⓒ $\sqrt{73}$ ⓓ $\sqrt{113}$

10. Use the graph in Exercise 9. Find the midpoint of the line segment connecting the points P and Q.

ⓐ $\left(\dfrac{-3}{2}, 4\right)$ ⓑ $\left(\dfrac{-7}{2}, 2\right)$

ⓒ $\left(\dfrac{-3}{2}, 2\right)$ ⓓ $\left(\dfrac{-7}{2}, 4\right)$

11. Choose the missing reason in the following proof that for all real numbers a and b, $-(a + b) = (-a) + (-b)$.

STATEMENTS

1. a and b are real numbers

2. $-(a + b) = (-1)(a + b)$

3. $ = (-1)a + (-1)b$

4. $ = (-a) + (-b)$

REASONS

1. Given

2. Multiplication property of -1

3. _____?_____

4. Multiplicative property of -1

(A) Definition of subtraction

(B) Associative property of addition

(C) Inverse property of addition

(D) Distributive property

(E) None of these

12. Which graph best represents the function $y = 3\sqrt{x} - 2$?

(A)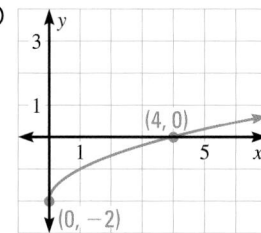

(B)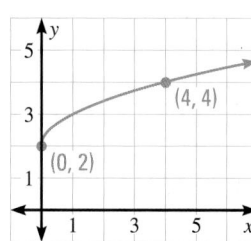

(C)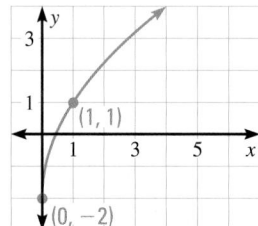

(D)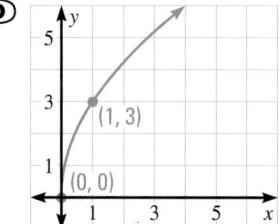

13. Which of the following triangles *is* a right triangle?

(A)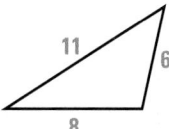

(B)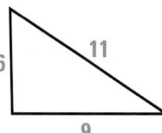

(C)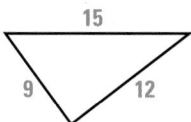

(D)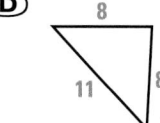

Write the sentence as an equation or an inequality. Then use mental math to solve the equation or the inequality. (1.4–1.5)

1. The quotient of m and 7 is greater than or equal to 16.

2. The sum of 4 and the second power of b is equal to 104.

3. The distance t you travel by train is 3 times the distance d you live from the train station. You drive 3 miles to get from your house to the train station.

Evaluate the expression for the given value of the variable. (2.2–2.6, 2.8)

4. $3 + x + (-4)$ when $x = 5$ **5.** $2x + 12 - 5$ when $x = 9$ **6.** $3.5 - (-x)$ when $x = 1.5$

7. $-(-3)^2(x)$ when $x = 7$ **8.** $6x(x + 2)$ when $x = 2$ **9.** $(8x + 1)(-3)$ when $x = 1$

10. $\frac{1}{4}\left|(x)(x)(-x)\right|$ when $x = 4$ **11.** $\frac{x^2 + 4}{6}$ when $x = 8$ **12.** $(-5)\left(-\frac{3}{4}x\right)$ when $x = 6$

Solve the equation. Round your solution to the nearest hundredth. (3.1–3.4, 3.6)

13. $-\frac{2}{9}(x - 5) = 12$ **14.** $7x - (3x - 2) = 38$ **15.** $\frac{1}{3}x + 7 = -7x - 5$

16. $8(x + 3) - 2x = 4(x - 8)$ **17.** $11 + 6.23x = 7 + 5.51x$ **18.** $-3(2.9 - 4.1x) = 9.2x + 6$

In Exercises 19 and 20, use the graph. (4.7, 5.3, 5.6)

19. Write an equation of a line passing through the point $(2, -2)$ and parallel to the line shown.

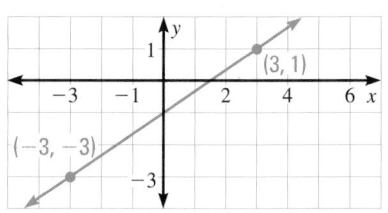

20. Write an equation of a line passing through the point $(-4, 2)$ and perpendicular to the line shown. Graph the equation in the same coordinate plane to check your answer.

Determine whether the relation is a function. If it is a function, give the domain and the range. (4.8)

21.

Input	Output
-1	-1
1	-1
3	1
5	3

22.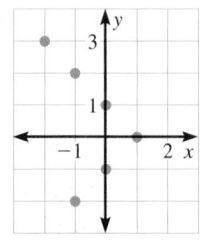

23.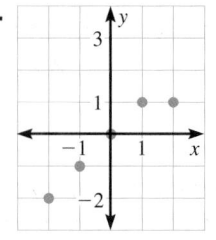

24.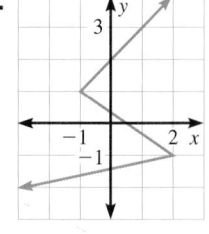

Write in standard form the equation of the line described below. (5.1–5.2)

25. Slope $= \frac{4}{5}$, y-intercept $= -3$ **26.** $(-1, 2)$, $m = \frac{1}{3}$

Solve the inequality. Then graph the solution. (6.3–6.5)

27. $-3 < -4x + 9 \le 14$ **28.** $|3x + 16| + 2 < 10$ **29.** $3x - 4 > 5$ or $5x + 1 < 11$

Solve the linear system. (7.2–7.3)

30. $4y = 8x + 16$
$\quad\;\; 2y = 11x - 7$

31. $-2x + 3y = 15$
$\quad\;\; 10x - 11y = 9$

32. $y = 5x - 2$
$\quad\;\; 3x + 7y = 5$

Simplify. Then evaluate the expression when $a = 1$ and $b = 2$. (8.1–8.2, 8.4)

33. $\dfrac{b^8}{b^2}$ **34.** $3a^4 \cdot a^{-3}$ **35.** $(-a^3)(2b^2)^3$

36. $4b^3 \cdot (2 + b)^2$ **37.** $\dfrac{4a^{-3}b^3}{ab^{-2}}$ **38.** $\dfrac{(5ab^2)^{-2}}{a^{-3}b}$

Determine whether the equation has *two solutions*, *one solution*, or *no real solution*. Then solve the equation. (9.2, 9.6–9.7, 10.5)

39. $6x^2 + 8 = 34$ **40.** $4x^2 - 9x + 5 = 0$ **41.** $3x^2 + 6x + 3 = 0$

Completely factor the expression. (10.5–10.7)

42. $x^2 + 6x + 8$ **43.** $x^2 - 24x - 112$ **44.** $3x^2 + 17x - 6$

45. $4x^2 + 12x + 9$ **46.** $x^2 + 10x + 25$ **47.** $x^2 - 14x + 49$

Solve the equation. (10.4–10.8)

48. $(3x + 1)(2x + 7) = 0$ **49.** $6x^2 - x - 7 = 8$ **50.** $x^2 - 4x + 4 = 0$

51. $4x^2 + 16x + 16 = 0$ **52.** $x^3 + 5x^2 - 4x - 20 = 0$ **53.** $x^4 + 9x^3 + 18x^2 = 0$

Simplify the expression. (11.3–11.7)

54. $\dfrac{4x}{12x^2}$ **55.** $\dfrac{2x + 6}{x^2 - 9}$ **56.** $\dfrac{3x}{x^2 - 2x - 24} \cdot \dfrac{x - 6}{6x^2 + 9x}$

57. $\dfrac{x^2 - 6x + 8}{x^2 - 2x} \div (3x - 12)$ **58.** $\dfrac{4}{x + 2} + \dfrac{15x}{3x + 6}$ **59.** $\dfrac{3x}{x + 4} - \dfrac{x}{x - 1}$

Simplify the expression. (12.2)

60. $4\sqrt{7} + 3\sqrt{7}$ **61.** $9\sqrt{2} - 12\sqrt{8}$ **62.** $\sqrt{6}(5\sqrt{3} + 6)$ **63.** $\dfrac{11}{7 - \sqrt{3}}$

Solve the equation by completing the square. (12.5)

64. $x^2 + 24x = -3$ **65.** $x^2 - 12x = 19$ **66.** $x^2 + 20x = -7$

67. $x^2 - 6x - 13 = 0$ **68.** $x^2 + 16x - 1 = 0$ **69.** $x^2 + 22x + 5 = 0$

Find the distance between the two points. Round your solution to the nearest hundredth if necessary. Then find the midpoint of the line segment connecting the two points. (12.7–12.8)

70. $(3, 0), (-5, 4)$ **71.** $(2, 7), (4, 3)$ **72.** $(5, 1), (1, -5)$ **73.** $(6, 2), (-2, -3)$

74. $(-1, 2), (6, 9)$ **75.** $(0, 4), (10, 11)$ **76.** $(-5, -7), (5, 7)$ **77.** $(1, -1), (3, 10)$

Investigating the Golden Ratio

Materials
- graph paper
- metric ruler
- graphing calculator (optional)

OBJECTIVE Explore what the golden ratio is and how it is used.

Over the centuries, the *golden rectangle* has fascinated artists, architects, and mathematicians. For example, the golden rectangle was used in the original design of the Parthenon in Athens, Greece. A **golden rectangle** has the special shape such that when a square is cut from one end, the ratio of length to width of the remaining rectangle is equal to the ratio of length to width of the original rectangle.

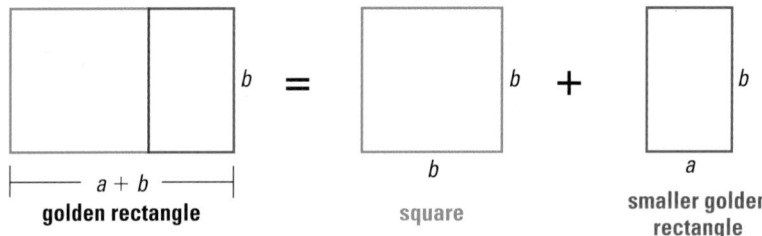

golden rectangle   square   smaller golden rectangle

INVESTIGATING THE GOLDEN RATIO

Before the pediment on top of the Parthenon in Athens was destroyed, the front of the building fit almost exactly into a golden rectangle.

From the picture, the large rectangle has a ratio of length to width $\frac{a + b}{b}$, while the small **b-by-a** rectangle that remains after cutting off the **b-by-b** square has a ratio of length to width $\frac{b}{a}$. For a golden rectangle, the ratio of length to width of the large rectangle is equal to the ratio of the small rectangle. In other words,

$$\frac{a + b}{b} = \frac{b}{a}.$$

Let $r = \frac{b}{a}$ represent the ratio of length to width of a golden rectangle. This ratio r is called the golden ratio. To derive the exact value of r, rewrite the equality above.

$\frac{a}{b} + 1 = \frac{b}{a}$	Rewrite $\frac{a + b}{b}$ as $\frac{a}{b} + 1$.
$\frac{1}{r} + 1 = r$	Substitute r for $\frac{b}{a}$.
$1 + r = r^2$	Multiply each side by r.
$r^2 - r - 1 = 0$	Write equation in standard form.
$r = \frac{1 + \sqrt{5}}{2}$ or $r = \frac{1 - \sqrt{5}}{2}$	Use quadratic equation to solve for r.

Since $r > 0$, the golden ratio r is given by $r = \frac{1 + \sqrt{5}}{2}$, or about 1.618034.

CONSTRUCTING GOLDEN RECTANGLES

❶ On graph paper, draw a **1-by-1** square.

❷ On one side of the square add another **1-by-1** square.

❸ Build a **2-by-2** square on the longest side of the 1-by-2 rectangle.

❹ Build a **3-by-3** square on the longest side of the 3-by-2 rectangle.

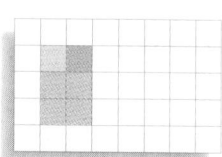 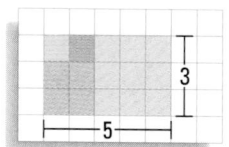

None of the rectangles in Steps 1–4 are golden rectangles. It is *not* possible to construct a golden rectangle with integer side lengths. However, it *is* possible to construct rectangles with integer side lengths whose ratios of length to width are very close to the golden ratio.

1. Continue the pattern from Steps 1–4 to draw the next four rectangles.

2. Copy and complete the table. If necessary, round to four decimal places.

length b	3	5	8	13	21	34
width a	2	3	5	8	13	21
$\dfrac{b}{a}$	1.5	1.6667	?	?	?	?

3. How do the ratios in your table compare to the golden ratio?

PRESENTING THE RESULTS

Write a report or make a poster to present your results. Include a sketch of a golden rectangle and include your answers to Exercises 1–3. Then describe what you learned about the golden ratio and the golden rectangle.

EXTENDING THE PROJECT

- The average chicken egg fits inside a golden rectangle. Measure the lengths and widths of six eggs and find the approximate ratio of length to width for each. Then find the average of these ratios.

- Find some rectangular objects that you think may have a length to width ratio close to the golden ratio. Measure them to see if they approximate golden rectangles. You might try a picture frame, a $1 bill, or a TV screen.

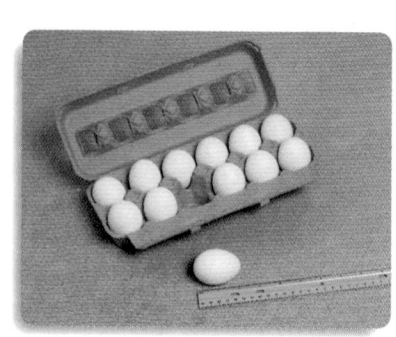

Contents of Student Resources

DECIMALS

To add and subtract decimals, you can use a vertical format. When you do this, line up the decimal places. Use zeros as placeholders as needed to help keep the decimal places aligned correctly. The steps are similar to those used for adding and subtracting whole numbers.

EXAMPLE Add 3.7 + 0.77 + 9.

SOLUTION Write the addition problem in vertical form. Line up the decimal points. Use zeros as placeholders.

$$\begin{array}{r} 3.70 \\ 0.77 \\ +\ 9.00 \\ \hline 13.47 \end{array}$$

ANSWER ▶ $3.7 + 0.77 + 9 = 13.47$

EXAMPLE Subtract 21.32 − 18.78.

SOLUTION Write the subtraction problem in vertical form. Line up the decimal points.

$$\begin{array}{r} 21.32 \\ -\ 18.78 \\ \hline 2.54 \end{array}$$

ANSWER ▶ $21.32 - 18.78 = 2.54$

Decimal multiplication is similar to multiplication with whole numbers. When multiplying decimals, you need to know where to put the decimal point in the product. The number of decimal places in the product is equal to the sum of the number of decimal places in the factors.

EXAMPLE Multiply 6.84 × 5.3.

SOLUTION Write the multiplication problem in vertical form. When multiplying decimals, you do not need to line up the decimal points.

$$\begin{array}{r} 6.84 \\ \times\ 5.3 \\ \hline 2052 \\ 34200 \\ \hline 36.252 \end{array}$$

6.84 two decimal places
× 5.3 one decimal place

36.252 three decimal places

ANSWER ▶ $6.84 \times 5.3 = 36.252$

You can divide decimals using long division. The steps for dividing decimals using long division are the same as the steps for dividing whole numbers using long division. When you use long division to divide decimals, line up the decimal place in the quotient with the decimal place in the the dividend. If there is a remainder, write zeros in the dividend as needed and continue to divide.

EXAMPLE   Divide 0.085 ÷ 0.2.

SOLUTION   Write the problem in long division form.

$$0.2\overline{)0.085}$$

Move the decimal points in the divisor and dividend the same number of places until the divisor is a whole number. Then divide.

$$0.2\overline{)0.085}$$

Move decimal points one place to the right.

Line up decimal place in quotient with decimal place in dividend.

Write a zero in dividend so you can continue to divide.

$$
\begin{array}{r}
0.425 \\
2\overline{)0.850} \\
\underline{0.8} \\
5 \\
\underline{4} \\
10 \\
\underline{10} \\
0
\end{array}
$$

ANSWER ▶ 0.085 ÷ 0.2 = 0.425

Practice

Find the sum.

1. 7.92 + 6.5

2. 12.36 + 9

3. 28.012 + 94.3

4. 19.9 + 93.8 + 5.992

5. 9.02 + 8 + 8.7

6. 2.25 + 7.789 + 4.32

Find the difference.

7. 3.42 − 2.4

8. 0.88 − 0.39

9. 2.91 − 0.452

10. 15 − 6.32 − 1.44

11. 10.24 − 3.1 − 0.07

12. 94.48 − 16.7 − 42.902

Find the product.

13. 6.25 × 6.5

14. 0.26 × 9.58

15. 0.15 × 24

16. 64 × 3.51

17. 183.62 × 2.834

18. 510.375 × 80.2

Find the quotient.

19. 133.6 ÷ 8

20. 57.3 ÷ 0.003

21. 231.84 ÷ 12.6

22. 100.38 ÷ 21

23. 84.4 ÷ 0.02

24. 2712.15 ÷ 35

25. You bought a shirt for $24, a pair of pants for $25.99, and a pair of shoes for $12.45. How much did you spend all together? If you give the cashier $70, how much change will you receive?

FACTORS AND MULTIPLES

The **natural numbers** are all the numbers in the sequence 1, 2, 3, 4, 5, ...
When two or more natural numbers are multiplied, each of the numbers is a
factor of the product. For example, **3** and **7** are factors of 21, because **3** • **7** = 21.
A **prime number** is a natural number that has exactly two factors, itself and 1.
To write the **prime factorization** of a number, write the number as a product of
prime numbers.

EXAMPLE **Write the prime factorization of 315.**

SOLUTION Use a tree diagram to factor
the number until all factors are prime
numbers. To determine the factors, test
the prime numbers in order.

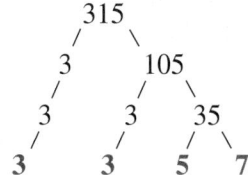

ANSWER▶ The prime factorization of 315
is 3 • 3 • 5 • 7, or 3^2 • 5 • 7.

A **common factor** of two natural numbers is a number that is a factor of both
numbers. For example, **7** is a common factor of 35 and 56, because 35 = 5 • **7**
and 56 = 8 • **7**. The **greatest common factor** (GCF) of two natural numbers is
the largest number that is a factor of both.

EXAMPLE **Find the greatest common factor of 180 and 84.**

SOLUTION First write the prime factorization of each number. Multiply the
common prime factors to find the greatest common factor.

180 = **2** • **2** • **3** • 3 • 5   84 = **2** • **2** • **3** • 7

ANSWER▶ The greatest common factor of 180 and 84 is 2 • 2 • 3 = 12.

A **common multiple** of two natural numbers is a number that is a multiple of
both numbers. For example, **42** is a common multiple of **6** and **14**, because
42 = **6** • 7 and **42** = **14** • 3. The **least common multiple** (LCM) of two natural
numbers is the smallest number that is a multiple of both.

EXAMPLE **Find the least common multiple of 24 and 30.**

SOLUTION First write the prime factorization of each number. The least
common multiple is the product of the common prime factors and all the
prime factors that are not common.

24 = **2** • 2 • 2 • **3**   30 = **2** • **3** • 5

ANSWER▶ The least common multiple of 24 and 30 is 2 • 3 • 2 • 2 • 5 = 120.

The **least common denominator** (LCD) of two fractions is the least common multiple of their denominators.

EXAMPLE Find the least common denominator of the fractions $\frac{5}{8}$ and $\frac{1}{6}$.

SOLUTION

Begin by finding the least common multiple of the denominators 8 and 6.

Multiples of 8: 8, 16, (24), 32, 40, 48, 56, 64, 72, . . .

Multiples of 6: 6, 12, 18, (24), 30, 36, 42, 48, 54, . . .

The least common multiple of 8 and 6 is 24.

ANSWER ▶ The least common denominator of $\frac{5}{8}$ and $\frac{1}{6}$ is 24.

Practice

List all the factors of the number.

1. 18 **2.** 10 **3.** 77 **4.** 35

5. 27 **6.** 100 **7.** 42 **8.** 49

Write the prime factorization of the number if it is not a prime number. If a number is prime, write *prime*.

9. 27 **10.** 24 **11.** 32 **12.** 61

13. 55 **14.** 68 **15.** 148 **16.** 225

List all the common factors of the pair of numbers.

17. 15, 22 **18.** 36, 54 **19.** 5, 20 **20.** 14, 21

21. 9, 36 **22.** 24, 25 **23.** 20, 55 **24.** 12, 30

Find the greatest common factor of the pair of numbers.

25. 25, 30 **26.** 32, 40 **27.** 17, 24 **28.** 35, 150

29. 14, 28 **30.** 65, 39 **31.** 102, 51 **32.** 128, 104

Find the least common multiple of the pair of numbers.

33. 5, 7 **34.** 7, 12 **35.** 16, 26 **36.** 5, 10

37. 9, 15 **38.** 12, 35 **39.** 6, 14 **40.** 20, 25

Find the least common denominator of the pair of fractions.

41. $\frac{1}{3}, \frac{11}{12}$ **42.** $\frac{4}{9}, \frac{7}{12}$ **43.** $\frac{1}{6}, \frac{3}{10}$ **44.** $\frac{5}{8}, \frac{9}{14}$

45. $\frac{3}{4}, \frac{9}{70}$ **46.** $\frac{7}{10}, \frac{13}{24}$ **47.** $\frac{1}{3}, \frac{8}{17}$ **48.** $\frac{4}{15}, \frac{27}{40}$

FRACTIONS

A fraction is in **simplest form** if its numerator and denominator have a greatest common factor of 1. To simplify a fraction, divide the numerator and denominator by their greatest common factor.

EXAMPLE   Simplify the fraction $\frac{28}{63}$.

SOLUTION   The greatest common factor of 28 and 63 is 7. Divide both the numerator and denominator by 7.

$$\frac{28}{63} = \frac{28 \div 7}{63 \div 7} = \frac{4}{9}$$

EXAMPLE   Rewrite the improper fraction $\frac{14}{3}$ as a mixed number.

SOLUTION   Begin by dividing 14 by 3. The remainder will be the numerator of the mixed number's fraction.

$$\frac{14}{3} \longrightarrow 3\overline{)14}^{\,4R2} \longrightarrow 4\frac{2}{3}$$

EXAMPLE   Rewrite the mixed number $5\frac{3}{7}$ as an improper fraction.

SOLUTION   To find the numerator of the improper fraction, multiply the whole number by the denominator and add the numerator of the fraction. The denominator of the improper fraction will be the same as the denominator of the mixed number.

$$5\frac{3}{7} = \frac{5 \cdot 7 + 3}{7} = \frac{38}{7}$$

Two numbers are **reciprocals** of each other if their product is 1. Every number except 0 has a reciprocal.

$$\frac{2}{3} \times \frac{3}{2} = 1, \text{ so } \frac{2}{3} \text{ and } \frac{3}{2} \text{ are reciprocals.}$$

To find the reciprocal of a number, write the number as a fraction. Then interchange the numerator and the denominator.

EXAMPLE   Find the reciprocal of $3\frac{1}{4}$.

SOLUTION $3\frac{1}{4} = \frac{13}{4}$ Write $3\frac{1}{4}$ as a fraction.

$\qquad\qquad \frac{13}{4} \implies \frac{4}{13}$ Interchange numerator and denominator.

ANSWER The reciprocal of $3\frac{1}{4}$ is $\frac{4}{13}$.

CHECK ✓ $3\frac{1}{4} \times \frac{4}{13} = \frac{13}{4} \times \frac{4}{13} = \frac{13 \times 4}{4 \times 13} = 1$

To add or subtract two fractions with the same denominator, add or subtract the numerators.

EXAMPLES   **a.** Add $\frac{3}{5} + \frac{4}{5}$.   **b.** Subtract $\frac{7}{10} - \frac{2}{10}$.

a. $\frac{3}{5} + \frac{4}{5} = \frac{3+4}{5}$ Add numerators.

$= \frac{7}{5}$, or $1\frac{2}{5}$ Simplify.

b. $\frac{7}{10} - \frac{2}{10} = \frac{7-2}{10}$ Subtract numerators.

$= \frac{5}{10}$ Simplify.

$= \frac{5}{2 \cdot 5}$ Factor.

$= \frac{1}{2}$ Simplify.

EXAMPLE

Find the least common denominator of the fractions $\frac{3}{5}$ and $\frac{1}{2}$. Then rewrite the fractions with the least common denominator.

SOLUTION

Begin by finding the least common multiple of the denominators 5 and 2.

Multiples of 5: 5, ⑩, 15, 20, 25, 30, 35, 40, . . .

Multiples of 2: 2, 4, 6, 8, ⑩, 12, 14, 16, 18, . . .

The least common multiple of 5 and 2 is 10. Now rewrite each fraction with a common denominator of 10.

$\frac{3}{5} = \frac{3 \cdot 2}{5 \cdot 2} = \frac{6}{10}$ Multiply by $\frac{2}{2}$.

$\frac{1}{2} = \frac{1 \cdot 5}{2 \cdot 5} = \frac{5}{10}$ Multiply by $\frac{5}{5}$.

To add or subtract two fractions with different denominators, write equivalent fractions with a common denominator.

EXAMPLE   Add $\frac{3}{5} + \frac{5}{6}$.

$\frac{3}{5} + \frac{5}{6} = \frac{18}{30} + \frac{25}{30}$ Use the LCD, 30.

$= \frac{18 + 25}{30}$ Add numerators.

$= \frac{43}{30}$, or $1\frac{13}{30}$ Simplify.

To add or subtract mixed numbers, you can first rewrite them as fractions.

EXAMPLE Subtract $3\frac{2}{3} - 2\frac{1}{4}$.

$$3\frac{2}{3} - 2\frac{1}{4} = \frac{11}{3} - \frac{9}{4}$$ Rewrite mixed numbers as fractions.

$$= \frac{44}{12} - \frac{27}{12}$$ Use the LCD, 12.

$$= \frac{44 - 27}{12}$$ Subtract numerators.

$$= \frac{17}{12}, \text{ or } 1\frac{5}{12}$$ Simplify.

To multiply two fractions, multiply the numerators and multiply the denominators.

EXAMPLE Multiply $\frac{3}{4} \times \frac{5}{6}$.

$$\frac{3}{4} \times \frac{5}{6} = \frac{3 \times 5}{4 \times 6}$$ Multiply numerators and multiply denominators.

$$= \frac{15}{24}$$ Simplify.

$$= \frac{\cancel{3} \cdot 5}{\cancel{3} \cdot 8}$$ Factor numerator and denominator.

$$= \frac{5}{8}$$ Simplify fraction to simplest form.

To divide by a fraction, multiply by its reciprocal.

EXAMPLES **a.** Divide $\frac{3}{4} \div \frac{5}{6}$.   **b.** Divide $2\frac{1}{2} \div 4\frac{1}{6}$.

a. $\dfrac{3}{4} \div \dfrac{5}{6} = \dfrac{3}{4} \times \dfrac{6}{5}$ The reciprocal of $\frac{5}{6}$ is $\frac{6}{5}$.

$$= \frac{3 \times 6}{4 \times 5}$$ Multiply numerators and denominators.

$$= \frac{18}{20} = \frac{9}{10}$$ Simplify.

b. $2\dfrac{1}{2} \div 4\dfrac{1}{6} = \dfrac{5}{2} \div \dfrac{25}{6}$ Write mixed numbers as fractions.

$$= \frac{5}{2} \times \frac{6}{25}$$ The reciprocal of $\frac{25}{6}$ is $\frac{6}{25}$.

$$= \frac{5 \times 6}{2 \times 25}$$ Multiply numerators and denominators.

$$= \frac{30}{50} = \frac{3}{5}$$ Simplify.

Practice

Find the reciprocal of the number.

1. 7

2. $\frac{1}{14}$

3. $\frac{7}{12}$

4. $\frac{5}{8}$

5. $\frac{1}{20}$

6. 100

7. $\frac{5}{13}$

8. $\frac{6}{7}$

9. $1\frac{1}{5}$

10. $2\frac{3}{5}$

11. $\frac{3}{9}$

12. $\frac{12}{17}$

13. $6\frac{2}{5}$

14. $10\frac{1}{3}$

15. $\frac{2}{7}$

16. $4\frac{3}{4}$

Add or subtract. Write the answer as a fraction or a mixed number in simplest form.

17. $\frac{1}{6} + \frac{4}{6}$

18. $\frac{5}{8} - \frac{3}{8}$

19. $\frac{4}{9} - \frac{1}{9}$

20. $\frac{5}{12} + \frac{3}{12}$

21. $\frac{1}{2} + \frac{1}{8}$

22. $\frac{3}{5} - \frac{1}{10}$

23. $\frac{7}{10} + \frac{1}{3}$

24. $\frac{15}{24} - \frac{7}{12}$

25. $5\frac{1}{8} - 2\frac{3}{4}$

26. $1\frac{3}{7} + \frac{1}{2}$

27. $4\frac{3}{8} - 2\frac{5}{6}$

28. $\frac{3}{7} + \frac{3}{4}$

29. $7\frac{1}{2} + \frac{7}{10}$

30. $5\frac{5}{9} - 2\frac{1}{3}$

31. $4\frac{5}{8} - 1\frac{3}{16}$

32. $9\frac{2}{5} + 3\frac{1}{3}$

Multiply or divide. Write the answer as a fraction or a mixed number in simplest form.

33. $\frac{1}{2} \times \frac{1}{2}$

34. $\frac{2}{3} \times \frac{4}{5}$

35. $\frac{5}{8} \times \frac{4}{15}$

36. $\frac{3}{7} \times \frac{7}{9}$

37. $\frac{3}{4} \times \frac{8}{9}$

38. $1\frac{2}{3} \times \frac{3}{5}$

39. $3 \times 2\frac{5}{9}$

40. $5\frac{1}{4} \times 1\frac{1}{7}$

41. $\frac{7}{8} \div \frac{3}{4}$

42. $\frac{5}{12} \div \frac{1}{2}$

43. $\frac{4}{5} \div \frac{2}{3}$

44. $\frac{11}{16} \div 1\frac{1}{2}$

45. $4\frac{1}{2} \div \frac{3}{4}$

46. $2\frac{1}{4} \div 1\frac{1}{3}$

47. $3\frac{2}{5} \div 4$

48. $7\frac{1}{5} \div 2\frac{1}{4}$

Add, subtract, multiply, or divide. Write the answer as a fraction or a mixed number in simplest form.

49. $\frac{15}{16} - \frac{1}{8}$

50. $\frac{5}{9} \times 1\frac{1}{2}$

51. $\frac{12}{13} \div \frac{12}{13}$

52. $\frac{24}{25} + \frac{1}{5}$

53. $5\frac{1}{2} - \frac{1}{8}$

54. $\frac{3}{10} \div \frac{1}{5}$

55. $\frac{7}{8} \times \frac{4}{9}$

56. $\frac{1}{3} + \frac{1}{6}$

57. $4\frac{1}{4} \times \frac{2}{3}$

58. $9\frac{2}{5} + 3\frac{1}{2}$

59. $\frac{4}{5} \div \frac{1}{2}$

60. $6\frac{5}{7} - 2\frac{1}{5}$

61. $\frac{9}{10} + \frac{3}{8}$

62. $8\frac{1}{2} \times \frac{1}{4}$

63. $\frac{11}{15} \times \frac{3}{8}$

64. $\frac{4}{7} \div \frac{4}{5}$

WRITING FRACTIONS AND DECIMALS

A fraction can be written as a decimal by dividing the numerator by the denominator. If the division stops with an exact quotient, then the decimal form of the number is a **terminating decimal**. If the resulting quotient includes a decimal digit or group of digits that repeats over and over, then the decimal form of the number is a **repeating decimal**.

EXAMPLES Write the fraction as a decimal. **a.** $\dfrac{9}{20}$ **b.** $\dfrac{7}{11}$

SOLUTION

Divide the numerator by the denominator.

a. $20\overline{)9.00}$ quotient 0.45

ANSWER▶ $\dfrac{9}{20} = 0.45$, a terminating decimal.

b. $11\overline{)7.000000\ldots}$ quotient $0.636363\ldots$

ANSWER▶ $\dfrac{7}{11} = 0.636363\ldots$, a repeating decimal. Write a repeating decimal with a bar over the digits that repeat: $\dfrac{7}{11} = 0.\overline{63}$.

EXAMPLES Write the decimal as a fraction. **a.** 0.12 **b.** $0.\overline{18}$

SOLUTION

a. To write a terminating decimal as a fraction, use the name for the last place to the right of the decimal as the denominator. The first place to the right is tenths, the second place is hundredths, and so on.

$0.12 = \dfrac{12}{100}$ Write as hundredths.

$ = \dfrac{3}{25}$ Simplify.

ANSWER▶ $0.12 = \dfrac{3}{25}$

b. $x = 0.181818\ldots$ Let x represent the repeating decimal.

$\begin{aligned}100x &= 18.181818\ldots\\ -x &= 0.181818\ldots\end{aligned}$ Multiply x by 10^n where n is the number of digits that repeat. (Here, $n = 2$.)

$99x = 18$ Subtract x from $100x$ to eliminate repeating decimal.

$x = \dfrac{18}{99}$ Divide each side by 99.

$ = \dfrac{2}{11}$ Simplify.

ANSWER▶ $0.\overline{18} = \dfrac{2}{11}$

Practice

Write the fraction as a decimal.

1. $\frac{1}{4}$ **2.** $\frac{7}{10}$ **3.** $\frac{2}{25}$ **4.** $\frac{41}{50}$

5. $\frac{1}{3}$ **6.** $\frac{4}{9}$ **7.** $\frac{10}{11}$ **8.** $\frac{27}{37}$

Write the decimal as a fraction. Simplify if possible.

9. 0.5   **10.** 0.16   **11.** 0.289   **12.** 0.1234

13. $0.\overline{7}$ **14.** $0.\overline{15}$ **15.** $0.6\overline{13}$ **16.** $0.5\overline{840}$

FRACTIONS, DECIMALS, AND PERCENTS

To write a percent as a decimal, move the decimal point two places to the left and remove the percent symbol.

EXAMPLES   Write the percent as a decimal.

a. $85\% = 85\% = 0.85$

b. $3\% = 03\% = 0.03$

c. $427\% = 427\% = 4.27$

d. $12.5\% = 12.5\% = 0.125$

To write a percent as a fraction in simplest form, first write the percent as a fraction with a denominator of 100. Then simplify if possible.

EXAMPLES   Write the percent as a fraction or a mixed number.

a. $71\% = \frac{71}{100}$

b. $10\% = \frac{10}{100} = \frac{1}{10}$

c. $4\% = \frac{4}{100} = \frac{1}{25}$

d. $350\% = \frac{350}{100} = \frac{7}{2} = 3\frac{1}{2}$

To write a decimal as a percent, move the decimal point two places to the right and add a percent symbol.

EXAMPLES   Write the decimal as a percent.

a. $0.93 = 0.93 = 93\%$

b. $1.47 = 1.47 = 147\%$

c. $0.025 = 0.025 = 2.5\%$

d. $0.005 = 0.005 = 0.5\%$

To write a fraction as a percent, first determine whether the denominator of the fraction is a factor of 100. If it is, rewrite the fraction with a denominator of 100. If not, divide the numerator by the denominator.

EXAMPLES **Write the fraction as a percent.**

a. $\dfrac{17}{25}$ ⟶ 25 is a factor of 100, so write $\dfrac{17}{25} = \dfrac{17 \cdot 4}{25 \cdot 4} = \dfrac{68}{100} = 68\%$.

b. $\dfrac{1}{8}$ ⟶ 8 is not a factor of 100, so divide: $1 \div 8 = 0.125 = 12.5\%$.

c. $\dfrac{1}{6}$ ⟶ 6 is not a factor of 100, so divide: $1 \div 6 = 0.1666\ldots \approx 0.167$
$= 16.7\%$.

You should memorize the relationships in this chart.

Equivalent percents, decimals, and fractions		
$1\% = 0.01 = \dfrac{1}{100}$	$33\dfrac{1}{3}\% = 0.\overline{3} = \dfrac{1}{3}$	$66\dfrac{2}{3}\% = 0.\overline{6} = \dfrac{2}{3}$
$10\% = 0.1 = \dfrac{1}{10}$	$40\% = 0.4 = \dfrac{2}{5}$	$75\% = 0.75 = \dfrac{3}{4}$
$20\% = 0.2 = \dfrac{1}{5}$	$50\% = 0.5 = \dfrac{1}{2}$	$80\% = 0.8 = \dfrac{4}{5}$
$25\% = 0.25 = \dfrac{1}{4}$	$60\% = 0.6 = \dfrac{3}{5}$	$100\% = 1$

Practice

Write the percent as a decimal and as a fraction or a mixed number in simplest form.

1. 63% **2.** 7% **3.** 24% **4.** 35% **5.** 17%

6. 125% **7.** 45% **8.** 250% **9.** $33.\overline{3}\%$ **10.** 96%

11. 62.5% **12.** 725% **13.** 5.2% **14.** 0.8% **15.** 0.12%

Write the decimal as a percent and as a fraction or a mixed number in simplest form.

16. 0.39 **17.** 0.08 **18.** 0.12 **19.** 1.5 **20.** 0.72

21. 0.05 **22.** 2.08 **23.** 4.8 **24.** 0.02 **25.** 3.75

26. 0.85 **27.** 0.52 **28.** 0.9 **29.** 0.005 **30.** 2.01

Write the fraction or mixed number as a decimal and as a percent.

31. $\dfrac{7}{10}$ **32.** $\dfrac{13}{20}$ **33.** $\dfrac{11}{25}$ **34.** $\dfrac{3}{10}$ **35.** $\dfrac{3}{8}$

36. $2\dfrac{3}{4}$ **37.** $5\dfrac{1}{8}$ **38.** $\dfrac{19}{20}$ **39.** $\dfrac{7}{8}$ **40.** $3\dfrac{7}{25}$

COMPARING AND ORDERING NUMBERS

When you compare two numbers *a* and *b*, *a* is either *less than*, *equal to*, or *greater than b*. To compare two whole numbers or decimals, compare the digits of the two numbers from left to right. Find the first place in which the digits are different.

a is less than *b*.	$a < b$
a is equal to *b*.	$a = b$
a is greater than *b*.	$a > b$

EXAMPLES

Compare the two numbers. Write the answer using <, >, or =.

a. 27.52 and 27.39

b. -4.5 and -4.25

SOLUTION

a. 27.52 and 27.39

ANSWER ▶ $5 > 3$, so $27.52 > 27.39$.

You can picture this on a number line. The numbers on a number line increase from left to right.

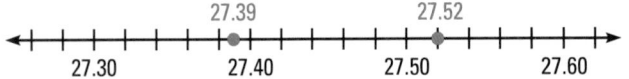

27.52 is *greater* than 27.39.

27.52 is to the *right* of 27.39.

b. Begin by graphing -4.5 and -4.25 on a number line.

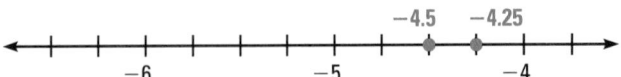

-4.5 is *less* than -4.25.

-4.5 is to the *left* of -4.25.

ANSWER ▶ From the number line, -4.5 is to the left of -4.25, so $-4.5 < -4.25$.

To compare fractions that have the same denominator, compare the numerators. If the fractions have different denominators, first rewrite the fractions to produce equivalent fractions with a common denominator.

EXAMPLE
Write the numbers $\frac{3}{4}, \frac{7}{8}$, and $\frac{5}{12}$ in order from least to greatest.

SOLUTION

The LCD of the fractions is 24.

$$\frac{3}{4} = \frac{3 \cdot 6}{4 \cdot 6} = \frac{18}{24} \qquad \frac{7}{8} = \frac{7 \cdot 3}{8 \cdot 3} = \frac{21}{24} \qquad \frac{5}{12} = \frac{5 \cdot 2}{12 \cdot 2} = \frac{10}{24}$$

Compare the numerators: $10 < 18 < 21$, so $\frac{10}{24} < \frac{18}{24} < \frac{21}{24}$, or $\frac{5}{12} < \frac{3}{4} < \frac{7}{8}$.

ANSWER ▶ In order from least to greatest, the fractions are $\frac{5}{12}, \frac{3}{4}$, and $\frac{7}{8}$.

EXAMPLE Compare $4\frac{3}{4}$ and $4\frac{2}{3}$. Write the answer using <, >, or =.

SOLUTION The whole number parts of the mixed numbers are the same, so compare the fraction parts.

The LCD of $\frac{3}{4}$ and $\frac{2}{3}$ is 12.

$$\frac{3}{4} = \frac{3 \cdot 3}{4 \cdot 3} = \frac{9}{12} \qquad \frac{2}{3} = \frac{2 \cdot 4}{3 \cdot 4} = \frac{8}{12}$$

Compare the numerators: $9 > 8$, so $\frac{9}{12} > \frac{8}{12}$, or $\frac{3}{4} > \frac{2}{3}$.

ANSWER ▶ Since $\frac{3}{4} > \frac{2}{3}$, it follows that $4\frac{3}{4} > 4\frac{2}{3}$.

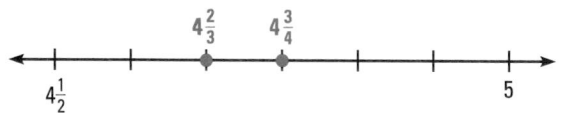

$4\frac{3}{4}$ is *greater* than $4\frac{2}{3}$.

$4\frac{3}{4}$ is to the *right* of $4\frac{2}{3}$.

Practice

Compare the two numbers. Write the answer using <, >, or =.

1. 12,428 and 15,116

2. 905 and 961

3. $-140{,}999$ and $-142{,}109$

4. -16.82 and -14.09

5. 0.40506 and 0.00456

6. 23.03 and 23.3

7. 1005.2 and 1050.7

8. 932,778 and 934,112

9. -0.058 and -0.102

10. $\frac{7}{13}$ and $\frac{3}{13}$

11. $17\frac{1}{4}$ and $17\frac{2}{8}$

12. $\frac{7}{10}$ and $\frac{3}{4}$

13. $-\frac{5}{9}$ and $-\frac{15}{27}$

14. $-\frac{1}{2}$ and $-\frac{3}{8}$

15. $\frac{1}{8}$ and $\frac{1}{9}$

16. $\frac{4}{5}$ and $\frac{2}{3}$

17. $42\frac{1}{5}$ and $41\frac{7}{8}$

18. 508.881 and 508.793

19. 32,227 and 32,226.5

20. $\frac{5}{8}$ and $\frac{2}{3}$

21. $-17\frac{5}{6}$ and $-17\frac{5}{7}$

Write the numbers in order from least to greatest.

22. 1207, 1702, 1220, 1772

23. $-45{,}617, -45{,}242, -40{,}099, -40{,}071$

24. $-23.12, -23.5, -24.0, -23.08, -24.01$

25. 9.027, 9.10, 9.003, 9.3, 9.27

26. 4.07, 4.5, 4.01, 4.22

27. $\frac{1}{3}, \frac{5}{6}, \frac{3}{8}, \frac{5}{4}$

28. $\frac{3}{5}, \frac{3}{2}, \frac{3}{4}, \frac{3}{10}, \frac{3}{7}$

29. $1\frac{2}{5}, \frac{7}{4}, \frac{5}{3}, 1\frac{1}{8}, \frac{15}{16}$

30. $-14\frac{7}{9}, -15\frac{1}{3}, -14\frac{5}{6}, -15\frac{1}{4}$

31. $-\frac{7}{8}, -\frac{5}{4}, -1\frac{1}{3}, -\frac{5}{12}$

32. You need a piece of trim that is $6\frac{5}{8}$ yards long for a craft project. You have a piece of trim that is $6\frac{3}{4}$ yards long. Is the trim you have long enough?

The **perimeter** P of a figure is the distance around it.

EXAMPLES

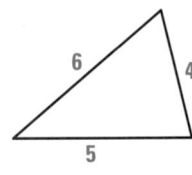

$$P = 6 + 5 + 4$$
$$= 15$$

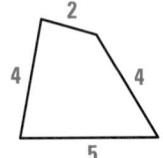

$$P = 4 + 2 + 4 + 5$$
$$= 15$$

$$P = \ell + w + \ell + w$$
$$= 2\ell + 2w$$

EXAMPLE Find the perimeter of a rectangle with length 14 centimeters and width 6 centimeters.

SOLUTION $P = 2\ell + 2w = (2 \times 14) + (2 \times 6) = 28 + 12 = 40$

ANSWER ▶ The perimeter is 40 centimeters.

A **regular polygon** is a polygon in which all the angles have the same measure and all the sides have the same length. The perimeter of a regular polygon can be found by multiplying the length of a side by the number of sides.

EXAMPLES

regular (equilateral) triangle

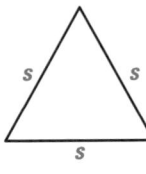

$$P = 3s$$

square

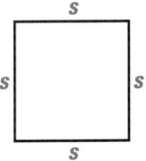

$$P = 4s$$

regular pentagon

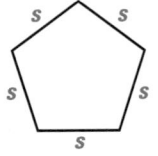

$$P = 5s$$

The **area** A of a figure is the number of square units enclosed by the figure.

EXAMPLES

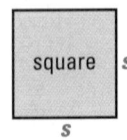

$$A = \text{length} \times \text{width}$$
$$= \ell \times w$$
$$= \ell w$$

$$A = \text{side} \times \text{side}$$
$$= s \times s$$
$$= s^2$$

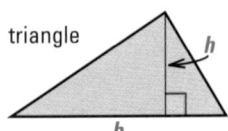

$$A = \frac{1}{2} \times \text{base} \times \text{height}$$
$$= \frac{1}{2} \times b \times h$$
$$= \frac{1}{2}bh$$

Volume is a measure of how much space is occupied by a solid figure. Volume is measured in cubic units.

One such unit is the cubic centimeter (cm^3). It is the amount of space occupied by a cube whose length, width, and height are each 1 centimeter.

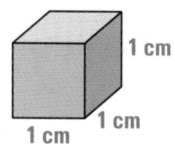
1 cm
1 cm
1 cm

EXAMPLES

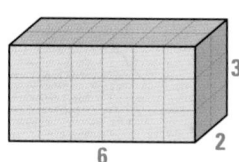
6
2
3

$V = 6 \times 2 \times 3$
$= 36$ cubic units

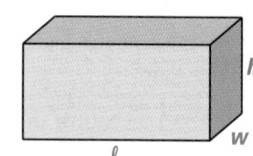
h
w
ℓ

$V = \ell \times w \times h$

EXAMPLE Find the volume of a rectangular prism with length 8 feet, width 5 feet, and height 9 feet.

SOLUTION $V = \ell \times w \times h = 8 \times 5 \times 9 = 360$

ANSWER ▶ The volume is 360 cubic feet (ft^3).

Practice

Find the perimeter.

1.
10
7
7
10

2.
0.5 in.
0.75 in.
0.75 in.
0.5 in.

3.
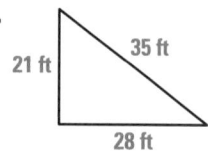
21 ft
35 ft
28 ft

4.
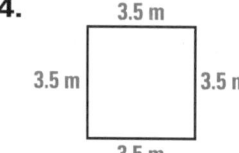
3.5 m
3.5 m
3.5 m
3.5 m

5. a square with sides of length 18 ft

6. a rectangle with length 6 m and width 7 m

Find the area.

7. a square with sides of length 29 yd

8. a rectangle with length 7 km and width 4 km

9. a square with sides of length 3.5 in.

10. a rectangle with length 24 ft and width 6 ft

11. a triangle with base 8 in. and height 5 in.

12. triangle with base 7.2 cm and height 5.3 cm

Find the volume.

13. a cube with sides of length 25 ft

14. a cube with sides of length 4.2 cm

15. a rectangular prism with length 15 yd, width 7 yd, and height 4 yd

16. a rectangular prism with length 7.3 cm, width 5 cm, and height 3.2 cm

17. a rectangular prism with length 5.3 in., width 4 in., and height 10 in.

ESTIMATION

You can use estimation to provide a quick answer when an exact answer is not needed. You also can use estimation to check if your answer is reasonable. Three methods of estimation are rounding, front-end estimation, and using compatible numbers.

To round, decide to which place you are rounding.

- If the digit to the right of that place is less than 5, round down.
- If the digit to the right of that place is greater than or equal to 5, round up.

EXAMPLE Estimate the difference of 688 and 52 by rounding to the nearest ten.

SOLUTION

$$
\begin{array}{rcl}
688 & \longrightarrow & 690 \\
-\ 52 & \longrightarrow & -\ 50 \\
\hline
 & & 640
\end{array}
$$

Round 688 to the nearest ten.
Round 52 to the nearest ten.
Subtract.

ANSWER ▶ The difference of 688 and 52 is about 640.

EXAMPLE Estimate the quotient of 110.23 and 10.85 by rounding to the nearest whole number.

SOLUTION

$$
110.23 \div 10.85 \longrightarrow 11\overline{)110}^{\,10}
$$

Round 110.23 and 10.85 to the nearest whole numbers and divide.

ANSWER ▶ The quotient of 110.23 and 10.85 is about 10.

To use **front-end estimation**, add the front digits. Then estimate the sum of the remaining digits, and add that sum to the front-end sum.

EXAMPLE Use front-end estimation to estimate the cost of 3 shirts marked $14.96, $11.78, and $8.25.

SOLUTION

Add the front digits.	Estimate what's left.
$14.96	$0.96 } about $1
$11.78	$0.78 } about $1
+ $8.25	$0.25 }
$33	$2

ANSWER ▶ The cost of the shirts is about $33 + $2 = $35.

There are two methods to estimate products and quotients. You can use rounding or compatible numbers. **Compatible numbers** are numbers that are easy to compute mentally.

EXAMPLE Use compatible numbers to estimate the product of 116.11 and 41.09.

SOLUTION

$$
\begin{array}{rl}
116.11 \longrightarrow & 115 \\
\underline{\times\ 41.09} \longrightarrow & \underline{\times\ 40} \\
& 4600
\end{array}
$$

Use compatible numbers 115 and 40 since they are easy to multiply.

ANSWER ▶ The product of 116.11 and 41.09 is about 4600.

You can estimate the area of a figure by placing it on a grid. Count the number of squares that are completely covered by the figure. Then count the number of squares that are partially covered. You can assume that on average a partially covered square is about half covered. So you can estimate the total area of the figure by adding the number of squares that are totally covered to one-half the number of squares that are partially covered.

EXAMPLE Estimate the area of the figure shown to the nearest square unit.

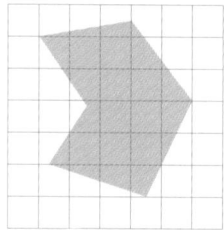

SOLUTION

First count the number of squares that are completely covered.

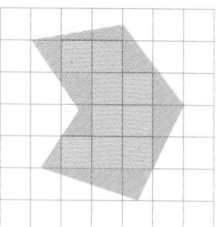

Then count the number of squares that are partially covered.

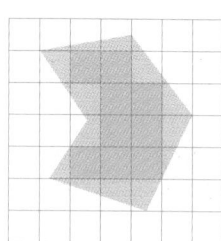

There are 9 squares that are completely covered.

There are 18 squares that are partially covered.

So an estimate for the area of the figure can be calculated as follows:

$$
\text{Area} = 9 + \frac{1}{2}(18) = 9 + 9 = 18
$$

ANSWER ▶ The area of the figure is approximately 18 square units.

Practice

Round to the nearest ten or hundred to estimate the sum or difference.

1. 36 + 11

2. 249 + 782

3. 1585 + 791

4. 16 + 23 + 74

5. 108 + 92 + 345

6. 1023 + 5062 + 3873

7. 58 − 39

8. 1375 − 911

9. 2014 − 389

10. 65 − 42 − 12

11. 1059 − 238 − 111

12. 8375 − 3847 − 1224

Use front-end estimation to estimate the sum.

13. 15.98 + 6.46

14. 62.36 + 44.68

15. 156.22 + 324.72

16. 533.2 + 37.2

17. 912.14 + 428.13

18. 588.61 + 120.37

19. 24.22 + 4.53 + 12.31

20. 16.1 + 34.2 + 25.2

21. 59.31 + 71.21 + 78.47

22. 113.73 + 97.1 + 65.18

23. 88.9 + 86.19 + 92.14

24. 0.4 + 120.46 + 584.53

Use rounding to estimate the product or quotient.

25. 52 × 48

26. 27 × 414

27. 602 × 53

28. 42 × 6.1

29. 10.34 × 2.69

30. 108.8 × 435

31. 642 ÷ 219

32. 121 ÷ 57

33. 838 ÷ 22

34. 77 ÷ 3.84

35. 58.9 ÷ 14

36. 40.32 ÷ 1.25

Use compatible numbers to estimate the product or quotient.

37. 74.94 × 11.6

38. 397.25 × 41.37

39. 3997.63 × 18.87

40. 536.2 × 22.1

41. 498.75 × 13.55

42. 2465.83 × 68.52

43. 68.66 ÷ 2.96

44. 995.88 ÷ 102.34

45. 523.12 ÷ 51.87

46. 948.68 ÷ 47.96

47. 1487.81 ÷ 28.65

48. 148.64 ÷ 14.71

Estimate the area of the figure to the nearest square unit.

49.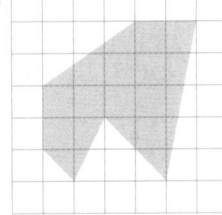

50.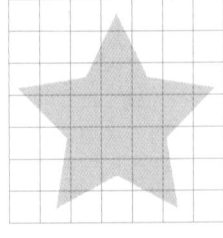

51.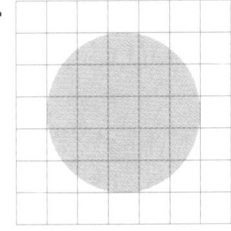

52.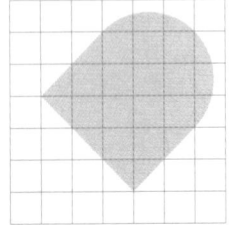

53.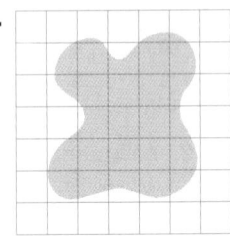

54.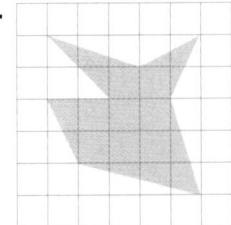

DATA DISPLAYS

A **bar graph** can be used to display data that fall into distinct categories. The bars in a bar graph are the same width. The height or length of each bar is determined by the data it represents and by the scale you choose.

EXAMPLE

In 1998, baseball player Mark McGwire hit a record 70 home runs. The table shows the locations to which the home runs were hit. Draw a bar graph to display the data. ▶ Source: *Stats Inc.*

Field location	Number of runs
left	31
left-center	21
center	15
right-center	3
right	0

❶ Choose a scale. Since the data range from 0 to 31, make the scale increase from 0 to 35 by fives.

❷ Draw and label the axes. Mark intervals on the vertical axis according to the scale you chose.

❸ Draw a bar for each category.

❹ Give the bar graph a title.

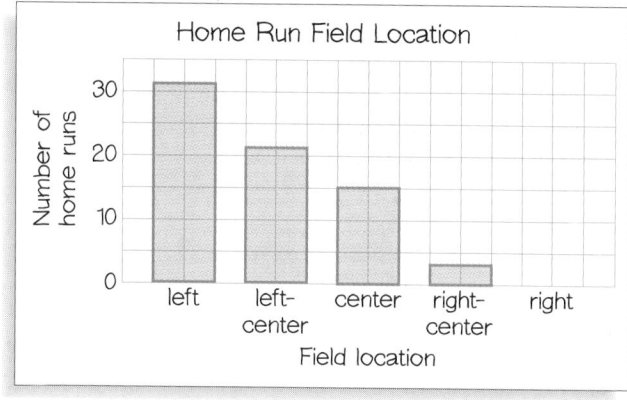

A **histogram** is a bar graph that shows how many data items occur within given intervals. The number of data items in an interval is the **frequency**.

EXAMPLE The table shows the distances of McGwire's home runs. Draw a histogram to display them.

Distance (ft)	Frequency
300–350	4
351–400	24
401–450	27
451–500	11
501–550	4

SOLUTION Use the same method you used for drawing the bar graph above. However, do not leave spaces between the bars.

❶ Since the frequencies range from 4 to 27, make the scale increase from 0 to 30 by fives.

❷ Draw and label the axes. Mark intervals on the vertical axis.

❸ Draw a bar for each category. Do not leave spaces between the bars.

❹ Give the histogram a title.

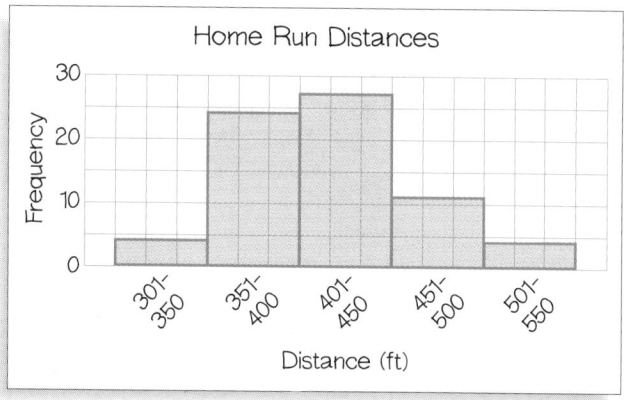

A **line graph** can be used to show how data change over time.

EXAMPLE

A science class recorded the highest temperature each day from December 1 to December 14. The temperatures are given in the table. Draw a line graph to display the data.

Date	1	2	3	4	5	6	7
Temperature (°F)	40	48	49	61	24	35	34

Date	8	9	10	11	12	13	14
Temperature (°F)	42	41	40	22	20	28	30

❶ Choose a scale.

❷ Draw and label the axes. Mark evenly spaced intervals on both axes.

❸ Graph each data item as a point. Connect the points.

❹ Give the line graph a title.

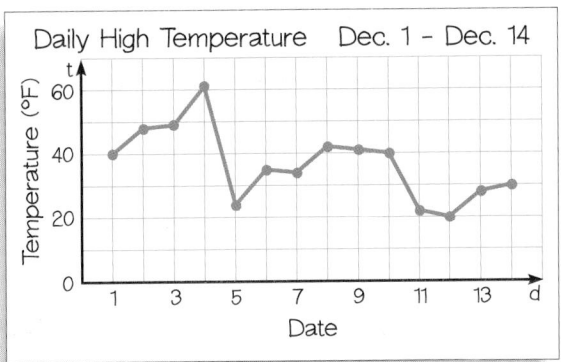

A **circle graph** can be used to show how parts relate to a whole and to each other.

EXAMPLE

The table shows the number of sports-related injuries treated in the hospital emergency room in one year. Draw a circle graph to display the data.

Related sport	Number of injuries
basketball	56
football	34
skating/hockey	22
track and field	10
other	28

❶ Find the total number of injuries.

$$56 + 34 + 22 + 10 + 28 = 150$$

To find the degree measure for each sector of the circle, write a fraction comparing the number of injuries to the total. Then multiply the fraction by 360°. For example:

Football: $\frac{34}{150} \cdot 360° = 81.6°$

❷ Draw a circle. Use a protractor to draw the angle for each sector.

❸ Label each sector.

❹ Give the circle graph a title.

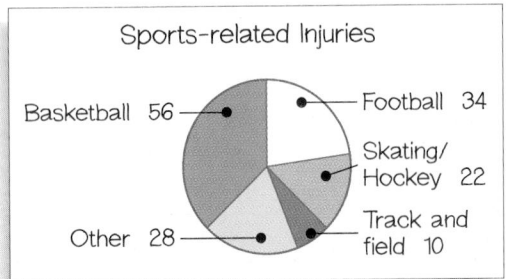

Practice

In 1998, baseball player Sammy Sosa hit 66 home runs. The tables show the field locations and distances of his home runs. ▶ Source: *Stats Inc.*

1. The location data range from 10 to 22. The scale must start at 0. Choose a reasonable scale for a bar graph.

2. Draw a bar graph to display the field locations of Sosa's home runs.

3. The distance data range from 1 to 16. The scale must start at 0. Choose a reasonable scale for a histogram.

4. Draw a histogram to display the distances of Sosa's home runs.

Field location	Number of runs
left	12
left-center	22
center	10
right-center	11
right	11

For Exercises 1 and 2

Distance (ft)	Frequency
326–350	5
351–375	12
376–400	14
401–425	16
426–450	14
451–475	1
476–500	4

For Exercises 3 and 4

5. There are 150 runs at a ski resort: 51 expert runs, 60 intermediate runs, and 39 beginner runs. Draw a circle graph to display the data.

6. A patient's temperature (in degrees Fahrenheit) was taken every 3 hours from 9 A.M. until noon of the following day. The temperature readings were 102°F, 102°F, 101.5°F, 101.1°F, 100°F, 101°F, 101.5°F, 100°F, 99.8°F, and 99°F. Draw a line graph to display the data.

Choose an appropriate graph to display the data. Draw the graph.

7.

Value of One Share of Company stock						
Year	1994	1995	1996	1997	1998	1999
Value ($)	15	18	16	12	10	15

8.

Passenger Car Stopping Distance (dry road)				
Speed (mi/h)	35	45	55	65
Distance (ft)	160	225	310	410

9.

Fat in One Tablespoon of Canola Oil	
Type of fat	Number of grams
saturated	22
polyunsaturated	10
monounsaturated	11

▶ Source: U.S. Department of Agriculture

10.

Enrollment in Capital City Schools by Age					
Age	4–6	7–9	10–12	13–15	16–18
Enrollment	912	2556	4812	2232	1502

MEASURES OF CENTRAL TENDENCY

A **measure of central tendency** for a set of numerical data is a single number that represents a "typical" value for the set. Three important measures of central tendency are the *mean*, the *median*, and the *mode*.

- The **mean**, or average, of a data set is the sum of the values in the set divided by the number of values in the set.

- The **median** of a data set with an odd number of values is the middle value when the values are written in numerical order. The median of a data set with an even number of values is the mean of the two middle values when the values are written in numerical order.

- The **mode** of a data set is the value or values in the set that occur most often. If no value occurs more often than any of the others, there is no mode.

EXAMPLE Find the mean, median, and mode of the following data set.

10, 12, 7, 11, 20, 7, 8, 19, 9, 5

SOLUTION

To find the mean, divide the sum of the data values by the number of data values.

$$\text{Mean} = \frac{10 + 12 + 7 + 11 + 20 + 7 + 8 + 19 + 9 + 5}{10} = \frac{108}{10} = 10.8$$

Since there are an even number of values, find the median by writing the data values in numerical order and finding the mean of the two middle values.

$$5, 7, 7, 8, \mathbf{9}, \mathbf{10}, 11, 12, 19, 20 \qquad \text{Median} = \frac{9 + 10}{2} = \frac{19}{2} = 9.5$$

The mode is the number that occurs most often in the data set.

$$\text{Mode} = 7$$

Practice

Find the mean, median, and mode(s) of the data set.

1. 0, 0, 0, 0, 0, 1, 2, 2, 4, 4

2. 3, 1, 1, 8, 2, 1, 3, 5, 3

3. 10, 15, 20, 25, 30, 35, 40, 45, 50

4. 14, 10, 45, 38, 60, 14, 23, 35, 68, 50

5. 376, 376, 386, 393, 487, 598, 737, 745, 853

6. 101, 76, 52, 50, 26, 7, 13, 1000

PROBLEM SOLVING

One of your primary goals in mathematics should be to become a good problem solver. It will help to approach every problem with an organized plan.

STEP ① **UNDERSTAND THE PROBLEM.** Read the problem carefully. Organize the information you are given and decide what you need to find. Determine whether some of the information given is unnecessary, or whether enough information is given. Supply missing facts, if possible.

STEP ② **MAKE A PLAN TO SOLVE THE PROBLEM.** Choose a strategy. (Get ideas from the list given on page 782.) Choose the correct operations. Decide whether a graphing calculator or a computer is necessary.

STEP ③ **CARRY OUT THE PLAN TO SOLVE THE PROBLEM.** Use the strategy and any technology you have chosen. Estimate before you calculate, if possible. Do any calculations that are needed. Answer the question that the problem asks.

STEP ④ **CHECK TO SEE IF YOUR ANSWER IS REASONABLE.** Reread the problem and see if your answer agrees with the given information.

EXAMPLE **How many segments can be drawn between 7 points, no three of which lie on the same line?**

① You are given a number of points, along with the information that no three points lie on the same line. You need to determine how many segments can be drawn between the points.

② Some strategies to consider are: draw a diagram, solve a simpler problem and look for a pattern.

③ Consider the problem for fewer points.

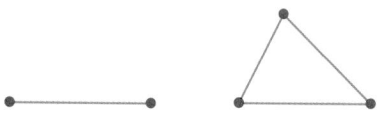

2 points
1 segment

3 points
3 segments

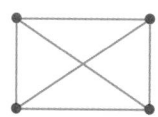

4 points
6 segments

5 points
10 segments

Look for a pattern. Then continue the pattern to find the number of segments for 7 points.

Number of points	2	3	4	5	6	7
Number of segments	1	3	6	10	15	21

$\llcorner$+2$\lrcorner\llcorner$+3$\lrcorner\llcorner$+4$\lrcorner\llcorner$+5$\lrcorner\llcorner$+6$\lrcorner$

ANSWER ▶ Given 7 points, no three of which lie on the same line, 21 segments can be drawn between the points.

④ You can check your solution by making a sketch.

In **Step 2** of the problem solving plan, you may want to consider the following strategies.

PROBLEM SOLVING STRATEGIES

- **Guess, check, and revise.**   When you do not seem to have enough information.

- **Draw a diagram or a graph.**   When words describe a picture.

- **Make a table or an organized list.** When you have data or choices to organize.

- **Use an equation or a formula.**   When you know a relationship between quantities.

- **Use a proportion.**   When you know that two ratios are equal.

- **Look for a pattern.**   When you can examine several cases.

- **Break the problem into simpler parts.** When you have a multi-step problem.

- **Solve a simpler problem.**   When easier numbers help you understand a problem.

- **Work backward.**   When you are looking for a fact leading to a known result.

Practice

1. Tasha bought salads at $2.75 each and cartons of milk at $.80 each. The total cost was $16.15. How many of each did Tasha buy?

2. A rectangular garden is 45 feet long and has perimeter 150 feet. Rows of plants are planted 3 feet apart. Find the area of the garden.

3. If five turkey club sandwiches cost $18.75, how much would seven sandwiches cost?

4. How many diagonals can be drawn from one vertex of a 12-sided polygon?

5. Nguyen wants to arrive at school no later than 7:25 A.M. for his first class. It takes him 25 minutes to shower and dress, 15 minutes to eat breakfast, and at least 20 minutes to get to school. What time should he plan to get out of bed?

6. There are 32 players in a single-elimination chess tournament. That is, a player who loses once is eliminated. Assuming that no ties are allowed, how many games must be played to determine a champion?

7. Andrea, Betty, Joyce, Karen, and Paula are starters on their school basketball team. How many different groups of three can be chosen for a newspaper photo?

8. Carl has $135 in the bank and plans to save $5 per week. Jean has $90 in the bank and plans to save $10 per week. How many weeks will it be before Jean has at least as much in the bank as Carl?

9. The Peznolas are planning to use square tiles to tile a kitchen floor that is 18 feet long and 15 feet wide. Each tile covers one square foot. A carton of tiles costs $18. How much will it cost to cover the entire kitchen floor?

Extra Practice

Chapter 1, Volume 1

Evaluate the expression for the given value of the variable. *(Lesson 1.1)*

1. $15a$ when $a = 7$

2. $7 + x$ when $x = 15$

3. $\dfrac{c}{4}$ when $c = 32$

Evaluate the expression for the given value(s) of the variable(s). *(Lesson 1.2)*

4. $3y^2$ when $y = 5$

5. $(4x)^3$ when $x = 2$

6. $6x^4$ when $x = 4$

7. $a^4 - 5$ when $a = 3$

8. $(x + 2)^3$ when $x = 4$

9. $(c - d)^2$ when $c = 10$ and $d = 3$

Evaluate the expression. *(Lesson 1.3)*

10. $33 - 12 \div 4$

11. $10^2 \div 4 + 6$

12. $10^2 \div (4 + 6)$

13. $2 + 21 \div 3 - 6$

14. $3 + 7 \cdot 35 \div 5$

15. $15 \div (6 - 1) - 2$

16. $[(5 \cdot 8) + 8] \div 16$

17. $\dfrac{9 \cdot 7^2}{5 + 8^2 - 6}$

Use mental math to solve the equation. *(Lesson 1.4)*

18. $x + 7 = 13$

19. $n - 4 = 8$

20. $3y = 21$

21. $\dfrac{m}{4} = 6$

Check to see if the given value of the variable is or is not a solution of the inequality. *(Lesson 1.4)*

22. $y + 10 < 22$; $y = 12$

23. $6n \geq 25$; $n = 5$

24. $3t \leq 12$; $t = 4$

25. $4 + x \geq 11$; $x = 6$

26. $48 \div g < 4$; $g = 16$

27. $a - 5 > 3$; $a = 9$

Write the sentence as an equation or an inequality. Let *x* represent the number. *(Lesson 1.5)*

28. The product of a number and 4 is less than or equal to 36.

29. 16 is the difference of 20 and a number.

30. **SPORTS** Your friend's score in a game is 48. This is twice your score. Write a verbal model that relates your friend's score to your score. What is your score? *(Lesson 1.6)*

31. **WIRELESS INDUSTRY** The table shows the estimated number of cellular telephone subscribers (in millions) in the United States. Make a bar graph and a line graph of the data. *(Lesson 1.7)*

Year	1993	1994	1995	1996	1997	1998	1999
Subscribers (millions)	13	19	28	38	49	61	76

▶ Source: Cellular Telecommunications Industry Association

Make an input-output table for the function. Use 0, 1, 2, 3, 4, and 5 as values for *x*. *(Lesson 1.8)*

32. $y = 8 - 2x$

33. $y = 7x + 1$

34. $y = 3(x - 4)$

Chapter 2, Volume 1

Graph the numbers on a number line. Then write two inequalities that compare the numbers. *(Lesson 2.1)*

1. $-7, 8$

2. $3, -5$

3. $-4, -7$

4. $0, -3$

Evaluate the expression. *(Lesson 2.2)*

5. $\left|-3\right|$

6. $-\left|4\right|$

7. $\left|8.5\right|$

8. $\left|-\dfrac{3}{4}\right|$

Find the sum. *(Lesson 2.3)*

9. $-3 + 8$

10. $18 + 27$

11. $5 + (-7)$

12. $-4 + (-11)$

13. $-4 + 13 + (-6)$

14. $15 + (-12) + (-4)$

15. $-2 + (-9) + 8$

16. $17 + (-5) + 15$

Find the difference. *(Lesson 2.4)*

17. $-8 - 5$

18. $-3 - (-7)$

19. $4.1 - 6.3$

20. $-\dfrac{2}{5} - \dfrac{3}{5}$

21. $6 - 13$

22. $5 - (-2)$

23. $-10 - (-3.5)$

24. $-2 - 14$

Evaluate the expression. *(Lesson 2.4)*

25. $-6 - (-3) - 4$

26. $-15 - 4 - 12$

27. $2 - 5 - (-18)$

Find the product. *(Lesson 2.5)*

28. $-6(-7)$

29. $-5(90)$

30. $4(-1.5)$

31. $-14\left(-\dfrac{3}{7}\right)$

32. $(-4)^3$

33. $-(3)^4$

34. $-(-2)^5$

35. $3(-8)(-2)$

WHALES In Exercises 36 and 37, suppose a whale is diving at a rate of about 6 feet per second. *(Lesson 2.5)*

36. Write an algebraic model for the displacement d (in feet) of the whale after t seconds.

37. What is the whale's change in position after diving for 15 seconds?

Use the distributive property to rewrite the expression without parentheses. *(Lesson 2.6)*

38. $6(y + 5)$

39. $4(a - 6)$

40. $(3 + w)2$

41. $(4x + 3)2$

42. $-3(r - 5)$

43. $-(2 + t)$

44. $(x + 4)(-6)$

45. $(y - 3)1.5$

Simplify the expression by combining like terms if possible. If not possible, write *already simplified*. *(Lesson 2.7)*

46. $3x + 7x$

47. $8r - r^2$

48. $6 + 2y - 3$

49. $w + 2w + 4w - 4$

50. $7 + 5r - 6 + 4r$

51. $m^2 + 3m - 2m^2 - m$

Find the quotient. *(Lesson 2.8)*

52. $18 \div (-2)$

53. $-48 \div 12$

54. $16 \div \left(-\dfrac{4}{5}\right)$

55. $\dfrac{-22}{-\frac{1}{3}}$

Chapter 3, Volume 1

Solve the equation. *(Lesson 3.1)*

1. $y - 6 = 8$ **2.** $5 + n = -10$ **3.** $3 = r - 14$ **4.** $-4 = 5 + q$

5. $8 = x - (-1)$ **6.** $t - 4 = -7$ **7.** $m + 6 = 9$ **8.** $-2 = r - (-5)$

Use division to solve the equation. *(Lesson 3.2)*

9. $7x = 35$ **10.** $-15m = 150$ **11.** $6a = 3$ **12.** $-144 = -12t$

Use multiplication to solve the equation. *(Lesson 3.2)*

13. $\dfrac{x}{5} = -4$ **14.** $\dfrac{y}{10} = -\dfrac{2}{5}$ **15.** $-\dfrac{g}{6} = -14$ **16.** $\dfrac{t}{-8} = -\dfrac{3}{8}$

Solve the equation. *(Lesson 3.3)*

17. $6x + 8 = 32$ **18.** $2x - 1 = 11$ **19.** $4m + 8m - 2 = 22$

20. $2x - 3(x + 4) = -1$ **21.** $\dfrac{1}{3}(m - 1) = -5$ **22.** $\dfrac{2}{5}(n + 3) = 4$

Solve the equation. *(Lesson 3.4)*

23. $-6 + 5x = 8x - 9$ **24.** $8r + 1 = 23 - 3r$ **25.** $2w + 3 = 3w + 1$

26. $3a + 12 = 4a - 2a + 1$ **27.** $5x + 6 = 2x + x + 2$ **28.** $6d - 2d = 10d + 6$

Solve the equation. *(Lesson 3.5)*

29. $4(a + 3) = 3(a + 5)$ **30.** $8(r - 2) + 6 = 2(r + 1)$

31. $6(x - 1) = 5(2x + 3) - 15$ **32.** $\dfrac{1}{2}(4q + 12) = 2 + 3(6 - q)$

Solve the equation. Round the result to the nearest hundredth. Check the rounded solution. *(Lesson 3.6)*

33. $-26x - 59 = 135$ **34.** $18.25d - 4.15 = 2.75d$ **35.** $2.3 - 4.8w = 8.2w + 5.6$

In Exercises 36 and 37, use the distance formula $d = rt$. *(Lesson 3.7)*

36. Solve the formula for rate r.

37. You ride your bike for 3 hours and travel 36 miles. Use the formula you wrote in Exercise 36 to find your average speed.

Find the unit rate. *(Lesson 3.8)*

38. 33 ounces in 6 cans of juice   **39.** Earn $50.75 for working 7 hours

40. Hike 10.5 miles in 3 hours   **41.** 16 grams of protein in 8 granola bars

Solve the percent problem. *(Lesson 3.9)*

42. How much money is 40% of $800?   **43.** 15% of 320 meters is what length?

44. 24 is what percent of 60?   **45.** What number is 30% of 150?

Chapter 4, Volume 1

Plot and label the ordered pairs in a coordinate plane. *(Lesson 4.1)*

1. $A(2, 4)$, $B(-2, 0)$, $C(5, -2)$ **2.** $A(4, 4)$, $B(0, -2)$, $C(-3, -3)$ **3.** $A(4, -4)$, $B(2.5, 5)$, $C(-3, 2)$

4. $A(0, -1)$, $B(1, -3)$, $C(3, 1)$ **5.** $A(-4, -2)$, $B(-2, 4)$, $C(4, 0)$ **6.** $A(-3, -4)$, $B(1, -1)$, $C(-1, 1)$

Use a table of values to graph the equation. *(Lesson 4.2)*

7. $y = 5x + 1$ **8.** $y = -2x + 4$ **9.** $4x + y = -8$ **10.** $2y - x = -1$

11. $y - 2x = -5$ **12.** $y = 3x - 1$ **13.** $y = -2x + 1$ **14.** $5y - 10x = 20$

Graph the equation. *(Lesson 4.3)*

15. $y = -2$ **16.** $x = 3$ **17.** $x = -\dfrac{1}{2}$ **18.** $y = 5$

Find the *x*-intercept of the line. *(Lesson 4.4)*

19. $5x + y = -5$ **20.** $2x - y = 6$ **21.** $6y + 2x = 12$ **22.** $8x + 2y = -16$

Find the *y*-intercept of the line. *(Lesson 4.4)*

23. $y = 2x - 5$ **24.** $y = 2x + 14$ **25.** $y = 6 - 3x$ **26.** $10x - 15y = 30$

Find the slope of the line that passes through the points. *(Lesson 4.5)*

27. $(6, 1)$ and $(-4, 1)$ **28.** $(2, 2)$ and $(-1, 4)$ **29.** $(-4, 2)$ and $(-3, -5)$

30. $(4, 5)$ and $(2, 2)$ **31.** $(3, 6)$ and $(3, -1)$ **32.** $(0, 6)$ and $(3, 0)$

In Exercises 33–40, the variables *x* and *y* vary directly. Use the given values to write an equation that relates *x* and *y*. *(Lesson 4.6)*

33. $x = 6$, $y = 18$ **34.** $x = 4$, $y = 1$ **35.** $x = 8$, $y = -7$ **36.** $x = -1$, $y = -20$

37. $x = -2$, $y = -2$ **38.** $x = 8$, $y = -4$ **39.** $x = 2$, $y = -6$ **40.** $x = 5$, $y = 2$

Write the equation in slope-intercept form. Then graph the equation. *(Lesson 4.7)*

41. $x - y = 1$ **42.** $-3x + 2y = 6$ **43.** $x + y + 4 = 0$

44. $2x - 4y + 6 = 0$ **45.** $2x + 2y + 2 = 4y$ **46.** $5x - 3y + 2 = 14 - 4x$

Determine whether the relation is a function. If it is a function, give the domain and the range. *(Lesson 4.8)*

47.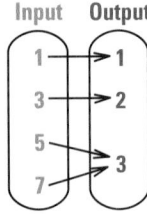

48.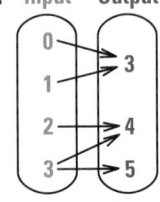

49.

Input	Output
4	-2
0	0
4	2
2	4

Chapter 5, Volume 1

Write in slope-intercept form the equation of the line described below.
(Lesson 5.1)

1. $m = 2, b = 1$ **2.** $m = -3, b = -2$ **3.** $m = \frac{1}{2}, b = -3$ **4.** $m = -4, b = 0$

Write in point-slope form the equation of the line that passes through the given point and has the given slope. *(Lesson 5.2)*

5. $(-1, 0), m = 3$ **6.** $(5, 2), m = -2$ **7.** $(3, 6), m = 0$ **8.** $(-2, 1), m = -5$

9. $(-3, -1), m = 4$ **10.** $(1, 5), m = 8$ **11.** $(2, -1), m = \frac{1}{2}$ **12.** $(-4, 3), m = -\frac{1}{3}$

Write in slope-intercept form the equation of the line that passes through the given points. *(Lesson 5.3)*

13. $(3, -2)$ and $(5, 4)$ **14.** $(5, 1)$ and $(0, -6)$ **15.** $(-2, -1)$ and $(4, -4)$

16. $(-1, 7)$ and $(5, 7)$ **17.** $(-3, 5)$ and $(-6, 8)$ **18.** $(5, 2)$ and $(1, 4)$

Write in standard form an equation of the line that passes through the given point and has the given slope. *(Lesson 5.4)*

19. $(5, -2), m = 3$ **20.** $(-2, 5), m = 5$ **21.** $(-4, 3), m = -\frac{5}{6}$ **22.** $(5, 7), m = \frac{3}{4}$

23. $(0, 8), m = -7$ **24.** $(-1, -7), m = 4$ **25.** $(3, 6), m = -2$ **26.** $(4, 5), m = -5$

In Exercises 27–29, use the following information. You buy $10.00 worth of apples and oranges. The apples cost $.80 a pound and the oranges cost $1.00 a pound. *(Lesson 5.5)*

27. Write an equation in standard form that represents the different amounts (in pounds) of apples A and oranges R that you could buy.

28. Copy the table. Then use the linear equation to complete the table.

Pounds of apples, A	0	1	2	3	4	5
Pounds of oranges, R	?	?	?	?	?	?

29. Plot the points from the table and sketch the line.

Determine whether the lines are perpendicular. *(Lesson 5.6)*

30. $y = x - 2,\ y = -x + 4$ **31.** $y = \frac{1}{4}x - 5,\ y = -\frac{1}{4}x + 5$

32. $y = \frac{1}{2}x - 1,\ y = -2x + 2$ **33.** $3y = -2x + 12,\ y = -\frac{3}{2}x - 12$

Write in slope-intercept form the equation of the line passing through the given point and perpendicular to the given line. *(Lesson 5.6)*

34. $(1, 2),\ y = x + 2$ **35.** $(-1, 4),\ y = \frac{3}{4}x - 1$ **36.** $(3, -2),\ y = 1$

Chapter 6, Volume 1

Solve the inequality. Then graph the solution. *(Lesson 6.1)*

1. $x + 1 < 2$ **2.** $r + 5 > -4$ **3.** $3 \geq y - 4$ **4.** $8 + t \leq -2$

Solve the inequality. Then graph the solution. *(Lesson 6.2)*

5. $9x \geq 36$ **6.** $5w < -15$ **7.** $\dfrac{k}{9} \leq 2$ **8.** $-\dfrac{2}{3}n > 4$

Solve the inequality. *(Lesson 6.3)*

9. $2x + 5 > 3$ **10.** $-3x - 7 < 2$ **11.** $4(x + 5) \geq 10$

12. $3x + 8 \geq -2x + 3$ **13.** $4(x - 2) \leq 3x + 1$ **14.** $-(x + 5) < -4x - 11$

Write an inequality that represents the statement. Then graph the inequality. *(Lesson 6.4)*

15. x is greater than -5 and less than 2.

16. x is greater than or equal to 4 and less than 6.

17. x is less than or equal to 5 and greater than -3.

18. x is less than 6 and greater than or equal to -1.

Solve the inequality. Then graph the solution. *(Lesson 6.4)*

19. $3 \leq x + 4 < 8$ **20.** $-36 < 6x < 12$ **21.** $-2 < 2x - 4 \leq 10$ **22.** $0 \leq 5x - 6 < 9$

Solve the inequality. Then graph the solution. *(Lesson 6.5)*

23. $x - 3 \leq -2 \ or \ x + 2 > 6$ **24.** $x + 1 > 4 \ or \ 2x + 3 \leq 5$

25. $2x + 1 > 9 \ or \ 3x - 5 < 4$ **26.** $-4x + 1 \geq 17 \ or \ 5x - 4 > 6$

Solve the equation and check your solutions. If the equation has no solution, write *no solution*. *(Lesson 6.6)*

27. $|x| = 14$ **28.** $|x| = -10$ **29.** $|x| = 12$

30. $|5x| = 15$ **31.** $|10 + x| = 4$ **32.** $|x - 8| = 2$

33. $|5x - 3| = 2$ **34.** $|2x + 3| = 9$ **35.** $|x - 4| + 4 = 7$

Solve the inequality. Then graph and check the solution. *(Lesson 6.7)*

36. $|x| \geq 2$ **37.** $|x| \leq 8$ **38.** $|x - 5| < 10$

39. $|6x| \leq 30$ **40.** $|4 + x| > 8$ **41.** $|4x + 5| \geq 3$

42. $|10 - 4x| \leq 2$ **43.** $|6x - 5| + 1 < 8$ **44.** $|3x + 4| - 6 \geq 14$

Graph the inequality in a coordinate plane. *(Lesson 6.8)*

45. $y \geq -2$ **46.** $x - y \leq 0$ **47.** $x + y \geq 5$ **48.** $4y + x < 4$

49. $x - 3y \leq 0$ **50.** $3y - 2x < 6$ **51.** $5x - 3y > 9$ **52.** $2y - x > 10$

Chapter 7, Volume 2

Estimate the solution of the linear system graphically. Then check the solution algebraically. *(Lesson 7.1)*

1. $y = 5$
$x = -2$

2. $x = 0$
$y = 3x + 7$

3. $x + y = 10$
$x - y = -2$

4. $-2x + 4y = 12$
$5x - 2y = 10$

Use the substitution method to solve the linear system. *(Lesson 7.2)*

5. $x = 5y$
$2x + 3y = -13$

6. $y = -2x$
$x + y = 7$

7. $x + y = 9$
$x - y = 3$

8. $2a + 3b = 3$
$a - 6b = -6$

9. $-s - t = -5$
$3s + 4t = 16$

10. $5x - 8y = -17$
$3x - y = 5$

11. $2m + n = 7$
$4m + 3n = -1$

12. $5a + b = 4$
$7a + 5b = 11$

Use linear combinations to solve the linear system. Then check your solution. *(Lesson 7.3)*

13. $x + y = 6$
$x - y = 2$

14. $3x + 3y = 6$
$2x - 3y = 4$

15. $4x - 5y = 10$
$2x + 5y = -10$

16. $2x + 8y = 9$
$x - y = 0$

17. $-x + y = -15$
$x + 4y = 5$

18. $2x + 3y = 15$
$3y + 5x = 12$

19. $y = 2x - 3$
$3x - 5y = 1$

20. $-4x - 15 = 5y$
$2y = 11 - 5x$

Choose a solution method to solve the linear system. Explain your choice, and then solve the system. *(Lesson 7.4)*

21. $x - 2y = -10$
$3x + y = 5$

22. $5x + 3y = 15$
$4x - 3y = 12$

23. $y = -2x - 6$
$y = -4$

24. $x + y = 8$
$x - y = 4$

25. $2x - 3y = 6$
$x + y = 3$

26. $2x + y = -8$
$6x + y = -2$

27. $5x - y = 10$
$2x + y = 4$

28. $-4x + 3y = 1$
$-8x + 4y = -4$

29. STUDENT THEATER You sell 20 tickets for admission to your school play and collect a total of $104. Admission prices are $6 for adults and $4 for students. How many of each type of ticket did you sell? *(Lesson 7.4)*

Use the graphing method to tell how many solutions the system has. *(Lesson 7.5)*

30. $x + y = 4$
$2x + 3y = 9$

31. $x + y = 6$
$3x + 3y = 3$

32. $x + 2y = 5$
$3x - 15 = -6y$

33. $12x - y = 5$
$-8x + y = -5$

34. $y = -3x$
$6y - x = 38$

35. $2x - 3y = 3$
$6x - 9y = 9$

36. $3x + 6 = 7y$
$x + 2y = 11$

37. $3x - 8y = 4$
$6x - 42 = 16y$

Graph the system of linear inequalities. *(Lesson 7.6)*

38. $y \geq 0$
$x \leq 0$

39. $y > x + 1$
$y < x + 3$

40. $x \geq 1$
$y + x \leq 5$

41. $y + 2 < -x$
$2y - 4 > 3x$

42. $x < 5$
$x \geq 1$
$y \geq -2$
$y < 7$

43. $y > x - 4$
$y \geq -x - 1$
$y \leq 0$

44. $y > x - 3$
$y < x + 2$
$x \leq 3$

45. $3x - 1 < 5$
$-x + y \leq 10$
$-5x + 2 < 12$

Chapter 8, Volume 2

Simplify the expression. *(Lesson 8.1)*

1. $7^2 \cdot 7^3$

2. $(2^3)^4$

3. $(12x)^3$

4. $(-3cd)^4$

5. $(m^3)^2$

6. $(4r)^2 \cdot r$

7. $(7x^2)^2 \cdot 2x^3$

8. $(3x)^3(-5y)^2$

Rewrite as an expression with positive exponents. *(Lesson 8.2)*

9. x^{-4}

10. $2x^{-2}$

11. $x^{-3}y^{-2}$

12. $\dfrac{2}{x^{-2}}$

13. $\dfrac{4x}{y^{-5}}$

14. $\dfrac{3y^{-3}}{x^{-1}}$

15. $(4y^{-2})^2$

16. $\dfrac{2}{(5x)^{-2}}$

Graph the exponential function. *(Lesson 8.3)*

17. $y = 5^x$

18. $y = -3^x$

19. $y = \left(\dfrac{1}{4}\right)^x$

20. $y = 2\left(\dfrac{1}{3}\right)^x$

Simplify the quotient. *(Lesson 8.4)*

21. $\dfrac{2^{11}}{2^8}$

22. $x^5 \cdot \dfrac{1}{x^4}$

23. $\left(\dfrac{2}{3}\right)^4$

24. $\left(\dfrac{x}{4}\right)^{-2}$

25. $\dfrac{(-4)^2}{(-4)^5}$

26. $\dfrac{a^3}{a^4}$

27. $\left(\dfrac{3}{8}\right)^{-1}$

28. $\left(\dfrac{4}{x}\right)^3$

Simplify the expression. Use only positive exponents. *(Lesson 8.4)*

29. $\dfrac{2x^4y^2}{xy} \cdot \dfrac{3x^2y}{4x}$

30. $\dfrac{16r^5s^9}{-2rs^2} \cdot \dfrac{r^2s}{-8}$

31. $\left(\dfrac{3x^2z^4}{2xz}\right)^3$

32. $\dfrac{3x^2y}{2x} \cdot \dfrac{2y^2}{x^2y}$

33. $\dfrac{4a^{-1}b^3}{a^4b^{-2}} \cdot \left(\dfrac{3a}{ab}\right)^{-2}$

34. $\dfrac{(a^2)^4}{(a^5)^4}$

Write the number in decimal form. *(Lesson 8.5)*

35. 4.813×10^{-6}

36. 3.11×10^4

37. 8.4162×10^{-2}

38. 9.43×10^0

39. 5.0645×10^1

40. 1.2468×10^{-3}

41. 2.34×10^{-8}

42. 6.09013×10^{10}

Write the number in scientific notation. *(Lesson 8.5)*

43. 5280

44. 0.0378

45. 11.38

46. 33,000,000

47. 827.66

48. 0.208054

49. 16.354

50. 0.000891

51. 3.95

52. 78.4

53. 0.008

54. 67,000

INTEREST You deposit $1100 in an account that pays 5% interest compounded yearly. Find the balance at the end of the given time period. *(Lesson 8.6)*

55. 1 year

56. 10 years

57. 15 years

58. 25 years

59. DEPRECIATION A piece of equipment originally costs $120,000. Its value decreases at a rate of 10% per year. Write an exponential decay model to represent the decreasing value of the piece of equipment. *(Lesson 8.7)*

Chapter 9, Volume 2

Evaluate the expression. Give the exact value if possible. Otherwise, approximate to the nearest hundredth. *(Lesson 9.1)*

1. $\sqrt{3}$

2. $\sqrt{625}$

3. $-\sqrt{100}$

4. $\pm\sqrt{676}$

5. $\sqrt{15}$

6. $-\sqrt{125}$

7. $\sqrt{220}$

8. $\pm\sqrt{90}$

Solve the equation or write *no solution*. Write the solutions as integers if possible. Otherwise, write them as radical expressions. *(Lesson 9.2)*

9. $x^2 = 25$

10. $4x^2 - 8 = 0$

11. $x^2 = -16$

12. $x^2 + 1 = 1$

13. $3x^2 - 48 = 0$

14. $6x^2 + 6 = 4$

15. $2x^2 - 6 = 0$

16. $x^2 - 4 = -3$

17. FALLING OBJECT A ball is dropped from a bridge 80 feet above a river. How long will it take for the ball to hit the surface of the water? Round your solution to the nearest tenth. *(Lesson 9.2)*

Simplify the expression. *(Lesson 9.3)*

18. $\sqrt{60}$

19. $\sqrt{88}$

20. $\sqrt{250}$

21. $\sqrt{112}$

22. $\sqrt{\dfrac{11}{16}}$

23. $\dfrac{\sqrt{20}}{\sqrt{5}}$

24. $2\sqrt{\dfrac{9}{2}}$

25. $\dfrac{1}{3}\sqrt{27}$

Sketch the graph of the function. Label the coordinates of the vertex. *(Lesson 9.4)*

26. $y = 3x^2$

27. $y = x^2 - 4$

28. $y = -x^2 - 2x$

29. $y = x^2 - 6x + 8$

30. $y = 4x^2 + 4x - 5$

31. $y = x^2 - 2x + 3$

32. $y = -x^2 + 3x + 2$

33. $y = -3x^2 + 12x - 1$

Solve the equation algebraically. Check your solution by graphing. *(Lesson 9.5)*

34. $x^2 - 6x = -5x$

35. $x^2 + 5x = -6$

36. $x^2 - 3x = 4$

37. $x^2 + 3x = 10$

38. $x^2 - 9 = 0$

39. $-2x^2 + 4x + 6 = 0$

Write the quadratic equation in standard form. Then solve using the quadratic formula. *(Lesson 9.6)*

40. $x^2 + x = 12$

41. $x^2 - 12 = 4x$

42. $3x^2 + 11x = 4$

43. $-x^2 + 5x = 4$

44. $x^2 - 3x - 4 = -6$

45. $-x^2 - 5x = 6$

46. $x^2 - 8 = 7x$

47. $10 - 2x^2 = -x$

Determine whether the equation has *two solutions*, *one solution*, or *no real solution*. *(Lesson 9.7)*

48. $3x^2 + 14x - 5 = 0$

49. $4x^2 + 12x + 9 = 0$

50. $x^2 + 10x + 9 = 0$

51. $2x^2 + 8x + 8 = 0$

52. $5x^2 + 125 = 0$

53. $x^2 - 2x + 35 = 0$

54. $2x^2 - x - 3 = 0$

55. $-3x^2 + 5x - 6 = 0$

Sketch the graph of the inequality. *(Lesson 9.8)*

56. $y > -x^2 + 4$

57. $y \geq 4x^2$

58. $y < 5x^2 + 10x$

59. $y \leq -x^2 + 4x + 5$

Chapter 10, Volume 2

Use a vertical format or a horizontal format to add or subtract. *(Lesson 10.1)*

1. $(7x^2 - 4) + (x^2 + 5)$ **2.** $(3x^2 - 2) - (2x - 6x^2)$ **3.** $(8x^2 - 3x + 7) + (6x^2 - 4x + 1)$

4. $(-z^3 + 3z) + (-z^2 - 4z - 6)$ **5.** $(5x^2 + 7x - 4) - (4x^2 - 2x)$ **6.** $(3a + 2a^4 - 5) - (a^3 + 2a^4 + 5a)$

Find the product. *(Lesson 10.2)*

7. $x(4x^2 - 8x + 7)$ **8.** $-3x(x^2 + 5x - 5)$ **9.** $5b^2(3b^3 - 2b^2 + 1)$ **10.** $(t + 9)(2t + 1)$

11. $(d - 1)(d + 5)$ **12.** $(3z + 4)(5z - 8)$ **13.** $(x + 3)(x^2 - 2x + 6)$ **14.** $(3 + 2s - s^2)(s - 1)$

Find the product. *(Lesson 10.3)*

15. $(x + 9)^2$ **16.** $(-c - d)^2$ **17.** $(a - 2)(a + 2)$ **18.** $(-7 + m)(-7 - m)$

19. $(4x + 5)^2$ **20.** $(5p - 6q)^2$ **21.** $(2a + 3b)(2a - 3b)$ **22.** $(10x - 5y)(10x + 5y)$

Solve the equation. *(Lesson 10.4)*

23. $(x + 3)(x + 6) = 0$ **24.** $(x - 11)^2 = 0$ **25.** $(z - 1)(z + 5) = 0$ **26.** $w(w - 4) = 0$

27. $(6n - 9)(n - 7) = 0$ **28.** $3(x + 2)^2 = 0$ **29.** $(2d - 2)(4d - 8) = 0$ **30.** $x(3x + 1) = 0$

Find the *x*-intercepts and the vertex of the graph of the function. Then sketch the graph of the function. *(Lesson 10.4)*

31. $y = (x - 8)(x - 6)$ **32.** $y = (x + 4)(x - 4)$ **33.** $y = (x - 5)(x - 7)$ **34.** $y = (x + 1)(x + 6)$

35. $y = (-x + 5)(x - 9)$ **36.** $y = (-x + 1)(x + 5)$ **37.** $y = (x - 3)(x + 1)$ **38.** $y = (-x - 3)(x + 7)$

Solve the equation by factoring. *(Lesson 10.5)*

39. $x^2 + 6x + 9 = 0$ **40.** $x^2 + 2x - 35 = 0$ **41.** $x^2 - 12x = -36$ **42.** $-x^2 - 4x = 3$

43. $x^2 - 15x = -54$ **44.** $-x^2 + 14x = 48$ **45.** $x^2 - 2x = 24$ **46.** $x^2 - 5x + 4 = 0$

Solve the equation by factoring. *(Lesson 10.6)*

47. $2x^2 + x - 6 = 0$ **48.** $2x^2 + 7x = -3$ **49.** $9x^2 + 24x = -16$ **50.** $20x^2 + 23x + 6 = 0$

51. $4x^2 - 5x = 6$ **52.** $3x^2 - 5 = -14x$ **53.** $3x^2 - 17x = 56$ **54.** $12x^2 + 46x - 36 = 0$

Factor the expression. *(Lesson 10.7)*

55. $x^2 - 1$ **56.** $9b^2 - 81$ **57.** $121 - x^2$ **58.** $12 - 27x^2$

59. $t^2 + 2t + 1$ **60.** $x^2 + 20x + 100$ **61.** $64y^2 + 48y + 9$ **62.** $20x^2 - 100x + 125$

Factor the expression completely. *(Lesson 10.8)*

63. $x^4 - 9x^2$ **64.** $m^3 + 11m^2 + 28m$ **65.** $x^4 + 4x^3 - 45x^2$ **66.** $x^3 + 2x^2 - 4x - 8$

67. $-3y^3 - 15y^2 - 12y$ **68.** $x^3 - x^2 + 4x - 4$ **69.** $7x^6 - 21x^4$ **70.** $8t^3 - 3t^2 + 16t - 6$

71. GEOMETRY The width of a box is 2 feet less than the length. The height is 8 feet greater than the length. The box has a cubic volume of 96 cubic feet. What are the dimensions of the box? *(Lesson 10.8)*

Chapter 11, Volume 2

Solve the equation. Check your solutions. *(Lesson 11.1)*

1. $\dfrac{9}{m} = \dfrac{15}{10}$

2. $\dfrac{x}{2} = \dfrac{8}{x}$

3. $\dfrac{3}{5} = \dfrac{x+2}{6}$

4. $\dfrac{12}{8} = \dfrac{5+t}{t-3}$

5. $\dfrac{c^2-16}{c+4} = \dfrac{c-4}{3}$

6. $\dfrac{x+15}{16} = \dfrac{-9}{x-10}$

The variables x and y vary directly. Use the given values to write an equation that relates x and y. *(Lesson 11.2)*

7. $x = 4, y = 12$

8. $x = 5, y = 10$

9. $x = 16, y = 4$

10. $x = 21, y = 7$

The variables x and y vary inversely. Use the given values to write an equation that relates x and y. *(Lesson 11.2)*

11. $x = 3, y = 5$

12. $x = 7, y = 1$

13. $x = 4, y = \dfrac{1}{2}$

14. $x = 5.5, y = 6$

Simplify the expression. If not possible, write *already in simplest form*. *(Lesson 11.3)*

15. $\dfrac{12x^4}{42x}$

16. $\dfrac{5x^2-15x^3}{10x}$

17. $\dfrac{x+6}{x^2+7x+6}$

18. $\dfrac{x^2-8x+15}{x-3}$

19. $\dfrac{8x^2}{12x^3}$

20. $\dfrac{6}{x+2}$

21. $\dfrac{4-y}{y^2-16}$

22. $\dfrac{x^2-9x+18}{x^2-4x-12}$

Write the product in simplest form. *(Lesson 11.4)*

23. $\dfrac{3x}{5} \cdot \dfrac{15}{18x}$

24. $\dfrac{z^2+5z+6}{z^2+z} \cdot \dfrac{z}{z+3}$

25. $\dfrac{10x^2}{x^2-25} \cdot (x-5)$

Write the quotient in simplest form. *(Lesson 11.4)*

26. $\dfrac{1}{4x} \div \dfrac{6x}{16}$

27. $\dfrac{5x}{x^2-6x+9} \div \dfrac{x}{x-3}$

28. $\dfrac{x^2+5x-36}{x^2-81} \div (x^2-16)$

Simplify the expression. *(Lesson 11.5)*

29. $\dfrac{3}{5x} + \dfrac{2}{5x}$

30. $\dfrac{3x}{x+2} + \dfrac{4x-1}{x+2}$

31. $\dfrac{x}{x-1} - \dfrac{3x+2}{x-1}$

32. $\dfrac{6x}{2x-1} - \dfrac{3}{2x-1}$

Simplify the expression. *(Lesson 11.6)*

33. $\dfrac{5}{x^2} - \dfrac{3}{x}$

34. $\dfrac{8}{3x} - \dfrac{x+2}{9x^2}$

35. $\dfrac{x-1}{x+8} + \dfrac{4}{x-3}$

36. $\dfrac{x+1}{3x^2} + \dfrac{3}{4x}$

37. $\dfrac{5x+3}{x^2-25} + \dfrac{5}{x-5}$

38. $\dfrac{4x-1}{3x+2} - \dfrac{3x}{x-4}$

Solve the equation. Check your solutions. *(Lesson 11.7)*

39. $\dfrac{4}{x} = \dfrac{3}{25}$

40. $\dfrac{1}{x-3} = \dfrac{5}{x+9}$

41. $\dfrac{-2}{3x} = \dfrac{4+x}{6}$

42. $\dfrac{4}{x} + \dfrac{2}{3} = \dfrac{6}{x}$

43. $\dfrac{x}{x-5} - \dfrac{11}{x-5} = 7$

44. $\dfrac{5}{x-1} + 1 = \dfrac{4}{x^2+3x-4}$

Chapter 12, Volume 2

Find the domain of the function. Then sketch its graph and find the range.
(Lesson 12.1)

1. $y = 8\sqrt{x}$ **2.** $y = \sqrt{5x}$ **3.** $y = \sqrt{x} - 5$ **4.** $y = \sqrt{x} + 1$

5. $y = \sqrt{x-2}$ **6.** $y = \sqrt{x+3}$ **7.** $y = \sqrt{3x+2}$ **8.** $y = \sqrt{4x-3}$

Simplify the expression. *(Lesson 12.2)*

9. $3\sqrt{5} + 2\sqrt{5}$ **10.** $8\sqrt{7} - 15\sqrt{7}$ **11.** $2\sqrt{8} + 3\sqrt{32}$ **12.** $\sqrt{20} - \sqrt{45} + \sqrt{80}$

13. $\sqrt{3}(7 - \sqrt{6})$ **14.** $(4 + \sqrt{10})^2$ **15.** $\dfrac{4}{\sqrt{24}}$ **16.** $\dfrac{3}{5 - \sqrt{2}}$

Solve the equation. Check for extraneous solutions. *(Lesson 12.3)*

17. $\sqrt{x} - 11 = 0$ **18.** $\sqrt{2x-1} + 4 = 7$ **19.** $\sqrt{x} + 10 = 2$

20. $12 = \sqrt{3x+1} + 7$ **21.** $x = \sqrt{4x-3}$ **22.** $4\sqrt{x} + 5 = 21$

Evaluate the expression. *(Lesson 12.4)*

23. $4^{2/3} \cdot 4^{4/3}$ **24.** $(27^{1/2})^{2/3}$ **25.** $(8^{1/4})^8$ **26.** $(2^2 \cdot 3^2)^{1/2}$

Simplify the variable expression. *(Lesson 12.4)*

27. $x^{1/4} \cdot x^{1/2}$ **28.** $(x^2)^{1/4}$ **29.** $(x \cdot y^{1/3})^6 \cdot \sqrt{y}$ **30.** $(x \cdot x^{1/3})^{3/4}$

Solve the quadratic equation by completing the square. *(Lesson 12.5)*

31. $x^2 + 10x = 56$ **32.** $x^2 + 2x = 3$ **33.** $x^2 + 6x + 8 = 0$

34. $x^2 - 12x = 13$ **35.** $x^2 - 6x = 16$ **36.** $x^2 - 10x - 39 = 0$

Find the missing length of the right triangle if *a* and *b* are the lengths of the legs and *c* is the length of the hypotenuse. *(Lesson 12.6)*

37. $a = 1, b = 1$ **38.** $a = 1, c = 2$ **39.** $b = 6, c = 10$

40. $a = 7, b = 10$ **41.** $b = 15, c = 25$ **42.** $a = 30, c = 50$

Find the distance between the two points. Round your solution to the nearest hundredth if necessary. *(Lesson 12.7)*

43. $(7, -6), (-1, -6)$ **44.** $(5, 2), (5, -4)$ **45.** $(12, -7), (-4, 2)$ **46.** $(-4, -5), (-8, 9)$

47. $(5, 8), (0, -3)$ **48.** $(10, -1), (4, 11)$ **49.** $(-3, -8), (-1, -4)$ **50.** $(12, 11), (9, 15)$

Find the midpoint of the line segment connecting the given points. Then show that the midpoint is the same distance from each point. *(Lesson 12.8)*

51. $(0, 4), (4, 5)$ **52.** $(-3, 3), (6, -1)$ **53.** $(1, 0), (4, -4)$ **54.** $(0, 0), (3, -2)$

55. $(-2, 0), (2, 8)$ **56.** $(3, 7), (-5, -9)$ **57.** $(6, 2), (4, 10)$ **58.** $(4, -6), (-8, 3)$

59. INDIRECT PROOF Use an indirect proof to prove that the following conclusion is true. If $xy = 0$, then either $x = 0$ or $y = 0$. *(Lesson 12.9)*

End-of-Course Test

The End-of-Course Test covers both Volumes 1 and 2. Exercises 1-6 and 9-12 cover Volume 1. The remaining exercises cover Volume 2.

VARIABLES, EXPRESSIONS, AND PROPERTIES

Evaluate the variable expression when $a = 7$, $b = 2$, $c = -4$, and $d = 1$.

1. $a^2 - 3b + bc$ **2.** $|c + d|$ **3.** $-d - (-c)$ **4.** $-6\left(\dfrac{2}{3}\right)(d)$

5. $\dfrac{b - c}{d}$ **6.** $a(b + 2d)$ **7.** $c^3 d$ **8.** $5(2^{-4})$

Simplify the expression. Name each property that you used.

9. $-ab + ba$ **10.** $0 + \sqrt{2}$ **11.** $5(x + 4)$ **12.** $-1 \cdot n + 0 \cdot n$

13. $7^{-3} \cdot 7^5 \cdot 7^3$ **14.** $(2y^2)^4$ **15.** $\dfrac{a^6}{a^9}$ **16.** $\left(\dfrac{3}{x}\right)^{-3}$

LINEAR EQUATIONS AND INEQUALITIES

Solve the equation or inequality.

17. $4s - 6 = 18$ **18.** $0.2b - 1.3 \geq 6.7$ **19.** $\dfrac{1}{3}p - 1 < 11$

20. $4m - 2(5 - m) = 14$ **21.** $9 + \dfrac{1}{2}k = 14$ **22.** $7(a + 5) = -(2a + 1)$

23. $0.15x + 5.01 = 1.44$ **24.** $-7 > 5 - 2y$ **25.** $0 \leq 1 - c \leq \dfrac{2}{3}$

26. $4t < -12$ or $-t < -4$ **27.** $|2 - x| = 1$ **28.** $|2n + 5| > 3$

LINEAR SYSTEMS

Solve the system of linear equations. Then check your solution.

29. $4x - y = 6$
$x + 3y = 8$

30. $5p + 3q = 4$
$7p + 2q = 21$

31. $6a - 9b = 18$
$b = \dfrac{2}{3}a + 2$

Graph the system of linear inequalities.

32. $2x + 3y > -6$
$y \geq 3x - 13$

33. $x + 4y > 0$
$y \geq 0$

34. $3x - y \geq 1$
$y \geq x$

QUADRATIC EQUATIONS AND INEQUALITIES

Solve the quadratic equation. Write the exact solution.

35. $a^2 + 5 = 37$

36. $x^2 + 2x = 35$

37. $2v^2 - 6v - 9 = 0$

38. Sketch the graph of $y < x^2 + 3x$.

POLYNOMIALS AND FACTORING

Add, subtract, or multiply.

39. $(t^2 + 3t - 2) - (t + 6)$

40. $(x + 2) + (x^2 - 6x - 1)$

41. $(x + 2)(x^2 - 6x - 1)$

42. $(9c - 5)(9c + 5)$

Factor the expression completely.

43. $y^2 + y - 30$

44. $z^3 - 3z^2 + 2z$

45. $8 + 27n^3$

RATIONAL EXPRESSIONS AND EQUATIONS

Write the expression in simplest form.

46. $\dfrac{x^2 - 6x + 9}{4x - 12}$

47. $\dfrac{x^2 - 7x + 6}{2x - 12} \cdot \dfrac{4x}{3x - 3}$

48. $\dfrac{6k^2}{4k + 8} \div \dfrac{4k^3}{k^2 - 4}$

49. $\dfrac{3x}{x^2 - 3x} - \dfrac{9}{x^2 - 3x}$

50. $\dfrac{4}{9z} - \dfrac{z + 1}{6z^2}$

51. $\dfrac{x}{x - 2} + \dfrac{x - 2}{x - 1}$

Solve the equation.

52. $\dfrac{d}{d + 4} = \dfrac{d - 5}{d + 1}$

53. $\dfrac{1}{2} + \dfrac{2}{s} = \dfrac{15}{4s}$

54. $\dfrac{n}{n - 1} + \dfrac{2}{n + 1} = 2$

RADICAL EXPRESSIONS AND EQUATIONS

Simplify the expression.

55. $\sqrt{18} \cdot \sqrt{2}$

56. $\sqrt{98} \cdot \sqrt{8}$

57. $2\sqrt{6}(5 - \sqrt{6})$

58. $\dfrac{8}{2 + \sqrt{3}}$

59. $4^{5/2} \cdot 4^{1/2}$

60. $(100^2)^{1/4}$

Solve the equation. Check for extraneous solutions.

61. $\sqrt{x} + 4 = 0$

62. $\sqrt{4x - 3} = 3$

63. $\sqrt{x + 2} = x$

Table of Symbols

Symbol		Page
$\cdot$, $(a)(b)$	multiplied by or times ($\times$)	3
a^n	nth power of a	9
$\ldots$	continues on	9
$(\;)$	parentheses	10
$[\;]$	brackets	10
$=$	equal sign, is equal to	24
$\stackrel{?}{=}$	Is this statement true?	24
$\neq$	is not equal to	24
$<$	is less than	26
$\leq$	is less than or equal to	26
$>$	is greater than	26
$\geq$	is greater than or equal to	26
$^\circ$	degree(s)	67
$-a$	the opposite of a	71
$|a|$	absolute value of a	71
$\dfrac{1}{a}$	reciprocal of a, $a \neq 0$	113

Symbol		Page
$\approx$	is approximately equal to	163
$\dfrac{a}{b}$	ratio of a to b, or $a{:}b$	177
$\dfrac{a}{b}$	rate of a per b, where a and b are measured in different units	177
$\%$	percent	183
(x, y)	ordered pair	203
m	slope	229
k	constant of variation	236
b	y-intercept	243
$f(x)$	the value of f at x	254
π	pi, an irrational number approximately equal to 3.14	445
a^{-n}	$\dfrac{1}{a^n}$, $a \neq 0$	449
$c \times 10^n$	scientific notation, where $1 \leq c < 10$ and n is an integer	469
$\sqrt{a}$	the positive square root of a when $a > 0$	499
$\pm$	plus or minus	499

Table of Formulas

Geometric Formulas

Perimeter of a polygon	$P = a + b + \ldots + z$ where $a, b, \ldots, z$ = side lengths
Area of a triangle	$A = \frac{1}{2}bh$ where b = base and h = height
Area of a square	$A = s^2$ where s = side length
Area of a rectangle	$A = \ell w$ where ℓ = length and w = width
Area of a trapezoid	$A = \frac{1}{2}h(b_1 + b_2)$ where h = height and b_1, b_2 = bases
Volume of a cube	$V = s^3$ where s = edge length
Volume of a rectangular prism	$V = \ell wh$ where ℓ = length, w = width, and h = height
Circumference of a circle	$C = \pi d$ where $\pi \approx 3.14$ and d = diameter $C = 2\pi r$ where $\pi \approx 3.14$ and r = radius
Area of a circle	$A = \pi r^2$ where $\pi \approx 3.14$ and r = radius
Surface area of a sphere	$S = 4\pi r^2$ where $\pi \approx 3.14$ and r = radius
Volume of a sphere	$V = \frac{4}{3}\pi r^3$ where $\pi \approx 3.14$ and r = radius

Other Formulas

Average speed	$r = \frac{d}{t}$ where r = average rate or speed, d = distance, and t = time

Algebraic Formulas

Slope formula	$m = \frac{y_2 - y_1}{x_2 - x_1}$ where m = slope and (x_1, y_1) and (x_2, y_2) are two points
Quadratic formula	The solutions of $ax^2 + bx + c = 0$ are $x = \frac{-b \pm \sqrt{b^2 - 4ac}}{2a}$ when $a \neq 0$ and $b^2 - 4ac \geq 0$.
Pythagorean theorem	$a^2 + b^2 = c^2$ where a, b = length of the legs and c = length of the hypotenuse of a right triangle
Distance formula	The distance between (x_1, y_1) and (x_2, y_2) is $\sqrt{(x_2 - x_1)^2 + (y_2 - y_1)^2}$.
Midpoint formula	The midpoint between (x_1, y_1) and (x_2, y_2) is $\left(\frac{x_1 + x_2}{2}, \frac{y_1 + y_2}{2} \right)$.

TABLES

Table of Properties

Basic Properties

	Addition	**Multiplication**
Closure	$a + b$ is a unique real number.	ab is a unique real number.
Commutative	$a + b = b + a$	$ab = ba$
Associative	$(a + b) + c = a + (b + c)$	$(ab)c = a(bc)$
Identity	$a + 0 = a, 0 + a = a$	$a(1) = a, 1(a) = a$
Property of zero	$a + (-a) = 0$	$a(0) = 0$
Property of negative one		$(-1)a = -a$ or $a(-1) = -a$
Distributive		$a(b + c) = ab + ac$ or $(b + c)a = ba + ca$

Properties of Equality

Addition	If $a = b$, then $a + c = b + c$.
Subtraction	If $a = b$, then $a - c = b - c$.
Multiplication	If $a = b$, then $ca = cb$.
Division	If $a = b$ and $c \neq 0$, then $\dfrac{a}{c} = \dfrac{b}{c}$.

Properties of Exponents

Product of Powers	$a^m \cdot a^n = a^{m + n}$
Power of a Power	$\left(a^m\right)^n = a^{m \cdot n}$
Power of a Product	$(a \cdot b)^m = a^m \cdot b^m$
Quotient of Powers	$\dfrac{a^m}{a^n} = a^{m - n}, a \neq 0$
Power of a Quotient	$\left(\dfrac{a}{b}\right)^m = \dfrac{a^m}{b^m}, b \neq 0$
Negative Exponent	$a^{-n} = \dfrac{1}{a^n}, a \neq 0$
Zero Exponent	$a^0 = 1, a \neq 0$

Properties of Radicals

Product Property	$\sqrt{ab} = \sqrt{a} \cdot \sqrt{b}$
Quotient Property	$\sqrt{\dfrac{a}{b}} = \dfrac{\sqrt{a}}{\sqrt{b}}, b \neq 0$

Properties of Proportions

Reciprocal	If $\dfrac{a}{b} = \dfrac{c}{d}$, then $\dfrac{b}{a} = \dfrac{d}{c}$.
Cross-multiplying	If $\dfrac{a}{b} = \dfrac{c}{d}$, then $ad = bc$.

Special Products and Their Factors

Sum and Difference Pattern	$(a + b)(a - b) = a^2 - b^2$
Square of a Binomial Pattern	$(a + b)^2 = a^2 + 2ab + b^2$ $(a - b)^2 = a^2 - 2ab + b^2$

Properties of Rational Expressions

Multiplication	$\dfrac{a}{b} \cdot \dfrac{c}{d} = \dfrac{ac}{bd}$
Division	$\dfrac{a}{b} \div \dfrac{c}{d} = \dfrac{a}{b} \cdot \dfrac{d}{c}$
Addition	$\dfrac{a}{c} + \dfrac{b}{c} = \dfrac{a + b}{c}, \dfrac{a}{b} + \dfrac{c}{d} = \dfrac{ad + bc}{bd}$
Subtraction	$\dfrac{a}{c} - \dfrac{b}{c} = \dfrac{a - b}{c}, \dfrac{a}{b} - \dfrac{c}{d} = \dfrac{ad - bc}{bd}$

Using the Table

EXAMPLE **1**

Find 54^2.

Solution

Find 54 in the numbers' column. Read across that line to the squares' column.
So, $54^2 = 2916$.

No.	Square	Sq. Root
51	2601	7.141
52	2704	7.211
53	2809	7.280
54	2916	7.348
55	3025	7.416

EXAMPLE **2**

Find a decimal approximation of $\sqrt{54}$.

Solution

Find 54 in the numbers' column. Read across that line to the square roots' column.
This number is a three-decimal place approximation of $\sqrt{54}$, so $\sqrt{54} \approx 7.348$.

No.	Square	Sq. Root
51	2601	7.141
52	2704	7.211
53	2809	7.280
54	2916	7.348
55	3025	7.416

EXAMPLE **3**

Estimate $\sqrt{3000}$.

Solution

Find the two numbers in the squares' column that 3000 is between. Read across these two lines to the numbers' column; $\sqrt{3000}$ is between 54 and 55, but closer to 55. So, $\sqrt{3000} \approx 55$. A more accurate approximation can be found using a calculator: 54.772256.

No.	Square	Sq. Root
51	2601	7.141
52	2704	7.211
53	2809	7.280
54	2916	7.348
55	3025	7.416

TABLES

Table of Squares and Square Roots

No.	Square	Sq. Root	No.	Square	Sq. Root	No.	Square	Sq. Root
1	1	1.000	51	2601	7.141	101	10,201	10.050
2	4	1.414	52	2704	7.211	102	10,404	10.100
3	9	1.732	53	2809	7.280	103	10,609	10.149
4	16	2.000	54	2916	7.348	104	10,816	10.198
5	25	2.236	55	3025	7.416	105	11,025	10.247
6	36	2.449	56	3136	7.483	106	11,236	10.296
7	49	2.646	57	3249	7.550	107	11,449	10.344
8	64	2.828	58	3364	7.616	108	11,664	10.392
9	81	3.000	59	3481	7.681	109	11,881	10.440
10	100	3.162	60	3600	7.746	110	12,100	10.488
11	121	3.317	61	3721	7.810	111	12,321	10.536
12	144	3.464	62	3844	7.874	112	12,544	10.583
13	169	3.606	63	3969	7.937	113	12,769	10.630
14	196	3.742	64	4096	8.000	114	12,996	10.677
15	225	3.873	65	4225	8.062	115	13,225	10.724
16	256	4.000	66	4356	8.124	116	13,456	10.770
17	289	4.123	67	4489	8.185	117	13,689	10.817
18	324	4.243	68	4624	8.246	118	13,924	10.863
19	361	4.359	69	4761	8.307	119	14,161	10.909
20	400	4.472	70	4900	8.367	120	14,400	10.954
21	441	4.583	71	5041	8.426	121	14,641	11.000
22	484	4.690	72	5184	8.485	122	14,884	11.045
23	529	4.796	73	5329	8.544	123	15,129	11.091
24	576	4.899	74	5476	8.602	124	15,376	11.136
25	625	5.000	75	5625	8.660	125	15,625	11.180
26	676	5.099	76	5776	8.718	126	15,876	11.225
27	729	5.196	77	5929	8.775	127	16,129	11.269
28	784	5.292	78	6084	8.832	128	16,384	11.314
29	841	5.385	79	6241	8.888	129	16,641	11.358
30	900	5.477	80	6400	8.944	130	16,900	11.402
31	961	5.568	81	6561	9.000	131	17,161	11.446
32	1024	5.657	82	6724	9.055	132	17,424	11.489
33	1089	5.745	83	6889	9.110	133	17,689	11.533
34	1156	5.831	84	7056	9.165	134	17,956	11.576
35	1225	5.916	85	7225	9.220	135	18,225	11.619
36	1296	6.000	86	7396	9.274	136	18,496	11.662
37	1369	6.083	87	7569	9.327	137	18,769	11.705
38	1444	6.164	88	7744	9.381	138	19,044	11.747
39	1521	6.245	89	7921	9.434	139	19,321	11.790
40	1600	6.325	90	8100	9.487	140	19,600	11.832
41	1681	6.403	91	8281	9.539	141	19,881	11.874
42	1764	6.481	92	8464	9.592	142	20,164	11.916
43	1849	6.557	93	8649	9.644	143	20,449	11.958
44	1936	6.633	94	8836	9.695	144	20,736	12.000
45	2025	6.708	95	9025	9.747	145	21,025	12.042
46	2116	6.782	96	9216	9.798	146	21,316	12.083
47	2209	6.856	97	9409	9.849	147	21,609	12.124
48	2304	6.928	98	9604	9.899	148	21,904	12.166
49	2401	7.000	99	9801	9.950	149	22,201	12.207
50	2500	7.071	100	10,000	10.000	150	22,500	12.247

TABLES

Table of Measures

Time

60 seconds (sec) = 1 minute (min)
60 minutes = 1 hour (h)
24 hours = 1 day
7 days = 1 week
4 weeks (approx.) = 1 month

$\left.\begin{array}{l}\text{365 days}\\\text{52 weeks (approx.)}\\\text{12 months}\end{array}\right\}$ = 1 year

10 years = 1 decade
100 years = 1 century

Metric

Length

10 millimeters (mm) = 1 centimeter (cm)
$\left.\begin{array}{l}\text{100 cm}\\\text{1000 mm}\end{array}\right\}$ = 1 meter (m)
1000 m = 1 kilometer (km)

Area

100 square millimeters = 1 square centimeter
(mm^2) (cm^2)
$10,000\ cm^2$ = 1 square meter (m^2)
$10,000\ m^2$ = 1 hectare (ha)

Volume

1000 cubic millimeters = 1 cubic centimeter
(mm^3) (cm^3)
$1,000,000\ cm^3$ = 1 cubic meter (m^3)

Liquid Capacity

1000 milliliters (mL) = 1 liter (L)
1000 L = 1 kiloliter (kL)

Mass

1000 milligrams (mg) = 1 gram (g)
1000 g = 1 kilogram (kg)
1000 kg = 1 metric ton (t)

Temperature — Degrees Celsius (°C)

0°C = freezing point of water
37°C = normal body temperature
100°C = boiling point of water

United States Customary

Length

12 inches (in.) = 1 foot (ft)
$\left.\begin{array}{l}\text{36 in.}\\\text{3 ft}\end{array}\right\}$ = 1 yard (yd)
$\left.\begin{array}{l}\text{5280 ft}\\\text{1760 yd}\end{array}\right\}$ = 1 mile (mi)

Area

144 square inches $(in.^2)$ = 1 square foot (ft^2)
$9\ ft^2$ = 1 square yard (yd^2)
$\left.\begin{array}{l}\text{43,560 ft}^2\\\text{4840 yd}^2\end{array}\right\}$ = 1 acre (A)

Volume

1728 cubic inches $(in.^3)$ = 1 cubic foot (ft^3)
$27\ ft^3$ = 1 cubic yard (yd^3)

Liquid Capacity

8 fluid ounces (fl oz) = 1 cup (c)
2 c = 1 pint (pt)
2 pt = 1 quart (qt)
4 qt = 1 gallon (gal)

Weight

16 ounces (oz) = 1 pound (lb)
2000 lb = 1 ton (t)

Temperature — Degrees Fahrenheit (°F)

32°F = freezing point of water
98.6°F = normal body temperature
212°F = boiling point of water

Glossary

absolute value (p. 71) The distance between zero and the point representing a real number on the number line. The symbol $|a|$ represents the absolute value of a number a.

absolute value equation (p. 355) An equation of the form $|ax + b| = c$.

absolute value inequality (p. 361) An inequality that has one of these forms: $|ax + b| < c$, $|ax + b| \le c$, $|ax + b| > c$, or $|ax + b| \ge c$.

addition property of equality (p. 140) If $a = b$, then $a + c = b + c$.

addition property of inequality (p. 324) If $a > b$, then $a + c > b + c$ and if $a < b$, then $a + c < b + c$.

algebraic model (p. 36) An expression, equation, or inequality that uses variables to represent a real-life situation.

associative property of addition (p. 79) The way three numbers are grouped when adding does not change the sum. For any real numbers a, b, and c, $(a + b) + c = a + (b + c)$.

associative property of multiplication (p. 94) The way three numbers are grouped when multiplying does not change the product. For any real numbers a, b, and c, $(ab)c = a(bc)$.

axiom (p. 740) A rule that is accepted as true without proof. An axiom is also called a *postulate*.

axis of symmetry of a parabola (p. 521) The vertical line passing through the vertex of a parabola or the line dividing a parabola into two symmetrical parts that are mirror images of each other.

bar graph (p. 43) A graph that represents a collection of data by using horizontal or vertical bars whose lengths allow the data to be compared.

base (p. 9) In exponential notation, the number or variable that undergoes repeated multiplication. For example, 4 is the base in the expression 4^6.

base number of a percent equation (p. 183) The number that is the basis for comparison in a percent equation. The number b in the verbal model "a is p percent of b."

binomial (p. 569) A polynomial consisting of two terms.

closure property of real number addition (p. 78) The sum of any two real numbers is again a real number.

closure property of real number multiplication (p. 93) The product of any two real numbers is again a real number.

coefficient (p. 107) If a term of an expression consists of a number multiplied by one or more variables, the number is the coefficient of the term.

commutative property of addition (p. 79) The order in which two numbers are added does not change the sum. For any real numbers a and b, $a + b = b + a$.

commutative property of multiplication (p. 94) The order in which two numbers are multiplied does not change the product. For any real numbers a and b, $ab = ba$.

completing the square (p. 716) The process of rewriting a quadratic equation so that one side is a perfect square trinomial.

compound inequality (p. 342) Two inequalities connected by the word *and* or the word *or*.

conclusion (p. 120) The *then* part of an if-then statement is called the conclusion.

conjecture (p. 741) A statement that is thought to be true but has not been proved.

constant function (p. 218) A function of the form $y = b$, where b is some number.

constant of variation (p. 236, p. 639) The constant in a variation model. It is equal to $\dfrac{y}{x}$ in the case of direct variation, and xy in the case of inverse variation.

converse of a statement (p. 726) A related statement in which the hypothesis and conclusion are interchanged. The converse of the statement "If p, then q" is "If q, then p."

converse of the Pythagorean theorem (p. 726) If a triangle has side lengths a, b, and c such that $a^2 + b^2 = c^2$, then the triangle is a right triangle.

coordinate plane (p. 203) The coordinate system formed by two real number lines that intersect at a right angle.

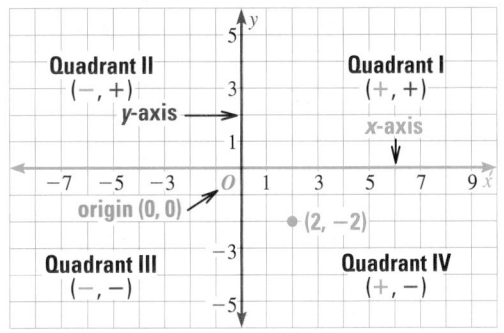

counterexample (p. 73) An example used to show that a given statement is false.

cross product property (p. 634) In a proportion, the product of the extremes equals the product of the means. If $\frac{a}{b} = \frac{c}{d}$, then $ad = bc$.

cube root (p. 710) If $b^3 = a$, then b is a cube root of a.

data (p. 42) Information, facts, or numbers used to describe something.

decay factor (p. 482) The expression $1 - r$ in the exponential decay model where r is the decay rate. *See also* exponential decay.

decay rate (p. 482) In an exponential decay model, the proportion by which the quantity decreases each time period. *See also* exponential decay.

decimal form (p. 469) A number written with place values corresponding to powers of ten. For example, 100, 14.2, and 0.007 are in decimal form.

deductive reasoning (p. 120) Using facts, definitions, rules, or properties to reach a conclusion.

degree of a monomial (p. 568) The sum of the exponents of each variable in the monomial. The degree of $5x^2y$ is $2 + 1 = 3$.

degree of a polynomial in one variable (p. 569) The largest exponent of that variable.

direct variation (p. 236) The relationship between two variables x and y for which there is a nonzero number k such that $y = kx$, or $\frac{y}{x} = k$. The variables x and y *vary directly.*

discriminant (p. 540) The expression $b^2 - 4ac$ where a, b, and c are coefficients of the quadratic equation $ax^2 + bx + c = 0$; the expression inside the radical in the quadratic formula.

distance formula (p. 730) The distance d between the points (x_1, y_1) and (x_2, y_2) is
$$d = \sqrt{(x_2 - x_1)^2 + (y_2 - y_1)^2}.$$

distributive property (pp. 100, 101) For any real numbers a, b, and c, $a(b + c) = ab + ac$, $(b + c)a = ba + ca$, $a(b - c) = ab - ac$, and $(b - c)a = ba - ca$.

division property of equality (p. 140) If $a = b$ and $c \neq 0$, then $\frac{a}{c} = \frac{b}{c}$.

division property of inequality (pp. 330, 331) If $a > b$ and $c > 0$, then $\frac{a}{c} > \frac{b}{c}$ and if $a < b$, then $\frac{a}{c} < \frac{b}{c}$. If $a > b$, and $c < 0$, then $\frac{a}{c} < \frac{b}{c}$ and if $a < b$, then $\frac{a}{c} > \frac{b}{c}$.

domain of a function (p. 49) The collection of all input values of a function.

equation (p. 24) A statement formed by placing an equal sign between two expressions.

equivalent equations (p. 132) Equations that have the same solution(s).

equivalent inequalities (p. 324) Inequalities that have the same solution(s).

evaluate an expression (p. 4) Find the value of an expression by substituting a specific numerical value for each variable, and simplifying the result.

exponent (p. 9) In exponential notation, the number of times the base is used as a factor. For example, 6 is the exponent in the expression 4^6.

exponential decay (p. 482) A quantity displays exponential decay if it decreases by the same proportion r in each time period t. If C is the initial amount, the amount at time t is given by $y = C(1 - r)^t$, where r is called the decay rate, $0 < r < 1$, and $(1 - r)$ is called the decay factor.

exponential function (p. 455) A function of the form $y = ab^x$, where $b > 0$ and $b \neq 1$.

exponential growth (p. 476) A quantity displays exponential growth if it increases by the same proportion r in each unit of time. If C is the initial amount, the amount after t units of time is given by $y = C(1 + r)^t$, where r is called the growth rate and $(1 + r)$ is called the growth factor.

extraneous solution (p. 705) A trial solution that does not satisfy the original equation.

extremes of a proportion (p. 633) In the proportion $\frac{a}{b} = \frac{c}{d}$, a and d are the extremes.

factor a polynomial completely (p. 617) To write a polynomial as the product of monomial and prime factors.

factor a trinomial (p. 595) Write the trinomial as the product of two binomials.

factored form of a polynomial (p. 588) A polynomial that is written as the product of two or more factors.

formula (p. 171) An algebraic equation that relates two or more variables.

function (p. 48) A rule that establishes a relationship between two quantities, the input and the output. There is exactly one output for each input.

function form (p. 211) A two-variable equation is written in function form if one of its variables is isolated on one side of the equation. The isolated variable is the output and is a function of the input.

GLOSSARY

function notation (p. 254) A way to describe a function by means of an equation. For the equation $y = f(x)$ the symbol $f(x)$ denotes the output and is read as "the value of f at x" or simply as "f of x."

graph of an equation in two variables (p. 211) The set of all points (x, y) that are solutions of the equation.

graph of an inequality in one variable (p. 323) The set of points on the number line that represent all the solutions of the inequality.

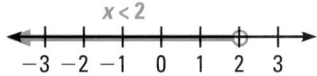

graph of a number (p. 65) The point on a number line that corresponds to a number.

graph of a quadratic inequality (p. 547) The graph of all ordered pairs (x, y) that are solutions of the inequality.

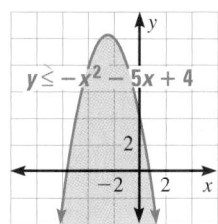

grouping symbols (p. 10) Symbols such as parentheses ( ) and brackets [ ] that indicate the order in which operations should be performed. Operations within the innermost set of grouping symbols are done first.

growth factor (p. 476) The expression $1 + r$ in the exponential growth model where r is the growth rate. *See also* exponential growth.

growth rate (p. 476) In an exponential growth model, the proportion by which the quantity increases each unit of time.

hypotenuse (p. 724) The side opposite the right angle in a right triangle.

hypothesis (p. 120) The *if* part of an if-then statement.

identity (p. 153) An equation that is true for all values of the variable.

identity property of addition (p. 79) The sum of a number and 0 is the number. For any real number a, $a + 0 = 0 + a = a$.

identity property of multiplication (p. 94) The product of a number and 1 is the number. For any real number a, $1 \cdot a = a$.

if-then statement (p. 120) A form of statement used in deductive reasoning where the *if* part is the hypothesis and the *then* part is the conclusion.

indirect proof (p. 742) A type of proof in which a statement is assumed false. If this assumption leads to an impossibility, then the original statement has been proved to be true.

inductive reasoning (p. 119) Making a general statement based on several observations.

inequality (p. 26) A statement formed by placing an inequality symbol, such as <, between two expressions.

input (p. 48) A value in the domain of a function.

input-output table (p. 48) A table used to describe a function by listing the outputs for several different inputs.

integers (p. 65) The numbers $\ldots -3, -2, -1, 0, 1, 2, 3, \ldots$.

inverse operations (p. 133) Two operations that undo each other, such as addition and subtraction.

inverse property of addition (p. 79) The sum of a number and its opposite is 0: $a + (-a) = 0$.

inverse variation (p. 639) The relationship between two variables x and y for which there is a nonzero number k such that $xy = k$, or $y = \dfrac{k}{x}$. The variables x and y are said to *vary inversely*.

leading coefficient (p. 505) For a quadratic equation in standard form, $ax^2 + bx + c = 0$ where $a \neq 0$, a is the leading coefficient.

least common denominator, LCD (p. 663) The least common multiple of the denominators of two or more fractions.

left-to-right rule (p. 16) When operations have the same priority, you perform them in order from left to right.

legs of a right triangle (p. 724) The two sides of a right triangle that are not opposite the right angle.

like terms (p. 107) Terms that have the same variables with each variable of the same kind raised to the same power. For example, $3x^2y$ and $-7x^2y$ are like terms.

line graph (p. 44) A graph that uses line segments to connect data points. Line graphs are especially useful for showing changes in data over time.

linear combination of two equations (p. 402) An equation obtained by (1) multiplying one or both equations by a constant and (2) adding the resulting equations.

linear equation in one variable (p. 134) An equation in which the variable appears only to the first power.

linear equation in *x* and *y* (p. 210) An equation that can be written in the form $Ax + By = C$, where A and B are not both zero.

linear function of *x* (p. 254) A function of the form $f(x) = mx + b$.

linear inequality in *x* and *y* (p. 367) An inequality that can be written in one of these forms: $ax + by < c$, $ax + by \leq c$, $ax + by > c$, or $ax + by \geq c$.

linear model (p. 298) A linear equation or function that is used to model a real-life situation.

linear system (p. 389) Two or more linear equations in the same variables. This is also called a system of linear equations.

means of a proportion (p. 633) In the proportion $\frac{a}{b} = \frac{c}{d}$, b and c are the means.

midpoint of a line segment (p. 736) The point on the segment that is equidistant from its endpoints.

midpoint formula (p. 736) The midpoint between (x_1, y_1) and (x_2, y_2) is $\left(\frac{x_1 + x_2}{2}, \frac{y_1 + y_2}{2} \right)$.

modeling (p. 36) Representing real-life situations by means of equations or inequalities.

monomial (pp. 568, 569) A number, a variable, or a product of a number and one or more variables with whole number exponents; a polynomial with only one term.

multiplication property of equality (p. 140) If $a = b$, then $ca = cb$.

multiplication property of inequality (pp. 330, 331) If $a > b$ and $c > 0$, then $ac > bc$ and if $a < b$, then $ac < bc$. If $a > b$ and $c < 0$, then $ac < bc$ and if $a < b$, then $ac > bc$.

multiplicative property of negative one (p. 94) The product of a number and -1 is the opposite of the number: $-1 \cdot a = -a$.

multiplicative property of zero (p. 94) The product of a number and 0 is 0. That is, $0 \cdot a = 0$.

negative number (p. 65) A number less than zero. *See also* real number line.

negative square root (p. 499) The negative number that is a square root of a positive number. For example, the negative square root of 9 is -3.

numerical expression (p. 3) An expression that represents a particular number.

opposites (p. 71) Two numbers that are the same distance from zero on a number line but on opposite sides of zero.

order of operations (p. 15) The rules for evaluating an expression involving more than one operation.

ordered pair (p. 203) A pair of numbers used to identify a point in a coordinate plane. The first number is the *x*-coordinate and the second number is the *y*-coordinate. *See also* coordinate plane.

origin (p. 203) The point in a coordinate plane where the horizontal axis intersects the vertical axis. The point (0, 0). *See also* coordinate plane.

output (p. 48) A value in the range of a function.

parabola (p. 520) The U-shaped graph of a quadratic function, $y = ax^2 + bx + c$ where $a \neq 0$.

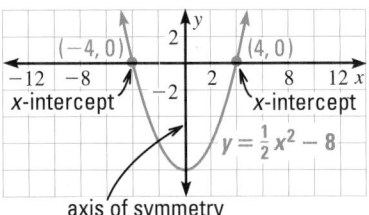

parallel lines (p. 245) Two different lines in the same plane that do not intersect. (Identical lines are sometimes considered to be parallel.)

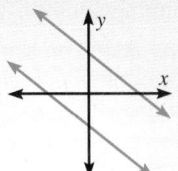

percent (p. 183) A ratio that compares a number to 100.

perfect square trinomials (p. 609) Trinomials of the form $a^2 + 2ab + b^2$ and $a^2 - 2ab + b^2$; perfect square trinomials can be factored as the squares of binomials.

perpendicular lines (p. 306) Two lines in a plane are perpendicular if they intersect at a right, or 90°, angle. If two nonvertical lines are perpendicular, the product of their slopes is -1.

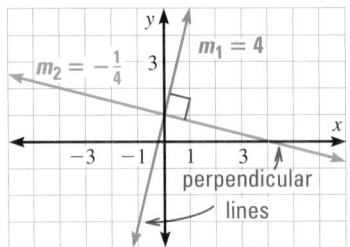

point of intersection (p. 389) A point (a, b) that lies on the graphs of two or more equations is a point of intersection for the graphs.

point-slope form (p. 278) An equation of a nonvertical line in the form $y - y_1 = m(x - x_1)$ where the line passes through a given point (x_1, y_1) and the line has a slope of m.

polynomial (p. 569) A monomial or a sum of monomials. *See* monomial.

positive number (p. 65) A number greater than zero.

positive square root, or principal square root (p. 499) The square root of a positive number that is itself positive. For example, the positive square root of 9 is 3.

postulate (p. 740) A rule that is accepted as true without proof. A postulate is also called an *axiom*.

power (p. 9) An expression of the form a^b or the value of such an expression. For example, 2^4 is a power, and since $2^4 = 16$, 16 is the fourth power of 2.

power of a power property (pp. 444, 445) To find a power of a power, multiply the exponents. For any real number a and integers m and n, $(a^m)^n = a^{mn}$.

power of a product property (p. 444) To find a power of a product, find the power of each factor and multiply. For any real numbers a and b and integer m, $(ab)^m = a^m \cdot b^m$.

power of a quotient property (pp. 462, 463) To find a power of a quotient, find the power of the numerator and the power of the denominator and divide. For any integer m and real numbers a and b, where $b \neq 0$,

$$\left(\frac{a}{b}\right)^m = \frac{a^m}{b^m}.$$

prime polynomial (p. 617) A polynomial that is not the product of factors with integer coefficients and of lower degree.

product of powers property (pp. 443, 445) To multiply powers having the same base, add the exponents. For any real number a and integers m and n, $a^m \cdot a^n = a^{m+n}$.

product property of radicals (p. 511) If a and b are real numbers such that $a \geq 0$ and $b \geq 0$, then $\sqrt{ab} = \sqrt{a} \cdot \sqrt{b}$.

properties of equality (p. 140) The rules of algebra used to transform equations into equivalent equations.

proportion (p. 633) An equation stating that two ratios are equal.

Pythagorean theorem (p. 724) If a right triangle has legs of lengths a and b and hypotenuse of length c, then $a^2 + b^2 = c^2$.

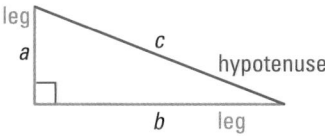

quadrant (p. 204) One of four regions into which the axes divide a coordinate plane.

quadratic equation (p. 505) An equation that can be written in the standard form $ax^2 + bx + c = 0$, where $a \neq 0$.

quadratic formula (p. 533) A formula used to find the solutions of a quadratic equation $ax^2 + bx + c = 0$ when $a \neq 0$ and $b^2 - 4ac \geq 0$:

$$x = \frac{-b \pm \sqrt{b^2 - 4ac}}{2a}.$$

quadratic function (p. 520) A function that can be written in the standard form $y = ax^2 + bx + c$, where $a \neq 0$.

quadratic inequality (p. 547) An inequality that can be written in one of the forms $y < ax^2 + bx + c$, $y \leq ax^2 + bx + c$, $y > ax^2 + bx + c$, or $y \geq ax^2 + bx + c$.

quotient of powers property (pp. 462, 463) To divide powers having the same base, subtract the exponents. For any real number $a \neq 0$ and integers m and n, $\frac{a^m}{a^n} = a^{m-n}$.

quotient property of radicals (p. 512) If a and b are real numbers such that $a \geq 0$ and $b > 0$, then

$$\sqrt{\frac{a}{b}} = \frac{\sqrt{a}}{\sqrt{b}}.$$

radical expression, or radical (p. 501) An expression written with a radical symbol.

radicand (p. 499) The number or expression inside a radical symbol.

range of a function (p. 49) The collection of all output values of a function.

rate of a per b (p. 177) The relationship $\frac{a}{b}$ of two quantities a and b that are measured in different units.

rate of change (p. 298) The quotient of two different quantities that are changing. In a linear model, the slope gives the rate of change of one variable with respect to the other.

ratio of a to b (p. 177) The relationship $\frac{a}{b}$ of two quantities a and b.

rational equation (p. 670) An equation that contains rational expressions.

rational exponent (p. 711) For any integer n and real number $a \geq 0$, the nth root of a is denoted $a^{1/n}$ or $\sqrt[n]{a}$. Let $a^{1/n}$ be an nth root of a, m be a positive integer and $a \geq 0$. Then $a^{m/n} = (a^{1/n})^m = (\sqrt[n]{a})^m = \sqrt[n]{a^m}$.

rational expression (p. 646) A fraction whose numerator and denominator are nonzero polynomials.

rational function (p. 678) A rational function is a function that is a quotient of polynomials.

rational number (p. 646) A number that can be written as the quotient of two integers.

real number line (p. 65) A line whose points correspond to the real numbers.

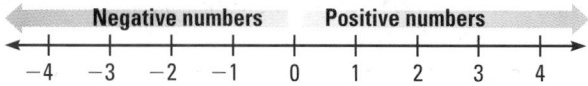

real numbers (p. 65) The set of numbers consisting of the positive numbers, the negative numbers, and zero. (The real numbers can also be thought of as the set of ali decimals, finite or infinite in length.)

reciprocals (p. 113) Two numbers are reciprocals if their product is 1. If $\frac{a}{b}$ is a nonzero number, then its reciprocal is $\frac{b}{a}$.

relation (p. 252) Any set of ordered pairs.

roots of a quadratic equation (p. 527) The solutions of a quadratic equation.

rounding error (p. 164) The error produced when a decimal expansion is limited to a specified number of digits to the right of the decimal point.

scatter plot (p. 205) A coordinate graph containing points that represent a set of ordered points; used to analyze relationships between two real-life quantities.

scientific notation (p. 469) A number expressed in the form $c \times 10^n$, where $1 \leq c < 10$ and n is an integer.

simplified expression (p. 108) An expression is simplified if it has no grouping symbols and if all the like terms have been combined.

simplest form of a radical expression (p. 511) An expression that has no perfect square factors other than 1 in the radicand, no fractions in the radicand, and no radicals in the denominator of a fraction.

slope (pp. 229, 230) The ratio of the vertical rise to the horizontal run between any two points on a line.

The slope is $m = \dfrac{(y_2 - y_1)}{(x_2 - x_1)}$.

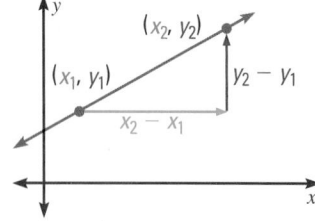

slope-intercept form (p. 243) A linear equation written in the form $y = mx + b$. The slope of the line is m. The y-intercept is b. See also slope and y-intercept.

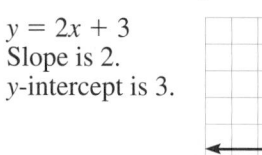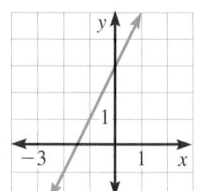

$y = 2x + 3$
Slope is 2.
y-intercept is 3.

solution of an equation or inequality (p. 24) A number that, when substituted for the variable in an equation or inequality, results in a true statement.

solution of an equation in two variables (p. 210) An ordered pair (x, y) that makes the equation true.

solution of a linear system in two variables (p. 389) An ordered pair (x, y) that makes each equation in the system a true statement.

solution of a system of linear inequalities in two variables (p. 424) An ordered pair that is a solution of each inequality in the system.

square root (p. 499) If $b^2 = a$, then b is a square root of a. Square roots can be written with a radical symbol, $\sqrt{}$.

square root function (p. 692) The function defined by the equation $y = \sqrt{x}$, for $x \geq 0$.

standard form of an equation of a line (p. 291) A linear equation of the form $Ax + By = C$, where A and B are not both zero.

standard form of a polynomial in one variable (p. 569) A polynomial whose terms are written in decreasing order, from largest exponent to smallest exponent.

standard form of a quadratic equation (p. 505) An equation in the form $ax^2 + bx + c = 0$, where $a \neq 0$.

subtraction property of equality (p. 140) If $a = b$, then $a - c = b - c$.

subtraction property of inequality (p. 324) If $a > b$, then $a - c > b - c$ and if $a < b$, then $a - c < b - c$.

system of linear equations (p. 389) Two or more linear equations in the same variables. This is also called a linear system.

system of linear inequalities (p. 424) Two or more linear inequalities in the same variables. This is also called a system of inequalities.

terms of an expression (p. 87) The parts that are added to form an expression. For example, in the expression $5 - x$, the terms are 5 and $-x$.

theorem (p. 724) A statement that has been proven to be true.

trinomial (p. 569) A polynomial of three terms.

unit analysis (p. 178) Using the units for each variable in a real-life problem to determine the units for the answer.

unit rate (p. 177) A rate expressing the amount of one given quantity per unit of another quantity, such as miles per gallon.

values (p. 3) The numbers a variable represents.

variable (p. 3) A letter used to represent a range of numbers.

variable expression (p. 3) A symbolic form made up of constants, variables, and operations.

verbal model (p. 36) An expression that uses words to describe a real-life situation.

vertex of a vertically oriented parabola (p. 521) The lowest point on the graph of a parabola opening up or the highest point on the graph of a parabola opening down. *See also* parabola.

vertical motion models (p. 535) Models that give the height of an object as a function of time. They include the case of a falling object.

whole numbers (p. 65) The positive integers together with zero.

x-axis (p. 203) The horizontal axis in a coordinate plane. *See also* coordinate plane.

x-coordinate (p. 203) The first number in an ordered pair. *See also* ordered pair.

x-intercept (p. 222) The x-coordinate of a point where a graph crosses the x-axis.

y-axis (p. 203) The vertical axis in a coordinate plane. *See also* coordinate plane.

y-coordinate (p. 203) The second number in an ordered pair. *See also* ordered pair.

y-intercept (p. 222) The y-coordinate of a point where a graph crosses the y-axis.

zero-product property (p. 588) If the product of two factors is zero, then at least one of the factors must be zero.

English-to-Spanish Glossary

This Glossary contains terms from both Volumes 1 and 2. Page numbers for Volume 1 are in black and page numbers for Volume 2 are in blue.

absolute value (p. 71) valor absoluto Distancia existente entre el cero y el punto que representa en la recta numérica un número real. El símbolo $|a|$ representa el valor absoluto de un número a.

absolute value equation (p. 355) ecuación de valor absoluto La de la forma $|ax + b| = c$.

absolute value inequality (p. 361) desigualdad de valor absoluto Aquella que presenta una de estas formas: $|ax + b| < c$, $|ax + b| \leq c$, $|ax + b| > c$, ó $|ax + b| \geq c$.

addition property of equality (p. 140) propiedad de igualdad en la suma Si $a = b$, entonces $a + c = b + c$.

addition property of inequality (p. 324) propiedad de desigualdad en la suma Si $a > b$, entonces $a + c > b + c$ y si $a < b$, entonces $a + c < b + c$.

algebraic model (p. 36) modelo algebraico Expresión, ecuación o desigualdad que usa variables para representar una situación de la vida real.

associative property of addition (p. 79) propiedad asociativa de la suma La agrupación que tengan tres números al sumarse no altera la suma. Para todos los números reales a, b, y c, $(a + b) + c = a + (b + c)$.

associative property of multiplication (p. 94) propiedad asociativa de la multiplicación La agrupación que tengan tres números al multiplicarse no altera el producto. Para todos los números reales a, b, y c, $(ab)c = a(bc)$.

axiom (p. 740) axioma Regla que se acepta como cierta sin demostración. Al axioma se le llama también *postulado*.

axis of symmetry of a parabola (p. 521) eje de simetría de una parábola Recta vertical que pasa por el vértice de una parábola o la recta que divide la parabola en dos partes simétricas, las cuales son reflejos exactos entre sí.

bar graph (p. 43) gráfica de barras La que representa un conjunto de datos mediante barras horizontales o verticales y cuya longitud permite la comparación de esos datos.

base (p. 9) base En notación exponencial, el número o variable que sostiene multiplicación repetida. Por ejemplo, 4 es la base en la expresión 4^6.

base number of a percent equation (p. 183) número base de una ecuación de porcentajes El número de una ecuación de porcentajes que es la base de una comparación. El número b en el modelo verbal "a es el p por ciento de b".

binomial (p. 569) binomio Polinomio que consiste de dos términos.

closure property of real number addition (p. 78) propiedad de cierre de la suma de números reales La suma de dos números reales cualesquiera es otra vez un número real.

closure property of real number multiplication (p. 93) propiedad de cierre de la multiplicación de números reales El producto de dos números reales cualesquiera es otra vez un número real.

coefficient (p. 107) coeficiente Si un término de una expresión consta de un número multiplicado por una o más variables, entonces ese número es el coeficiente del término.

commutative property of addition (p. 79) propiedad conmutativa de la suma El orden de dos números al sumarse no altera la suma. Para todos los números reales a y b, $a + b = b + a$.

commutative property of multiplication (p. 94) propiedad conmutativa de la multiplicación El orden de dos números al multiplicarse no altera el producto. Para todos los números reales a y b, $ab = ba$.

completing the square (p. 716) completar cuadrados Proceso de escribir una ecuación cuadrática de manera que uno de sus miembros sea un trinomio cuadrado perfecto.

compound inequality (p. 342) desigualdad compuesta Dos desigualdades unidas entre sí mediante la palabra y u o.

conclusion (p. 120) conclusión La parte del *entonces* en un enunciado de si-entonces.

conjecture (p. 741) conjetura Enunciado que se considera probable sin que haya sido demostrado.

constant function (p. 218) función constante La de la forma $y = b$, donde b es un número.

constant of variation (p. 236, p. 639) constante de variación Constante de un modelo de variación. Es equivalente a $\frac{y}{x}$ en el caso de una variación directa y a xy en el caso de una variación inversa.

converse of a statement (p. 726) recíproco de un enunciado Afirmación relacionada en la que se intercambian la hipótesis y la conclusión. El recíproco del enunciado "Si p, entonces q" es "Si q, entonces p".

converse of the Pythagorean theorem (p. 726) recíproco del teorema de Pitágoras Si un triángulo tiene lados de longitudes a, b, y c tales que $a^2 + b^2 = c^2$, entonces es un triángulo rectángulo.

coordinate plane (p. 203) **plano de coordenadas** El sistema de coordenadas formado por dos rectas numéricas reales que al cortarse configuran un ángulo recto.

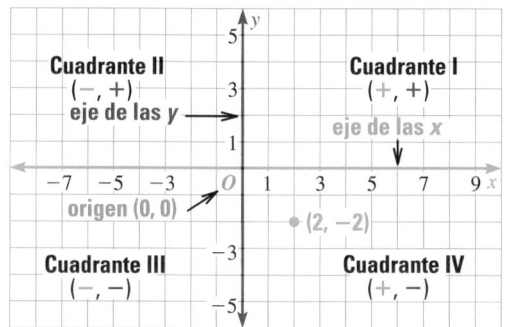

counterexample (p. 73) **contraejemplo** Ejemplo que sirve para mostrar la falsedad de un enunciado dado.

cross product property (p. 634) **propiedad de los productos cruzados** En una proporción, el producto de los extremos es igual al de los medios. Si $\frac{a}{b} = \frac{c}{d}$, entonces $ad = bc$.

cube root (p. 710) **raíz cúbica** Si $b^3 = a$, entonces b es una raíz cúbica de a.

data (p. 42) **datos** Informaciones, hechos o números que sirven para describir algo.

decay factor (p. 482) **factor de decrecimiento** La expresión $1 - r$, en el modelo de decrecimiento exponencial donde r es la tasa de decrecimiento. *Ver también* decrecimiento exponencial.

decay rate (p. 482) **tasa de decrecimiento** La proporción de un modelo de decrecimiento exponencial en la cual disminuye la cantidad durante cada período de tiempo. *Ver también* decrecimiento exponencial.

decimal form (p. 469) **forma decimal** Número escrito con valores relativos que corresponden a potencias de diez. Por ejemplo, 100, 14.2 y 0.007 están expresados en forma decimal.

deductive reasoning (p. 120) **razonamiento deductivo** Empleo de hechos, definiciones, reglas o propiedades para sacar una conclusión.

degree of a monomial (p. 568) **grado de un monomio** Suma de los exponentes de cada una de las variables del monomio. El grado de $5x^2y$ es $2 + 1 = 3$.

degree of a polynomial in one variable (p. 569) **grado de un polinomio de una variable** Mayor exponente de esa variable.

direct variation (p. 236) **variación directa** Relación entre dos variables x e y para la cual hay un número k distinto a cero tal que $y = kx$, ó $\frac{y}{x} = k$. Las variables x e y *varían directamente* entre sí.

discriminant (p. 540) **discriminante** La expresión $b^2 - 4ac$ donde a, b y c son coeficientes de la ecuación cuadrática $ax^2 + bx + c = 0$; la expresión del radical de la fórmula cuadrática.

distance formula (p. 730) **fórmula de la distancia** La distancia d que hay entre los puntos (x_1, y_1) y (x_2, y_2) es $d = \sqrt{(x_2 - x_1)^2 + (y_2 - y_1)^2}$.

distributive property (pp. 100, 101) **propiedad distributiva** Para todos los números reales a, b y c, $a(b + c) = ab + ac$, $(b + c)a = ba + ca$, $a(b - c) = ab - ac$ y $(b - c)a = ba - ca$.

division property of equality (p. 140) **propiedad de igualdad en la división** Si $a = b$ y $c \neq 0$, entonces $\frac{a}{c} = \frac{b}{c}$.

division property of inequality (pp. 330, 331) **propiedad de desigualdad en la división** Si $a > b$ y $c > 0$, entonces $\frac{a}{c} > \frac{b}{c}$ y si $a < b$, entonces $\frac{a}{c} < \frac{b}{c}$. Si $a > b$, y $c < 0$, entonces $\frac{a}{c} < \frac{b}{c}$ y si $a < b$, entonces $\frac{a}{c} > \frac{b}{c}$.

domain of a function (p. 49) **dominio de una función** Conjunto de todos los valores de entrada de una función.

equation (p. 24) **ecuación** Enunciado formado por dos expresiones unidas entre sí mediante el signo de igual.

equivalent equations (p. 132) **ecuaciones equivalentes** Las que tienen la misma solución o soluciones.

equivalent inequalities (p. 324) **desigualdades equivalentes** Aquellas que tienen la misma solución o soluciones.

evaluate an expression (p. 4) **evaluar una expresión** Hallar el valor de una expresión mediante la sustitución de cada variable por un valor numérico específico y la simplificación del resultado.

exponent (p. 9) **exponente** En notación exponencial, el número de veces que la base se usa como factor. Por ejemplo, 6 es el exponente en la expresión 4^6.

exponential decay (p. 482) **decrecimiento exponencial** Una cantidad presenta un decrecimiento exponencial cuando disminuye en una misma proporción r durante cada período de tiempo t. Si C es la cantidad inicial, la existente tras transcurrir el tiempo t viene dada por $y = C(1 - r)^t$, donde r es la tasa de decrecimiento, $0 < r < 1$, y $(1 - r)$ el factor de decrecimiento.

exponential function (p. 455) **función exponencial** La de la forma $y = ab^x$, donde $b > 0$ y $b \neq 1$.

exponential growth (p. 476) **crecimiento exponencial** Una cantidad presenta un crecimiento exponencial cuando aumenta en una misma proporción r durante cada unidad de tiempo. Si C es la cantidad inicial, la existente después de t unidades de tiempo viene dada por $y = C(1 + r)^t$, donde r es la tasa de crecimiento y $(1 + r)$ el factor de crecimiento.

extraneous solution (p. 705) **solución extraña** Solución de prueba que no satisface la ecuación original.

extremes of a proportion (p. 633) **extremos de una proporción** En la proporción $\frac{a}{b} = \frac{c}{d}$, a y d son los extremos.

factor a polynomial completely (p. 617) **descomponer un polinomio en todos sus factores** Escribir un polinomio como producto de factores monómicos y primos.

factor a trinomial (p. 595) **descomponer un trinomio en factores** Escribir el trinomio como producto de dos binomios.

factored form of a polynomial (p. 588) **forma factorial de un polinomio** Polinomio escrito como producto de dos o más factores.

formula (p. 171) **fórmula** Ecuación algebraica que relaciona dos o más variables.

function (p. 48) **función** Regla que establece una relación entre dos cantidades: la de entrada y la de salida. A cada entrada le corresponde una sola salida.

function form (p. 211) **forma de función** Una ecuación de dos variables está expresada en forma de función si una de sus variables está aislada en un miembro de la ecuación. La variable aislada es la salida que además está en función de la entrada.

function notation (p. 254) **notación de función** Forma de describir una función por medio de una ecuación. Para la ecuación $y = f(x)$, el símbolo $f(x)$ indica la salida y se lee "el valor de f en x" o simplemente "f de x".

graph of an equation in two variables (p. 211) **gráfica de una ecuación de dos variables** Conjunto de todos los puntos (x, y) que son soluciones de la ecuación.

graph of an inequality in one variable (p. 323) **representación gráfica de una desigualdad de una variable** Conjunto de puntos de la recta numérica que representan todas las soluciones de la desigualdad.

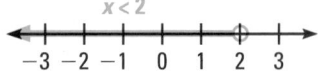

graph of a number (p. 65) **representación gráfica de un número** Punto situado en una recta numérica que corresponde a un número.

graph of a quadratic inequality (p. 547) **gráfica de una desigualdad cuadrática** Gráfica de todos los pares ordenados (x, y) que son soluciones de la desigualdad.

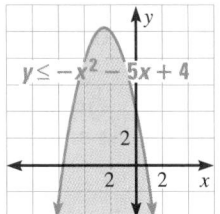

grouping symbols (p. 10) **signos de agrupación** Signos como los paréntesis ( ) o los corchetes [ ] que indican el orden en que deben realizarse las operaciones. Se efectúan primero las operaciones de los signos de agrupación situados más en el interior.

growth factor (p. 476) **factor de crecimiento** La expresión $1 + r$, en el modelo de crecimiento exponencial donde r es la tasa de crecimiento. *Ver también* crecimiento exponencial.

growth rate (p. 476) **tasa de crecimiento** La proporción de un modelo de crecimiento exponencial en la cual aumenta la cantidad durante cada unidad de tiempo.

hypotenuse (p. 724) **hipotenusa** El lado opuesto al ángulo recto de un triángulo rectángulo.

hypothesis (p. 120) **hipótesis** La parte del *si* en un enunciado de si-entonces.

identity (p. 153) **identidad** Ecuación que es cierta para todos los valores de la variable.

identity property of addition (p. 79) **propiedad de identidad de la suma** La suma de un número y 0 es igual a ese número. Para todo número real a, $a + 0 = 0 + a = a$.

identity property of multiplication **(p. 94)** **propiedad de identidad de la multiplicación** El producto de un número y 1 es igual a ese número. Para todo número real a, $1 \cdot a = a$.

if-then statement **(p. 120)** **enunciado de si-entonces** Tipo de enunciado que se emplea en el razonamiento deductivo y en el cual la parte del *si* es la hipótesis y la parte del *entonces* la conclusión.

indirect proof **(p. 742)** **prueba indirecta** Tipo de pruebas en que se supone que el enunciado es falso. Si mediante esa suposición se da una imposibilidad, entonces la certeza del enunciado original queda demostrada.

inductive reasoning **(p. 119)** **razonamiento inductivo** Formulación de un enunciado general basándose en varias observaciones.

inequality **(p. 26)** **desigualdad** Enunciado compuesto de dos expresiones unidas entre sí mediante un signo de desigual como <.

input **(p. 48)** **entrada** Un valor en el dominio de una función.

input-output table **(p. 48)** **tabla de entradas y salidas** La que describe una función mediante la presentación de las salidas correspondientes a varias entradas diferentes.

integers **(p. 65)** **números enteros** Los números . . . $-3, -2, -1, 0, 1, 2, 3, \ldots$.

inverse operations **(p. 133)** **operaciones inversas** Dos operaciones que se anulan mutuamente como son la suma y la resta.

inverse property of addition **(p. 79)** **propiedad del elemento inverso de la suma** La suma de un número y su opuesto es igual a 0: $a + (-a) = 0$.

inverse variation **(p. 639)** **variación inversa** La relación entre dos variables x e y para la cual hay un número k distinto a cero tal que $xy = k$ ó $y = \dfrac{k}{x}$.

Se dice que las variables x e y *varían inversamente* entre sí.

leading coefficient **(p. 505)** **coeficiente dominante** En una ecuación cuadrática expresada en forma normal, $ax^2 + bx + c = 0$, donde $a \neq 0$, a es el coeficiente dominante.

least common denominator, LCD **(p. 663)** **mínimo común denominador, mcd** El menor de los múltiplos comunes a los denominadores de dos o más fracciones.

left-to-right rule **(p. 16)** **regla de izquierda a derecha** Las operaciones de igual prioridad se efectúan de izquierda a derecha.

legs of a right triangle **(p. 724)** **catetos de un triángulo rectángulo** Los dos lados de un triángulo rectángulo que no están opuestos al ángulo recto.

like terms **(p. 107)** **términos semejantes** Aquellos que tienen iguales variables y en los que cada una de éstas está elevada a igual potencia. Por ejemplo, $3x^2y$ y $-7x^2y$ son términos semejantes.

line graph **(p. 44)** **gráfica lineal** La que utiliza segmentos de recta para unir puntos de datos. Es de mucha utilidad para indicar los cambios producidos en los datos a lo largo del tiempo.

linear combination of two equations **(p. 402)** **combinación lineal de dos ecuaciones** Ecuación obtenida (1) al multiplicar una o ambas ecuaciones por una constante y (2) al sumar las ecuaciones resultantes.

linear equation in one variable **(p. 134)** **ecuación lineal con una variable** Una ecuación en que la variable viene elevada sólo a la primera potencia.

linear equation in x and y **(p. 210)** **ecuación lineal con x e y** La que puede escribirse en la forma $Ax + By = C$, donde A y B no son ambos cero.

linear function of x **(p. 254)** **función lineal de x** Función de la forma $f(x) = mx + b$.

linear inequality in x and y **(p. 367)** **desigualdad lineal con x e y** La que puede escribirse en una de estas formas: $ax + by < c$, $ax + by \leq c$, $ax + by > c$, ó $ax + by \geq c$.

linear model **(p. 298)** **modelo lineal** Una ecuación o función lineal que sirve para representar una situación de la vida real.

linear system **(p. 389)** **sistema lineal** Dos o más ecuaciones lineales con las mismas variables. Se le denomina también sistema de ecuaciones lineales.

means of a proportion **(p. 633)** **medios de una proporción** En la proporción $\dfrac{a}{b} = \dfrac{c}{d}$, b y c son los medios.

midpoint of a line segment **(p. 736)** **punto medio de un segmento de recta** El punto del segmento que es equidistante de los extremos.

midpoint formula (p. 736) **fórmula del punto medio** El punto medio entre (x_1, y_1) y (x_2, y_2) es $\left(\dfrac{x_1 + x_2}{2}, \dfrac{y_1 + y_2}{2}\right)$.

modeling (p. 36) **hacer un modelo** La representación de situaciones de la vida real por ecuaciones o desigualdades.

monomial (pp. 568, 569) **monomio** Número, variable o producto de un número y una o más variables con exponentes que sean enteros positivos o cero; polinomio de un solo término.

multiplication property of equality (p. 140) **propiedad de igualdad en la multiplicación** Si $a = b$, entonces $ca = cb$.

multiplication property of inequality (pp. 330, 331) **propiedad de desigualdad en la multiplicación** Si $a > b$ y $c > 0$, entonces $ac > bc$ y si $a < b$, entonces $ac < bc$. Si $a > b$ y $c < 0$, entonces $ac < bc$ y si $a < b$, entonces $ac > bc$.

multiplicative property of negative one (p. 94) **propiedad multiplicativa del uno negativo** El producto de un número y -1 es igual al opuesto de ese número: $-1 \cdot a = -a$.

multiplicative property of zero (p. 94) **propiedad multiplicativa del cero** El producto de un número y 0 es igual a 0. Es decir, $0 \cdot a = 0$.

negative number (p. 65) **número negativo** Número menor que cero. *Ver también* recta numérica real.

negative square root (p. 499) **raíz cuadrada negativa** Número negativo que es una raíz cuadrada de un número positivo. Por ejemplo, la raíz cuadrada negativa de 9 es -3.

numerical expression (p. 3) **expresión numérica** La que representa un número determinado.

opposites (p. 71) **opuestos** Dos números situados a igual distancia del cero en una recta numérica pero en lados opuestos del mismo.

order of operations (p. 15) **orden de las operaciones** Reglas para evaluar una expresión relacionada con más de una operación.

ordered pair (p. 203) **par ordenado** Par de números empleados para identificar un punto situado en un plano de coordenadas. El primer número es la coordenada x y el segundo la coordenada y. *Ver también* plano de coordenadas.

origin (p. 203) **origen** Punto de un plano de coordenadas donde el eje horizontal corta al vertical. El punto (0, 0). *Ver también* plano de coordenadas.

output (p. 48) **salida** Un valor en el recorrido de una función.

parabola (p. 520) **parábola** Gráfica en forma de U de una función cuadrática, $y = ax^2 + bx + c$ donde $a \neq 0$.

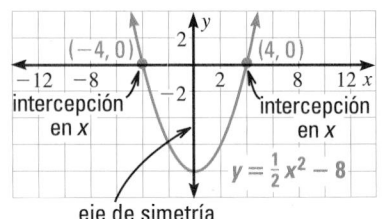

parallel lines (p. 245) **rectas paralelas** Dos rectas diferentes del mismo plano que no se cortan. (A veces se consideran paralelas las rectas idénticas.)

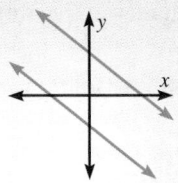

percent (p. 183) **porcentaje** Razón que relaciona un número con 100.

perfect square trinomials (p. 609) **trinomios cuadrados perfectos** Los de la forma $a^2 + 2ab + b^2$ y $a^2 - 2ab + b^2$; este tipo de trinomios pueden descomponerse en factores como cuadrados de binomios.

perpendicular lines (p. 306) **rectas perpendiculares** Dos rectas situadas en un plano son perpendiculares si al cortarse forman un ángulo recto, o sea de 90°. Si dos rectas no verticales son perpendiculares, el producto de sus pendientes es -1.

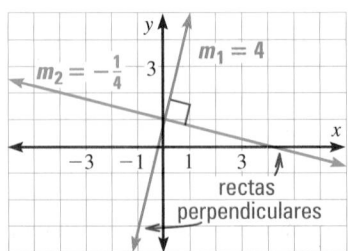

point of intersection (p. 389) **punto de intersección** Un punto (a, b) situado en las gráficas de dos o más ecuaciones es un punto de intersección de esas gráficas.

point-slope form (p. 278) **ecuación punto pendiente de una recta** Ecuación de una recta no vertical de la forma $y - y_1 = m(x - x_1)$, donde la recta pasa por un punto dado (x_1, y_1) y la recta tiene pendiente m.

polynomial (p. 569) **polinomio** Monomio o suma de monomios. *Ver* monomio.

positive number (p. 65) **número positivo** Número mayor que cero.

positive square root, or principal square root (p. 499) **raíz cuadrada positiva, o raíz cuadrada principal** Raíz cuadrada de un número positivo que resulta también positiva. Por ejemplo, la raíz cuadrada positiva de 9 es 3.

postulate (p. 740) **postulado** Regla que se acepta como cierta sin demostración. Al postulado se le llama también *axioma*.

power (p. 9) **potencia** Expresión de la forma a^b o valor de ese tipo de expresiones. Por ejemplo, 2^4 es una potencia, y como $2^4 = 16$, 16 es la cuarta potencia de 2.

power of a power property (pp. 444, 445) **propiedad de la potencia de una potencia** Para hallar una potencia de otra se multiplican los exponentes. Para todo número real a y para los números enteros m y n, $\left(a^m\right)^n = a^{mn}$.

power of a product property (p. 444) **propiedad de la potencia de un producto** Para hallar la potencia de un producto se halla la potencia de cada factor y se multiplica. Para todos los números reales a y b y para el número entero m, $(ab)^m = a^m \cdot b^m$.

power of a quotient property (pp. 462, 463) **propiedad de la potencia de un cociente** Para hallar la potencia de un cociente se halla la potencia del numerador y la del denominador y se divide. Para todo número entero m y todos los números reales a y b, donde $b \neq 0$, $\left(\dfrac{a}{b}\right)^m = \dfrac{a^m}{b^m}$.

prime polynomial (p. 617) **polinomio primo** El que no es el producto de factores con coeficientes de número entero y de grado menor.

product of powers property (pp. 443, 445) **propiedad del producto de potencias** Para multiplicar potencias de igual base se suman los exponentes. Para todo número real a y para los números enteros m y n, $a^m \cdot a^n = a^{m+n}$.

product property of radicals (p. 511) **propiedad del producto de radicales** Si a y b son números reales tales que $a \geq 0$ y $b \geq 0$, entonces $\sqrt{ab} = \sqrt{a} \cdot \sqrt{b}$.

properties of equality (p. 140) **propiedades de igualdad** Reglas de álgebra que sirven para transformar ecuaciones en otras equivalentes.

proportion (p. 633) **proporción** Ecuación estableciendo la igualdad de dos razones.

Pythagorean theorem (p. 724) **teorema de Pitágoras** Si un triángulo rectángulo tiene catetos de longitudes a y b y la hipotenusa de longitud c, entonces $a^2 + b^2 = c^2$.

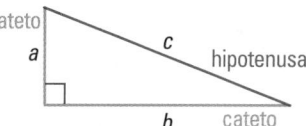

quadrant (p. 204) **cuadrante** Una de las cuatro regiones en que los ejes dividen al plano de coordenadas. *Ver también* plano de coordenadas.

quadratic equation (p. 505) **ecuación cuadrática** La que puede escribirse en la forma normal $ax^2 + bx + c = 0$, donde $a \neq 0$.

quadratic formula (p. 533) **fórmula cuadrática** Aquella que sirve para hallar las soluciones de una ecuación cuadrática $ax^2 + bx + c = 0$ cuando $a \neq 0$ y $b^2 - 4ac \geq 0$: $x = \dfrac{-b \pm \sqrt{b^2 - 4ac}}{2a}$.

quadratic function (p. 520) **función cuadrática** La que puede escribirse en la forma normal $y = ax^2 + bx + c$, donde $a \neq 0$.

quadratic inequality (p. 547) **desigualdad cuadrática** Aquella que puede escribirse de una de estas formas: $y < ax^2 + bx + c$, $y \leq ax^2 + bx + c$, $y > ax^2 + bx + c$, ó $y \geq ax^2 + bx + c$.

quotient of powers property (pp. 462, 463) **propiedad del cociente de potencias** Para dividir potencias de igual base se restan los exponentes. Para todo número real $a \neq 0$ y para los números enteros m y n, $\dfrac{a^m}{a^n} = a^{m-n}$.

quotient property of radicals (p. 512) **propiedad del cociente de radicales** Si a y b son números reales tales que $a \geq 0$ y $b > 0$, entonces $\sqrt{\dfrac{a}{b}} = \dfrac{\sqrt{a}}{\sqrt{b}}$.

radical expression, or radical (p. 501) **expresión radical, o radical** Expresión escrita con el signo radical.

radicand (p. 499) **radicando** Número o expresión que aparece debajo del signo radical.

range of a function (p. 49) **recorrido de una función** Conjunto de todos los valores de salida de una función.

rate of _a_ per _b_ (p. 177) **relación de _a_ por _b_** Relación $\frac{a}{b}$ de dos cantidades _a_ y _b_ que se miden con unidades diferentes.

rate of change (p. 298) **tasa de variación** Cociente de dos cantidades diferentes que cambian. En un modelo lineal, la pendiente indica la tasa de variación de una variable con respecto a la otra.

ratio of _a_ to _b_ (p. 177) **razón de _a_ a _b_** Relación $\frac{a}{b}$ de dos cantidades _a_ y _b_.

rational equation (p. 670) **ecuación racional** Aquella que contiene expresiones racionales.

rational exponent (p. 711) **exponente racional** Para todo número entero _n_ y para el número real $a \geq 0$, la raíz enésima de _a_ es denotada por $a^{1/n}$ ó $\sqrt[n]{a}$. Sea $a^{1/n}$ una raíz enésima de _a_, _m_ un número entero positivo y $a \geq 0$. Entonces $a^{m/n} = \left(a^{1/n}\right)^m = \left(\sqrt[n]{a}\right)^m = \sqrt[n]{a^m}$.

rational expression (p. 646) **expresión racional** Fracción que tiene por numerador y denominador polinomios distintos a cero.

rational function (p. 678) **función racional** Función que es el cociente de polinomios.

rational number (p. 646) **número racional** El que puede escribirse como cociente de dos números enteros.

real number line (p. 65) **recta numérica real** Recta cuyos puntos corresponden a los números reales.

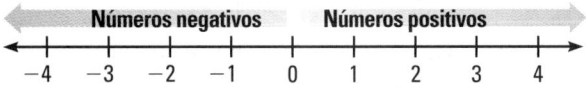

real numbers (p. 65) **números reales** Conjunto de números compuesto por los positivos, los negativos y cero. (Se puede considerar que los números reales son el conjunto de todos los decimales finitos o infinitos.)

reciprocals (p. 113) **recíprocos** Dos números cuyo producto es 1. Si $\frac{a}{b}$ es un número distinto a cero, entonces su recíproco es $\frac{b}{a}$.

relation (p. 252) **relación** Conjunto cualquiera de pares ordenados.

roots of a quadratic equation (p. 527) **raíces de una ecuación cuadrática** Soluciones de una ecuación cuadrática.

rounding error (p. 164) **error de redondeo** El producido tras limitar la expansión de un decimal a un número específico de enteros a la derecha del punto decimal.

scatter plot (p. 205) **diagrama de dispersión** Gráfica de coordenadas cuyos puntos representan un conjunto de pares ordenados; es de utilidad para analizar las relaciones entre dos cantidades reales.

scientific notation (p. 469) **notación científica** Número expresado en la forma $c \times 10^n$, donde $1 \leq c < 10$ y _n_ es un número entero.

simplified expression (p. 108) **expresión simplificada** Aquella que carece de signos de agrupación y tiene combinados todos los términos semejantes.

simplest form of a radical expression (p. 511) **expresión radical en su mínima expresión** La que no tiene en el radicando factores de raíz exacta distintos a 1 ni fracciones, además de no tener radicales en el denominador de una fracción.

slope (p. 229, 230) **pendiente** Razón de la distancia vertical a la distancia horizontal existente entre dos puntos cualesquiera de una recta. La pendiente es $m = \frac{(y_2 - y_1)}{(x_2 - x_1)}$.

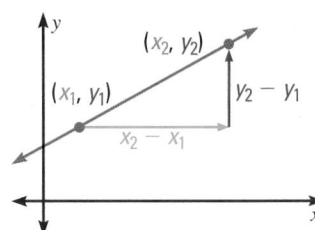

slope-intercept form (p. 243) **ecuación pendiente intercepción de una recta** Ecuación lineal escrita en la forma $y = mx + b$. La pendiente de la recta es _m_ y la intercepción en _y_ es _b_. _Ver también_ pendiente _e_ intercepción en _y_.

$y = 2x + 3$
La pendiente es 2.
La intercepción
en _y_ es 3.

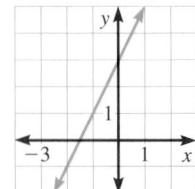

solution of an equation or inequality (p. 24) **solución de una ecuación o desigualdad** Número que cumple una ecuación o desigualdad al sustituir a la variable de la misma.

solution of an equation in two variables (p. 210) **solución de una ecuación de dos variables** Par ordenado (x, y) que cumple la ecuación.

solution of a linear system in two variables (p. 389) **solución de un sistema lineal de dos variables** Par ordenado (x, y) que satisface cada ecuación del sistema.

solution of a system of linear inequalities in two variables (p. 424) **solución de un sistema de desigualdades lineales de dos variables** Par ordenado que cumple cada desigualdad del sistema.

square root (p. 499) **raíz cuadrada** Si $b^2 = a$, entonces b es una raíz cuadrada de a. Las raíces cuadradas pueden escribirse con el signo radical, $\sqrt{\ }$.

square root function (p. 692) **función de raíz cuadrada** La definida por la ecuación $y = \sqrt{x}$, para $x \geq 0$.

standard form of an equation of a line (p. 291) **forma usual de la ecuación de una recta** Ecuación lineal de la forma $Ax + By = C$, donde A y B no son ambos cero.

standard form of a polynomial in one variable (p. 569) **forma usual de un polinomio de una variable** Polinomio cuyos términos están escritos en orden descendente, del exponente mayor al menor.

standard form of a quadratic equation (p. 505) **forma usual de una ecuación cuadrática** Ecuación de la forma $ax^2 + bx + c = 0$, donde $a \neq 0$.

subtraction property of equality (p. 140) **propiedad de igualdad en la resta** Si $a = b$, entonces $a - c = b - c$.

subtraction property of inequality (p. 324) **propiedad de desigualdad en la resta** Si $a > b$, entonces $a - c > b - c$, y si $a < b$, entonces $a - c < b - c$.

system of linear equations (p. 389) **sistema de ecuaciones lineales** Dos o más ecuaciones lineales que tienen las mismas variables. Se le llama también sistema lineal.

system of linear inequalities (p. 424) **sistema de desigualdades lineales** Dos o más desigualdades lineales que tienen las mismas variables. Se le llama también sistema de desigualdades.

terms of an expression (p. 87) **términos de una expresión** Partes que se unen para formar una expresión. Por ejemplo, en la expresión $5 - x$, los términos son 5 y $-x$.

theorem (p. 724) **teorema** Afirmación cuya certeza ha sido demostrada.

trinomial (p. 569) **trinomio** Polinomio de tres términos.

unit analysis (p. 178) **análisis por unidades** Usar las unidades de cada variable de un problema real para así determinar las unidades de la solución.

unit rate (p. 177) **tasa unitaria** Relación que expresa la magnitud de una cantidad dada por unidad de otra cantidad como, por ejemplo, millas por galón.

values (p. 3) **valores** Números que representa una variable.

variable (p. 3) **variable** Letra empleada para representar una gama de números.

variable expression (p. 3) **expresión algebraica** Forma simbólica compuesta por constantes, variables y operaciones.

verbal model (p. 36) **modelo verbal** Expresión que emplea palabras para describir una situación de la vida real.

vertex of a vertically oriented parabola (p. 521) **vértice de una parábola orientada verticalmente** Punto inferior de la gráfica de una parábola que abre hacia arriba o punto superior de la gráfica de una parábola que abre hacia abajo. *Ver también* parábola.

vertical motion models (p. 535) **modelos de movimiento vertical** Aquellos que dan la altura de un objeto como una función del tiempo. Incluyen el caso de un objeto que cae.

whole numbers (p. 65) **números naturales** Números enteros positivos y cero.

x-axis (p. 203) **eje de las x** Eje horizontal de un plano de coordenadas. *Ver también* plano de coordenadas.

x-coordinate (p. 203) **coordenada x** Primer número de un par ordenado. *Ver también* par ordenado.

x-intercept (p. 222) **intercepción en x** Coordenada x de un punto donde una gráfica cruza al eje de las x.

y-axis (p. 203) **eje de las y** Eje vertical de un plano de coordenadas. *Ver también* plano de coordenadas.

y-coordinate (p. 203) **coordenada y** Segundo número de un par ordenado. *Ver también* par ordenado.

y-intercept (p. 222) **intercepción en y** Coordenada y de un punto donde una gráfica cruza al eje de las y.

zero-product property (p. 588) **propiedad del producto cero** Si el producto de dos factores es cero, entonces al menos uno de ellos debe ser cero.

Index

This Index contains terms from both Volumes 1 and 2. Page numbers for Volume 1 are in black and page numbers for Volume 2 are in blue. Page numbers for material included in both volumes are in red.

to solve inequalities, 330–335, 375

to solve linear equations, 138–143, 189

by zero, 115, 116, 117

Division property of inequality, 330–334

Division rule, 113

Dobbs, John Wesley, 637

Domain

of a constant function, 218

definition of, 49

division by zero and, 115, 116, 117

of an exponential function, 457

of a radical function, 691, 692

E

End-of-Course Test, *See* Assessment

Enrichment, *See* Challenge exercises; Extension

Equality, properties of, 140

Equation(s), *See also* Formulas; Functions; Graphs; Linear equations; Modeling; Polynomials; Quadratic equations

absolute value, 72–76, 354–360, 377

addition and subtraction of linear, 132–137, 189, 402–407

checking solutions of, 24–29, 56–57

compound interest, 477

cubic, 619, 621–622

decimal, 163–169, 191

definition of, 24

direct variation, 236–240, 261, 639–640, 642–644, 681–682

equivalent, 132

exponential decay, 482

exponential growth, 476

of horizontal lines, 293, 295

identity, 153, 154, 155

for linear functions, 50–54, 58

using mental math to solve, 25, 27, 28

quadratic, 505–510, 553

radical, 704–709, 748

rational, 670–676, 684

repeated factor, 589–593

solution of, 24

systems of, 386–436

transforming, 132, 138

translating words into, 31–35, 57

with variables on both sides,

150–162, 190

of vertical lines, 293, 295

Equivalent equations, 132

Error analysis, 104, 110, 116, 142, 147, 155, 161, 296, 328, 334, 340, 400, 405, 420, 427, 453, 466, 509, 514, 544, 571, 591, 602, 607, 620, 655, 661, 667, 702, 707

Estimation, *See also* Prediction

area, 5, 422, 775–776

compatible numbers and, 775–776

exercises, 83, 334, 468, 544

using exponential models, 483, 486, 493

front-end, 774, 776

using a graph, 46, 244, 321, 390, 393, 395, 431, 497, 530

using linear models, 298–304, 316

of roots of a quadratic equation, 532

rounding and, 774, 776

using slope-intercept form, 243, 244, 248

of square root, 500–504

Expanded form, 99–105

Exponential decay, 482–487, 492

Exponential function(s)

comparing to linear functions, 475

decay, 482–487, 492

evaluating, 455–461, 490

graph of, 455–461, 490

growth, 476–481, 484, 492

Exponential growth, 475–481, 484, 492

Exponent(s), 9–14, 56, *See also* Exponential functions

division properties of, 462–468, 490–491

grouping symbols and, 10–11

multiplication properties of, 441–448, 489

rational, 710–714, 748

scientific notation and, 469–474

zero and negative, 449–454, 464–468, 489–490

Expression(s)

absolute value, 71–76, 122

addition, 78–83

combining like terms in, 107–112, 124

describing patterns with, 22–23

distributive property and, 99–105, 123

division, 113–117, 124

equivalent, 99

evaluating, 4–8, 55, 381

exponential, 9–14, 56, 443–454, 462–468

with fraction bars, 16, 19

multiplication, 93–98, 123

order of operations and, 15–21

radical, 501–504

rational

adding and subtracting, 658–669, 683–684

factoring, 647–650, 671–676

multiplying and dividing, 652–657, 683

simplifying, 646–650, 682

with rational exponents, 710–714

simplified, 107–112

square root, 500–504

subtraction, 86–91, 122

terms of, 87–91

translating words into, 30–35, 57

value of, 4

variable, 94–98

variables and, 3–8

Extension exercises, 120, 199, 385, 563

Extension: Inductive and Deductive Reasoning, 119–120

Extraneous solution, 705–709

Extra Practice for Chapters, 1–12, 783–794

Extremes of a proportion, 633

F

Factored cubic equation, 589–593

Factored form of a polynomial, 588–593, 624

Factoring, rational expressions, 647–650, 671–676

Factoring a polynomial

$ax^2 + bx + c$, 602–608, 625

cubic, 616–622, 626

special products, 609–615, 618–620, 626

$x^2 + bx + c$, 594–601, 625

Factor(s), 761

prime, 495, 761

FOIL pattern, 576, 578, 603

Formula(s)

area, 172, 174–175, 192, 516, 772

Celsius/Fahrenheit temperature, 171, 174

Continued

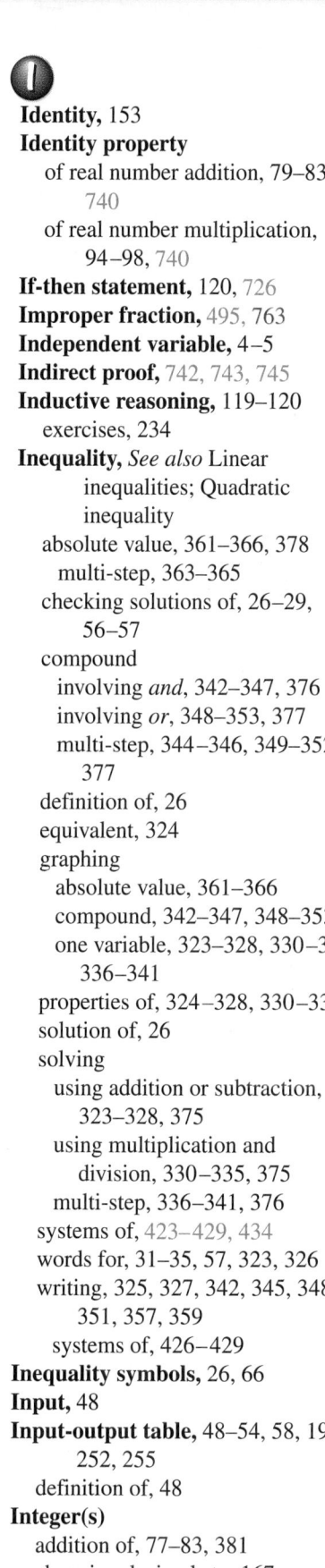

INDEX

theorem, 741
Luyendyk, Arie, 4

Maintaining Skills, *See* Reviews
Manipulatives, 22–23, 77, 84–85,
99, 131, 150, 228, 305, 384,
567, 594, 715, 722–723
Mathematical model, *See* Modeling
McGwire, Mark, 777
Mean, 780
Means of a proportion, 633
Measurement
area, 5, 7, 11, 12, 13, 127, 172,
174–175, 577, 579
distance, 3, 4, 7, 8, 38, 46, 129, 173
perimeter, 5, 6, 7, 22–23
temperature, 65, 67, 171, 174
volume, 11, 13, 14, 437

Measures, Table of, 802
Median, 780
Mental math
calculations using the distributive
property, 102, 103, 104
exercises, 70, 83, 98, 118, 155, 156
solving equations with, 25, 27, 28,
32, 74

Midpoint
definition, 736
formula, 736–739, 750, 798
Mixed number(s)
improper fractions and, 495, 763
operations with, 765
Mixture problems, 673, 675, 676
Mode, 780
Modeling, *See also* Graphs;
Manipulatives; Reasoning;
Tables; Technology Activities
using absolute value
equations, 357
inequalities, 372
addition of integers, 77
algebraic model, 36–40, 50, 57,
95, 109, 117, 134, 145, 159,
165, 183–185, 191, 214, 226,
300, 338, 372, 379, 391, 398,
400, 406, 409, 410, 411, 570,
583, 666, 672, 700
using algebra tiles, 77, 84–85, 99,
131, 150
using an area model, 100, 103,
105, 583, 586

completing the square, 715
using compound inequalities, 343,
346, 350, 352
using a constant function, 218, 220
using a cubic model, 619, 621
definition of, 36
using direct or inverse variation,
641, 643–645
direct variation, 236–240
using the discriminant, 545
using the distributive property,
102, 104, 105
equivalent expressions, 99
using exponential decay, 482–483,
485–487, 593
using exponential growth,
476–481, 593
using an exponential model, 457,
459, 467
using a falling object model, 507,
508, 509
using a function, 109, 111
using an inequality, 338, 340, 341
using linear equations, 134,
136–137, 140, 142, 145, 159,
161–162, 165, 167–169, 191,
214, 226, 285, 289, 290,
298–303
using linear inequalities, 371, 372
using a linear model, 244, 248,
298–303, 316, 338, 340, 341
using multiplication properties of
exponents, 445, 447
using negative exponents, 453
negative slope, 271, 273–274
patterns, 22–23
using percent, 183–185, 187
using polynomials, 570, 572, 577,
579, 584, 586
using proportions, 635, 637
using a quadratic model, 524, 525,
528, 530, 544, 590, 592, 598,
600, 601, 605, 607, 612, 614,
718, 720
using radical functions, 694, 696,
694–697
using radicals, 513, 515, 516, 700,
702, 706, 708, 709
using rates, 177–182
using rational equations, 672–673,
675, 676
using rational expressions, 650,
661, 666, 668
using ratios, 177–182

using real number addition, 80, 82
using real number multiplication,
95, 97
using real number subtraction, 88,
90, 91
using a scatter plot, 205, 207
using scientific notation, 471, 473
using slope-intercept form, 271,
273–274
subtraction of integers, 84–85
using systems of linear equations,
387, 391, 393, 398, 400, 406,
407, 409–414
unit analysis, 8, 178, 179, 181
verbal model, 36–40, 50, 57, 95,
109, 117, 134, 140, 145, 159,
165, 183–185, 191, 214, 226,
300, 338, 372, 391, 398, 400,
406, 409, 410, 411, 570, 583,
666, 672, 700
using vertical motion models, 535,
537, 538, 557, 605, 607, 613,
614, 621
Monomial, 568
Multicultural connections, 36, 40,
52, 60, 179, 193, 257, 289,
406, 407, 473, 503, 530, 600,
633, 635, 637, 643
Multiple representations, 30–35,
36–40, 43, 44, 48, 49, 50, 57,
78, 84–85, 86, 95, 99, 100,
109, 117, 127, 132, 134, 140,
145, 150, 159, 165, 178, 183,
184, 185, 205, 211, 212, 214,
216–218, 223, 224, 226,
229–232, 237, 238, 244,
250–251, 269–271, 278–280,
285–287, 291–293, 300,
307–308, 313–315, 323–327,
338, 342–345, 348–351,
361–363, 365, 367–370, 372,
374, 376–378, 390–393, 398,
409, 410, 411, 417, 418, 483,
484, 490, 518–519, 520, 521,
522, 528, 547–549, 554, 555,
556, 570, 583, 590, 597, 611,
641, 666, 672, 693, 694, 700,
736, 737, 747, 767–769, 777,
778
Multiplication
axioms of, 740
cross multiplying, 634–638, 670,
674–676
Continued

Credits

Houser/CORBIS; **592** Allen E. Morton/Visuals Unlimited; **595** Orion Press/Tony Stone Images; **598** Rachel Epstein/PhotoEdit; **600** Richard Vogel/Liaison Agency, Inc.; **603** Charles & Josette Lenars/CORBIS; **607** Vandystadt/Allsport; **609** David Young-Wolff/PhotoEdit; **612** Tony Freeman/PhotoEdit; **614** Mike Powell/Allsport (l); Darren Carroll/Duomo (r); **616** Ben Klaffke; **619** Dave Schiefelbein; **621** Alan Klehr/Tony Stone Images; **630, 631** Phillip Gould/CORBIS; **633** Wolfgang Kaehler/CORBIS; **635** Louis Mazzatenta/National Geographic Image Collection; **637** Robert Ginn/PhotoEdit (l); Cordelia Williams (r); **639** Linc Cornell/Stock Boston; **643** Chris Arend/Alaska Stock Images; **646** AFP/CORBIS; **650** AFP/CORBIS; **652** Raymond Gehman/CORBIS; **658** S B Photography/Tony Stone Images; **661** Zigy Kaluzny/Tony Stone Images; **663** Ron Dorsey/Stock Boston; **668** Joseph Pobereskin/Tony Stone Images; **670** Karl Weatherly/CORBIS; **675** John W. McDonough/Sports Illustrated Picture Collection; **688, 689** Rex A. Butcher/Tony Stone Images; **692** Louis Mazzatenta/National Geographic Image Collection; **696** Peter Menzel/Tony Stone Images; **698** Jeff Greenberg/Visuals Unlimited; **702** John Bova/Photo Researchers, Inc.; **704** Art Montes De Oca/FPG International; **706** Jeff Persons/Stock Boston; **708** Mike Powell/Allsport; **710** Tony Duffy/Allsport; **715** RMIP/Richard Haynes (all); **716, 718** Norbert Wu; **724** Tony Duffy/Allsport; **730** Doug Pensinger/Allsport; **734** Bob Daemmrich/PNI/PictureQuest; **736** Bob Daemmrich/The Image Works; **737** David Young-Wolff/PhotoEdit; **740** John Neubauer/PhotoEdit; **742** Dennis MacDonald/PhotoEdit; **756** Werner Forman/CORBIS; **757** RMIP/Richard Haynes.

Illustration

Steve Cowden **641, 700, 720, 732**
Laurie O'Keefe **238, 357, 401, 537 (r)**
School Division, Houghton Mifflin Company **666**
Doug Stevens **365, 577, 605, 708 (t)**

Selected Answers

Pre-Course Practice

DECIMALS (p. xx) **1.** 21.1 **3.** 67.95 **5.** 15.105 **7.** 66.3
9. 76.304 **11.** 729.008 **13.** 3.7 **15.** 0.35

FACTORS AND MULTIPLES (p. xx) **1.** 1, 2, 3, 4, 6, 12
3. 1, 2, 3, 6, 9, 18, 27, 54 **5.** $2 \cdot 3^3$ **7.** $5 \cdot 7$ **9.** 1, 2, 4
11. 1, 2, 7, 14 **13.** 4 **15.** 3 **17.** 6 **19.** 2 **21.** 36
23. 42 **25.** 48 **27.** 900 **29.** 24 **31.** 60 **33.** 28 **35.** 54

FRACTIONS (p. xxi) **1.** $\frac{1}{8}$ **3.** $\frac{5}{9}$ **5.** $\frac{1}{2}$ **7.** $1\frac{1}{5}$ **9.** $\frac{5}{9}$
11. $\frac{19}{24}$ **13.** $\frac{3}{10}$ **15.** $\frac{9}{10}$ **17.** $\frac{1}{2}$ **19.** 6 **21.** $1\frac{1}{2}$ **23.** $13\frac{31}{40}$
25. $1\frac{1}{3}$ **27.** $1\frac{1}{4}$

FRACTIONS, DECIMALS, AND PERCENTS (p. xxi) **1.** 0.08,
$\frac{2}{25}$ **3.** 0.38, $\frac{19}{50}$ **5.** 1.35, $1\frac{7}{20}$ **7.** 0.064, $\frac{8}{125}$ **9.** 44%,
$\frac{11}{25}$ **11.** 13%, $\frac{13}{100}$ **13.** 160%, $1\frac{3}{5}$ **15.** 660%, $6\frac{3}{5}$
17. 0.6, 60% **19.** 0.68, 68% **21.** 5.2, 520% **23.** 3.063,
306.3%

COMPARING AND ORDERING NUMBERS (p. xxii)
1. $13{,}458 < 14{,}455$ **3.** $-8344 > -8434$ **5.** $0.58 > 0.578$
7. $\frac{15}{16} > \frac{9}{10}$ **9.** $\frac{9}{24} = \frac{3}{8}$ **11.** $-2\frac{11}{16} > -3\frac{2}{9}$ **13.** 1075,
1507, 1705, 1775 **15.** $-0.205, -0.035, -0.019, -0.013$
17. $\frac{2}{7}, \frac{5}{11}, \frac{1}{2}, \frac{5}{8}$ **19.** $-\frac{4}{2}, -\frac{3}{2}, -\frac{4}{3}, -\frac{2}{3}$ **21.** $\frac{7}{5}, 1\frac{3}{5}, \frac{5}{3}, 1\frac{4}{5}$

PERIMETER, AREA, AND VOLUME (p. xxii) **1.** 10 m
3. 22.6 km **5.** 95 ft **7.** 3.92 in.^{2} **9.** 39,304 ft^3
11. 78.65 mm^3

DATA DISPLAYS (p. xxiii) **1.** *Sample answer:* 0 to 60 by
tens: 0, 10, 20, 30, 40, 50, 60 **3.** *Sample answer:* 0 to
25 by fives: 0, 5, 10, 15, 20, 25
5. *Sample answer:* bar graph

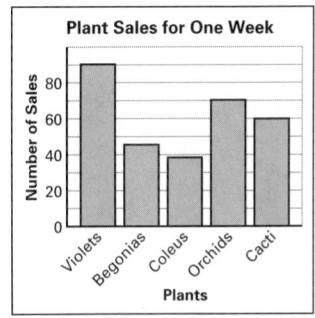

MEASURES OF CENTRAL TENDENCY (p. xxiii) **1.** 4.9; 5; 7
3. 52.1; 53; no mode

Chapter 1

STUDY GUIDE (p. 2) **1.** B **2.** A **3.** B **4.** A

1.1 GUIDED PRACTICE (p. 6) **7.** *p* minus 4, subtraction
9. 8 times *x*, multiplication **11.** 1 **13.** $\frac{1}{11}$ **15.** 54

1.1 PRACTICE AND APPLICATIONS (pp. 6–8) **21.** 20
23. 2 **25.** 20 **27.** 9 **29.** 70 **31.** 6 **33.** 260 mi
35. 40 ft **37.** 340 mi **39.** 240 ft **41.** 64 m **43.** 10 m^2
45. 6 yd^2 **49.** 4 h **53.** 9.48 **55.** 15 **57.** $\frac{1}{6}$ **59.** 23.9
61. 11.1508 **63.** 53.55 **65.** 13.405

1.2 GUIDED PRACTICE (p. 12) **5.** B **7.** A **9.** 9 **11.** 36

1.2 PRACTICE AND APPLICATIONS (pp. 12–14) **13.** 2^3
15. 9^5 **17.** 3^4 **19.** 5^2; 25 **21.** 16 **23.** 64 **25.** 1 **27.** 0
29. 729 **31.** 32 **33.** 125 **35.** 371,293 **37.** 35,831,808
39. 531,441 **41.** 29 **43.** 9 **45.** 20 **47.** 6 **49.** 15,625
51. 100,000 **53.** 8 m^3 **55.** 2^3, 8 cubic units **57.** 4^3,
64 cubic units **65.** 18 **67.** 45 **69.** 9 **71.** 28 **73.** 3
75. 9 **77.** 5 **79.** $\frac{3}{10}$ **81.** $\frac{6}{7}$ **83.** 9 **85.** 3 **87.** 7
89, 91, and 93. Estimates may vary. **89.** about 0.3; 0.27
91. about 5; 4.764 **93.** about 6; 6.325

1.3 GUIDED PRACTICE (p. 18) **3.** 60 **5.** 12 **7.** 17
9. 23 **11.** 4 **13.** 246 **15.** 3

1.3 PRACTICE AND APPLICATIONS (pp. 18–21) **17.** 34
19. 1 **21.** 82 **23.** 300 **25.** 42 **27.** 11 **29.** 16 **31.** 48
33. 14 **35.** 46 **37.** 3 **39.** $\frac{1}{2}$ **41.** 128 **47.** 35($230 +
$300 + $40 + $15 + $100 + $200) − $2000 **49.** $\frac{3}{4}x^2$
51. 2($7) + $5 + 2($4) **59.** 8 **61.** 162 **63.** 11 **65.** z^6
67. 81 **69.** 900 **71.** composite; 1, 3, 9 **73.** composite;
1, 2, 19, 38 **75.** composite; 1, 2, 5, 10, 25, 50 **77.** prime

QUIZ 1 (p. 21) **1.** 18 **2.** 14 **3.** 32 **4.** 9 **5.** 5 **6.** 16
7. 6 **8.** 54 **9.** 216 **10.** 200 mi **11.** 2000 mi **12.** 20 mi
13. 6^3 **14.** 4^5 **15.** $(5y)^3$ **16.** 3^3 **17.** $(2x)^4$ **18.** 8^2
19. 64 ft^3 **20.** 2 **21.** $\frac{1}{3}$ **22.** $\frac{1}{2}$

1.4 GUIDED PRACTICE (p. 27) **9.** not a solution
11. solution **13.** not a solution **15.** solution **17.** not a
solution **19.** solution **21.** not a solution **23.** solution
25. solution

1.4 PRACTICE AND APPLICATIONS (pp. 27–29) **27.** not a
solution **29.** solution **31.** solution **33.** solution **35.** 5
37. 8 **39.** 9 **41.** 21 **43.** 2 **45.** 5 **47.** 6 **51.** solution
53. not a solution **55.** solution **57.** 34 boxes or more
59. 7, 2, 1 **65.** 16 **67.** 2 **69.** 7^2 **71.** 9^6 **73.** $(8d)^3$
75. 12 **77.** 3 **79.** 9 **81.** 9 **83.** 5.6 **85.** 0.457
87. 758.95 **89.** 0.3 **91.** 4.10

1.5 GUIDED PRACTICE (p. 33) **3.** B   **5.** A

7. $x + 10 = 24$ **9.** $\dfrac{20}{n} \le 2$

1.5 PRACTICE AND APPLICATIONS (pp. 33–35)

11. $10 - x$ **13.** $x + 9$ **15.** $\dfrac{x}{50}$ **17.** $x + 18$ **19.** $x - 7$

25. $x + 10 \ge 44$ **27.** $35 < 21 - x$ **29.** $7x = 56$

31. $\dfrac{35}{x} = 7$ **33.** $28 - x = 18; 10$ **35.** $\dfrac{49}{x} = 7; 7$

37. $110 = 55t; 2$ h   **43.** solution   **45.** not a solution

47. 0.28 **49.** 0.4 **51.** 0.45 **53.** 0.174

QUIZ 2 (p. 35) **1.** solution   **2.** not a solution   **3.** solution
4. solution   **5.** not a solution   **6.** solution   **7.** solution
8. not a solution   **9.** solution   **10.** $8x = 32$; 4 units

11. $\dfrac{x}{9} < 17$ **12.** $10x = 50$ **13.** $y + 10 \ge 57$

14. $y - 6 = 15$

1.6 PRACTICE AND APPLICATIONS (pp. 39–41) **5.** 20 min
7. walking speed $= 4$ (mi/h), time to walk home $= t$,
distance to home $= 1$ (mi)   **9.** $t = \dfrac{1}{4}$ h or 15 min

11. original length $+$ number of days $\cdot$ growth rate $=$
total length   **17.** number of weeks worked $= 8$,
amount saved each week $= m$ ($), price of stereo with
CD $= 480$ ($)   **19.** $60   **25.** 1000   **27.** 14   **29.** 12

31. solution   **33.** $0.25l + 0.50(100) = 100; 200$ **35.** $1\dfrac{3}{4}$

37. $2\dfrac{1}{6}$ **39.** $2\dfrac{1}{3}$ **41.** $2\dfrac{1}{7}$ **43.** $4\dfrac{1}{2}$ **45.** $6\dfrac{2}{3}$

1.7 GUIDED PRACTICE (p. 45) **3.** false   **5.** false

1.7 PRACTICE AND APPLICATIONS (pp. 45–47) **7.** Player 4;
Player 1   **9.** 1990; 2000   **11.** about 150 ft   **13.** The
braking distance at that speed is about 300 ft. You need
to have time to react to any emergency and still allow
time for your car to travel that distance while stopping.
15. the 6 years from 1991 to 1996   **17.** 1998

19. *Sample answer:*
I chose a line graph
because line graphs are
useful in showing
changes over time.
23. 42 in., 98 in.²
25. 56 ft, 84 ft²
27. solution
29. not a solution
31. solution
33. not a solution
35. $<$ **37.** $>$
39. $=$ **41.** $>$
43. $=$

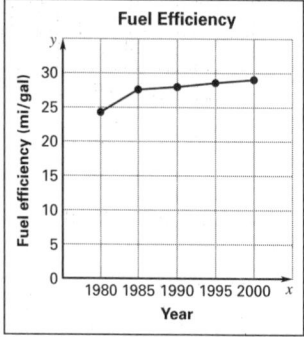
Fuel Efficiency

1.8 GUIDED PRACTICE (p. 51)

5.

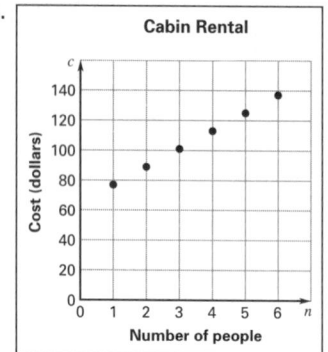
Cabin Rental

1.8 PRACTICE AND APPLICATIONS (pp. 51–54)

7.

Input x	0	1	2	3	4	5
Output y	5	11	17	23	29	35

9.

Input x	0	1	2	3	4	5
Output y	21	28	35	42	49	56

11.

Input x	0	1	2	3	4	5
Output y	75	70	65	60	55	50

13.

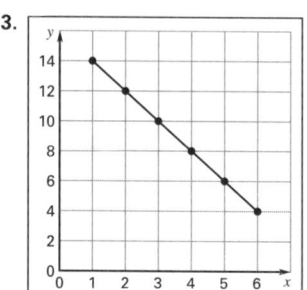

15.

Input t	0	5	10	15	20	25	30
Output d	0	1	2	3	4	5	6

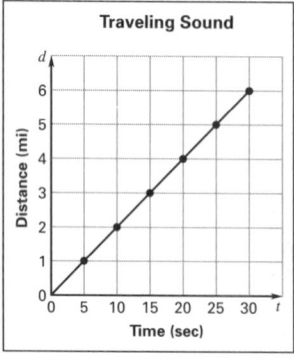
Traveling Sound

17. no   **19.** no

21.

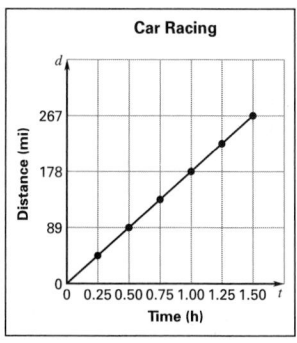

Car Racing

23. a. $d = 11t$

b.

Input t	7	14	28
Output d	77	154	308

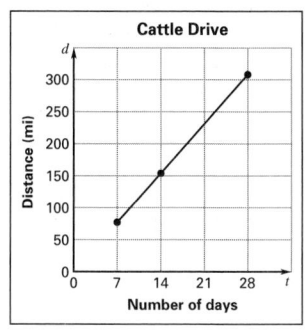

Cattle Drive

c. 100 days

25.

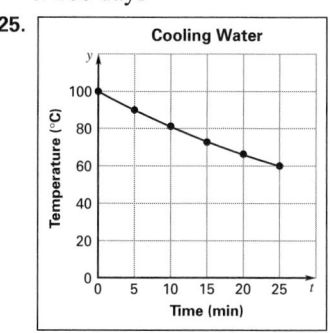

Cooling Water

31. 64 **33.** 15 **35.** 45 **37.** $\dfrac{72}{x} > 7$ **39.** $\dfrac{1}{2}$ **41.** $4\dfrac{1}{3}$

43. $\dfrac{3}{8}$ **45.** 3

QUIZ 3 (p. 54) **1.** 6 bottles

2.

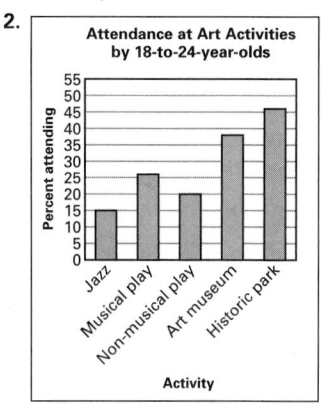

Attendance at Art Activities by 18-to-24-year-olds

3. *Sample answer:* Attending historic parks was most popular; attending a jazz concert is about a third as popular as attending a historic park. Since the percents total more than 100%, some 18-to-24-year-olds attend more than one kind of arts activity.

4. *Sample table:*

Input t	0	1	2	3	4
Output h	200	225	250	275	300

5.

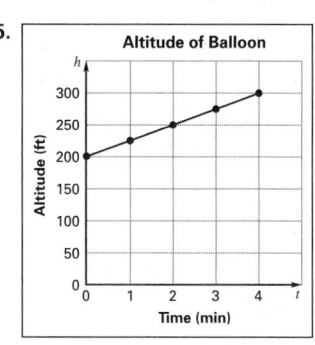

Altitude of Balloon

6. $h \geq 200$ and $h \leq 300$

CHAPTER SUMMARY AND REVIEW (pp. 55–58) **1.** 20 **3.** 6
5. 10 **7.** 6 miles **9.** 525 miles **11.** 26 m **13.** 6^3
15. 16 **17.** 33 **19.** 54 **21.** 3 **23.** $\dfrac{17}{4}$ **25.** solution
27. solution **29.** 3 **31.** 16 **33.** 10 **35.** $x + 30$
37. $x - 9$
39. $48.9 + 55.1 < 53.5 + 53.3$; $104 < 106.8$; yes

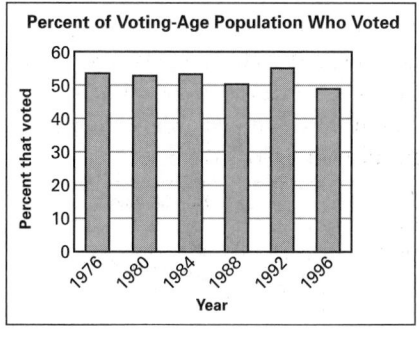

Percent of Voting-Age Population Who Voted

MAINTAINING SKILLS (p. 61) **1.** 2.7 **3.** 12.1 **5.** 5.806
7. 4.244 **9.** 155.8 **11.** 0.99
13–20.

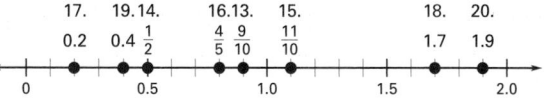

Chapter 2

1. B   **2.** A   **3.** D   **4.** C

2.1 GUIDED PRACTICE (p. 68)

3.

5.

7. >   **9.** >   **11.** $-8, -3, -2, 1, 2$ **13.** $-9, -7, -\frac{1}{5}, \frac{5}{4}, 2$

2.1 PRACTICE AND APPLICATIONS (pp. 68–70)

15.

19.

23. $-2 < 3, 3 > -2$ **25.** $-6 < -1, -1 > -6$
27. $-4 < 0, 0 > -4$ **29.** $10 < 11, 11 > 10$
35.

39.

43.

45. $-3.0, -0.3, -0.2, 0, 0.2, 2.0$ **47.** $-5.2, -5.1, -\frac{10}{4},$
$3.4, 4.1, \frac{9}{2}$ **49.** $-\frac{7}{2}, -2.6, -\frac{1}{2}, 0, \frac{1}{2}, 4.8$ **51.** >   **53.** -8

55.

57. Pollux, Altair, Spica, Regulus, Deneb   **59.** Regulus
63. 4 ft^2 **65.** 81 cm^2 **67.** 4   **69.** 5   **71.** 3   **73.** $65.9°$,
$67.5°, 69.1°, 69.9°, 72.3°$ **75.** $64.3 \le T \le 72.3$
77. $5 \cdot 7$ **79.** 2^6 **81.** prime   **83.** $2^4 \cdot 3^2$

2.2 GUIDED PRACTICE (p. 74) **3.** -1 **5.** 2.4   **7.** 12
9. -5.1 **11.** $8, -8$ **13.** $5.5, -5.5$ **15.** False. *Sample*
counterexample: if $a = -2$, then $-a = -(-2) = 2$,
which is greater than -2.

2.2 PRACTICE AND APPLICATIONS (p. 74–76) **17.** -8
19. 10   **21.** 3.8   **23.** $\frac{1}{9}$ **25.** 7   **27.** -3 **29.** 0.8   **31.** $\frac{2}{3}$
33. $4, -4$ **35.** no solution   **37.** $3.7, -3.7$ **39.** $\frac{11}{2}, -\frac{11}{2}$
41. Mercury: 1080; Mars: 288   **43.** negative
45. positive   **47.** -6 ft/sec   **49.** 400 ft/min   **51.** False:
Sample counterexample: The opposite of $-a$ is a.
If $-a = 5$, then $a = -5$, which is negative.   **53.** true

61. 3   **63.** 75   **65.** 3   **67.** $x + 8 = 17$ **69.** $9y < 6$
71. $-6 < -2, -2 > -6$ **73.** $-3 < 0.4, 0.4 > -3$
75. $-10 < -\frac{1}{10}, -\frac{1}{10} > -10$ **77.** $\frac{5}{9}$ **79.** $\frac{2}{3}$ **81.** $\frac{1}{2}$

2.3 GUIDED PRACTICE (p. 81) **5.** $-5 + 9 = 4$ **7.** -10
9. 7   **11.** -10 **13.** 7

2.3 PRACTICE AND APPLICATIONS (pp. 81–83) **19.** -6
21. -11 **23.** -4 **25.** 6   **27.** 7   **29.** -11 **31.** 3
33. -31 **35.** -35 **37.** commutative property
39. property of opposites   **41.** 10   **43.** 0   **45.** 5   **47.** 4
49. $-2\frac{4}{7}$ **51.** -81.14 **53.** 356.773   **55.** two strokes
under par   **59.** 4^2 **61.** x^3 **63.** 33   **65.** 4   **67.** 24
69. solution   **71.** not a solution   **73.** not a solution
75. 9300   **77.** 100   **79.** 2900

QUIZ 1 (p. 83) **1.** $-2 < 7, 7 > -2$ **2.** $-3 < -2$,
$-2 > -3$ **3.** $-6 < 1, 1 > -6$ **4.** $-10, -8, -3, 2, 9$
5. $-7, -5.2, 3.3, 5, 7.1$ **6.** $-1, -\frac{2}{5}, 0, \frac{1}{10}, 2$ **7.** 5
8. 13   **9.** -0.56 **10.** no solution   **11.** $2.7, -2.7$
12. $-\frac{3}{5}, \frac{3}{5}$ **13.** -13 **14.** -6 **15.** 4   **16.** -7 **17.** -2
18. 0   **19.** yes

2.4 GUIDED PRACTICE (p. 89) **3.** -7 **5.** 7   **7.** -1
9. $3\frac{1}{2}$ **11.** $12, -5x$ **13.** $-12y, 6$

2.4 PRACTICE AND APPLICATIONS (pp. 89–91)
15. 9   **17.** -11 **19.** 39   **21.** 36   **23.** 9.2   **25.** -1.2
27. 3   **29.** $-4\frac{1}{2}$ **31.** -1 **33.** 31   **35.** -43
37. 10.2   **39.** 1   **41.** $1\frac{1}{10}$ **43.** 14, 13, 12, 11
45. $-6.5, -7.5, -8.5, -9.5$ **47.** $-2\frac{1}{2}, -1\frac{1}{2}, -\frac{1}{2}, \frac{1}{2}$
49. $-x, -7$ **51.** $9, -28x$ **53.** $a, -5$ **55.** up 275 ft
57. $-7301 - 662 - 1883 + 77 - 1311 + 8021; -3059$
65. 35   **67.** 41   **69.** 64   **71.** true
73.

75.

79. 0.04   **81.** 0.0338   **83.** 19.176

2.5 GUIDED PRACTICE (p. 96) **7.** -35 **9.** -1 **11.** $5t^4$
13. 40

2.5 PRACTICE AND APPLICATIONS (pp. 96–98) **15.** yes
17. -28 **19.** -12.6 **21.** $-\frac{4}{3}$ **23.** -216 **25.** -49
27. -54 **29.** 97.2   **31.** $-\frac{3}{2}$ **33.** $-7x$ **35.** $-5a^3$
37. $-10r^2$ **39.** $-2x^2$ **41.** -48 **43.** -147 **45.** 41
47. true   **49.** False. *Sample counterexample:* $3 > 2$,
but $3 \cdot 0 = 2 \cdot 0$ **51.** -20 ft   **53.** $d \approx -300t$
55. about 150 ft   **63.** 2   **65.** 4   **67.** 12

69.

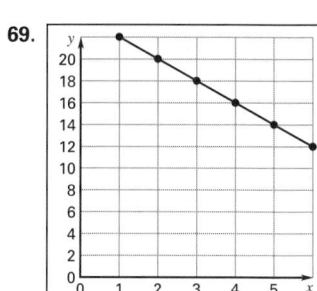

71. 2 **73.** –9 **75.** 7.2 **77.** 10.43 **79.** 12, $-z$
81. $4w, -11$ **83.** $-7x, 4x$ **85.** 20 **87.** 150 **89.** 10,920

2.6 GUIDED PRACTICE (p. 103) **5.** $12(x + 5); 12x + 60$
7. D **9.** B **11.** $4(1) + 4(0.15); 4 + 0.6; 4.6$

2.6 PRACTICE AND APPLICATIONS (pp. 103–106)
13. $3(4 + x) = 12 + 3x$ **15.** $(x + 5)(11) = 11x + 55$
17. $3x + 12$ **19.** $7 + 7t$ **21.** $12 + 6u$ **23.** $4y + 2$
25. $12 + 18a$ **27.** $1.3x + 2.6$ **29.** $5y - 10$ **31.** $63 - 9a$
33. $28 - 4m$ **35.** $10 - 30t$ **37.** $18x - 18$
39. $-9.3u - 2.4$ **41.** $-3r - 24$ **43.** $-1 - s$
45. $-y - 9$ **47.** $-24a - 18$ **49.** $-6y + 5$
51. $-13.8 + 42w$ **53.** forgot to distribute $9(3) - 9(5)$;
-18 **55.** 24.44 **57.** 27.60 **59.** 5.80 **61.** -12.30
63. -22.10 **65.** -54.95 **67.** \$19.96 **69.** \$10.45
71. $200(x + 225); 200x + 45,000$ **73.** 60,000 yd³
79. $\frac{12}{5}$ **81.** 3 **83.** 5 **85.** identity property of addition
87. associative property of addition **89.** 12 **91.** 3
93. $-1\frac{1}{3}$ **95.** $\frac{1}{4}$ **97.** $\frac{1}{2}$ **99.** $\frac{41}{50}$ **101.** $\frac{24}{25}$

QUIZ 2 (p. 106) **1.** $-15, -13, -11, -9$ **2.** 30, 28, 26, 24
3. $-3\frac{1}{4}, -1\frac{1}{4}, \frac{3}{4}, 2\frac{3}{4}$ **4.** $2x, -9$ **5.** $8, -x$ **6.** $-10x, 4$
7. $-0.25, 0.12, -0.12, -0.13$ **8.** -63 **9.** 30
10. -2800 **11.** 10.8 **12.** -3 **13.** 270 **14.** $11x + 22$
15. $60 - 5y$ **16.** $-12a + 16$ **17.** \$49.90

2.7 GUIDED PRACTICE (p. 110) **3.** $6r$ **5.** -8
7. $4a^2 + 3a - 5$ **9.** $18f + 4$ **11.** $-11m - 20$
13. $9x - 27$

2.7 PRACTICE AND APPLICATIONS (pp. 110–112) **15.** $3a, 5a$
17. $m, 6m$ **19.** $-6w, -3w$ **21.** $-7m$ **23.** $2c - 5$
25. $6r - 7$ **27.** already simplified **29.** $6p^2 + 4p - 2$
31. $-27 - 4y$ **33.** $-11 - 6r$ **35.** $10m + 19$
37. $2c + 48$ **39.** 7 is not a like term with $3x$ and $-2x$;
$x + 7 = 16$ **41.** $x + (x - 7) + x + (x - 7); 4x - 14$
43. $2(x + 2) + (x + 4) + 2(x + 2) + (x + 4); 6x + 16$
47. 15,675 tons **49.** $T = -45c + 480$ **51.** $1.06x + 21.2$
59. about 35% **61.** 9 **63.** -6 **65.** -14.1 **67.** -180
69. -3 **71.** 29.88 **73.** $\frac{2}{10}, \frac{4}{10}, \frac{5}{10}, \frac{6}{10}, \frac{9}{10}$
75. $\frac{1}{4}, \frac{3}{8}, \frac{4}{8}, \frac{3}{4}, \frac{7}{8}$ **77.** $\frac{2}{6}, \frac{4}{6}, \frac{3}{4}, \frac{2}{2}, \frac{5}{2}$
79. $\frac{3}{8}, \frac{8}{8}, 1\frac{2}{8}, \frac{12}{8}, 2\frac{1}{8}$ **81.** $\frac{11}{15}, \frac{4}{5}, \frac{5}{6}, 2\frac{2}{3}, 2\frac{7}{10}$

2.8 GUIDED PRACTICE (p. 116) **3.** $\frac{1}{32}$ **5.** $-\frac{5}{1}$ or -5
7. -4 **9.** -2 **11.** 2 **13.** all real numbers except $x = 4$
15. all real numbers except $x = 0$

2.8 PRACTICE AND APPLICATIONS (pp. 116–118)
17. multiply by reciprocal; -27 **19.** -3 **21.** -1
23. -5 **25.** 2 **27.** -12 **29.** $-\frac{5}{6}$ **31.** 12 **33.** -48
35. $-\frac{1}{9}$ **37.** $-\frac{3}{2}$ **39.** $-\frac{1}{3}$ **41.** 4 **43.** $6x - 3$
45. already simplified **47.** $11 + 2t$ **49.** all real numbers
except $x = -2$ **51.** all real numbers **53.** -10.5 m/sec
57. 24 **59.** 5 **61.** 10 **63.** $2x \geq 7$ **65.** -21 **67.** -19.9
69. $4\frac{1}{4}$ or $\frac{17}{4}$ **71.** $<$ **73.** $<$ **75.** $>$ **77.** $<$

QUIZ 3 (p. 118) **1.** $3x, -7x$ **2.** $6a$ and $9a$, -5 and 10
3. $-5p, -p$ **4.** $-26t$ **5.** $7 + 2d$ **6.** $g^2 - 8g$ **7.** $3a - 4$
8. $3p - 9$ **9.** $5 - 3w$ **10.** -5 **11.** 16 **12.** -32
13. $\frac{98}{9}$ **14.** -54 **15.** $\frac{1}{8}$ **16.** $5 - 2x$ **17.** already
simplified **18.** $3x - 2$ **19.** all real numbers except
$x = -2$ **20.** all real numbers **21.** all real numbers
except $x = 0$

CH. 2 EXTENSION (pp. 119–120)

EXERCISES (p. 120) **1.** inductive reasoning **3.** inductive
reasoning **5.** 64, 128, 256

CHAPTER SUMMARY AND REVIEW (pp. 121–124) **1.** -6,
$-4, -3, 1, 2, 5$ **3.** $-2, -1, -\frac{1}{2}, \frac{2}{3}, 1, 4, 6$ **5.** 5
7. -45 **9.** -9.1 **11.** $3\frac{1}{2}$ **13.** -12 **15.** 5 **17.** -8
19. 19 **21.** -11.2 **23.** $-3\frac{1}{4}$ **25.** 600 **27.** 4.2
29. -14 **31.** $-3f$ **33.** $-12t^2$ **35.** $-81b^2$ **37.** $9y + 54$
39. $6 - 2w$ **41.** $-3t - 33$ **43.** $-6x + 60$ **45.** $9a$
47. $3 + f$ **49.** $4t + 2$ **51.** -4 **53.** 10 **55.** $-\frac{2}{3}$ **57.** -9

MAINTAINING SKILLS (p. 127) **1.** 25 **3.** 100
5.

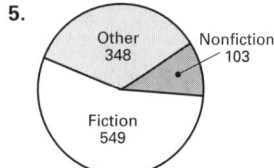

Other 348   Nonfiction 103   Fiction 549

Chapter 3

3.1 GUIDED PRACTICE (p. 135) **7.** -1 **9.** -17 **11.** 4
13. 3 **15.** -3 **17.** addition

3.1 PRACTICE AND APPLICATIONS (pp. 135–137)
19. subtract 28 **21.** add 3 **23.** subtract -12 **25.** 9
27. -5 **29.** 10 **31.** 8 **33.** -4 **35.** 24 **37.** -15
39. -24 **41.** $\frac{3}{5}$ **43.** 0 **45.** 5 **47.** 6 **49.** 3 **51.** 1

53. 20 cm **55.** B; 8 **57.** 6463 seats **59.** 10,534 acres; $4218 + 3800 + 2764 - 248 = x$ **61.** Simplify with subtraction rule; subtract 2 from both sides. **65.** $5x = 160$ **67.** $36 - k = 15$ **69.** $4x + 8$ **71.** $-5y - 20$ **73.** $-2x + 12$ **75.** $\frac{4}{7}$ **77.** $\frac{3}{32}$ **79.** $\frac{4}{7}$ **81.** 1

3.2 GUIDED PRACTICE (p. 141) **7.** -1 **9.** 32 **11.** 28 **13.** -6 **15.** 60 mi/h

3.2 PRACTICE AND APPLICATIONS (pp. 141–143)
17. divide by 5 **19.** divide by -4 **21.** multiply by 7 **23.** -8 **25.** -6 **27.** 11 **29.** $\frac{9}{10}$ **31.** -10 **33.** 30 **35.** 84 **37.** $\frac{4}{3}$ **39.** 0 **41.** 12 **43.** 18 **45.** -45 **47.** multiply by $-\frac{4}{3}$; -8 **49.** $\frac{3}{8} \cdot p = 3.30$; $8.80 **51.** 13 **57.** $27 - 8x$ **59.** $-2x + 6$ **61.** $12y + 15$ **63.** 8 **65.** -19 **67.** 2 **69.** A; 18 **71.** 10 **73.** 5 **75.** 9 **77.** 3

3.3 GUIDED PRACTICE (p. 147) **7.** 2 **9.** -1 **11.** 2 **13.** 25 **15.** -9 **17.** 19

3.3 PRACTICE AND APPLICATIONS (pp. 147–149) **19.** 2 **21.** 14 **23.** 2 **25.** 3 **27.** 5 **29.** -3 **31.** 3 **33.** 9 **35.** 14 **37.** 11 **39.** 6 **41.** 5 and $3x$ are not like terms, so $3x$ cannot be subtracted from 5; $-\frac{5}{3}$ **43.** Subtract 3 from each side; multiply each side by 2; divide each side by 5. **45.** 14 months **55.** a^6 **57.** 4^3 **59.** t^3 **61.** 10 **63.** 47 **65.** 14 **67.** < **69.** < **71.** < **73.** <

QUIZ 1 (p. 149) **1.** 21 **2.** -17 **3.** -7 **4.** -1 **5.** 282 **6.** 5 **7.** B **8.** $6x = 72$; $12 **9.** 9 **10.** 2 **11.** 2 **12.** 1 **13.** -25 **14.** 14 **15.** 9 min

3.4 GUIDED PRACTICE (p. 154) **9.** one solution, -1 **11.** one solution, 7 **13.** identity **15.** B

3.4 PRACTICE AND APPLICATIONS (pp. 154–156) **17.** subtract x from each side **19.** add $8x$ to each side **21.** 3 **23.** 3 **25.** 2 **27.** $\frac{3}{7}$ **29.** -8 **31.** 4 **33.** -2 **35.** $3x - 12x = -9x$; $x = -5$ **37.** one solution, 2 **39.** one solution, -1 **41.** one solution, -5 **43.** no solution **45.** one solution **47.** 121 hours **49.** 25 sec; the gazelle would probably be safe since the cheetah begins to tire after 20 seconds. **57.** 144 miles **59.** 8 **61.** 216 **63.** 144 **65.** 10 **67.** yes **69.** -4 **71.** 12 **73.** -23 **75.** 0 **77.** 90 **79.** 2000 **81.** 9 **83.** 8 **85.** 3910

3.5 GUIDED PRACTICE (p. 160) **11.** -5 **13.** -2 **15.** -6 **17.** 2

3.5 PRACTICE AND APPLICATIONS (pp. 160–162) **19.** 19 **21.** 14 **23.** 3 **25.** 21 **27.** -1 **29.** -4 **31.** -1 **33.** $\frac{1}{2}$ **35.** 1 **37.** $3x - 12 + 2x = 6 - x$, $6x - 12 = 6$, $6x = 18$, $x = 3$ **39.** $-4(3 - n) = -12 + 4n$, $8(4n - 3) = 32n - 24$; $n = \frac{3}{7}$ **43.** C, $x = 25$; you will need to use the gym more than 25 times to justify the

cost of the yearly fee. **51.** 400,000 km; 700,000 km; 1,100,000 km; 1,900,000 km **55.** 36 **57.** -77 **59.** $3w^2 - w$ **61.** $s + 11t$ **63.** $-6m - m^2$ **65.** 11.5 **67.** 6.42 **69.** 22.49

3.6 GUIDED PRACTICE (p. 166) **7.** 23.4 **9.** -13.9 **11.** 56.1 **13.** 8.8 **15.** 6.82 **17.** 4.22 **19.** $12

3.6 PRACTICE AND APPLICATIONS (pp. 166–169) **21.** 5.78 **23.** 7.57 **25.** 4.33 **27.** 0.77 **29.** 2.22 **31.** 0.94 **33.** 0.42 **35.** -2.63 **37.** $M = 150 + 0.38x$ **39.** 1.0 **41.** 1.9 **43.** $162 + 30 = 71n$, where n is the number of buses needed **45.** Round up to 3 buses; you need enough buses to seat all the students and adults. **51.** $697.45
53.

Input t	2	3	4	5	6
Output A	18	23	28	33	38

55. 3 **57.** $-\frac{4}{5}$ **59.** -5.6 **61.** 16 **63.** 14 **65.** $13\frac{6}{7}$ **67.** $25\frac{9}{16}$ **69.** 11

QUIZ 2 (p. 169) **1.** no solution **2.** one solution **3.** identity **4.** no solution **5.** -3 **6.** -7 **7.** 10 **8.** 1 **9.** 5 **10.** 4 **11.** -1 **12.** 19 **13.** 8 **14.** 13 **15.** You need to use the bike for at least 10 hours to justify the cost of the helmet. **16.** -1.14 **17.** -0.68 **18.** 1.63 **19.** 0.36 **20.** -5.03 **21.** -2.23 **22.** 7

3.6 TECHNOLOGY (p. 170) **1.** 12.3 **3.** 5.3

3.7 GUIDED PRACTICE (p. 174) **3.** $r = s + t$ **5.** $y = \frac{x}{3}$ **7.** $y = 2x - 4$ **9.** $w = \frac{A}{l}$

3.7 PRACTICE AND APPLICATIONS (pp. 174–176) **11.** $C = \frac{5}{9}(F - 32)$ **13.** $w = \frac{A}{l}$; $w = 4$ **15.** $l = \frac{A}{w}$; $l = 16$ **17.** 18 cm^2 **19.** 16.67 cm^3 **21.** 6 min **23.** 30 ft **27.** solution **29.** not a solution **31.** not a solution **33.** not a solution **35.** solution **37.** 28% **39.** $\frac{3}{7}$ **41.** $\frac{2}{9}$ **43.** $\frac{1}{2}$ **45.** $\frac{7}{8}$

3.8 GUIDED PRACTICE (p. 180) **5.** $\frac{4}{5}$ **7.** $\frac{2}{3}$ **9.** 0.05 mi/min **11.** 231 miles

3.8 PRACTICE AND APPLICATIONS (pp. 180–182) **13.** $\frac{1}{4}$ **15.** $\frac{3}{5}$ **17.** $\frac{11}{3}$ **19.** $\frac{4}{5}$ **21.** $\frac{5}{8}$ **23.** 15 mi/day **25.** $.40/can **27.** 8 oz/serving **29.** miles **33.** 24 months **35.** 21.2 hours **37.** 2 km **39.** 21 mi/hr **41.** 12 min **43.** $91 **49.** $4 > -3$; $-3 < 4$ **51.** $-6 < 3$; $3 > -6$ **53.** 1.43 **55.** 75 ft **57.** 18 **59.** 21 **61.** 162 **63.** 490

3.9 GUIDED PRACTICE (p. 186) **7.** 175% **9.** 72 **11.** $a = 0.06(10)$

3.9 PRACTICE AND APPLICATIONS (pp. 186–188)

17. 20   **19.** 30.8 ft   **21.** 10   **23.** 84 ft   **25.** $1000
27. 200   **29.** 480%   **31.** 30%   **33.** 20%
35. no; A: 30%(60) = $18 discount, cost = $42;
B: 20%(60) = $12, cost = $48, 10%(48) = 4.8,
final cost = $48 − $4.80 = $43.20   **37.** 21%   **39.** 27%
41. $a = 3b$; *Sample answer:* $a = 30, b = 10, p = 300$
45. $21x = 105; x = 5$ **47.** 32   **49.** −16   **51.** 217, 270,
2017, 2170, 2701   **53.** 5.09, 5.1, 5.19, 5.9, 5.91

QUIZ 3 (p. 188)   **1.** $t = \dfrac{d}{r}$ **2.** $h = \dfrac{2A}{b}$ **3.** $v = \dfrac{m}{d}$

4. $\dfrac{7 \text{ days}}{1 \text{ week}}$ **5.** $\dfrac{1 \text{ ft}}{12 \text{ in.}}$ **6.** 300 students/school   **7.** 240 hours
8. $5.75   **9.** $5.75 = p(23); p = 0.25$, or 25%

CHAPTER SUMMARY AND REVIEW (pp. 189–192)

1. 11   **3.** −8   **5.** −9   **7.** −3   **9.** 1   **11.** 2   **13.** one
solution; 2   **15.** one solution; 5   **17.** one solution, −2
19. $12 + n = 6 + 2n; n = 6$; the plants will be the
same height after 6 weeks.   **21.** 1.08   **23.** $l = \dfrac{V}{wh}$
25. $b = P - a - c$ **27.** 85 mi

MAINTAINING SKILLS (p. 195)

1.

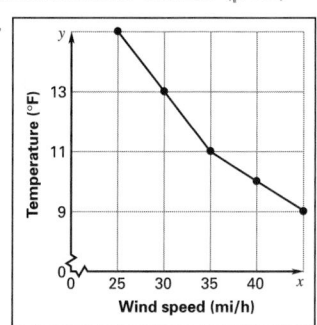

CUMULATIVE PRACTICE (pp. 196–197)   **1.** 8   **3.** 41   **5.** 216

7. 5   **9.** 7   **11.** 57   **13.** not a solution   **15.** solution
17. not a solution   **19.** $x^3 - 8$ **21.** $-3x < 12$
23.

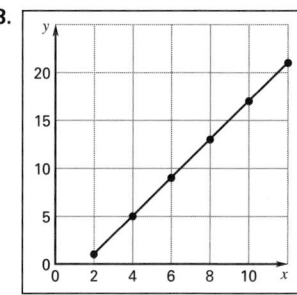

25. <   **27.** >   **29.** <   **31.** <   **33.** $-5y^3$ **35.** $-4 + 2t$
37. $4x - 6$ **39.** $43x + 25$ **41.** −30 ft; negative; downward
velocity is negative.   **43.** $15(x + 6) = 15x + 90$
45. −9   **47.** 18   **49.** 0   **51.** $\dfrac{3}{2}$ **53.** $3(50) + 2n = 750$;
300 rolls   **55.** −20.33   **57.** −2.30   **59.** −1.22
61. 10 cm   **63.** $45.50

Chapter 4

STUDY GUIDE (p. 202)   **1.** B   **2.** B   **3.** D

4.1 GUIDED PRACTICE (p. 206)

5.

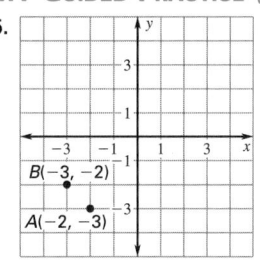

7. always   **9.** always

4.1 PRACTICE AND APPLICATIONS (pp. 206–208)

11. $A(2, 4), B(0, -1), C(-1, 0), D(-2, -1)$
13.

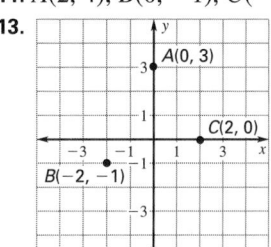

15.

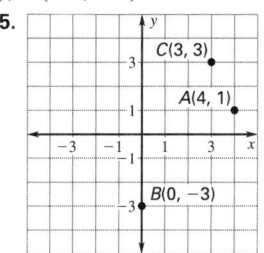

19. IV   **21.** I   **23.** III   **25.** III   **27.** pounds; inches
31. Gas mileage decreases as weight increases.
33.

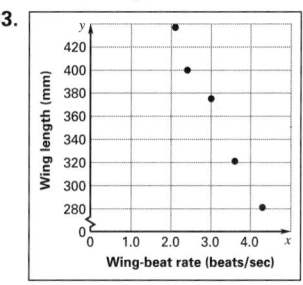

35. As wing-beat rate increases, the wing length
decreases.   **41.** 7   **43.** 3   **45.** 39   **47.** −13   **49.** 1.07
51. $\dfrac{2}{3}$ **53.** 5   **55.** 1   **57.** 5   **59.** $2\dfrac{1}{3}$ **61.** $7\dfrac{4}{15}$ **63.** $\dfrac{5}{11}$
65. $5\dfrac{5}{7}$

4.2 GUIDED PRACTICE (p. 213)   **3.** solution   **5.** solution

7. $y = -x - 2$ **9.** $y = -2x + 4$ **11.** *Sample answer:*
$(0, 7), (-1, 2), (1, 12)$
13.

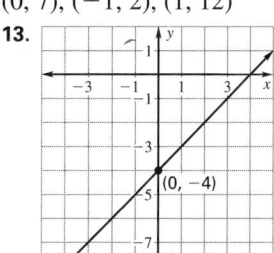

15.

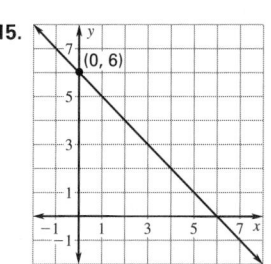

17. not solution **19.** solution **21.** not solution

23. $y = -\frac{2}{3}x + 2$ **25.** $y = -x + \frac{19}{5}$ **27.** $y = -x - 5$

29. $y = -\frac{3}{2}x - \frac{3}{2}$ *Sample answers given for 31–39*

31. $(0, -5), (1, -2), (-1, -8)$ **33.** $(0, -6), (1, -8),$
$(-1, -4)$ **35.** $(0, 3), (3, 1), (-3, 5)$ **37.** $(0, 5), (2, 0),$
$(4, -5)$ **39.** $(0, -4), \left(1, -\frac{17}{3}\right), (3, -9)$

43. 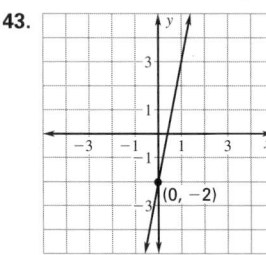 **47.**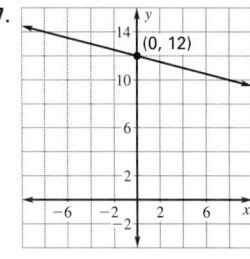

49. $7.1x + 10.1y = 800$ **51.** about 48 minutes **53.** The boiling temperature of water decreases as altitude increases.

55.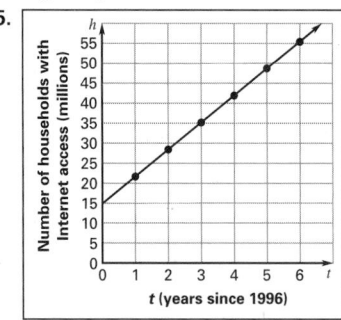

61. -12 **63.** 6 **65.** $-14x + 6y$ **67.** $-5t^3 - 9r$
69. $-3k^3 + h$ **71.** -15 **73.** 63 **75.** 63% **77.** 2%
79. 127% **81.** 860%

5. 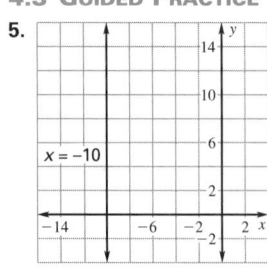 **7.**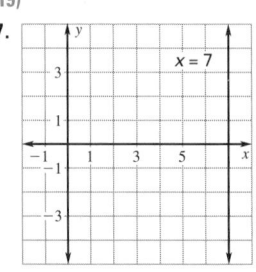

9. $x = 3$ **11.** sometimes **13.** always

15. not solution **17.** not solution *Sample answers given for 19–23:* **19.** $\left(\frac{1}{2}, 0\right), \left(\frac{1}{2}, 2\right), \left(\frac{1}{2}, -2\right)$

21. $(0, -5), (3, -5), (-3, -5)$ **23.** $(0, 7), (-2, 7),$
$(-3, 7)$

25. 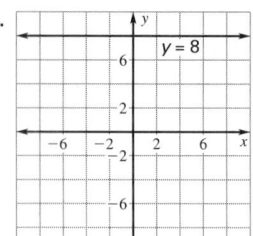 **27.**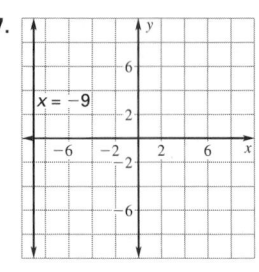

31. $x = -4$ **33. a.** $H = 110$; domain: 0–5; range: 110
b. $H = 160$; domain: 0–10; range: 160 **37.** 7 **39.** 8
41. 10 **43.** 5 **45.** 15 **47.** $21; \frac{15}{21}, \frac{14}{21}$ **49.** $21; \frac{15}{21}, \frac{4}{21}$
51. $26; \frac{24}{26}, \frac{5}{26}$ **53.** $60; \frac{9}{60}, \frac{28}{60}$

1. 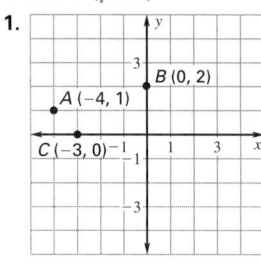 **2.**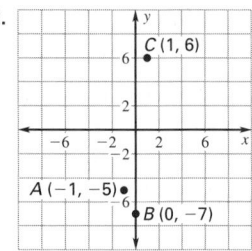

3. 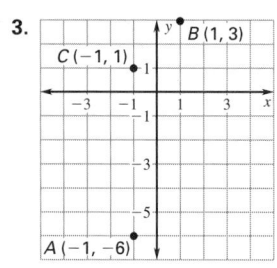 **4.**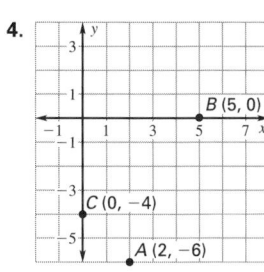

5. I **6.** III **7.** IV **8.** II **9.** $y = -2x$ **10.** $y = \frac{5}{2}x - 10$
11. $y = -\frac{1}{2}x - 4$ **12.** *Sample answer:* $(0, -6),$
$(1, -4), (2, -2)$

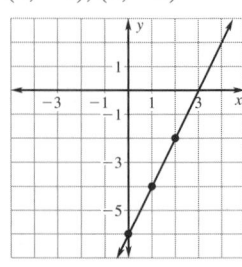

13. *Sample answer:*
$(0, 1), (1, 5), (-1, -3)$ **14.** *Sample answer:*
$(0, 2), (1, -4), (-1, 8)$

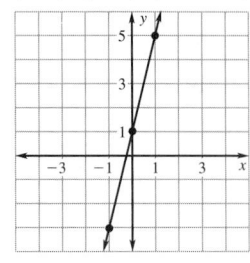 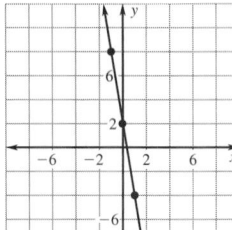

15. Sample answer:
(0, 12), (3, 3), (6, −6)

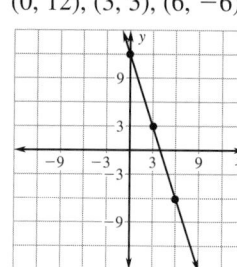

16. Sample answer:
(0, 5), (1, −5), (2, −15)

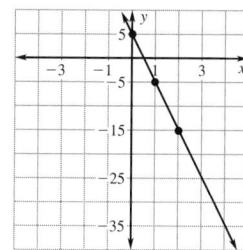

17. Sample answer:
(0, −2), (3, 6), (−3, −10)

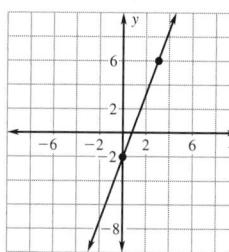

18.

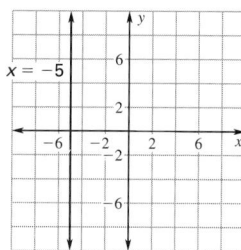

19.

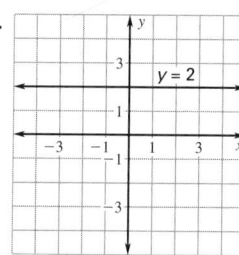

20.

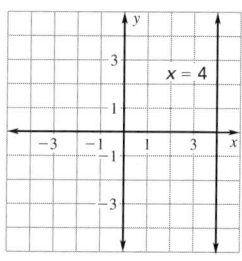

4.4 GUIDED PRACTICE (p. 225) **3.** 6 **5.** −3 **7.** −2
9. *x*-intercept = −2,
y-intercept = 2

11. *x*-intercept = 2,
y-intercept = −4

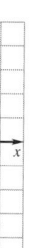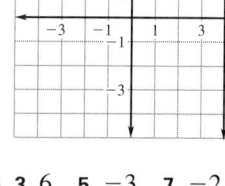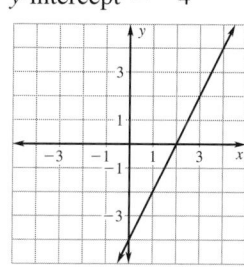

13. *x*-intercept = −3, *y*-intercept = 3

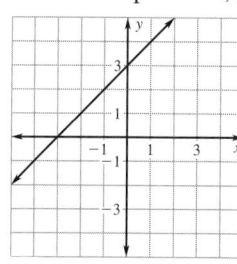

4.4 PRACTICE AND APPLICATIONS (pp. 225–227)
15. *x*-intercept = 2, *y*-intercept = 3
17. *x*-intercept = −4, *y*-intercept = −1 **19.** −2 **21.** 19
23. 6 **25.** −12 **27.** −2 **29.** 26 **31.** −4
33.

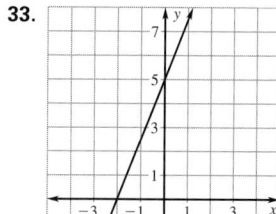

35.

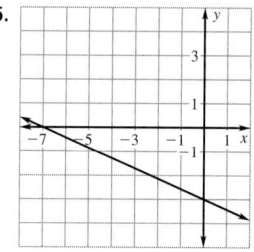

41.

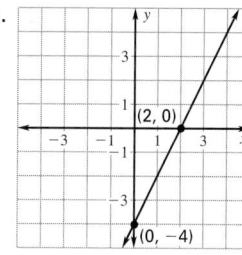

45.

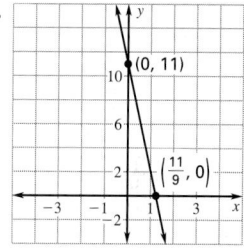

49. 7.5; if students get in free, the adult ticket price needs
to be $7.50. **53.** about 189,000 **57.** −4 **59.** −5
61. $\frac{5}{3}$ **63.** −17 **65.** 6 **67.** −2 **69.** −60 **71.** $\frac{1}{4}$
75. $1.65 **77.** $8.36 **79.** $3.15 **81.** $5.11

4.5 GUIDED PRACTICE (p. 233) **5.** positive **7.** negative
9. zero **11.** undefined

4.5 PRACTICE AND APPLICATIONS (pp. 233–235)
13. $-\frac{3}{2}$ **15.** $\frac{1}{2}$ **17.** $\frac{3}{4}$ **19.** −1 **21.** 1 **23.** $\frac{1}{2}$ **25.** $-\frac{1}{4}$
27. $-\frac{3}{2}$ **29.** neither **31.** zero **33.** neither **35.** $\frac{3}{2}$
39. $\frac{1}{5}$; it represents how the rise changes with respect to
the run. **41.** 6% **45.** 5 **47.** 4 **49.** $y = 2x + 9$
51. $y = 4x + 5$ **53.** $y = -\frac{5}{2}x - \frac{5}{2}$ **55.** true **57.** false
59. true

4.6 GUIDED PRACTICE (p. 239) **3.** $\frac{1}{9}$ **5.** $\frac{1}{7}$ **7.** $y = 5x$
9.

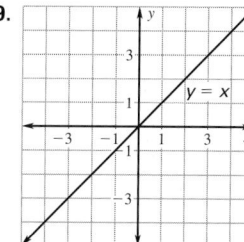

11.

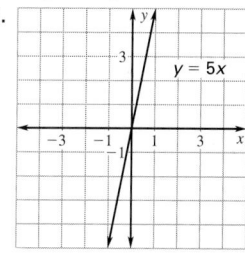

4.6 PRACTICE AND APPLICATIONS (pp. 239–241) **13.** 12
15. 25 **17.** $y = 5x$ **19.** $y = 6x$ **21.** $y = -\frac{1}{3}x$
23. $y = -10x$ **25.** yes, direct variation

27.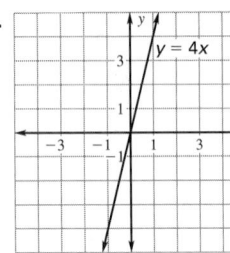

29.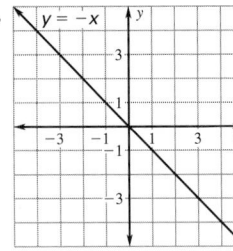

18.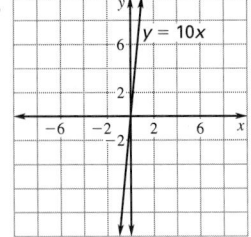

31. yes; line through origin **33.** no; line does not pass through origin **35.** 17 min **37.** about 16 in. **41.** 2

43. -5 **45.** -3 **47.** $y = -\frac{2}{5}x + \frac{12}{5}$ **49.** solution

51. solution **53.** solution **55.** 66 **57.** 56 **59.** 3570

Quiz 2 (p. 241)

1.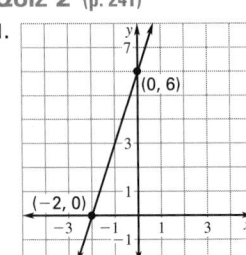

2.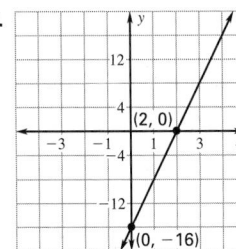

3.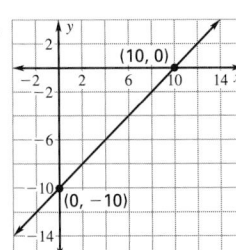

4.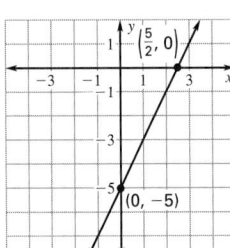

5.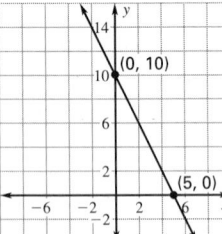

6.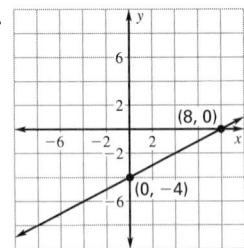

7. $\frac{2}{5}$ **8.** $\frac{2}{5}$ **9.** $\frac{7}{9}$ **10.** 2 **11.** 0 **12.** -1 **13.** $y = 3x$

14. $y = 8x$ **15.** $y = 4x$

16.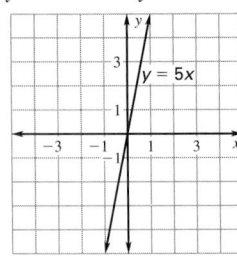

17.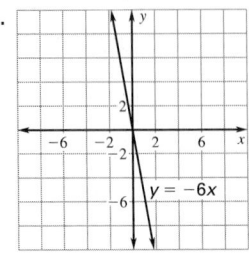

19. 10,500 bolts

4.7 Guided Practice (p. 246) **3.** $m = 2, b = 1$
5. $m = 5, b = -3$ **7.** $m = -1, b = 15$ **9.** B

4.7 Practice and Applications (pp. 246–249)

11. $y = x + 9$ **13.** $y = 2x - 10$ **15.** $y = \frac{1}{2}x - 6$
17. $m = 6, b = 4$ **19.** $m = 2, b = -9$ **21.** $m = 9,$
$b = 0$ **23.** $m = -3, b = 6$ **25.** $m = 2, b = 4$

27.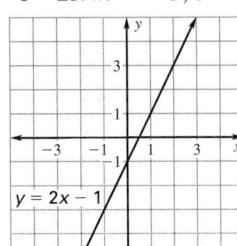

29.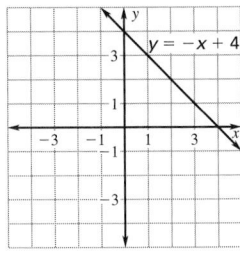

31.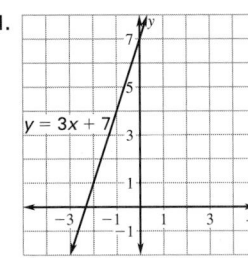

33.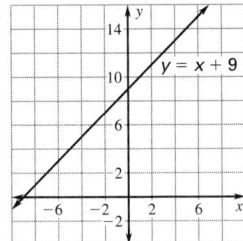

35.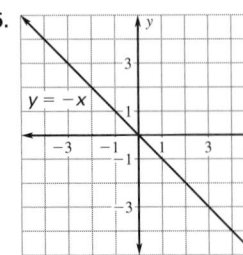

37.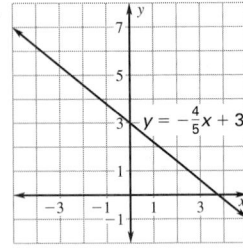

39.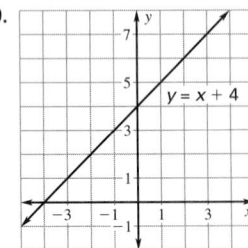

41.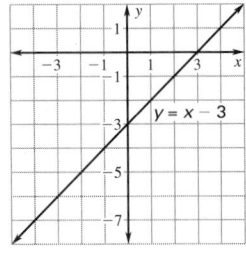

47. $m = -\dfrac{4}{3}$, $b = 4$ **49.** parallel; same slope, $m = -3$
51. parallel; same slope, $m = 1$ **53.** not parallel;
different slopes **55. (1)** $\dfrac{9}{70}$ **(2)** $\dfrac{1}{7}$ **63.** line a and
line b **71.** 5 **73.** 12 **75.** 6 **77.** -5
79. Atomic weight $\approx 2 \times$ Atomic number **81.** $\dfrac{13}{40}$
83. $1\dfrac{23}{36}$ **85.** $1\dfrac{13}{56}$ **87.** $1\dfrac{1}{21}$

4.8 GUIDED PRACTICE (p. 255) **3.** -22 **5.** 8
7. function; domain: 10, 20, 30, 40, 50; range: 100, 200,
300, 400, 500 **9.** not a function **11.** not a function

4.8 PRACTICE AND APPLICATIONS (pp. 255–258)
13. function; domain: 1, 2, 3, 4; range: 2, 3, 4, 5
15. not a function **17.** function; domain: 0, 2, 3, 4;
range: 1, 2, 3, 4 **19.** function **21.** function **23.** function
25. 6, 0, -6 **27.** 1, -5, -11 **29.** 11, 1, -9
31. 23, 7, -9 **33.** 4, -6, -16

37. 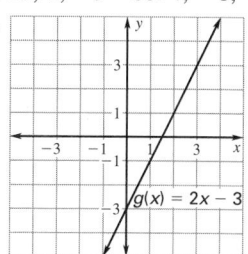 **39.**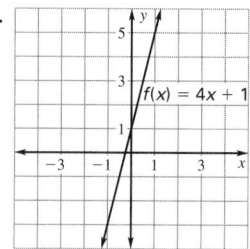

43. 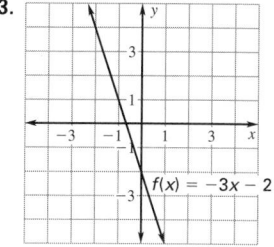 **45.**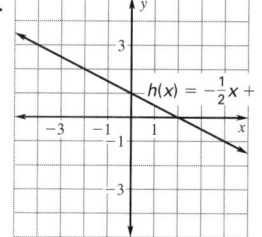

47. -1 **49.** -3 **51.** not a function
53. function; domain: -2, 0, 1, 2; range: -2, 0, 1, 2
55.

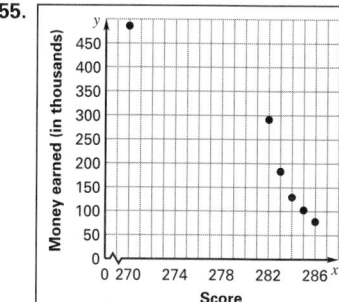

Yes. *Sample explanation:* For each input, there is exactly
one output. (The score 285 occurs twice, but the prize
money is the same each time.) Domain: 270, 282, 283,
284, 285, 286; range: 486,000, 291,600, 183,600,
129,600, 102,600, 78,570

57. 1500 miles **59.** $f(t) \approx 5.88t$ **63.** 6 **65.** $\dfrac{1}{3}$
67. no solution **69.** -1 **71.** -4 **73.** 0 **75.** $-\dfrac{3}{5}$
77. $\dfrac{1}{2}$ **79.** $\dfrac{2}{3}$

QUIZ 3 (p. 258) **1.** $y = 3x + 4$; $m = 3$, $b = 4$
2. $y = -x + 2$; $m = -1$, $b = 2$ **3.** $y = -2x + 6$;
$m = -2$, $b = 6$ **4.** $y = -\dfrac{5}{8}x + 4$; $m = -\dfrac{5}{8}$, $b = 4$
5. $y = \left(\dfrac{4}{3}\right)x - 8$; $m = \dfrac{4}{3}$, $b = -8$
6. $y = 1$; $m = 0$, $b = 1$
7. 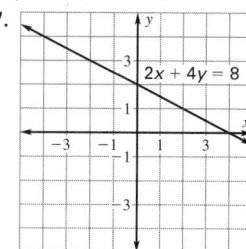 **8.**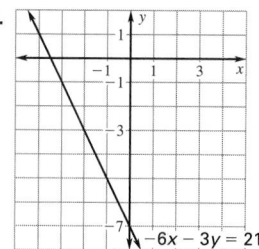

9.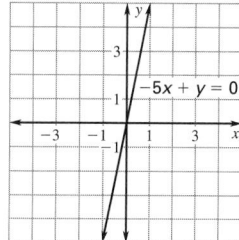

10. not parallel **11.** not parallel **12.** -24, 0, 32
13. 6, -9, -29 **14.** -9, 3, 19 **15.** -21, -12, 0
16. 4.2, 0, -5.6 **17.** $\dfrac{3}{4}$, 0, -1
18. 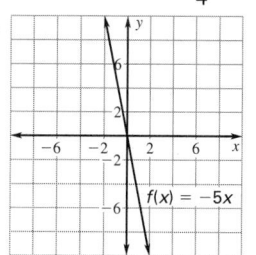 **19.**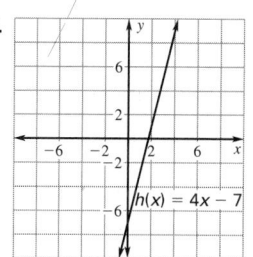

20.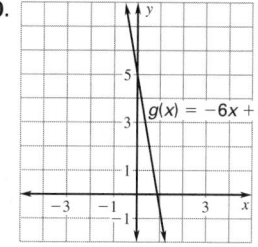

CHAPTER SUMMARY AND REVIEW (pp. 259–262)

1. Quadrant I **3.** Quadrant II

Graph for Ex. 1 and 3 **5.**

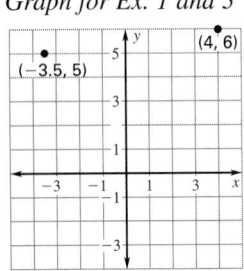

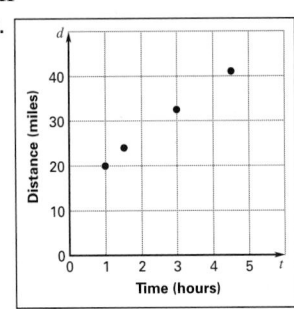

7.

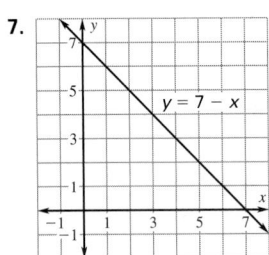

9.

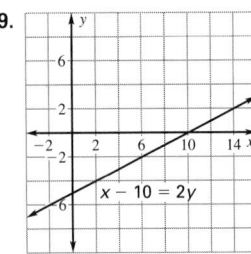

11.

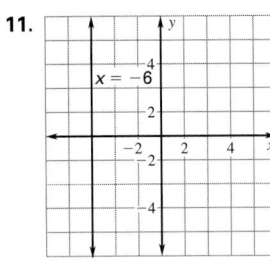

13.

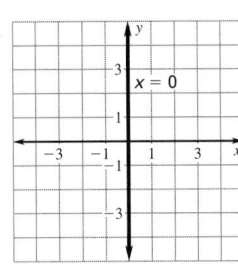

15.

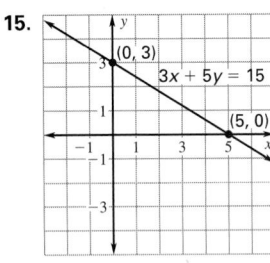

17.

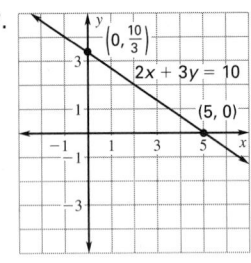

19. 0 **21.** undefined **23.** $y = -\frac{1}{3}x$ **25.** $y = 3.5x$

27. $y = -2x + 6$ **29.** $y = \frac{2}{3}x - 4$

31.

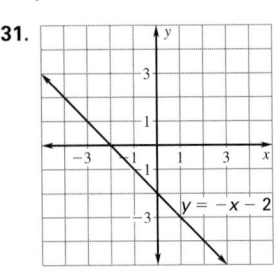

33.

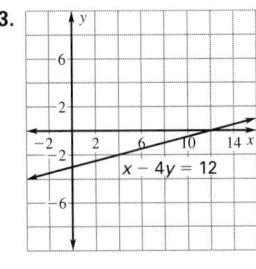

35. -9

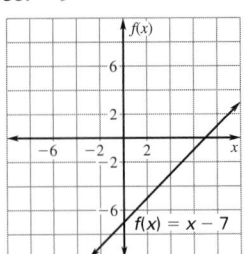

37. 11

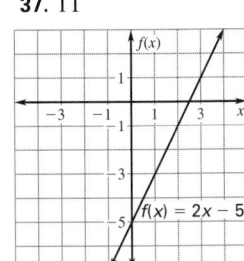

39. function; domain: $-1, 0, 1$; range: 2, 4, 6

41. function; domain: $-2, 0, 2$; range: 6

MAINTAINING SKILLS (p. 265) **1.** $\frac{1}{2}$ **3.** $\frac{1}{9}$ **5.** $\frac{5}{4}$ **7.** $\frac{1}{10}$

9. 0 **11.** -11 **13.** -11

Chapter 5

STUDY GUIDE (p. 268) **1.** C **2.** C **3.** B

5.1 GUIDED PRACTICE (p. 272) **5.** no **7.** $y = x$

9. $y = -x + 3$ **11.** $y = 5x + 5$

5.1 PRACTICE AND APPLICATIONS (pp. 272–275)

13. $y = 3x + 2$ **15.** $y = 6$ **17.** $y = \frac{2}{5}x + 7$

19. $y = -x - \frac{2}{5}$ **21.** $y = -\frac{1}{5}x + \frac{2}{3}$ **23.** $m = -\frac{1}{2}$;
$b = 1$ **25.** $m = \frac{3}{2}$; $b = 2$ **27.** $m = -\frac{2}{3}$; $b = -1$

29. $y = -3x - 1$ **31.** $y = -x + 1$ **33.** $y = 2x - 1$

41. 13.16 sec **43.** *Sample answer:* The prediction may
be unrealistic because athletes may be unable to continue
the downward trend. **45.** All three lines have the same

slope, $\frac{1}{2}$. **47.** $y = x + 63.64$, $y = -x - 63.64$,
$y = x - 63.64$ **49.** $y = -x + 63.64$ **53.** 92 min
57. 3 **59.** -1 **61.** -1 **63.** *Sample answer:* $(-1, -3)$,
$(0, -4)$, $(1, -5)$ **65.** *Sample answer:* $(0, 7)$, $(-1, 12)$,
$(1, 2)$ **67.** *Sample answer:* $(-3, 4)$, $(0, 3)$, $(3, 2)$

69. 3; 5

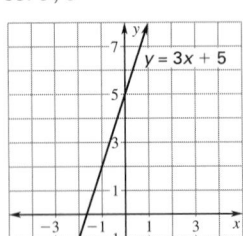

71. -2; 3

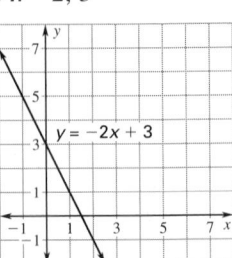

73. 5; -6

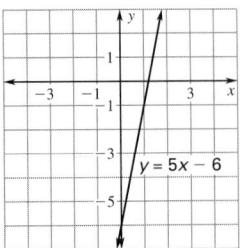

75. $\dfrac{3}{4}$ **77.** $\dfrac{31}{50}$ **79.** $\dfrac{1}{200}$ **81.** $1\dfrac{7}{25}$ **83.** $\dfrac{3}{50}$

5.2 GUIDED PRACTICE (p. 281)   **3.** $y - 4 = 4(x - 3)$
5. $y - 4 = \dfrac{1}{2}(x - 3)$ **7.** $y - 2 = 3(x - 2)$
9. $y = \dfrac{1}{2}x - \dfrac{5}{2}$ **11.** $y = x$ **13.** $y = \dfrac{1}{4}x + \dfrac{9}{4}$

5.2 PRACTICE AND APPLICATIONS (pp. 281–284)
15. $y - 2 = \dfrac{1}{2}(x - 1)$ **17.** $y + 3 = \dfrac{1}{3}(x + 1)$
19. $y + 4 = -(x - 4)$ **21.** $y - 2 = -5(x + 6)$
23. $y + 2 = 2(x + 8)$ **25.** $y - 4 = 6(x + 3)$
27. $y + 1 = 0(x - 8)$; $y = -1$ **29.** $y - 4 = 2(x - 1)$;
$y = 2x + 2$ **31.** $y + 5 = -2(x + 5)$; $y = -2x - 15$
33. $y - 1 = -\dfrac{1}{3}(x + 1)$; $y = -\dfrac{1}{3}x + \dfrac{2}{3}$ **35.** $y = 2x - 2$
37. $y = \dfrac{1}{3}x - \dfrac{8}{3}$ **39.** $y = -9x - 5$ **41.** $y = 2x - 1$
43. $y = -x - 4$ **45.** 55.25 psi   **53.** yes   **55.** yes   **57.** no

61.
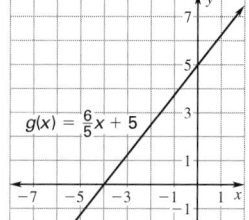

63.

65. $\dfrac{5}{18}$ **67.** $\dfrac{3}{10}$ **69.** $\dfrac{1}{21}$ **71.** $\dfrac{5}{12}$

QUIZ 1 (p. 284)   **1.** $y = -2x + 1$ **2.** $y = 5x$
3. $y = -\dfrac{2}{3}x + 1$ **4.** $y = x - 2$ **5.** $y = 2x + 3$
6. $y - 7 = -2(x - 7)$ **7.** $y + 2 = 3(x + 8)$
8. $y = -\dfrac{1}{2}x$ **9.** $y = x + 1$ **10.** $y = 4$ **11.** $y = -4x$
12. $y = 4x - 4$ **13.** $y = -\dfrac{1}{3}x - 4$ **14.** $y = -2x + 5$
15. $y = \dfrac{3}{7}x - \dfrac{13}{7}$

5.3 GUIDED PRACTICE (p. 288)   **3.** $y = -\dfrac{4}{3}x + 2$
5. $y = \dfrac{5}{3}x - \dfrac{1}{3}$ **7.** $y = -\dfrac{2}{3}x$

5.3 PRACTICE AND APPLICATIONS (pp. 288–290)
9. $y - 3 = -\dfrac{1}{2}(x - 2)$ or $y - 4 = -\dfrac{1}{2}x$
11. $y + 10 = \dfrac{7}{6}x$ or $y - 4 = \dfrac{7}{6}(x - 12)$
13. $y - 1 = -(x - 1)$ or $y - 2 = -x$
15. $y - 6 = x + 8$ or $y - 1 = x + 13$ **17.** $y - 5 = 0$
19. $y = \dfrac{15}{4}x + 16$ **21.** $y = 4x + 1$ **23.** $y = 2$
25. $y = -\dfrac{3}{2}x + 3$ **27.** $y = \dfrac{8}{3}x + \dfrac{2}{3}$ **29.** $y = -2x + 1$
31. $y = -3x + 14$ **33.** point-slope form; $y = x - 2$
35. point-slope form; $y = \dfrac{4}{5}x - \dfrac{1}{5}$ **43.** -5 **45.** 4
47. $\dfrac{17}{2}$ **49.** $\dfrac{1}{3}$ **51.** $7\dfrac{19}{24}$ **53.** $8\dfrac{23}{24}$ **55.** $26\dfrac{5}{6}$ **57.** $6\dfrac{17}{18}$

5.4 GUIDED PRACTICE (p. 294)   **3.** $2x - y = 9$ or
$-2x + y = -9$ **5.** $3x - 4y = 0$ **7.** $5x - y = 7$
9. $3x + y = 10$ **11.** $3x + 5y = 15$ **13.** $x = -2$

5.4 PRACTICE AND APPLICATIONS (pp. 294–297)
15. $5x + y = 2$ **17.** $-4x + y = -9$ or $4x - y = 9$
19. $3x + 8y = 0$ **21.** $2x - y = -19$ **23.** $3x + y = 1$
25. $5x - y = 17$ **27.** $2x - 5y = -41$ **29.** $x + 3y = 16$
31. $2x - 3y = -6$ **33.** $2x + y = 1$ **35.** $x + y = -3$
37. $x + 10y = 27$ **39.** $y = -2$ **41.** $x = 4$ **43.** $x = -3\dfrac{1}{2}$
45. $x = 9$ **47.** $y = 10$ **49.** $-x + y = 4$ **51.** $x + y = 7$
53. $4x + 3y = -8$ **55.** Only the right side was
multiplied by 3.

57.

63. -5 **65.** -42 **67.** $\dfrac{21}{2}$ or 10.5

69.
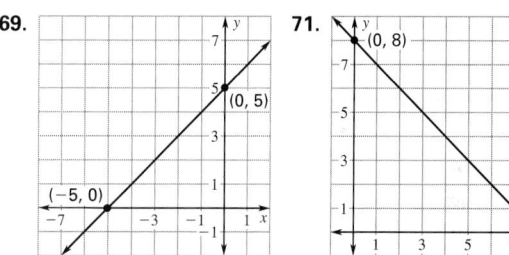

71.

73. \$908   **75.** \$14,098   **77.** \$0   **79.** \$12,346

QUIZ 2 (p. 297)   **1.** $y = -\dfrac{1}{5}x - 1$ **2.** $y = 3x - 16$
3. $y = 4$ **4.** $y = -4x + 3$ **5.** $y = \dfrac{1}{3}x - \dfrac{1}{3}$
6. $3x + y = 9$ **7.** $-x + 2y = 8$ **8.** $-2x + 5y = -5$
9. $2x - y = 4$ **10.** $x + 2y = 6$ **11.** $2x - 5y = -23$
12. $2x - y = -2$ **13.** $x + 2y = 2$ **14.** $y = 3$

5.5 GUIDED PRACTICE (p. 301)   **3.** C; the slope, 1.5,
represents the amount paid for each unit produced per
hour.   **5.** B; the slope, 0.32, represents the amount paid
per day for each mile driven.

5.5 PRACTICE AND APPLICATIONS (pp. 301–304)   **7.** 124
9. $y = 124t$ **11.** about 3.2 hours   **13.** 10
15.
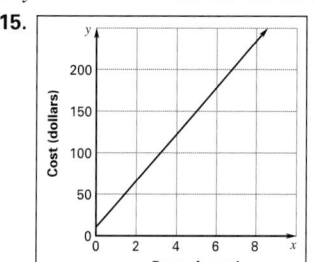

17. 2 days **19.** (1, 48.9) **21.** about 67 cents
23. *Sample answer:* about 51 cents **25.** $5x + 7y = 315$
27. $2x + y = 102$ **29.** 62; 52; 42; 32; 22
31. $2C + 1.25B = 10$ **33.** *Sample answer:* 4500 years
37. 0 **39.** -50 **41.** 3 feet **43.** $\frac{3}{7}$; *Sample answer:* The
slope is the rise divided by the run of the ramp.
45. $y = -2x + 3$ **47.** $y = \frac{4}{3}x - 3$ **49.** $y = 2$ **51.** $>$
53. $<$ **55.** $=$ **57.** $=$

5.6 GUIDED PRACTICE (p. 309) **3.** yes **5.** no
7. $y = x + 3$; the product of the slopes of the lines is
$(1)(-1) = -1$, so the lines are perpendicular.
9. $y = 2x - 8$

5.6 PRACTICE AND APPLICATIONS (pp. 309–312) **11.** no
13. yes **15.** yes **17.** $y = -x - 2, y = x - 3$; yes
19. $y = -3, x = -2$; yes **21.** $y = -\frac{1}{3}x - \frac{8}{3}$; the
product of the slopes of the lines is $\left(-\frac{1}{3}\right)(3) = -1$, so
the lines are perpendicular. **23.** $y = 4x - 23$; the
product of the slopes of the lines is $(4)\left(-\frac{1}{4}\right) = -1$, so
the lines are perpendicular. **25.** $y = \frac{2}{3}x$; the product of
the slopes of the lines is $\left(\frac{2}{3}\right)\left(-\frac{3}{2}\right) = -1$, so the lines
are perpendicular. **27.** $y = -x - 2$ **29.** $y = x - 1$
31. $y = -2x + 5$ **33.** $y = -\frac{8}{7}x + 3$ **35.** $x = -2$
37. $y = -\frac{3}{2}x + 2$ **39.** $y = \frac{1}{4}x - 6$ **41.** always
43. always **45.** $y = \frac{4}{3}x + 3, y = -\frac{3}{4}x + \frac{3}{2}$ **49.** $-6k - 8$
51. $6x + 12y + 2$ **53.** $\frac{13}{3}$
55. horizontal **57.** vertical

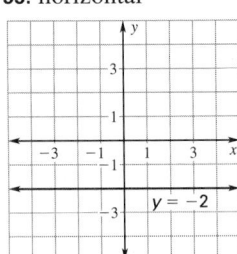
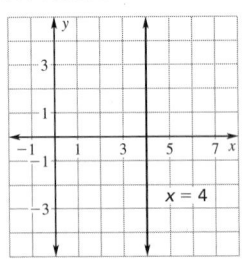

59. $\frac{7}{10}$ **61.** $\frac{2}{3}$ **63.** $\frac{8}{27}$ **65.** 7 **67.** $\frac{7}{13}$ **69.** $\frac{2}{21}$

QUIZ 3 (p. 312) **1.** $7x + 3y = 42$ **2.** $y = -\frac{7}{3}x + 14$;
14, 7, 0

3.
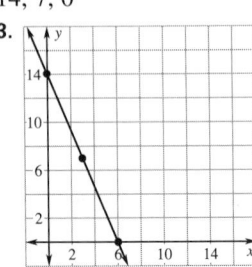

4. yes **5.** yes **6.** $y = x + 1$; The product of the slopes of
the lines is $(1)(-1) = -1$, so the lines are perpendicular.
7. $y = -\frac{4}{3}x - 4$; The product of the slopes of the lines is
$\left(-\frac{4}{3}\right)\left(\frac{3}{4}\right) = -1$, so the lines are perpendicular.
8. $y = -2x + 11$

CHAPTER SUMMARY AND REVIEW (pp. 313–316)
1. $y = 6x - 4$ **3.** $y = -8x + 8$ **5.** $y = \frac{3}{2}x$
7. $y = 2x - 2$ **9.** $y = -x - 4$ **11.** $y + 1 = \frac{5}{2}(x + 3)$;
$y = \frac{5}{2}x + \frac{13}{2}$ **13.** $y - 3 = 5(x + 2)$ or $y = 5x + 13$
15. $y = 3x + 5$ **17.** $y = -8x + 12$ **19.** $y = \frac{16}{9}x$
21. $y = -1$ **23.** $y = 7, x = -1$ **25.** $y = -6, x = -8$
27. $2x + y = 7$ **29.** \$1,489,200 **31.** 6; 4; 2; 0 **33.** yes
35. $y = -2x$

MAINTAINING SKILLS (p. 319)
1.

-21 -14 -7 0 7 14 21 28

3.

0 30 60 90 120 150

5. $<$ **7.** $>$ **9.** $>$ **11.** $>$ **13.** $>$

Chapter 6

STUDY GUIDE (p. 322) **1.** C **2.** B **3.** C **4.** B

6.1 GUIDED PRACTICE (p. 326) **3.** open **5.** solid
7. solid **9.** left **11.** left **13.** left

6.1 PRACTICE AND APPLICATIONS (pp. 326–328)
15. all real numbers less than 8 **17.** all real numbers
greater than or equal to 21 **19.** solution **21.** solution
29. subtract 11 **31.** subtract 6 **33.** add 3
41. $x < 2$ **45.** $p \geq 11$

-4 -2 0 2 4 $\qquad$ 4 6 8 10 12

49. $-2 > c$ **55.** $c < 14$

-4 -2 0 2 4 $\qquad$ 8 10 12 14 16

57. $r > 0.11$
59. $d > 16.3$

0 5 10 15 20

61. subtract 4 from each side; $x < -3$ **65.** 6 **67.** 14
69. 32 **71.** 3 **73.** -1 **75.** $y = -x + 3$ **77.** $y = -x + 2$
79. $y = 2x - 1$ **81.** $y = -\frac{1}{3}x + \frac{10}{3}$ **83.** $y = \frac{2}{5}x + \frac{36}{5}$
85. -3 **87.** $-\frac{32}{7}$ **89.** $-\frac{15}{8}$ **91.** -1 **93.** $\frac{1}{9}$ **95.** $\frac{8}{5}$

6.2 GUIDED PRACTICE (p. 333) **3.** multiply by 5; do not
reverse **5.** divide by 4; do not reverse **7.** multiply
by -6; reverse **9.** not equivalent **11.** equivalent
13. not equivalent

6.2 Practice and Applications (pp. 333–335)
15. multiply by 3; do not reverse **17.** multiply by 2; do not reverse **19.** divide by -7; reverse **21.** divide by -3; reverse **23.** solution **25.** solution **27.** Not equivalent; $12y > -24$ is equivalent to $y > -2$. **29.** equivalent **31.** equivalent **33.** Reverse the inequality sign when dividing by -3; $x \leq -5$.
35. $p < 4$

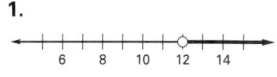

37. $j \leq -18$

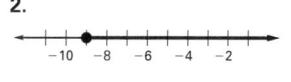

39. $n > -60$

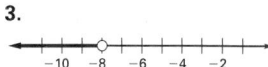

43. $a \geq 20$

47. $d < 5$; $1.999 \approx 2$

49. $a \leq -18$; $5.91 \approx 6$

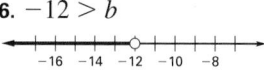

51. always **53.** never **55.** $20n \geq 25{,}000$; $n \geq 1250$ **57.** 31 or fewer rides **63.** -14 **65.** 0 **67.** 2 **69.** -4
71. -27 **73.** 9 **75.** -1 **77.** -2 **79.** $b = \dfrac{2A}{h}$
81. $A(4, -2)$, $B(2, 1)$, $C(-3, -3)$, $D(0, 0)$ **83.** 1, 2, 4, 5, 7, 10, 14, 20, 28, 35, 70, 140 **85.** 1, 2, 3, 4, 6, 8, 9, 12, 16, 18, 24, 36, 48, 72, 144 **87.** 1, 5, 17, 25, 85, 425 **89.** 1, 3, 9, 13, 19, 39, 57, 117, 171, 247, 741, 2223

6.3 Guided Practice (p. 339) **3.** not multistep; subtract 2 **5.** not multistep; divide by -4 **7.** multistep; subtract 12, divide by 5 **9.** multistep; subtract 2, multiply by 2 **11.** multistep; subtract $2w$, subtract 2, divide by 4

6.3 Practice and Applications (pp. 339–341)
13. 14, 14; -7; -7; 7 **15.** subtract 11, divide by -2 and reverse inequality **17.** subtract 22, divide by 3 **19.** divide by 6, add 2; or distribute 6, add 12, divide by 6
21. $x < 5$ **23.** $\dfrac{7}{6} \leq x$ **25.** $x \geq -8$ **27.** $x \geq -3$
33. $x < 12$ **35.** $6 \leq x$ **37.** $x \leq -1$ **39.** $x > \dfrac{1}{2}$
41. $x > -\dfrac{14}{3}$ **43.** In line 2, distribute the 4 over -1 and distribute 3 over 1; $f > -\dfrac{7}{2}$. **45.** $n \leq 16$; you may purchase up to 16 tickets. **47.** $0.75t + 14 \leq 18.50$
49. $2x + 18 > 26$; $x > 4$ m **51.** $\dfrac{1}{2}(8x) < 12$, $x < 3$ ft
55. 3 **57.** 3 **59.** $h = 4 + a$ **61.** \$77.48 **63.** $\dfrac{9}{7}$ **65.** $\dfrac{15}{4}$

Quiz 1 (p. 341)
1.

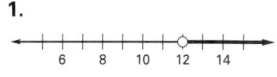

2.

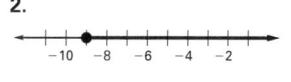

3.

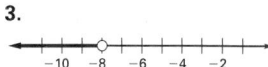

4. $a < 5$

5. $m \leq -8$

6. $-12 > b$

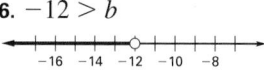

7. $z \geq -21$

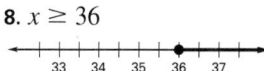

8. $x \geq 36$

9. $-7 < k$

10. $h \geq 52$ **11.** 8 or fewer plays **12.** $-2 \geq x$
13. $x \leq -3$ **14.** $x < 2$ **15.** $x > -2$ **16.** $7 \geq x$
17. $17 \leq x$

6.4 Guided Practice (p. 345) **3.** A **5.** $(4 + x)$ is greater than 7 and less than 8. **7.** $(-8 - x)$ is greater than or equal to 4 and less than 7. **9.** $-4 \leq x \leq 4$

6.4 Practice and Applications (pp. 345–347)
11. x is greater than or equal to -23 and less than or equal to -7. **13.** x is greater than or equal to -4 and less than 19. **15.** $2 < x < 3$ **17.** $-2 \leq x < 2$
19. $0 \leq x < 5$ **21.** $-4 < x \leq -2$

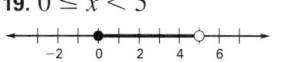

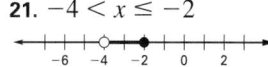

23. $85 \leq f \leq 1100$ **25.** $15 \leq f \leq 50{,}000$
27. $85{,}000 \leq c \leq 2{,}600{,}000$
29. $12 < x \leq 14$ **35.** $-4 \leq x \leq 3$

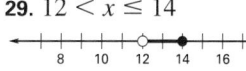

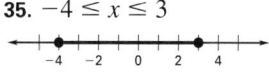

37. $4 < x < 7$ **39.** $-2 < x \leq 10$

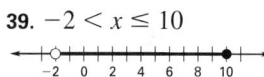

41. $-16 \leq x < -14$ **43.** $2 < x \leq 4$

51. 24 **53.** 2 **55.** 20 **57.** -6 **59.** -8 **61.** 16
63. -12 **65.** -7 **67.** more than 25 times
69. 262 million **71.** 37.5% **73.** $33\dfrac{1}{3}\%$ **75.** 75%
77. 84%

6.5 Guided Practice (p. 351) **3.** B **5.** A **7.** all real numbers less than 10 or greater than 13
9. $x < -6$ or $x > -1$

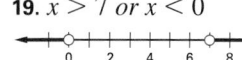

6.5 Practice and Applications (pp. 351–353) **11.** all real numbers less than or equal to 15 or greater than or equal to 31 **13.** all real numbers less than or equal to -7 or greater than 11 **15.** $x \leq -3$ or $x > 0$
17. $x \leq 7$ or $x \geq 8$
19. $x > 7$ or $x < 0$ **21.** $x \leq -2$ or $x > 5$

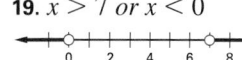

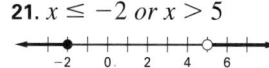

23. $x \geq -1 \text{ or } x \leq -4$

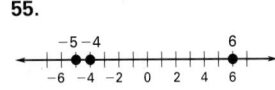

25. $x < -6 \text{ or } x \geq -2$

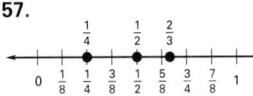

29. $x < 10 \text{ or } x > 12$; solution   **31.** $x \leq -3 \text{ or } x > 2$; not a solution

33. $x < -2 \text{ or } x \geq 4$

35. $x > 6 \text{ or } x < -3$

37. $x < -2 \text{ or } x \geq 1$

39. $x < -8 \text{ or } x \geq -2$

41.

Input t	0	0.5	1	1.5	2
Output v	−4	−2	0	2	4

The velocity of the yo-yo decreases until it reaches the bottom of the string and then as the yo-yo ascends, the velocity increases. At 1 second, the yo-yo has reached the bottom and has a velocity of 0. From then, it rises and gains speed.

43. $t \leq 32 \text{ or } t \geq 212$ **45.** $y < 11 \text{ or } y \geq 65$

49.

Input x	0	1	2	3	4
Output y	2	5	8	11	14

51.

Input x	0	1	2	3	4
Output y	5	4	3	2	1

53.

Input x	0	1	2	3	4
Output y	−4	−2	0	2	4

55.

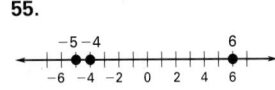

57.

59. 1.20   **61.** 6.65   **63.** −0.29

65. $9 < x$

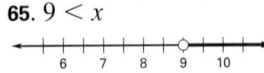

67. $x \geq 25$

71. $x < -8$

73. 28   **75.** 221   **77.** 28,000   **79.** 5400   **81.** 11,000

6.6 GUIDED PRACTICE (p. 358)   **3.** 2   **5.** none

7. $x - 4 = 10, x - 4 = -10$

9. $3x + 2 = 6, 3x + 2 = -6$

6.6 PRACTICE AND APPLICATIONS (pp. 358–360)

11. 9, −9   **13.** no solution   **15.** 100, −100   **17.** 7, −3
19. 12, −12   **21.** 10, −2   **23.** 3.5, −3.5   **25.** 10, −4
27. 18, −18   **29.** always   **31.** always   **33.** 6, −5
35. −1, −4   **37.** 8, −1   **39.** 11, −7   **45.** *Sample answer:* $|x - 2| = 8$ **47.** midpoint: 92.95 million miles; distance: 1.55 million miles

53.

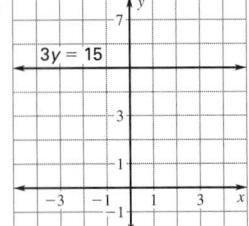

55. $y = -5x + 20$ **57.** $y = 4x - 12$ **59.** $y = -2x - 1$
61. 48,000   **63.** 47,500   **65.** 47,509.13

QUIZ 2 (p. 360)

1. $3 < x < 12$

2. $-9 < x \leq 7$

3. $-4 \leq x \leq -2$

4. $x > 5 \text{ or } x < -5$

5. $x < -9 \text{ or } x > -4$

6. $x < -1 \text{ or } x > 5$

7. $-128.6 < T < 136$ **8.** 14, −14   **9.** no solution
10. 33, −15   **11.** −9, −21   **12.** 18, −6   **13.** 7, −11
14. *Sample answer:* $|x - 7.5| = 10.5 \text{ or } |2x - 15| = 21$

6.7 GUIDED PRACTICE (p. 364)   **5.** not a solution
7. solution

6.7 PRACTICE AND APPLICATIONS (pp. 364–366)
9. $x > 1, x < -1$; or   **11.** $x - 1 \leq 9, x - 1 \geq -9$; and
13. $10 + 7x \geq 11, 10 + 7x \leq -11$; or
15. $-15 < x < 15$ **19.** $x \geq 30 \text{ or } x \leq -10$

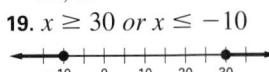

21. $x > 12 \text{ or } x < -4$ **25.** $-16 \leq x \leq -2$

27. never   **29.** always
31. $-2 < x < 1$ **37.** $x > 1 \text{ or } x < -\dfrac{7}{2}$

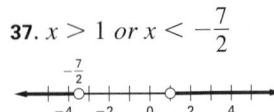

39. $x \geq 8 \text{ or } x \leq -2$ **41.** $0 \leq x \leq 6$

43. $t < 3 \text{ or } t > 7$ **45.** orange   **51.** all real numbers except 4   **53.** \$38   **55.** *Sample answers:* $(-12, 0)$, $(-12, 3), (-12, -4)$ **57.** *Sample answers:* $\left(\dfrac{2}{3}, 0\right)$, $\left(\dfrac{2}{3}, 1\right), \left(\dfrac{2}{3}, 5\right)$ **59.** function   **61.** not a function

63. $5\dfrac{11}{18}$ **65.** $11\dfrac{5}{18}$ **67.** $19\dfrac{3}{8}$

6.8 GUIDED PRACTICE (p. 370)
5. B **7.** to the right
9. solution **11.** not a solution **13.** not a solution

6.8 PRACTICE AND APPLICATIONS (pp. 370–373)
15. Both $(0, 0)$ and $(-1, -1)$ are solutions. **17.** $(0, 0)$ is a solution; $(2, 0)$ is not a solution. **19.** Neither $(0, 0)$ nor $(2, -4)$ are solutions. **23.** solid **25.** dashed **27.** $y = x$; solid **29.** $y = \frac{1}{2}x - 8$; solid **31.** $y = -2x - 3$; dashed **33.** solid

35. yes

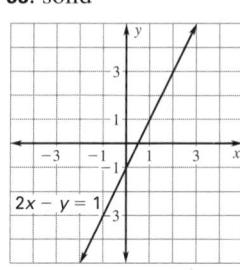
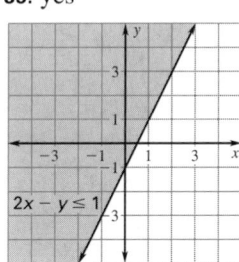

37.
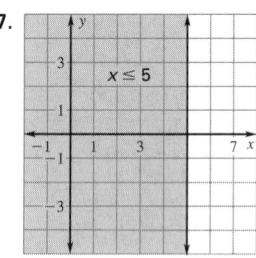

41.
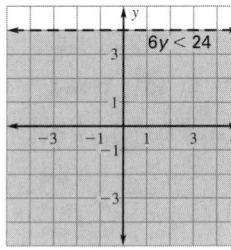

45.
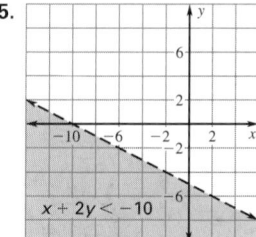

49.
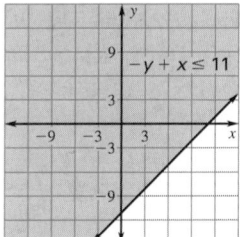

51. *Sample answer:* $(1, 3), (2, 2), (3, 1)$
53. $y \leq -2x + 3200$

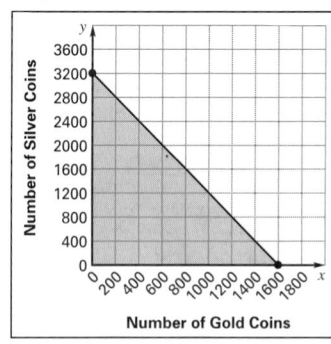

57. 15 **59.** 69 **61.** 30°C **63.** $m = \frac{1}{2}, b = -2$
65. $m = -3, b = 7$ **67.** $m = 0, b = 5$ **69.** 52%

QUIZ 3 (p. 373)
1. $x \geq 18 \ or \ x \leq -18$
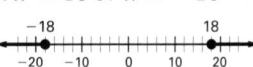

2. $x > 5 \ or \ x < 3$
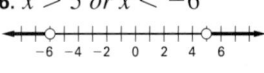

3. $-9 < x < -5$
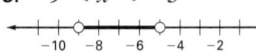

4. $1 \leq x \leq 7$

5. $-16 \leq x \leq 9$
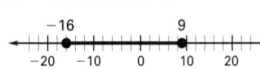

6. $x > 5 \ or \ x < -6$

7. $t < 0.75 \ or \ t > 2.25$ **8.** Both $(0, -1)$ and $(2, 2)$ are solutions. **9.** $(0, 0)$ is not a solution; $(-4, 1)$ is a solution. **10.** $(2, 1)$ is not a solution; $(-1, 2)$ is a solution. **11.** $(1, -1)$ is a solution; $(2, -3)$ is not a solution.

12.
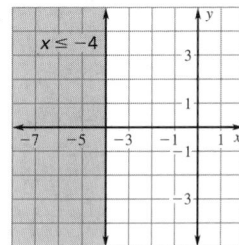

13.
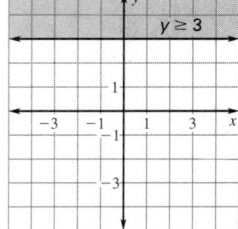

14.
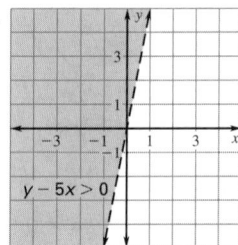

15.
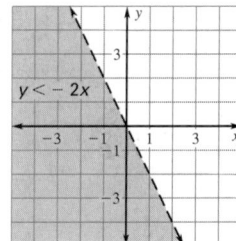

16.
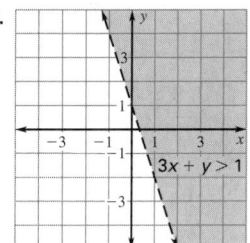

17.
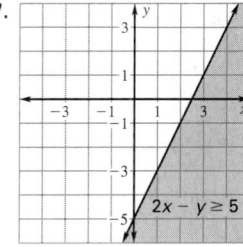

6.8 TECHNOLOGY (p. 374)
1.
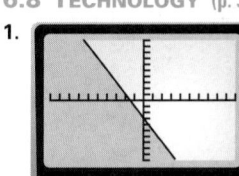

3.
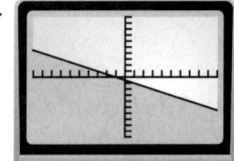

5.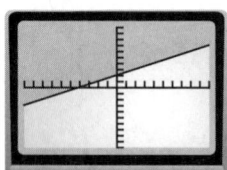

7.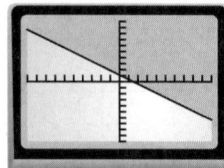

9.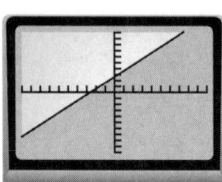

11.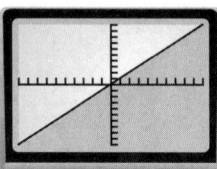

13. $y > x$

CHAPTER SUMMARY AND REVIEW (pp. 375–378)

1. $x \leq 2$

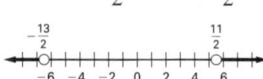

3. $2 < x$

5. $8 < x$

7. $27 \leq p$

9. $n \leq -6$

11. $t \leq 56$

13. $x \geq 2$ **15.** $x \geq 5$ **17.** $x < -\frac{1}{3}$ **19.** $x \geq 1$

21. $x \leq 13$

23. $-1 \leq x \leq 5$

25. $2 < x < 4$

27. $8 \leq x < 40$

29. $x \leq -5 \text{ or } x > -2$

31. $x \leq 1 \text{ or } x > 7$

33. $x < 2 \text{ or } x > 10$

35. no solution   **37.** $9, -9$ **39.** no solution
41. $-2 \leq x \leq 2$ **43.** $2 \leq x \leq 18$

45. $-3 < x < 5$ **47.** $-2 < x < 10$

49. $x < -\frac{13}{2} \text{ or } x > \frac{11}{2}$

51.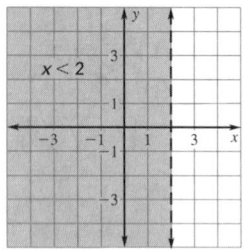

53.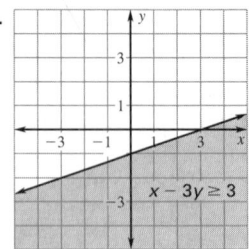

$x - 3y \geq 3$

55.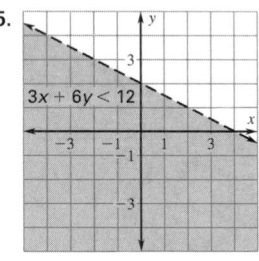

$3x + 6y < 12$

MAINTAINING SKILLS (p. 381) **1.** 70   **3.** 37   **5.** 69   **7.** 51
9. -17 **11.** 7   **13.** 3   **15.** 7

CUMULATIVE PRACTICE (pp. 382–383) **1.** 7   **3.** 45   **5.** 3
7.

Input n	0	1	2	3	4	5	6
Output C	65	66	67	68	69	70	71

9. 2.5   **11.** -18 **13.** 4.6   **15.** 83°F   **17.** $18 + 3x$
19. $-15 + 5t$ **21.** $11b + 7$ **23.** $6y + 6$ **25.** -18
27. 24   **29.** -4 **31.** 10   **33.** 75   **35.** 1   **37.** 12.5 cm³
39. 52 mi/h   **41.** 25 ft/sec

43.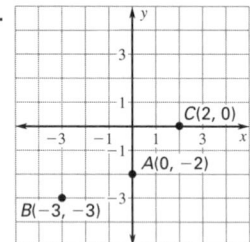

45.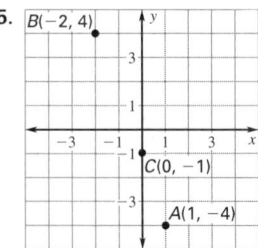

47. The sales of catfish have increased since 1990, although not consistently. There are points clustered around sales of $370 to $380 million.

49.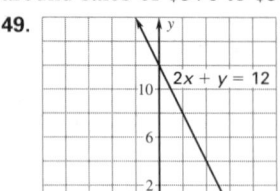

51.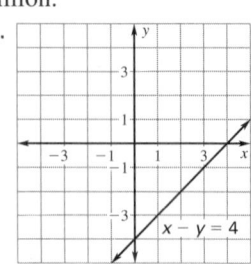

53.

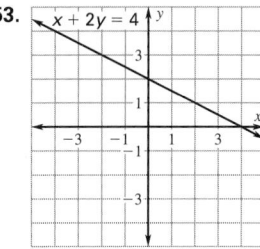

$x + 2y = 4$

55. $y = -2x + 5$ **57.** $y = 4x + 1$ **59.** $y = x + 1$
61. $y = \frac{1}{4}x - \frac{7}{4}$ **63.** $y = -3x - 4$
65. $y - 4 = x - 1$ or $y - 6 = x - 3$
67. $y + 7 = -8(x + 1)$ or $y - 1 = -8(x + 2)$
69. $y - 7 = \frac{3}{4}(x - 4)$ or $y - 10 = \frac{3}{4}(x - 8)$
71. $x < 2$ **73.** $x \geq -7$ **75.** $x > 4$ **77.** $-5 \leq x \leq 2$
79. $x > 4$ or $x \leq -2$ **81.** $-6 \leq x \leq 1$

Chapter 7

Study Guide (p. 388) **1.** C **2.** B **3.** A **4.** D

7.1 Guided Practice (p. 392) **3.** $y = x - 2$;
$y = -2x + 10$ **5.** (4, 2)

7.1 Practice and Applications (pp. 392–394)
7. solution **9.** not a solution **11.** not a solution **13.** (4, 5)
15. (3, 0) **17.** (6, −6) **19.** (−3, −5) **21.** (−4, −5)
23. (1, 4) **25.** 125,000 miles **27.** 14 years **33.** 4
35. 5 **37.** −2 **39.** $y = x + 7$ **41.** $y = -2x - 9$
43. $y = -3x + 2$ **45.** 4.764 **47.** 2 **49.** 10

7.1 Technology (p. 395) **1.** (−3.5, 2.5)
3. (−0.8, −2.05)

7.2 Guided Practice (p. 399) **3.** Equation 2; y has a
coefficient of −1 **5.** $x = 1$ **7.** (−5, 18) **9.** (1, 3)

7.2 Practice and Applications (pp. 399–401)
11. Equation 2; m has a coefficient of 1, no constant.
13. Equation 2; x and y have coefficients of 1.
15. Equation 2; x has a coefficient of 1. **17.** (9, 5)
19. (4, −2) **21.** (−1, 5) **23.** (0, 0) **25.** (−7, 4)
27. $\left(-\frac{7}{2}, -\frac{13}{2}\right)$ **29.** 30 11-inch softballs and 50 12-inch
softballs **31.** $3375 in ABC and $1125 in XYZ
33. 1200 meters uphill, 1000 meters downhill **39.** −2x
41. 26
43.

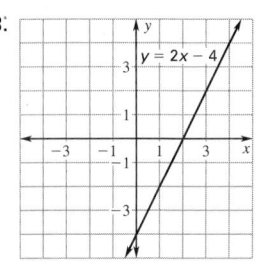

$y = 2x - 4$

45.

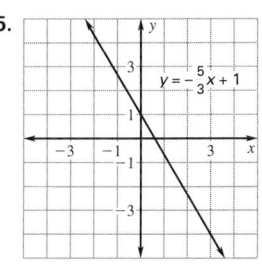

$y = -\frac{5}{3}x + 1$

47.

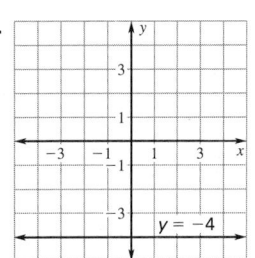

$y = -4$

49. $-19 \leq x \leq 9$

51. $x < 1$ or $x > 3$

53. 1, 3 **55.** 1, 3 **57.** 1, 2, 3, 6 **59.** 1, 3

7.3 Guided Practice (p. 405) **3.** $9x + 7x = 16x$;
$24 + 8 = 32$; Solution: (2, 2) **5.** *Sample answer:*
multiply equation 2 by −4, then add and solve for x.
Solution: (1, −1)

7.3 Practice and Applications (pp. 405–408)
7. (−3, 7) **9.** (2, 0) **11.** (3, 5) **13.** (−8, 6) **15.** (3, 0)
17. (3, 2) **19.** (2, 0) **21.** $\left(\frac{7}{2}, 5\right)$ **23.** (21, −3)
25. (8, −1) **27.** (3, −4) **29.** $\left(-79, -\frac{61}{5}\right)$ **31.** (1, 2)
33. (1, 0) **35.** (2, 1) **37.** (2, 0) **39.** (3, 2) **41.** (2, 0)
43. about 3 cubic centimeters **45.** There are 15,120 men
and 20,000 rolls of cotton. **49.** $y = 3x + 10$
51. $y = -3x + 30$ **53.** $y = x - 1$ **55.** (1, 3) is a
solution; (2, 0) is not a solution. **57.** (−3, −2)
59. (10, −2) **61.** true **63.** true **65.** false

Quiz 1 (p. 408) **1.** (3, −4) **2.** (0, 0)
3. (6, 8) **4.** (1, 9) **5.** (−1, 3) **6.** (−6, 10) **7.** (6, 8)
8. (5, 1) **9.** $\left(-\frac{1}{2}, \frac{1}{2}\right)$ **10.** (2, −1) **11.** (0, 1) **12.** (2, 1)
13. Four compact discs were bought at $10.50 each and
6 were bought at $8.50 each.

7.4 Guided Practice (p. 412) **3.** (7.5, 0.5)
5. You would have to sell $600,000 of merchandise.
7. $10d$

7.4 Practice and Applications (pp. 412–414)
9. (0, 2) **11.** (3, 6)

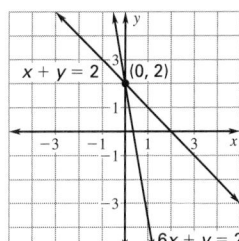

$x + y = 2$ (0, 2) $6x + y = 2$

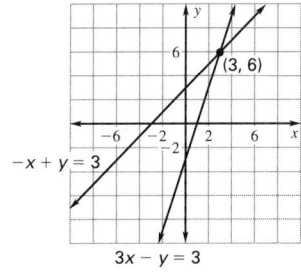

(3, 6) $-x + y = 3$ $3x - y = 3$

13. *Sample answer:* Multiplication and addition. No variable can be easily isolated. **15.** *Sample answer:* Substitution. Equation 2 can be solved for x or y. **17.** *Sample answer:* Substitution. Equations 1 or 2 can be solved for x. **19.** $(3, 3)$ **21.** $\left(\dfrac{4}{15}, \dfrac{6}{5}\right)$ **23.** $(-2, 1)$

25. $(-3, 2)$ **31.** 6 pea plants, 7 broccoli plants **33.** about $(1.6, 6474)$ **39.** parallel; $m = 4$ for both lines **41.** not parallel; different slopes

43.
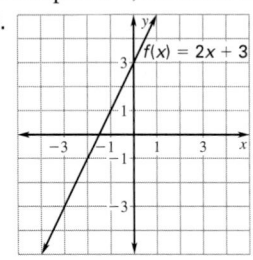

47.
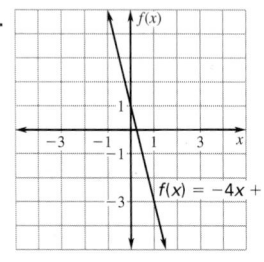

49. $1\dfrac{1}{5}$ **51.** $1\dfrac{11}{72}$ **53.** $\dfrac{23}{30}$ **55.** $\dfrac{25}{32}$

7.5 GUIDED PRACTICE (p. 420)

5. No solution; the two equations represent parallel lines.

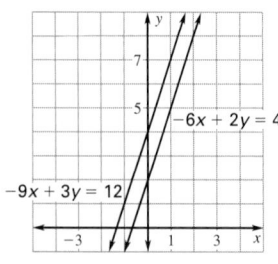

7. no solution **9.** one solution; $(5, 12)$

7.5 PRACTICE AND APPLICATIONS (pp. 420–422)

17. no solution **19.** no solution **21.** one solution **23.** Infinitely many solutions; multiplying Equation 1 by 4 yields Equation 2. **25.** infinitely many solutions; one line **27.** infinitely many solutions; one line **29.** no solution; parallel lines **31.** No; there are infinitely many solutions for the system. **33.** Yes, $14.98. *Sample explanation:* The solution of the system $4x + 2y = 99.62$ and $8x + y = 139.69$ is $(14.98, 19.85)$. **39.** about 4:27 P.M.

41.
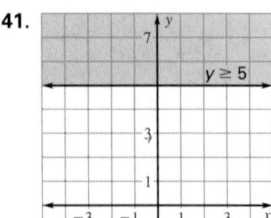

43.
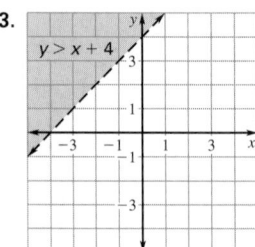

45.
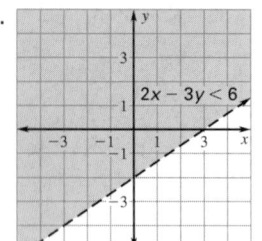

47. $20; \dfrac{25\pi}{4}$ **49.** $20; 20$

7.6 GUIDED PRACTICE (p. 427)

3.
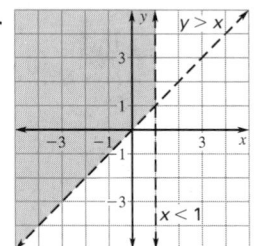

5. The student graphed $y \ge 1$, instead of $y > -1$; graphed $x \le 2$, instead of $x \ge 2$; graphed $y \le x - 4$, instead of $y > x - 4$. **7.** $y \le -x, x > -2$

7.6 PRACTICE AND APPLICATIONS (pp. 427–430)

13.
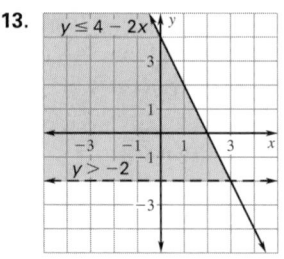

15.
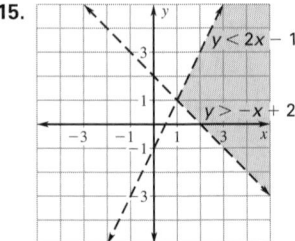

19.
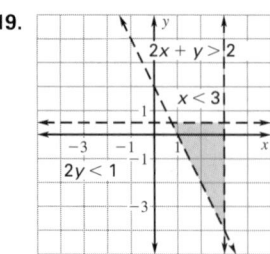

21.
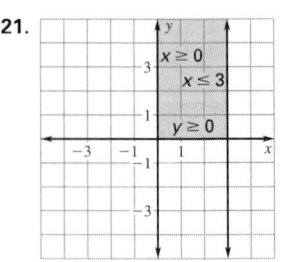

25. *Sample answer:* $2y - x \le 4, 2y - x \ge -4$ **27.** *Sample answer:* $y \ge 0, y \le -x + 2, y \le x + 2$ **29.** *Sample answer:* $y \ge 0, 3y \le -5x, 4y \le 5x + 35$ **31.** $b + c \ge 240; b < c; 5b + 3c \le 1200$

35.
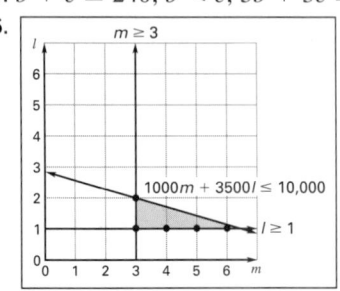

37. $b + c \le 20$, $5b + 6c \ge 90$ **39.** *Sample answer:*
5 hours babysitting and 15 hours as a cashier; 15 hours
babysitting and 5 hours as a cashier **41.** $y \ge 0$, $x \ge 0$,
$y \le -x + 4$ **45.** 243 **47.** 137 **49.** 62 **51.** 49
53. -60 **55.** 38 5-point questions and 30 2-point
questions **57.** 9.25 **59.** 2.8 **61.** 3.8 **63.** 6.875

QUIZ 2 (p. 430) **1.** $l = 8$ ft, $w = 3$ ft **2.** premium gas costs
$1.57/gallon, regular gas costs $1.35/gallon **3.** no
solution **4.** one solution; (0, 1) **5.** infinitely many
solutions

6. 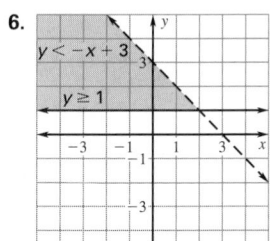 **7.**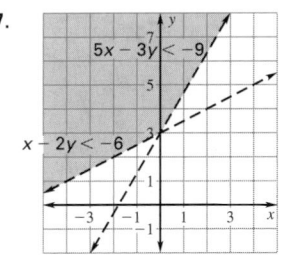

8.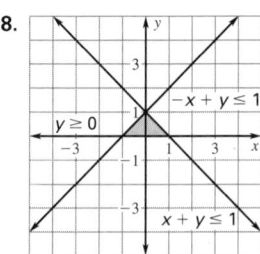

9. *Sample answer:* $x + 2y \le 4$, $-x + y \ge -1$

CHAPTER SUMMARY AND REVIEW (pp. 431–434)

1. $(9, -3)$ **3.** $(0, 1)$ **5.** $\left(4, -\dfrac{1}{2}\right)$ **7.** $(0, 3)$ **9.** $\left(\dfrac{5}{8}, \dfrac{3}{2}\right)$
11. $\left(\dfrac{1}{2}, 0\right)$ **13.** $\left(-\dfrac{83}{14}, \dfrac{39}{14}\right)$ **15.** $(3, -5)$ **17.** $(-1, 1)$
19. 2 regular movies; 3 new releases **21.** no solution

23. 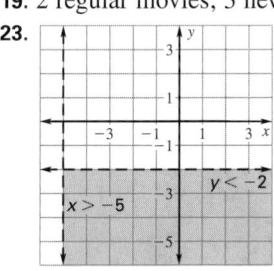 **25.**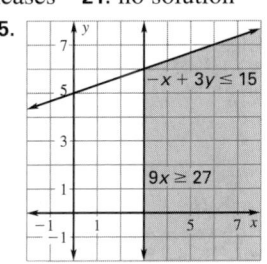

27.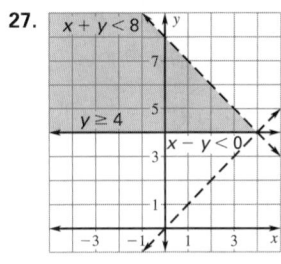

MAINTAINING SKILLS (p. 437) **1.** 125 **3.** 9 **5.** 0.47
7. 0.035 **9.** 61% **11.** 200%

Chapter 8

STUDY GUIDE (p. 440) **1.** A **2.** C **3.** D **4.** D **5.** A

8.1 GUIDED PRACTICE (p. 446) **5.** $(-5)^6$ **7.** 2^{12} **9.** y^{20}
11. $16n^4$

8.1 PRACTICE AND APPLICATIONS (pp. 446–448) **13.** 5
15. 18 **17.** 7 **19.** 4^9 **21.** $(-2)^6$ **23.** x^9 **25.** 3 **27.** 12
29. 9 **31.** 2^6 **33.** $(-4)^{15}$ **35.** c^{80} **37.** 441 **39.** 576
41. $64d^6$ **43.** $64m^6n^6$ **45.** $-r^5s^5t^5$ **47.** < **49.** <
51. > **53.** $-4x^7$ **55.** r^8s^{12} **57.** $18x^5$ **59.** $a^4b^4c^6$
61. $V = 36\pi a^3 \approx 113.1 a^3$ **63.** 8, or 8 to 1 **65.** $2^1 = 2$,
$2^2 = 4$, $2^3 = 8$ **67.** $2^{30} = 1{,}073{,}741{,}824$ pennies
75. 10,000 **77.** $\dfrac{1}{25}$ **79.** $\dfrac{45}{4}$

83. 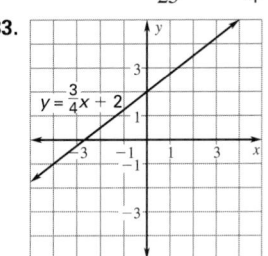 **85.**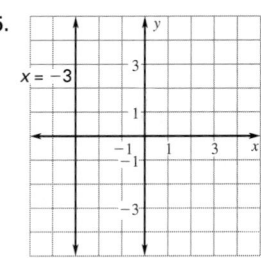

87. $x < 7$ **89.** $x \le 1$ **91.** $x \ge \dfrac{7}{4}$ **93.** true **95.** false; 10
97. false; 1

8.2 GUIDED PRACTICE (p. 452) **3.** 1 **5.** 64 **7.** 2
9. $\dfrac{1}{16}$ **11.** 0.0016 **13.** 0.0156 **15.** $\dfrac{1}{m^2}$ **17.** $3c^5$

8.2 PRACTICE AND APPLICATIONS (pp. 452–454) **19.** $\dfrac{1}{2}, \dfrac{1}{5}$,
$\dfrac{1}{6}$ **21.** 1 **23.** $\dfrac{1}{16}$ **25.** $-\dfrac{1}{343}$ **27.** 256 **29.** $\dfrac{1}{8}$ **31.** $\dfrac{1}{36}$
33. 64 **35.** $\dfrac{1}{9}$ **37.** $\dfrac{1}{400}$ **39.** $\dfrac{1}{16}$ **41.** 0.0313 **43.** 0.0016
45. 0.0625 **47.** 0.0714 **49.** The 5 should not be raised
to a negative power; $\dfrac{5}{x^3}$. **51.** $\dfrac{1}{x^5}$ **53.** $\dfrac{y^4}{x^2}$ **55.** x^2
57. $x^{10}y^4$ **59.** $\dfrac{1}{64x^3}$ **61.** $\dfrac{216}{x^9}$ **63.** about 5.31 million
people **73.** 4 **75.** 2 **77.** $\dfrac{27}{2} = 13.5$ **79.** -9
81. 15 **83.** -15
85. $-13 < x < -5$ **87.** $-6 \le x \le 1$

89. $x > 2$ *or* $x < -\dfrac{20}{3}$

91. $\left(-\dfrac{5}{3}, -1\right)$ **93.** $(5, 0)$ **95.** $(2, 3)$ **97.** *Sample
answer:* $\dfrac{6}{10}, \dfrac{9}{15}, \dfrac{12}{20}$ **99.** *Sample answer:* $\dfrac{2}{16}, \dfrac{3}{24}, \dfrac{4}{32}$
101. *Sample answer:* $\dfrac{30}{32}, \dfrac{45}{48}, \dfrac{60}{64}$
103. *Sample answer:* $\dfrac{50}{64}, \dfrac{75}{96}, \dfrac{100}{128}$

8.3 GUIDED PRACTICE (p. 458)

3.

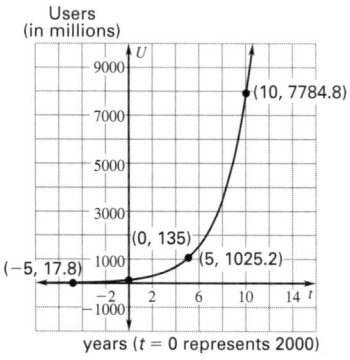

$y = 4^x$

5. domain: all real numbers; range: all positive real numbers

8.3 PRACTICE AND APPLICATIONS (pp. 458–460)
7. yes; $2^0 = 1$ **9.** no; $2(3)^0 = 2$ **11.** yes; $\left(\frac{1}{8}\right)^0 = 1$ **13.** no; $7\left(\frac{1}{5}\right)^0 = 7$

15.

x	-2	-1	0	1	2	3
$y = 3^x$	$\frac{1}{9}$	$\frac{1}{3}$	1	3	9	27

17.

x	-2	-1	0	1	2	3
$y = 5(4)^x$	$\frac{5}{16}$	$\frac{5}{4}$	5	20	80	320

19.

x	-2	-1	0	1	2	3
$y = \left(\frac{1}{6}\right)^x$	36	6	1	$\frac{1}{6}$	$\frac{1}{36}$	$\frac{1}{216}$

21.

x	-2	-1	0	1	2	3
$y = 2\left(\frac{1}{7}\right)^x$	98	14	2	$\frac{2}{7}$	$\frac{2}{49}$	$\frac{2}{343}$

23. 55.90 **25.** 45.25 **27.** 0.00 **29.** 1.06

35.

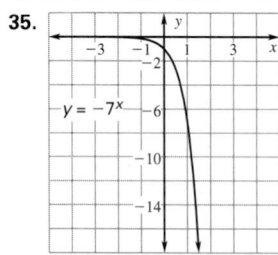

$y = -7^x$

37.

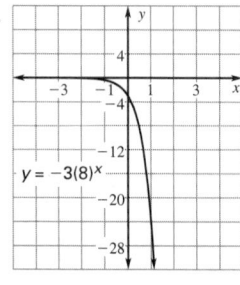

$y = -3(8)^x$

39.

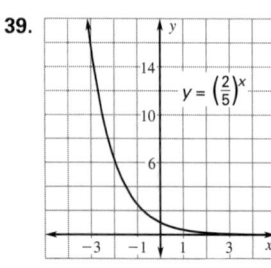

$y = \left(\frac{2}{5}\right)^x$

41.

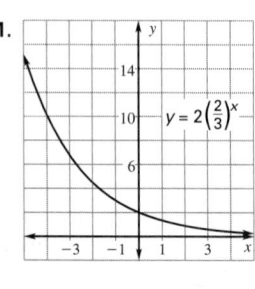

$y = 2\left(\frac{2}{3}\right)^x$

43. domain: all real numbers; range: all negative real numbers **45.** domain: all real numbers; range: all negative real numbers **47.** domain: all real numbers; range: all positive real numbers **49.** domain: all real numbers; range: all positive real numbers

51.

Year	1995	2000	2005	2010
t	-5	0	5	10
U (in millions)	17.8	135	1025.2	7784.8

Users
(in millions)

(10, 7784.8)

(0, 135)

(−5, 17.8) (5, 1025.2)

years ($t = 0$ represents 2000)

55. 0.38 **57.** -0.46 **59.** -1.91 **61.** $8x + y = 4$
63. $7x - 8y = 0$ **65.** $3x + 16y = 9$ **67.** 1 solution
69. no solution **71.** infinitely many solutions
73. $-5, -4, 6$ **75.** $-3\frac{4}{5}, -2\frac{3}{4}, -2\frac{1}{5}$ **77.** 3.001, 3.01, 3.25

QUIZ 1 (p. 460) **1.** 59,049 **2.** 64 **3.** 1600 **4.** 36 **5.** $\frac{1}{25}$
6. 1 **7.** r^{13} **8.** k^8 **9.** $9d^2$ **10.** $\frac{2}{x^3 y^9}$ **11.** $\frac{a^{10} b^{12}}{5}$
12. $\frac{1}{m^7 n^7}$ **13.** about \$1008; about \$2177

14.

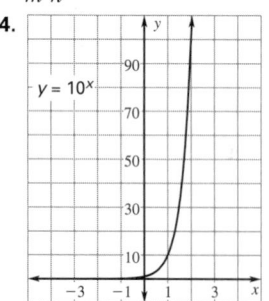

$y = 10^x$

15.

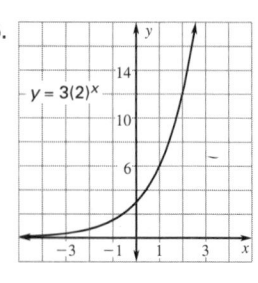

$y = 3(2)^x$

16.

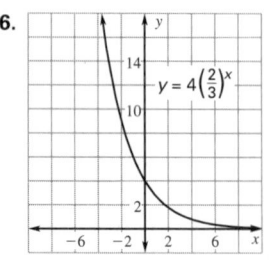

$y = 4\left(\frac{2}{3}\right)^x$

8.3 TECHNOLOGY (p. 461)

1. 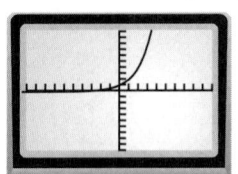 **3.**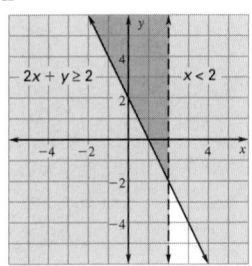

5.

7. *Sample answer:* For $a > 1$, the graph of $y = a^x$ is a curve that passes through $(0, 1)$ and increases to the right. The graph of $y = -a^x$ passes through $(0, -1)$ and decreases to the right. Both graphs approach the x-axis to the left.

8.4 GUIDED PRACTICE (p. 465)

3. 125 **5.** -32 **7.** x^3
9. $\dfrac{1}{m^6}$ **11.** $\dfrac{1}{32}$ **13.** $\dfrac{256}{81}$ **15.** $\dfrac{25}{m^2}$ **17.** $\dfrac{m^6}{n^{10}}$

8.4 PRACTICE AND APPLICATIONS (pp. 465–468)

19. 4
21. 11 **23.** 6 **25.** 125 **27.** 1 **29.** $\dfrac{1}{x}$ **31.** $\dfrac{1}{x^3}$ **33.** 1296
35. 3 **37.** 10 **39.** $\dfrac{1}{625}$ **41.** $-\dfrac{8}{27}$ **43.** $\dfrac{81}{x^4}$ **45.** $\dfrac{x^5}{y^5}$
47. $\left(\dfrac{6a}{b^2}\right)^3 = \dfrac{6^3 a^3}{b^6} = \dfrac{216a^3}{b^6}$ **49.** $5x^3 y^3$ **51.** $6a^8 b^3$
53. $\dfrac{96x^4}{y}$ **55.** $\dfrac{2y^9}{3x^3}$ **57.** $\dfrac{9x^2 y^2}{2}$ **59.** ≈ 0.437 **61.** $200,$
$160, 128, 102, 82, 66, 52$ **63.** product of powers property; quotient of powers property; product of powers property; canceling a common factor   **69.** $100,000$ **71.** 1
73. $y = \dfrac{1}{2}x + 4$ **75.** $y = -x - 8$ **77.** $y = -x + 3$
79. solution   **81.** not a solution   **83.** $(8, 4)$ **85.** $(4, 3)$
87. $(9, -1)$ **89–93.** Estimates may vary.   **89.** 450
91. 80.5 **93.** 1750

8.5 GUIDED PRACTICE (p. 472)

3. 430 **5.** 0.05
7. 0.245 **9.** 6.9×10^6 **11.** 9.9×10^{-1}
13. 2.05×10^{-2} **15.** 2×10^{-11}

8.5 PRACTICE AND APPLICATIONS (pp. 472–474)

17. right, 2   **19.** left, 7   **21.** 8000 **23.** $21,000$
25. $433,000,000$ **27.** 0.009 **29.** 0.098
31. 0.00000000011 **33.** in scientific notation
35. 9×10^2 **37.** 8.8×10^7 **39.** 9.52×10^1
41. 1×10^{-1} **43.** 6×10^{-6} **45.** 8.5×10^{-3}
47. 1.23×10^9 **49.** 1.5×10^5 **51.** 7.0×10^{-4}
53. 2.7×10^7 **55.** 4.0×10^{-2} **57.** $1.09926 \times 10^6;$
$1,099,260$ **59.** $1.5 \times 10^{-11}; 0.000000000015$
61. $\approx 7.9626 \times 10^{-19}; \approx 0.00000000000000000079626$

63. 0.00098 **65.** 2×10^{-23} **67.** about $\$18.12$ per square mile   **69.** about $(4.87 \times 10^{14})\pi$ km^3 or about 1.53×10^{15} km^3 **73.** no solution

75. 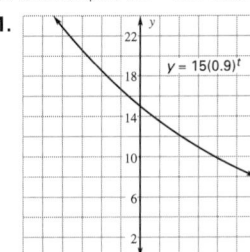   **77.**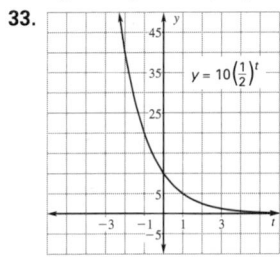

79. 212% **81.** 67.4% **83.** 7.567

QUIZ 2 (p. 474)

1. 7776 **2.** $\dfrac{1}{x^2}$ **3.** $-\dfrac{343}{8}$ **4.** $\dfrac{b^5}{a^5}$ **5.** $\dfrac{4}{3y^9}$
6. $30x^2$ **7.** $-\dfrac{25b^6}{a^3}$ **8.** $\dfrac{16m^4}{81n^4}$ **9.** $\dfrac{4x^3 y^7}{5}$ **10.** $\dfrac{243}{w^2 z^{11}}$
11. $5,000,000,000$ **12.** $4,800$ **13.** $33,500$ **14.** 0.000007
15. 0.011 **16.** 0.0000208 **17.** 1.05×10^2
18. 9.9×10^4 **19.** 3.07×10^7 **20.** 2.5×10^{-1}
21. 4×10^{-4} **22.** 6.7×10^{-6}

8.6 GUIDED PRACTICE (p. 479)

3. 0.04 **5.** about $\$608$

8.6 PRACTICE AND APPLICATIONS (pp. 479–481)

7. $C = 100, r = 0.5$ **9.** $C = 7.5, r = 0.75$
11. $y = 310,000(1.15)^t$; $y =$ population, $t =$ number of years   **13.** $y = 10,000(1.25)^{10}$; $y =$ profit, $t =$ number of years after 1990 ($t \le 10$)   **15.** $y = 15,000(1.3)^{15}$; $y =$ profit, $t =$ number of years after 1990 ($t \le 15$)
17. $\$2231.39$ **19.** $\$4489.99$ **21.** $\$382.88$ **23.** $\$510.51$
25. $\$1466.01$ **27.** $\$1770.44$ **29.** $3, 4$ **31.** 2 **33.** 3
35. about 13.2 L/min, 46.3 L/min, 86.5 L/min   **45.** 5
47. -2 **49.** -7 **51.** 4 **53.** 2^4 **55.** 3^7 **57.** r^6
59. $\dfrac{1}{4}$ **61.** $\dfrac{1}{8}$

8.7 GUIDED PRACTICE (p. 485)

3. $\$6185.20$ **5.** $\$4266.98$
7. C   **9.** exponential decay   **11.** exponential decay

8.7 PRACTICE AND APPLICATIONS (pp. 485–488)

13. $18;$ 0.11 **15.** $0.5; 0.625$ **17.** $y = 100,000(0.98)^t$
19. $y = 100(0.91)^t$ **21.** $y = 70(0.99)^t$ **23.** about $\$11,192$
25. about $\$8372$ **27.** about 229 mg   **29.** $y = 64(0.5)^t$

31.   **33.**

35. $y = 22,000(0.91)^t$; about $\$10,300$
37. $y = 10,500(0.9)^t$; about $\$3700$
39. $302, 239, 189, 150, 119$ **41.** about 106 miles

45. exponential decay; 0.98   **47.** exponential decay; $\frac{2}{3}$

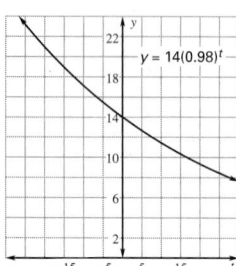

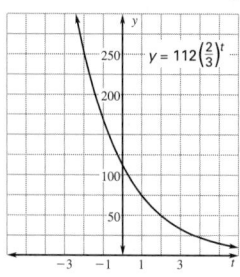

49. exponential growth; $\frac{5}{4}$

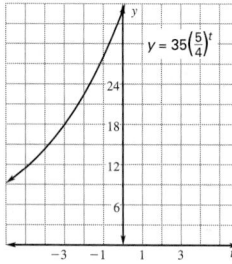

51. *Sample answer:* As b increases, the curve becomes steeper or more vertical.   **57.** 24   **59.** 72   **61.** -0.92
63. -0.64 **65.** $y - 5 = 3(x - 2)$ **67.** $y + 4 = 4(x + 1)$
69. $y - 7 = -6(x + 1)$ **71.** 2.5   **73.** 0.2   **75.** 5.5

QUIZ 3 (p. 488) **1.** $270   **2.** $314.93   **3.** $367.33
4. $462.73   **5.** 1600 raccoons   **6.** about $12,422
7. about $10,286   **8.** about $9360   **9.** about $5841
10. $y = 20,000(0.92)^t$; about $13,200
11. exponential decay; 0.1   **12.** exponential growth; 1.2

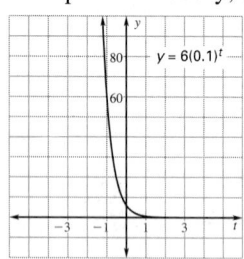

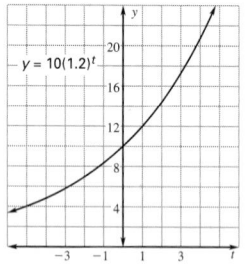

13. exponential growth; 4.5   **14.** exponential decay; 0.1

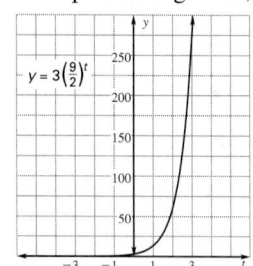

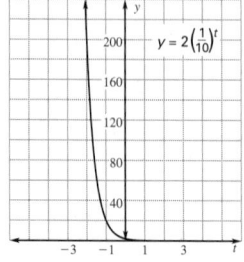

CHAPTER SUMMARY AND REVIEW (pp. 489–492) **1.** 128
3. 4096   **5.** $81x^4$ **7.** $8p^4$ **9.** 1   **11.** $\frac{1}{49}$ **13.** $\frac{x^6}{y^6}$ **15.** $\frac{b^5}{a^2}$

17.

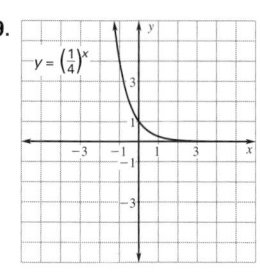

19.

21. $\frac{1}{3}$ **23.** $\frac{16}{81}$ **25.** $9y$ **27.** $\frac{8a^6b^{12}}{125}$ **29.** 70   **31.** 0.0002
33. 5.2×10^7 **35.** 9×10^{-3} **37.** 1.5×10^7
39. 1.44×10^7 **41.** 7×10^8 **43.** $y = 2(1.05)^t$
45. $y = 125(0.97)^t$

MAINTAINING SKILLS (p. 495) **1.** 2^3 **3.** $3 \cdot 5 \cdot 7$ **5.** $2\frac{5}{8}$
7. $1\frac{12}{15}$

Chapter 9

STUDY GUIDE (p. 498) **1.** B   **2.** D   **3.** C

9.1 GUIDED PRACTICE (p. 502) **5.** ± 11 **7.** -2
9. irrational   **11.** rational   **13.** 14.66, -2.66
15. 13.31, -9.31

9.1 PRACTICE AND APPLICATIONS (pp. 502–504) **17.** The positive and negative square roots of 16 are 4 and -4.
19. The positive square root of 225 is 15.   **21.** The negative square root of 289 is -17.   **23.** The positive square root of 1 is 1.   **25.** 12   **27.** 14   **29.** ± 7 **31.** -16
33. 20   **35.** 11   **37.** -1 **39.** 13   **41.** no   **43.** no
45. yes   **47.** no   **49.** no   **51.** no   **53.** 2.24   **55.** 3.61
57. -7 **59.** ± 1 **61.** ± 3.87 **63.** -4.47 **65.** 3   **67.** 0
69. 6   **71.** 7   **73.** 7   **75.** 10.24, 5.76   **77.** -0.34, -11.66
79. -11.24, -2.76 **81.** 5.13, -1.80 **83.** -2.90, 0.57
85. m is a perfect square   **87.** False. *Sample counterexample:* the square root of 0 is 0.   **95.** $(2, -2)$
97. 116 adult tickets and 208 student tickets
99. $(-4, -19)$ **101.** $(5, -6)$ **103.** $0.5\overline{3}$ **105.** 0.875
107. 0.3125   **109.** 0.4   **111.** $0.\overline{8}$ **113.** 0.9

9.2 GUIDED PRACTICE (p. 508) **3.** 2   **5.** 0   **7.** 2   **9.** ± 7
11. $\pm\sqrt{7}$ **13.** no real solution   **15.** 1.7 sec   **17.** 3.5 sec

9.2 PRACTICE AND APPLICATIONS (pp. 508–510) **19.** ± 1
21. no real solution   **23.** ± 15 **25.** ± 11 **27.** ± 16
29. ± 7 **31.** ± 8 **33.** ± 4 **35.** $\pm\sqrt{2}$ **37.** ± 3 **39.** no real solution   **41.** ± 5 **43.** $\pm\sqrt{3}$ **45.** ± 6 **47.** $\pm\sqrt{14}$
49. The equation has no real solution.   **51.** ± 1.41
53. ± 2.83 **55.** ± 1.84 **57.** True; the solutions of $x^2 = c$ are $\sqrt{c}$ and $-\sqrt{c}$.   **59.** $h = -16t^2 + 96$ **61.** 0.40 mm
63. 0.15 mm   **65.** 0.12 mm   **67.** 5,500,400; 22,582,900; 73,830,400   **71.** -18 **73.** 12   **75.** 5; 6   **77.** 8; 2
79. $x \geq -2$ **81.** $x < 2$ **83.** 8×10^{-7} **85.** 8.721×10^3
87. $\frac{2}{3}$ **89.** $\frac{1}{3}$ **91.** $\frac{5}{6}$ **93.** $\frac{3}{4}$

9.3 GUIDED PRACTICE (p. 514) **5.** D **7.** B **9.** 6

11. $2\sqrt{15}$ **13.** $\dfrac{\sqrt{15}}{4}$ **15.** $\dfrac{\sqrt{10}}{5}$

9.3 PRACTICE AND APPLICATIONS (pp. 514–517)

17. no; radical in the denominator **19.** yes **21.** $2\sqrt{11}$

23. $3\sqrt{2}$ **25.** $3\sqrt{3}$ **27.** $10\sqrt{2}$ **29.** $5\sqrt{5}$ **31.** 12 **33.** $\dfrac{1}{2}$

35. $\dfrac{2}{5}$ **37.** $\dfrac{6}{5}$ **39.** $\dfrac{\sqrt{11}}{9}$ **41.** $\dfrac{3}{4}$ **43.** $\dfrac{\sqrt{5}}{9}$

45. $\sqrt{20} = \sqrt{4 \cdot 5} = 2\sqrt{5}$ **47.** $\dfrac{\sqrt{5}}{5}$ **49.** $\dfrac{\sqrt{2}}{2}$ **51.** $\dfrac{\sqrt{3}}{3}$

53. $\dfrac{\sqrt{10}}{5}$ **55.** $\dfrac{\sqrt{11}}{11}$ **57.** $\dfrac{5\sqrt{3}}{3}$ **59.** 20 **61.** $-6\sqrt{3}$

63. -12 **65.** -1 **67.** $3\sqrt{6}$ **69.** $-3\sqrt{10}$ **71.** $\dfrac{\sqrt{15}}{5}$

73. $2\sqrt{5}$ **75.** $70\sqrt{2}$ m/sec **77.** No; ratio of speeds is the square root of the ratio of depths. **79.** 98

81. Multiplication; square

93. 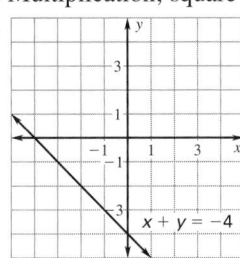 **95.**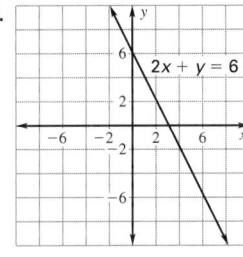

97. $81x^4$ **99.** 144 **101.** $64x^2y^2$ **103.** $-a^3b^3c^3$

105. domain: all real numbers; range: all negative real numbers **107.** $\dfrac{1}{4}$ **109.** $\dfrac{3}{8}$ **111.** $\dfrac{2}{189}$ **113.** $\dfrac{1}{10}$

QUIZ 1 (p. 517) **1.** 9 **2.** -5 **3.** 4 **4.** -2 **5.** ± 1 **6.** 10

7. ± 7 **8.** 11 **9.** ± 8 **10.** $\pm\sqrt{63}$ or $\pm 3\sqrt{7}$ **11.** $\pm\sqrt{6}$

12. no real solution **13.** ± 4 **14.** ± 5 **15.** $3\sqrt{2}$

16. $2\sqrt{15}$ **17.** $\sqrt{3}$ **18.** -9 **19.** $4\sqrt{30}$ **20.** $\dfrac{2\sqrt{3}}{3}$

21. $\dfrac{\sqrt{5}}{3}$ **22.** $\dfrac{1}{2}$ **23.** $\dfrac{\sqrt{5}}{4}$ **24.** $2\sqrt{2}$ **25.** $\dfrac{\sqrt{6}}{3}$ **26.** $\dfrac{6\sqrt{5}}{5}$

9.4 GUIDED PRACTICE (p. 523) **3.** up **5.** down **7.** up

9. axis of symmetry: **11.** axis of symmetry:
$x = 0$ $x = 0$

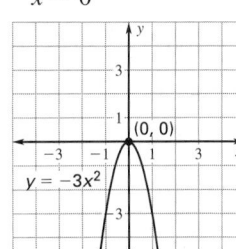 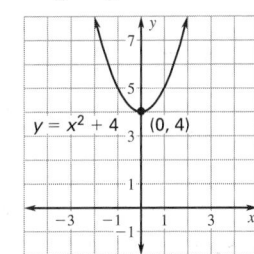

13. axis of symmetry:
$x = 1$

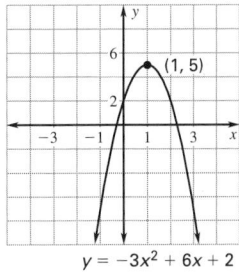

9.4 PRACTICE AND APPLICATIONS (pp. 523–525) **15.** up

17. down **19.** down **21.** down **23.** down

25.
$(0, 0)$

x	-2	-1	0	1	2	3
y	24	6	0	6	24	54

27.
$\left(\dfrac{5}{2}, -\dfrac{25}{2}\right)$

x	0	1	2	$\dfrac{5}{2}$	3	4	5
y	0	-8	-12	$-\dfrac{25}{2}$	-12	-8	0

29.
$\left(-\dfrac{1}{6}, 3\dfrac{5}{6}\right)$

x	-2	-1	$-\dfrac{1}{6}$	0	1	2
y	24	8	$3\dfrac{5}{6}$	4	12	32

31.
$\left(-\dfrac{1}{2}, 9\right)$

x	-3	-2	-1	$-\dfrac{1}{2}$	0	1	2
y	-16	0	8	9	8	0	-16

37. 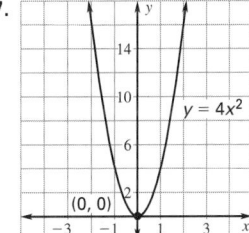 **39.**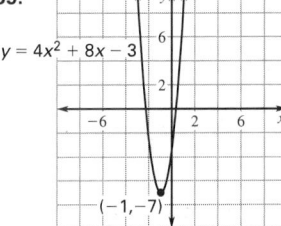

41. 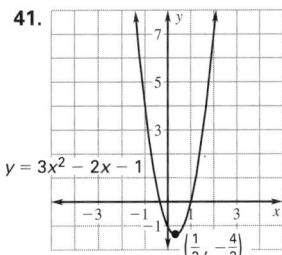 **43.**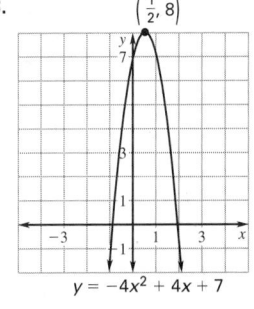

45. $\left(\dfrac{15}{32}, \dfrac{609}{64}\right)$; this point represents the highest point on the path of the basketball. At $\dfrac{15}{32} \approx 0.47$ sec the ball reaches its high point of $\dfrac{609}{64} \approx 9.52$ ft. **47.** 10 ft

55. 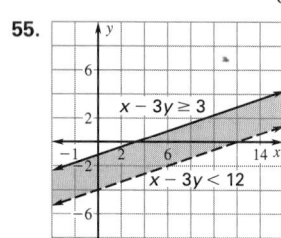 **57.**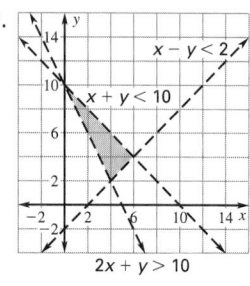

59. $(-5)^9$ **61.** x^8 **63.** m^8 **65.** 2^5 **67.** $\dfrac{4}{15}, \dfrac{1}{3}, \dfrac{2}{5}$

69. $\dfrac{3}{4}, \dfrac{7}{8}, \dfrac{9}{10}$

9.5 GUIDED PRACTICE (p. 529) **3.** B **5.** A **7.** ± 1
9. ± 4 **11.** 2, 5

9.5 PRACTICE AND APPLICATIONS (pp. 529–531)
13. $x^2 - 6x + 6 = 0$ **15.** $3x^2 - x - 5 = 0$
17. $6x^2 - 12x = 0$ **19.** $-3, 1$ **23.** $-3, 1$ **25.** $-3, 1$
27. $-1, 5$ **29.** $-5, 1$ **31.** $-3, 2$ **33.** $-1, 2$ **35.** ± 5
37. ± 5 **39.** ± 4 **41.** ± 9 **43.** ± 2 **45.** ± 3 **47.** $-4, 1$
49. $-4, 8$ **51.** 10 sec **55.** pasta: \$5.95; salad: \$1.95
57. (3, 2), one solution **59.** $\left(-\dfrac{7}{2}, 6\right)$; one solution
61. no solution **63.** 4 **65.** 0 **67.** 2 **69.** -9 **71.** $2\sqrt{6}$
73. $10\sqrt{2}$ **75.** $\sqrt{3}$ **77.** $\dfrac{20\sqrt{3}}{3}$ **79.** $>$ **81.** $>$ **83.** $<$ **85.** $<$

9.5 TECHNOLOGY (p. 532) **1.** $-1, 2$ **3.** $-0.77, 2.27$ **5.** 2

9.6 GUIDED PRACTICE (p. 536) **5.** $2x^2 - 16x + 32 = 0$; $a = 2, b = -16, c = 32$ **7.** $-7, 1$ **9.** -6
11. $\dfrac{-1 \pm \sqrt{13}}{6}$ **13.** $2x^2 + x - 6 = 0; -2, \dfrac{3}{2}$
15. $x^2 - x - 2 = 0; -1, 2$ **17.** $x^2 - 4x + 3 = 0; 1, 3$

9.6 PRACTICE AND APPLICATIONS (pp. 536–539)
19. $3x^2 - 3x - 6 = 0; a = 3, b = -3, c = -6$
21. $x^2 - 5x + 6 = 0; a = 1, b = -5, c = 6$
23. $3x^2 - 24x + 45 = 0; a = 3, b = -24, c = 45$
25. $k^2 - \dfrac{1}{4} = 0; a = 1, b = 0, c = \dfrac{-1}{4}$
27. $\dfrac{2}{3}x^2 + 2x - \dfrac{1}{3} = 0; a = \dfrac{2}{3}, b = 2, c = -\dfrac{1}{3}$ **29.** 9
31. 1 **33.** 169 **35.** 148 **37.** 21 **39.** 39 **41.** $-1, -10$
43. $-\dfrac{4}{3}, 2$ **45.** $-1.30, -0.26$ **47.** $-1.87, 13.87$
49. $2x^2 - 4x - 30 = 0; -3, 5$ **51.** $x^2 + 6x - 5 = 0$;
$-3 \pm \sqrt{14}$ **53.** $2x^2 - 5x - 7 = 0; -1, \dfrac{7}{2}$
55. $x^2 - 2x - 3 = 0; -1, 3$ **57.** $2x^2 - 2x - 12 = 0$;
$-2, 3$ **59.** $-2, -3$ **61.** $-2, -8$ **63.** $-1, 4$ **65.** $-3, 1$
67. 2.30 sec **69.** 2.21 sec **71.** 0.92 sec **73.** 0.4 sec

75. 1.4 sec **77.** 5.7 sec **79.** about 5.04 sec **81.** A
83. D **85.** -27 **91.**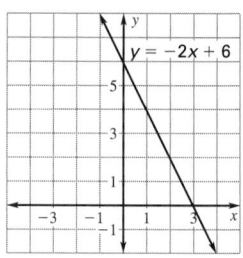

93. $x \le -5$

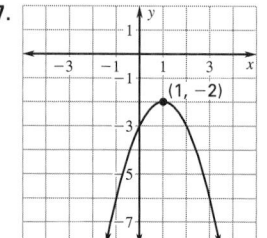

94. $x > 16$

96. $>$ **97.** $<$ **99.** $<$ **101.** $<$

QUIZ 2 (p. 539) **1.** up **2.** up **3.** down **4.** up **5.** down
6. down

7. 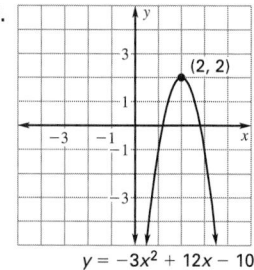 **8.**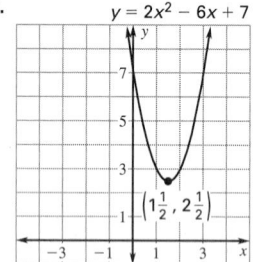

9.

10. $-2, 5$ **11.** 6 **12.** $-1, -3$ **13.** -3 **14.** $-6, -\dfrac{1}{2}$
15. $-2, 8$ **16.** $\dfrac{3}{2}, 2$ **17.** $1.17, -2.84$ **18.** $1.55, -0.22$

9.7 GUIDED PRACTICE (p. 543) **5.** one solution **7.** B
9. A **11.** 2

9.7 PRACTICE AND APPLICATIONS (pp. 543–545)
13. 49 **15.** -40 **17.** 0 **19.** -111 **21.** -40
23. no solution **25.** two solutions **27.** no solution
29. two solutions **31.** two solutions **33.** one solution
35. 60 **37.** It crosses the x-axis at two distinct points.
39. 0 **41.** 0 **43.** 1 **47.** domain: $0 \le t \le 5$;
range: $9.29 \le P \le 161.49$ **49.** about 8.5 years
53. $1 \le x < 4$ **55.** $-3 < x < 5$

 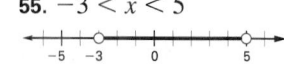

57.

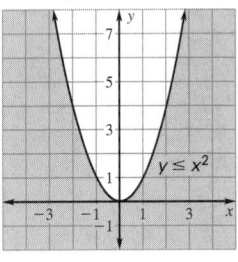

$y - 4x < 0$

59. 0.06   **61.** 0.01   **63.** 0.0018

9.8 GUIDED PRACTICE (p. 550)   **3.** inside   **5.** outside
7. $(0, 0)$, yes; $(1, -2)$, no

9.

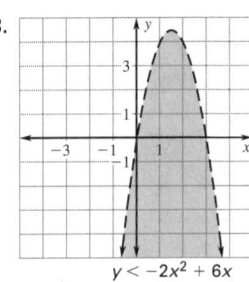

$y \leq x^2$

11.

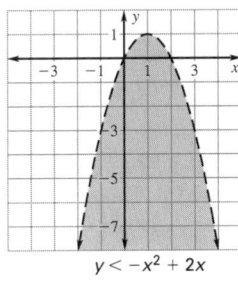

$y < -x^2 + 2x$

13.

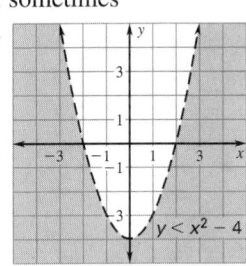

$y < -2x^2 + 6x$

9.8 PRACTICE AND APPLICATIONS (pp. 550–552)   **15.** yes
17. no   **19.** no   **21.** outside   **23.** inside   **25.** sometimes
27. sometimes

33.

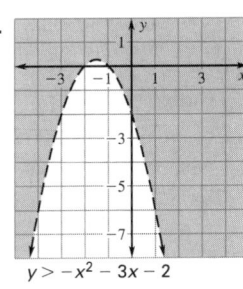

$y < x^2 - 4$

35.

$y > -x^2 - 3x - 2$

37.

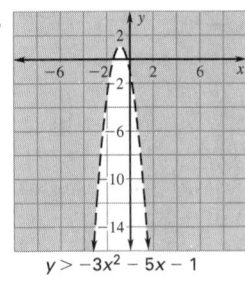

$y > -3x^2 - 5x - 1$

41. $y = 7x$ **43.** $y = \frac{1}{2}x$ **45.** $y = -2x$

48.

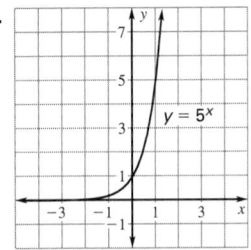

$y = 5^x$

50.

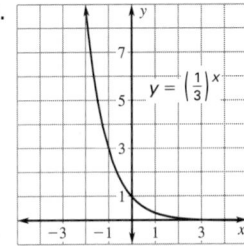

$y = \left(\frac{1}{3}\right)^x$

52.

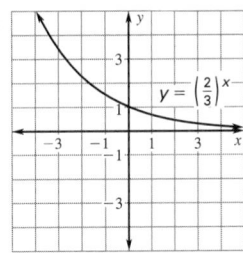

$y = \left(\frac{2}{3}\right)^x$

53. $\frac{1}{25}$ **55.** $\frac{9}{20}$ **57.** $\frac{3}{100}$ **59.** $\frac{6}{25}$ **61.** $3\frac{9}{10}$ **63.** $1\frac{3}{4}$
65. $\frac{91}{100}$ **67.** $\frac{1}{4}$

QUIZ 3 (p. 552)   **1.** two solutions   **2.** one solution   **3.** no
solution   **4.** No. *Sample answer:* the vertical motion
model is $h(t) = -16t^2 + 50t + 5$. If you let $h(t) = 45$
and solve for t, you have the quadratic equation
$-16t^2 + 50t - 40 = 0$. The discriminant has a value of
$2500 - 2560 = -60$, so there are no solutions.
5. A   **7.** B

8.

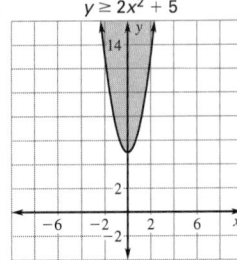

$y \geq 2x^2 + 5$

9.

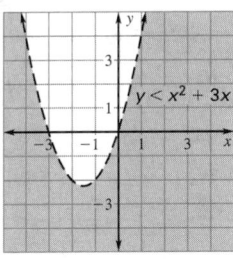

$y < x^2 + 3x$

10.

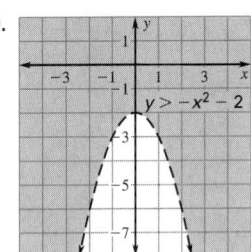

$y > -x^2 - 2$

11.

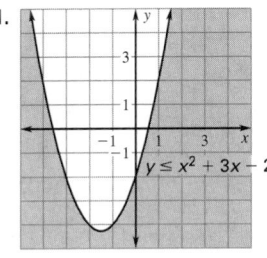

$y \leq x^2 + 3x - 2$

12.

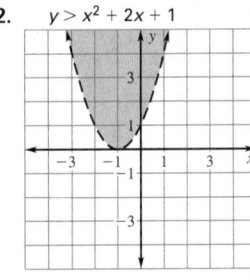

$y > x^2 + 2x + 1$

13.

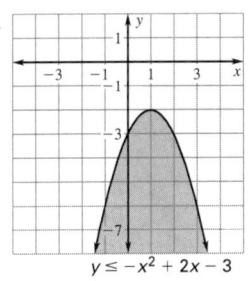

$y \leq -x^2 + 2x - 3$

SUMMARY AND REVIEW (pp. 553–556) **1.** -2 **3.** 10
5. ± 12 **7.** ± 4 **9.** $3\sqrt{5}$ **11.** $\dfrac{\sqrt{6}}{2}$

13.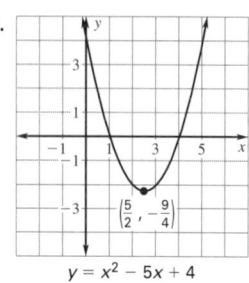
$y = x^2 - 5x + 4$

15.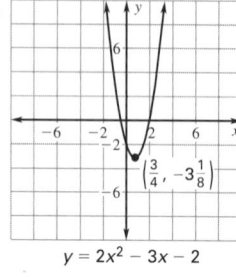
$y = 2x^2 - 3x - 2$

17. $5, 1$ **19.** $1, \dfrac{1}{3}$ **21.** $\dfrac{1}{2}, \dfrac{3}{5}$ **23.** two solutions **25.** 2 **27.** 1

29.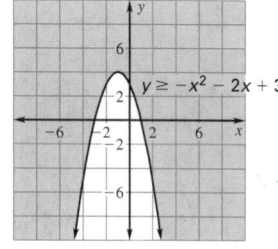
$y \geq -x^2 - 2x + 3$

MAINTAINING SKILLS (p. 559) **1.** $16x - 96$ **3.** $5m - 65$
5. $30a + 80$ **7.** $21m + 6n$ **9.** $2x + 10$

CHAPTERS 1–9 CUMULATIVE PRACTICE (p. 560–561)
1. No. Each input value can only have one output value.
5 has two. **3.** $3x - 6$ **5.** $9 + 2h$ **7.** $1.25x = 60$;
48 pretzels **9.** 360 **11.** 400% **13.** $-3; \dfrac{1}{2}$ **15.** $\dfrac{14}{5}; 14$
17. $-2; -28$ **19.** Yes; slope of both lines is 4.
21. $y = -x + 10$ **23.** $y = -2x - 2$ **25.** $y = -\dfrac{1}{2}x + \dfrac{9}{2}$
27. $3x - 5y = -6$ **29.** $-2x + 7y = 15$ **31.** $x + 4y = 24$
33. $m \leq -9$ **35.** $t \leq -8$ **37.** $y \geq 14$ **39.** $y > -4$
41. $k \geq 7$ **43.** $(2, 6)$ **45.** $(-5, -4)$ **47.** $\left(1, -\dfrac{1}{2}\right)$

49. 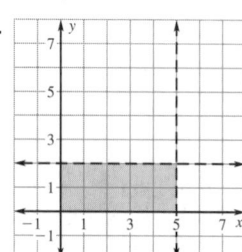 **51.**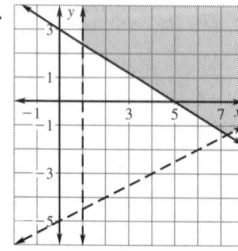

53. x^9 **55.** $64t^2$ **57.** 243 **59.** $\dfrac{1}{16}$ **61.** $\dfrac{x^4 y^8}{4}$ **63.** $\dfrac{9x^3}{y}$
65. 1.5×10^3 **67.** 6×10^{10} **69.** 8×10^0 **71.** $2\sqrt{10}$
73. $6\sqrt{2}$ **75.** $\dfrac{\sqrt{21}}{2}$ **77.** $3\sqrt{2}$ **79.** $\dfrac{\sqrt{10}}{10}$ **81.** $\dfrac{\sqrt{6}}{3}$

83.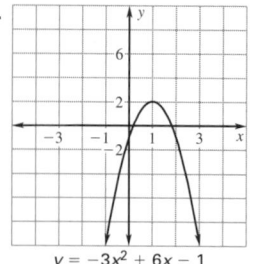
$y = -3x^2 + 6x - 1$

85.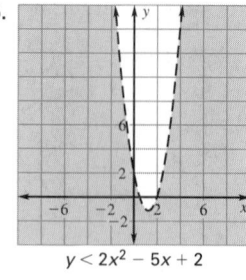
$y < 2x^2 - 5x + 2$

87. No. Discriminant for $-16t^2 + 100t - 180 = 0$ is
-1520, so there is no real solution.

Chapter 10

STUDY GUIDE (p. 566) **1.** B **2.** C **3.** D

10.1 GUIDED PRACTICE (p. 571) **3.** linear binomial
5. quadratic binomial **7.** cubic trinomial **9.** $-3x^2$
and $-5x$ are not like terms; $9x^3 - 3x^2 - 5x - 2$
11. $3x - 16$ **13.** $4x^2 - 7x - 2$

10.1 PRACTICE AND APPLICATIONS (pp. 571–573)
15. always **17.** sometimes **19.** always **21.** 4
23. 4 **25.** $20m^3$; cubic monomial **27.** -16; constant
monomial **29.** $11y^3 - 14$; cubic binomial
31. $7b^3 - 4b^2$; cubic binomial **33.** $-6x^3 + 4x^2 - 6$
35. $-7m^2 + 7m - 3$ **37.** -6 **39.** $3x^2 - 5$
41. $z^3 + 1$ **43.** $-n^3 + 3n^2 + 3n - 5$
45. $25x^3 + 8x + 2$ **47.** $x^2 + 2x + 2$ **49.** $-3x^2 + 6$
51. $1.5x^2 + 60x$ **53.** $A = 1.381t^2 + 3.494t + 235.325$
59. $5x - 2$ **61.** $-15x + 9$ **63.** $-7x - 55$ **65.** 32
67. 256 **69.** 256 **71.** 1.295 **73.** 4 **75.** $1\dfrac{5}{8}$
77. $3\dfrac{7}{10}$ **79.** $12\dfrac{19}{28}$ **81.** $3\dfrac{3}{14}$ **83.** $15\dfrac{31}{72}$

10.2 GUIDED PRACTICE (p. 578) **3.** $(x + 3), (x + 3)$
5. 3 **7.** 20 **9.** $-8x^2 - 14x$ **11.** $-12x^4 - 8x^3 + 24x^2$
13. $y^2 + 6y - 16$ **15.** $w^2 + 2w - 15$
17. $8x^2 - 29x - 12$ **19.** $x^2 + x - 56$

10.2 PRACTICE AND APPLICATIONS (pp. 578–580)
21. $-8x^2 + 20x$ **23.** $2x^3 - 16x^2 + 2x$
25. $12w^5 - 8w^4 - 4w^3$ **27.** $t^2 + 13t + 40$
29. $d^2 - 2d - 15$ **31.** $2y^2 + 5y + 2$ **33.** $3s^2 + 5s - 2$
35. $8y^2 - 18y + 7$ **37.** $y^2 - 3y - 40$
39. $2w^2 + 5w - 25$ **41.** $2x^2 - 3x - 135$
43. $6z^2 + 25z + 14$ **45.** $10t^2 + 9t - 9$
47. $63w^2 - 143w + 60$ **49.** $d^3 - 7d^2 + 4d + 30$
51. $6x^3 + x^2 - 8x + 6$ **53.** $a^3 + 4a^2 - 19a + 14$
55. $4y^3 + 45y^2 - 38y - 24$ **57.** $21x^2 + 100x + 100$
59. $R = -3.15t^2 - 6.21t + 989.12$, in millions of dollars
61. $2x^2 + 7x + 3$ **65.** $49x^2$ **67.** $\dfrac{4}{25}y^2$ **69.** 9^8 **71.** b^7
73. $432t^4$ **75.** $-108x^3 y^5$ **77.** two solutions **79.** two
solutions **81.** one solution **83.** two solutions **85.** two
solutions

87.

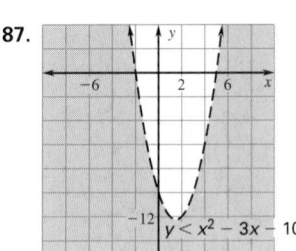

$y < x^2 - 3x - 10$

89. $0.0\overline{3}$ **91.** 2 **93.** $\dfrac{27}{8}$ **95.** $\dfrac{87}{92}$ **97.** 2

10.3 GUIDED PRACTICE (p. 585) **3.** $x^2 - 12x + 36$
5. $p^2 + 12p + 36$ **7.** $t^2 - 36$ **9.** F; $9x^2 + 24x + 16$
11. T

10.3 PRACTICE AND APPLICATIONS (pp. 585–587) **13.** yes
15. no **17.** yes **19.** yes **21.** yes **23.** $x^2 - 25$
25. $4m^2 - 4$ **27.** $9 - 4x^2$ **29.** $x^2 + 10x + 25$
31. $9x^2 + 6x + 1$ **33.** $16b^2 - 24b + 9$ **35.** $x^2 - 16$
37. $9x^2 - 6x + 1$ **39.** $4y^2 - 25$ **41.** $a^2 - 4b^2$
43. $9x^2 - 16y^2$ **45.** $81 - 16t^2$ **47.** false;
$a^2 + 4ab + 4b^2$ **49.** true **51.** $(x + 3)^2 = x^2 + 6x + 9$;
square of a binomial **53.** $(2x + 4)^2 = 4x^2 + 16x + 16$;
square of a binomial **55.** $9x^2 - 24x + 16$ in.^{2}
57. 25% normal feathers; 50% mildly frizzled;
25% extremely frizzled **61.** x **63.** $\dfrac{15x^2}{y}$

65.

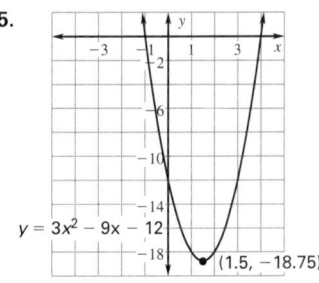

$y = 3x^2 - 9x - 12$

$(1.5, -18.75)$

67. $\dfrac{1}{4}$ **69.** $\dfrac{4}{9}$ **71.** $\dfrac{1}{27}$ **73.** $\dfrac{27}{64}$

QUIZ 1 (p. 587) **1.** 2 **2.** 0 **3.** 3 **4.** 5 **5.** $3x^2 + 5x + 9$
6. $-6x^3 - 14x^2 + 2x - 2$ **7.** $3t^2 - 13t + 14$
8. $6x^3 + 3x^2 + 4x + 3$ **9.** $x^2 + 7x - 8$
10. $y^2 + 11y + 18$ **11.** $-12x^5 + 11x^4 - 3x^2$
12. $4x^2 - 49y^2$ **13.** $16n^2 - 49$ **14.** $2x^3 - 3x^2 - 6x + 8$
15. $x^2 - 36$ **16.** $16x^2 - 9$ **17.** $25 - 9b^2$
18. $4x^2 - 49y^2$ **19.** $9x^2 + 36x + 36$
20. $64x^2 + 96x + 36$

10.4 GUIDED PRACTICE (p. 591) **3.** No; 2 and -5 are
solutions, 3 is not. **5.** no **7.** yes **9.** $-1, -3$ **11.** 7

13.

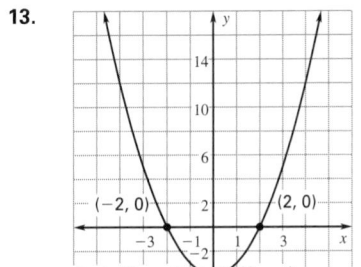

$(-2, 0)$ $(2, 0)$
$y = (x + 2)(x - 2)$ $(0, -4)$

10.4 PRACTICE AND APPLICATIONS (pp. 591–593)
15. $-8, 6$ **17.** -3 **19.** -7 **21.** $-2, -3$ **23.** 17
25. -9 **27.** $20, -15$ **29.** $-1, -2, 4$ **31.** $-5, 6$
33. $-8, -9, 12$ **35.** $8, -\dfrac{1}{2}, -2$

41. x-intercepts: $(-5, -3)$; **45.** x-intercepts: $(-4, -3)$;
vertex: $(-4, -1)$ vertex: $(-3.5, -0.25)$

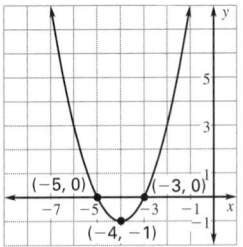

$(-5, 0)$ $(-3, 0)$
$(-4, -1)$

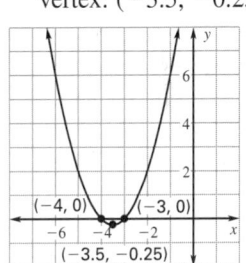

$(-4, 0)$ $(-3, 0)$
$(-3.5, -0.25)$

47. $(0, -14)$ **49.** 630 ft **51.** 200 m **55.** 0.04443
57. 1,250,000 **59.** 9,960,000 **61.** 81,700,000
63. $x^2 - 64$ **65.** $6x^2 + 19x - 7$ **67.** $24x^2 - x - 3$
69. $x^2 + 20x + 100$ **71.** exponential decay;
$y = P(0.84)^t$ where $P = $ the average price of the computer
in 1996, and t is the number of years since 1996.
73. exponential decay; $y = N(0.97)^t$ where N is the
number of members in 1996 and t is the number of years
since 1996. **75.** 1, 2, 3, 4, 6, 12 **77.** 1, 2, 3, 6, 9, 18
79. 1, 3, 17, 51 **81.** 1, 2, 3, 4, 6, 9, 12, 18, 36
83. 1, 2, 4, 8, 16, 32, 64 **85.** 1, 2, 3, 4, 6, 7, 12, 14, 21,
28, 42, 84

10.5 GUIDED PRACTICE (p. 599) **3.** A **5.** C **7.** 5, -1
9. always **11.** never

10.5 PRACTICE AND APPLICATIONS (pp. 599–601)
15. $(z + 1)(z + 5)$ **17.** $(b + 8)(b - 3)$ **19.** $(r + 4)(r + 4)$
21. $(m - 10)(m + 3)$ **23.** $(b + 8)(b - 5)$ **25.** 2, -7
27. $-1, -15$ **29.** 6, -9 **31.** 4, 11 **33.** 5, -13
35. 8, -7 **37.** $-4, -8$ **39.** 2, 15 **41.** 3, -6
43. base: 8 ft, height: 5 ft **45.** 305 m by 550 m **51.** 15
53. 1 **55.** 18 **57.** $y^2 + 5y - 36$ **59.** $-3w^2 + 3w + 60$
61. $20t^2 - 62t + 30$ **63.** $-2, -3$ **65.** 6, 9 **67.** 1, $-\dfrac{1}{2}$
69. $-4, 3, \dfrac{1}{2}$ **71.** 11.056 **73.** 11.86 **75.** 20.9204
77. 114.8106

10.6 GUIDED PRACTICE (p. 606) **3.** -6 **5.** $10x^2$ **7.** D
9. C   **11.** $(2x + 1)(x - 2)$ **13.** $(3x - 4)(4x - 1)$
15. $(3x - 4)(x + 2)$ **17.** $\frac{1}{2}, -8$

10.6 PRACTICE AND APPLICATIONS (pp. 606–608)
23. $(3t + 1)(t + 5)$ **25.** $(2a + 1)(3a + 1)$
27. $(6b + 1)(b - 2)$ **29.** $3(x + 1)(2x - 5)$
31. $(2z - 1)(z + 10)$ **33.** $(4x + 7)(x + 5)$
35. $(3c - 4)(c - 11)$ **37.** $(2t + 7)(3t - 10)$
39. $(2y - 5)(4y - 3)$ **41.** Incorrectly factored:
$3y^2 - 16y - 35 = (3y + 5)(y - 7)$; solutions are $-\frac{5}{3}, 7$.
43. $\frac{3}{7}, 1$ **45.** $\frac{1}{4}, 5$ **47.** $\frac{13}{5}, -2$ **49.** $\frac{1}{2}, \frac{3}{2}$ **51.** $\frac{5}{2}, \frac{7}{4}$
53. $\frac{3}{7}, -\frac{1}{4}$ **55. a.** $h = -16t^2 + 8t + 8$ **b.** 1 sec; yes
57. 2 sec; the other solution of $\frac{3}{4}$ second is the time it
takes for the T-shirt to leave the cannon and go up to a
height of 30 feet. You would probably catch the T-shirt
as it fell.   **61.** $\left(-\frac{49}{12}, -\frac{11}{2}\right)$ **63.** $16t^2 - 8t + 1$
65. $9x^2 + 30x + 25$ **67.** $121 - 132x + 36x^2$ **69.** $\frac{4}{33}$
71. $\frac{5}{27}$ **73.** $\frac{16}{35}$ **75.** $\frac{5}{4}$

QUIZ 2 (p. 608)   **1.** -5 **2.** -4 **3.** $-\frac{7}{2}, 4$ **4.** $0, \frac{2}{5}$
5. $5, -\frac{1}{2}$ **6.** $0, -4, 7$
7. x-intercepts: $2, -2$;   **8.** x-intercepts: $-3, -5$;
 vertex: $(0, -4)$ vertex: $(-4, -1)$

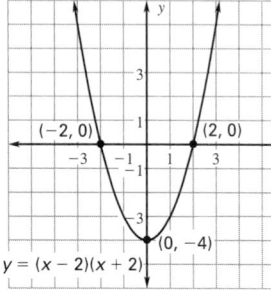
$y = (x - 2)(x + 2)$

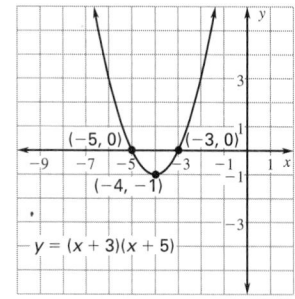
$y = (x + 3)(x + 5)$

9. x-intercepts: $1, -3$; vertex: $(-1, -4)$

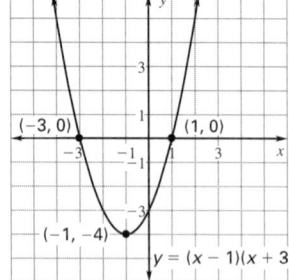
$y = (x - 1)(x + 3)$

10. $(y + 4)(y - 1)$ **11.** $(w + 11)(w + 2)$
12. $(n + 19)(n - 3)$ **13.** cannot be factored
14. $(b - 8)(b + 2)$ **15.** $(r - 7)(r + 4)$
16. $(m - 9)(m + 5)$ **17.** $(x + 6)(x + 11)$
18. $(r - 43)(r + 2)$ **19.** $1, -6$ **20.** $-1, -25$ **21.** $5, 9$

22. $-9, -2$ **23.** $-\frac{1}{2}, -5$ **24.** $\frac{1}{3}, 1$ **25.** $-\frac{2}{3}, 4$
26. $-\frac{3}{2}$ **27.** $-\frac{7}{3}, -\frac{2}{5}$

10.7 GUIDED PRACTICE (p. 613)   **3.** $(b + 5)^2$
5. $(w - 8)^2$ **7.** $6(y - 2)(y + 2)$ **9.** $(2x - 1)^2$ **11.** -3
13. 7   **15.** 3   **17.** 3 sec

10.7 PRACTICE AND APPLICATIONS (pp. 613–615)
19. $(q - 8)(q + 8)$ **21.** $(3c - 1)(3c + 1)$
23. $(9 - x)(9 + x)$ **25.** $(w - 3y)(w + 3y)$ **27.** $(x + 4)^2$
29. $(b - 7)^2$ **31.** $(3x + 1)^2$ **33.** $(5n - 2)^2$
35. $4(2w - 5)^2$ **37.** $(a - 2b)^2$ **39.** $4(n - 3)(n + 3)$
41. $5(c + 2)^2$ **43.** $9(3t^2 + 2t + 1)$ **45.** $3(k - 10)(k - 3)$
47. $4(b - 5)^2$ **49.** $4(2w + 5)^2$ **51.** $-\frac{1}{2}$ **53.** 4   **55.** 6
57. $\frac{7}{4}$ **59.** 5 sec   **61.** $S = 2D^2$; about 2.12 in.
63. 1 sec   **65.** 16 ft   **69.** solution   **71.** not a solution
73. $(1, -1)$ **75.** $(0, 0)$ **77.** $(2, 2)$ **79.** $6\sqrt{6}$ **81.** $10\sqrt{2}$
83. $\frac{2\sqrt{7}}{7}$ **85.** 8   **87.** $\frac{7 \pm 4\sqrt{7}}{9}$ **89.** $\frac{9 \pm \sqrt{557}}{14}$
91. $2^2 \cdot 5$ **93.** $3 \cdot 19$ **95.** $2^4 \cdot 5$ **97.** $2^3 \cdot 3 \cdot 5$
99. $3 \cdot 5 \cdot 23$ **101.** $2^3 \cdot 3 \cdot 5^2$

10.8 GUIDED PRACTICE (p. 620)   **3.** When factoring
out $-2b$, the remaining factor is $(b^2 - 6b + 7)$;
answer is $-2b(b - 7)(b + 1)$.   **5.** $3x^2(x^2 + 2)$
7. $(x - 1)(x^2 + x + 1)$ **9.** $(3x + 1)(9x^2 - 3x + 1)$
11. $2b(b - 3)(b + 3)$ **13.** $3t(t + 3)^2$ **15.** $x(x - 4)(x + 4)$

10.8 PRACTICE AND APPLICATIONS (pp. 620–622)
17. $6v(v^2 - 3)$ **19.** $3x(1 - 3x)$ **21.** $4a^2(1 - 2a^3)$
23. $5x(3x^2 - x - 2)$ **25.** $3d(6d^5 - 2d + 1)$
27. $(a + b)(a + 3)$ **29.** $(5x + 1)(2x - 3)$
31. $(10x - 7)(x - 1)$ **33.** $(c - 2)(c^2 + 2c + 4)$
35. $(m - 5)(m^2 + 5m + 25)$ **37.** $2y(y - 6)(y + 1)$
39. $4t(t - 6)(t + 6)$ **41.** $(c^3 - 12)(c + 1)$
43. $3(x + 10)(x^2 - 10x + 100)$ **45.** $-3, -4$ **47.** $9, -3$
49. $0, \frac{1}{2}, -\frac{1}{2}$ **51.** $-\frac{3}{4}, 3$ **53.** $\frac{-5 \pm \sqrt{17}}{4}$ **55.** $\frac{2 \pm 2\sqrt{43}}{12}$
57. 3 sec   **59.** $h, l = h - 3, w = h - 9$ **61.** $h = 12$ in.,
$l = 9$ in., $w = 3$ in.   **65.** $x < 1$ **67.** $-3, 3$ **69.** $7, -19$
72.

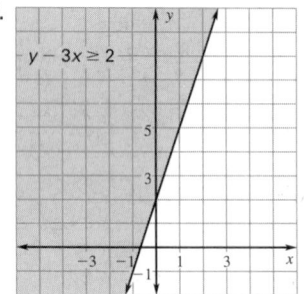
$y - 3x \geq 2$

75. $-\frac{1}{7}$ **77.** $\frac{4}{7}$ **79.** $-\frac{8}{21}$ **81.** $-\frac{4}{35}$

QUIZ 3 (p. 622) **1.** $(7x - 8)(7x + 8)$; difference of squares
2. $(11 - 3x)(11 + 3x)$; difference of squares
3. $(2t + 5)^2$; perfect square trinomial
4. $2(6 - 5y)(6 + 5y)$; difference of squares
5. $(3y + 7)^2$; perfect square trinomial   **6.** $3(n - 6)^2$;
perfect square trinomial   **7.** 4   **8.** -4 **9.** $0, 3, -12$
10. $3x^2(x + 4)$ **11.** $3x(2x + 1)$ **12.** $9x^3(2x - 1)$
13. $2x(4x^4 + 2x - 1)$ **14.** $2x(x - 2)(x - 1)$
15. $(x^2 + 4)(x + 3)$ **16.** $4(x - 5)(x^2 + 5x + 25)$
17. $0, \dfrac{5}{6}, -\dfrac{5}{6}$ **18.** 2

CHAPTER SUMMARY AND REVIEW (pp. 623–626)
1. $3x - 5$ **3.** $2x^2 + 5x + 7$ **5.** $x^3 + 2x^2 + 2x - 2$
7. $6a^3 - 15a^2 + 3a$ **9.** $a^2 + 3a - 40$
11. $d^3 - d^2 - 16d - 20$ **13.** $x^2 - 225$
15. $x^2 + 4x + 4$ **17.** $(2x + 2)^2 = 4x^2 + 8x + 4$; square
of a binomial   **19.** 2, 3   **21.** $\dfrac{3 \pm \sqrt{29}}{10}$ **23.** $0, -9, 12$
25. $-\dfrac{1}{3}, 4$ **27.** $(x + 6)(x + 4)$ **29.** $(m - 10)(m + 2)$
31. $-8, 4$ **33.** $(3x + 1)(4x + 1)$ **35.** $(4r - 3)(r + 2)$
37. $-\dfrac{1}{2}, 1$ **39.** $\dfrac{1}{2}, -4$ **41.** $\dfrac{1}{4}, -\dfrac{1}{4}$ **43.** $10, -10$
45. $-\dfrac{2}{5}$ **47.** $5y^2(y^2 - 4y + 2)$ **49.** $(y^2 - 2)(3y - 4)$
51. $(3b + 1)(9b^2 - 3b + 1)$ **53.** $5, -5$

MAINTAINING SKILLS (p. 629) **1.** $\dfrac{1}{4}, \dfrac{2}{5}$ **3.** $\dfrac{1}{3}, \dfrac{1}{2}, \dfrac{5}{6}$ **5.** $\dfrac{3}{10}$,
$\dfrac{13}{20}, \dfrac{3}{4}$ **7.** $\dfrac{5}{6}, \dfrac{5}{4}, 1\dfrac{1}{3}$ **9.** $1\dfrac{1}{12}$ **11.** $\dfrac{29}{35}$ **13.** $\dfrac{11}{30}$ **15.** $5\dfrac{1}{3}$

Chapter 11

STUDY GUIDE (p. 632) **1.** B   **2.** B   **3.** D

11.1 GUIDED PRACTICE (p. 636) **3.** 3   **5.** $\dfrac{1}{7}$ **7.** 6   **9.** no
11. yes (assuming $a, c \neq 0$)

11.1 PRACTICE AND APPLICATIONS (pp. 636–638)
13. $\dfrac{32}{9}$ **15.** 35   **17.** 3   **19.** $\dfrac{45}{8}$ **21.** $\dfrac{5}{2}$ **23.** $\dfrac{1}{3}$ **25.** ± 8
27. 10   **29.** $-\dfrac{5}{3}$ **31.** $-5, 2$ **33.** 2, 5   **35.** $4, \dfrac{5}{2}$
37. about 7.5 ft high and 5.4 ft wide   **39.** 6.875 in.
45. $y + 3 = -4(x - 5)$ **47.** $2x + y = 26$
49. $3x - 4y = -29$ **51.** $12x + y = 84$ **53.** 8   **55.** 100
57. $3\sqrt{2}$ **59.** $4\sqrt{5}$ **61.** 54   **63.** $\sqrt{7}$

65.

Decimal	0.78	0.2	$0.\overline{6}$	0.073	0.03	0.48
Percent	78%	20%	$66\dfrac{2}{3}\%$	7.3%	3%	48%
Fraction	$\dfrac{39}{50}$	$\dfrac{1}{5}$	$\dfrac{2}{3}$	$\dfrac{73}{1000}$	$\dfrac{3}{100}$	$\dfrac{12}{25}$

11.2 GUIDED PRACTICE (p. 642) **3.** Direct variation; the
graph is a line passing through the origin.   **5.** Inverse
variation; the graph represents $y = \dfrac{4}{x}$.   **7.** neither
9. inverse variation   **11.** $y = \dfrac{24}{x}$

11.2 PRACTICE AND APPLICATIONS (pp. 642–644)
13. $y = 4x$ **15.** $y = 3x$ **17.** $y = \dfrac{1}{9}x$ **19.** $y = \dfrac{21}{x}$
21. $y = \dfrac{22}{x}$ **23.** $y = \dfrac{13}{x}$ **25.** $y = \dfrac{27}{x}$
27. inversely   **29.** directly

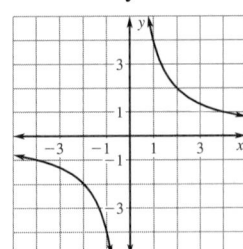

31. inverse variation   **33.** inverse variation   **35.** 116 lb
37. about 0.36 pounds per square inch   **39.** 2.2°   **45.** 4.5
47. 1   **49.** 5.5   **51.** yes   **53.** yes   **55.** $(x + 7)(x - 2)$
57. $(5x - 6)(x - 9)$ **59.** $5x^2(3x + 2)(x - 4)$
61. about 1.36 to 1   **63.** $\dfrac{2}{3}$ **65.** 2   **67.** $9\dfrac{7}{15}$ **69.** $1\dfrac{28}{55}$

11.2 TECHNOLOGY (p. 645) **1.** directly; 0.825; $y = 0.825x$

11.3 GUIDED PRACTICE (p. 649) **5.** $\dfrac{1}{8c}$ **7.** already in
simplest form   **9.** $\dfrac{2n}{3n^2 + 10}$ **11.** $y^4 - 1$ **13.** $3y + 1$
15. $x + 1$

11.3 PRACTICE AND APPLICATIONS (pp. 649–651) **17.** $3x$
19. $\dfrac{7}{25x^2}$ **21.** $\dfrac{4}{3}$ **23.** $\dfrac{t^2}{t + 2}$ **25.** $\dfrac{7}{12 + x}$ **27.** $\dfrac{7 - x^2}{6}$
29. -1 **31.** $\dfrac{x - 4}{x - 3}$ **33.** $\dfrac{x + 1}{x + 6}$ **35.** $2x - 1$ **37.** $-\dfrac{1}{x}$
39. $-\dfrac{1}{2y}$ **41.** $-\dfrac{1}{y + 3}$ **43.** $a - 2$ **45.** $x - 8$
47. $-\dfrac{4(11x - 738)}{5(x + 40)}$; 3.6 lb per in.^{2} **51.** $-\dfrac{1}{3}$ **53.** $\dfrac{24}{49}$
55. $\dfrac{9y}{20}$ **57.** $4m^3$ **59.** $\dfrac{8c^2}{3}$

61. 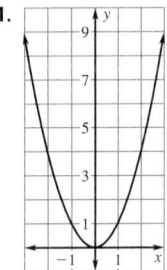   **63.**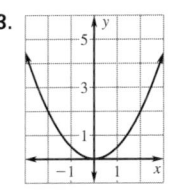

65.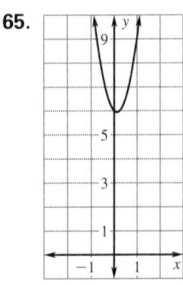

67. 2.387   **69.** 111.4   **71.** 0.02

QUIZ 1 (p. 651) **1.** 8 **2.** $\dfrac{27}{7}$ **3.** 4 **4.** $1, -\dfrac{5}{3}$ **5.** $y = 4x$

6. $y = \dfrac{3}{5}x$ **7.** $y = \dfrac{3}{2}x$ **8.** $y = \dfrac{24}{x}$ **9.** $y = \dfrac{16}{x}$ **10.** $y = \dfrac{7.5}{x}$

11. $\dfrac{3x}{2}$ **12.** $\dfrac{x-4}{x+6}$ **13.** $-\dfrac{1}{x+4}$ **14.** $\dfrac{5}{11+x}$ **15.** $x+4$

16. $2x+3$

11.4 GUIDED PRACTICE (p. 655) **3.** $\dfrac{1}{2x^2}$ **5.** $\dfrac{x}{(x+5)^2}$

7. $\dfrac{1}{4}$ **9.** The solver should have multiplied the first expression by the reciprocal of the second expression;

$\dfrac{x+3}{x-3} \div \dfrac{4x}{x^2-9} = \dfrac{x+3}{x-3} \cdot \dfrac{x^2-9}{4x} =$

$\dfrac{(x+3)(x+3)(x-3)}{(x-3)(4x)} = \dfrac{(x+3)^2}{4x}.$

11.4 PRACTICE AND APPLICATIONS (pp. 655–657) **11.** x

13. $\dfrac{6}{35x}$ **15.** $-\dfrac{1}{4(x-7)}$ **17.** $\dfrac{z(z+1)}{10(z-7)}$ **19.** 3 **21.** x

23. $\dfrac{c-8}{4c^2(c+1)}$ **25.** $9x$ **27.** $2(y-3)$ **29.** $x+3$ **31.** $5x$

33. $\dfrac{5}{6x}$ **35.** $\dfrac{x+2}{2(x-2)}$ **37.** $\dfrac{x(x-6)}{x+3}$ **39.** $\dfrac{x(2x+1)}{2(x-1)^2}$

41. $-\dfrac{x+6}{5x^2}$ **43.** $\dfrac{1}{(2y+3)(y-2)}$

45. $\dfrac{4x+3}{(x-1)(4x-3)(x+1)}$ **47.** $\dfrac{x+3}{x+1}$ **49.** The ratio approaches 1.

55.

Input x	2	3	4	5	6
Output y	11	12	13	14	15

57. $-19 < x < 5$ **59.** $x \le -46 \text{ or } x \ge 20$
61. $x < -22 \text{ or } x > 12$ **63.** $-3 \pm 2\sqrt{3}$ **65.** $-\dfrac{5}{3}, -2$
67. $\dfrac{1}{2}, -\dfrac{5}{3}$ **69.** $2x^2 + 11x - 18$
71. $16p^3 + 11p^2 - 8p + 8$ **73.** 0.85 **75.** 1.74
77. 1.125 **79.** 1.12

11.5 GUIDED PRACTICE (p. 660) **3.** $\dfrac{5(y+2)}{y+3}$ **5.** $\dfrac{7}{3r}$

7. $-\dfrac{5}{c^2-4}$ **9.** $-\dfrac{12}{y-2}$ **11.** $\dfrac{2}{r+4}$

11.5 PRACTICE AND APPLICATIONS (pp. 660–662)

13. $\dfrac{7}{x+7}$ **15.** 2 **17.** $\dfrac{1}{2}$ **19.** $\dfrac{t+14}{3t}$ **21.** $\dfrac{2-5x}{3x-1}$ **23.** 2

25. $\dfrac{a-1}{a-5}$ **27.** $\dfrac{x+5}{x+2}$ **29.** $\dfrac{2x+3}{x+1}$ **31.** $\dfrac{y-3}{y-7}$ **33.** The solver multiplied the rational expressions rather than adding them; $\dfrac{y+2}{y+3} + \dfrac{y-4}{y+3} = \dfrac{2y-2}{y+3}.$ **35.** $\dfrac{3x+9}{x-9}$

37. $-\dfrac{2}{x-3}$ **39.** $\dfrac{2(3x-4)^2}{x^2}$ **41.** $\dfrac{14x}{x+1}$ **43.** 1 joule

45. $\dfrac{x}{x-10}$ joules **49.** $\dfrac{x^5}{y^6}$ **51.** $\dfrac{y^5}{2x^8}$ **53.** $\dfrac{1}{1296c^4}$ **55.** c^2d

57. $\dfrac{1}{p^2}$ **59.** $\dfrac{1}{a^5}$ **61.** m^{16} **63.** $-\dfrac{v^9}{8u^3}$ **65.** 1.6×10^2
67. 8.1×10^{-7} **69.** 1.6×10^{-3} **71.** 9, 11, 13 **73.** 42, 35, 27 **75.** $8, \dfrac{19}{2}, 11$

11.6 GUIDED PRACTICE (p. 667) **3.** $\dfrac{x}{3}$ **5.** $\dfrac{(x+2)(2x+7)}{(x+1)(2x+3)}$
7. -1

11.6 PRACTICE AND APPLICATIONS (pp. 667–669) **9.** 15
11. $7c^5$ **13.** $5b$ **15.** $90x^3$ **17.** $24y^2$ **19.** $21a^7 + 7a^6$
21. $8a^4 - 12a^3$ **23.** $\dfrac{155}{78x}$ **25.** $\dfrac{4x+5}{4}$ **27.** $\dfrac{7n^2+1}{30n}$

29. $\dfrac{63x-4}{14x^2}$ **31.** $-\dfrac{3x+1}{6x^2}$ **33.** $\dfrac{19x-11}{33x}$

35. $\dfrac{2(x^2-20)}{(x-10)(x+6)}$ **37.** $\dfrac{4x^2+17x+5}{(3x-1)(x+1)}$

39. $-\dfrac{x^2+14x-2}{(3x-1)(x-2)}$ **41.** $-\dfrac{5x(x-3)}{(x-1)(x+4)}$

43. $T = \dfrac{x}{10} + \dfrac{8-x}{20}$, where x is the number of miles in the woods.

45.

Distance (woods), x	0	2	4	6	8
Total time, T	0.4	0.5	0.6	0.7	0.8

47. $T = \dfrac{48x}{(x-2)(x+2)}$ **49.** $\dfrac{2(2x^2+x+1)}{(2x+1)(2x-1)}$ **51.** $\dfrac{3}{35}$
55. $y + 2 = 2(x+3)$ **57.** $y - 6 = \dfrac{1}{2}(x+3)$

59. $y = \dfrac{3}{7}(x-7)$ **61.** $\dfrac{1}{2x}$ **63.** $\dfrac{1}{2x^4}$ **65.** $\dfrac{1}{12x}$ **67.** $\dfrac{3p^2}{4q}$
69. $6x^2 - 5x + 7 = 0$ **71.** $3y^2 - y - 4 = 0$
73. $12x^2 + 5x - 7 = 0$ **75.** $|x - 8500| \le 1000$
77. 0.315 **79.** 0.296 **81.** -0.708 **83.** -0.545 **85.** 0.104
87. -0.514

11.7 GUIDED PRACTICE (p. 674) **3.** $3x$ **5.** $3x^3$ **7.** $6, -1$
9. 7 **11.** 2

11.7 PRACTICE AND APPLICATIONS (pp. 674–677) **13.** 28
15. 13 **17.** $\dfrac{1}{2}$ **19.** -7 **21.** $10, -2$ **23.** $0, 16$ **25.** $\dfrac{1}{3}$
27. 2 **29.** 2 **31.** $-\dfrac{6}{7}$ **33.** $\dfrac{2}{3}$ **35.** $3, -\dfrac{1}{4}$ **37.** $0, 3$
39. -12 **41.** $3, -2$ **43.** $7, -6$ **45.** -4 **47.** $3, 6$
49. about 6.43 hours, or 6 hours 26 minutes; about 128.57 hours, or 128 hours 34 minutes **51.** $1.00 per pound **53.** 7 dimes, 5 quarters **61.** 9, 8, 7, 6, 5
63. $0, -1, -4, -9, -16$ **65.** $0, \dfrac{1}{2}, 2, \dfrac{9}{2}, 8$ **67.** 36 **69.** 1
71. 125 **73.** $6\sqrt{2}$ **75.** $\sqrt{13}$ **77.** $\dfrac{3\sqrt{10}}{4}$ **79.** $\dfrac{21\sqrt{17}}{8}$
81. $3\sqrt{3}$ **83.** $3\sqrt{3}$ **85.** $\dfrac{7}{8}$ **87.** $\dfrac{31}{45}$ **89.** 1 **91.** $-\dfrac{7}{24}$
93. 1 **95.** $\dfrac{89}{220}$

QUIZ 2 (p. 677) **1.** $\dfrac{7x^2}{2}$ **2.** 10 **3.** $\dfrac{3}{2}$ **4.** $\dfrac{x-3}{x+2}$ **5.** $\dfrac{1}{x-7}$

6. $\dfrac{1}{x+1}$ **7.** $\dfrac{7x^2-7x+6}{(x+1)(x-1)}$ **8.** $\dfrac{x(x^2+2x-2)}{(x-3)(x+2)}$ **9.** 4

10. -2 **11.** 3 **12.** 130 **13.** $\dfrac{15}{x+2}; \dfrac{15}{x-2}$

14. $\dfrac{15}{x+2} + \dfrac{15}{x-2} = \dfrac{30x}{(x+2)(x-2)}$ **15.** 18 hours
16. about 1.71 hours, or 1 hour 43 minutes

EXTENSION EXERCISES (p. 680) **1.** $\dfrac{10}{x-9}$ **3.** $\dfrac{2x-1}{x^2}$

5. $\dfrac{x(11x+7)}{(x-7)(x+7)}$ **7.** $\dfrac{3x+5}{3x+7}$ **9.** $-\dfrac{x+3}{x^2}$

11. $-\dfrac{18}{(x+9)(x-9)}$ **13.** $\dfrac{3}{x(x+15)}$ **15.** $\dfrac{3(x-2)^2}{2x}$

17. $(x-2)^2$ **19.** $\dfrac{x(x+3)}{x+1}$ **21.** $\dfrac{x^2}{(2x+1)^2}$ **23.** $\dfrac{(x+5)^2}{(x+2)^2}$

25. $f(x) = \dfrac{1}{x-9}$ **27.** $g(x) = \dfrac{x}{2x+3}$

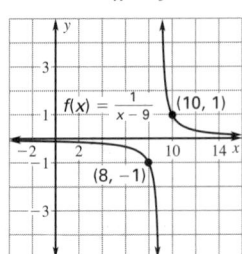

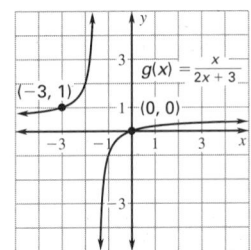

CHAPTER SUMMARY AND REVIEW (pp. 681–684) **1.** $\dfrac{8}{7}$

3. 4 **5.** $y = 5x$ **7.** $y = \dfrac{4}{5}x$ **9.** $y = 14x$ **11.** $y = \dfrac{36}{x}$

13. $y = \dfrac{450}{x}$ **15.** $y = \dfrac{22}{x}$ **17.** $\dfrac{x}{3x^2+1}$ **19.** $\dfrac{7x(x-2)}{3x+2}$

21. $\dfrac{x+2}{x+7}$ **23.** $\dfrac{x+7}{x-1}$ **25.** $\dfrac{y-8}{2y-3}$ **27.** $20x^2$

29. $\dfrac{8(2x+7)}{x-1}$ **31.** $9x$ **33.** $\dfrac{x+2}{x}$ **35.** 1 **37.** $\dfrac{x+2}{4}$

39. $\dfrac{4x-5}{x-2}$ **41.** $\dfrac{1}{6}$ **43.** $-4, 2$ **45.** no solution

MAINTAINING SKILLS (p. 687) **1.** $\dfrac{4\sqrt{2}}{7}$ **3.** $\dfrac{\sqrt{5}}{3}$ **5.** $\dfrac{11\sqrt{3}}{12}$

7. $2\sqrt{2}$ **9.** $(a-9)^2$ **11.** $(y-11)^2$ **13.** $(15+r)^2$ or
$(r+15)^2$ **15.** $(2x+5)^2$ **17.** $(4-7x)^2$ or $(7x-4)^2$

Chapter 12

STUDY GUIDE (p. 690) **1.** D **2.** A **3.** B

12.1 GUIDED PRACTICE (p. 695) **3.** 0, 4, 5.7, 6.9, 8
5. 4, 7, 8.2, 9.2, 10 **7.** 1.4, 1.7, 2, 2.2, 2.4 **9.** domain:
all nonnegative real numbers; range: all nonnegative
real numbers **11.** domain: all nonnegative real numbers;
range: all real numbers ≥ -10 **13.** domain: all real
numbers ≥ -5; range: all nonnegative real numbers
15. all nonnegative real numbers

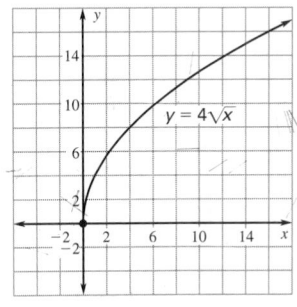

17. all real numbers ≥ -1

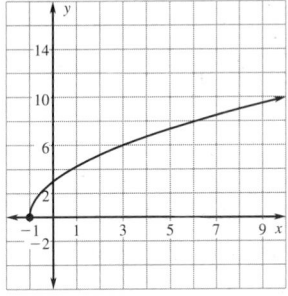

19. 1200 gal/min

12.1 PRACTICE AND APPLICATIONS (pp. 695–697)
21. -10 **23.** 6 **25.** 6 **27.** 4
29. All nonnegative real numbers. *Sample table:*

x	0	1	4	9
$y = 6\sqrt{x}$	0	6	12	18

31. All real numbers $\geq \dfrac{10}{3}$. *Sample table:*

x	$\dfrac{10}{3}$	$\dfrac{11}{3}$	4	5	6
$y = \sqrt{(3x-10)}$	0	1	≈ 1.4	≈ 2.2	≈ 2.8

33. All nonnegative real numbers. *Sample table:*

x	0	1	4	9	16
$y = 4 + \sqrt{x}$	4	5	6	7	8

35. All real numbers ≥ -9. *Sample table:*

x	-9	-8	-5	0	7
$y = \sqrt{x+9}$	0	1	2	3	4

37. All nonnegative real numbers. *Sample table:*

x	0	1	4	9
$y = x\sqrt{x}$	0	1	8	27

39. incorrect statement; $S = 42$ mph
41. domain: all nonnegative
real numbers; range: all
nonnegative real numbers

47. domain: all nonnegative
real numbers; range: all
real numbers ≥ -3

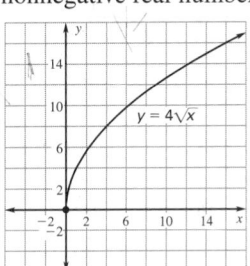

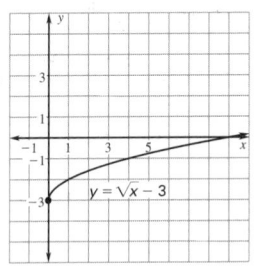

49. domain: all nonnegative real numbers; range: all real numbers ≤ 6

55. domain: all real numbers $\geq -\dfrac{5}{2}$; range: all nonnegative real numbers

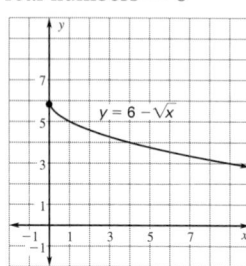

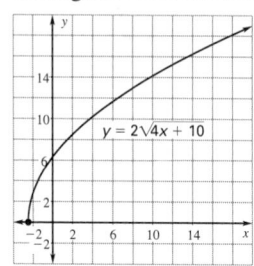

57. twice as fast **63.** $2\sqrt{15}$ **65.** $6\sqrt{10}$ **67.** $2\sqrt{5}$
69. $\sqrt{11}$ **71.** $-1.24, 3.24$ **73.** $-3.30, 0.30$
75. $0.19, 1.31$ **77.** $3x^2 + 5x - 28$
79. $10x^2 - 33x + 27$ **81.** $2x^3 + x^2 + x - 1$ **83.** $\dfrac{8}{3}$
85. $\dfrac{x}{x+1}$ **87.** $\dfrac{1}{2}$ **89.** 24 **91.** 35 **93.** 0.2635

12.2 GUIDED PRACTICE (p. 701) **3.** $4 + 6\sqrt{5}$ **5.** $5\sqrt{6}$
7. $16 + 6\sqrt{7}$ **9.** $\dfrac{4\sqrt{13}}{13}$ **11.** $\dfrac{3\sqrt{10}}{5}$

12.2 PRACTICE AND APPLICATIONS (pp. 701–703)
13. $7\sqrt{7}$ **15.** $-\sqrt{3}$ **17.** $\sqrt{3} + 5\sqrt{5}$ **19.** $5\sqrt{2}$
21. $\sqrt{5}$ **23.** $12\sqrt{5}$ **25.** 15 **27.** $3\sqrt{10}$ **29.** $6 - \sqrt{6}$
31. $4\sqrt{5} + 5$ **33.** $5\sqrt{6} + 3$ **35.** -12 **37.** 5 **39.** 33
41. $\dfrac{5\sqrt{7}}{7}$ **43.** $\dfrac{\sqrt{3}}{4}$ **45.** $\dfrac{\sqrt{30}}{3}$ **47.** $\dfrac{12 - 2\sqrt{3}}{11}$
49. $\dfrac{2 - \sqrt{2}}{2}$ **51.** $\dfrac{3\sqrt{5} + 5}{4}$ **53.** $\sqrt{12}$ and $\sqrt{13}$ are not like terms; $\sqrt{12} + \sqrt{13} = 2\sqrt{3} + \sqrt{13}$ **55.** You ran $16\sqrt{5} - 32 \approx 3.78$ ft/sec faster. **61.** 43.75% **63.** 147
65. $-5, 3$ **67.** $13, -2$ **69.** $-\dfrac{2}{3}, -1$ **71.** -30
73. All nonnegative real numbers. *Sample table:*

x	0	1	4	9	16
$y = \sqrt{x} - 3$	-3	-2	-1	0	1

75. All nonnegative real numbers. *Sample table:*

x	0	1	4	9	16
$y = 6\sqrt{x}$	0	6	12	18	24

77. All real numbers ≥ -3. *Sample table:*

x	-3	-2	1	6	13
$y = \sqrt{x+3}$	0	1	2	3	4

79. $>$ **81.** $=$ **83.** $>$ **85.** $<$ **87.** $<$ **89.** $=$ **91.** $<$
93. $>$ **95.** $<$

12.3 GUIDED PRACTICE (p. 707) **3.** 64 **5.** 196 **7.** 36
9. no solution **11.** 4 **13.** 25 **15.** 3 **17.** 3

12.3 PRACTICE AND APPLICATIONS (pp. 707–709)
19. 1 **21.** 100 **23.** 256 **25.** 6 **27.** 3 **29.** $\dfrac{1}{3}$ **31.** 48
33. Line 2 should be $(\sqrt{x})^2 = 7^2$; $x = 49$. **35.** 75
37. about 28.4 lb/in.² **39.** *Sample answer:* $\sqrt{2x - 20} = 4$
41. 36 **43.** no solution **45.** no solution **47.** 7
49. no solution **51.** 3 **53.** 3 **55.** 270 m/sec²
57. false; $\sqrt{36} \neq -6$ **61.** $\pm\sqrt{11}$ **63.** ±2 **65.** $\pm\sqrt{3}$
67. $4x^2 - 12x + 9$ **69.** $9x^2 - 25y^2$
71. $4a^2 - 36ab + 81b^2$ **73.** $(x - 6)^2$ **75.** $\dfrac{9}{19}$ **77.** $\dfrac{10}{13}$
79. $\dfrac{50}{57}$ **81.** $\dfrac{9}{34}$

QUIZ 1 (p. 709)
1. domain: all nonnegative real numbers; range: all nonnegative real numbers
2. domain: all real numbers ≥ 9; range: all nonnegative real numbers

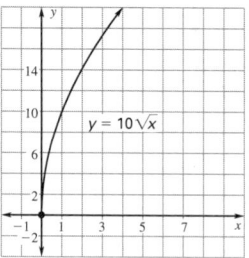

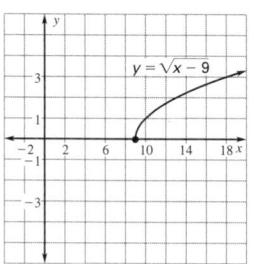

3. domain: all real numbers $\geq \dfrac{1}{2}$; range: all nonnegative real numbers
4. domain: all nonnegative real numbers; range: all real numbers ≥ -2

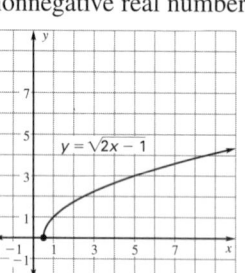

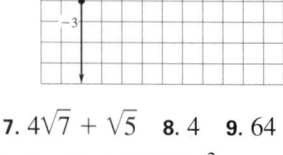

5. $18\sqrt{10}$ **6.** $3\sqrt{6} + 3$ **7.** $4\sqrt{7} + \sqrt{5}$ **8.** 4 **9.** 64
10. $-\dfrac{1}{3}$ **11.** 6 **12.** 7 **13.** 3 **14.** 1.78 lb/in.²

12.4 GUIDED PRACTICE (p. 713) **3.** 7 **5.** 125 **7.** 27
9. 729

12.4 PRACTICE AND APPLICATIONS (pp. 713–714)
11. $11^{1/3}$ **13.** $16^{5/2}$ **15.** $\sqrt{7}$ **17.** $\left(\sqrt[3]{8}\right)^7$ **19.** 100 **21.** 2
23. 16 **25.** 81 **27.** 25 **29.** 256 **31.** 16 **33.** 36 **35.** 20
37. 64 **39.** $x^{5/6}$ or $\left(\sqrt[6]{x}\right)^5$ **41.** $x^{1/2}y^{1/2}$ or $\sqrt{xy}$ **43.** y^2
45. sometimes **49.** $\pm2\sqrt{14}$ **51.** ±6 **53.** $\pm\dfrac{2\sqrt{5}}{5}$
55. $-4, 8$ **57.** prime **59.** composite; $3 \cdot 5^2$
61. composite; $2 \cdot 3^2$ **63.** composite; $3 \cdot 23$

12.5 GUIDED PRACTICE (p. 719)   **3.** 100   **5.** 25   **7.** 121

9. $\dfrac{3 \pm \sqrt{41}}{2}$ **11.** $-5 \pm \sqrt{35}$ **13.** $-13, -1$

15. $-\dfrac{2}{3}, -5$ **17.** $\dfrac{5 \pm \sqrt{85}}{6}$ **19.** $\pm\dfrac{\sqrt{6}}{3}$

12.5 PRACTICE AND APPLICATIONS (pp. 719–721)
21. 16   **23.** 121   **25.** 400   **27.** 9   **29.** 2, 6   **31.** $2, -8$
33. $-5 \pm \sqrt{37}$ **35.** $3, -13$ **37.** 2, 22   **39.** $1 \pm \sqrt{6}$
41. $2 \pm \sqrt{5}$ **43.** $-7 \pm \sqrt{51}$ **45.** $-5 \pm 2\sqrt{7}$
47. $-11 \pm 2\sqrt{30}$ **49.** $-4 \pm \sqrt{22}$ **51.** $-10 \pm 7\sqrt{2}$
53. $6 \pm \sqrt{39}$ **55.** $1 \pm \sqrt{5}$ **57.** about 12.25 ft by 12.25 ft
59. Base is about 6.8 ft; height is about 17.6 ft.   **61.** ± 3
63. $-7, 2$ **65.** $-3, \dfrac{4}{3}$ **67.** $3 \pm \sqrt{2}$ **69.** $-\dfrac{1}{2}, -3$
71. $12 \pm 5\sqrt{6}$ **73.** no solution   **75.** about 8.6 ft
81. (4, 0)   **83.** ± 7 **85.** ± 9 **87.** $\pm 4\sqrt{10}$ **89.** no
solution   **91.** no solution   **93.** $3, -1$ **95.** $-4, 8$
97. $-5, -6$ **99.** 3   **101.** $(x + 5)(x - 4)$ **103.** $(x + 2)^2$
105. $(2x - 3)(x + 1)$ **107.** $\dfrac{3}{5}$ **109.** $\dfrac{11}{100}$ **111.** $\dfrac{1}{100}$
113. $\dfrac{3}{100}$ **115.** $\dfrac{3}{8}$

12.6 GUIDED PRACTICE (p. 727)   **3.** $c = 25$ **5.** $a = 8$
7. $a = 60$ **9.** $b = 16$ **11.** 6, 8

12.6 PRACTICE AND APPLICATIONS (pp. 727–729)
13. $b = \sqrt{7} \approx 2.65$ **15.** $a = 2\sqrt{10} \approx 6.32$
17. $b = 5\sqrt{3} \approx 8.66$ **19.** $c = 2\sqrt{17} \approx 8.25$
21. $a = \sqrt{91} \approx 9.54$ **23.** $b = \sqrt{33} \approx 5.74$
25. $x - 6 = 18, x = 24$ **27.** $x = 5, x + 5 = 10$
29. $x = 1, \sqrt{2}x = \sqrt{2}$ **31.** about 127.3 ft
33. about 12.2 in.   **35.** about 4.9 ft   **37.** right triangle;
$5^2 + 12^2 = 13^2$ **39.** right triangle; $11^2 + 60^2 = 61^2$
41. not a right triangle; $3^2 + 9^2 \neq 10^2$ **43.** not a right
triangle; $6^2 + 9^2 \neq 11^2$

47. 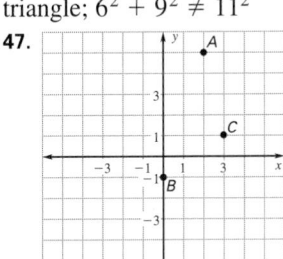   **49.**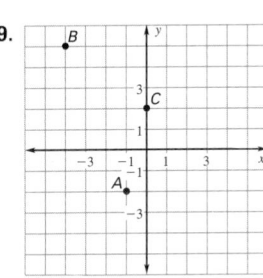

51. zero   **53.** two   **55.** two   **57.** 35   **59.** 50   **61.** 51

QUIZ 2 (p. 729)   **1.** 2   **2.** 42   **3.** 9   **4.** $3 \pm \sqrt{2}$
5. $-2 \pm \sqrt{5}$ **6.** $-1 \pm \sqrt{3}$ **7.** not a right triangle;
$6^2 + 9^2 \neq 11^2$ **8.** right triangle; $12^2 + 35^2 = 37^2$
9. right triangle; $1^2 + 1^2 = (\sqrt{2})^2$ **10.** 2000 ft

12.7 GUIDED PRACTICE (p. 733)   **3.** 7.62   **5.** right
triangle   **7.** not a right triangle   **9.** 25 yd

12.7 PRACTICE AND APPLICATIONS (pp. 733–735)
11. 12.08   **13.** 8.60   **15.** 4.24   **17.** 9   **19.** 21.26

21. 16.16   **23.** 12.73   **25.** right triangle   **27.** not a right
triangle   **29.** right triangle   **31.** $AB = 4\sqrt{2} \approx 5.66$,
$BC = \sqrt{17} \approx 4.12$, $CA = 5$ **33.** 269 mi
35. about 670 mi   **37.** about 457 mi
43. $9(3x - 4)(3x + 4)$ **45.** $(x + 6)^2$
47. $(3x + 1)^2$ **49.** $2(6 - 5p)(6 + 5p)$
51. $3y(y + 6)(y - 1)$ **53.** $2x^2(x - 2)(x + 2)$
55. $\dfrac{x}{7}$ **57.** $4x$ **59.** $\dfrac{7 - x}{4x}$ **61.** $x + 6$ **63.** $9a - 36$
65. $\dfrac{x + 12}{x}$ **67.** $\dfrac{13}{x}$ **69.** $\dfrac{43}{12x}$ **71.** 40%   **73.** $33.\overline{3}\%$
75. 62.5%   **77.** 4%

12.8 GUIDED PRACTICE (p. 738)   **3.** $\left(\dfrac{3}{2}, 3\right)$ **5.** $(-4, 0)$
7. (0, 5)   **9.** (2, 1); $d = \sqrt{17} \approx 4.12$ **11.** (3, 4);
$d = \sqrt{5} \approx 2.24$ **13.** $(-1, 7); d = \sqrt{5} \approx 2.24$

12.8 PRACTICE AND APPLICATIONS (pp. 738–739)
15. (3, 3)   **17.** (3, 3)   **19.** $\left(-\dfrac{1}{2}, \dfrac{1}{2}\right)$ **21.** $\left(-\dfrac{5}{2}, -\dfrac{3}{2}\right)$
23. $\left(-\dfrac{5}{2}, -4\right)$ **25.** $\left(\dfrac{1}{2}, 1\right); d = \dfrac{\sqrt{5}}{2} \approx 1.12$ **27.** (3, −2);
$d = \sqrt{13} \approx 3.61$ **29.** $\left(-1, \dfrac{5}{2}\right); d = \dfrac{\sqrt{97}}{2} \approx 4.92$
31. $(-2, 5); d = \sqrt{193} \approx 13.89$ **33.** $\left(\dfrac{5}{2}, 8\right), (7, 1)$,
$\left(-\dfrac{17}{2}, 1\right)$ **35.** (39.95° N, 115.35° W)   **37.** (1, 1)
or 1 mi east and 1 mi north of the starting point, $\sqrt{13}$, or
3.61 mi   **39.** $\left(\dfrac{1}{3}, -\dfrac{1}{9}\right)$ **41.** (2, −1)   **43.** $\left(\dfrac{3}{2}, 0\right)$; one
45. $=$ **47.** $<$

12.9 GUIDED PRACTICE (p. 743)   **3.** identity property
of multiplication   **5.** distributive property   **7.** identity
property of addition

12.9 PRACTICE AND APPLICATIONS (p. 744–746)
9. inverse property of addition; identity property of
addition   **13.** *Sample answer:* $a = 3, b = 2$
15. *Sample answer:* $a = 3, b = 2$ **17.** Yes; the map
cannot be colored with three different colors so that no
two countries that share a border have the same color.
27. 10,000   **29.** 20   **31.** 2 solutions   **33.** 1 solution
35. no real solution   **37.** not a solution   **39.** solution
41. $2\dfrac{3}{4}$ **43.** $\dfrac{11}{12}$ **45.** $-\dfrac{7}{8}$

QUIZ 3 (p. 746)   **1.** right triangle   **2.** right triangle
3. 13.42; (4, −3)   **4.** 7.21; (4, −8)   **5.** 16.12; (4, −7)
6. 16; (−8, 0)   **7.** 6; (0, 4)   **8.** 10.30; $\left(-\dfrac{3}{2}, \dfrac{5}{2}\right)$
9. *Sample answer:* $a = 2, b = 3, c = -5$ **10.** *Sample
answer:* $a = 2, b = 3$

1. domain: all nonnegative real numbers; range: all nonnegative real numbers **3.** domain: all nonnegative real numbers; range: all real numbers ≥ 3

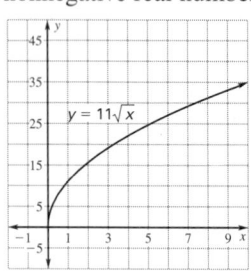
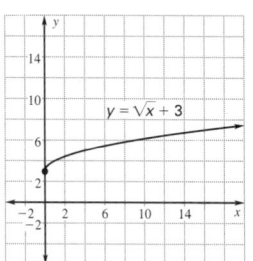

5. $3\sqrt{5} - \sqrt{3}$ **7.** $6\sqrt{2} - 8\sqrt{3}$ **9.** $\dfrac{48 + 8\sqrt{7}}{29}$

11. no solution **13.** 26 **15.** 9 **17.** 16 **19.** 16 **21.** 22

23. $2 \pm 2\sqrt{3}$ **25.** $8 \pm 2\sqrt{14}$ **27.** $\dfrac{1 \pm \sqrt{13}}{2}$

29. $c = 2\sqrt{13}$ **31.** $b = 5$, $2b + 2 = 12$ **33.** not a right triangle; $10^2 + 14^2 \neq 17^2$ **35.** 9.49 **37.** 10.77

39. $(2, -1)$ **41.** $\left(-\dfrac{1}{2}, -\dfrac{13}{2}\right)$

43. *Sample answer:*

$(c)(-b) = (c)[(-1)(b)]$ Multiplication property of -1

$= [(c)(-1)](b)$ Associative property of multiplication

$= [(-1)(c)](b)$ Commutative property of multiplication

$= (-1)[(c)(b)]$ Associative property of multiplication

$= -cb$ Multiplication property of -1

CHAPTERS 1–12 CUMULATIVE PRACTICE (pp. 754–755)

1. $\dfrac{m}{7} \geq 16$; $m \geq 112$ **3.** $t = 3d$; $t = 9$ mi **5.** 25

7. -63 **9.** -27 **11.** $\dfrac{34}{3}$ **13.** -49 **15.** -1.64

17. -5.56 **19.** *Sample answer:* $y = \dfrac{2}{3}x - \dfrac{10}{3}$

21. function; domain: $-1, 1, 3, 5$; range: $-1, 1, 3$

23. function; domain: $-2, -1, 0, 1, 2$; range: $-2, -1, 0, 1$ **25.** $4x - 5y = 15$

27. $-\dfrac{5}{4} \leq x < 3$

29. $x > 3$ or $x < 2$

31. $(24, 21)$ **33.** b^6; 64 **35.** $-8a^3b^6$; -512 **37.** $\dfrac{4b^5}{a^4}$; 128 **39.** 2 solutions; $\pm\dfrac{\sqrt{39}}{3}$ **41.** 1 solution; -1

43. $(x - 28)(x + 4)$ **45.** $(2x + 3)^2$ **47.** $(x - 7)^2$

49. $-\dfrac{3}{2}, \dfrac{5}{3}$ **51.** -2 **53.** $0, -3, -6$ **55.** $\dfrac{2}{x - 3}$

57. $\dfrac{1}{3x}$ **59.** $\dfrac{2x^2 - 7x}{(x + 4)(x - 1)}$ **61.** $-15\sqrt{2}$ **63.** $\dfrac{77 + 11\sqrt{3}}{46}$

65. $6 \pm \sqrt{55}$ **67.** $3 \pm \sqrt{22}$ **69.** $-11 \pm 2\sqrt{29}$

71. 4.47; $(3, 5)$ **73.** 9.43; $\left(2, -\dfrac{1}{2}\right)$ **75.** 12.21; $\left(5, 7\dfrac{1}{2}\right)$

77. 11.18; $\left(2, 4\dfrac{1}{2}\right)$

Skills Review Handbook

DECIMALS (p. 760) 1. 14.42 **3.** 122.312 **5.** 25.72
7. 1.02 **9.** 2.458 **11.** 7.07 **13.** 40.625 **15.** 3.6
17. 520.37908 **19.** 16.7 **21.** 18.4 **23.** 4220
25. $62.44; $7.56

FACTORS AND MULTIPLES (p. 762) 1. 1, 2, 3, 6, 9, 18
3. 1, 7, 11, 77 **5.** 1, 3, 9, 27 **7.** 1, 2, 3, 6, 7, 14, 21, 42
9. 3^3 **11.** 2^5 **13.** $5 \cdot 11$ **15.** $2^2 \cdot 37$ **17.** 1 **19.** 1, 5
21. 1, 3, 9 **23.** 1, 5 **25.** 5 **27.** 1 **29.** 14 **31.** 51
33. 35 **35.** 208 **37.** 45 **39.** 42 **41.** 12 **43.** 30
45. 140 **47.** 51

FRACTIONS (p. 766) 1. $\dfrac{1}{7}$ **3.** $\dfrac{12}{7}$, or $1\dfrac{5}{7}$ **5.** 20 **7.** $\dfrac{13}{5}$, or $2\dfrac{3}{5}$ **9.** $\dfrac{5}{6}$ **11.** 3 **13.** $\dfrac{5}{32}$ **15.** $\dfrac{7}{2}$, or $3\dfrac{1}{2}$ **17.** $\dfrac{5}{6}$ **19.** $\dfrac{1}{3}$

21. $\dfrac{5}{8}$ **23.** $1\dfrac{1}{30}$ **25.** $2\dfrac{3}{8}$ **27.** $1\dfrac{13}{24}$ **29.** $8\dfrac{1}{5}$ **31.** $3\dfrac{7}{16}$

33. $\dfrac{1}{4}$ **35.** $\dfrac{1}{6}$ **37.** $\dfrac{2}{3}$ **39.** $7\dfrac{2}{3}$ **41.** $1\dfrac{1}{6}$ **43.** $1\dfrac{1}{5}$ **45.** 6

47. $\dfrac{17}{20}$ **49.** $\dfrac{13}{16}$ **51.** 1 **53.** $5\dfrac{3}{8}$ **55.** $\dfrac{7}{18}$ **57.** $2\dfrac{5}{6}$ **59.** $1\dfrac{3}{5}$

61. $1\dfrac{11}{40}$ **63.** $\dfrac{11}{40}$

WRITING FRACTIONS AND DECIMALS (p. 768) 1. 0.25
3. 0.08 **5.** $0.\overline{3}$ **7.** $0.\overline{90}$ **9.** $\dfrac{1}{2}$ **11.** $\dfrac{289}{1000}$ **13.** $\dfrac{7}{9}$ **15.** $\dfrac{613}{999}$

FRACTIONS, DECIMALS, AND PERCENTS (p. 769) 1. 0.63; $\dfrac{63}{100}$ **3.** 0.24; $\dfrac{6}{25}$ **5.** 0.17; $\dfrac{17}{100}$ **7.** 0.45; $\dfrac{9}{20}$ **9.** $0.\overline{3}$; $\dfrac{1}{3}$

11. 0.625; $\dfrac{5}{8}$ **13.** 0.052; $\dfrac{13}{250}$ **15.** 0.0012; $\dfrac{3}{2500}$ **17.** 8%; $\dfrac{2}{25}$ **19.** 150%; $\dfrac{3}{2}$ **21.** 5%; $\dfrac{1}{20}$ **23.** 480%; $4\dfrac{4}{5}$

25. 375%; $3\dfrac{3}{4}$ **27.** 52%; $\dfrac{13}{25}$ **29.** 0.5%; $\dfrac{1}{200}$ **31.** 0.7; 70% **33.** 0.44; 44% **35.** 0.375; 37.5% **37.** 5.125; 512.5% **39.** 0.875; 87.5%

COMPARING AND ORDERING NUMBERS (p. 771)
1. $12{,}428 < 15{,}116$ **3.** $-140{,}999 > -142{,}109$
5. $0.40506 > 0.00456$ **7.** $1005.2 < 1050.7$
9. $-0.058 > -0.102$ **11.** $17\dfrac{1}{4} = 17\dfrac{2}{8}$ **13.** $-\dfrac{5}{9} = -\dfrac{15}{27}$
15. $\dfrac{1}{8} > \dfrac{1}{9}$ **17.** $42\dfrac{1}{5} > 41\dfrac{7}{8}$ **19.** $32{,}227 > 32{,}226.5$
21. $-17\dfrac{5}{6} < -17\dfrac{5}{7}$ **23.** $-45{,}617; -45{,}242; -40{,}099;$
$-40{,}071$ **25.** 9.003, 9.027, 9.10, 9.27, 9.3 **27.** $\dfrac{1}{3}, \dfrac{3}{8},$
$\dfrac{5}{6}, \dfrac{5}{4}$ **29.** $\dfrac{15}{16}, 1\dfrac{1}{8}, 1\dfrac{2}{5}, \dfrac{5}{3}, \dfrac{7}{4}$ **31.** $-1\dfrac{1}{3}, -\dfrac{5}{4}, -\dfrac{7}{8}, -\dfrac{5}{12}$

PERIMETER, AREA, AND VOLUME (p. 773) **1.** 34
3. 84 ft **5.** 72 ft **7.** 841 yd^2 **9.** 12.25 in.^{2} **11.** 20 in.^{2}
13. 15,625 ft^3 **15.** 420 yd^3 **17.** 212 in.^{3}

ESTIMATION (p. 776) **1–53.** Estimates may vary. **1.** 50
3. 2400 **5.** 500 **7.** 20 **9.** 1600 **11.** 700 **13.** 22.5
15. 481 **17.** 1340 **19.** 41 **21.** 209 **23.** 267 **25.** 2500
27. 30,000 **29.** 30 **31.** 3 **33.** 40 **35.** 4 **37.** 750
39. 80,000 **41.** 7000 **43.** 23 **45.** 10 **47.** 50 **49.** 16
51. 19 **53.** 18

DATA DISPLAYS (p. 779) **1–10.** Sample answers are given.
1. 0 to 25 by fives **3.** 0 to 20 by fives
5.

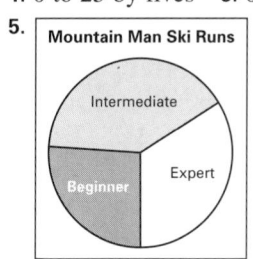

Mountain Man Ski Runs

7.

Company Stock

9.

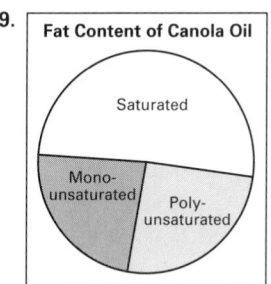

Fat Content of Canola Oil

MEASURES OF CENTRAL TENDENCY (p. 780)
1. 1.3; 0.5; 0 **3.** 30; 30; no mode **5.** ≈550.1; 487; 376

PROBLEM SOLVING (p. 782) **1.** 5 salads, 3 cartons of milk
3. $26.25 **5.** no later than 6:25 A.M. **7.** 10 groups
9. The problem cannot be solved; not enough information
is given.

Extra Practice

CHAPTER 1 (p. 783) **1.** 105 **3.** 8 **5.** 512 **7.** 76 **9.** 49
11. 31 **13.** 3 **15.** 1 **17.** 7 **19.** 12 **21.** 24 **23.** solution
25. not a solution **27.** solution **29.** $16 = 20 - x$

31.

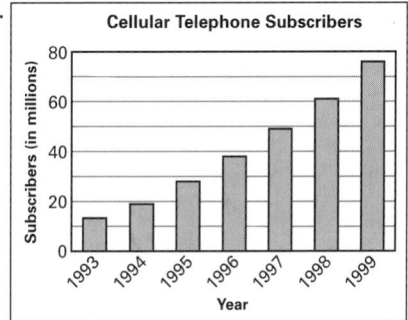

Cellular Telephone Subscribers

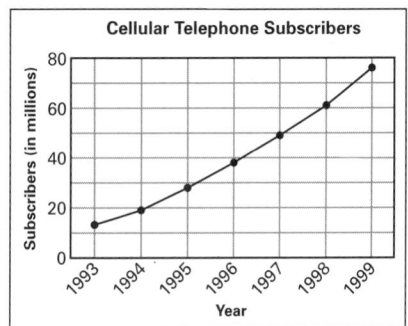

Cellular Telephone Subscribers

33.

Input x	0	1	2	3	4	5
Output y	1	8	15	22	29	36

CHAPTER 2 (p. 784)
1. $-7 < 8, 8 > -7$ **3.** $-4 > -7, -7 < -4$

5. 3 **7.** 8.5 **9.** 5 **11.** -2 **13.** 3 **15.** -3 **17.** -13
19. -2.2 **21.** -7 **23.** -6.5 **25.** -7 **27.** 15
29. -450 **31.** 6 **33.** -81 **35.** 48 **37.** -90 ft
39. $4a - 24$ **41.** $8x + 6$ **43.** $-2 - t$ **45.** $1.5y - 4.5$
47. already simplified **49.** $7w - 4$ **51.** $-m^2 + 2m$
53. -4 **55.** 66

CHAPTER 3 (p. 785) **1.** 14 **3.** 17 **5.** 7 **7.** 3 **9.** 5
11. $\frac{1}{2}$ **13.** -20 **15.** 84 **17.** 4 **19.** 2 **21.** -14 **23.** 1
25. 2 **27.** -2 **29.** 3 **31.** $-\frac{3}{2}$ **33.** -7.46 **35.** -0.25
37. 12 mi/hr **39.** $7.25/hr **41.** 2 g/bar **43.** 48 m
45. 45

CHAPTER 4 (p. 786)

1. 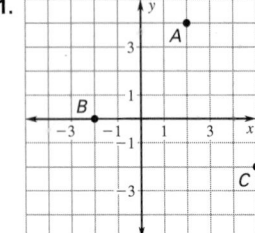   **3.**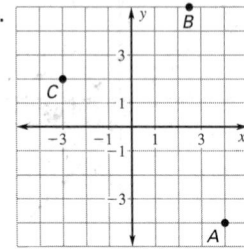

5. 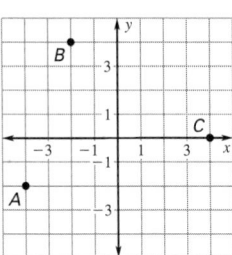   **7.**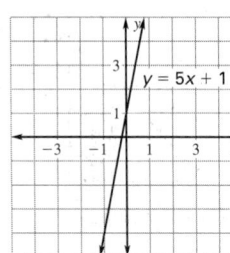

9. 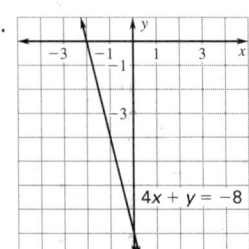   **11.**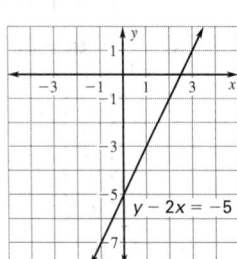

13. 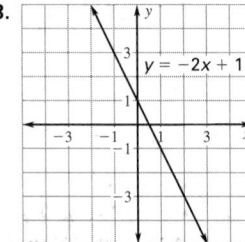   **15.**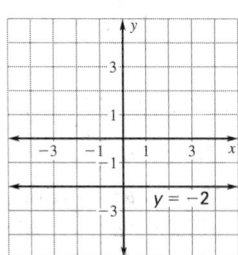

17.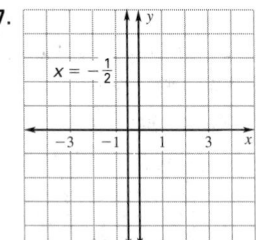

19. -1 **21.** 6   **23.** -5 **25.** 6   **27.** 0   **29.** -7
31. undefined   **33.** $y = 3x$ **35.** $y = -\dfrac{7}{8}x$ **37.** $y = x$
39. $y = -3x$

41. 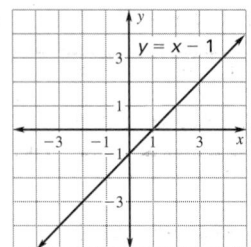   **43.**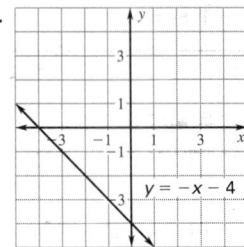

45.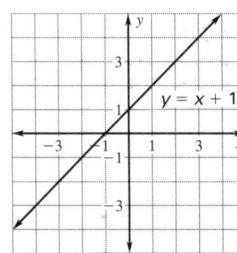

47. function; domain is 1, 3, 5, 7 and range is 1, 2, 3
49. not a function

CHAPTER 5 (p. 787)   **1.** $y = 2x + 1$ **3.** $y = \dfrac{1}{2}x - 3$
5. $y = 3(x + 1)$ **7.** $y - 6 = 0(x - 3)$
9. $y + 1 = 4(x + 3)$ **11.** $y + 1 = \dfrac{1}{2}(x - 2)$
13. $y = 3x - 11$ **15.** $y = -\dfrac{1}{2}x - 2$ **17.** $y = -x + 2$
19. $3x - y = 17$ **21.** $5x + 6y = -2$
23. $7x + y = 8$ **25.** $2x + y = 12$
27. $4A + 5R = 50,\ 0.80A + 1.00R = 10.00$
29.

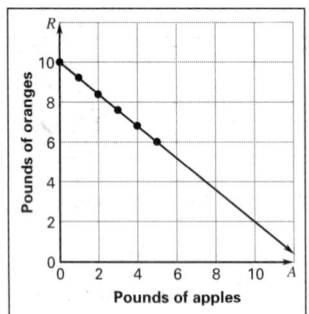

31. not perpendicular   **33.** not perpendicular
35. $y = -\dfrac{4}{3}x + \dfrac{8}{3}$

CHAPTER 6 (p. 788)

1. $x < 1$ **3.** $7 \geq y$

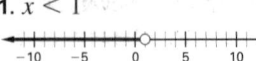   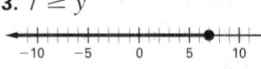

5. $x \geq 4$ **7.** $k \leq 18$

   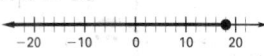

9. $x > -1$ **11.** $x \geq -2\dfrac{1}{2}$ **13.** $x \leq 9$
15. $-5 < x < 2$ **17.** $-3 < x \leq 5$

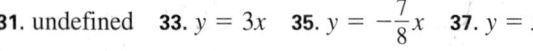   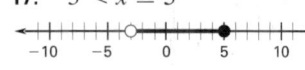

19. $-1 \le x < 4$

21. $1 < x \le 7$

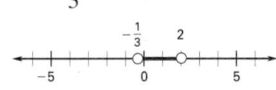

23. $x \le 1 \text{ or } x > 4$

25. $x < 3 \text{ or } x > 4$

27. $-14, 14$ **29.** $-12, 12$ **31.** $-14, -6$ **33.** $\frac{1}{5}, 1$

35. $1, 7$

37. $-8 \le x \le 8$ **39.** $-5 \le x \le 5$

41. $x \le -2 \text{ or } x \ge -\frac{1}{2}$ **43.** $-\frac{1}{3} < x < 2$

45.

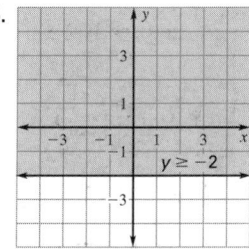

47.

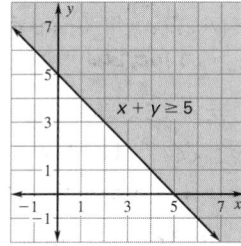

49.

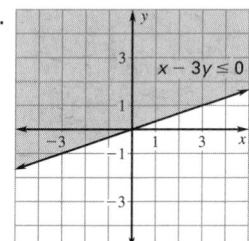

51.

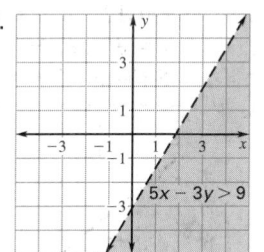

CHAPTER 7 (p. 789) **1.** $(-2, 5)$ **3.** $(4, 6)$ **5.** $(-5, -1)$

7. $(6, 3)$ **9.** $(4, 1)$ **11.** $(11, -15)$ **13.** $(4, 2)$

15. $(0, -2)$ **17.** $(13, -2)$ **19.** $(2, 1)$ **21.** *Sample answer:*
substitution, because it is easy to solve for x; $(0, 5)$
23. *Sample answer:* substitution, because the equations
are already solved for y; $(-1, -4)$ **25.** *Sample answer:*
linear combinations, because it is easy to eliminate y;
$(3, 0)$ **27.** *Sample answer:* linear combinations, because
it is easy to eliminate y; $(2, 0)$ **29.** 12 adult tickets and
8 student tickets   **31.** none   **33.** one   **35.** infinitely many
37. none

39.

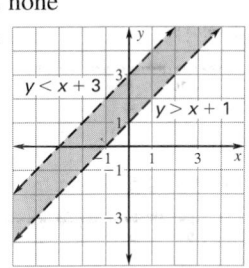

41.

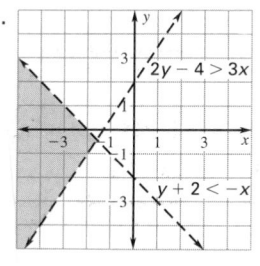

43.

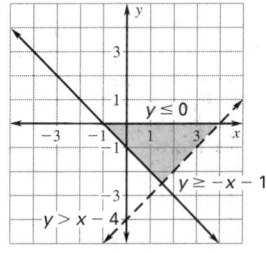

45.

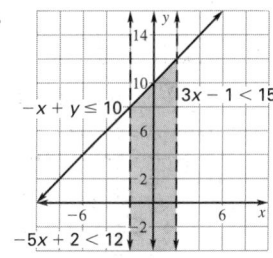

CHAPTER 8 (p. 790) **1.** $16,807$ **3.** $1728x^3$ **5.** m^6 **7.** $98x^7$

9. $\frac{1}{x^4}$ **11.** $\frac{1}{x^3 y^2}$ **13.** $4xy^5$ **15.** $\frac{16}{y^4}$

17.

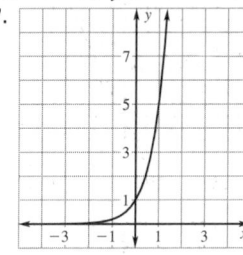

19.

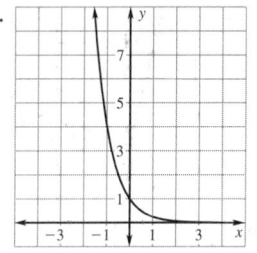

21. 8 **23.** $\frac{16}{81}$ **25.** $-\frac{1}{64}$ **27.** $\frac{8}{3}$ **29.** $\frac{3x^4 y^2}{2}$

31. $\frac{27x^3 z^9}{8}$ **33.** $\frac{4b^7}{9a^5}$ **35.** 0.000004813 **37.** 0.084162

39. 50.645 **41.** 0.0000000234 **43.** 5.28×10^3

45. 1.138×10^1 **47.** 8.2766×10^2 **49.** 1.6354×10^1

51. 3.95×10^0 **53.** 8×10^{-3} **55.** $\$1155$ **57.** $\$2286.82$

59. $y = 120,000(0.90)^t$

CHAPTER 9 (p. 791) **1.** 1.73 **3.** -10 **5.** 3.87 **7.** 14.83

9. ± 5 **11.** no real solution   **13.** ± 4 **15.** $\pm \sqrt{3}$

17. 2.2 sec   **19.** $2\sqrt{22}$ **21.** $4\sqrt{7}$ **23.** 2 **25.** $\sqrt{3}$

27.

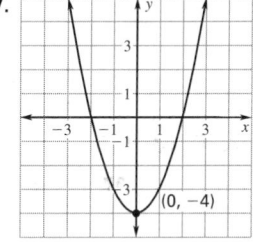

29.

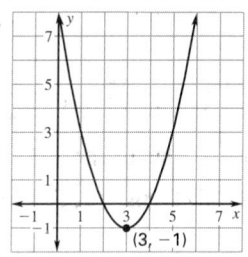

31.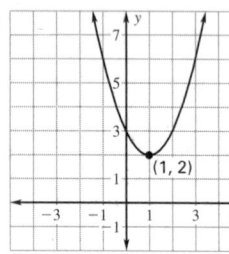

33.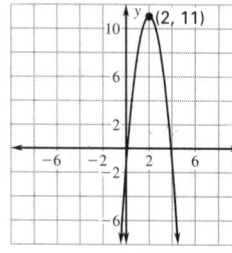

35. $-3, -2$ **37.** $-5, 2$ **39.** $-1, 3$
41. $x^2 - 4x - 12 = 0; -2, 6$
43. $x^2 - 5x + 4 = 0; 1, 4$ **45.** $x^2 + 5x + 6 = 0;$
$-3, -2$ **47.** $2x^2 - x - 10 = 0; -2, \dfrac{5}{2}$ **49.** one solution

51. one solution **53.** no real solution **55.** no real solution

57.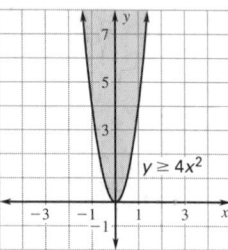

59.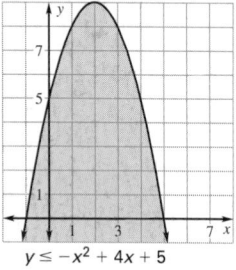

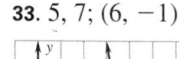

CHAPTER 10 (p. 792) **1.** $8x^2 + 1$ **3.** $14x^2 - 7x + 8$
5. $x^2 + 9x - 4$ **7.** $4x^3 - 8x^2 + 7x$
9. $15b^5 - 10b^4 + 5b^2$ **11.** $d^2 + 4d - 5$
13. $x^3 + x^2 + 18$ **15.** $x^2 + 18x + 81$ **17.** $a^2 - 4$
19. $16x^2 + 40x + 25$ **21.** $4a^2 - 9b^2$ **23.** $-6, -3$
25. $-5, 1$ **27.** $\dfrac{3}{2}, 7$ **29.** $1, 2$
31. $6, 8; (7, -1)$ **33.** $5, 7; (6, -1)$

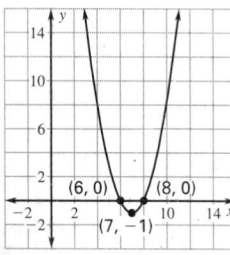 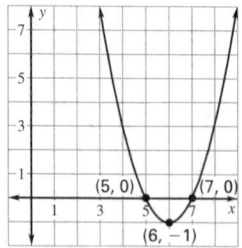

35. $5, 9; (7, 4)$ **37.** $-1, 3; (1, -4)$

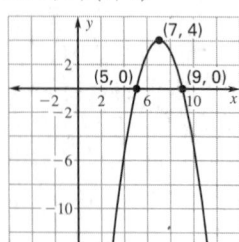 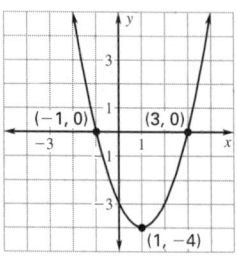

39. -3 **41.** 6 **43.** $6, 9$ **45.** $-4, 6$ **47.** $-2, \dfrac{3}{2}$ **49.** $-\dfrac{4}{3}$
51. $-\dfrac{3}{4}, 2$ **53.** $-\dfrac{7}{3}, 8$ **55.** $(x + 1)(x - 1)$
57. $(11 + x)(11 - x)$ **59.** $(t + 1)^2$ **61.** $(8y + 3)^2$

63. $x^2(x + 3)(x - 3)$ **65.** $x^2(x + 9)(x - 5)$
67. $-3y(y + 1)(y + 4)$ **69.** $7x^4(x^2 - 3)$
71. 4 ft by 2 ft by 12 ft

CHAPTER 11 (p. 793) **1.** 6 **3.** $1\dfrac{3}{5}$ **5.** 4 **7.** $y = 3x$
9. $y = \dfrac{1}{4}x$ **11.** $y = \dfrac{15}{x}$ **13.** $y = \dfrac{2}{x}$ **15.** $\dfrac{2x^3}{7}$ **17.** $\dfrac{1}{x + 1}$
19. $\dfrac{2}{3x}$ **21.** $-\dfrac{1}{y + 4}$ **23.** $\dfrac{1}{2}$ **25.** $\dfrac{10x^2}{x + 5}$ **27.** $\dfrac{5}{x - 3}$ **29.** $\dfrac{1}{x}$
31. $-\dfrac{2(x + 1)}{x - 1}$ **33.** $\dfrac{5 - 3x}{x^2}$ **35.** $\dfrac{x^2 + 35}{(x - 3)(x + 8)}$
37. $\dfrac{2(5x + 14)}{(x + 5)(x - 5)}$ **39.** $33\dfrac{1}{3}$ **41.** -2 **43.** 4

CHAPTER 12 (p. 794)
1. domain: all nonnegative real numbers; range: all nonnegative real numbers
3. domain: all nonnegative real numbers; range: all real numbers ≥ -5

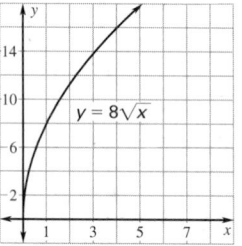 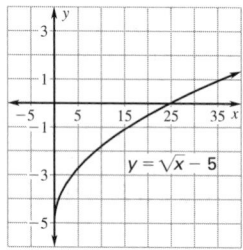

5. domain: all real numbers ≥ 2; range: all nonnegative real numbers
7. domain: all real numbers $\geq -\dfrac{2}{3}$; range: all nonnegative real numbers

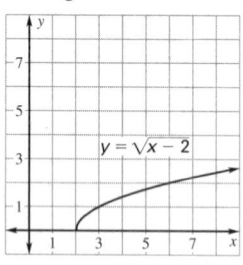 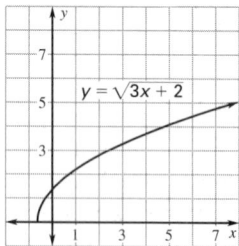

9. $5\sqrt{5}$ **11.** $16\sqrt{2}$ **13.** $7\sqrt{3} - 3\sqrt{2}$ **15.** $\dfrac{\sqrt{6}}{3}$ **17.** 121
19. no solution **21.** $1, 3$ **23.** 16 **25.** 64 **27.** $x^{3/4}$
29. $x^6 y^{5/2}$ **31.** $-14, 4$ **33.** $-4, -2$ **35.** $-2, 8$ **37.** $\sqrt{2}$
39. 8 **41.** 20 **43.** 8 **45.** 18.36 **47.** 12.08 **49.** 4.47
51. $(2, 4.5); d = \sqrt{4.25}$ **53.** $(2.5, -2); d = 2.5$
55. $(0, 4); d = 2\sqrt{5}$ **57.** $(5, 6); d = \sqrt{17}$ **59.** *Sample answer:* Assume $xy = 0$ and both $x \neq 0$ and $y \neq 0$. If $xy = 0$ and $x \neq 0$, then $y = \dfrac{0}{x} = 0$, but this is impossible since $y \neq 0$. Therefore if $xy = 0$, either $x = 0$ or $y = 0$.